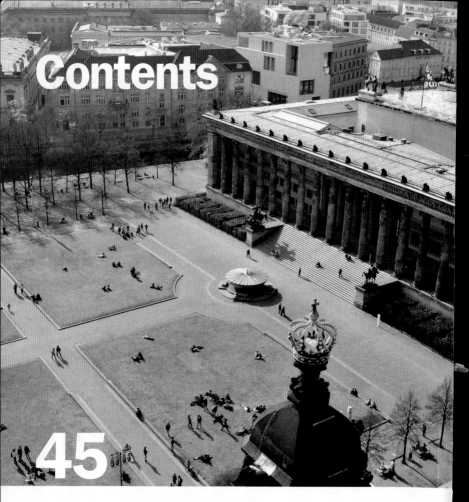

Contents

45

72

203

155

278

Time Out Berlin

Editorial
Editor Tommy Tannock
Consultant Editor Arsalan Mohammad
Copy Editor Cath Phillips
Listings Editor Tim Eve
Proofreader John Watson

Editorial Director Sarah Guy
Group Finance Manager Margaret Wright

Design
Art Editor Christie Webster
Designers Kei Ishimaru, Darryl Bell
Group Commercial Senior Designer Jason Tansley

Picture Desk
Picture Editor Jael Marschner
Deputy Picture Editor Ben Rowe
Picture Researcher Lizzy Owen

Advertising
Managing Director St John Betteridge

Marketing
Senior Publishing Brand Manager Luthfa Begum
Head of Circulation Dan Collins

Production
Production Controller Katie Mulhern-Bhudia

Time Out Group
Founder Tony Elliott
Chief Executive Officer Tim Arthur
Managing Director Europe Noel Penzer
Publisher Alex Batho

Contributors
The Editor would like to thank Silke Neumann, Annika von Taube, Johannes Christian Schön and all contributors to previous editions of *Time Out Berlin*, whose work forms the basis for parts of this book

Maps JS Graphics Ltd (john@jsgraphics.co.uk)

Cover and pull-out map photography Masterfile

Back cover photography Clockwise from top left: anweber/Shutterstock.com; ilolab/Shutterstock.com; Morenovel/Shutterstock.com; Courtesy 25hours Hotel Bikini Berlin; Funny Solution Studio/Shutterstock.com

Photography Pages 2/3, 14/15 ilolab/Shutterstock.com; 4 (top), 45, 96 Lucian Milasan/Shutterstock.com; 4 (bottom), 10, 17 (left), 72, 85, 146, 207, 256 360b/Shutterstock.com; 5 (top), 200, 203 Monika Rittershaus; 5 (bottom left), 155 Benjamin Pritzkuleit; 5 (bottom right), 278 Menachim Czertok; 13 (top), 35, 93, 94, 122, 126, 134 (top), 160, 220 Jael Marschner; 13 (bottom), 102 Occity/Shutterctock.oom; 14 (top), 24 (bottom) pavel dudek/Shutterstock.com; 14 (bottom), 15 (top) Matyas Rehak/Shutterstock.com; 15 (bottom), 38/39 Morenovel/Shutterstock.com; 16 (top), 53, 170 T.W. van Urk/Shutterstock.com; 16 (bottom), 98 Jorg Hackemann/Shutterstock.com; 17 (right) Jo Chambers/Shutterstock.com; 20 © Günter Wicker; 22/23 (bottom) alex_bendea/Shutterstock.com; 23 De Visu/Shutterstock.com; 24 (top) Mag Mac/Shutterstock.com; 25 (top), 60 (top) Steve Herud; 25 (bottom) Dominik Wojcik; 26/27 (top) Funny Solution Studio/Shutterstock.com; 26/27 (bottom) Lienhard Schulz/Wikimedia Commons; 28 (top) Sebastian Greuners; 30 Jana Schoenknecht/Shutterstock.com; 31 cinemafestival/Shutterstock.com; 32/33, 41, 68, 79, 88 (bottom), 135, 145, 156/157, 180 (bottom), 194, 270 Elan Fleisher; 34/35 Ppictures/Shutterstock.com; 38, 108, 240, 260 WorldWide/Shutterstock.com; 46, 57 Sean Pavone/Shutterstock.com; 47, 48, 50, 82/83, 101, 134 (bottom) Virginia Rollison; 49 turtix/Shutterstock.com; 54 ken schluchtmann/dirk daehmlow; 59 Jens Ziehe; 60 (bottom) Ailine Liefeld; 62 (left) © BrooksWalkerPhoto.com; 62 (right) © Heike Ollertz + Brooks Walker; 68/69, 74 (left) Eldad Carin/Shutterstock.com; 74 (right), 94/95 Eddy Galeotti/Shutterstock.com; 77 Jennifer Martin; 80 hafakot/Shutterstock.com; 81, 103 (left), 105, 128, 137, 139, 191 Britta Jaschinski; 99 anyaivanova/Shutterstock.com; 107 (top) © kai abresch photography; 108/109, 142 pio3/Shutterstock.com; 110 hans engbers/Shutterstock.com; 114 andersphoto/Shutterstock.com; 116 vvoe/Shutterstock.com; 118 Ulf Büschleb; 121 Rudolf Tepfenhart; 123, 129, 196, 197 Camille Blake; 126/127 carol.anne/Shutterstock.com; 140, 141 Nina Strassguetl; 143 LensTravel/Shutterstock.com; 144 (bottom) Flik47/Shutterstock.com; 146/147 -jkb-/Wikimedia Commons; 150 Tommy Tannock; 154 BenBuschfeld/Wikimedia Commons; 164 © Wolfgang Scholvien/Visit Berlin; 166/167, 177 Jan Bitter; 168 gary yim/Shutterstock.com; 171 Ulrich Sülflow; 172 Naturschutzzentrum Ökowerk Berlin; 173 Caterina Gili; 174 taniavolobueva/Shutterstock.com; 175 Everett/REX_Shutterstock; 178, 179 Marek Szandurski/Shutterstock.com; 182 Paolo Brand; 198 Clovis Bouhier; 206 Libertinus/Wikimedia Commons; 208 A.Savin/Wikimedia Commons; 210 (left) © Julia Sievert; 210 (right) Rebecca Sampson; 211 Joe Goergen; 214/215 Ventura/Shutterstock.com; 226/227 Narongsak Nagadhana/Shutterstock.com; 228/229, 238 Roger Viollet/Getty Images; 231 Print Collector/Getty Images; 237 © Lebrecht Music and Arts Photo Library/Alamy; 243 Popperfoto/Getty Images; 245 Gamma-Keystone/Getty Images; 255 Claudio Divizia/Shutterstock.com; 258 © adam eastland/Alamy; 265 (bottom) Michael Tewes

The following images were supplied by the featured establishments: 51, 67, 73, 76, 82, 88 (top), 91, 106, 107 (bottom), 117, 133, 151, 152, 153, 163, 169, 176, 180 (top), 181, 183, 184, 187, 189, 192, 262/263, 264, 265 (top), 268, 271, 272, 273, 274, 275, 277, 279, 280

About the Guide

GETTING AROUND

Each sightseeing chapter contains a street map of the area marked with the locations of sights and museums (❶), restaurants and cafés (❶), bars and pubs (❶) and shops (❶). There are also street maps of Berlin at the back of the book, along with an overview map of the city. In addition, there's a detachable fold-out street map.

THE ESSENTIALS

For practical information, including visas, disabled access, emergency numbers, lost property, websites and local transport, see the Essential Information section. It begins on page 262.

THE LISTINGS

Addresses, phone numbers, websites, transport information, hours and prices are all included in our listings, as are selected other facilities. All of these were checked and correct at press time. However, business owners can alter their arrangements at any time, and fluctuating economic conditions can cause prices to change rapidly.

The very best venues in the city, the must-sees and must-dos in every category, have been marked with a red star (★). In the sightseeing chapters, we've also marked venues with free admission with a FREE symbol, and budget restaurants and cafés with a € symbol.

PHONE NUMBERS

The area code for Berlin is 030. When calling within Berlin you don't need to dial the area code; simply dial the number as listed in this guide. From outside Germany, dial your country's access code (00 from the UK, 011 from the US) or a plus symbol, followed by the German country code (49), then 30 for Berlin (dropping the initial zero) and the number. So, to reach the Deutsches Historiches Museum, dial +49 30 203 040. For more on phones, see page 291.

FEEDBACK

We welcome feedback on this guide, both on the venues we've included and on any other locations that you'd like to see featured in future editions. Please email us at guides@timeout.com.

Berlin's
Top **20**

From street food to majestic monuments, we count down the essentials.

❷

1 Reichstag
(page 98)

This neo-Baroque edifice housing the German Bundestag (Parliament) has survived wars, Nazis, fire, bombing and the country's division, only to return renovated and a symbol of a new era in German politics. A tour around the iconic dome, designed by Sir Norman Foster, is thoroughly recommended.

❶

2 Brandenburger Tor
(page 40)

Berlin's long-suffering victory arch. Now back to its former glory and a must-see on any Berlin itinerary, the Brandenburg Gate is a mammoth monument to unity. Ironically, it has served as a visual flashpoint for much of the trauma to have beset Germany in the 20th century, standing alone in no-man's-land during the DDR era.

3 Museumsinsel
(page 44)

Berlin's Museumsinsel – home to five of the city's oldest museums – is practically a work of art in itself. Awarded UNESCO World Heritage status, the Mitte complex incorporates the Altes Museum, Alte Nationalgalerie, Bode-Museum, Neues Museum and Pergamonmuseum.

4 Tiergarten
(page 96)

This vast park in the heart of the city comes into its own during spring and summer, when you can happily lose yourself amid its woodlands, lakes and miles of greenery.

5 Denkmal für die ermordeten Juden Europas
(page 48)

Architect Peter Eisenman's memorial to the victims of the Holocaust is sobering, chilling and intentionally disorienting. A beautiful sculptural statement that invites visitors in, only to create a feeling of unease, it's rightfully acclaimed as an essential part of the city.

6 Sowjetisches Ehrenmal am Treptower Park
(page 145)

One of Berlin's most awesome public monuments, this memorial to Soviet soldiers killed in World War II, located out in former East Berlin, is as bombastic and intimidating as you would expect.

7 Haus am Checkpoint Charlie
(page 142)

Once the flashpoint between East and West, today the former Checkpoint Charlie border crossing offers tacky souvenir stalls, coachloads of trippers, and actors pretending to be US and Soviet guards. But it also features this intriguing little museum.

8 Tempelhofer Feld
(page 154)

The vast 1920s airport west of Neukölln now stands empty, while the surrounding airfields and runways have become a huge park for cycling, kite-flying and open-air festivals.

9 Gedenkstätte Berlin-Hohenschönhausen
(page 92)

Former inmates of this Stasi internment facility lead chilling tours through the depths of their former jail, describing the horrors inflicted on them by the DDR's notorious secret police.

10 East Side Gallery

(page 84)
One of the few remaining strips of the Berlin Wall still standing, and still festooned with the graffiti murals that became iconic across the world.

11 Jüdisches Museum

(page 142)
Daniel Libeskind's beautiful, yet deliberately oppressive, building houses a masterful museum devoted to the turbulent history of Judaism in Germany.

12 Berlin's art scene

A city of artists and art-lovers, Berlin has a wonderful variety of gallery spaces – from pop-ups in former East Berlin apartments to the colossal monoliths of Museumsinsel. Probably the best time to get an overview of the scene is the Gallery Weekend (p27), which takes place at the end of April.

13 Currywurst

Berlin and Hamburg have long gently tussled over ownership of this ubiquitous street-food snack: a chopped pork sausage smothered in ketchup and curry powder. You're never more than a few minutes from one in Berlin. To see what all the fuss is about, head to Konnopke's Imbiss (p77), the oldest sausage stand in the city.

14 Zoologischer Garten
(page 105)

From elephants to monkeys and all manner of weird, wild and wonderful fauna in between, this world-class zoological garden, founded in 1841, makes for a fantastic family day out.

15 KaDeWe
(page 188)

The legendary department store is more than a century old and has stood at the heart of the city's shopping district through thick and thin. Today, it's as opulent as ever, especially the food hall on the sixth floor.

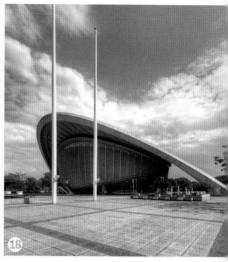

18 Haus der Kulturen der Welt
(page 98)

Germany's national centre for international contemporary arts, with a special focus on non-European cultures and societies. Housed in a modernist masterpiece in the centre of Tiergarten, HKW covers art, music, dance, theatre and much more.

16 River Spree

Winding through the centre of Berlin, the Spree is a fantastic way to navigate Berlin via boat. There's no shortage of tour operators (p111) and even the humble city travelcard can get you on a number of services plying the various waterways.

17 Internationale Filmfestspiele Berlin
(page 31)

The Berlinale (founded in 1951) is the world's most popular film festival, in terms of audience attendance figures. A major fixture on the global cultural calendar, it sees unlovely Potsdamerplatz transformed into a glittering stage of glamour, excitement and major movie stars each February.

19 Döner kebabs

It's said that the humble döner was invented in Berlin in the early 1970s, by Turkish fast-food mogul Mehmet Aygun. Given the city's sizeable Turkish population and profusion of related eateries, this could well be true. Aficionados swear by the kebabs at Imren Grill (p150) in Neukölln.

20 The lakes
(page 163)

It's the height of summer, the sun's beating down – where is everyone? They've packed a bike, a basket of beer and a towel on to the S-Bahn and headed out to one of the many hundreds of lakes, large and small, that surround the city.

Berlin Today

The city's very popularity is a problem.

TEXT: ARSALAN MOHAMMAD

It's perhaps ironic that Berlin's new mayor, former urban development senator Michael Müller, was hitherto best known for his controversial plans to redevelop the historic Tempelhof airport site. Ironic, as it was largely the debacle surrounding the city's long-awaited new Brandenburg airport that finally did for previous incumbent Klaus Wowereit, who bowed out of office prematurely in August 2014. Aware that the city largely blamed him for the multiple failures of the new airport project – he referred to it in his resignation statement as his 'greatest defeat' – the once hugely popular 'Wowi' decided to jump before he was pushed. It marks the end of a colourful chapter in Berlin politics. Wowereit's mayoralty covered the chaotic, second post-reunification decade of modern Berlin, a turbulent period for a city still recovering from its 40-year fracture.

AIRPORT DISASTER!

How not to build a new flight hub.

Berlin's new Brandenburg airport (BER) was due to open in 2011. It was to be the jewel in the crown of the gleaming 21st-century metropolis. Instead, though, an increasingly ludicrous series of errors, mistakes and general cock-ups – a 2013 report identified 66,500 problems – have beset the project, leaving the city struggling on with its two overwhelmed hubs, Tegel and Schönefeld, and suffering an acute case of egg-on-face as the capital's plans for a capacious, ultra-modern airport teeter on the brink of ruin.

With the city torn between shame, embarrassment and Berlin cynicism, new mayor Michael Müller has been charged with getting the project firmly back on track. The fact that the BER board of directors was headed up by none other than (now former) mayor Klaus Wowereit and Brandenburg state premier Matthias Platzeck, rather than anyone with proven project management, construction or technical experience, demonstrates clearly the perils of putting politicians in charge.

So what went wrong? The first major blunder was the fire system. Given that smoke and hot air rise, the system of underground smoke exhaust shafts proved wildly impractical. It turned out that the chief planner, Alfredo di Mauro, wasn't actually a qualified engineer – merely a lowly technical draughtsman. 'Everyone thought I was an engineer,' di Mauro explained to the media. 'I just didn't contradict them.' Siemens and Bosch are now responsible for a new – and usable – fire-protection system.

Then there was BER technical chief Horst Amann, who was roundly pilloried in the media when he confessed that no one on the building site could work out how to switch the airport's lights off. 'We haven't progressed far enough with our lighting system that we can control it,' Amann told *Spiegel Online*. He was promptly turfed out. Another ex-technical director is facing trial on corruption charges, having allegedly accepted around half a million euros in bribes from a prospective contractor.

The projected capacity of 27 million passengers a year also proved a challenge too far. It was only after check-in desks and luggage carousels were installed that it was discovered there was nowhere near enough of them. The air-conditioning was also below par, meaning that the vast IT network could overheat and shut down at any time.

Still, BER is doing its best to put a positive spin on things. Until the airport is completed – hopefully by the second half of 2017, and within its now-estimated €5-€7 billion budget, more than twice the original – Berliners can enjoy (for a modest price) bike tours of the deserted runways and check-in areas, packed lunch included.

The unfinished airport.

TOURIST TOWN

Although Wowereit failed to turn the capital into the sort of economic powerhouse Europe's most muscular nation expects, it seems that Berlin has fulfilled his early promise of remaining 'poor but sexy'. Well, certainly still poor. The 'sexy' – Berlin's louche, legendary bohemia – is increasingly under threat from developers, agents of the dread gentrification and mass tourism. All of which were encouraged by the former mayor.

Even had he achieved nothing else, Wowereit can point to the phenomenal boom in tourism that flourished under his watch. In 2014 alone, 12 million visitors landed in Berlin, making the German capital one of the three most popular travel destinations in Europe. As local artist Sven Johne recently told broadcaster Deutsche Welle, 'Why do the tourists come? For Hitler, the Wall, clubbing!'

It's still very early into Michael Müller's mayoralty to pronounce judgement, but this rather austere character is already something of a contrast to his ebullient predecessor. Wowereit's time in office was characterised by his easygoing persona and fervent promotion of the city as a cosmopolitan, artist-friendly destination. A familiar presence at celebrity and cultural events, Wowereit symbolised the Berlin of the early 2000s perfectly. But today, the city faces a new set of challenges. Müller – a former printer and union man, known for his rather colourless, bureaucratic personality and finicky attention to detail – talks of affordable housing, social policy, cutting the city's perilous €6-billion-plus debt through prudent fiscal strategies, and assuaging the national humiliation of the stalled Brandenburg airport project (see p20 **Airport Disaster!**).

In a city perpetually at war with itself over how best to present and conserve its cultural cachet, he has already stepped into the long-festering argument about the city's €595-million Humboldt Forum, concerning the future use of the reconstructed City Palace. Müller proposes scrapping the current plan to turn it into a vast library and suggests making it a museum about the history of Berlin instead.

GENTRIFICATION TO ZOMBIEFICATION

If you're looking to provoke a lively reaction in any Berliner, merely bring up the issue of gentrification. The Wowereit era saw a gradual smoothing out of the city's rougher edges –

> *'If you're looking to provoke a lively reaction in any Berliner, merely bring up the issue of gentrification.'*

to the distress of those who romanticised the city's innate shabbiness – and yuppies, foreign property speculators and wealthy young Americans and European expats swarmed into town, seduced by the city's comparatively low property prices and rents.

Those living in Prenzlauer Berg, Neukölln, Kreuzberg and Mitte found themselves under siege. Between 2009 and 2011, rents increased by an average of eight per cent – in some of the most popular districts, hikes hit an astonishing 25 per cent, twice the national average. Even the effervescent Wowereit had to concede: 'The city is not as cheap as it used to be.' Nevertheless, he was publicly irritated by those who saw the rise in rents as an out-and-out negative. 'We have to decide whether we want to keep these low standards or take the city forward,' he said, while stipulating that he didn't want Berlin to become like New York or London, where 'normal' earners can't afford to live near the city centre.

Again, the new mayor heralds a new era. In spring 2015, the German parliament agreed measures to control sharp rent rises in areas under housing pressure. At the same time, Müller announced a programme to protect the city's cherished art scene, planning the creation of 2,000 new studio spaces for self-employed artists by 2020. All this is an attempt to placate those who bewail the furious rate of gentrification. Long-term residents express nostalgia, anger and bitterness at the erosion of the idiosyncratic nooks and crannies of their city. It remains to be seen whether Müller's actions can ameliorate the impact of speculators, developers and expats.

As they continue to flock in search of affordable bohemia, many of those who were responsible for creating it in the first place are now finding themselves – along with Berlin's native elderly and impoverished – priced out of their own city.

Itineraries

*Plot your perfect trip
to the capital with our
step-by-step planner.*

9AM

Day 1

9AM Sprawling **Tiergarten** park (p95), in the heart of Berlin, is the city's soul. Acres of greenery, lakes and trees can easily swallow up a sunny day, but if you're eager to get exploring, head to the **Siegessäule** (Victory Column; p99) in the centre. This 67m (220ft) monument was constructed in 1873 to commemorate Prussian victories against the Austrians, Danish and French. From the monument, head down Lichtensteinallee for a hearty breakfast at the delightfully bucolic **Café am Neuen See** (p99), a café, beer garden and brasserie rolled into one. Retrace your steps to the Siegessäule and head east on Strasse des 17 Juni – named in honour of the 1953 East German uprising – to the **Brandenburg Gate** (p40). One of the city's most recognisable icons, it has survived war, the Berlin Wall and reunification, and now stands as a dual symbol of Prussian might and the city's indomitable spirit.

11AM From the Brandenburg Gate, go past Pariser Platz – home to the famous **Adlon Hotel** (p265), where the Nazi high command and Michael Jackson's baby once hung out – and turn on to Ebertstrasse. Here, you can follow the old course of the Berlin Wall (look for the narrow strip of paving stones marking the route) past the **Denkmal für die ermordeten Juden Europas** (Memorial to the Murdered

NOON

Clockwise from left:
Tiergarten; **Sony Center**; **Adlon Hotel**.

Jews of Europe; p48). This powerful remembrance work consists of 2,711 concrete blocks spread across a 19,000sq m undulating surface in the heart of the city.

NOON Continuing down Ebertstrasse will bring you to **Potsdamer Platz** (p102). This was once a bustling hub, boasting Europe's first set of traffic lights (a replica set is still visible), before it fell into no-man's-land desolation during the DDR era. Today, it's home to an array of modern malls, cinemas and tower blocks. At the Kollhoff Tower, you can get an express lift up to the **Panoramapunkt** observation decks (p105) on the 24th and 25th floors for an awesome 360-degree view of the city. For mega-mall fans, the vast **Sony Center** (p102) houses an IMAX, a multiplex and the **Legoland Discovery Centre** (p169). A short stroll south of Potsdamer Platz, **Joseph-Roth-Diele** (p106) is a traditional book café serving good-value lunches.

11AM

2PM Heading east along Leipziger Strasse leads you to one of the city's major retail drags, **Friedrichstrasse** (p45). Here, you'll find the infamous Checkpoint Charlie crossing point between East and West Berlin. Today, it's a tourist mess of souvenir shops, kebab joints and coachloads of visitors. But it's still worth visiting the mini-museum at the **Haus am Checkpoint Charlie** (p142).

4PM Heading down Friedrichstrasse towards Kreuzberg brings you to the rather unlovely Hallesches Tor district. However, it's worth persevering as hip boutiques and cafés are mushrooming in this bleak neighbourhood. One of the newest can be found inside **Hallesches Haus** (Tempelhofer-Ufer 1, www. hallescheshaus.com). What makes this simple café all the more enticing is the fact that it's situated within a mini-complex containing a flower shop, an artisan furniture workshop and an emporium selling quirky, locally made gifts. The café serves fabulous coffee (courtesy of Tom's Kaffeerösterei) and simple, healthy dishes.

7PM Kreuzberg (p126) is the city's rough, ready and vibrant quarter – a fun mix of shops, bars, clubs and restaurants that reflect the district's multicultural population. Kottbusser Tor is Kreuzberg's hub. From here, walk down Kottbusser Damm to **Maybachufer** (where a legendary Turkish market takes place every Friday morning selling all manner of spices, herbs and fresh produce; p139). Then, enjoy an early-evening ramble along the Landwehrkanal, which bisects the southern half of the city and is lined with dozens of attractive hostelries for frequent refreshment opportunities. Looking for somewhere to soak up the beer? Make a beeline for **Mustafa's Gemüse Kebap** (p138), easily the most popular kebab stall in town.

Day 2

9AM There's no shortage of breakfast spots around Berlin – you can take your choice from some vegan 'clean food' at **Laauma** (Sonntagstrasse 26, Friedrichshain, www.laauma. com) to Russian mixed plates at **Gorki Park** (Weinbergsweg 25, Prenzlauer Berg, www. gorki-park.de). One of the city's morning joints *du jour* is **Chipps** (Jägerstrasse 35, Mitte, www.chipps.eu). It's a temple to the humble egg, available in countless permutations – omelettes in 'The Morning After' to scrambled in 'Perfect Gentleman' – alongside quirky twists on the usual breakfast fare.

10AM

10AM Now head east along Jägerstrasse, take a left on to Niederlagstrasse and you'll soon be at **Museumsinsel** (Museum Island; p44), Berlin's UNESCO-certified museum quarter. This is one of the city's most visited attractions and it's easy to see why – the group of five major museums makes for an immersive cultural experience. In the shadow of the Berlin Cathedral, you'll find the **Altes Museum** (p47), next to the Lustgarten. North from there are the **Neues Museum** (p50) and the **Alte Nationalgalerie** (p47). Finally, on the Kupfergraben side of the island, you'll find the **Pergamonmuseum** (p50) and the **Bode-Museum** (p48).

NOON After a morning's museum-hopping, wander a few steps northwards across Monbijoupark to the open-air Hackescher Markt, a historic enclave of shops, cafés and a regular open-air market. If the weather's fine, there's a multitude of outdoor lunch

NOON

spots to explore, as well as the maze-like warren of courtyards containing stalls, shops and more cafés in the Jugendstil **Hackesche Höfe** (p54) complex.

2PM From here, you're close to Alexanderplatz, the former hub of East Berlin during the DDR era. Remnants of the brutalist architecture of the day remain – most notably in

6PM

9PM

Clockwise from top left: **Altes Museum**; **Mogg & Melzer**; **Neues Odessa Bar**; **Hackesche Höfe**.

6PM As you mooch around Mitte, you'll soon notice that not only is the district home to some of the city's most exciting and unusual shops, it's also a gallery heartland. Along Auguststrasse you'll discover some of the coolest art spots in town, including dynamic arts centre **KW** (Kunst-Werke; p65). Nearby is the **ME Collectors Room** (Auguststrasse 68, Mitte, www.me-berlin.com), a private museum showing off Berlin collector Thomas Olbricht's collection of contemporary art. And further down, you'll come to the **Jüdische Mädchenschule** building (Auguststrasse 11-13, Mitte, www.maedchenschule.org), home now to the Michael Fuchs and CWC galleries. The building also houses the Pauly Saal bar and restaurant – a Michelin-starred dining spot. If you fancy something a little more down-and-dirty, the excellent **Mogg & Melzer** (p61) Jewish restaurant serves up the hugest, juiciest salt-beef sandwiches this side of Lower Manhattan.

9PM Mitte's nightlife isn't for the faint-hearted, but if you're up for dingy, shabby bars and pubs full of music, noise, eccentric locals and noisy artists, Torstrasse's mile of bars and clubs is the place to end the night in a haze of cocktails and dancing. Try the **Neues Odessa Bar** (p79) or the newer **Chelsea Bar** (p63). If you fancy rubbing shoulders with the locals in a cosier environment, the tiny **Lois** bar (Linienstrasse 60, Mitte) is an old favourite with Mitte-ites looking for wine, low lights and long summer evenings at the pavement tables.

the shape of the **Fernsehturm** TV tower (p58), completed in 1969. It's worth braving the queues for a ride up to the observation deck and a coffee in the revolving café.

4PM Mitte's classy boutiques attract fashionistas from around the world to the area around Mulackstrasse and Alte Schönhauser Strasse, a ten-minute walk from Alexanderplatz. **Starstyling Berlin** (Mulackstrasse 4,

Mitte, www.starstyling.net) is bright, colourful and chic; **Lala Berlin** (p66) delivers cutting-edge French couture; **C'est Tout** (Mulackstrasse 26, Mitte, www.cesttout.de) is a popular Berlin brand; and **Filippa K** (Alte Schönhauser Strasse 11, Mitte, www.filippa-k.com) is famed for its clean Scandinavian cuts. Among the boutiques are pop-up outlets and flagship stores from the likes of Hugo Boss and Fred Perry.

Diary

Your guide to what's happening when.

There's hardly a day in the year when there isn't some sort of do on in Berlin – whether it's the twice-yearly fashion week, the rowdy May Day Riots (Kreuzberg's very own rite of spring), the flag-waving public holiday commemorating German reunification or Lange Nacht der Museen, which sees museums and exhibitions stay open into the small hours. Music festivals are particularly numerous, covering everything from early music to the latest avant-garde creations, and from pop to jazz. In summer, the Karneval der Kulturen and the Christopher Street Day Parade celebrate the city's cultural diversity, while the prestigious Berlin International Film Festival, or Berlinale, sprinkles a little stardust over the wintry city each February.

Above: **Karneval der Kulturen**.
Below: **Gallery Weekend**.

Spring

MaerzMusik – Festival für aktuelle Musik
Various venues (254 890, www.berlinerfestspiele.de). **Date** late Mar.
A holdover from the more culture-conscious days of the old East Germany, this ten-day contemporary music festival invites international avant-garde composers and musicians to present new works.

Gallery Weekend
Various venues (2844 4387, www.gallery-weekend-berlin.de). **Date** late Apr.
Around 40 galleries time their openings for the last weekend in April, making for an arty extravaganza attended by leading dealers and ordinary art-lovers.

May Day Riots
Around Kottbusser Tor, Kreuzberg. *U8, U12 Kottbusser Tor.* **Date** 1 May.
An annual event since 1987, when Autonomen engaged in violent clashes with police. The riots have quietened in recent years, but Kreuzberg is still lively on May Day. There are lots of street parties and music as well as protests.

Theatertreffen Berlin
Various venues (254 890, www.berlinerfestspiele.de). **Date** May.
A jury picks out ten of the most innovative and controversial new theatre productions from companies across Germany, Austria and Switzerland, and the winners come to Berlin to perform their pieces over two weeks in May.

Deutschland Pokal-Endspiele
Information & tickets: Deutscher Fussball-Bund (tickets@dfb.de). Venue: Olympiastadion, Olympischer Platz 3, Charlottenburg (300 633). U12 Olympia-Stadion or S5 Olympiastadion. **Date** late May.
The domestic football cup final has been taking place at the Olympiastadion every year since 1985. It regularly attracts some 65,000 fans, and tickets are very hard to come by.

Karneval der Kulturen
Kreuzberg (6097 7022, www.karneval-berlin.de). **Date** May/June.
Inspired by London's Notting Hill Carnival and intended as a celebration of Berlin's ethnic and cultural diversity, this long holiday weekend (always Pentecost) centres on a 'multi-kulti' parade (on the Sunday) involving dozens of floats, hundreds of musicians and thousands of spectators.

ILA Berlin Air Show
Berlin ExpoCenter Airport, Messestrasse 1, Schönefeld (3038 2014, www.ila-berlin.de). S9, S45 Flughafen Berlin-Schönefeld, or bus 742. **Date** late May/early June.

Berlin Philharmonie
at the Waldbühne.

This popular biennial event – the next is in 2016 – is held over six days at Schönefeld airport. It features around 1,000 exhibitors from 40 countries, with aircraft of all kinds, and a serious focus on space travel.

Summer

Berlin Philharmonie at the Waldbühne
Waldbühne, Am Glockenturm, Charlottenburg (administration 8107 5230, box office 0180 533 2433, www.berliner-philharmoniker.de). S5 Pichelsberg then shuttle bus. **Tickets** €23 €75. **Date** June/July.
The Philharmonie ends its season with an open-air concert that sells out months in advance. Over 20,000 Berliners light the atmospheric 'forest theatre' with candles once darkness falls.

Deutsch-Französisches Volksfest
Zentraler Festplatz, Kurt-Schumacher-Damm, Reinickendorf (213 3290, www.deutsch-franzoesisches-volksfest.de). U6 Kurt-Schumacher-Platz. **Tickets** €2; free under-14s. **Date** mid June-mid July.
A survivor from the days when this area was the French Sector, the month-long German-French Festival offers fairground rides, French music and cuisine, and Bastille Day fireworks.

Fête de la Musique
Various venues (4171 5289, www.fetedela musique.de). **Date** 21 June.
A regular summer solstice happening since 1995, this music extravaganza of bands and DJs takes place across the city. The selection is mixed, with everything from heavy metal to *schlager*.

Lesbisch-Schwules Stadtfest
Nollendorfplatz & Motzstrasse, Schöneberg (2147 3586, www.regenbogenfonds.de). U3, U4, U12 Nollendorfplatz. **Date** late June.

Silvester. *See p30.*

The Lesbian & Gay Street Fair takes over Schöneberg every year, filling several blocks in West Berlin's gay quarter. Participating bars, clubs, food stands and musical acts make this a dizzying, non-stop event that also serves as a kick-off for the following week's Christopher Street Day Parade (*see below*).

Christopher Street Day Parade
2362 8632, www.csd-berlin.de. **Date** Sat in late June.
Originally organised to commemorate the 1969 riots outside the Stonewall Bar on Christopher Street in New York, this fun and flamboyant parade has become one of the summer's most enjoyable and inclusive street parties, attracting straights as well as gays. Check the website for details of the route.

Berlin Fashion Week
Various venues (399 800, www.fashion-week-berlin.com). **Date** early July & late Jan.
OK, so it's not quite Paris. But Berlin's twice-yearly style shindig is slowly being taken a little more seriously. Bread & Butter, an international trade fair for streetwear and urbanwear, takes place at the same time in the former Tempelhof airport. There's a late-night shopping night and plenty of parties too.

Classic Open Air
Gendarmenmarkt, Mitte (3157 5413, www.
classicopenair.de). U6 Französische Strasse.
Tickets €39-€102. **Date** early July.
Big names usually open this concert series held over
five days in one of Berlin's most beautiful squares.

Deutsch-Amerikanisches Volksfest
Heidestrasse 30, Tiergarten (0163 390 0930,
www.deutsch-amerikanisches-volksfest.de).
U6 Reinickendorferstrasse or U55, S5, S7, S75
Hauptbahnhof, then shuttle bus. **Tickets** €2;
free under-14s. **Date** July/Aug.
Established by the US forces stationed in West
Berlin, the German-American Festival lasts about
three weeks and offers a tacky but popular mix of
carnival rides, cowboys doing lasso tricks, candy
floss, hot dogs and Yankee beer.

Tanz im August
Various venues (2590 0427, www.tanzimaugust.de).
Tickets €15-€35. **Date** Aug.
This three-week event is Germany's leading modern
dance festival, with big-name participants.

Internationales Berliner Bierfestival
Karl-Marx-Allee, from Strausberger Platz to
Frankfurter Tor, Friedrichshain (6576 3560,
www.bierfestival-berlin.de). U5 Frankfurter Tor.
Admission free. **Date** Aug.
Describing itself as 'the world's longest beer garden'
and nearly 20 years old, this two-dayer showcases
hundreds of beers from over 80 countries, bringing
conviviality to the city's premier Stalinist boulevard.

Young.euro.classic
Konzerthaus, Gendarmenmarkt 2, Mitte
(0180 556 8100, www.young-euro-classic.de).
U6 Französische Strasse. **Tickets** €12. **Date** Aug.
This summer concert programme brings together
youth orchestras from around Europe for two weeks.

Lange Nacht der Museen
Various venues (2474 9888, www.lange-nacht-
der-museen.de). **Tickets** €18; €12 reductions.
Date last Sat in Aug.
Around 100 museums, collections, archives and
exhibition halls stay open into the early hours of the
morning, with special events, concerts, readings, lectures and performances. A ticket gets you free travel
on special shuttle buses and regular public transport.

Autumn

Musikfest Berlin
Various venues (254 890, www.berlinerfestspiele.de).
Date Sept.
This major classical music festival, held over the
space of three weeks, presents more than 70 works
by 25 composers. Orchestras, instrumental and vocal

ensembles, and numerous soloists take part, with
many from abroad (Sweden, Denmark, Israel, the UK
and the States in recent years).

Internationales Literaturfestival Berlin
Various venues (2787 8620, www.literatur
festival.com). **Date** Sept.
A major literary event, with readings, symposiums
and discussions over ten days, drawing well-known
authors and rising stars from around the world.

Berlin Marathon
Throughout the city (www.bmw-berlin-marathon.
com). **Date** last Sun in Sept.

PUBLIC HOLIDAYS

On public holidays (*feiertagen*) it can
be difficult to get things done in Berlin.
However, most cafés, bars and restaurants
stay open – except on Christmas Eve,
when almost everything closes.

New Year's Day
1 Jan

Good Friday
Mar/Apr

Easter Monday
Mar/Apr

May Day
1 May

Ascension Day
May/June

Whit Monday
May/June

Day of German Unity
3 Oct

Day of Prayer &
National Repentance
3rd Wed in Nov

Christmas Eve
24 Dec

Christmas Day
25 Dec

Boxing Day
26 Dec

Fewer than 300 people took part in the inaugural Berlin Marathon in 1974; now, it's one of the biggest and most popular road races in the world with more than 40,000 runners, plus a million spectators lining the route to cheer them on.

Tag der deutschen Einheit
Date 3 Oct.
The Day of German Unity is a public holiday commemorating the day two Germanies became one, back in 1990. Head to the Brandenburg Gate to join the party.

Festival of Lights
Various venues (www.festival-of-lights.de/en). **Date** mid Oct.
Berlin's world-famous sights and monuments (most are situated in the city centre) become the canvas for spectacular light and video projections. The illuminations are switched on at 7pm nightly.

JazzFest Berlin
Various venues (254 890, www.berlinerfestspiele.de). **Date** 1st wknd in Nov.
A wide range of jazz from an array of internationally renowned artists, and a fixture since 1964. The concurrent Fringe Jazz Festival (organised by JazzRadio) showcases less established acts.

Berliner Märchentage
Various venues (2809 3603, www.berliner-maerchentage.de). **Date** Nov.
The fortnight-long Berlin Fairytale Festival celebrates tales from around the world with some 400 storytelling and music events in a carnival atmosphere. The theme varies each year: in 2014 (the festival's 25th anniversary), it was stories from the UK; in 2015, Arabian fairy tales.

Festival of Lights.

Winter

Christmas Markets
Kaiser-Wilhelm-Gedächtniskirche, Breitscheidplatz, Charlottenburg (213 3290, www.weihnachtsmarkt-deutschland.de). U9, U12, S5, S7, S75 Zoologischer Garten. **Open** 11am-10pm daily. **Date** Dec.
Traditional markets spring up across Berlin during the Christmas season, offering toys, mulled wine and gingerbread. This is one of the biggest.

Berliner Silvesterlauf
Grunewald (3012 8820, www.berliner-silvesterlauf.de). S5 Messe Süd. **Date** 31 Dec.
A Berlin tradition for decades, the New Year's Eve Run starts off in Grunewald at the intersection of Waldschulallee and Harbigstrasse.

Silvester
Date 31 Dec.
Given Berliners' enthusiasm for tossing firecrackers out of windows, New Year's Eve is always going to be vivid, noisy and hazardous. Thousands celebrate at the Brandenburger Tor. Thousands more trek up to the Teufelsberg at the northern tip of Grunewald or the Viktoriapark in Kreuzberg to watch the fireworks across the city. *Photo p28.*

Grüne Woche
Messegelände am Funkturm, Messedamm 22, Charlottenburg (3038 2267, www.gruenewoche.de). U12 Kaiserdamm, or S5 Messe Süd, or S41, S42, S46 Messe Nord. **Tickets** €12. **Date** Jan.
Dedicated to food, agriculture and horticulture, the best thing about this ten-day show is the opportunity to eat and drink from the far corners of Germany and across the planet.

Ultraschall Berlin – Festival für Neue Musik
Various venues (ultraschallberlin.de). **Tickets** €15-€18; €70 festival pass. **Date** mid Jan.
Ultrasound Berlin focuses on new music played in high-profile venues by some of the world's leading specialist ensembles. Concerts are broadcast live, and there are talks by composers and other events.

Transmediale
Haus der Kulturen der Welt, John-Foster-Dulles-Allee 10, Tiergarten (2474 9761, www.transmediale.de). U55, S5, S7, S75 Hauptbahnhof. **Date** late Jan/early Feb.
One of the world's largest international festivals for media art and digital culture, with exhibitions and screenings from artists working in video, TV, computer animation, internet and other visual media.

Berlin International Film Festival
Various venues (259 200, www.berlinale.de). **Tickets** €7-€16; €100 festival pass. **Date** mid Feb.
See p31 **Hurrah for Berlinale.**

HURRAH FOR BERLINALE

One of the world's most influential – and most enjoyable – film festivals.

For more than 60 years, the **Berlin International Film Festival** (Internationale Filmfestspiele Berlin; *see p30*) has been the city's biggest cultural event, as well as one of the world's three most prominent film festivals. Born out of the Cold War, it developed from a propaganda showcase, supported by the Allies, into a genuine meeting place – and frequent collision point – for East and West. Whether it was the 1959 French boycott over Stanley Kubrick's indictment of war, *Paths of Glory*, the jury revolt over the pro-Vietnamese film *OK* in 1970 or the 1979 Eastern Bloc walkout over the depiction of Vietnamese people in *The Deer Hunter*, the festival's drama was never confined to the screens. The years following the fall of the Berlin Wall were particularly exciting: the mood and energy of the festival reflected the joy and chaos of the changing city.

Now settled comfortably into Potsdamer Platz, the festival has taken on more of the glamour and celebrity of its two major rivals, Cannes and Venice. At the same time, festival director Dieter Kosslick has concentrated on creating a more open and energetic atmosphere to the proceedings.

What remains the same, however, is the chance to see arguably the widest and most eclectic mix of any film festival anywhere. Every February, it seems like the entire city turns out to see hundreds of films, presented in eight sections, the most important of which are as follows:

International Competition

Recent years have seen a rise in star attendance. The downside to this is that the selection is becoming more conservative. Concentrating on big-budget productions from all over the world, with a heavy (and often heavily criticised) accent on the US, these films often make it to general release. Entries compete for the Gold and Silver Bears, announced at the closing night gala.

International Forum of Young Cinema

Some devotees claim this is the real Berlin festival, the place where discoveries are made. Born out of the revolt that dissolved the Competition in 1970, the Forum provides challenging and eclectic fare that you won't see elsewhere.

Panorama

Originally intended to showcase films that fell outside the guidelines of the Competition, Panorama shines a spotlight on world independent movies, gay and lesbian works and political films.

Perspektive Deutsches Kino

Perspektive reflects the festival's increased focus on the latest in German cinema. The newest of the festival's sections, it has emerged as a big audience favourite, helped by the fact that all films are shown with English subtitles. If you think German cinema has a bad rep, this is where to break down the stereotypes.

Retrospective

Perhaps the festival's best bet for sheer moviegoing pleasure. The Retrospective often concentrates on the mainstream, but it's an opportunity to experience classics and rarities on the big screen. Themes have ranged from great directors such as Louis Buñuel, Fritz Lang and William Wyler, to subjects such as 1950s glamour girls, production design, Hollywood mavericks and even Nazi entertainment films.

Buying tickets

Tickets can be bought up to three days in advance (four days for Competition repeats) at the main ticket office in the Potsdamer Platz Arkaden (Alte Potsdamer Strasse, Tiergarten, 259 2000), and at Kino International and Urania. Tickets are also available for online booking. On the day of performance, they must be bought at the theatre box office; last-minute tickets are often available. Queues for advance tickets can be long and online tickets can go fast, so plan well ahead.

Films are usually shown three times. Prices range from €8 to €20. From January onwards, check for updates and programme information at www.berlinale.de.

Berlin's Best

Get to the heart of the city with our selection of highlights.

Sightseeing

BERLIN LANDMARKS
Brandenburger Tor p40
Berlin's long-suffering victory arch.
Fernsehturm p58
Looming over Alexanderplatz is this symbol of Soviet-era technology.
Olympiastadion p120
The site of the infamous 1936 Olympics.
Reichstag p98
The German parliament, renovated and updated for the 21st century.
Schloss Charlottenburg p121
Historic royal palace with gorgeous gardens.

WAR MEMORIALS
Denkmal für die ermordeten Juden Europas p48
Stunning Holocaust memorial in the city centre.
Gruselkabinett p142
A World War II bunker recast as a fairground house of horror.
Kaiser-Wilhelm-Gedächtnis-Kirche p114
A jagged, broken spire, damaged in World War II.
Siegessäule p99
Magnificent monument to Prussian military victories.
Sowjetisches Ehrenmal am Treptower Park p145
Awe-inspiring Soviet war memorial.

Fernsehturm.

Topographie des Terrors p143
Subterranean former
command centre of the
Nazi state police.

LIFE IN THE DDR
DDR Museum p56
From Trabants to covert
surveillance, in an interactive
family museum.
East Side Gallery p84
Graffiti-clad riverside
stretch of the Berlin Wall.
**Forschungs- und
Gedenkstätte
Normannenstrasse
(Stasi Museum)** p92
Former police HQ of the
notorious Stasi regime.
**Gedenkstätte Berlin-
Hohenschönhausen** p92
Take a guided tour of this
Stasi internment camp.
**Haus am Checkpoint
Charlie** p142
Museum at the world-famous
border crossing.

CITY MUSEUMS
**Deutsches Historisches
Museum** p49
Germany from 100 BC
to the present day.
**Deutsches Technikmuseum
Berlin** p142
Triumphs of German
engineering.
Jüdisches Museum p142
A dynamic journey through
Jewish culture, society
and history.
Märkisches Museum p58
Whirl through the turbulent
history of Berlin.
Museum für Naturkunde p50
Natural history wonders
and lots of dinosaurs.
Neues Museum p50
The home of the famed bust
of Nefertiti, and much more.
Pergamonmuseum p50
The Ishtar Gate and artefacts
from across the Hellenic and
Islamic worlds.

Eating & drinking

GERMAN/AUSTRIAN
Austria p138
The best wiener schnitzel
in the city, say locals.
Café Einstein p105
A slice of Berlin history
right on your plate.
Florian p116
Old-fashioned bistro
serving quality southern
German cooking.
Gugelhof p76
Alsatian specialities in
gargantuan portions.
Henne p132
Serving their sole dish of
chicken for over a century.
Mutzenbacher p88
Hipsterish twists on
Austrian classic dishes.
Schwarzer Hahn p88
Regional German cuisine.
Spätzle & Knödel p89
The depth and diversity of
Bavarian noodle culture.

SMALL AND QUIRKY
Il Casolare p132
Grumpy waiters, punk-
rock flyers on the walls,
superlative pizzas.
Dottir p51
Icelandic-inspired cooking
at one of the city's newest
culinary gems.
Imren Grill p150
The finest kebabs
in a city of döners.
Konnopke's Imbiss p77
Berlin's most venerable
sausage stand.
Mogg & Melzer p61
New York-style pastrami
and matzo ball soup in
arty surroundings.

ASIAN EATS
Kimchi Princess p133
Korean delights in a
wonderfully kitsch spot.

Schloss Charlottenburg. *See p32.*

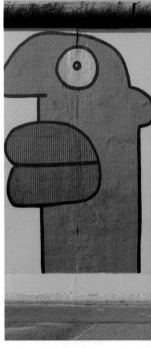

Monsieur Vuong p61
Insanely popular Mitte
noodle house.
Sasaya p77
Japanese restaurant with
high-quality fresh fish.
Si An p78
Stylish Vietnamese
noodles.

BLOWOUTS
Borchardt p51
Distinguished dining in a
historic Mitte institution.
Hugos p106
Michelin-starred
opulence in this wonderfully
decadent restaurant.
**Les Solistes by Pierre
Gagnaire** p117
The legendary chef's
Berlin outpost serving
seasonal French
haute cuisine.
Weinbar Rutz p52
Middle European
contemporary classics
from Michelin-starred
chef Marco Müller.

Shopping

UNIQUELY BERLIN
**Ampelmann Galerie
Shop** p64
Get your own little green
and red men.
**Erich Hamann Bittere
Schokoladen** p123
Berlin's oldest
chocolate factory.
KaDeWe p118
Still the city's luxury
department store.
RSVP p66
A blissful oasis of
old-school stationery.
Taschen p119
The flagship store from the
Berlin-based publishers.
Weichardt Brot p123
Get your biodynamic Berlin
bloomers and cakes here.

FASHION
DSTM p65
Slinky black leather designs
from Canadian-born
designer Jen Gilpin.

LaLa Berlin p66
Fashionistas worldwide
covet Leyla Piedayesh's
knitwear designs.
Mykita p66
Berlin's home-grown
sunglasses brand is
a global success story.
Shusta p66
Heaven for shoe-nerds.

Nightlife

DIVE BARS
8MM p78
Scuzzy indie-rock stalwart
in Prenzlauer Berg.
Barbie Deinhoff's p134
Small, neon gay/trannie bar.
Chelsea Bar p63
One of the newest
additions to the sleazy
Torstrasse strip.
Kingsize p63
Tiny and always rammed.

East Side Gallery. *See p33.*

Schwarze Traube.

Neue Odessa Bar p79
Hipster central, and
some ace cocktails.
Supamolly p89
The famous punk-era
watering hole soldiers on.

BERLIN FAVES
Green Door p125
Actor and musician
Fritz Müller's legendary
cocktail spot.
Lebensstern p107
Notoriously, Quentin
Tarantino's favourite
Berlin bar.
Luzia p135
The perfect spot for
a drink with friends at
any time.
Paris Bar p116
An art-lover's paradise.
Schwarze Traube p135
Founded and run by
an award-winning
cocktail magician.

Tausend p64
The daddy of Berlin's
elegant nightspots.
Würgeengel p136
A fixture on the Berlin
scene: old-school
atmosphere and fab drinks.

Art

KEY INSTITUTIONS
Alte Nationalgalerie p47
Neoclassical, Romantic,
Biedermeier and
Impressionist works
on Museum Island.
Berlinische Galerie p141
An appealingly angular
building with modern art,
photography and architecture.
Gemäldegalerie p104
Superb Dutch and Flemish
work in this museum of
European art from the
13th to 18th centuries.

**Hamburger Bahnhof –
Museum für Gegenwart** p49
Star exhibitions and a
permanent collection of
work by Joseph Beuys.
**Haus der Kulturen
der Welt** p98
Global arts, music, dance
and theatre.

CONTEMPORARY ART
Alexander Levy p144
An emphasis on emerging
and idiosyncratic artists.
**Contemporary Fine
Arts** p52
A mix of edgier younger names
and well-known German and
European artists.
**C/O Berlin Amerika
Haus** p114
The revived C/O photography
gallery's new outpost.
Johann König p144
Leading Berlin gallerist
with a diverse and
challenging programme.
**KW Institute for
Contemporary Art** p65
The epicentre of the Berlin
contemporary art scene.
Peres Projects p90
Some of the most controversial
and must-see shows in Berlin.
Sprüth Magers p67
Vast gallery space of
local and international
names to watch.

Explore

Mitte

Historically, the centre, Mitte – meaning 'middle' – floundered in a no-man's-land between East and West. But now, as extensive construction continues apace, Mitte is right back in the swing of things. It contains many of Berlin's biggest sights: the Brandenburg Gate (Brandenburger Tor), the TV Tower (Fernsehturm) and the magnificent UNESCO World Heritage Site of Museum Island (Museumsinsel), which is in the midst of an epic overhaul, scheduled to be fully completed in 2025. But there's much more to this area than ticking off the sights – galleries abound, as do cool shops. As for nightlife, take your pick from fine dining at the likes of Borchardt and Grill Royal to the bar scene that stretches down Torstrasse, and the late-night kebab mecca of Rosenthalerplatz.

Denkmal für die ermordeten Juden Europas.

Don't Miss

1 Brandenburger Tor Berlin's long-suffering victory arch now back to its former glory (p40).

2 Grill Royal Meat and people-watching *par excellence* at this city institution (p52).

3 Denkmal für die ermordeten Juden Europas This sea of standing stones serves as a graphic memorial to the Holocaust (p48).

4 Neues Museum View Nefertiti's bust in this neoclassical museum restored by David Chipperfield (p50).

5 Departmentstore Quartier 206 Splurge in an art deco-tiled luxury department store (p52).

HISTORIC MITTE

From before the domination of the Hohenzollerns through to the Weimar Republic, and from the Third Reich to the GDR, the entire history of Berlin can be found on or around the celebrated street of **Unter den Linden**. Originally laid out to connect the town centre with the king's hunting grounds of Tiergarten and running east from the Brandenburger Tor to Museumsinsel, the street got its name from the *Linden* (lime trees) that shaded its central walkway. Hitler, concerned that the trees obscured the view of his parades, had them felled, but they were later replanted.

During the 18th and 19th centuries, the Hohenzollerns erected baroque and neoclassical buildings along their capital's showcase street. The side streets were laid out in a grid by Great Elector Friedrich Wilhelm for his Friedrichstadt district. It was primarily a residential street for nobles' palaces until German reunification in 1871, when it was transformed into a bustling commercial avenue befitting Berlin's new status as a *Weltstadt*. By the 1900s, contemporary commentators were already comparing it to Paris for its decadent nightlife scene – including its rampant sex trade.

Brandenburger Tor & Pariser Platz

The focal point of Unter den Linden's western end is the **Brandenburger Tor** (Brandenburg Gate). Constructed in 1791, and designed by Carl Gotthard Langhans after the Propylaea gateway into ancient Athens, the gate was built as a triumphal arch celebrating Prussia's capital city. It was initially called the Friedenstor (Gate of Peace) and is the only city gate remaining from Berlin's original 18. (Today, only a few U-Bahn station names recall the other city gates, such as Frankfurter Tor or Schlesisches Tor).

The **Quadriga** statue, a four-horse chariot driven by Victory and designed by Johann Gottfried Schadow, sits on top of the gate. It has had an eventful life. When Napoleon conquered Berlin in 1806, he carted the Quadriga off to Paris and held it hostage until his defeat in 1814. The Tor was badly damaged during World War II and, during subsequent renovations, the GDR removed the Prussian Iron Cross and turned the Quadriga around so that the chariot faced west. The current Quadriga is actually a 1958 copy of the 18th-century original, and was stranded in no-man's-land for 30 years. It saw further repair after some overly exuberant youths climbed up on the Tor to celebrate the fall of the Wall. The Iron Cross was replaced and the Quadriga was turned back to face into Mitte again.

West of the gate stretches the vast expanse of the **Tiergarten** (*see p96*), Berlin's central park. Just to the north is the phoenix-like Reichstag, while ten minutes' walk south is the even more dramatically reconceived **Potsdamer Platz** complex.

Immediately east of the Brandenburger Tor is **Pariser Platz**, which was given its name in 1814 when Prussia and its allies conquered Paris. This square, enclosed by embassies and bank buildings, was once seen as Berlin's *Empfangssaal* – its reception room. Foreign dignitaries would ceremoniously pass through on their way to visit tyrants and dictators in their palaces, and today this remains the area where you'll still see enormous limos carting around politicians and diplomats. In 1993, it was decided the Tor looked a little exposed, so plans were drawn up to revive Pariser Platz, with new buildings on the same scale as the old ones, featuring conservative exteriors and contemporary interiors. Some old faces are back on the historical sites they occupied before World War II: the reconstructed **Adlon** hotel (*see p265*) is now at its old address, as is the **British Embassy**, around the corner at Wilhelmstrasse 70-71.

On the south-west corner of the square – the last building to complete the Pariser Platz puzzle – is the underwhelming **US Embassy**. Since a return to its old address was announced in 1993, construction was delayed first by budgetary miscalculation, then by various problems attendant on new US State Department regulations stipulating a minimum 30-metre (98-foot) security zone around US embassies. The design was adjusted, streets were moved, and America is now securely back on the block. Meanwhile, Wilhelmstrasse is closed to traffic for a block south of the square because of security provisions for the British Embassy.

While outwardly conforming to aesthetic restrictions, many of the straightforward exteriors front flights of fancy within. Frank Gehry's **DG Bank** at no.3 has a huge, biomorphic interior dome hidden behind its regular façade. The **Dresdner Bank** opposite is virtually hollow, thanks to another interior atrium. Next door, Christian de Portzamparc's **French Embassy** features a space-saving 'vertical garden' on the courtyard wall, and 'french windows' extending over two storeys.

Directly to the south of Pariser Platz is the vast **Denkmal für die ermordeten Juden Europas** (Memorial to the Murdered Jews of Europe). Designed by Peter Eisenmann (from an original plan with sculptor Richard Serra), it's a city-block-size field of concrete slabs, arranged in rows but sloping in different directions on uneven ground. Conceived in 1993, the project became mired in controversy. The winning design of the initial competition was rejected by then Chancellor Kohl, and there was no end of argument over the second competition,

REMEMBER, REMEMBER

There are many victims to memorialise.

Nowhere is the vexed question of Germany's relationship to its past dramatised more intensely than in the startling proliferation of memorials at the heart of Berlin.

The centrepiece, of course, is the memorial to Jewish Holocaust victims – the **Denkmal für die ermordeten Juden Europas** (*see p48*). No debate about the intersection of history, architecture and the form of Berlin's reunified cityscape lumbered on so long or conjured so much controversy as the one that engendered this grid of concrete blocks. The idea of some kind of central memorial had been around since the 1980s opening on the site of the Gestapo headquarters of what is now the **Topographie des Terrors** (*see p143*).

In 1993, the **Neue Wache** (*see p44*), a memorial to the 'victims of fascism and militarism' under the Communists, was recast as one to the 'victims of war and violent rule'. This involved installing an enlarged replica of Käthe Kollwitz's statue, *Mother with Dead Son*. There were immediate protests that this put murdered victims on the same level as dead perpetrators, and memorialised them in a form contrary to Jewish tradition. Chancellor Kohl then promised that a memorial would be erected solely for Jewish victims of the Holocaust.

The winning design of a 1995 competition was a concrete slab the size of two football fields, bearing the names of all 4.2 million identified Holocaust victims. But the cliché of equating the enormity of the crime with the size of the memorial was widely criticised. Kohl rejected the design. A second competition in 1998 produced a design by Peter Eisenmann and Richard Serra (who pulled out for personal reasons) involving 4,000 columns – what eventually got built is a scaled-down version.

Meanwhile, representatives of other persecuted groups – Gypsies, gays, the mentally or physically disabled, prisoners of war, political prisoners, forced labourers and blacks – all pointed to the inadequacy of a memorial for Jewish victims alone. Roma groups argued that the extermination of their people should not be separated from that of the Jews, but then refused to share a memorial with homosexuals. In 2008, a memorial to gay victims of the Nazis, **Denkmal für die im Nationalsozialismus verfolgten Homosexuellen**, designed by Michael Elmgreen and Ingar Dragset, was

Topographie des Terrors

unveiled on the edge of the Tiergarten. It's a lone concrete slab and includes a small window through which a video of two men kissing can be viewed. After criticism by lesbian groups, this will now be rotated every two years with a video of two women.

Disagreements between Roma groups, meanwhile, have delayed construction of a memorial to Gypsy victims of the Nazis. The fountain by Israeli memorial specialist Dani Karavan will be sited on the corner of the Tiergarten closest to the Reichstag, just behind an impromptu memorial to people killed going over the Wall, and not far from the **Sowjetisches Ehrenmal** (Soviet War Memorial; *see p96*). And on another corner of the Tiergarten, in the parking area behind the Philharmonie, is a memorial to the mentally and physically disabled victims of the Nazis' T4 euthanasia programme.

There's more to come. Currently under discussion are memorials for those who died during the expulsion of Germans from Poland and Czechoslovakia after World War II, for those who were persecuted for deserting the German army and for those who died while serving in the Bundeswehr. And conservatives are now asking for a memorial plaque to the victims of 1970s terrorist group, the RAF (aka the Baader-Meinhof gang).

Keen for something positive to stand in this increasingly baleful landscape, the latest idea is a 'Monument to Germany's Liberty and Unity' – an interactive 'site of joy' that will celebrate German unity. In 2011, Berlin finally settled on an unusual design – a 55-metre (180-foot), dish-shaped see-saw that can hold up to 1,400 people at any one time. Called *Bürger in Bewegung* (*Citizens in Motion*), it is due to be built on the site of the old GDR parliament building on Schloss Platz.

EXPLORE

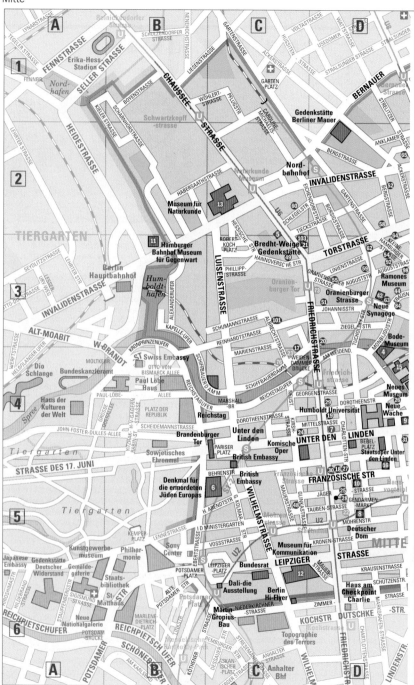

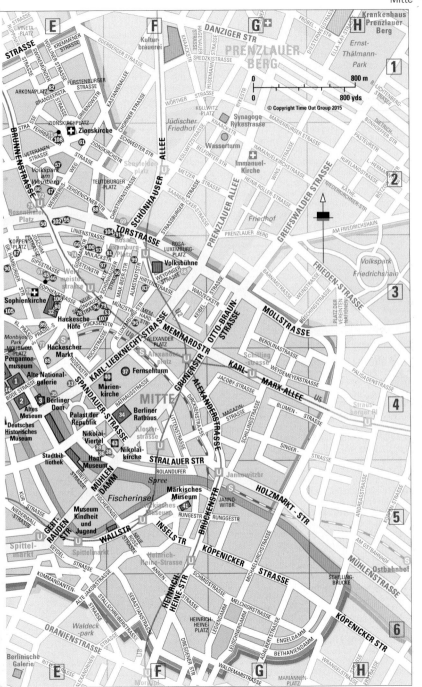

including rows over location (the chosen site has no particular link to the Holocaust), function (should such a monument draw a line under history or seek to stimulate debate and discussion?), delivery (one of the companies involved in construction was subsequently removed due to links with Degesch, wartime Zyklon B producers) and content (many feel the memorial should honour all victims of the Holocaust, not only Jewish ones).

In the wake of this memorial, assorted other victim memorials have been built or are planned (*see p41* **Remember, Remember**). The first has already appeared on the other side of Ebertstrasse: Elmgreen and Dragset's **Denkmal für die im Nationalsozialismus verfolgten Homosexuellen** (Monument to the Homosexuals Persecuted During National Socialism). It looks like one of the slabs from the Jewish Denkmal, but contains a video installation.

Between the Denkmal and the Leipziger Platz/Potsdamer Platz complex is an area filled with representations from Germany's various *Länder*. If you want to visit the site of Hitler's World War II bunker, head to the car park on the corner of In den Ministergärten and Gertrud-Kolmar-Strasse. There is nothing to see there these days other than an information board detailing in English and German the history of the Führerbunker, but it's chilling nonetheless.

East along Unter den Linden

Heading east along Unter den Linden, passing the 1950s Stalinist wedding cake-style **Russian Embassy** on your right, and, on the next block, the box office of the **Komische Oper** (*see p202*), you'll reach the crossroads with Friedrichstrasse, once a café-strewn focus of Weimar Berlin.

On the other side of the junction, on the right, housed in the ground floor of a 1920s building that's now occupied by Deutsche Bank, is the **KunstHalle**, displaying items from the bank's massive collection. Facing the art gallery across Unter den Linden stands the **Staatsbibliotek** (open to all, and there's a small café), usually filled with students from the **Humboldt-Universität**. The university's grand old façade has been restored, as have the two statues of the Humboldts (founder Wilhelm and his brother Alexander), between which booksellers set up tables in good weather.

Across the street is **Bebelplatz**, site of the notorious Nazi book-burning, commemorated by Micha Ullmann's subterranean monument set into the Platz itself. The glass has become pretty scratched, unfortunately, and it can be hard to see through. Dominating the square's eastern side is the **Staatsoper** (*see p202*), built in neoclassical style by Georg Wenzeslaus von Knobelsdorff in 1741-43. The present building

closed for extensive renovations in autumn 2010 and is, unsurprisingly, behind schedule and over budget, with an optimistic reopening date of 2015. Meanwhile, the company is squatting at the Schiller Theatre in Charlottenburg, ironically just down the road from its big west Berlin rival, the Deutsche Oper.

Just south of the Staatsoper (and also designed by Knobelsdorff, in 1747) is **Sankt-Hedwigs-Kathedrale**, a curious circular Roman Catholic church, inspired by the Pantheon in Rome. A minute's walk east of here is another church, **Friedrichswerdersche Kirche**. This imposing brick structure, which was designed by Karl Friedrich Schinkel, was completed in 1831. It was badly damaged in World War II, but reopened in the late 1980s as a homage to its architect. Structural problems meant it closed again in 2012 – and remains shut. Across the Schinkelplatz lies the **Bauakademie**, or at least plastic sheeting picturing it – the architect's proto-modernist School of Architecture was demolished for a GDR ministry, but is now being lobbied for reconstruction.

On the west side of Bebelplatz is Rocco Forte's **Hotel de Rome** (*see p266*), occupying what used to be the East German central bank, and the late 18th-century **Alte Bibliotek**. Alongside that, in the centre of Unter den Linden, stands a restored equestrian statue of Frederick the Great.

On the north side of Unter den Linden, the **Neue Wache** (New Guardhouse), constructed by Schinkel in 1816 18, originally served as a guardhouse for the royal residences in the area. Today, it is a hauntingly plain memorial to the 'victims of war and tyranny', with an enlarged reproduction of a Käthe Kollwitz sculpture, *Mother with Dead Son*, at its centre. Beneath this are the remains of an unknown soldier and an unknown concentration camp victim, surrounded by earth from World War II battlefields and concentration camps.

Next to it, to the east, is the Baroque **Zeughaus**, a former armoury with a deceptively peaceful pink façade. Following renovations that were completed in 2006, it once again houses the **Deutsches Historisches Museum**. The new wing by IM Pei hosts changing exhibitions and has a fine café.

This whole last eastern stretch of Unter den Linden is supposed to undergo further heritage restoration, in line with the eventual rebuilding of the nearby Stadtschloss by the Italian architect Frank Stella.

Museumsinsel

The eastern end of Unter den Linden abuts the island in the Spree where Berlin was 'born' and the site of the original town, Cölln. The northern part, with its excellent collection of museums and

Deutsches Historisches Museum. See p49

galleries, is known as Museumsinsel (Museum Island), while the southern half (much enlarged by landfill), once a neighbourhood for the city's fishermen (and known as Fischerinsel), is now dominated by a clutch of grim tower blocks.

The five Museumsinsel museums (the Pergamonmuseum, Altes Museum, Alte Nationalgalerie, Bode-Museum and Neues Museum) are all now open after undergoing a massive restoration programme, though works are set to continue for some years yet. Such is the importance of the site that it was added to UNESCO's World Cultural Heritage list in 1999. If you want to visit all five, it's much cheaper to get the the combined Museumsinsel ticket.

The **Pergamonmuseum**, one of Berlin's main attractions, is a showcase for three huge and important examples of ancient architecture: the Hellenistic Pergamon Altar (part of a Greek temple complex from what is now western Turkey), the Babylonian Gate of Ishtar and the Roman Market Gate of Miletus. The museum also contains the Museum für Islamische Kunst (Museum of Islamic Art).

Schinkel's superb **Altes Museum**, from 1830, has a small permanent collection, hosts some excellent temporary exhibitions, and for now houses a new exhibition on the ancient world, including sections on the Romans and Etruscans. The renovated **Alte Nationalgalerie** has once again become home to a wide-ranging collection of 19th-century painting and sculpture.

The **Neues Museum**, rebuilt by British architect David Chipperfield, reopened in 2009 as a home to the Ägyptisches Museum and Charlottenburg's Museum für Vor- und Frühgeschichte (Prehistory and Early History Museum). Instead of rebuilding an exact copy, Chipperfield has created new architecture within the liminal spaces of the old that couldn't be saved.

Dominating the Museumsinsel skyline is the huge, bombastic **Berliner Dom**. It's worth climbing right up to the cathedral's dome for fine views over the city. In front of here, bounded on one side by the neoclassical colonnade of the Altes Museum, is the **Lustgarten**, an elegant green square.

Across the main road bisecting the island is where the GDR's parliament complex once stood. The original palace, the Stadtschloss, home to the Hollenzoherns since 1451, saw the overthrow of the Kaisers and the failed 1918 Spartacist uprising, and was badly damaged in World War II. Instead of rebuilding it, the GDR demolished it in 1950 as a sign of Prussian militarism, and Erich Hoenecker built his 1970s showpiece Palast der Republik there, which grew to be loved by East Berliners.

After lengthy arguments and occupations, the asbestos-ridden Palast was finally demolished in 2009 and, at the time of writing, the new Stadtschloss is set to be completed in 2019. It will house the Humboldt Forum, a cultural centre dealing with non-European art. Opposite the new development will be the new monument to German unity – a gigantic rocking dish (*see p41* **Remember, Remember**). Temporarily squatting on the site is the much-maligned **Humboldt Box** (Schlossplatz 5, 01805 030 707 premium line, www.humboldt-box.com), which houses a tourist information centre, restaurant and viewing platform from which to see the construction site.

South of Unter den Linden

What the Kurfürstendamm was in post-war West Berlin, **Friedrichstrasse** had been and is trying to be again: the city's glitziest shopping street. Like Unter den Linden, the north–south street (starting at Mehringplatz in Kreuzberg

Friedrichstrasse

and ending at Oranienburger Tor in Mitte) was laid out as part of the baroque, late 17th-century expansion of the city.

The liveliest, sleekest stretch of the street is that between **Checkpoint Charlie** (*see p142*) and Friedrichstrasse station. A huge amount of money has been poured into redevelopment here, with office buildings and upmarket shops and malls galore, although it's a pretty soulless place. Look out for the all-glass façade of the modernist-style **Galeries Lafayette** (no.75), the acute angles of the expressionist **Quartier 206** (nos.71-74) and the monolithic geometric mass of **Quartier 205** (nos.66-70). Otherwise, there are luxury-car showrooms, and boutiques for Mont Blanc, Cartier and countless other high-class concerns.

Just to the east of this stretch lies the square of **Gendarmenmarkt**, one of the high points of Frederick the Great's vision for the city. Here, two churches – the **Französischer Dom**, home to the **Hugenottenmuseum**; and the **Deutscher Dom** – frame the **Konzerthaus** (*see p202*), the home base of the Deutsches Symphonie-Orchester Berlin.

Just west of Friedrichstrasse, on Leipziger Strasse, is the **Museum für Kommunikation**. Many other interesting sights are close by, over the Mitte border with Kreuzberg. For these, *see pp126-145* **Kreuzberg & Treptow**.

North of Unter den Linden

The continuation of Friedrichstrasse north of Unter den Linden is less appealing and lively than its southern stretch. Friedrichstrasse station once had an interior notable mostly for its ability to confuse. Its role as the only East–West border crossing point open for all categories of citizen involved a confusing warren of passageways and interior partitions. Today, it is open and full of shops.

Following the line of the train tracks east along Georgenstrasse, you'll come upon the **Berliner Antik & Flohmarkt** – a succession of antiques stores, bookshops and cafés in the *Bogen* ('arches'), underneath the railway.

The building just to the north of the railway station is known as the **Tränenpalast** (Palace Tears). This was where departing visitors left their Eastern friends and relations who could not follow them through the border. In autumn 2011, the building reopened as a museum commemorating the division of Berlin (Reichstagsufer 17, open 9am-7pm Tue-Fri, 10am-6pm Sat, Sun, admission free).

Across Friedrichstrasse stands the **Admiralspalast** (*see p204*), a landmark theatre from 1910 that reopened in 2006 after eight years of darkness. A survivor of wartime bombing, the building contains a 1,600-seat theatre used over the decades for everything from Broadway transfers to the Staatsoper. There are also two smaller performance spaces and a restored Roman-style bathhouse turned 21st-century spa.

Crossing the river on the wrought-iron Weidendammer Brücke, a left turn on Schiffbauerdamm brings you to the **Berliner Ensemble** (*see p208*), with its bronze statue of Bertolt Brecht, who directed the company from 1948 to 1956, surrounded by quotations from his works. *Die Dreigroschenoper* (*The Threepenny Opera*) was premiered here on 31 August 1928. The theatre's canteen, down some steps in the backyard, is open to the public, and is a great place to grab a cheap bite to eat. There are also various congenial bars and less touristy restaurants along the riverfront, beyond which this neighbourhood begins to merge into what is now the government quarter.

Back on Friedrichstrasse stands the **Friedrichstadtpalast** (*see p212*), a large variety venue that was an entertainment hotspot during the GDR days, since it took

EXPLORE

hard currency; it still pulls the crowds today, albeit mostly grannies from out of town. Further north is the **Brecht-Weigel-Gedenkstätte**, home to Bertolt Brecht (until his death in 1956) and his iconic actor wife Helene Weigel. Both are buried in the **Dorotheenstädtische Friedhof** (open 8am-dusk daily) next door, along with the architect Schinkel, the author Heinrich Mann and the philosopher Hegel.

Two worthwhile museums are five and ten minutes' walk from here: the **Museum für Naturkunde** (Natural History Museum) and the **Hamburger Bahnhof – Museum für Gegenwart** (Hamburg Station – Museum of Contemporary Art), which puts on excellent temporary exhibitions within the atmospheric confines of a former railway station.

Sights & Museums

Alte Nationalgalerie

Bodestrasse 1-3 (266 424242, www.smb.museum/ang). U6, S1, S2, S5, S7, S25, S75 Friedrichstrasse, or S5, S7, S75 Hackescher Markt. **Open** 10am-6pm Tue, Wed, Fri-Sun; 10am-8pm Thur. **Admission** €8; €4 reductions. Museumsinsel ticket €18; €9 reductions. **Map** p43 E4 **❶**

With its ceiling and wall paintings, fabric wallpapers and marble staircase, the Old National Gallery is a sparkling home to one of the largest collections of 19th-century art and sculpture in Germany. Friedrich Stüler was commissioned to design the building to house the collection of wealthy industrialist JHW Wagener in 1861, who donated it to the Prussian state. The 440 paintings and 80 sculptures span the period from Goethe's to the early Modern, with Romantic German artists such as Adolph Menzel, Caspar David Friedrich, Max Liebermann and Carl Spitzweg well represented. There are also some first-rank works from Manet, Monet and Rodin. Although the gallery is worth a visit, don't expect to see any kind of definitive German national collection.

Altes Museum

Lustgarten (266 424242, www.smb.museum/am). U6, S1, S2, S5, S7, S25, S75 Friedrichstrasse, or S5, S7, S75 Hackescher Markt. **Open** 10am-6pm Tue, Wed, Fri-Sun; 10am-8pm Thur. **Admission** €10; €5 reductions. Museumsinsel ticket €18; €9 reductions. **Map** p43 E4 **❷**

Opened as the Royal Museum in 1830, the Old Museum originally housed all the art treasures on Museumsinsel. It was designed by Schinkel and is considered one of his finest buildings, with a particularly magnificent entrance rotunda, where vast neon letters declare that 'All Art has been Contemporary'. Now that the Egyptian galleries have moved into the Neues Museum round the corner, this building houses a new exhibition on ancient worlds, with an excellent look at the

Etruscans and Romans on the top floor. The main floor shows off the collection of classical antiquities, including a world-class selection of Greek art, pride of place going to the superlative third-century bronze, *The Praying Boy*.

Berliner Dom

Lustgarten 1 (2026 9136, guided tours 2026 9119, www.berliner-dom.de). U6, S1, S2, S5, S7, S25, S75 Friedrichstrasse, or S5, S7, S75 Hackescher Markt. **Open** *Apr-Sept* 9am-7pm Mon-Sat; noon-8pm Sun. *Oct-Mar* 9am-7pm Mon-Sat; noon-7pm Sun. **Admission** €7; €4 reductions; free under-18s. **Map** p43 E4 **❸**

The dramatic Berlin Cathedral, which celebrated its centenary in 2005, is now finally healed of its war wounds. Built in Italian Renaissance style, it was destroyed during World War II and remained a ruin until 1973, when extensive restoration work began. It has always looked fine from the outside, but now that the internal work is complete, it is fully restored to its former glory. Crammed with detail and containing dozens of statues of eminent German Protestants, its lush 19th-century interior is hardly the perfect acoustic space for the frequent concerts that are held here (even on the colossal organ), but it's worth a visit to see the crypt containing around 90 sarcophagi of notables from the Hohenzollern dynasty, or to clamber up for splendid views from the cupola. Call to book a guided tour. *Photo p48.*

Alte Nationalgalerie.

EXPLORE

Bode-Museum

*Monbijoubrücke (266 424242, www.smb.museum/
bm). U6, S1, S2, S5, S7, S25, S75 Friedrichstrasse,
or S5, S7, S75 Hackescher Markt.* **Open** 10am-6pm
Tue, Wed, Fri-Sun; 10am-8pm Thur. **Admission**
€8; €4 reductions. Museumsinsel ticket €18; €9
reductions. **Map** p42 D4 ④

Built by Berlin architect Ernst Eberhard von Ihne in
1904, the Bode-Museum reopened after a thorough
renovation in 2006. It was originally intended
by Wilhelm von Bode as a home for art from the
beginnings of Christendom, and now contains the
Byzantine Collection, Sculpture Collection and the
Numismatic Collection. The neo-Baroque great
dome, the basilica hall and the glorious cupola
have been carefully restored to keep up with
modern curatorial standards, but they retain their
magnificence. Most impressively, despite having
one of the world's largest sculpture collections and
more than half a million pieces in the coin collection,
the museum somehow retains a totally uncluttered
feel, and the sculptures stand free from off-putting
glass cases. In particular, make sure you look out for
the wall-length Apse Mosaic from AD 545 and the
14th-century Mannheim High Altar.

Berliner Dom. *See p47.*

Brecht-Weigel-Gedenkstätte

*Chausseestrasse 125 (200 571 844, www.adk.de/
de/archiv/gedenkstaetten). U6 Oranienburger
Tor.* **Open** *Guided tours* (every 30mins) 2-3.30pm
Tue; 5-6.30pm Thur; 10am-3.30pm Sat; 11am-
6pm Sun; and by appointment. **Admission**
€5; €2.50 reductions. **No credit cards.**
Map p42 C3 ⑤

Brecht's home from 1948 until his death in 1956 has
been preserved exactly as he left it. Tours of the
house (phone in advance for an English tour) give
interesting insights into the life and reading habits
of the playwright. The window at which he worked
overlooked the grave of Hegel in the neighbouring
cemetery. Brecht's wife, actress Helene Weigel,
continued living here until her death in 1971. The
Brecht archives are kept upstairs.

★ FREE Denkmal für die ermordeten Juden Europas

*Cora-Berliner-Strasse 1 (2639 4336, www.
holocaust-denkmal.de). U2, S1, S2, S25 Potsdamer
Platz.* **Open** *Field of stelae* 24hrs daily. *Information
centre* Apr-Sept 10am-8pm daily. Oct-Mar 10am-
7pm daily. **Admission** free. **Map** p42 C5 ⑥

After many years of controversy, Peter Eisenmann's
'field of stelae' – 2,711 of them, arranged in
undulating rows on 19,704sq m (212,000sq ft) of
ground – with its attendant information centre to
memorialise the Murdered Jews of Europe, was
opened in 2005. Each of the concrete slabs has its
own foundation, and they tilt at differing angles.
The effect is (no doubt deliberately) reminiscent
of the packed headstones in Prague's Old Jewish
Cemetery. There's no vantage point or overview; to
fully engage with the structure you need to walk into
it. It's spooky in places, especially on overcast days
and near the middle of the monument, where it's
easy to feel a sense of confinement. The information
centre is at the south-east corner of the site, mostly
underground. It's like a secular crypt, containing a
sombre presentation of facts and figures about the
Holocaust's Jewish victims.

Deutsche Bank KunstHalle

*Unter den Linden 13-15 (202 0930, www.
deutsche-bank-kunsthalle.de). U6 Französische
Strasse.* **Open** 10am-8pm daily **Admission** €4;
€3 reductions; free under-12s. Free to all Mon.
Map p42 D4 ⑦

Deutsche Bank took over management of this space
from the Guggenheim in April 2013 and now holds
four shows a year, with guest curators invited to
build exhibitions from the banks's vast corporate
art collection.

FREE Deutscher Dom

*Gendarmenmarkt, entrance in Markgrafenstrasse
(2273 0431). U2, U6 Stadtmitte.* **Open** *May-
Sept* 10am-7pm Tue-Sun. *Oct-Apr* 10am-6pm
Tue-Sun. *Guided tours* every half hour 11am-5pm;

Denkmal für die ermordeten Juden Europas.

call first for English- or French-speaking guide. **Admission** free. **Map** p42 D5 ⑧

The neoclassical domed tower of this church – and the identical tower of the Französischer Dom on the other side of the square – were built in 1780-85 by Carl von Gontard for Frederick the Great, in imitation of Santa Maria in Montesanto and Santa Maria del Miracoli in Rome. The Deutscher Dom was intended for Berlin's Lutheran community. The dome is topped by a 7m (23ft) gilded statue representing Virtue. Badly damaged by Allied bombing in the war, the church and tower burned down in 1943, and were restored in the 1980s and '90s.

Inside is a permanent exhibition on the history of Germany's parliamentary system, from the 1848 revolution through the suspension of parliamentary politics by the Nazis, up to the present day. Visitors are encouraged to consider the role of parliaments throughout the modern world, but there are no translations, so to get much out of this without a guided tour your German must be up to scratch.

Deutsches Historisches Museum

Zeughaus, Unter den Linden 2 (203 040, www.dhm.de). U6 Französische Strasse. **Open** 10am-6pm daily. **Admission** €8; €4 reductions; free under-18s. **Map** p42 D4 ⑨

The permanent exhibition in the Zeughaus provides an exhaustive blast through German history from 100 BC to the present day, divided chronologically into significant eras. The museum originally had trouble raising the funds to buy historical objects, but there's enough here now for the exhibits to work on their own, without the need for an overarching narrative. German nationalism becomes the focus once you enter the 19th century, and, later on, more than one room is dedicated to the Nazi era. The DHM has succeeded admirably in looking the past straight in the eye, although the attempt to be impartial means that it's sometimes factual

to the extreme. Temporary exhibitions are housed in the gorgeous IM Pei building. *Photo p45.*

Französischer Dom & Hugenottenmuseum

Gendarmenmarkt (229 1 760, www.franzoesischer-dom.de). U2, U6 Stadtmitte. **Open** *Church* noon-5pm Mon-Sat; after service-5pm Sun. *Tower* 10am-6pm Tue-Sun. **Admission** *Church* free. *Tower* €3; €1 reductions. **No credit cards.** **Map** p42 D5 ⑩

Built in the early 18th century for Berlin's 6,000-plus-strong French Protestant community, the church (known as the Französischen Friedrichstadtkirche) was later given a baroque domed tower, as was the Deutscher Dom across the square. The tower, with its fine views over Mitte, is purely decorative and unconsecrated – and not part of the modest church, which has a separate entrance at the western end.

An exhibition on the history of the French Protestants in France and Berlin-Brandenburg is displayed within the building. The museum chronicles the religious persecution suffered by Calvinists (note the bust of Calvin on the outside of the church) and their subsequent immigration to Berlin after 1685, at the behest of the Hohenzollerns. The development of the Huguenot community is also detailed, with paintings, documents and artefacts. One part of the museum is devoted to the church's history, particularly the effects of World War II – it was bombed during a Sunday service in 1944 and remained a ruin until the mid 1980s.

★ Hamburger Bahnhof – Museum für Gegenwart

Invalidenstrasse 50-51 (3978 3439, www.hamburgerbahnhof.de). U55, S5, S7, S75 Hauptbahnhof. **Open** 10am-6pm Tue, Wed, Fri-Sun; 10am-8pm Thur. **Admission** (incl temporary exhibitions) €10; €5 reductions. **Map** p42 B3 ⑪

EXPLORE

Hamburger Bahnhof – Museum für Gegenwart. See p49.

This contemporary art museum opened in 1997 within this vast, grand neoclassical ex-train station. Outside is a stunning fluorescent light installation by Dan Flavin. Inside, the biggest draw is the controversial Friedrich Christian Flick Collection: some 2,000 works from around 150 artists (mainly from the late 20th century), with key pieces by Bruce Nauman and Martin Kipperberger. Flick, from a steel family whose fortune was earned partly from Nazi-era slave labour, paid for the refurbishment of the adjacent Rieckhalle warehouse to house the (many large-scale) works, which are doled out in temporary, themed exhibitions. There are other shows too – Tomás Saraceno installed a network of interactive gigantic bouncy balloons for his Cloud Cities show – plus one of Berlin's best art bookshops.

Museum für Kommunikation

Leipziger Strasse 16 (202 940, www.mfk-berlin.de). U2 Mohrenstrasse, or U2, U6 Stadtmitte. **Open** 9am-8pm Tue; 9am-5pm Wed-Fri; 10am-6pm Sat, Sun. **Admission** €4; €2 reductions; free under-17s. **No credit cards. Map** p42 C6 ⑫

A direct descendant of the world's first postal museum (founded in 1872), this collection covers a bit more than mere stamps. It traces the development of telecommunications up to the internet era, though philatelists might want to head straight to the basement and ogle the 'Blue Mauritius', one of the world's rarest stamps.

★ Museum für Naturkunde

Invalidenstrasse 43 (2093 8551, www.naturkunde museum-berlin.de). U6 Naturkundemuseum. **Open** 9.30am-6pm Tue-Fri; 10am-6pm Sat, Sun. **Admission** €5; €3 reductions. **Map** p42 C2 ⑬

Berlin's recently renovated Natural History Museum is a real trove. The biggest (literally) draw is the skeleton of a Brachiosaurus dinosaur, which weighed 50 tons at death and is as high as a four-storey house. 'Oliver' – as the dinosaur is nicknamed – is one of the world's largest known land animals

and was discovered in the early 1900s. Don't miss the creepy *Forschungssammlungen* (research collections), which show off some of the museum's store of over a million pickled animals suspended in jars of alcohol. Berlin's most famous polar bear, Knut, who died in 2011, is now stuffed and on display.

★ Neues Museum

Bodestrasse 1 (266 424242, www.smb.museum/nm). U6, S1, S2, S5, S7, S25, S75 Friedrichstrasse, or S5, S7, S75 Hackescher Markt. **Open** 10am-6pm Tue, Wed, Fri-Sun; 10am-8pm Thur. Entry by timed ticket. **Admission** €12; €6 reductions. Museumsinsel ticket €18; €9 reductions. **Map** p43 F4 ⑭

Reopened in 2009 after extensive remodelling, this stunning building houses the Egyptian Museum & Papyrus Collection, the Museum of Prehistory & Early History and artefacts from the Collection of Classical Antiquities. The most famous object is the bust of the Egyptian queen, Nefertiti (which Germany refuses to return to Egypt despite repeated requests), and the skull of a Neanderthal from Le Moustier. The Museum für Vor- und Frühgeschichte (Prehistory & Early History), which traces the evolution of *Homo sapiens* from 1,000,000 BC to the Bronze Age, has among its highlights reproductions (and some originals) of Heinrich Schliemann's famous treasure of ancient Troy, including works in ceramic and gold, as well as weaponry. Look out also for the sixth-century BC grave of a girl buried with a gold coin in her mouth. Information is available in English. Entry is within a half-hour ticketed time slot, so book online to skip the queues.

★ Pergamonmuseum

Am Kupfergraben (266 424242, www.smb. museum/pm). U6, S1, S2, S5, S7, S25, S75 Friedrichstrasse, or S5, S7, S75 Hackescher Markt. **Open** 10am-6pm Mon-Wed, Fri-Sun; 10am-8pm Thur. **Admission** €12; €6 reductions. Museumsinsel ticket €18; €9 reductions. **Map** p42 D4 ⑮

One of the world's major archaeological museums, the Pergamon should not be missed. Its treasures, comprising the Antikensammlung (Collection of Classical Antiquities) and the Vorderasiatisches Museum (Museum of Near Eastern Antiquities), contain three major draws. The star attraction is the Hellenistic Pergamon Altar, dating from 170-159 BC; huge as it is, the museum's partial reconstruction is only a third of the original's size. In an adjoining room, and even more architecturally impressive, is the towering Roman Market Gate of Miletus (29m/95ft wide and almost 17m/ 56ft high), erected in AD 120. This leads through to the third of the big attractions: the extraordinary blue and ochre tiled Gate of Ishtar and the Babylonian Processional Street, dating from the reign of King Nebuchadnezzar (605-562 BC). There are plenty of other gems to see, including some stunning Assyrian reliefs.

The Pergamon is also now home to the Museum für Islamische Kunst (Museum of Islamic Art), which takes up some 14 rooms in the southern wing. The wide-ranging collection includes applied arts, crafts, books and architectural details from the eighth to the 19th centuries. Entrance to the museum is included in the overall admission price, as is an excellent audio guide.

▶ *The Pergamonmuseum is currently undergoing renovation in stages, which means the Pergamon Altar is closed until 2019.*

Barcomi's. *See p59.*

FREE Sankt-Hedwigs-Kathedrale

Bebelplatz (203 4810, www.hedwigs-kathedrale. de). U2 Hausvogteiplatz, or U6 Französische Strasse. **Open** 10am-5pm Mon-Sat; 1-5pm Sun. **Admission** free. *Guided tours* €1.50. **Map** p42 D5 ⑯

Constructed in 1747 for Berlin's Catholic minority, this circular Knobelsdorff creation was bombed out during the war and only reconsecrated in 1963. Its modernised interior contains a split-level double altar with a ribbed dome. The crypt holds the remains of Bernhard Lichtenberg, who preached here against the Nazis, was arrested, and died while being transported to Dachau in 1943.

Restaurants & Cafés

€ Berliner Ensemble Kantine

Bertolt-Brecht-Platz 1 (2840 8117). U6, S1, S2, S5, S7, S25, S75 Friedrichstrasse. **Open** 9am-midnight Mon-Sat; 4pm-midnight Sun. **Main courses** €3-€5. **Map** p42 C4 ⑰ German

Eat passable, hearty German fare with the jovial cast and crew at the canteen of Brecht's Berliner Ensemble. It's tucked around the back of the theatre, down some steps in the courtyard. The three daily specials cost around €5 or less, and always include a good veggie option.

Borchardt

Französische Strasse 47 (8188 6262). U6 Französische Strasse. **Open** 11.30am-late daily. **Main courses** €20-€40. **Map** p42 D5 ⑱ Brasserie

The original Borchardt opened next door at no.48 in the late 19th century. It became *the* place for politicians and society folk, but was destroyed in World War II. Now, Roland Mary and Marina Richter have reconstructed a highly fashionable, Maxim's-inspired bistro. People come not for the respectable French food, but for the clannish atmosphere, where you can often spot a film star or politico. Ideal if you fancy a dozen oysters and a fillet of pike-perch or beef after a cultural evening nearby.

Dottir

Mittelstrasse 40 (330 060 760, www.dottir berlin.com). U6, S1, S2, S5, S7, S25, S75 Friedrichstrasse. **Open** 6pm-late Tue-Sat. **Map** p42 D4 ⑲ Scandinavian

One of the latest hotspots to hit Berlin, this tiny restaurant was launched in early 2015 by the team behind such acclaimed Berlin institutions as Grill Royal (*see p52*) and Pauly Saal. Chef Victoria Eliasdottir (daughter of artist Olafur Eliasson) serves chic New Nordic cuisine, with the accent on light, fresh flavours cut with Icelandic-influenced pickles and vinegars. It's located in one of the last remaining unrenovated buildings in the district, and has managed to keep its impeccable 1950s shabby-chic charm intact.

EXPLORE

Grill Royal

Friedrichstrasse 105B (2887 9288, www.grill royal.com). U6, S1, S2, S5, S7, S25, S75 Friedrichstrasse. **Open** 6pm-1am daily. **Main courses** €15-€55. **Map** p42 D3 ⑳ **Steakhouse**

One of the city's best-known venues, nestled on the riverside, Grill Royal is a stylish, friendly and profoundly meaty experience. Not for vegetarians or those on a diet or budget, Grill is as compelling for its people-watching potential as it is for its (stoutly priced) steaks, seafood and accoutrements. The meat is sourced from local suppliers as well as Argentina, Ireland and Australia. The walls are adorned with rather striking soft-porn art from the owner's collection. Reservations essential.

★ Weinbar Rutz

Chausseestrasse 8 (2462 8760, www.rutz-weinbar. de). U6 Naturkundemuseum. **Open** 6.30-10.30pm Tue-Sat. **Main courses** €12.50-€25. **Set meal** €115-€170 6-10 courses. **Map** p42 C3 ㉑ **German**

The impressive ground-floor bar has a whole wall showcasing wines from around the globe – the best of the best. There are hearty meals in the bar downstairs (pig's stomach with sauerkraut and mustard-seed sauce, anyone?), while the second-floor restaurant serves a limited nouvelle menu from Michelin-starred chef Marco Müller, all of it beautifully presented. Booking essential.

Bars & Pubs

Newton Bar

Charlottenstrasse 57 (2029 5421, www.newton-bar.de). U6 Französische Strasse. **Open** 10am-late daily. **Map** p42 D5 ㉒

Homage seems to be Berlin's preferred method for naming bars, and here iconoclastic fashion photographer Helmut Newton is immortalised. For those unfamiliar with his pictures of statuesque models, an entire wall of this large bar is dedicated to a series of his black and white nudes. Stick to the classics, martinis or a good single malt, settle into the cosy seating and watch the world go by from the heated terrace with a view on to Gendarmenmarkt.

Ständige Vertretung

Schiffbauerdamm 8 (282 3965, www.staev.de). U6, S1, S2, S5, S7, S25, S75 Friedrichstrasse. **Open** 9am-1.30am daily. **Map** p42 C4 ㉓

The knick-knack-filled Ständige commemorates the still controversial decision to move the German capital from Bonn to Berlin after reunification. Ständige Vertretung – 'permanent representation' – was the name West and East Germany used to describe the special consulates they kept in each other's countries, not wanting to legitimise the other by calling it an embassy. Due to the pub's proximity to the government quarter, you get the odd politician popping in for some draught Kölsch. There's a lovely terrace by the river in summer.

Shops & Services

Berlin Story

Unter den Linden 40 (2045 3842, www.berlin-story.de). U6 Französische Strasse. **Open** 10am-7pm Mon-Sat; 10am-6pm Sun. **Map** p42 C4 ㉔ **Books & music**

You won't find a better selection of Berlin-related books in German and English: everything from novels with Berlin settings to non-fiction volumes on the history and culture of the city. Historical maps, posters, DVDs, CDs and souvenirs are also available.

Brille 54

Friedrichstrasse 71 (2094 6060, www.brille54.de). U6 Französische Strasse. **Open** 10am-7pm Mon-Fri; 10am-6pm Sat. **Map** p42 D5 ㉕ **Fashion**

This small, sleek space in Quartier 206 was designed by hot young local architects Plajer & Franz. Lots of smart international brands are found here, including Lindberg, Thom Browne and Oliver Peoples.

Other locations Rosenthaler Strasse 36, Mitte (2804 0818); Kurfürstendamm 50, Charlottenburg (882 6696).

Contemporary Fine Arts

Am Kupfergraben 10 (288 7870, www.cfa-berlin. com). U6, S1, S2, S3, S5, S7, S75 Friedrichstrasse. **Open** 11am-6pm Tue-Fri; 11am-4pm Sat. **No credit cards. Map** p42 D4 ㉖ **Gallery**

Bruno Brunnet, Nicole Hackert and Philipp Haverkampf's gallery is among the swishest in Berlin. The museum-like space (designed by David Chipperfield) over two floors frequently shows major stars such as Georg Baselitz and Norbert Schwontkowski, alongside YBA luminaries (Cecily Brown, Chris Ofili) and well-known German artists (Daniel Richter, Jonathan Meese).

Corner Berlin

Französische Strasse 40 (2067 0940, www. thecornerberlin.de). U6 Französische Strasse. **Open** 10.30am-7.30pm Mon-Fri; 10am-7pm Sat. **Map** p42 D5 ㉗ **Fashion/Homewares**

Typically plush surroundings for this luxury 'lifestyle' shop. There's designer nightclub clobber for both sexes: Rick Owens biker jackets and studded Christian Louboutin slippers for the boys; silken Lanvin tunics and Balenciaga handbags for the girls. Plus an incongruous section of beautiful modernist antique furniture by the likes of Arne Jacobsen and Charles Eames.

Other locations Wielandstrasse 29, Charlottenburg (8892 1261); Markgrafenstrasse 45, Kreuzberg (2067 4973).

★ Departmentstore Quartier 206

Friedrichstrasse 71 (2094 6500, www.dsq206. com). U6 Französische Strasse. **Open** 11am-8pm Mon-Fri; 10am-6pm Sat. **Map** p42 D5 ㉘ **Department store**

EXPLORE

Departmentstore Quartier 206

This ultra-luxe store occupies the first floor of IM Pei studio's neo-art deco building known for its elaborate Byzantine-style tiled flooring. Definitive pieces are carefully selected from cult labels such as Alexander Wang and Vivienne Westwood, alongside cosmetics and furnishings from the likes of perfumier Jul et Mad and craftsman Alexander Lamont. The rest of the building contains branded boutiques from Wolford, Bottega Veneta and more.

Dussmann das KulturKaufhaus
Friedrichstrasse 90 (2025 1111, www. kulturkaufhaus.de). U6, S1, S2, S5, S7, S25, S75 Friedrichstrasse. **Open** 9am-midnight Mon-Fri; 9am-11.30pm Sat. **Map** p42 D4 ❷ **Books & music**
Intended as a 'cultural department store', this spacious five-floor retailer has books, magazines, CDs and DVDs. You can borrow reading glasses (€10 deposit) or a portable CD player (€50 deposit) for the time you're in the store. The huge English-language section has an excellent selection of cookbooks and travel literature.

Galeries Lafayette
Friedrichstrasse 76-78 (209 480, www. galerieslafayette.de). U6 Französische Strasse. **Open** 10am-8pm Mon-Sat. **Map** p42 D5 ❸
Department store
The most famous of Paris's *grand magasins* built itself a Berlin outpost in the mid 1990s when the city underwent a post-reunification construction boom. Fashion-wise, it caters across the board, with sophisticated labels such as Ferragamo and Agnès B for genteel Charlottenburg mums, while French rock-chic from Sandro and the Kooples caters for a younger crowd. As to be expected, the food halls are excellent, if a little less spectacular than at KaDeWe, with a fine butcher selling Charolais beef and capons from Burgundy. *Photo p54.*

Schinkel Pavilion
Oberwallstrasse 1 (2088 6444, www.schinkelpavillon.de). U2 Hausvogteiplatz. **Open** 2-8pm Thur, Fri; noon-6pm Sat, Sun. **Map** p42 D4 ❶ **Gallery**
This gallery space is in the gardens of the Kronprinzenpalais, which itself lays claim to being the world's first contemporary art institution: the palace displayed work by Berlin's expressionists from 1918 until the Nazis closed it down for showing 'degenerate' art. Today, the octagonal pavilion with its wall-to-ceiling glass, designed to DDR specifications in 1969, happily shows all manner of installation, sculpture and performance art, cheerily degenerate or not. Philippe Parreno, Douglas Gordon and James Franco have all appeared recently.

ALEXANDERPLATZ & THE SCHEUNENVIERTEL

The Scheunenviertel

If the area south of Friedrichstrasse station is the commercial face of Mitte, the Scheunenviertel (stretching around the north bank of the River Spree, running east from Friedrichstrasse to Hackescher Markt) is the area in its final throes of bohemian gentrification.

Today, this is one of Berlin's main nightlife districts and art quarters, littered with bars and galleries. Once far enough out of town that it was safe to build the highly flammable hay barns (*Scheunen*) here, this was also historically the centre of Berlin's immigrant community, including many Jews from Eastern Europe.

EXPLORE

IN THE KNOW STOLPERSTEINE

Walking around Berlin, you may stumble across a brass-plated cobblestone with writing engraved on it – this is a *Stolpersteine* (literally 'stumbling block'), set down to remember a victim of the Holocaust in front of their house.

Remarkably, these are the work of a private citizen: artist Gunter Hemnig, who casts and installs each one. Since 1992, he's put in over 40,000 of them across Europe, with close to 3,000 in Berlin alone, the majority commemorating Jewish victims, but also Roma, homosexuals and victims of euthanasia. Touchingly, the cost of each one is covered by private donation, usually from the current residents of the building, who do the research and add the name to a searchable database (www.stolpersteine.eu). The stone will usually tell you a person's name, date of birth and where they were murdered.

Galeries Lafayette. *See p53.*

During the 1990s, it again began to attract Jewish immigrants, including both young Americans and Orthodox Jews from the former Soviet Union; now, Berlin has the fastest-growing Jewish population in Europe.

In the 1990s, the Scheunenviertel became a magnet for squatters with access to the list of buildings supposedly wrecked by lazy urban developers, who had ticked them off as 'gone' in order to meet quotas but had actually left them standing. With many other buildings in disrepair, rents were cheap, and the new residents soon learned how to take advantage of city subsidies for opening galleries and other cultural spaces. Result: the Scheunenviertel became Berlin's hottest cultural centre.

The first of these art-squats was Tacheles, on the western end of Oranienburger Strasse, the spine of the Scheunenviertel. Built in 1907, the building originally housed an early attempt at a shopping mall. It had stood vacant for years when squatted by artists after the Wall came down. It then became a rather arrogant arbiter of hip in the neighbourhood, with studios and performance spaces, a cinema and several edgy bars and discos, and eventually became one of Berlin's most popular tourist attractions. In 2012, the final group of artists left after much protest, following the occupants of the bars, restaurants and other art studios, who had previously agreed to take a €1m pay-off from developers.

Ironically, the original gentrifiers are now victims of their own success, with luxury flats forcing out even mainstream institutions: the photography museum **C/O Gallery** (*see p114*), which was housed in the magnificent red-brick Postführamt just down the road, was forced out in 2012. It's now moved to the west, as commentators predict a shift in the cultural locus to Schöneberg and Charlottenburg as development here runs rampant.

Across Tucholskystrasse, at Oranienburger Strasse 32, is an entrance to the **Heckmann Höfe** (the other is on Auguststrasse), a series of courtyards that have been delightfully restored to accommodate shops and restaurants. The free-standing building, with the firm's coat of arms in the pavement in front of it, was once the stables.

A little further down the block stands the **Neue Synagoge**, with its gleaming golden Moorish-style dome. Turning into Grosse Hamburger Strasse, you'll find yourself surrounded by Jewish history. On the right, on the site of a former old-people's home, there's a memorial to the thousands of Berlin Jews who were forced to congregate here before being shipped off to concentration camps. Behind the memorial is a park that was once Berlin's oldest Jewish cemetery; the only gravestone left is that of the father of the German Jewish renaissance, Moses Mendelssohn, founder of

the city's first Jewish school, next door at no.27. A rash of post-reunification anti-Semitism by empowered East German skinheads led to all synagogues and Jewish institutions being put under 24-hour guard. That the school has such a heavy security presence, even today, only adds to the poignancy of this place.

Located across the street at nos.15-16 is the **Missing House**, a memorial by Christian Boltanski, in which the walls of a bombed-out house have the names and occupations of former residents inscribed on the site of their vanished apartments. A little further on, the **Sophienkirche** (from which nearby Sophienstrasse gets its name) is one of Berlin's few remaining baroque churches. It is set back from the street behind wrought-iron fences, and, together with the surrounding ensemble, is one of the prettiest architectural sites in the city. The interior is a little disappointing, however.

Just north of the synagogue is the new **Ramones Museum**, run by Flo Hayler, probably the biggest fan of the New York band.

At the end of Oranienburger Strasse, at the corner of Rosenthaler Strasse, is the famous **Hackesche Höfe**. Built in 1906-07, these form a complex of nine interlinking Jugendstil courtyards with elegant ceramic façades. The Höfe symbolise Berlin's new Mitte: having miraculously survived two wars, the forgotten, crumbling buildings were restored in the mid 1990s using the old plans. Today, they house an upmarket collection of shops, galleries, theatres, cafés, restaurants and cinemas, which get rammed with tourists.

A few doors up Rosenthaler Strasse is a tumbledown alley alongside the Central cinema, in which a workshop for the blind was located during World War II. Its owner managed to stock it fully with 'blind' Jews, and helped them escape or avoid the camps. Now it houses

EXPLORE

alternative galleries, bars and shops. In the same complex is the **Anne Frank Zentrum**, home to a multimedia exhibition that tells the life story of the young Dutch diarist who was murdered in Bergen-Belsen. Across the street from the Hackesche Höfe, and under the S-Bahn arches, there are further bars, restaurants and shops.

There are still more fashionable bars and shops along **Rosenthaler Strasse** and around the corner on **Neue Schönhauser Strasse**, as well as some good sandwich and coffee bars. This area has settled into being Berlin's hip centre, with many cool little shops. Most of the original houses have now been renovated and the gaps left by wartime bombing have been filled in by slick new buildings or ergonomic playgrounds. Even the *Plattenbauten*, the East German prefabs, have been spruced up, although, in their higher-rise form, they continue to curse Berlin's suburbs.

Leading off Rosenthaler Strasse, **Sophienstrasse** is Mitte's most picturesque street. Built in the 18th century, it was restored in 1987 for the city's 750th anniversary, with craftworkers' ateliers that have replicas of old merchants' metal signs hanging outside them. This pseudo-historicism has now become part of a more interesting mix of handicraft shops. The brick façade of the Handwerker Verein at no.18 is particularly impressive. If you wander into the courtyard (as you can with most courtyards that aren't private), you'll find the **Sophiensaele** (*see p211*), an interesting performing-arts space in an old ballroom. The Sophiensaele was also the location of the first German Communist Party HQ.

At nos.20-21 are the **Sophie-Gips Höfe**, which came into being when wealthy art patrons Erika and Rolf Hoffmann were denied permission to build a gallery in Dresden for their collection of contemporary art. Instead, they bought this complex between Sophienstrasse and Gipsstrasse, restored it, and installed the art here – in the **Sammlung Hoffman** – along with their spectacular private residence.

Running between the west end of Oranienburger Strasse and Rosenthaler Strasse, **Auguststrasse** was the original core of Berlin's eastern gallery district; it was here that the whole Mitte scene began almost two decades ago. Important venues include Thomas Olbricht's 'me Collectors Room' and the redeveloped **Jüdische Mädchenschule** complex (nos. 11-13), containing such art spaces as Michael Fuchs Galerie, CWC Gallery and the Eigen Art Lab. Across the road, the **KW Institute for Contemporary Art** is a polarising bellwether of the Berlin art scene, but usually has something worth seeing. Known as Mitte's 'Art Mile', the street makes for a good afternoon's stroll.

Alexanderplatz & Around

Visitors who have read Alfred Döblin's raucous novel *Berlin Alexanderplatz* or seen Fassbinder's masterful television adaptation may arrive here and wonder what this dead space is. What happened was that, in the early 1970s, Erich Hönecker decided that this historic area should reflect the glories of socialism, and tore it all down. He replaced it with a masterpiece of Commie kitsch: wide boulevards; monotonous white buildings filled with cafés and shops (though to a degree these took their cue from modernist structures dating from the Weimar era, such as the block between the south-west side of the square and the station); and, of course, the impressive golf-ball-on-a-knitting-needle, the **Fernsehturm** (Television Tower; *see p58* and *p57* **Tower of the Hour**). The goofy clock topped with the 1950s-style atom design signals the time in (mostly) former socialist lands; water cascades from the Brunnen der Völkerfreundschaft ('Fountain of the Friendship of Peoples').

The original 1990s plans to replace most of Alexanderplatz with a dozen or so skyscrapers based on New York's Rockefeller Center, among which the Fernsehturm would remain standing, met mass resistance due to surrounding GDR apartment buildings having to be demolished. These plans are unlikely to come to fruition, but there are rumblings of a Frank Gehry-designed rotating apartment block. For now, though, the Kaufhaus department store on the north-west of the square has been expanded and has lost its 1970s façade, while the 22,000 square metres (237,000 square feet) of new shopping space on the north-east corner has ruined the square's Communist-era sightlines and obscured the view across Grunerstrasse of the domed **Kongresshalle** and the **Haus des Lehrers** with its first-floor frieze – two of Berlin's finest examples of GDR architecture. Beyond them is Alexa, a giant new mall that no one likes.

One of the few survivors from pre-war Alexanderplatz sits in the shadow of the Fernsehturm: the **Marienkirche**, Berlin's oldest parish church, dating from the 13th century. Later 15th-century (the tower) and 18th-century (the upper section) additions enhance the building's harmonious simplicity.

Just south of here stands the extravagant **Neptunbrunnen**, an 1891 statue of the trident-wielding sea god, surrounded by four female figures representing the Elbe, Rhine, Oder and Vistula rivers. It was moved here from the Stadtschloss when the Communists demolished it in 1950. Overlooking Neptune from the south-east is the huge red-brick bulk of the **Berliner Rathaus** (Berlin Town Hall), while to the south-west is the open space of Marx-Engels Forum,

EXPLORE

one of the few remaining monuments to the old boys – the huge statue of Karl and Fred begs you to take a seat on Marx's lap. On Spandauer Strasse, behind the Radisson Hotel, is the entrance to the **AquaDom & Sea Life**, one of Mitte's more eccentric attractions, and round the corner on the river is the hardly more sensible **DDR Museum**.

For a vague impression of what this part of the city might have looked like before Allied bombers and the GDR did their work, take a stroll around the Nikolaiviertel, just south of Alexanderplatz. This is Berlin's oldest quarter, centred around the **Nikolaikirche** (dating from 1220). The GDR's reconstruction involved bringing the few undamaged buildings from this period together into what is essentially a fake assemblage of history. There are a couple of historic residences, including the **Knoblauchhaus** and the **Ephraim-Palais**. You'll also find Enlightenment big shot Gottfried Lessing's house, cafés (including a reconstruction of Zum Nussbaum, a contender for the oldest bar in Berlin) and expensive shops. On the southern edge of the district is the **Hanf Museum** (Hemp Museum).

Long before the infamous Wall, Berlin had another one: the medieval **Stadtmauer** (City Wall) of the original 13th-century settlement. There's almost as much left of this wall (a couple of minutes' walk east of the Nikolaiviertel, on Littenstrasse/Waisenstrasse) as there is of the more recent one. Built along the wall by the junction with Parochialstrasse is the extremely old restaurant **Zur Letzten Instanz**, which takes its name from the neighbouring law courts. There has been a restaurant on this site since 1621, Napoleon supposedly having stopped off here for refreshment. Just over the Spree from here is the church-like red-brick **Märkisches Museum**, which houses a rambling, but not unappealing, collection tracing the history of the city, and the small neighbouring **Köllnischer Park**. The park's bearpit is home to Schnute and Maxi, Berlin's two flesh-and-blood brown bears – and official symbols of the city.

Sights & Museums

Anne Frank Zentrum
Rosenthaler Strasse 39 (288 865 610, www. annefrank.de). U8 Weinmeisterstrasse. **Open** 10am-6pm Tue-Sun. **Admission** €5; €3 reductions; €12 families; free under-10s. **No credit cards.** **Map** p43 E3 ㉜
This permanent exhibition about the life and death of Anne Frank opened in 2006 and is a co-project with the Anne Frank House in Amsterdam. Pictures, collages, films and special objects describe the world of the diarist and her family in the context of National Socialism, the persecution of the Jews and World War II.

AquaDom & Sea Life
Spandauer Strasse 3 (992 800, www.visitsealife. com/berlin). S5, S7, S75 Hackescher Markt. **Open** 10am-6pm daily. **Admission** €17.50; €12.50 reductions. **Map** p43 E4 ㉝
Billed as two attractions in one, both involving lots of water and plenty of fish. Sea Life leads you through 13 themed aquaria offering fish in different habitats. The AquaDom is the world's largest free-standing aquarium – a space age tuboid that looks like it might have just landed from some alien planet. A lift takes you up through the middle of this giant cylindrical fishtank – a million litres of saltwater that is home to 2,500 colourful creatures, and enfolded by the atrium of the Radisson Blu hotel (*see p267*). Unfortunately, only the staff are allowed to scuba-dive through the tank to feed the fish.

FREE Berliner Rathaus
Rathausstrasse 15 (guided tours 9026 2411). U2, U5, U8, S5, S7, S75 Alexanderplatz. **Open** 9am-6pm Mon-Fri. *Guided tours* by appointment. **Admission** free. **Map** p43 F4 ㉞
This magnificent building was constructed of terracotta brick during the 1860s in an Italian Renaissance pastiche. The history of Berlin up to that point is illustrated in a series of 36 reliefs on the façade. During Communist times, it served as East Berlin's town hall – which made its old nickname, Rotes Rathaus ('Red Town Hall'), and the colour of the façade, doubly fitting. West Berlin's city government workers moved here from their town hall, Rathaus Schöneberg, in 1991. Entry is restricted to small parts of the building; bring some ID.

DDR Museum
Karl Liebknecht Strasse 1 (847 123 731, www. ddr-museum.de). S5, S7, S75 Hackescher Markt. **Open** 10am-8pm Mon-Fri, Sun; 10am-10pm Sat. **Admission** €6; €4 reductions. **Map** p43 E4 ㉟
Bright blue neon signage and a Trabant in the window welcome you into 'one of Europe's most interactive museums!' This is Ostalgia in action. Touchscreens, sound effects and even the 'DDR Game' mean that the more distasteful aspects of East German life are cheerfully glossed over. The museum is essentially a collection of GDR memorabilia, from travel tickets to Palast der Republik serviettes. Climb inside the Trabi or sit on a GDR couch in a GDR living room where you can watch GDR TV. Even the much feared Stasi get the interactive family treatment too – you can pretend to be a Stasi officer and listen in on a bugged flat. Take it all with a large pinch of salt.

Ephraim-Palais
Poststrasse 16 (2400 2162, www.stadtmuseum.de). U2, U5, U8, S5, S7, S75 Alexanderplatz. **Open** 10am-6pm Tue, Thur-Sun; 10am-8pm Wed. **Admission** €5; €3 reductions; free under-18s. Free 1st Wed of mth. **No credit cards. Map** p43 E4 ㊱

TOWER OF THE HOUR

Berliners have learned to love the Fernsehturm.

Most great cities have their iconic landmarks, the kind of thing film directors shoehorn in to quickly show a change of location. Eiffel Tower in the background? Ooh la la, it's Paris. Big Ben? It's London. Sydney Harbour Bridge? Time to head Down Under. And these days, a Berlin establishing shot will have the **Fernsehturm** (*see p58*) poking out somewhere in it.

It was not always so. The Nazis had envisaged Germania, a city stuffed with landmarks, with oversized triumphal arches and mountainous meeting halls, but by the late 1940s there was little left that said 'Berlin' save rubble and ruin. In 1950, the East Berlin authorities blew up what was left of the old Prussian Stadtschloss, an act widely regarded as one of cultural barbarism, and started thinking about a new landmark to fill the void at the city's heart. While they pondered, another dilemma arose. The new medium of television demanded that a transmission tower be built in the eastern part of Berlin to provide a service to compete with the powerful signals already emanating from the West.

The winning design was by architect Herbert Henselmann, who in 1958 had come up with a plan for an overhaul of Berlin's medieval centre: the now-open area between the Spree and Alexanderplatz. Part of his vision was for a 'tower of signals'. The inspiration for Henselmann's designs was the new mania for space travel that followed the launch of Sputnik, the first artificial satellite, in October 1957. Henselmann's tower would have a tapering shaft, to represent a rocket soaring into the sky; and at the very top would be a bright, socialist-red sphere to represent a satellite.

Construction began in 1965, and the Fernsehturm finally opened on 7 October 1969 – the 20th anniversary of the founding of the GDR. It marked the very centre of the city in the manner of a medieval church tower, allowed the second GDR TV station to commence broadcasting, and advertised the thrusting triumph of socialism in a form visible for miles around, in particular all over West Berlin. Equipped with a viewing platform at 203 metres (668 feet) and a revolving restaurant one floor above it, it was also a handy tourist attraction.

Its simple, ball-on-spike shape was also a boon to East Berlin's graphic designers. At last, the city had a politically neutral but versatile symbol that could be used in all sorts of different ways. Soon it was making appearances on tourist brochures and party calendars, commemorative stamps and political posters, city maps and menu covers, shopping bags and official invitations. Easily anthropomorphised with a smiley face added to the ball, and often depicted with garlands of flowers, it also served as a perfect canvas for literature addressed to socialist youth. In the heyday of East Berlin, it was as inescapable as a graphic icon as it was as a towering landmark.

The Fernsehturm nearly didn't survive reunification: it was so closely associated with the outgoing Communist regime that there were calls to tear it down. But it remains useful and is still a major tourist draw. And now that bananas and free speech are sufficiently plentiful, Berliners have once again learned to love the thing. The restaurant still revolves, and the tower is still the fourth-tallest free-standing structure in Europe. What more could you ask of an icon?

EXPLORE

Built in the 15th century as a lavish townhouse, remodelled in late baroque style in the 18th century, demolished by the Communists, and then rebuilt by them close to its original location for the 750th anniversary of Berlin in 1987, the Ephraim-Palais is today home to temporary exhibitions about Berlin's history drawn from the city's collection. Soft chandelier lighting and parquet floors lend a refined air to the place.

★ Fernsehturm

Panoramastrasse 1A (242 3333, www. berlinerfernsehturm.de). U2, U5, U8, S5, S7, S75 Alexanderplatz. **Open** *Mar-Oct* 9am-midnight daily. *Nov-Feb* 10am-midnight daily. **Admission** €12.50; €8 reductions; free under-3s. **Map** p43 F4 ③

Built in the late 1960s at a time when relations between East and West Berlin were at their lowest ebb, the 365m (1,198ft) Television Tower – its ball-on-spike shape visible all over the city – was intended as an assertion of Communist dynamism and modernity. A shame, then, that such television towers were a West German invention. A shame too that they had to get Swedish engineers to build the thing. Communist authorities were also displeased to note a particular phenomenon: when the sun shines on the tower, reflections on the ball form the shape of a cross. Berliners dubbed this phenomenon 'the Pope's revenge'. Nevertheless, the authorities were proud enough of their tower to make it one of the central symbols of the East German capital, and today it is one of Berlin's most popular graphic images. Take an ear-popping trip in the lift to the observation platform at the top: a great way to orient yourself early on a visit to Berlin. The view is unbeatable by night or day – particularly looking westwards, where you can take in the whole of the Tiergarten and surrounding area. If heights make you hungry, take a twirl in the revolving restaurant, which offers an even better view. There are usually queues to get up there, however. *See also p57* **Tower of the Hour**.

Hanf Museum

Mühlendamm 5 (242 4827, www.hanfmuseum.de). U2, U5, U8, S5, S7, S75 Alexanderplatz. **Open** 10am-8pm Tue-Fri; noon-8pm Sat, Sun. **Admission** €4.50, €3 reductions; free under-10s. **No credit cards. Map** p43 F4 ③

The world's largest hemp museum aims to teach the visitor about the uses of the plant throughout history, as well as touching on the controversy surrounding it. The café (doubling as a video and reading room) serves cakes made with hemp, as well as those without it.

FREE Knoblauchhaus

Poststrasse 23 (240 020 171, www.knoblauchhaus. de). U2, U5, U8, S5, S7, S75 Alexanderplatz. **Open** 10am-6pm Tue-Sun. **Admission** free. **Map** p43 E4 ③

This neoclassical mid 18th-century townhouse was once home to the influential Knoblauch family and contains an exhibition about some of their more prominent members. However, the real draw is the house's striking interior. The first floor contains an exhibition about the increasingly sophisticated middle-class tastes of post-Napoleonic Germany, while the second floor hosts temporary exhibitions about 19th-century cultural history.

FREE Marienkirche

Karl-Liebknecht-Strasse 8 (2475 9510, www. marienkirche-berlin.de). U2, U5, U8, S5, S7, S75 Alexanderplatz. **Open** 10am-6pm daily. **Admission** free. **Map** p43 F4 ④

Begun in 1270, the Marienkirche is one of Berlin's few remaining medieval buildings. Just inside the door is a wonderful 'Dance of Death' fresco dating from 1485, and the 18th-century Walther organ here is considered his masterpiece. Marienkirche hit the headlines in 1989 when the East German civil rights movement chose it for one of their first sit-ins, since churches were among the few places where people could congregate without state permission.

Märkisches Museum

Am Köllnischen Park 5 (240 020 171, www. stadtmuseum.de). U2 Märkisches Museum. **Open** 10am-6pm Tue-Sun. **Admission** €5; €3 reductions. Free 1st Wed of mth. **Map** p43 F5 ④

This extensive, curious and somewhat old-fashioned museum traces the history of Berlin through a wide range of historical artefacts. Different sections examine themes such as Berlin as a newspaper city, women in Berlin's history, city guilds, intellectual Berlin and the military. There are models of the city at different times, and some good paintings, including works by members of the Brücke group. It ends with a particularly charming section about traditional toys, with plenty of hands-on exhibits.

Neue Synagoge

Centrum Judaicum, Oranienburger Strasse 28-30 (8802 8316, www.centrumjudaicum.de). S1, S2, S25 Oranienburger Strasse. **Open** *Mar-Oct* 10am-8pm Mon, Sun; 10am-6pm Tue-Thur; 10am-2pm Fri. *Nov-Feb* 10am-6pm Mon-Thur, Sun; 10am-2pm Fri. **Admission** €3.50; €3 reductions. **No credit cards. Map** p42 D3 ④

Built in 1857-66 as the Berlin Jewish community's showpiece, it was the New Synagogue that was attacked during Kristallnacht in 1938, but not too badly damaged – Allied bombs did far more harm in 1945. The façade remained intact and the Moorish dome has been rebuilt. Inside is a permanent exhibition about Jewish life in Berlin and a glassed-in area protecting the ruins of the sanctuary.

Nikolaikirche

Nikolaikirchplatz (240 020 171, www. stadtmuseum.de). U2, U5, U8, S5, S7, S75

Sammlung Hoffman.

Alexanderplatz. **Open** 10am-6pm daily.
Admission €5; €3 reductions; free under-18s.
Free 1st Wed of mth. **Map** p43 F4 ㊸
Inside Berlin's oldest congregational church is
an interesting collection chronicling the city's
development until 1648. Old tiles, tapestries, and
stone and wood carvings – even punishment devices
– are on display. There are fascinating photos of
wartime damage, plus examples of how the stones
melted together in the heat of bombardment.

Ramones Museum
*Krausnickstrasse 23 (7552 8890, www.ramones
museum.com). S1, S2, S25 Oranienburger Strasse.*
Open noon-10pm daily. **Admission** €3.50.
No credit cards. Map p42 D3 ㊹
Run by a German Ramones' maniac, Flo Hayler,
this compact museum houses a vast collection of
memorabilia, including childhood photos, gig set
lists, flyers and concert T-shirts. There are also
movie screenings, acoustic shows, Ramones-related
special events and a small in-house record label.

Sammlung Hoffman
*Sophienstrasse 21 (2849 9121, www.sophie-
gips.de). U8 Weinmeisterstrasse.* **Open** (by
appointment only) 11am-4pm Sat. **Admission**
€8. **No credit cards. Map** p43 E3 ㊺
Erika and Rolf Hoffmann's private collection of
international contemporary art includes a charming
floor installation by Swiss video artist Pipilotti Rist,
a luxurious art library, and work by Lucio Fontana,
Frank Stella, Douglas Gordon, Felix Gonzalez-
Torres and AR Penck. The Hoffmans offer guided
tours every Saturday by appointment – felt slippers
supplied. Every summer, the entire display changes.

Restaurants & Cafés

Barcomi's
*Sophie-Gips-Höfe, Sophienstrasse 21 (2859
8363, www.barcomis.de). U8 Weinmeisterstrasse.*
Open 9am-9pm Mon-Sat; 10am-9pm Sun. **Map**
p43 E3 ㊻ **Café**

Berlin's very own domestic goddess, Cynthia
Barcomi, opened her first café, in Kreuzberg, back in
1997 – an age in reunified Berlin years. The American
expat brought her nation's sweet treats to Berlin,
doling out blueberry pancakes and whoopee pies as
well as bagels. She now supplies baked goods all over
town, and has two bestselling cookbooks under her
belt. The café is situated in a quiet courtyard near
Hackescher Markt, and locals flock to the outdoor
tables to escape the tourist hubbub. *Photo p51.*
Other location Bergmannstrasse 21,
Kreuzberg (694 8138).

€ Café Fleury
*Weinbergsweg 20 (4403 4144). U8 Rosenthaler
Platz.* **Open** 8am-10pm Mon-Sat; 10am-8pm
Sun. **Main courses** €3-€11. **No credit cards.**
Map p43 E2 ㊼ **Café**
This wildly popular French café at the bottom of the
hill up to Prenzlauer Berg provides the perfect perch
from which to people-watch over a buttery croissant
and café au lait. A variety of cakes, tarts, salads and
baguettes are offered for lunch.

Café Nö!
*Glinkastrasse 23 (201 0871, www.cafe-noe.de).
U6 Französische Strasse.* **Open** noon-1am Mon-
Fri; 7pm-1am Sat. **Main courses** €6.50-€13.50.
Map p42 C5 ㊽ **Wine bar**
This unassuming but right-on wine bar with
simple and wholesome meals is owned by a former
GDR rock musician now continuing his family's
gastronomy tradition. Given the mostly bland or
overpriced restaurants in the neighbourhood, this
is a genuine pearl. Snacks include the shaved Swiss
cheese tête de moine and anchovy crostini; more
substantial fare includes Alsatian *flammkuchen*, and
maultaschen (ravioli) with spinach.

Chicago-Williams
*Hannoverschestrasse 2 (2804 2422, www.
chicago williamsbbq.com). U6 Oranienburger
Tor.* **Open** 5pm-midnight daily. **Main courses**
€9.50-€25. **Map** p42 C3 ㊾ **Barbecue**

At Berlin's first real attempt at aping a Southern-style barbecue shack, platters of smoked meats come piled high on plastic trays. The unctuous ribs are a particular highlight, but pulled pork, pastrami, steak and other favourites are all available. There's an extensive menu of craft beers, IPAs, pale ales and dark beers – surprisingly, all produced in small batches by German brewers, who are usually notoriously pilsener-centric. The place gets rowdy as the night progresses, when the owner starts firing out complimentary Jäger shots.

€ CôCô

Rosenthalerstrasse 2 (2463 0595, www.co-co.net).
U8 Rosenthaler Platz. Open 11am-10pm Mon-Thur; 11am-midnight Fri, Sat; noon-10pm Sun.
Main courses €4-€7. **No credit cards.**
Map p43 E2 ⑩ **Vietnamese**
There's been a *banh mi* explosion in Berlin. Contending for the title of Perfect Sandwich, this Vietnamese speciality combines fatty pâté and roast pork slices, offset by coriander and zingy pickled daikon and carrot, all in an airy-light baguette (rice flour is used to combat the humidity in Vietnam). CôCô's choice of sandwich fillings includes *banh mi thit nuong* (with lemongrass meatballs) and *banh mi chay* (with tofu), as well as the classic variety – all are made to order at the bar. If the sun's out, take your sandwich to the nearby Weinbergpark and munch in peace on the hillside.

House of Small Wonder

Johannisstrasse 20 (2758 2877, www.house ofsmallwonder.de). U6 Oranienburger Tor.
Open 9am-5pm Mon-Fri; 10am-4pm Sat, Sun. **Main courses** €8-€10. **Map** p42 D3 ⑪ **Japanese**
What happens when you take Japanese food, give it an American twist and bring it to the heart of Berlin? You get the House of Small Wonder. Opened by husband and wife team Shaul Margulies and Motoko Watanbe, the café is based on their successful Brooklyn joint, with a menu that offers unlikely juxtapositions of Eastern and Western flavours. All in a lovely, airy and suitably eccentric setting.

Katz Orange

Bergstrasse 22 (983 208 430, www.katzorange. com). U8 Rosenthaler Platz. **Open** 6pm-3.30am Mon-Sat. **Main courses** €17-€26. **Map** p42 D2 ⑫ **Modern German**
Set off the street in a handsome 19th-century red-brick ex-brewery, Katz Orange is a grown-up restaurant for locavore dining with an excellent late-night cocktail bar attached. They take pains to source local produce from trusted farmers and suppliers to create a short menu of seasonal dishes. Try the zander (a sustainable river fish, better known as pike-perch) with mushroom ravioli or share the signature pork neck dish, cooked sous-vide for 12 hours then crisped up under the grill.

Mogg & Melzer.

Lebensmittel im Mitte

Rochstrasse 2 (2759 6130). U8 Weinmeisterstrasse. **Open** noon-4pm, 5-11pm Mon-Sat. **Main courses** €6.50-€22. **No credit cards. Map** p43 F3 ⑬ **German/Austrian**
This deli/restaurant is a little journey into the joys of southern German and Austrian cuisine. The deli at the front offers fine cheeses, rustic bread, organic veg, sausages and even Austrian pumpkin-seed oil. But you can also settle on to long wooden benches beneath the antlers on the wall, and dine on high-fat, carb-loaded dishes such as *Leberkäse*, tongue, rösti and cheese *Spätzle* accompanied by a broad selection of southern German and Austrian wines or Bavarian beer. Laptops not allowed.

★ Das Lokal

Linienstrasse 160 (2844 9500, http://lokal-berlin. blogspot.co.uk). S1, S2, S25 Oranienburger Strasse. **Open** 6pm-midnight Mon, Sat, Sun; noon-4pm, 6pm-midnight Tue-Fri. **Main courses** €14-€25. **Map** p42 D3 ⑭ **Modern German**
Das Lokal comes from fine heritage: it opened while the much-loved Kantine was being redesigned alongside David Chipperfield's studio. The weekly changing seasonal menu might feature starters of pigeon with chestnuts, mussels in broth or asparagus croquettes – all designed to demonstrate

the superior flavour of well-sourced produce. It's also an oasis for offal dishes and game, with which Berlin's surrounding forests abound.

★ Mogg & Melzer

Auguststrasse 11-13 (330 060 770, www. moggandmelzer.com). U6 Oranienburger Tor. **Open** 8am-late Mon-Fri; 10am-late Sat, Sun. **Main courses** €8.50-€12.50. **Map** p42 D3 ⑤ **Deli**
This New York-style deli is a lunchtime hotspot for local galleristas, where all the necessaries are pitch-perfect: the pickles pack a hefty crunch; fresh coleslaw is just the right side of creamy-sour; and the toasted rye bread reveals a fluffy interior. Yet all play second fiddle to the thick wodge of smoky goodness that is their pastrami meat. The menu features classics such as the Reuben, topped with melted 'Swiss' cheese, sauerkraut and a special dressing, plus matzo ball soup and cream cheese bagels.

Monsieur Vuong

Alte Schönhauser Strasse 46 (3087 2643, www.monsieurvuong.de). U8 Weinmeisterstrasse. **Open** noon-midnight daily. **Main courses** €7-€9. **No credit cards. Map** p43 F3 ⑤ **Vietnamese**
With its central Mitte location, chic interiors and flawless pho stock, Monsieur Vuong has set a template for plenty of passable copycats. It offers two daily specials (usually something saucy with rice or noodles), plus a short regular menu of noodle salads and pho soups – a large bowl of broth with glass noodles, topped with chicken or beef and crunchy beansprouts, a generous helping of chopped coriander and a squirt of lime. You can't book, but the experienced staff keep the place turning over at a head-spinning rate.

Nola's am Weinberg

Veteranenstrasse 9 (4404 0766, www.nola.de). U8 Rosenthaler Platz. **Open** 10am-1am daily. **Main courses** €9-€17. **Map** p43 E2 ⑤ **Swiss**
This former park pavilion has a fabulous terrace overlooking the park slope, as well as a bar and dining room. Expect artery-hardening Swiss fare, such as venison goulash with mushrooms and spinach noodles, or cheese and spinach rösti topped with a fried egg. On Sundays, they do a magnificently generous brunch buffet.

Noto

Torstrasse 173 (2009 5387, www.noto-berlin.com). U8 Rosenthaler Platz. **Open** 6pm-midnight Mon-Sat. **Main courses** €14.50-€28.50. **Map** p42 D2 ⑤ **Haute cuisine**
Noto exemplifies contemporary Berlin dining: a laid-back setting, with the chef-owner cooking traditional German produce made modern through creative techniques. The succinct menu changes weekly, zipping from cocoa and pumpkin ravioli in a rabbit ragoût to the signature dish of veal spare ribs in an Asian-style sweet marinade.

Princess Cheesecake

Tucholskystrasse 37 (2809 2760, www. princess-cheesecake.de). U2 Senefelderplatz. **Open** 10am-7pm daily. **Map** p42 D3 ⑤ **Café**
A perfect pit stop during a day's Auguststrasse gallery-hopping, Princess Cheesecake is where you can try the venerable 'Kaffee und Kuchen' tradition – Germany's equivalent of afternoon tea. Decor takes equally from minimalism as it does from the baroque, and the cakes are accordingly clean-lined but opulent in flavour. Try a classic baked cheesecake or one of the more adventurous numbers such as 'Mi Cariño Suave', laden with candied almonds and toffee and topped with quark cream.

Reinstoff

Edison-Höfe, Schlegelstrasse 26C (3088 1214, www.reinstoff.eu). U6 Naturkundemuseum. **Open** 7pm-midnight Tue-Sat. **Set meal** €100-€160 5-8 courses. **Map** p42 C2 ⑥ **Haute cuisine**
Since winning a second Michelin star, this extremely slick restaurant tucked away in a courtyard near Nordbahnhof has hiked its prices. Chef Daniel Achilles uses meticulously sourced, mostly organic, ingredients to create 'taste adventures'. You choose from two menus: the *ganznah* (quite near) and *weiterdraussen* (far away), each playing with the notion of taste memory and texture, but utilising a distinctly different palette of ingredients. Typical dishes are brown crab from the Dutch coast of Oosterschelde, served with chicory and hibiscus, followed by teriyaki venison saddle, cooked in lotus, ginger and brown sugar.

€ Sababa

Kastanienallee 50-51 (4050 5401, www.sababa hummus.de). U2 Senefelderplatz, or U8 Rosenthaler Platz. **Open** 11am-10pm daily. **Main courses** €5-€9. **No credit cards. Map** p43 E2 ⑥ **Israeli**
Israeli chef Ze'ev brings a taste of one of the Middle East's reviving culinary features – rich and creamy houmous – plus plenty of pitta to mop it up with. You'll also find *shakshuka*, a breakfast favourite of two eggs baked in tomato sauce; zingy salads; and assorted omelettes including a Persian version that is stuffed full of fresh herbs.

Schwarzwaldstuben

Tucholskystrasse 48 (2809 8084). S1, S2, S25 Oranienburger Strasse. **Main courses** €7-€14.50. **Open** 9am-midnight daily. **No credit cards. Map** p42 D3 ⑥ **German**
Some of the best German cooking comes from Swabia, but Swabian restaurants tend to be filled with teddy bears and knick-knacks. This place, however, is casually chic, and wears its mounted deer head ironically. Food is excellent: the soups are hearty; stellar main courses include the *Schäuffele* with sauerkraut and potatoes; and the *Flammkuchen* (a sort of German pizza) is good. Another plus is the popular Rothaus Tannenzapfle beer on tap.

EXPLORE

€ Tadshikische Teestube

KunstHof, Oranienburger Strasse 27 (204 1112, www.tadshikische-teestube.de). S1, S2, S25, Oranienburger Strasse, or U6 Oranienburger Tor. **Open** 4pm-midnight Mon-Fri; noon-midnight Sat, Sun. **Main courses** €4-€12. **Map** p42 D3 ⓿ **Café**

Originally the Soviet pavilion at the 1974 Leipzig Fair, this charming Tajik tearoom was lovingly preserved and for many years operated out of the grander Palais on the Moat. It's had to move – but a new owner has arrived to continue this Berlin oddity at a new location in an old art gallery. Remove your shoes, lounge around on the plushly carpeted floors and enjoy a full Russian tea service with sweet buckwheat pancakes on the side.

★ Trois Minutes sur Mer

Torstrasse 166 (6730 2052, www.3minutes surmer.de). U8 Rosenthaler Platz. **Open** 11.30am-midnight Mon-Fri; 10am-midnight Sat, Sun. **Main courses** €16-€23.50. **Map** p42 D2 ⓿ **French**

Here, the traditional Parisian bistro aesthetic (art deco bar stools, paper tablecloths) sits alongside Nouveau Berlin touches (GDR light fittings and funky red bar stools). Excellent fish options, such as red mullet and bream, come impeccably cooked, all crisp skin and translucent flesh. There are also more gutsy dishes: a reduced coq au vin, and escargots de bourgogne dripping in garlic butter. Presentation is visually spare, any jus neatly daubed and portions squared off; the suckling pig dish a geometric wonder. Start with some foie gras pâté (ethical stance dependent) and end with the tarte tatin. Booking advised.

ULA-Berlin

Anklamer Strasse 8 (8937 9570, www.ulaberlin. jimdo.com). S1, S2, S25 Nordbahnhof. **Open** 6pm-midnight Tue-Sun. **Main courses** €13.50-€29. **Map** p42 D2 ⓿ **Japanese**

Head to ULA for an elegant alternative to budget sushi joints. The kitchen is headed by Taro Fujita, who was previously chef at the Japanese ambassador's residence and was trained in Kyoto's ornate techniques. The high-concept menu and fine sakés are matched by the sleek, black interior. As well as sushi, there are saké tasting menus, complex Kaiseki-style dishes and luxury specialities such as *sukiyaki* (hotpot) with stone-grilled wagyu beef.

Weinbar Al Contadino Sotto le Stelle

Gormannstrasse 10 (2759 2102, www.alcontadino. eu). U8 Weinmeisterstrasse. **Open** 6pm-midnight Tue-Sat. **Main courses** €13.50-€22.50. **Map** p43 E3 ⓿ **Italian**

Skip the overpriced main restaurant and instead head to the cosy wine bar for some of the city's best Emilia-Romagnan cooking, which follows Slow Food guidelines for sourcing produce. Start, perhaps, with octopus in green sauce, or ricotta and cauliflower *malfatti* (dumplings), followed by handmade chestnut tagliatelle or roast veal in milk sauce. Otherwise, just order a bottle of crisp Veneto Soave and share antipasti from the bar menu.

Bars & Pubs

Altes Europa

Gipsstrasse 11 (2809 3840, www.alteseuropa.com). U8 Weinmeisterstrasse. **Open** noon-1am daily. **No credit cards. Map** p43 E3 ⓿

Trois Minutes sur Mer.

The gentle minimalism of the decor – big picture windows, basic furnishings and nothing but a few old maps and prints on the walls – is a relief in an increasingly touristy neighbourhood, and this inviting place is good for anything from a mid-afternoon drink to a rowdier night out with friends. The bar serves light meals, Ukrainian vodka and draught Krusovice in both dark and light varieties to a mixed, youngish crowd.

★ Bar 3

Weydingerstrasse 20 (9700 5106). U2 Rosa-Luxemburg-Platz. **Open** 9pm-late Tue-Sat. **No credit cards. Map** p43 F3 ⑱

Located in a backstreet off Torstrasse, this cosy bar is a favourite of Mitte media types. With a large horseshoe-shaped bar dominating the room, it's bar stools or standing only, as this place seriously packs out with a slick, bespectacled clientele and the occasional actor or celebrity. The house wine is very good. Or try the Kölsch beer from Cologne – tradition dictates that it's served in a tiny glass, constantly refilled by the barman until you abandon it half-full or lay a beer mat over the top.

Chelsea Bar

Torstrasse 59 (0176 3225 2652, www.thechelsea bar.info). U2 Rosa-Luxemburg-Platz. **Open** 7pm-late daily. **Map** p43 F2 ⑲

A recent addition to the thriving Torstrasse scene, Chelsea Bar is an appealingly scuzzy, down-at-heel joint that's yet to be overrun by the city's hipsters (as with the infamous Neues Odessa bar down the street). A basic menu, art-rock sounds, frequent live music and nightly DJs meld into an ambience happily reminiscent of an old-school Berlin dive bar.

Cordobar

Grosse Hamburger Strasse 32 (2758 1215, www.cordobar.net). S1, S2, S25 Oranienburger Strasse, or U8 Rosenthaler Platz. **Open** 5pm-2am Tue-Sat. **Map** p43 E3 ⑩

The Parisian-wine-bar-with-small-plates model has become extremely popular in recent years, and Mitte finally has an excellent example. The Cordobar is owned by Austrian sommelier Willi Shlögl and friends (including film director Jan-Ole Gerster), so the list focuses on southern German and Austrian wines, with many unsulphured 'natural' bottles. Hot and cold dishes such as blood-sausage pizza or smoked eel with brussels sprouts, are also available.

Kapelle

Zionskirchplatz 22-24 (4434 1300, www.cafe-kapelle.de). U8 Rosenthaler Platz. **Open** 9am-3am daily. **No credit cards. Map** p43 E2 ⑪

A comfortable, high-ceilinged café-bar at the corner of the Zionskirchplatz, Kapelle takes its name from Die Rote Kapelle, 'the Red Orchestra'. This was a clandestine anti-fascist organisation, and in the 1930s and '40s the Kapelle's basement was a

secret meeting place for the Resistance. Come here for tidy breakfasts featuring organic meat and unpasteurised milk from nearby farms.

Kim

Brunnenstrasse 10 (no phone, www.kim-in-berlin. com). U8 Rosenthaler Platz. **Open** 9pm-late daily. **No credit cards. Map** p43 E2 ⑫

A veteran of the Mitte scene, Kim has been a favourite with twentysomething art-scenesters since it opened in 2007, although its ramshackle atmosphere and charm was somewhat neutralised by a makeover a year or so ago. The door is unmarked: look for an all-glass façade and crowds of people sporting billowy monochrome clothing. Cheap drinks and a rotating roster of neighbourhood DJs add to the don't-give-a-damn aesthetic.

Kingsize

Friedrichstrasse 112B (no phone, www.kingsize bar.de). U6 Oranienburger Tor. **Open** 9pm-7am Wed-Sat. **Map** p42 D3 ⑬

This is one of the tiniest dive bars in Berlin, and traditionally the place where late-night adventures begin. Be prepared to be shoved, jostled and pushed about the minuscule interior. The place really reaches maximum capacity on Wednesday when local gallerist Martin Kwade runs his Artist's Night, with random DJs culled from across Berlin's art underground. The party gets going after midnight and continues until way past dawn.

Maxime

Gormannstrasse 25 (6583 3962, www.vins-cochonneries.com). U8 Weinmeisterstrasse. **Open** 6pm-1am Tue-Sat. **Map** p43 E3 ⑭

Another excellent new 'natural' wine bar, this time from the French team behind the much-missed HBC and local vintner Maxime Boillat. There's a rotating menu of around 20 wines by the glass, as well as an extensive list of bottles from France, Spain and Italy. Naturally, where there's wine, there's cheese – supplied by the renowned French *affineur* Bernard Antony, with pungent raw-milk brillat-savarin and bûche des pyrénées on offer.

Mein Haus am See

Brunnenstrasse 197-198 (2388 3561, www.mein-haus-am-see.blogspot.com). U8 Rosenthaler Platz. **Open** 9am-late daily. **No credit cards. Map** p43 E2 ⑮

This hugely popular split-level joint is situated a stone's throw from busy Rosenthaler Platz and is a great alternative to the tired Sankt Oberholz. The owners' slightly vapid claim is that 'it's not a bar, it's not a club, it's something sexier in between', but it's certainly hard to categorise. There are exhibitions, readings, DJs and it almost never closes, so whether you want another beer, a sobering coffee or a panino at 4.30am, this is the place to come. Excellent breakfasts too.

EXPLORE

Tausend

Schiffbauerdamm 11 (2758 2070, www. tausend berlin.com). U6, S1, S2, S5, S7, S25, S75 Friedrichstrasse. **Open** 9pm-late Tue-Sat. **Map** p42 C4 ⓰

With its unmarked entrance – look for the iron door under the train overpass – and strict entrance policy, this grown-up bar is as exclusive as Berlin gets. This is where the well-heeled come to be seen sipping innovative drinks in a tubular, steel-ceilinged interior lit by eerily eye-like 3D installations. Try a bracing wasabi cocktail in summer or a malt whisky served with local pine honey in winter. Go late, look sharp. Skip the Backroom Cantina restaurant and its fussy fusion menu.

Trust

Neue Promenade 10 (no phone, www.trust-berlin.com). S5, S7, S75 Hackescher Markt. **Open** 10pm-5am Thur-Sat. **No credit cards**. **Map** p43 E3 ⓱

The old Torstrasse dive bar space has now been replaced by this sprawling Hackescher Markt location, but the old rules still apply. All spirits are sold in Trust-branded bottles and the idea is to band together with friends (especially if just made at the bar) to booze the night away. It's owned by Cookie, a local club legend, and one of the Weekend founders, so come to see the ritzy Mitte crowds letting their hair down, but watch out for the moody doorman. Local DJs usually spin on weekends.

Shops & Services

14 oz. Berlin

Neue Schönhauser Strasse 13 (4920 3750, www.14oz-berlin.com). U8 Weinmeisterstrasse. **Open** 1-8pm Mon-Sat. **Map** p43 E3 ⓲ **Fashion**

This menswear (mainly) shop caters for the rugged high-end heritage look, dealing primarily in the

kind of rigid blue denim you're never supposed to wash, but also stocking quality leather footwear from English cobblers Trickers and eye-wateringly expensive Nigel Cabourne jackets.

Other locations Kurfürstendamm 194, Charlottenburg (8892 1814); Memhardstrasse 7, Mitte (2847 8578).

Acne Studios

Weinmeisterstrasse 2 (9700 5187, www.acne studios.com). U8 Weinmeisterstrasse. **Open** 11am-8pm Mon-Sat. **Map** p43 E3 ⓳ **Fashion**

Sweden's Acne just keeps going from strength to strength, having completed its transformation from cult jeans label to fully-fledged global empire with its slinky draping and quality materials. The bulbous white Berlin flagship store, hidden behind a crumbling shopfront, features skin-tight jeans, fine knitwear and silken evening wear for both men and women.

Ampelmann Galerie Shop

Rosenthaler Strasse 40-41 (4404 8801, www.ampelmann.de). S5, S7, S75 Hackescher Markt. **Open** 9.30am-8pm Mon-Sat (summer until 10pm); 10.30am-7pm Sun. **Map** p43 E3 ⓴ **Gifts & souvenirs**

You'll find a huge variety of stuff emblazoned with the old East's enduring symbol, the jaunty red and green traffic-light men (*see left* **In the Know**). As you can see from the number of shops dotted around the city, they've become unofficial city mascots and have even started colonising West Berlin road crossings too.

Other locations DomAquarée, Karl-Liebknecht-Strasse 1, Mitte (2758 3238); Potsdamer Platz Arkaden, Alte Potsdamer Strasse 7, Tiergarten (2592 5691); Markgrafenstrasse 37, Kreuzberg (4003 9095).

APC

Mulackstrasse 36 (2844 9192, www.apc.fr). U2 Rosa-Luxemburg-Platz, or U8 Weinmeisterstrasse. **Open** 11.30am-7.30pm Mon-Fri; noon-6pm Sat. **Map** p43 F3 ㉛ **Fashion**

Tucked away on a side street that boasts Mitte's finest couture shops, this popular Parisian brand offers mens- and womenswear essentials: chunky woollens, leather boots and Japanese denim jeans. **Other locations** Fasanenstrasse 22, Charlottenburg (8870 8544).

Arkonaplatz Flohmarkt

Arkonaplatz (786 9764, www.troedelmarkt-arkonaplatz.de). U8 Bernauer Strasse. **Open** 10am-4pm Sun. **Map** p43 E1 ㉜ **Market**

A broad array of retro gear – ranging from vinyl to clothing, books to trinkets, bikes to coffee tables – is all available here at moderate prices. The golden rule of flea markets applies at Arkonaplatz: the best stuff gets snapped up early.

IN THE KNOW
AMPELMÄNNCHEN

Wondering why pedestrian traffic lights have much jauntier little red and green men than in other cities? Both are wearing hats, and the green man has a very purposeful stride. They are *Ampelmännchen*, a hangover from East Germany, which had different traffic lights from West Germany. In the euphoria following the collapse of Communism, the *Ampelmännchen* started to die out and be replaced by their more straight-laced western counterparts – until Ostalgie struck and a campaign was launched to bring them back. Due to their marketability as souvenirs, you can now see them on both sides of the reunified city.

Blush

*Rosa-Luxemburg-Strasse 22 (2809 3580,
www.blush-berlin.com). U2 Rosa-Luxemburg-
Platz, or U8 Weinmeisterstrasse.* **Open** noon-
8pm Mon-Fri; noon-7pm Sat. **Map** p43 F3
❽ **Accessories**
There's all sorts of silk and lace goodies at this
lingerie shop, including underwear, pyjamas and
even hot water bottle covers. Imports from France
and Italy, as well as German brands.

★ Bonbon Macherei

*Oranienburger Strasse 32 (4405 5243,
www.bonbonmacherei.de). S1, S2, S25
Oranienburger Strasse.* **Open** noon-8pm
Wed-Sat. **No credit cards. Map** p42 D3
❸ **Food & drink**
A nostalgic candy shop that offers sweet, sour and
everything in between. You can watch Katja Kolbe
and Hjalmar Stecher produce their boiled sweets in
the on-site workshop using vintage equipment and
traditional recipes. High quality at reasonable prices.

Buchhandlung Walther König

*Burgstrasse 27 (2576 0980, www.buchhandlung-
walther-koenig.de). S5, S7, S75 Hackescher
Markt.* **Open** 10am-8am Mon-Sat. **Map** p43 E4
❺ **Books & music**
Cologne-based Walther König is Germany's top art
publisher, with several branches dotted throughout
Europe; it also stocks the bookshops at Berlin's
museums. This flagship store by Museumsinsel
heaves with beautifully reproduced catalogues and
a comprehensive range of critical-theory literature.
These books would make a handsome gift for the art-
lover in your life.

Civilist

*Brunnenstrasse 13 (8561 0715, www.civilist
berlin.com). U8 Rosenthaler Platz.* **Open**
noon-8pm Mon-Fri; 11am-6pm Sat. **Map**
p43 E2 ❻ **Accessories**
No self-respecting Berlin skater would be seen in
anything other than a Civilist wool beanie. This
neatly designed shop is run by the local *Lodown*
magazine crew, focusing on limited-edition
collaborations and mature skate labels including
HUF and aNYthing. There's a special Nike SB shop
a few doors down.

Do You Read Me?

*Auguststrasse 28 (6954 9695, www.doyou
readme.de). U8 Rosenthaler Platz, or S1, S2,
S25 Oranienburger Strasse.* **Open** *Summer*
10am-9.30pm Mon-Sat. *Winter* 10am-7.30pm
Mon-Sat. **Map** p43 E3 ❼ **Books & music**
On Mitte's main art drag, this small shop's shelves
heave with glossy picks of global fashion, style,
art and design print media. The magazines are
attractively presented, and there's a small selection
of books in the back.

★ DSTM

*Torstrasse 161 (4920 3750, www.dstm.co).
U8 Rosenthaler Platz.* **Open** 1-8pm Mon-Sat.
Map p43 E2 ❽ **Fashion**
There's plenty of young Berlin designers cutting
their chops at boutiques around the city, but
Canadian-born Jen Gilpin's label, Don't Shoot
The Messenger, is the definitive city look. Local
influences can be read from all over: shades of
Marlene Dietrich's austere raunchiness and even the
complex fastenings of fetish-ware are apparent in
the billowy clothing, made mostly in fine black silk
and leather. Angular cutouts offer glimpses of flesh,
and sleek shapes are conjured by inventive draping
that proves Gilpin's skilled technique.

Fun Factory

*Oranienburger Strasse 92 (2804 6366, www.
funfactory.com). S5, S7, S75 Hackescher Markt.*
Open 11am-8pm Mon-Thur; 11am-9pm Fri, Sat.
Map p43 E3 ❾ **Sex shop**
Berlin's temple to adult toys lies slap-bang in the
middle of Hackescher Markt's central shopping
area. With an interior designed by American futurist
Karim Rashid, the two-floor shop caters to a mixed
gay/straight crowd of all stripes. Staff are extremely
helpful if advice is needed.

Galerie Eigen Art

*Auguststrasse 26 (280 6605, www.eigen-art.
com). U8 Rosenthaler Platz, or S1, S2, S25
Oranienburger Strasse.* **Open** 11am-6pm
Tue-Sat. **Map** p43 E3 ❿ **Gallery**
A stalwart of the old Auguststrasse art strip, this
is where man-about-town Gerd Harry 'Judy' Lybke
continues his longstanding relationship with New
Leipzig School star painters Matthias Weischer
and Neo Rauch. It's a far cry from Lybke's Leipzig
living-room gallery in the early 1980s. There's also a
'lab' space for younger artists at the Mädchenschule
down the road.

Happy Shop

*Torstrasse 67 (0157 7847 3620 mobile, www.
happyshop-berlin.com). U2 Rosa-Luxemburg-
Platz.* **Open** 11am-7pm Tue-Sat. **Map** p43 F2
❶ **Fashion**
A dash of Technicolor fun in monochromatic
Mitte, this spacious boutique features a cool op-art
façade, racks and mannequins dangling from the
ceiling, and a selection of wonderfully unique pieces
by funky Japanese designer Tsumori Chisato and
Bernhard Wilhelm.

KW Institute for Contemporary Art

*Auguststrasse 69 (243 4590, www.kw-berlin.de). U6
Oranienburger Tor, or S1, S2, S25 Oranienburger
Strasse.* **Open** noon-7pm Tue, Wed, Fri-Sun;
noon-9pm Thur. **Admission** €6; €4 reductions.
Map p42 D3 ❷ **Gallery**

EXPLORE

Housed in a former margarine factory, KW has been a major non-profit showcase since the early 1990s. It gets involved with other local galleries and projects, such as Berlin Art Week and the cheerfully never-less-than-controversial Berlin Biennale. Ellen Blumenstein took over as head curator in 2013. The courtyard (great for social events) was designed by American artist Dan Graham.

LaLa Berlin
Mulackstrasse 7 (2576 2924, www.lalaberlin.com). U8 Weinmeisterstrasse. **Open** noon-8pm Wed-Sat. **Map** p43 E3 ③ **Fashion**
Iranian-born Leyla Piedayesh knocks out stylish and cosy knitwear at her Mitte boutique. She's got a shop in Copenhagen too and has become well known across the Atlantic, not least due to famous fans such as Claudia Schiffer, Cameron Diaz and Jessica Alba.

Made in Berlin
Neue Schönhauser Strasse 19 (2123 0601). U8 Weinmeisterstrasse. **Open** 11am-8pm Mon-Sat. **Map** p43 E3 ④ **Fashion**
Another branch of the Kleidermarkt clothes empire, where the 'better stuff' supposedly goes – vintage Barbour, Burberry and Lacoste, for example. It's still pretty cheap, though, and offers a ton of great no-name 1980s gear. Every Tuesday between noon and 3pm, you'll get a 20% discount.
Other location Friedrichstrasse 114A, Mitte (2404 8900).

Moebel Horzon
Torstrasse 106 (0176 6273 0874, www. modocom.de). U8 Rosenthaler Platz. **Open** varies. **No credit cards. Map** p43 E2 ⑤ **Homewares**
Artist? Writer? Businessman? It's hard to define what Rafael Horzon really does. But the fact is that he invented simple shelves that are easy on the eye and can be admired in his Mitte showroom.

Mykita
Rosa-Luxemburg-Strasse 6 (6730 8715, www.mykita.com). U2, U5, U8, S5, S7, S75 Alexanderplatz. **Open** 11am-8pm Mon-Fri; noon-6pm Sat. **Map** p43 F3 ⑥ **Accessories**
This Berlin-based glasses label has been a mainstay for fashion-conscious locals since 2004, but the brand has hit the big time since some of its more experimental frames were picked up by the likes of Lady Gaga. Creators Philipp Haffmans and Harald Gottschling present their handmade prescription frames and sunglasses on stark, industrial shelving in this beautifully lit, ultra-minimalist store.

Das Neue Schwarz
Mulackstrasse 38 (2787 4467, www.dasneue schwarz.de). U2 Rosa-Luxemburg-Platz, or U8 Weinmeisterstrasse. **Open** 11am-8pm Mon-Sat. **Map** p43 E3 ⑦ **Fashion**

Mulackstrasse is full of expensive designer boutiques, so Das Neue Schwarz ('the new black') is a great alternative for those looking for a (relative) bargain. The hand-selected stock offers almost-new designer pieces from past seasons, most still with tags. There's stuff for both boys and girls: chunky Céline handbags, flashy Bernard Willhelm bomber jackets, Chloé wedges and Dries Van Noten suits, to name just a few.

Oona
Auguststrasse 26 (2804 5905, www.oona-galerie. de). S1, S2, S25 Oranienburger Strasse, or U8 Rosenthaler Platz. **Open** 2-6pm Tue-Fri; 1-6pm Sat. **Map** p42 D3 ⑨ **Accessories**
In addition to its permanent collection, this 'gallery for contemporary jewellery' features work by young creatives from Japan, Australia and elsewhere in Europe. The gallery and artists choose a special theme and work with architects, photographers and interior designers to develop a concept. A mix of precious and non-precious materials means there's a corresponding mix of price tags.

★ Pro QM
Almstadtstrasse 48-50 (2472 8520, www.pro-qm.de). U2 Rosa-Luxemburg-Platz. **Open** 11am-8pm Mon-Sat. **Map** p43 F3 ⑨ **Books & music**
This art bookshop has the rarified design of a white cube, but don't let that put you off – inside the ambience is extremely welcoming, with staff encouraging lengthy browsing. There's a particularly strong selection of urban and critical theory, in both German and English, as well as an active schedule of talks by artists, writers and architects.

RSVP
Mulackstrasse 14 (2809 4644, www.rsvp-berlin.de). U8 Weinmeisterstrasse. **Open** noon-7pm Mon-Thur; noon-8pm Fri, Sat. **Map** p43 E3 ⑩ **Gifts & souvenirs**
Stationery for the aesthete: art deco scissors, exotic erasers, weighty Rivoli writing paper, Polish notebooks and Koh-I-Noor mechanical pencils.

Sammlung Boros
Reinhardtstrasse 20 (no phone, www.sammlung-boros.de). U6 Oranienburger Tor. **Open** by appointment. **No credit cards. Map** p42 C3 ⑪ **Gallery**
More akin to a museum than an actual gallery, this concrete World War II bunker has been transformed into a 3,000sq m space containing the formidable collection of advertising mogul Christian Boros and his wife Karen. Works on view include contemporary greats such as Olafur Eliasson and Sarah Lucas, as well as a healthy selection of contemporary local and international names that have caught Boros's beady eye. Tours are on weekends by appointment only; book well in advance through the website.

EXPLORE

Mykita.

Shusta

Rosenthaler Strasse 72 (7621 9780, www.shusta. de). U8 Rosenthaler Platz. **Open** *11am-8pm Mon-Sat.* **Map** p43 E2 ⑩ **Accessories**
In this high-ceilinged store, you'll find stylish leather shoes imported from all over the world by Tedros and Fidel, the shop's very cool and friendly owners. A separate door leads upstairs to classic men's shoes, as well as some women's clothing.

Smart Deli

Chausseestrasse 5 (2068 7037, www.smartdeli. org). U6 Oranienburger Tor. **Open** *10am-10pm Mon-Sat.* **Map** p42 C3 ⑩ **Food & drink**
Most Asian food stores in Berlin sell South-east Asian and Chinese goodies, so this is one of the best places to buy specific Japanese products such as the cult Kewpie mayonnaise and curry paste.

Soto

Torstrasse 72 (2576 2070, www.sotostore.com). U2 Rosa-Luxemburg-Platz. **Open** *noon-8pm Mon-Fri; 11am-8pm Sat.* **Map** p43 F2 ⑩ **Fashion**
One for the boys, with a curated selection of cult labels on offer: limited-edition Flyknit Nikes, soft woollen slacks from Norse Projects or fine knitwear from Acne. Complete the look with a pair of tortoiseshell shades from Italy's Super 4 and something from their extensive accessories range, from spotty socks to chunky headphones.

Sprüth-Magers

Oranienburger Strasse 18 (2888 4030, www. spruethmagers.com). S5, S7, S75 Hackescher Markt. **Open** *11am-6pm Tue-Sat.* **Map** p43 E3 ⑩ **Gallery**
This is now the main space for Cologne powerhouses Monika Sprüth and Philomene Magers (alongside their London gallery). They've been key in developing the careers of such international figures

as Peter Fischli and David Weiss, Andreas Gursky and Cindy Sherman. With the emphasis still on emerging artists, shows vary between big hitters such as Gary Hume and younger artists.

Whisky & Cigars

Sophienstrasse 8-9 (282 0376, www.whisky-cigars.de). S5, S7, S75 Hackescher Markt. **Open** *11am-7pm Mon-Fri; 11am-6pm Sat.* **Map** p43 E3 ⑩ **Food & drink**
Two friends with a love of single malts are behind this shop, which stocks 450 whiskies, plus cigars from Cuba, Jamaica and Honduras, among other sources. Regular tastings too.

Wood Wood

Rochstrasse 4 (2804 7877, www.woodwood.dk). U2, U5, U8, S5, S7, S75 Alexanderplatz. **Open** *noon-8pm Mon-Fri; noon-7pm Sat.* **Map** p43 E3 ⑩ **Fashion**
An avant-garde design collective from Copenhagen, Wood Wood offers beautiful, angular and sometimes outrageous street fashion, sneakers and accessories by Japanese (or co-opted by Japan) designers, such as Sonia Rykiel, Comme des Garçons and White Mountaineering. Almost half the stock is Wood Wood's own, an explosion of prints, stitching and bright colours tempered by clean, classic cuts.

Zionskirchplatz Farmers' Market

Zionskirchplatz (394 4073). U2 Senefelderplatz, or U8 Rosenthaler Platz. **Open** *11am-6.30pm Thur.* **Map** p43 E2 ⑩ **Market**
Regional growers sell fresh fruit and vegetables, fresh fish, homemade jams, assorted breads, and organic cheese from Berliner Käsehandel. Farmers set up on the cobbled walkway surrounding one of Berlin's most beautiful churches, making this a truly picturesque market whatever the time of year.

EXPLORE

Prenzlauer Berg

Prenzlauer Berg is the district that has been most visibly transformed by Berlin's history. From 19th-century roots as a working-class district, it's become the most desirable neighbourhood for hip young families, the bijou children's clothing shops speaking nothing of its previous life as a centre of GDR dissidence or post-Wall bohemia. Even if there aren't many major museums or sights to visit, the area still has fine examples of late 19th-century civic architecture, Berlin's biggest flea market at the Mauerpark, and lots of great shopping. A blend of old and new, sleekly modern and charmingly quaint, Prenzlauer Berg is ideal for a weekend's exploring.

EXPLORE

"The Bird"

Bird.

Don't Miss

1 Mauerpark Flohmarkt Sunday bargain-hunting has become an institution at Berlin's liveliest flea market (p81).

2 Museum in the Kulturbrauerei For a taste of what GDR life was really like (p72).

3 Bonanza Need a caffeine fix? Head to Berlin's espresso mecca (p76).

4 Bird Knives and forks are positively discouraged at Berlin's best burger joint (p73).

5 Saint George's A proper bookshop, with leather sofas and a great selection in English (p81).

Gethsemanekirche.

Once a grey, depressing, working-class district, in the last two decades Prenzlauer Berg has had its façades renovated, its streets cleaned, and its buildings newly inhabited by everyone from Russian artists to office workers. Worlds away from its grim wartime depiction in Hans Fallada's chilling novel *Alone in Berlin*, galleries and cafés have sprouted, and century-old buildings have had coal heating replaced and private bathrooms installed. It's gone too far for some alternative types, but for many lifestyle émigrés from wealthier parts of Germany, there's no cooler part of town.

Laid out during the second half of the 19th century, Prenzlauer Berg was part of the city's Hobrecht-Plan expansion that coincided with the Gründerzeit – the building boom that followed German unification. It left behind wider streets and pavements, giving the area a distinctive, open look. Although a few buildings still await restoration, the newly scrubbed and painted streets give the impression of 19th-century boulevards.

The district's focal point is leafy **Kollwitzplatz**. The square is lined with bars, cafés and restaurants, and hosts an organic market on Thursdays. Knaackstrasse, heading south-east from Kollwitzplatz, brings you to one of the district's main landmarks, the **Wasserturm**. This water tower, constructed by English architect Henry Gill in 1852-75, provided running water for the first time in Germany. During the war, the Nazis used its basement as a prison and torture chamber. A plaque commemorates their victims; the tower has been converted into swanky apartments.

Opposite the Wasserturm on Rykestrasse is the **Synagoge Rykestrasse**, a neo-romanesque turn-of-the-20th-century structure that was badly damaged during Kristallnacht in 1938. After undergoing renovation in 1953, it was the only working synagogue in East Berlin. Now it stands peacefully in gentrified surrounds. Nearby, to the south-west of Kollwitzplatz,

is the **Jüdischer Friedhof**, Berlin's oldest Jewish cemetery, and fairly gloomy due to its closely packed stones and canopy of trees. The Impressionist painter Max Liebermann is buried here, and the tomb of famed soprano Sophie Löwe is, unusually, decorated with a carving of her face – usually prohibited by Judaism. To learn more about the district's history, look in at the **Prenzlauer Berg Museum**.

Moving on clockwise to the other side of Kollwitzplatz, Knaackstrasse extends north-west to the vast complex of the **Kulturbrauerei**, an old brewery that now houses a concert space, galleries, artists' studios, a market, a cinema and a museum. South-west from here, the area around Kastanienallee has plenty of good bars, shops and restaurants. To the north-east is the 'LSD' area – around Lychener Strasse, Stargarder Strasse and Dunckerstrasse – which is what passed for the GDR's druggy zone, and **Helmholtzplatz**, popular with young families.

East of here, on the other side of Prenzlauer Allee, is **Ernst-Thälmann-Park**, named after the leader of the pre-1933 German Communist Party. In its north-west corner stands the **Zeiss-Grossplanetarium**, a fantastic GDR space that once celebrated Soviet cosmonauts and is currently being renovated. On the Greifswalder Strasse side of the park, just north of the Danziger Strasse corner, is a bombastic 1980s statue of Ernst Thälmann himself, raising a Communist fist – after the Wall fell, only pre-GDR figures remained memorialised in street names and monuments. The statue was built with an amusing contemporary feature: a heated nose to melt any accumulating snow.

Sights & Museums

FREE Gethsemanekirche

Stargarder Strasse 77 (445 7745, www. gethsemanekirche.de). U2, S8, S9, S41, S42, S85 Schönhauser Allee. **Open** *Services* 11am Sun. **Admission** free. **Map** p71 A2 ●

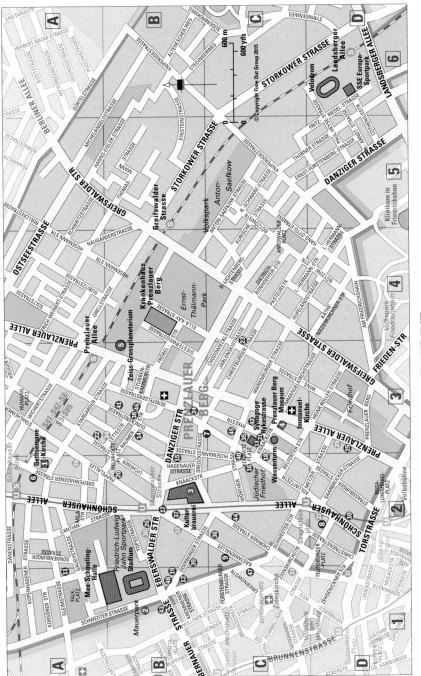

Situated just south of Schönhauser Allee S-Bahn, this striking neo-Gothic church built in August Orth's typical red-brick style – he also built the Zionskirche – is best known for its central role as a meeting place for GDR dissidents in the late 1980s. A statue outside commemorates their sacrifice.

FREE Mauerpark
Bernauer Strasse (no phone, www.mauerpark.info). U2 Eberswalder Strasse. **Open** 24hrs daily. **Admission** free. **Map** p71 B1 ➋
The site of an old train station, this area became a 'death strip' when the Wall went up, with a viewing platform for West Berliners to look into the East. It was turned into a community space in the 1990s, with two large sports halls, a graffiti-daubed section of the Wall and a home for the popular Sunday flea market. It's a lovely place to while away a summer afternoon among the drum circles, circus performers and assorted hippy types.

FREE Museum in the Kulturbrauerei
Kulturbrauerei, Schönhauser Allee 36 (4677 7790, www.hdg.de/berlin). U2 Eberswalderstrasse. **Open** 10am-6pm Tue, Wed, Fri-Sun; 10am-8pm Thur. **Admission** free. **Map** p71 B2 ➌
'Everyday Life in the GDR' is a fascinating permanent exhibition here, featuring hundreds of objects that show the contradictory nature of Communist life. Examples of leisure time include a Trabi roof-mounted tent, a mocked-up GDR living room and clothing customised to break the drab uniformity.

FREE Prenzlauer Berg Museum
Prenzlauer Allee 227 (902 953 917). U2 Senefelderplatz, or tram M2. **Open** 9am-7pm

Tue, Wed, Fri; noon-8pm Thur. **Admission** free. **Map** p71 C3 ➍
A small but interesting permanent exhibition (lots of old photos) examining local history and culture, with an emphasis on the area's development before and after the Wall went up. It's a little staid, though – the newer Museum in the Kulturbrauerei is more visually exciting.

Zeiss-Grossplanetarium
Prenzlauer Allee 80 (4218 4512, www.sdtb.de). S8, S9, S41, S42, S85 Prenzlauer Allee. **Map** p71 B3 ➎
This vast planetarium was constructed in 1987 as part of the city's 750th anniversary; at the time, its Cosmorama projector was one of the most advanced in Europe. It's currently undergoing a major refurbishment and should reopen in 2016.

Restaurants & Cafés

A Magica
Greifenhagener Strasse 54 (2280 8290, www.amagica.de). U2, S8, S9, S41, S42, S85 Schönhauser Allee. **Open** noon-midnight Mon-Fri; 4pm-midnight Sat, Sun (Oct-Mar 4-10pm Sat, Sun). **Main courses** €5-€9.50. **Map** p71 A2 ➏ **Pizza**
A real oasis of democratic Italian nosh, this pizzeria has been packing them in since 2007. It's a particular favourite for local young families, and for good reason: their Roman-style base is thin and flavoursome, and pizzas start at a mere €5. Or try the DIY option, building from a base of either tomato sauce, mint pesto or chickpea purée, then loading it with a long list of delicious toppings.

Wasserturm. *See p70.*

EXPLORE

Barn Roastery.

€ Anna Blume

Kollwitzstrasse 83 (4404 8749, www.cafe-anna-blume.de). U2 Eberswalder Strasse. **Open** 8am-midnight daily. **Main courses** €4-€12.50. **Map** p71 B3 ➐ Café

This café-cum-florist is named after a poem by Kurt Schwitters. There are expensive but high-quality pastries, plus sweet and savoury crêpes, soups and hot dishes. The terrace is lovely in summer, and the interior, not surprisingly, smells of flowers.

€ Antipodes

Fehrbelliner Strasse 5 (0176 3834 0118 mobile). U2 Senefelderplatz. **Open** 8am-5pm Wed-Fri; 9am-5pm Sat, Sun. **Main courses** €1.50-€8. **Map** p71 D2 ➑ Café

This tiny café doles out all-day breakfast classics such as eggs benedict and, as to be expected from Kiwi ownership, great coffee, whether creamy flat whites or punchy espressos. Cutesy but not overly precious decor and beaming service complete the welcoming atmosphere. There are daily soups and grilled sandwiches plus plenty of baked goodies if you fancy something more filling.

€ Babel

Kastanienallee 33 (4403 1318). U2 Eberswalder Strasse. **Open** 10am-1am daily. **Main courses** €3-€9. **No credit cards.** **Map** p71 C2 ➒ Lebanese

The crew at Babel have been throwing out Lebanese shawarma wraps for over a decade now, filled with the likes of grilled chicken, halloumi or crispy falafel. Although being on Prenzlauer Berg's most popular shopping street has meant prices have risen while portions have shrunk, their *teller* (plates) are still big enough to share, coming with a selection of fresh houmous, tabbouleh, pickled radish and their famous green chilli sauce.

€ Barn Roastery

Schönhauser Allee 8 (0151 2410 5136 mobile, www.thebarn.de). U8 Rosenthaler Platz. **Open** 8.30am-6pm Tue-Fri; 10am-6pm Sat, Sun. **No credit cards.** **Map** p71 D2 ➓ Café

The Barn is a shrine to the coffee bean. Owner Ralf Kueller has even made headlines for his serious approach: when he opened this second, more spacious branch (the original is in Mitte), customers were bemused by the industrial bollard set in the doorway. Ralf was taking a rather humourless stand against the area's 'yummy mummy' invasion by banning prams (and laptops and dogs), so there are no distractions from appreciation of the finished product. Australian baristas 'dial in' their own special blends, roasted on site in collaboration with London's Square Mile coffee roasters; try the pour-over Hario V60 for an alternative cupping method. **Other location** Auguststrasse 58, Mitte.

★ Bird

Am Falkplatz 5 (5105 3283, www.thebirdin berlin.com). U2, S8, S9, S41, S42, S85 Schönhauser Allee. **Open** 6pm-midnight Mon-Thur; 5pm- midnight Fri; noon-midnight Sat, Sun. **Main courses** €9.50-€40. **No credit cards.** **Map** p71 A1 ⓫ North American

Staff stick to the hard-bitten New Yorker stereotype and the restaurant gets rowdy: 'angry hour' runs 6-8pm daily, with a two-for-one offer on Schneider Weisse draught beer and 25-cent spicy chicken wings. The Bird's burgers are mighty: 250g of freshly minced meat smothered in molten cheese and caramelised onions, with a toasted English muffin perched jauntily atop the sloppy pile. Alongside this glistening beauty lies an enormous pile of hand-cut fries, one of the restaurant's highlights. **Other location** Kottbusserdamm 95, Neukölln (0170 2155 666 mobile).

EXPLORE

WALK THE WALL REMEMBERED

Once an iconic barrier between Cold War enemies, little remains today.

Most of the Berlin Wall was demolished between June and November 1990. What had become the symbol of the inhumanity of the East German regime was prosaically crushed and reused for roadfill.

This walk sets out to trace the course of a small stretch of the Wall on the northern border of Mitte. Along the way you can see some of the remnants – including the restored segment at the **Gedenkstätte Berliner Mauer** (*see p158*) – and gain an impression of how brutally the border carved its way through the city.

The starting point is Berlin's central station – **Hauptbahnhof**, in former West Berlin. Exit the station into Invalidenstrasse, turning right along the street. Continue eastwards, passing on your left a Wilhelmine building, now a regional court, and the railway station turned art gallery, **Hamburger Bahnhof – Museum für Gegenwart** (*see p49*).

A little further on is the **Sandkrugbrücke**, located on a former border crossing into East Berlin. A stone by the bridge commemorates Günter Litfin, the first person to be shot dead attempting to escape to West Berlin (in 1961). The **Invalidenhaus** on the eastern side long predates the Cold War. Built in 1747 to house disabled soldiers, it was used in East German times as a hospital, ministry of health and supreme court. Today, it houses the Bundesministerium für Wirtschaft und Arbeit (Federal Ministry of Economics and Labour). Keeping this complex on your right, turn down the canalside promenade, continuing along until you get to the **Invalidenfriedhof**.

The Wall once ran straight through this graveyard – and a section remains. Headstones of the graves in the 'death strip' were removed so as not to impair the sightlines of border guards. The graveyard is a fascinating microcosm of Berlin history. Metres from the splendid 19th-century tombs of Prussian generals, there is a plaque commemorating members of the anti-Hitler resistance. Victims of air raids and the Battle of Berlin are buried in an adjacent mass grave. And it was here in 1962 that West Berlin police shot dead an East Berlin border guard to save a 15-year-old boy who was in the process of escaping.

Just outside the graveyard is a former **watchtower** improbably standing in front of a new apartment building at the corner of Kieler Strasse. The observation post is closed in winter, but sometimes in summer you can look inside.

Between here and the corner of Chausseestrasse, few traces are left of the Wall, which ran roughly parallel to the canal before veering off to the right, close to the present helipad. At the end of Boyenstrasse, pavement markings indicating the Wall's former course briefly appear before vanishing under the new corner building.

Bernauer Strasse.

Bernauer Straße

1961

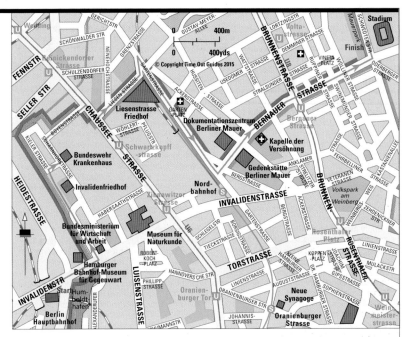

Looking down Chausseestrasse, note the line of powerful street lights indicating the site of another checkpoint. The **Liesenstrasse Friedhof** is the graveyard where 19th-century writer Theodor Fontane is buried. It was also part of East Berlin's border strip. A short section of the Wall appears before the railway bridge at the junction with Gartenstrasse.

The last leg of the walk takes you up Bernauer Strasse. Desperate scenes took place here in August 1961 as people jumped – three of them to their deaths – from the windows of houses that then stood on the street's eastern side. The buildings were in East Berlin, but the pavement before their doors was in the West. The iconic photo of a border guard leaping over barbed wire into the West was snapped days earlier at the street's northern end. In the 1960s and '70s, several tunnels were dug from cellars in this area and dozens escaped this way.

At the Gedenkstätte Berliner Mauer, you can gain an impression of what the border installation looked like – from below or above. The **Dokumentationszentrum** opposite, an information centre about the Wall, has a viewing platform. With in-depth documentation, testimony and recorded

memories available, the physical memorial becomes even more poignant. Steel rods delineate the Walls' route and, in a grassy former death strip, neat elements indicate the remains of submerged buildings, barriers, security features and other deterrents.

A little further on is the oval **Kapelle der Versöhnung** (Chapel of Reconciliation), built on the site of an older church that was left stranded in the death strip and finally blown up in 1985 by the East German authorities.

The old patrol road remains in places, as do some of the border illuminations – note, for instance, the lights on Swinemünder Strasse 20. The plasterwork on the building at the corner of Wolliner Strasse clearly reveals where the eastern side of the Wall abutted existing apartment blocks.

Between Wolliner and Schwedter Strasse, you can still see the turning circle once used by West Berlin buses. On the eastern side, the tram still comes to an abrupt halt in Eberswalder Strasse. Even so, it's hard to believe that this whole area was once part of the world's most heavily fortified border. In the **Mauerpark**, where there is a popular Sunday flea market (see p81), you can have one last stroll along the Wall before heading to the Eberswalder Strasse U-Bahn station.

★ € Bonanza

Oderberger Strasse 35 (0171 563 0795 mobile,
www.bonanzacoffee.de). U2 Eberswalder Strasse.
Open 8.30am-6pm Mon-Fri; 10am-6pm Sat, Sun.
No credit cards. Map p71 B1 **⑫ Café**
Bonanza serves some of the best coffee in Berlin. The
proprietors are concerned with every detail, from
relationships with suppliers to roasting the beans
in-house and getting the right steam temperature.
The bar is dominated by a highly sensitive handmade Synesso Cyncra machine, and seating is minimal. The flat white is smooth and divine. The cake
selection is small – pretty much just carrot cake and
brownies – but high grade.

Café Anita Wronski

Knaackstrasse 26-28 (442 8483). U2
Senefelderplatz. **Open** 9am-1am daily.
Main courses €6-€9. **No credit cards.**
Map p71 C3 **⑬ Café**
A friendly café on two levels, with scrubbed floors,
beige walls, hard-working staff and as many tables
crammed into the space as the laws of physics allow.
Brunches are serviceable, but there are plenty of
other cafés on this stretch if there's no room here.
Quiet in the afternoon, it's a good spot to sit and read.

€ Dairy

Raumerstrasse 12 (0176 2273 7551 mobile,
www.thedairy.de). U2 Eberswalder Strasse.
Open 8am-6pm Mon-Fri; 9am-6pm Sat, Sun.
Main courses €3-€7. **No credit cards.**
Map p71 B3 **⑭ Café**
One of the first places to open in the great wave
from Down Under, this Kiwi-run café does all sorts

of superb Anglo goodies, from scones and mince
pies, to more substantial lunch offerings of cottage
pie or avocado and chicken salad. Be warned, the
space is minuscule, though the little green oasis of
Helmholtzplatz is just outside.

€ Fischfabrik

Danziger Strasse 24 (6431 4581, www.
fischfabrikberlin.de). U2 Eberswalder Strasse.
Open 10am-10pm Mon-Sat; 2-10pm Sun.
Main courses €4.50-€10.50. **No credit
cards. Map** p71 B2 **⑮ Fish & chips**
For those craving some battered cod, this fish shop
does a pretty decent chip supper, with Sarson's malt
vinegar handily placed on every table. The fish is
as fresh as it gets in Berlin, nicely steamed within a
crispy shell, and the chips hit the spot even if they
aren't really cut thickly enough. Perfect with a glass
of the crisp house riesling.

Gugelhof

Knaackstrasse 37 (442 9229, www.gugelhof.de).
U2 Senefelderplatz. **Open** 4pm-midnight Mon-Fri;
10am-midnight Sat, Sun. **Main courses** €8-€21.
Map p71 C2 **⑯ Alsatian**
This restaurant pioneered the Kollwitzplatz scene in
the 1990s. Food is refined but filling, service formal
but friendly, and the furnishings comfortably worn.
The *Backöfe* – lamb, pork and beef marinated in riesling, stewed and served in an earthenware pot with
root veg and a bread-crust lid – displays the peasant flourishes of Alsace's regional cooking. There's
also a fine selection of Alsatian *tartes flambées*.
Breakfast is served until a leisurely 4pm at weekends. Reservations advised.

Bonanza.

EXPLORE

€ Konnopke's Imbiss
*Under U-Bahn tracks, Schönhauser Allee 44B,
at Danziger Strasse (442 7765). U2 Eberswalder
Strasse.* **Open** 9am-8pm Mon-Fri; 11.30am-8pm
Sat. **Currywurst** €2-€3.50. **No credit cards.**
Map p71 B2 🕖 **Imbiss**
This venerable sausage stand (refurbished a few
years ago) has been under the same family man-
agement since 1930. After coming up with a secret
recipe for ketchup (not available after the Wall was
erected), it was the first place to offer Currywurst
in East Berlin, and still serves probably the most
famous – if not the best – Currywurst in the city.
Expect a queue.
Other location Romain-Rolland-Strasse 16,
Pankow (4700 9099).

Lucky Leek
*Kollwitzstrasse 54 (6640 8710, www.lucky-leek.de).
U2 Senefelderplatz.* **Open** 6-11pm Wed-Sun.
Main courses €12-€17. **Set meal** £45-£66.
No credit cards. Map p71 C2 ⑮ **Vegan**
Chef Josita Hartanto started out at Charlottenburg's
haute-cuisine La Mano Verde, and has now carved
out quite a following for her inventive vegan food
(and published a cookbook in 2013). She's pushed
the boundaries through clever plating and textural
contrast, with dishes such as filo-spinach pockets
of seitan with macadamia dumpling and brus-
sels-sprout praline. Desserts are very inventive.

Oderquelle
*Oderbergerstrasse 27 (4400 8080,
www.oderquelle.de). U2 Eberswalder Strasse.*
Open 6pm-1am Mon-Sat; noon-1am Sun.
Main courses €10-€19.50. Map p71 B1
⑲ **Austrian/German**
This simple yet cosy Prenzlauer Berg classic might
be a tad more expensive than its rivals, but that's
because it's better than them. The menu is short
but changes regularly. Typical dishes are goose leg
stuffed with vegetables on red-wine risotto or vege-
table strudel in tomato sauce. It's particularly nice
in summer, when you can sit outside and watch the
world go by.

Osmans Töchter
*Papelallee 15 (3266 3388, www.osmans
toechter.de). U2 Eberswalder Strasse.* **Open**
5.30pm- midnight daily. **Main courses** €12.50-
€20.50. **No credit cards.** Map p71 B2 ⑳ **Turkish**
Although exposed light bulbs and mismatched
wooden chairs are verging on a Berlin cliché these
days, it's refreshing for a modern Turkish restaurant
to not have to resort to the usual cartoon orientalism.
The menu is notable primarily for its homeliness,
and a network of Turkish housewives helps produce the range of meze salads and dips, as well as
the *manti*, Turkish meat dumplings smothered in a
garlicky yoghurt sauce. The juicy swordfish kebab
is a particular draw.

Sauvage. *See p78.*

Pasternak
*Knaackstrasse 22-24 (441 3399, www.restaurant-
pasternak.de). U2 Senefelderplatz.* **Open** 9am-
1am daily. **Main courses** €11-€25. Map p71 C3
㉑ **Russian**
A small bar and restaurant that became home to
the wave of Russian immigrants, many of them
Jewish, following the fall of the Soviet Union. Food
focuses on Russian and Ashkenazi classics such as
sweet and sour brisket or beef stroganoff. The lively
atmosphere can get a little much sometimes – ask for
a table in the small side room.

★ Sasaya
*Lychener Strasse 50 (4471 7721, www.sasaya-
berlin.de). U2 Eberswalder Strasse.* **Open**
noon-3pm, 6-11.30pm Mon, Thur-Sun. **Sushi**
€1.50-€3 per roll. **No credit cards.** Map p71 A3
㉒ **Japanese**
Berlin's famously poor availability of fresh fish
poses a challenge for Japanese restaurants; there are
scores of pan-Asian places serving 'discount' sushi,
but the real thing is hard to come by. An authentic
menu and a bustling atmosphere have kept Sasaya
a long-term favourite. The sashimi is eye-poppingly
fresh, and they also serve fine cooked dishes such
as grilled horse mackerel and *kakuni* (braised pork
belly). For a real taste of the ocean, try one of the
dressed seaweed salads. Booking essential.

Sauvage

Winsstrasse 30 (3810 0025, www.sauvageberlin. com). S8, S9, S41, S42, S85 Greifswalder Strasse, or tram M2, M4, M10. **Open** 6pm-midnight Wed-Fri; 11am-3.30pm, 6pm-midnight Sat, Sun. **Main courses** €21-€32. **No credit cards.** **Map** p71 C4 ㉓ **French**

Partners Rodrigo and Boris Leite-Poço were well ahead of the curve when they opened Europe's first Paleo restaurant in 2011. This primitivist diet rejects all forms of processed food (grains, refined fats, gluten and sugar), but still allows fun stuff in the form of natural fats and meat. Their original Neukölln location functions more as a bistro now, with this newer branch satisfying deeper caveman pockets. The kitchen uses local produce to turn out dishes such as hare terrine and salad or herb-crusted pikeperch with fennel and celeriac gratin. *Photo p 77.*
Other location Pflügerstrasse 25, Neukölln (5316 7547).

Si An

Rykestrasse 36 (4050 5775, www.sian-berlin.de). U2 Senefelderplatz, or tram M2, M10. **Open** noon-midnight daily. **Main courses** €8. **No credit cards.** **Map** p71 B3 ㉔ **Vietnamese**

Si An was one of the first Viet restaurants to really up the ante on decor while making an effort to cook everything fresh. There are various phos and usually some sort of combination of curry, rice and meats heaped with fresh herbs and vegetables. The approach has clearly paid off, as it now has a mini-empire of restaurants including Saigon streetfood specialist District Mot and tea house Chen Che.

La Soupe Populaire

Prenzlauer Allee 244 (4431 9680, www.lasoupe populaire.de). U2 Senefelderplatz. **Open** noon-2.30pm, 5.30-10.30pm Thur-Sat. **Main courses** €15-€24. **Map** p71 D3 ㉕ **German**

Michelin-starred local hero Tim Raue opened this high-end 'canteen' in order to serve local German classic dishes reimagined with trained polish. The restaurant is inside the hulking Bötzow brewery complex – all exposed piping and industrial walkways – overlooking a large art gallery, and a special menu is created for each new exhibition. Otherwise, stick to the classics such as *Senfei* (poached egg in a silky mustard sauce with caviar) or *Königsberger Klopse,* a Prussian favourite of delicate veal meatballs in a rich white sauce.

Les Valseuses

Eberswalder Strasse 28 (7552 2032, www. lesvalseuses.de). U2 Eberswalder Strasse. **Open** 6.30pm-midnight daily. **Main courses** €12.50-€24. **No credit cards.** **Map** p71 B2 ㉖ **French**

This modern French bistro (owned by some of the team behind Mitte's popular Themroc) is remarkably good value: the 200g steak frites with béarnaise is a very reasonable €13.50. The specials board of

French classics changes weekly – expect the likes of steak tartare with smoked garlic or chicken with lemon and green olives. Team your meal with a 'natural' wine from the Languedoc. Local baker Ma Patissière has her ovens in the back and provides the excellent desserts.

Bars & Pubs

8MM

Schönhauser Allee 177B (4050 0624, www. 8mmbar.com). U2 Senefelderplatz. **Open** 9pm-late daily. **No credit cards.** **Map** p71 D2 ㉗

Sometimes the 4/4 techno beat can seem inescapable in Berlin, so head to this one-room dive bar for an alternative. Weekends get raucous with DJs playing a mix of punk and new-wave staples, and the occasional touring band member getting behind the decks for a concert after-party. It's a relic from a previous generation of American expats (in Berlin's accelerated timescale, this means the early noughties), but Anglophones and indie locals still come here to booze into the small hours. Drinks are very reasonable, making it just the place for your umpteenth nightcap.

Beckett's Kopf

Pappelallee 64 (0162 237 9418 mobile, www. becketts-kopf.de). U2 Eberswalder Strasse. **Open** 8pm-late daily. **No credit cards.** **Map** p71 A2 ㉘

This long-running cocktail bar is an oasis of fine drink in rather sparsely served Prenzlauer Berg. It follows the classic 'speakeasy' model: enter via an unmarked door and find yourself in rooms draped in red velvet. You can breathe deeply on their chesterfield sofas, as one of the two rooms caters for non-smokers, a relative rarity in Berlin's bar scene. Try the Aviation, a paean to the classier days of air travel: a florid mix of gin, violet, maraschino and lemon. A grizzled portrait of playwright Samuel Beckett (not averse to a drink himself) keeps watch over proceedings.

★ Le Croco Bleu

Prenzlauer Allee 242 (0177 443 2359 mobile, www.lecrocobleu.com). U2 Senefelderplatz. **Open** 6pm-late Thur-Sat. **Map** p71 D3 ㉙

Le Croco Bleu is the baby of Berlin drinks king Gregor Scholl, who began his career at the Charlottenburg stalwart Paris Bar before opening cult favourite Rum Trader. Housed in the old machine rooms of the 19th-century Bötzow Brewery, its name derives from an apocryphal story about a pair of Berlin Zoo crocodiles who were given shelter in a basement pool at the end of World War II. Try the Acu Acu, a particularly potent blend of aged rums, orgeat (almond syrup) and absinthe.

★ Dr Pong

Eberswalder Strasse 21 (no phone, www.drpong. net). U2 Eberswalder Strasse. **Open** 8pm-late

Mon-Sat; 6pm/7pm-late Sun. **No credit cards.**
Map p71 B2 ㉚

Bring your table-tennis bat (or hire one for a €5 deposit) and prepare for drunken ping-pong carnage. The action doesn't start until around midnight, but then you can expect 30 or so players – some good, some bad – to surround the table in one almighty round-the-world session. There's a bar and, bizarrely, Twiglets for nourishment. Note that the opening hours are unreliable.

★ Neue Odessa Bar

Torstrasse 89 (0171 839 8991 mobile, www.neueodessabar.de). U8 Rosenthaler Platz.
Open 7pm-late daily. **No credit cards.**
Map p71 D1 ㉛

Acting as the unofficial hub for the hip 'SoTo' set – the area south of Torstrasse – this bar serves a mean cocktail. It's populated by local fashionistas and media-industry expats, who come here for further libations after doing the rounds of nearby gallery openings. DJs appear at weekends, but it can get very smoky, reflecting the buzz inside.

Prater

Kastanienallee 7-9 (448 5688, www.pratergarten. de). U2 Eberswalder Strasse. **Open** 6-11pm Mon-Sat; noon-11pm Sun. **No credit cards.**
Map p71 B2 ㉜

This rowdy beer garden, which lies across a courtyard from an old ballroom of the same name, has been doing Berliners a brisk service since 1852. The enthusiastic beer-swilling, big wooden tables and platefuls of *Bratwurst* and *Bretzeln* (pretzels) almost make you feel like you've been teleported down south to Munich. There's an indoor bar with a traditional German restaurant, but in summer you want to grab a house-brewed Pils and join the all-day buzz outdoors. Brunch is served from 10am to 4pm at the weekend.

Schwarze Pumpe

Choriner Strasse 76 (449 6939, www.schwarze pumpe-berlin.de). U2 Senefelderplatz, or U8 Rosenthaler Platz. **Open** 10am-1am daily.
No credit cards. Map p71 C1 ㉝

One of the first places to open after the Wall fell, Schwarze Pumpe is still a popular low-key neighbourhood bar, which has seen the street go from reclaimed derelict housing to luxury apartment living. It serves reasonably priced magnums of wine, draught beer and a decent menu of bar snacks.

Wohnzimmer

Lettestrasse 6 (445 5458, www.wohnzimmer-bar. de). U2 Eberswalder Strasse. **Open** 10am-late daily.
No credit cards. Map p71 B3 ㉞

Immediately behind the door of this shabbily elegant 'living room' is a bar-like structure assembled from kitchen cabinets and assorted GDR furniture. Even if not the bohemian destination it used to be, it still provides a sanctuary for hip young Helmholtzplatz mothers during the day, and for local barflies at night who come for the strong cocktails.

Shops & Services

D.nik

Wörther Strasse 14 (3064 8628, www.dnik-berlin.de). U2 Senefelderplatz. **Open** 10am-7pm Mon-Fri; 10am-6pm Sat. **Map** p71 C3 ㉟ **Children**

Prater.

Mauerpark Flohmarkt.

The name spells 'child' backwards in German. Stock is carefully selected to fit into a design aesthetic of using sustainable materials and allowing for ergonomic play. You'll find modular Tukluk, which can be folded into gigantic colourful geometric structures, playful furniture from young Swedish designers Little Red Stuga and cardboard building blocks.

★ Fein & Ripp
Kastanienallee 91-92 (4403 3250, www.fein undripp.de). U2 Eberswalder Strasse. **Open** noon-7pm Mon-Sat. **Map** p71 C2 ③ **Fashion**
A curious shop, which started out selling old stock discovered in a Swabian clothes factory – primarily cotton underwear in all shapes and sizes, from the 1920s to the '70s. They've now expanded into brands that continue traditional production methods: Frye's heavy leather prison boots, which come 'distressed', and Pike Brothers' stiff blue denim jeans. Unfortunately, dressing like a Depression-era hobo doesn't come cheap these days.

Filetstück
Schönhauser Allee 45 (4882 0304, www.filetstueck-berlin.de). U2 Eberswalder Strasse. **Open** noon-10pm Mon-Sat. **Map** p71 B2 ③ **Food & drink**
It's no news that Germans love pork, getting through close to 40kg of it a year per capita. Beef is comparatively expensive and not very good quality, something butcher Matthias Martens set out to change. Fridges parade sides of marbled beef sourced from trusted farms; these are then dry-aged for a minimum of three weeks in order to concentrate flavour and texture. The small adjoining restaurant grills steaks for those who can't wait to get home.

Goldhahn & Sampson
Dunckerstrasse 9 (no phone, www.goldhahn undsampson.de). U2 Eberswalder Strasse. **Open** 8am-8pm Mon-Fri; 9am-8pm Sat. **Map** p71 B3 ③ **Food & drink**

A charming deli that sells all sorts, from locally roasted Andraschko coffee to imported Japanese mayonnaise. There's also an assortment of international cookbooks and you can sign up to a wide range of specialist cookery classes, such as macaroon baking or festive Jewish cuisine.

Goo
Oderbergerstrasse 45 (4403 3737, www. paulsboutiqueberlin.de). U2 Eberswalder Strasse. **Open** noon-8pm Mon-Sat. **Map** p71 B2 ③ **Fashion**
This tiny store is easily overlooked, but it sets itself apart from the usual vintage shop by specialising in almost-new designer clobber from big labels such as Comme des Garçons, Wood Wood and Y-3. If you want the usual sneakers and sweatshirts, its bigger brother, Pauls Boutique, is at no.47.

Kollwitzplatz Farmers' Market
Kollwitzplatz (organic market 4433 9137, farmers' market 0172 327 8238 mobile). U2 Senefelderplatz. **Open** noon-7pm Thur; 9.30am-5pm Sat. **Map** p71 C2 ④ **Market**
The Saturday farmers' market is popular with gourmets stocking up on weekend food supplies and with locals out for a stroll and a snack. You'll find chocolates by Martin Franz, locally made tofu and amazing fresh pasta. A Turkish-run stand sells the best *Gözleme* in town; another offers delicious and inexpensive fish soup. The Thursday market is slightly smaller and exclusively organic.

★ Lunettes Brillenagentur
Dunckerstrasse 18 (4471 8050, www.lunettes-selection.com). S8, S9, S41, S42, S85 Prenzlauer Allee, or tram M2. **Open** noon-8pm Mon, Tue, Thur, Fri; 10am-8pm Wed; noon-6pm Sat. **Map** p71 B3 ④ **Accessories**
Owner Uta Geyer has a knack for getting her hands on hard-to-find vintage spectacles frames, ranging

EXPLORE

from sleek 1920s pieces to rockabilly cat-eyes, classic aviators to glitzy Jackie Os. Prices are affordable and they also do their own range of handmade frames, called Kollektion.

Manufacture Délicate

Rykestrasse 7 (6891 3699, www.manufacture-delicate.de). U2 Senefelderplatz, or tram M2. **Open** 7am-6pm Tue-Fri; 8am-6pm Sat, Sun. **Map** p71 C3 ㊷ **Food & drink**
A 2013 addition to the Prenzlauer Berg bakery scene, Manufacture Délicate distinguishes itself with a variety of hard-crust sourdough loaves, fruit tarts and sweet pastries. Owner Marko Vielle uses only natural yeasts and additives.

Mauerpark Flohmarkt

Bernauer Strasse 63-64 (0176 2925 0021 mobile). U8 Bernauer Strasse. **Open** 7am-5pm Sun. **Map** p71 B1 ㊸ **Market**
One of the biggest and busiest flea markets in Berlin, selling everything from local designer clothes to cardboard boxes of black-market CDs. Students and residents sell their things here; even if the market's massive popularity has meant prices creeping higher, you can still stumble upon a trove of rare records or vintage clothing.
▶ *This is also the venue for the immensely popular weekly outdoor singing session, Bearpit Karaoke, where thousands flock in summer to have a go on the mobile sound system.*

Saint George's.

★ Onkel Philipp's Spielzeugwerkstatt

Choriner Strasse 35 (449 0491, www.onkel-philipp. de). U2 Senefelderplatz. **Open** 9.30am-6.30pm Tue, Wed, Fri; 11am-8pm Thur; 11am-4pm Sat. **Map** p71 C2 ㊹ **Children**
Here's one for kids, both big and small: a toy-repair shop that's an Aladdin's cave of aged playthings, wooden toys, puzzles, trains, puppets and more. If you ask nicely, owner Philipp Schünemann lets you view his private GDR toy collection, a remote control unveiling a special surprise.

★ Saint George's

Wörther Strasse 27 (8179 8333, www.saint georgesbookshop.com). U2 Senefelderplatz, or tram M2. **Open** 11am-8pm Mon-Fri; 11am-7pm Sat. **Map** p71 C3 ㊺ **Books & music**
Founded by Paul and Daniel Gurner, twin brothers from England, Saint George's harks back to the heyday of London's Charing Cross Road. It's a sweet spot, where leather sofas coax readers to peruse at leisure. Housing around 10,000 English-language books, including plenty of biographies and contemporary fiction, it's also reliable for second-hand books in good condition.

Shakespeare & Sons

Raumerstrasse 36 (4000 3685, www.shakes books.de). U2 Eberswalder Strasse. **Open** 9am-8pm Mon-Sat; 10am-8pm Sun. **Map** p71 B3 ㊻ **Books & music**
Nothing to do with Paris's famous Shakespeare and Co, this place is the offshoot of a pair of bookshops in Prague. This branch supplies French as well as English books, both new and used, in every genre, but its unique selling point has to be the range of eastern European literature available in English translations. It's a cute space that encourages browsing. Note that there's a 10% discount on purchases costing over €50.

Temporary Showroom

Kastanienallee 36A (6220 4564, www.temporary showroom.com). U2 Senefelderplatz. **Open** 11am-7pm Mon-Sat. **Map** p71 C1 ㊽ **Fashion**
Both a boutique stocking cult labels and a creative agency for young European designers, the Temporary Showroom rotates its stock regularly. There's technical shoeware from Adidas's experimental SLVR line to go with your patterned tracksuit from Switzerland's Julian Zigerli.

VEB Orange

Oderbergerstrasse 29 (9788 6886, www. veborange.de). U2 Eberswalder Strasse. **Open** 11am-7pm Mon-Sat. **Map** p71 B1 ㊾ **Homewares/Fashion**
The tagline claims they sell 'everything but fruit' – and there is certainly a wide range of original 1960s and '70s furniture, lighting and clothes. Lots of polyester, Formica and GDR kitsch bargains to be found.

EXPLORE

Friedrichshain & Lichtenberg

Berlin's alternative squat community migrated to Friedrichshain in the 1990s and politicised this traditionally working-class district. Much of the area is pretty bleak, dominated by big Communist-era housing blocks – it was one of the hardest hit during World War II – and slashed through by railway tracks. This was historically an industrial district, and much of its southern part bordering the Spree contains the remains of industrial buildings. It's also home to East Berlin's first massive post-war civic building project – a broad boulevard built in the style of Moscow's Gorky Street that was originally named Stalinallee, and then Karl-Marx-Allee.

Lichtenberg isn't the most attractive of neighbourhoods, but it does contain a couple of key former Stasi strongholds and East Berlin Zoo.

Karl-Marx-Allee.

Don't Miss

1 **Karl-Marx-Allee** Look east on this formidable Stalinist avenue (p84).

2 **Gedenkstätte Berlin-Hohenschönhausen** Ex-inmates lead tours of this Stasi prison (p92).

3 **East Side Gallery** Colourful murals adorn what's left of the Wall (p84).

4 **Tierpark Berlin-Friedrichsfelde** Elephants play in this spacious zoo (p93).

5 **Café Schönbrunn** Where to go for a cold beer and wurst (p85).

Volkspark Friedrichshain

FRIEDRICHSHAIN

As Prenzlauer Berg and Mitte saw rents soar in
the 1990s, Berlin's alternative squat community
migrated to Friedrichshain and politicised this
traditionally working-class district. Much of the
area remains pretty bleak, dominated as it is by
big Communist-era housing blocks – it was one of
the hardest hit during World War II – and slashed
through by railway tracks. This was historically
an industrial district, and much of its southern
part bordering the Spree contains the remains
of industrial buildings. It's also home to East
Berlin's first massive post-war civic building
project – a broad boulevard built in the style of
Moscow's Gorky Street that was originally named
Stalinallee, and then (following Khrushchev's
de-Stalinisation policy) Karl-Marx-Allee.

The best way to get a feeling for both
Friedrichshain and the old GDR is to head east
from Alexanderplatz down Karl-Marx-Allee,
which is the site of the **Computerspiele
Museum** (Computer Games Museum) and
GDR icon Café Sybille. It's from Lichtenberger
Strasse onwards that the street truly impresses
in its Communist monumentalism, with rows
of grand apartment blocks draped in stone
and Meissen tiles stretching beyond the twin
towers of Frankfurter Tor.

South and east of Frankfurter Tor are the
shops, bars and restaurants of **Simon-Dach-
Kiez**, which, sadly, have turned the area's non-
conformist values into something of a boozy
tourist industry. There's also an excellent weekly
flea and farmers' market at **Boxhagener Platz**.

To the south, on Mühlenstrasse ('Mill Street';
the old mill is at no.8), along the north bank
of the Spree, is the **East Side Gallery**,
a stretch of former Wall that was turned into
a mural memorial in 1990. The industrial
buildings hereabouts have been renovated
and rechristened **Oberbaum City**, and are
now home to loft spaces, offices and studios. Both
Universal Music and MTV-Europe have moved
their German HQ here, as part of the ongoing
development of the vast **Mediaspree** complex,
which has met much opposition. As nightclubs
have been forced eastwards, some of Berlin's best
nightlife can be found around Ostkreuz at places
such as **Salon zur Wilden Renate** (*see p196*)
and the infamous **Homopatik** (*see p181*).

At the district's far north-west corner is the
Volkspark Friedrichshain. This huge park
is scattered with socialist-realist art, and has an
open-air stage, a fountain of fairy-tale characters
and the popular **Café Schönbrunn**. Graves of
fighters who fell in March 1848 in the battle for
German unity are here too. It's a popular gay
cruising zone at night.

Sights & Museums

Computerspiele Museum
*Karl-Marx-Allee 93A (6098 8577, www.
computerspielemuseum.de). U5 Weberwiese.*
Open 10am-8pm Mon, Wed-Sun. **Admission**
€8; €5 reductions. **Map** p86 D3 ❶
Today's video-game industry is now worth more than
the movie industry in dollar terms, and this excellent
museum traces its history, from early arcade classics
such as Pong to groundbreaking genre-definers such
as SimCity.

★ FREE East Side Gallery
*Mühlenstrasse (no phone, www.eastsidegallery-
berlin.de). U1, S5, S7, S75 Warschauer Strasse
or S5, S7, S75 Ostbahnhof.* **Open** 24hrs daily.
Admission free. **Map** p87 G3 ❷
One of Berlin's most photographed tourist sights,
this is the largest remaining section of Wall still
standing, where, in 1990, international artists
came together to produce 101 paintings across its
side. Dmitri Vrubel's striking portrait depicting
Brezhnev and Hönecker's kiss – a Soviet sign of

great respect – is easily its most iconic image. It was steadily defaced in the ensuing years, and controversy rages over its 2009 restoration, with certain artists objecting to copies being painted over their originals. Recent riverside developments even had the mighty David Hasselhoff leading the protests.

Restaurants & Cafés

Café Schönbrunn

Volkspark Friedrichshain (4530 56525, www. schoenbrunn.net). Bus 200. **Open** 10am-late daily. **Main courses** €9-€18.50. **Map** p86 B2 ❸ Café
Not for those afraid to walk in the park at night; but for everyone else, it's a favoured hangout. A couple of years ago, this lakeside place sold basic coffee and snacks to an elderly crowd. With a change of management, the food and music both improved dramatically. The unspectacular concrete front is unchanged, while the (new) lounge furniture is pure 1970s. On a sunny afternoon, older parkgoers take their first afternoon beer on the terrace next to the in-crowd having breakfast.

€ Café Sybille

Karl-Marx-Allee 72 (2935 2203, www.cafe-sibylle-berlin.de). U5 Weberwiese. **Open** 10am-8pm Mon-Wed; 10am-10pm Thur, Fri; noon-10pm Sat, Sun. **No credit cards. Map** p86 D2 ❹ Café
The perfect pit stop for doing some GDR sightseeing on the official Karl-Marx-Allee tour, this opened as a milk bar in the 1950s and was one of East Berlin's most popular cafés. They serve ice-cream sundaes, coffee, cake and, of course, beer. There's also a roof terrace accessible by reservation (€15 for groups of up to five) and a free exhibition on local history.

€ Dirty South

Krossener Strasse 18 (2936 0555, www. dirtysouthberlin.de). U5 Samariterstrasse. **Open** 5pm-4am Mon-Fri; noon-4am Sat, Sun. **Main courses** €4-€7.50. **No credit cards. Map** p87 F4 ❺ Tex-Mex
A Tex-Mex dive offering late-night cocktails and boozy brunches on weekends. Slightly incongruously, the decor is all Edwardian saloon, but the tacos, burritos and quesadillas with lashings of zesty salsa are excellent, as is the bloody mary.

€ Goodies

Warschauer Strasse 69 (0151 5376 3801 mobile, www.goodies-berlin.de). U1, S5, S7, S75 Warschauer Strasse. **Open** 7am-8pm Mon-Fri; 9am-8pm Sat, Sun. **Main courses** €3-€4.50. **No credit cards. Map** p87 E4 ❻ Vegetarian
If an excess of doner kebabs is getting you down, head to the original branch of the vegetarian Goodies chain, a great place to load up on superfood smoothies and tofu bagels. Friendly staff and comfy sofas facilitate lingering. Their outlets inside supermarket chain Veganz are, not surprisingly, vegan. **Other locations** throughout the city.

Kater Mikesch

Proskauerstrasse 13 (2804 1950, www.katermikesch.com). U5 Samariterstrasse or Frankfurter Tor. **Open** 5pm-midnight Mon-Fri; noon-midnight Sat, Sun. **Main courses** €6-€13.50. **No credit cards. Map** p86 D5 ❼ Czech
Hearty Bohemian specialities – goulash, dumplings (both bread and potato), paprika chicken and other Czech favourites – are served in this modern restaurant. The unfiltered Svijany beer on tap is excellent.

Berlin Wall remnants, Mediaspree.

EXPLORE

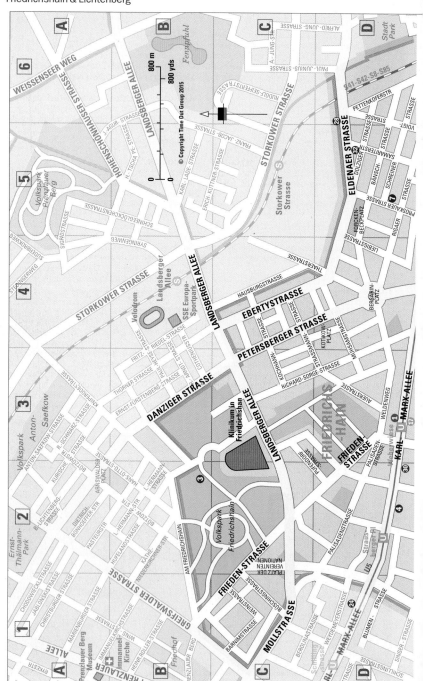

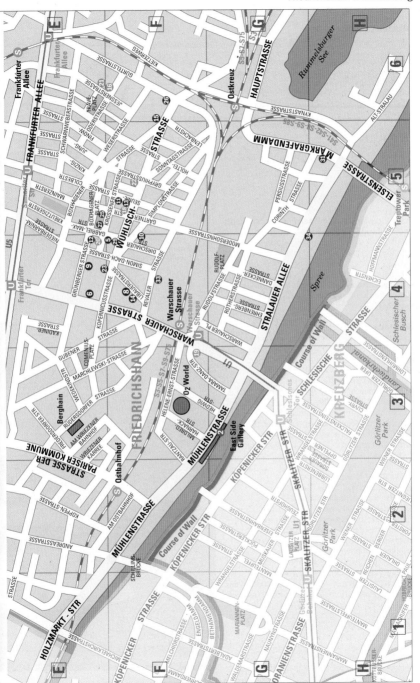

EXPLORE

Mutzenbacher

Libauerstrasse 11 (9561 6788, www.mutzenbacher-berlin.de). U1, S5, S7, S75 Warschauer Strasse. **Open** noon-midnight Mon-Fri; 10am-midnight Sat, Sun. **Main courses** €8.90-€15.50. **No credit cards.** Map p87 F4 **8** **Austrian**
Named after fictional Viennese prostitute Josephine Mutzenbacher, star of a famous 1906 erotic novel, this place offers inventive Austrian cuisine, in surroundings befitting Friedrichshain's punkier vibe. A mounted boar's head made from glass shards looks over as fetching waitstaff in Lederhosen bring out *Rindsvögerl* (braised beef rolls) with red cabbage or *Fleischkäse* (meatloaf).

€ Nil

Grünberger Strasse 52 (2904 7713, www.nil-imbiss.de). U5 Frankfurter Tor. **Open** 11am-midnight daily. **Main courses** €2-€4.50. **No credit cards.** Map p87 E4 **9** **Imbiss/Sudanese**
In a city full of vegetarians, Nil was an instant hit with its Sudanese spin on the falafel wrap: fried to order for extra crispness; plenty of fresh salad; and the magic ingredient, a creamy peanut sauce.
Other locations Oppelnerstrasse 4, Kreuzberg (4881 6414); Kottbusser Damm 21, Kreuzberg (no phone).

Schneeweiss

Simplonstrasse 16 (2904 9704, www.schneeweiss-berlin.de). U1, S5, S7, S75 Warschauer Strasse. **Open** 6pm-1am Mon-Fri; 10am-1am Sat, Sun. **Main courses** €13.50-€25.50. Map p87 F4 **10** **Southern German/Austrian**
This understated place, done out in minimalist white, offers 'Alpine' dishes – essentially a fusion of Italian, Austrian and south German ideas. There are daily lunch and dinner menus, plus a breakfast, and snacks, shakes and schnitzels throughout the day. Although upmarket for the area, it's great quality for the price and deservedly popular, so do book.

Schwarzer Hahn

Seumestrasse 23 (2197 0371, www.schwarzerhahn-heimatkueche.de). U5 Samariterstrasse or tram M13. **Open** 5.30-11pm Mon-Sat. **Main courses** €17-€22. **Set meal** €37 3 courses, €48 4 courses. **No credit cards.** Map p87 F5 **11** **Modern German**
Another example of what Berlin does so well – a great kitchen that's been discreetly knocking out fantastic regional German cuisine for years. It's excellent value for money, with two menus available (one is vegetarian), to be ordered either à la carte, or as a set menu. Try their pickled suckling-pig cheek with cauliflower and barley salad or the potato and chanterelle strudel.

Sigiriya

Grünberger Strasse 66 (2904 4208, www.restaurant-sigiriya.de). U5 Frankfurter Tor.

Schneeweiss.

Open noon-midnight daily. **Main courses** €7-€12. **No credit cards.** Map p87 E4 **⓬** **Sri Lankan**

Berlin is infamous for its bland Indian food – the German palate not being used to strong spicing – so Sigiriya is a hit with British expats for its authentic curries. They use organic or Neuland (free-range) meat and dairy, and do plenty of interesting vegetarian dishes, such as green mung-bean curry.

Spätzle & Knödel
Wühlischstrasse 20 (2757 1151, www.spaetzle knoedel.de). U1, S5, S7, S75 Warschauer Strasse or tram M13. **Open** 5-11pm Mon-Fri; 3-11pm Sat, Sun. **Main courses** €7-€14. **No credit cards.** Map p87 F5 **⓭** **Bavarian**

A bare-bones eaterie – literally a brick-walled room with wooden tables – catering to southern German appetites with plates piled high with cheesy Spätzle or dumplings, topped with a choice of goulash, roast pork or mushroom sauce.

€ Trattoria Libau
Libauer Strasse 10 (2576 8529). U1, S5, S7, S75 Warschauer Strasse. **Open** 4pm-midnight Tue-Sun. **Main courses** €7-€9.50. **No credit cards.** Map p87 F4 **⓮** **Italian**

A little Italian gem nestled among the cheap fast-food places around Warschauer Strasse station, serving Roman-style pizzas that are big enough to share, salads and the ubiquitous tiramisu, all at very reasonable prices. Service can be a little gruff.

€ Tres Cabezas
Boxhagener Strasse 74 (2904 7470, www.tres cabezas.de). S3, S5, S7, S41, S42, S75 Ostkreuz. **Open** 8.30am-7.30pm daily. **No credit cards.** Map p87 F6 **⓯** **Café**

Tres Cabezas is so much more than a cute neighbourhood café. Owner Robert Stock has control over every step of the production chain, from owning a Fairtrade plantation in Costa Rica to servicing the Kees van der Westen espresso machines they exclusively stock. Naturally, they pull a mean shot of their custom blends, which are freshly roasted on-site.

Bars & Pubs

★ Antlered Bunny
Oderstrasse 7 (6640 5300, www.auntbenny.com). S3, S5, S7, S41, S42, S75 Ostkreuz. **Open** 6pm-2am Tue-Sat. **No credit cards.** Map p87 F6 **⓰**

To see the strange Berlin custom of Indian restaurants serving takeaway cocktails, head to the touristy area around Boxenhagener Platz. Luckily, local hipsters have the Canadian siblings behind the excellent Aunt Benny to thank for remedying this situation with this capsule cocktail bar, which they've put in behind their café. The special menu offers drinks such as the Rosebud – Bulleit rye, rose syrup, maple syrup and calvados – and you can even get freshly shucked oysters on weekends.

CSA
Karl-Marx-Allee 96 (2904 4741, www.csa-bar.de). U5 Weberwiese. **Open** 7pm-late daily. **No credit cards.** Map p86 D3 **⓱**

This ultra-modern bar, housed in the old Czech Airlines building, has the feel of a futuristic airport lounge as dreamed up in the 1970s. The angular furniture and white plastic fittings contrast magnificently with its shabby location and the vast concrete sweep of Karl-Marx-Allee. The atmosphere is relaxed, the design-conscious crowd coming for the excellent drink selection.

Hops & Barley
Wühlischstrasse 22-23 (2936 7534, www.hops andbarley-berlin.de). U1, S5, S7, S75 Warschauer Strasse. **Open** 5pm-3am daily. **No credit cards.** Map p87 F5 **⓲**

Interesting hop varieties are used here to produce traditional German beers, such as the top-fermenting *Weiz* (wheat) and *Dunkles* (dark), as well as *Apfelwein* (apple wine – cider, to you and me), a drink rarely seen in Berlin pubs. The heavy wooden bar is matched with fine green and white tiling, with the large brewing kettles in pride of place along one side.

★ Monster Ronson's Ichiban Karaoke
Warschauer Strasse 34 (8975 1327, www. karaokemonster.de). U1, S5, S7, S75 Warschauer Strasse. **Open** 7pm-midnight daily. **No credit cards.** Map p87 F3 **⓳**

In 1999, Monster Ronson – aka Ron Rineck – moved to Berlin from Salt Lake City with just $7,000 to his name. His savings dwindled and he began sleeping in his car, then bought a second-hand karaoke machine and began throwing karaoke parties in squat houses all over Europe. Eventually, he saved up enough to open his very own karaoke bar, which is now packed out most nights. Aspiring divas can belt out songs in several different booths, some small and intimate, others with their own stage area, where transsexual hosts often compere on weekends.

Paule's Metal Eck
Krossener Strasse 15 (291 1624). U1, S5, S7, S75 Warschauer Strasse. **Open** 7pm-5am daily. **No credit cards.** Map p87 E4 **⓴**

Neither a typical heavy-metal bar nor remotely typical for this area, the Egyptian-themed Eck attracts a young crowd with relentless metal videos, a decent selection of beers, and both pool and table football. Non-working disco balls, overhead lighting in the shape of mummies, and formidable dragon busts deck an interior that's designed half like a gloomy mausoleum, half in pastiche medieval style.

Supamolly
Jessner Strasse 41 (2900 7294, www.supamolly.de). U5, S8, S9, S41, S42, S85 Frankfurter Allee. **Open** 8pm-late Tue-Sat. **No credit cards.** Map p87 E6 **㉑**

EXPLORE

With the few remaining Berlin squats now tourist sites, Supamolly soldiers on as a punk-music venue, bar, cinema and general activist meeting point. You're more likely to encounter itinerant South American musicians these days, although an old-guard of Berlin punks still turns out for the frequent ska and hardcore gigs. It retains its grimy charm, the walls daubed with graffiti and the candlelit bar welcoming all for cheap beer at all hours of the night.

Süss War Gestern

Wühlischstrasse 34 (0176 2441 2940 mobile). U5 Samariterstrasse or tram M13. **Open** 7pm-4am Mon, Tue; 7pm-5am Wed; 7pm-6am Thur; 7pm-8am Fri, Sat. **No credit cards**. **Map** p87 F5 ㉒

Berlin's nightlife can sometimes seem aggressively all-or-nothing, but this Friedrichshain DJ bar provides a welcome middle ground, with free entry, cheap beer and two floors with rotating DJs. There's space to dance every night, but you can just as well chill with TVs hooked up to Super Mario Bros.

Shops & Services

Big Brobot

Kopernikusstrasse 19 (7407 8388, www.big brobot.com). U5 Frankfurter Tor. **Open** 11am-8pm Mon-Fri; 11am-6pm Sat. **Map** p87 E4 ㉓ **Gifts & souvenirs**

A paradise for graphics nerds, with hundreds of collectible toys, comics and books on tattoo art or vintage typography. Big Brobot also stocks high-end skate labels such as Stüssy and Kid Robot. The refreshingly unpretentious staff are friendly.

Capitain Petzel

Karl-Marx-Allee 45 (2408 8130, www.capitain petzel.de). U5 Schillingstrasse. **Open** 11am-6pm Tue-Sat. **Map** p86 D1 ㉔ **Gallery**

Housed in a dramatic, Soviet-era modernist block, Capitain Petzel is a light, bright and airy space, which was used to showcase ideologically friendly art during the GDR era. Today, thanks to Cologne gallerist Gisela Capitain and her partner Friedrich Petzel, it offers an international range of contemporary artists, including John Stezaker, Wade Guyton, Martin Kippenburger and Sarah Morris.

Dollyrocker

Gärtnerstrasse 25 (5471 9606, www.dollyrocker. de). U5 Samariterstrasse. **Open** 11am-7pm Tue-Fri; 11am-4pm Sat. **No credit cards**. **Map** p87 E5 ㉕ **Children**

Designers (and mothers) Gabi Hartkopp and Ina Langenbruch upcycle high-quality textiles to create colourful and adorable clothing and accessories for kids aged up to seven. Under their sewing machines, a man's blouse becomes a boy's T-shirt, women's designer jeans become a girl's dress – each piece unique. Handmade leather shoes are also sold.

Fischsuppen

Boxhagenerstrasse 68 (2243 5039). S3, S5, S7, S41, S42, S75 Ostkreuz. **Open** 10am-10.30pm Mon-Sat; noon-9.30pm Sun. **No credit cards**. **Map** p87 F6 ㉖ **Food & drink**

Berlin's distinct lack of easily available fresh fish is usually blamed on its distance from the sea, but it's more likely down to local tastes traditionally preferring freshwater or pickled fish. This fishmonger covers these, plus more popular varieties of fresh fish, such as Alaskan salmon and Icelandic cod. There's also a small restaurant in the back.

Flohmarkt am Boxhagener Platz

Boxhagener Platz (fleamarket 0162 292 3066 mobile, farmers' market 0178 476 2242 mobile). U5 Samariterstrasse. **Open** 9am-3.30pm Sat; 10am-6pm Sun. **No credit cards**. **Map** p87 E5 ㉗ **Market**

The Boxi market used to be more of a makeshift affair, full of bric-a-brac and punk clothing, but, much like the surrounding area, it's got with the times, now offering a thriving farmers' market on Saturdays and craft fare on Sundays. Stock up on local organic vegetables while chomping on a *lahmacun* (Turkish flatbread) roll. On Sundays, you may find some very cheap vintage clothing.

Frische Paradies

Hermann-Blankenstein-Strasse 48 (390 8150, www.frischeparadies.de). S8, S9, S41, S42, S85 Storkower Strasse. **Open** 8am-8pm Mon-Fri; 8am-6pm Sat. **Map** p86 D6 ㉘ **Supermarket**

This sleek black monolith is a surprise, emerging from a series of nondescript warehouses in the industrial backwaters of Friedrichshain. Primarily a wholesale market for the restaurant trade, it's the place to come for gourmet ingredients: there's tinned produce, vegetables, spices and an enormous chiller section of vacuum-packed meats and exotic veg. **Other location** Morsestrasse 2, Charlottenburg (3908 1523).

▶ *On the first Monday of every month, get 15% off all produce.*

Olivia

Wühlischstrasse 30 (6050 0368, www.olivia-berlin. de). U1, S5, S7, S75 Warschauer Strasse. **Open** noon-7pm Mon-Sat; 1-6pm Sun. **No credit cards**. **Map** p87 F4 ㉙ **Food & drink**

A cutesy boutique of a chocolatier with beautiful hand-painted biscuits, lots of cocoa varieties and their signature cakes, which come baked in a jar. The Chilli Schokoladen Torte is recommended.

Peres Projects

Karl-Marx-Allee 82 (275 950 770, www.peres projects.com). U5 Weberwiese. **Open** 11am-6pm Tue-Sat. **No credit cards**. **Map** p86 D2 ㉚ **Gallery**

EXPLORE

Hip Californian curator Javier Peres has a talent for putting on transgressive shows that everyone talks about. He hit headlines with the Bruce LaBruce and Terence Koh show Blame Canada, a live installation of 'degenerate art' consisting of horizontal glory holes, with real (Viagra-assisted) penises poking down from the ceiling and up from the floor like stalactites and stalagmites.

Sake Kontor

Markgrafendamm 34 (2123 7601, www. sake-kontor.de). S3, S5, S7, S41, S42, S75 Ostkreuz. **Open** 10am-4pm Tue; noon-8pm Thur; noon-6pm Wed, Fri, Sat. **Map** p87 H5
㉛ Food & drink

Decked out in kiri wood, a traditional decorative timber reminiscent of cedarwood, this is Germany's only specialist saké shop and distributor. Run by Susanne Rost and her Japanese husband, they take pains to explain the complexity behind fine saké, where different grades of quality are measured by rice grain purity and filtration.

Stil Raum Berlin

Eldenaer Strasse 21 (4679 4857, www. stilraumberlin.de). S8, S9, S41, S42, S85 Storkower Strasse. **Open** noon-7pm Tue-Fri; noon-4pm Sat. **No credit cards. Map** p86 D5
㉜ Homewares

The owners of this beautiful furniture showroom make regular trips to Copenhagen and bring back Danish design classics. Berlin is mad for Scandinavian modernism, and there are a lot of cheap knock-offs about; head here for advice on the real deal, from designers such as Andreas Hansen and Ib Kofod-Larsen.

Urban Spree Bookshop & Gallery

Revaler Strasse 99 (7407 8597, www.urban spree.com). U1, S5, S7, S75 Warschauer Strasse. **Open** noon-midnight Mon-Thur, Sun; noon-3am Fri, Sat. **No credit cards. Map** p87 F4
㉝ Books & music/Gallery

Urban Spree is run by the team behind the now closed .HBC, its ground-floor space functioning as a gallery devoted to street art, graffiti and photography. There's also an excellent bookshop specialising in these topics, with limited editions and books from small publishers such as Fabulatorio. Gigs and performances also take place – *see p196* and *p206*.

Zigarren Herzog am Hafen

Stralauer Allee 9 (2904 7015, www.herzog-am-hafen.de). U1, S5, S7, S75 Warschauer Strasse. **Open** 11am-9pm Mon-Sat. **Map** p87 G4 **㉞ Gifts & souvenirs**

Swiss-born Max Herzog is the undisputed cigar king of Berlin, his flagship shop featuring the largest walk-in humidor in Germany. It has a dizzying variety of Habano cigars, categorised by box code and production date. There's a spacious lounge and terrace in which to sample your purchases.

EXPLORE

Urban Spree Bookshop & Gallery.

LICHTENBERG

Most of the neighbourhoods in the old East have little to offer the visitor, lumbered with a legacy of unemployment, squalid Plattenbau high-rise housing and lingering pockets of neo-Nazi support. East of Friedrichshain, Lichtenberg is famously unappealing, though it does contain the **Tierpark Berlin-Friedrichsfelde** (Berlin-Friedrichsfelde Zoo) and both the **Stasi Museum**, more properly known as the Forschungs- und Gedenkstätte Normannenstrasse, and the **Gedenkstätte Berlin-Hohenschönhausen**, a former Stasi prison turned chilling exhibit of state oppression. The **Museum Berlin-Karlshorst** documents the somewhat troubled history of Russian-German relations during the last century.

Sights & Museums

Forschungs- und Gedenkstätte Normannenstrasse (Stasi Museum)

Ruschestrasse 103 (553 6854, www.stasimuseum. de). U5, S8, S9, S41, S42, S85 Frankfurter Allee. **Open** 10am-6pm Mon-Fri; noon-6pm Sat, Sun. **Admission** €5; €4 reductions. **No credit cards.**
In what used to be part of the HQ of the Stasi, you can look around the former offices of secret police chief Erich Mielke – his old uniform still hangs in his wardrobe – and see displays of bugging devices and spy cameras concealed in books, plant pots and car doors. In early 2015, a new exhibition opened exploring the Stasi's structure, methods and activities, and

giving an insight into the most insidious police surveillance state in all of history. Tours are also offered of the Stasi Archives next door.

Gärten der Welt Marzahn

Eisenacher Strasse 99, Marzahn (700 906 699, www.gruen-berlin.de). S7 Marzahn then bus 195. **Open** 9am-sundown daily. **Admission** €4.
Originally built in 1986 as the GDR equivalent to the similar Britz gardens in Neukölln, this existed as an eastern peripheral oddity until the millennium, when it was turned into the sparkling collection of specialist gardens that exists today. The Chinese garden is the largest in Europe; and there are similarly authentic Korean, Balinese and Italian gardens. Kids will love the fiendish hedge maze.

★ Gedenkstätte Berlin-Hohenschönhausen

Gensler Strasse 66 (9860 8230, www.stiftung-hsh. de). Tram M5, M6. **Open** Guided tours (German) 11am, 1pm, 3pm Mon-Fri; 10am-4pm hourly Sat, Sun. (English) 2.30pm Wed, Sat, Sun. **Admission** €5; €2.50 reductions. **No credit cards.**
A sprawling former remand prison run by the Stasi, this building has a vicious history. First the site of a canteen for the Nazi social welfare organisation, it was turned into 'Special Encampment No.3' by the Soviets and later expanded by the MfS (Ministerium für Staatssicherheit; Stasi). The inmates were all political prisoners, from the leaders of the 1953 workers' uprising to critical students. Excellent and highly personal guided tours by ex-prisoners take 90 minutes. The experience is gut-wrenchingly bleak,

Gedenkstätte Berlin-Hohenschönhausen.

EXPLORE

Dong Xuan Center.

but a potent insight into how the Stasi operated. On one interrogator's office wall hangs a painting of a fairytale castle, beneath which prisoners underwent horrifying psychological interrogation.

FREE Mies van der Rohe Haus
Oberseestrasse 60 (9700 0618, www. miesvanderrohehaus.de). Tram M5, 27. **Open** 11am-5pm Tue-Sun. **Admission** free.
Ludwig Mies van der Rohe designed this L-shaped modernist gem in 1933 for Karl Lemke, the owner of a Berlin graphic-art and printing firm. Lemke and his wife lived here until 1945, when the Red Army stormed in and used it as a garage. From 1960 until the fall of the Wall, it was a laundry for the Stasi; these days, it hosts art exhibitions.

FREE Museum Berlin-Karlshorst
Zwieseler Strasse 4 (5015 0810, www.museum-karlshorst.de). S3 Karlshorst. **Open** 10am-6pm Tue-Sun. **Admission** free.
After the Soviets took Berlin, they commandeered this former German officers' club as HQ for the military administration. It was here, on the night of 8-9 May 1945, that German commanders signed the unconditional surrender, ending the war in Europe. This stern museum surveys over 70 years of German-Soviet relations. Divided into 16 rooms, with the surrender room left in its original state, it takes us through the wars (both World and Cold), plus assorted pacts, victories and capitulations. Buy an English guide, as the exhibits are labelled in German and Russian. English tours can be booked.

Tierpark Berlin-Friedrichsfelde
Am Tierpark 125 (515 310, www.tierpark-berlin. de). U5 Tierpark. **Open** Late Mar-mid Sept

9am-6pm daily. Mid Sept-late Mar 9am-5pm daily. **Admission** €12; €6-€8 reductions.
East Berlin's zoo is still one of Europe's largest, with an impressive amount of roaming space for the herd animals, although others are still kept in rather small cages. Residents include bears, big cats, elephants and penguins. One of the continent's biggest snake farms is also here. In the north-west corner is the baroque Schloss Friedrichsfelde.

Shops & Services

Dong Xuan Center
Herzbergstrasse 128-139 (5321 7480, www. dongxuan-berlin.de). Tram M8, 21. **Open** 10am-8pm Mon, Wed-Sun. **Food & drink**
Four cavernous warehouses stand on the former site of an enormous coal and graphite processing plant (it was demolished in the 1990s and the land underwent extensive 'detoxification'). Tradesmen hawk all sorts of wares for businesses affiliated with the Vietnamese community, from wholesale nail-salon supplies to glitzy chandeliers, but of most interest are the enormous food halls. The offal butchers and rare South-east Asian herbs will transport you straight to downtown Saigon.

Sammlung Haubrok
Herzbergstrasse 40-43 (0172 210 9525 mobile, www.haubrok.org). Tram M8, 21. **Open** By appointment. **Admission** €80 donation per group. **Gallery**
With over 750 works, spanning painting, sculpture, photography, video and conceptual pieces, Barbara and Axel Haubrok's collection is regarded as one of Berlin's best. They regularly stage exhibitions and loans to organisations around Germany.

Tiergarten

A slightly uncertain mish-mash of districts plus the grand green park that gives it its name, Tiergarten straddles the centre of Berlin; it's home to dozens of embassies as well as the iconic Reichstag parliament building. Tiergarten was once hemmed in on the east by the Wall, but these days it's right at the heart of things again, stretching from the futuristic Hauptbahnhof in the north to the Zoo in the south-west. South of the park is Potsdamer Platz, Berlin's rejuvenated commercial centre, as well as the museums and venues of the Kulturforum – including the spectacular modernist Philharmonie concert hall. Further south still, the rather unlovely former red-light drag of Potsdamer Strasse is experiencing something of a revival, as a score of galleries have relocated there in recent years, driven out of Mitte by sharply rising rents.

EXPLORE

Tiergarten.

Don't Miss

1 Gemäldegalerie Immerse yourself in the world of the Flemish Renaissance (p104).

2 Tiergarten Stroll through this ex-royal hunting ground and aim straight for the gleaming Siegessäule (p96).

3 Hugos Michelin-starred dining with a fantastic view (p106).

4 Joseph-Roth-Diele Talk art over a bottle of wine at this lovingly recreated intellectuals' café (p106).

5 Museum für Film und Fernsehen The story of Germany's long relationship with the moving image (p104).

THE PARK & THE REICHSTAG

A hunting ground for the Prussian electors since the 16th century, **Tiergarten** was opened to the public in the 18th century. It was badly damaged during World War II; in the desperate winter of 1945-46, almost all the surviving trees were cut down for firewood, and it wasn't until 1949 that Tiergarten started to recover. Today, though, joggers, nature lovers, gay cruisers and picnickers pour into the park in fair weather. There's no finer place from which to appreciate it all than the beer garden of the **Café am Neuen See** on Lichtensteinallee.

All roads entering the Tiergarten lead to the park's largest monument, the **Siegessäule** (Victory Column), which celebrates the last wars Germany managed to win. The park's main thoroughfare, **Strasse des 17 Juni** (the date of the East Berlin workers' strike of 1953), is one of the few pieces of Hitler's plan for 'Germania' that actually got built – a grand east–west axis, lined with Nazi lamp-posts and linking Unter den Linden to Neu-Westend. The Siegessäule was moved here from its original position in front of the Reichstag.

Towards the eastern end of Strasse des 17 Juni, just west of the Brandenburger Tor, stands the **Sowjetisches Ehrenmal** (Soviet War Memorial). Once the only piece of Soviet property in West Berlin, it was built in 1945-46 out of granite and marble from the ruins of Hitler's Neue Reichskanzlei, but posed a political problem. Standing in the British Zone, it was surrounded by a British military enclosure, which was in turn guarded by Berlin police – all to protect the monument and the two Soviet soldiers who stood guard. The tanks flanking it are supposed to have been the first two Soviet tanks into Berlin.

At the north-eastern corner of the park stands the **Reichstag**. Described by Kaiser Wilhelm II as the 'Imperial Monkey House', it hasn't had a happy history: the scene of Weimar squabblings, it was then left as a burnt-out ruin during the Third Reich, regarded by the Red Army as its main prize, and then stranded for decades beside the Wall dividing the Deutsches Volk whose representatives it was intended to house. But in 1999, Lord Norman Foster's brilliant refitting of the building was unveiled. His crowning achievement is the glass cupola: a trip to the top should be a must-do on any visitor's agenda.

When the decision was made in 1991 to make Berlin the German capital, the area north of the Reichstag was picked as the central location for new government buildings. Designed by Axel Schultes and Charlotte Frank, the immense Spreebogen complex, also known as the Band des Bundes, is built over a twist in the River Spree (*Bogen* means 'bend'). It crosses the river twice and the old East–West border once, symbolising the reunion of Berlin. The most notable new building is Schultes and Frank's **Bundeskanzleramt** (Federal Chancellery). Across the river to the north, rapid development is taking place round the hulking **Berlin Hauptbahnhof**. Berlin never had a central station before – now it has the biggest and most futuristic in Europe.

South of the Bundeskanzleramt's western end is the **Haus der Kulturen der Welt** (House of World Cultures), an impressive piece of modern architecture with a reflecting pool that contains a Henry Moore sculpture. Formerly known as the Kongresshalle and nicknamed the 'pregnant oyster', the HdKdW opened in 1957 as a gift from the United States and today hosts exhibits from cultures around the world.

Also on the park's northern boundary stands **Schloss Bellevue**, a minor palace from 1785 that's now the official residence of the German President. Across the river, a serpentine 718-apartment residence for Federal employees, nicknamed 'Die Schlange' (The Snake), winds across land that was formerly used as a goods yard. West of Schloss Bellevue is the post-war **Englischer Garten**, landscaped in the style of Capability Brown and filled with plants donated by the English royal family and various horticultural societies.

Just north of here, the smaller branch of the **Akademie der Künste** (*see p203*) has a varied programme of arts events and classical concerts. The district between the Akademie and the loop of the Spree is known as the **Hansaviertel**, a post-war housing project designed by a who's who of architects as part of the 1957 Interbau Exhibition for the 'city of tomorrow'. It's of great interest to lovers of concrete modernism, if a little desolate.

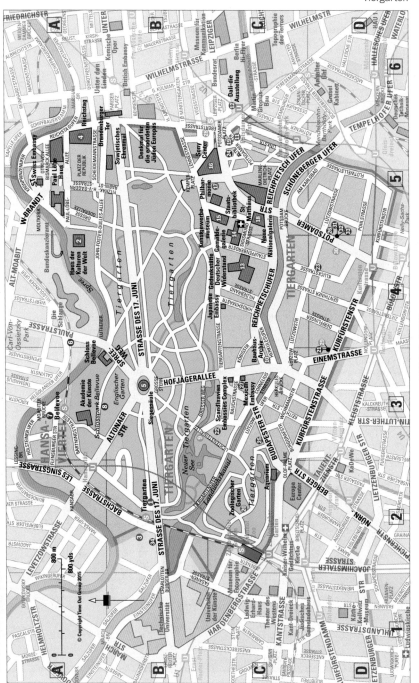

EXPLORE

Sights & Museums

FREE Gaslaternen-Freilichtmuseum Berlin

Strasse des 17 Juni (9025 4124, www.museums portal-berlin.de). S5, S7, S75 Tiergarten. **Open** 24hrs daily. **Admission** free. **Map** p97 B2 ❶

A charming little oddity right by the Tiergarten S-Bahn station, this open-air gas-lamp museum has over 90 examples of historic streetlights, all lovingly restored. Take a turn through here at night and bask in their historic glow.

Haus der Kulturen der Welt

John-Foster-Dulles-Allee 10 (3978 7175, www.hkw.de). S5, S7, S75 Bellevue. **Open** & admission varies. **Map** p97 A4 ❷

Set up in 1989 to promote the arts of developing countries, the 'House of World Cultures' features a lively programme of concerts (*see p207*), exhibitions and symposia centred around global cultural questions. Housed in Hugh Stubbins' oyster-like building, erected in 1957 as America's contribution to the Interbau Exhibition, this is a treasured Berlin cultural institution.

▶ *There's a decent café on the premises.*

Königliche Porzellan-Manufaktur Berlin

Wegelystrasse 1 (390 090, www.kpm-berlin.com). S5, S7, S75 Tiergarten. **Open** 10am-6pm Mon-Sat. **Admission** €10; €5 reductions. **Map** p97 B2 ❸

At first a closely guarded secret, porcelain was originally imported from China, but by the 16th century production had begun in Germany. Frederick the Great founded this factory in 1763. The solid red-brick building houses an extensive interactive exhibition that takes in the firm's history and production methods, and also gets hands-on in the workshop. Classic rococo and modernist designs are sold in the shop.

★ FREE Reichstag

Platz der Republik (2270, www.bundestag.de). U55, S1, S2, S25 Brandenburger Tor. **Open** 8am-midnight daily (last entry 10pm). **Admission** free. **Map** p97 A5 ❹

The imposing Reichstag was controversial from the beginning. Architect Paul Wallot struggled to find a style that would symbolise German national identity at a time – 1884-94, shortly after unification – when no such style or identity existed. It was burned on 17 February 1933; the Nazis blamed Dutchman Marius van der Lubbe, a Communist, and used it as an excuse to begin their seizure of power. But since its celebrated renovation by Lord Foster, the Reichstag again houses the Bundestag (Federal Parliament). Foster conceived of it as a 'dialogue between old and new': graffiti scrawled by Russian soldiers in 1945 has been left on view, and there has been no attempt to deny the building's turbulent history.

No dome appeared on Foster's original plans, but the German government insisted upon one as a sop to conservatives. Foster then insisted that unlike the structure's original dome (damaged in the war and demolished in the 1950s), the new dome must be open to visitors as a symbol of political transparency; due to the materials used, it ended up costing even more than a replica would have done. A lift whisks you up to the roof; from here, ramps lead to the top of the dome, from where there are fine views of the city. At the centre is a funnel of mirrors, angled so as to shed

Reichstag.

EXPLORE

light on the workings of democracy below, but also lending an almost funhouse effect to the dome. An excellent (free) audio guide points out all the surrounding landmarks.

A trip to the top of this open, playful and defiantly democratic space is a must, but note that you can't just rock up any more: following a series of terrorist threats in 2010, you must now book in advance by filling in an online form and suggesting three possible time-slots at least three working days in advance: www.bundestag.de/besuche/kuppel.html.

Siegessäule
Strasse des 17 Juni (391 2961). S5, S7, S75 Bellevue. **Open** *Summer* 9.30am-6.30pm Mon-Fri; 9.30am-7pm Sat, Sun. *Winter* 10am-5pm Mon-Fri; 10am-5.30pm Sat, Sun. **Admission** €3; €2.50 reductions; free under-5s. **No credit cards.** **Map** p97 B3 ⑤

Tiergarten's biggest monument was built in 1871-73 during Berlin's original transformation into the German capital, to commemorate Prussian campaigns against Denmark (1864), Austria (1866) and France (1870-71). Originally positioned in front of the Reichstag, it was moved by Hitler to form a centrepiece for the East–West axis connecting western Berlin with the palaces and ministries of Mitte. On top of the column is a gilded goddess of victory by Friedrich Drake; captured French cannons and cannonballs, sawn in half and gilded, decorate the column itself. Contemporary wags joked about the glum-looking Victoria as 'being the only woman in town without a man.' It's an arduous 285 steps up to the viewing platform.

Restaurants & Cafés

Balikci Ergün
Lüneburger Strasse 382 (397 5737). S5, S7, S75 Bellevue. **Open** 5pm-midnight Mon; 3pm-midnight Tue-Sun. **Main courses** €7-€12. **No credit cards.** **Map** p97 A4 ⑥ **Turkish**

Opened by a Turkish ex-football player, this is as close to an Anatolian fish shack as you'll find in Berlin. The formula is simple but effective: daily fresh fish charred on the grill, zingy side salads and plenty of cold beer. It's tucked away beneath a railway arch, and the ceiling is covered in notes from appreciative diners.

★ Konditorei Buchwald
Bartningallee 29 (391 5931), www.konditorei-buchwald.de). S5, S7, S75 Bellevue. **Open** 8am-6pm Mon-Fri; 9am-6pm Sun. **No credit cards.** **Map** p97 A3 ⑦ **German**

One Berlin institution (afternoon coffee and cake) celebrated by another: Buchwald, which has been pumping out the sugar and caffeine fix in style for over 160 years. The premises are charming and old-fashioned. The cakes are legendary. Arrive early afternoon, grab a table and savour the history.

Siegessäule.

Teehaus im Englischen Garten
Altonaer Strasse 2 (3948 0400), www.teehaus-tiergarten.com). S5, S7, S75 Bellevue. **Open** 10am-11pm daily. **Main courses** €7.50-€21.50. **No credit cards.** **Map** p97 A3 ⑧ **German**

This 1950s garden in the north-west of the Tiergarten was designed to commemorate Anglo-German relations during the blockade of Berlin, and is filled with trees donated by George VI. The charming thatched teahouse serves seasonal specialities such as venison stew or goose leg with dumplings.

Bars & Pubs

€ Café am Neuen See
Lichtensteinallee 2 (254 4930), www.cafeam neuensee.de). S5, S7, S75 Tiergarten. **Open** 9am-late daily. **No credit cards.** **Map** p97 B3 ⑨

Hidden away by a small lake in the western part of the Tiergarten, this café, beer garden and brasserie rolled into one is among Berlin's most idyllic spots. In summer, there are rowing boats for hire, and it's a fun and buzzy place to while away an afternoon, eating excellent stone-baked pizza washed down with big jugs of Pilsner – or, unusually for Berlin, cider.

EXPLORE

WALK BERLIN REVIVED

A city centre made anew.

The area around Potsdamer Platz, the Brandenburg Gate and the Reichstag has received special attention in the binding together of the city's two halves. This walk highlights the dramatic changes in what was once a no-man's-land.

The walk begins on the corner of Potsdamer Strasse and Eichhornstrasse, which feels like a border. To the west and south is the 1960s **Kulturforum**, home to a variety of cultural institutions that were placed on the edge of West Berlin in anticipation of reunification. To the east is a new and much denser commercial quarter. Designed and built in the 1990s, it's generally known as **Potsdamer Platz** (see p102), although the actual 'Platz' is three blocks. Here stands Keith Haring's sculpture *The Boxers*, part of the Daimler Contemporary's collection of art. Comprising two figures in primary blue and red, conjoined yet in conflict, it's befitting of both Berlin and this particular spot.

From here, walk down Eichhornstrasse, with the **Grand Hyatt** hotel (see p273) to your left. You'll see a spaceship-like contraption perched on the shoulder of a building ahead, apparently scanning the streets below but

actually another Daimler collection sculpture – Auk de Vries's *gelandet* ('landed'). At the point where this street opens into Marlene-Dietrich-Platz, in front of the Spielbank (casino), there's a third sculpture: Jeff Koons' *Balloon Flower*.

A couple of hundred metres along Alte Potsdamer Strasse on the right is the entrance to the Arkaden shopping mall. **Haus Huth** (see p102), the old building next to it at no.5, was the only surviving pre-war structure this side of Potsdamer Strasse when Renzo Piano planned the 75,000-square-metre site now known as the Daimler Viertel in the early 1990s. Slip through the passage between Haus Huth and the Arkaden, and you'll emerge into Fontaneplatz. The building to the right, with round towers inserted into its corners, is by Richard Rogers. And to the left stands Robert Rauschenberg's *Riding Bikes* – another Daimler-owned sculpture and, like the Haring piece, a symbol of two halves.

Bearing to the left will lead you into Potsdamer Platz itself. The green contraption by the junction is a replica of Europe's first traffic lights, erected here in 1924 when this was supposedly the world's busiest intersection. The borders of the British, American and Soviet occupation zones met at this point, meaning that even among the late 1940s ruins it remained a centre of commerce – no matter which direction the police approached, black market traders were able to escape into another zone. The Wall snuffed out all activity in the area for several decades, but with grand new entrances to the sub-surface station and an assortment of high-rises – notably the brick-clad **Kollhoff Tower** and the rounded **Bahn-Tower** that flank Potsdamer Strasse, forming a gateway from western Berlin – it once more feels like downtown. Ascend to the **Panoramapunkt** (see p105) for great views.

Cross Potsdamer Platz and duck left into Helmut Jahn's futuristic **Sony Center** (see p102), completely different from the more traditional cityscape of the Daimler Viertel. Taking the exit right of the fin-de-siècle artists' favourite, Café Josty, you'll pass the relocated remains of the 19th-century **Sheraton Berlin Grand Hotel Esplanade** (see p274).

The triangular area north of the Sony Center is called the Lenné Dreieck. During the Cold War, this land was politically part of East Berlin but lay west of the Wall, and was left as

overgrown wasteland. In 1988, it changed hands as part of an East–West agreement, but not before a squatters' camp had occupied it in order to protest against a planned new road. On the day it formally became West Berlin territory, police moved in to evict the squatters, 182 of whom used ladders to flee into the East. It was the single largest escape across the Wall and possibly the only one in an eastwards direction.

Turn right on Bellevuestrasse and left on Ebertstrasse, and you'll see the line of the Wall is marked by a double row of cobblestones. The buildings on the right are embassies of the German Länder, constructed on land once occupied by Hitler's Reichskanzlerei. Turn right down In den Ministergarten and, at the junction with Gertrude-Kolmar-Strasse, you'll find an information board about the Führerbunker, the last remaining tunnels of which were destroyed in the late 1980s. Turning left along Gertrude-Kolmar-Strasse brings you to Peter Eisenmann's **Denkmal für die ermordeten Juden Europas** (see p48). Get lost among its 2,711 concrete columns, ending up in Behrenstrasse on the other side.

The massive new **US Embassy** is on the corner of Ebertstrasse and Behrenstrasse. Next to it is the anarchistic rear façade of Frank Gehry's **DZ Bank** building. Gehry had to play along with the Pariser Platz conformity rule on the front side, but uses the building's rear quite differently.

Turn left on to Wilhelmstrasse to admire Michael Wilford's much-lauded **British Embassy**, one of the few unconventional buildings in the area. Turning left at the end of the block brings you into **Pariser Platz**, the square in front of the Brandenburg Gate. Laid out in 1732, from 1850 it was given a uniform, classical style, but was then destroyed in World War II. In 1993, the Berlin Senate decided to recreate it in classical style; on the left side, Günther Behnisch's glass-fronted **Akademie der Künste** defies those rules. And on the other side of the square, the French Embassy rebels against the statutes with slanted window jambs asymmetrically facing the Brandenburger Tor.

Walk through the **Brandenburger Tor** (see p40). Ahead in the distance is the **Siegessäule** (see p99) and to your right the **Reichstag** (see p98). Walk around to the front and queue to visit Norman Foster's wonderful cupola, before which lies a splendid view of all the new government buildings. Then circumnavigate Platz der Republik to the Bundeskanzleramt, Germany's answer to 10 Downing Street, admiring the new **Hauptbahnhof** on the skyline to the north, and the squat **Swiss Embassy** that has survived war and redevelopment. On the east side of Axel Schultes and Charlotte Frank's Kanzleramt is another piece of public art. A sculpture by Basque artist Eduardo Chillida, with two rusty forms reaching out for each other, it's called, simply, *Berlin*.

EXPLORE

EXPLORE

POTSDAMER PLATZ & SOUTH OF THE PARK

At the south-east corner of the Tiergarten is the resurrected **Potsdamer Platz**, intended to be the reunified city's new commercial centrepiece. In the 1920s, Potsdamer Platz was reckoned to be one of Europe's busiest squares. The first-ever traffic lights stood here (a replica can be seen today on the south side of the square). Like much of Berlin, it was bombed flat in World War II; during the Cold War, it became a grim no-man's-land bisected by the Wall. Fierce debate ensued over whether the redevelopment should adopt the typical scale of a 'European' city or go for an 'American' high-rise approach. A group of internationally renowned super-architects locked horns with the city's traditionalist building commissioner, Hans Stimmann. The result was a compromise: medium-height development except on Potsdamer Platz itself, where high-rises up to 90 metres (295 feet) were allowed but with a slightly more uniform look than the proposed experimental designs.

Opinions are mixed as to the success of the finished article, some architectural critics finding its non-nationalistic idiom too much like 'a nebulous international airport space'. During the Cold War, the area was not identified with either East or West – which makes it sound like a good candidate for a unifying centre. But it was really an isolated island of redevelopment, the new western side of Park am Gleisdreieck now finally linking it to Kreuzberg and Schöneberg. Even so, it's beginning to feel worn in, a natural part of a long-disjointed urban landscape.

Helmut Jahn's soaring **Sony Center**, surprisingly light in steel and glass, contains the Forum, an urban entertainment complex that in turn holds the **CineStar** multiplex (*see p176*), the more offbeat **Arsenal** cinema (*see p174*) and the **Museum für Film**. (There's another multiplex over the road in the Daimler quarter, the **CinemaxX**.) Served also by a clutch of new five-star hotels, including the **Ritz-Carlton** (*see p274*) and the **Grand Hyatt** (*see p273*), Potsdamer Platz is also now the main venue for the **Berlin International Film Festival** (*see p30*). But there's little to recommend in terms of eating, drinking or shopping. It's all franchise culture.

One of only two Potsdamer Platz buildings to survive World War II and the subsequent clearout was once here, on the Sony site: the **Kaisersaal Café** from the old Grand Hotel Esplanade, a listed building. When plans for the area solidified, the café was found to be in a bad position, so the whole structure was moved 75 metres (246 feet) to its present location on the building's north side, where it's been integrated into the apartment complex on Bellevuestrasse.

Sony Center.

The other major corporate presence at Potsdamer Platz is Daimler (formerly DaimlerChrysler), responsible for most of the development south of the Sony Center. One of the most admired of the area's buildings is Hans Kollhoff's triangular, brick-clad tower at Potsdamer Platz 1, which, together with the curved Deutsche Bahn tower over the road, forms the gateway to the area. It's the tallest building here; the **Panoramapunkt** platform up top offers fine views.

A few doors down the road at Alte Potsdamer Strasse 5 is **Haus Huth**, the only other building to survive from before World War II. For decades a lonely structure in the middle of overgrown wasteland, it now stands next to the three-storey Arkaden shopping mall. At the top is the **Daimler Contemporary** gallery, which exhibits works from the auto manufacturer's big-name art collection. The company has also positioned various contemporary sculptures around the quarter, including work by Jeff Koons, Robert Rauschenberg, Keith Haring and Nam June Paik (*see p100* **Walk: Berlin Revived**).

Immediately west of the Potsdamer Platz development is one of the city's major concentrations of museums, galleries and cultural institutions. Collectively known as the **Kulturforum** and built in anticipation of reunification, it was based on the designs of Hans Scharoun. Scharoun himself designed the **Staatsbibliotek** (State Library) and the gold **Philharmonie** (*see p202*), home to the Berlin Philharmonic; adjacent is the **Musikinstrumentenmuseum** (Musical Instrument Museum).

One block west is a low-rise museum complex. Its biggest draw is the **Gemäldegalerie** (Picture Gallery), but the **Kunstgewerbemuseum** (Museum of Decorative Art) is also worth a peek. Here too is the **Kunstbibliotek** (Art Library), and a decent café and shop. Next door is the **Matthäuskirche** (Matthias Church) and, to the south, the bold glass cube of the **Neue Nationalgalerie** (New National Gallery).

Between the north flank of the Kulturforum and the south flank of Tiergarten runs **Tiergartenstrasse**, the main drag of Berlin's revived diplomatic quarter. Part of Albert Speer's plan for 'Germania', the street originally contained the embassy buildings (designed by German architects) of Hitler's Axis allies. Damaged by bombing, they were largely abandoned, and Tiergartenstrasse became an eerie walk past decaying grandeur. But with the land often still owned by the respective governments, embassies were reconstructed at their old addresses during the diplomatic relocation from Bonn, and this area is now embassy row again.

The **Gedenkstätte Deutscher Widerstand** (Memorial to the German Resistance) lies south on Stauffenbergstrasse, a street named after the leader of the July 1944 plot to kill Hitler. At the corner of Stauffenbergstrasse and Reichpietschufer is **Shell House** (1932), a curvaceous expressionist masterpiece by Emil Fahrenkamp. Five minutes' walk west along the Landwehrkanal sits the gleaming white building of the **Bauhaus Archiv – Museum für Gestaltung** (Museum of Design); a further ten-minute walk leads to the less highbrow attractions of the **Zoologischer Garten & Aquarium** and the hub of West Berlin around Bahnhof Zoo and the Ku'damm.

Sights & Museums

Bauhaus Archiv – Museum für Gestaltung

Klingelhöferstrasse 13-14 (254 0020, www. bauhaus.de). U1, U2, U3, U4 Nollendorfplatz. **Open** 10am-5pm Mon, Wed-Sun. **Admission** Mon, Sat, Sun €7; €4 reductions. Wed-Fri €6; €3 reductions. **Map** p97 C3 ⑩

Walter Gropius, founder of the Bauhaus school, designed this elegant white building that now houses this absorbing design museum. The permanent exhibition presents a selection of furniture, ceramics, prints, sculptures, photographs and sketches created in the Bauhaus workshop between 1919 and 1933, when the school was closed down by the Nazis. There are also first-rate temporary exhibitions from the extensive archive, such as a show about Kandinsky's tenure as a teacher. An interesting gift shop sells design icons including the Bauhaus lamp by Wilhelm Wagenfeld.

FREE Daimler Contemporary

Haus Huth, Alte Potsdamer Strasse 5 (2594 1420, www.sammlung.daimler.com). U2, S1, S2, S25 Potsdamer Platz. **Open** 11am-6pm daily. Guided tours 4pm 1st Sat of mth. **Admission** free. **Map** p97 C5 ⑪

EXPLORE

Bauhaus Archiv – Museum für Gestaltung.

As you'd expect, Daimler's collection is serious stuff. It sticks to the 20th century, specifically abstract and geometric art; the collection numbers around 1,800 works from artists such as Josef Albers, Max Bill, Walter de Maria, Jeff Koons and Andy Warhol. The gallery rotates themed portions of the collection, typically 30-80 works at a time, and often stages joint shows with other private collections.

Dalí – Die Ausstellung

Leipziger Platz 7 (0700 325 423 7546, www. daliberlin.de). U2, S1, S2, S25 Potsdamer Platz. **Open** noon-8pm Mon-Sat; 10am-8pm Sun. **Admission** €12.50; €9.50 reductions; free under-6s. **Map** p97 C6 ⑫

There is no obvious reason why Berlin boasts a Salvador Dalí museum, let alone one as good as this. It was opened in 2009 to commemorate 20 years since both the fall of the Wall and the artist's death: the somewhat tenuous Berlin theme is that Dalí 'tore down walls in his art'. There are more than 400 Dalí originals on show – drawn from a pool of more than 2,000 works from private collections – including drawings, lithographs, etchings, woodcuts, illustrated books, documents and supporting works, original graphics and complete portfolios. As a purely commercial venture, the entrance fee is stiff.

⟨FREE⟩ Gedenkstätte Deutscher Widerstand

Stauffenbergstrasse 13-14 (2699 5000, www. gdw-berlin.de). U2, S1, S2, S25 Potsdamer Platz. **Open** 9am-6pm Mon-Wed, Fri; 9am-8pm Thur; 10am-6pm Sat, Sun. *Guided tours* 3pm Sun. **Admission** free. **Map** p97 C4 ⑬

The Memorial to the German Resistance chronicles the German resistance to National Socialism. The building is part of a complex known as the Bendlerblock, owned by the German military from its construction in 1911 until 1945. At the back is a memorial to the conspirators killed during their attempt to assassinate Hitler at this site on 20 July 1944. Regular guided tours are in German only, but you can book an English tour four weeks in advance.

★ Gemäldegalerie

Stauffenbergstrasse 40 (266 424242, www. smb.museum/gg). U2, S1, S2, S25 Potsdamer Platz. **Open** 10am-6pm Tue, Wed, Fri-Sun; 10am-8pm Thur. **Admission** €10; €5 reductions. **Map** p97 C5 ⑭

The Picture Gallery is a first-rate early European collection with many fine Italian, Spanish and English works on display, but the real highlights are the superb Dutch and Flemish pieces. Fans of Rembrandt can indulge themselves with around 20 paintings, the best of which include a portrait of preacher and merchant Cornelis Claesz Anslo and his wife, and an electric Samson confronting his father-in-law. Two of Franz Hals' finest works are here – the wild, fluid, almost impressionistic Malle

Babbe (Mad Babette) and the detailed portrait of the one-year-old Catharina Hooft and her nurse. Other highlights include a couple of unflinching portraits by Robert Campin (early 15th century), a version of Botticelli's *Venus Rising*, and Corregio's brilliant *Leda with the Swan*. Look out too for a pair of Lucas Cranach Venus and Cupid paintings and his *Fountain of Youth*. Pick up the excellent (free) English-language audio guide.

▶ *There are plans to move some of the collection to a new Bode-Museum annex in coming years.*

Kunstgewerbemuseum

Matthäikirchplatz 40 (266 424242, www.smb. museum/kgm). U2, S1, S2, S25 Potsdamer Platz. **Open** 10am-6pm Tue-Thur. **Admission** €8; €4 reductions. **Map** p97 C5 ⑮

The Museum of Decorative Art reopened in late 2014 after an extensive two-year revamp. There are some lovely items in its collection of European arts and crafts, stretching from the Middle Ages through Renaissance, Baroque and rococo to Jugendstil and art deco. New features include an impressive fashion gallery, covering 150 years of fashion history, and the design collection in the basement. **Other location** Schloss Köpenick, Schlossinsel, Köpenick (266 3666).

Museum für Film und Fernsehen

Sony Center, Potsdamer Strasse 2 (300 9030, www.deutsche-kinemathek.de). U2, S1, S2, S25 Potsdamer Platz. **Open** 10am-6pm Tue, Wed, Fri Sun; 10am-8pm Thur. **Admission** €7; €4.50 reductions. **No credit cards**. **Map** p97 C5 ⑯

Since 1963, the Deutsche Kinemathek has been amassing films, memorabilia, documentation and antique film apparatus. In 2000, all this stuff found a home in this roomy, well-designed exhibition space set over two floors in the Sony Center. Striking exhibits include the two-storey-high video wall of disasters from Fritz Lang's adventure films and a morgue-like space devoted to films from the Third Reich. On a lighter note, there's a collection of 'claymation' figures from Ray Harryhausen films, such as Jason and the Argonauts. But the main attraction is the Marlene Dietrich collection of personal effects, home movies and designer clothes. Exhibitions are often linked with film programming at the Arsenal cinema (*see p174*) downstairs.

Musikinstrumentenmuseum

Tiergartenstrasse 1 (254 810, www.sim.spk-berlin. de). U2, S1, S2, S25 Potsdamer Platz. **Open** 9am-5pm Tue, Wed, Fri; 9am-8pm Thur; 10am-5pm Sat, Sun. **Admission** €6; €3 reductions; free under-17s. **No credit cards**. **Map** p97 C5 ⑰

More than 3,200 string, keyboard, wind and percussion instruments (dating from the 16th century) are crammed into the small Musical Instrument Museum, located next to the Philharmonie. Among

Café Einstein.

the Kollhoff Tower. The building's north-east corner is precisely at the point where the borders of Tiergarten, Mitte and Kreuzberg all meet – and also on what was the line of the Wall. From this vantage point, you can peer through railings and the neighbouring postmodern high-rises at the landmarks of new Berlin. There are good views to the south and west; looking north, the DB Tower gets in the way.

Zoologischer Garten & Aquarium

Hardenbergplatz 8 (254 010, www.zoo-berlin.de). U2, U9, S5, S7, S75 Zoologischer Garten. **Open** *Zoo* Summer 9am-7pm daily. Winter 9am-5pm daily. *Aquarium* 9am-6pm daily. **Admission** *Zoo* €13; €6.50-€10 reductions. *Aquarium* €13; €6.50-€10 reductions. *Combined admission* €20; €10-€15 reductions. **Map** p97 C2 ⑳

Germany's oldest zoo was opened in 1841 to designs by Martin Lichtenstein and Peter Joseph Lenné. With almost 14,000 creatures, it's one of the world's largest and most important zoos, with more endangered species in its collection than any zoo in Europe except Antwerp's. It's beautifully landscaped, with lots of architectural oddities, and there are plenty of places for a coffee, beer or snack.

You can access the aquarium from within the zoo or through its own entrance on Olof-Palme-Platz by the Elephant Gate. More than 500 species are arranged over three floors, and it's a good option for a rainy day. On the ground floor are the fish (including some impressive sharks); on the first you'll find reptiles (the crocodile hall is the highlight); while insects and amphibians occupy the second. The dark corridors and liquid ambience, with tanks lit from within and curious aquatic creatures drifting by, can be as absorbing as an art installation.

Restaurants & Cafés

Café Einstein

Kurfürstenstrasse 58 (2639 1918, www.cafe einstein.com). U1, U2, U3, U4 Nollendorfplatz. **Open** 8am-midnight daily. **Main courses** €16.50-€24.50. **Map** p97 D3 ㉑ **Austrian**

For a taste of Old World decadence, visit this Nollendorfplatz institution. It's set in a neo-Renaissance villa built in the 1870s by a wealthy industrialist; red leather banquettes, parquet flooring and the crack of wooden chairs all contribute to the historic Viennese café experience. You could come for a bracing breakfast of herb omelette with feta cheese and spinach, or, in the afternoon, enjoy a classic apple strudel and a *Wiener Melange* (a creamy Austrian coffee), all served with a flourish by the charming uniformed waiters.

them are rococo musical clocks, for which 18th-century princes commissioned jingles from Mozart, Haydn and Beethoven. Museum guides play obsolete instruments such as the Kammerflugel; on Saturdays at noon, the largest Wurlitzer organ in Europe – salvaged from an American silent movie house – is cranked into action.

Neue Nationalgalerie

Potsdamer Strasse 50 (266 424242, www. smb.museum/nng). U2, S1, S2, S25 Potsdamer Platz. **Closed** until 2020. **Map** p97 C5 ⑱

The Neue Nationalgalerie, a stark glass and steel pavilion designed in the 1960s by Mies van der Rohe, was built to house German and international artworks from the 20th century. The collection features key pieces by Kirchner, Picasso, Gris and Léger. The Neue Sachlichkeit is well represented by paintings from George Grosz and Otto Dix, while the Bauhaus contribution includes work from Paul Klee and Wassily Kandinsky. The gallery is currently closed for a major renovation (the first in its history), masterminded by David Chipperfield under the guiding principle 'as much Mies as possible'. It should reopen in summer 2020.

Panoramapunkt

Kollhoff Tower, Potsdamer Platz 1, entrance on Alte Potsdamer Strasse (2593 7080, www. panoramapunkt.de). U2, S1, S2, S25 Potsdamer Platz. **Open** *Summer* 10am-6pm daily. *Winter* 10am-6pm daily. **Admission** €6.50; €5 reductions. **No credit cards. Map** p97 C5 ⑲

What's billed as 'the fastest elevator in Europe' shoots up to the 100m (328ft) viewing platform in

Cinco

Das Stue Hotel, Drakestrasse 1 (311 7220, www.5-cinco.com). S5, S7, S75 Tiergarten. **Open** 7-10.30pm Tue-Sat. **Main courses** €42-€55. **Set meal** €155. **Map** p97 C3 ㉒ **Spanish**

EXPLORE

Andreas Murkudis.

Chef Paco Pérez gained another Michelin star (his fifth) within Cinco's first year of opening. He supposedly keeps a camera trained on the kitchen 24/7, so he can quality-control all the way from Spain. The menu combines Catalan traditional cooking and the inventive plating of Spain's *nueva cocina*. Expect deconstructed classics such as *ajo blanco* (garlic soup) and Iberian suckling pig. Booking advised.

Edd's

Lützowstrasse 81 (215 5294, www.edds-thai restaurant.de). U1 Kurfürstenstrasse. **Open** 11.30am 3pm, 6pm-midnight Mon-Fri; 5pm-midnight Sat; 2pm-midnight Sun. **Main courses** €16.50-€24.50. **No credit cards. Map** p97 D4
㉓ Thai
Bookings are pretty much essential for this comfortable, elegant Thai, where a husband-and-wife team take care to use the freshest ingredients and a healthy amount of spice on their menu. Try the banana flower and prawn salad, or duck no.18, which is double-cooked and excellent.

Facil

Mandala, Potsdamer Strasse 3 (590 051 234, www.facil.de). U2, S1, S2, S25 Potsdamer Platz. **Open** noon-3pm, 7-11pm Mon-Fri. **Main courses** €56-€68. **Set meal** €108-€210. **Map** p97 C5
㉔ Haute cuisine
Upstairs at the plush Mandala hotel is a pavilion-like structure walled off by a row of verdant chestnut trees, its trim white furnishings and impeccable service perfectly complimenting Michael Kempf's complex cooking. Expect rustic ingredients such as veal hearts and salsify spun into culinary gold.

★ Hugos

Hotel InterContinental Berlin, Budapester Strasse 2 (2602 1263, www.hugos-restaurant.de). U2, U9, S5, S7, S75 Zoologischer Garten. **Open** 6.30-10.30pm Tue-Sat. **Set meal** €100-€155. **Map** p97 C3 **㉕ Haute cuisine**

One of Berlin's best restaurants right now, and with the awards to prove it. Chef Thomas Kammeier juxtaposes classic French technique – the silver Christofle cheese trolley is a sight to behold – with New German flair. Try the wagyu short rib, cooked sous-vide and served with buckwheat and truffles, or the perfectly poached turbot enriched with mussels, jerusalem artichoke and tarragon.

€ Joseph-Roth-Diele

Potsdamer Strasse 75 (2636 9884, www.joseph-roth-diele.de). U1 Kurfürstenstrasse. **Open** 10am-midnight Mon-Fri. **Main courses** €6-€10. **No credit cards. Map** p97 D5 **㉖ Café**
A traditional Berlin book café, just a short stroll south of Potsdamer Platz, which pays homage to the life and work of interwar Jewish writer Joseph Roth. It's an amiable place, decorated in ochre tones and with comfortable seating, offering tea, coffee, wine, beer, snacks and great-value lunch specials such as meatloaf with mash.

€ Nordic Embassies Canteen

Rauchstrasse 1 (305 0500, www.nordic embassies.org). U2, U9, S5, S7, S75 Zoologischer Garten. **Open** 1-3pm Mon-Fri. **Main courses** €4.50-€6.20. **No credit cards. Map** p97 C3
㉗ Scandinavian
The striking Nordic embassy complex, clad in maplewood and glass, houses an excellent lunch secret. The canteens of Berlin's civic buildings are all open to the public, so after 1pm you can tuck into the excellent subsidised food provided for the Scandinavian diplomats. The choice of a meat, fish and vegetarian dish changes daily.

Bars & Pubs

Curtain Club

Ritz-Carlton Hotel, Potsdamer Platz 3 (337 777, www.ritzcarlton.com). U2, S1, S2, S25 Potsdamer Platz. **Open** 6pm-late daily. **Map** p97 C5 **㉘**

Reeking of luxury, this wood-panelled and richly carpeted bar is slightly let down by its location in the ground-floor hotel foyer. Head barman Arnd Heissen specialises in essences; the Hypnose is a potent blend of rose petal-infused vodka and various aromatics. The rum tiki drinks come in comical skull-shaped ceramic mugs.

Lebensstern
Kurfürstenstrasse 58 (2639 1922, www.lebens-stern.de). U1, U2, U3, U4 Nollendorfplatz. **Open** 7pm-2am daily. **Map** p97 D3 ②
This smart bar above Café Einstein (*see p105*) became a second home for Quentin Tarantino when he was in Berlin to film *Inglourious Basterds*. He liked it so much, some scenes were even filmed here. If you can't find something among the list of 800 or so rums, there are over 200 gins to try. The cocktails are excellent too.

★ Victoria Bar
Potsdamer Strasse 102 (2575 9977, www.victoriabar.de). U1 Kurfürstenstrasse. **Open** 6.30pm-3am Mon-Thur, Sun; 6.30pm-4am Fri, Sat. **No credit cards. Map** p97 D4 ③
Owner Stefan Weber has a humorous art collection, so works by Sarah Lucas and Martin Kippenberger adorn the walls of this sleek bar, which strikes a perfect balance between modernist layout and antique

Nordic Embassies Canteen.

details. The drinks are superb. The menu is divided by liquor type: go fully decadent with an Alfonso, a mix of Dubonnet, sugar, bitters and champagne, or if you're feeling adventurous, try a Rosemary's Baby, an aged tequila sour with rosemary and sage.

Shops & Services

Andreas Murkudis
Potsdamer Strasse 81E (680 798 306, www.andreasmurkudis.com). U2, S1, S2, S25 Potsdamer Platz. **Open** 10am-8pm Mon-Sat. **Map** p97 D4 ③ **Fashion/Homewares**
The Murkudis brothers are a design duo with the Midas touch. This concept store (designed by one brother and housed in the former *Tagesspiegel* complex, whose move caused a mini-renaissance for Potsdamer Strasse a few years ago) is white, stark and immense, with neon strip lighting. Clothes (by the other brother, as well as the likes of Dries van Noten and Maison Martin Margiela) are immaculately displayed among items of contemporary furniture, porcelain and homewares.

★ BlainSouthern
Potsdamer Strasse 77-87 (644 931 510, www.blainsouthern.com). U2, S1, S2, S25 Potsdamer Platz. **Open** 11am-6pm Tue-Sat. **Map** p97 D4 ③ **Gallery**
The curator duo behind London's influential Haunch of Venison gallery set up in Berlin a few years ago. Their gallery – housed in the same complex as Andreas Murkudis – uses the vast space of the former *Tagesspiegel* printing hall to powerful effect. Big-name artists are shown here, such as Bill Viola, Damian Hirst and Berlin-based Douglas Gordon.

Galerie Guido W Baudach
Potsdamer Strasse 85 (3199 8101, www.guidowbaudach.com). U2, S1, S2, S25 Potsdamer Platz. **Open** 11am-6pm Tue-Sat. **Map** p97 D4 ③ **Gallery**
Originally named Maschenmode (and situated in an old East Berlin knitting factory), Baudach is one of Berlin's pioneering galleries. It joined the vast *Tagesspiegel* complex in 2013. The museum-quality shows and extensive resources cover influential contemporary German artists including Thomas Zipp, Andreas Hofer, Thilo Heinzmann and Andy Hope.

Kunst und Trödel Markt
Strasse des 17 Juni 110-114 (2655 0096, www.berliner-troedelmarkt.de). U2 Ernst-Reuter-Platz, or S5, S7, S75 Tiergarten. **Open** 10am-5pm Sat, Sun. **Map** p97 B2 ③ **Market**
This second-hand market lies on the stretch of road west of Tiergarten S-Bahn station. You'll find good-quality, early 20th-century objects (with prices to match) alongside a jumble of vintage clothing, old furniture, records and books. Interesting stuff, but the stalls get a little cramped.

EXPLORE

Charlottenburg & Schöneberg

The old heart of West Berlin runs all the way from the Tiergarten to Spandau, from Tegel Airport in the north to wealthy, residential Wilmersdorf in the south. Often derided as staid and stagnant in comparison to its edgier eastern neighbours, Charlottenburg is undeniably bourgeois – the fur coat/small dog quotient is high – but it's far from boring. As well as having some charming hotels and lovely squares, it boasts the magnificent Schloss Charlottenburg and the Kurfürstendamm shopping street. It's also where you'll find department store KaDeWe, Berlin's answer to Harrods. East of Wilmserdorf is Schöneberg, also well heeled and residential. Berlin's long-established gay scene is focused on its northern reaches.

EXPLORE

Olympiastadion.

Don't Miss

1 **Schloss Charlottenburg** The palace gardens have been restored to their Baroque glory (p121).

2 **Diener Tattersall** Ex-Prussian riding school turned 1950s bohemian hangout (p117).

3 **Manufactum** An upmarket craft department store (p118).

4 **Rogacki** Try the pickled herring at this time-warp deli (p123).

5 **Olympiastadion** The Olympic rings hover in the sky at this Nazi-era stadium (p120).

BAHNHOF ZOO & THE KU'DAMM

Immortalised in song by U2 and a centrepiece of the film *Christiane F*, **Bahnhof Zoo** (Zoo Station or Bahnhof Zoologischer Garten, to give it its full name) was long the main entry point to the West. During the Cold War, it was a spooky anomaly – slap in the middle of West Berlin but policed by the East, which controlled the intercity rail system – and a seedy hangout for junkies and winos. In the 1990s, attempts were made to spruce it up with chain stores and fast-food outlets, but since the opening of **Berlin Hauptbahnhof** it's been relegated to just another regional train stop.

The original building was designed in 1882 by Ernst Dircksen; the modern glass sheds were added in 1934. The surrounding area, with its sleaze and shopping, cinemas and crowds, is the gateway to the Kurfürstendamm, the main shopping street of western Berlin. The discos and meat markets along Joachimstaler Strasse are best avoided – the opening of the **Beate-Uhse Erotik-Museum** actually added a touch of class to the area. On the other side of Hardenbergplatz – the square outside **Bahnhof Zoo** – is the entrance to the **Zoologischer Garten** (*see p105*) itself, which is in Tiergarten. Fans of photography, in particular of Helmut Newton, shouldn't miss the **Museum für Fotografie** (Museum of Photography), behind the station.

The most notable landmark nearby is the fractured spire of the **Kaiser-Wilhelm-Gedächtnis-Kirche** (Kaiser Wilhelm Memorial Church) in Breitscheidplatz. Close by is the 22-storey **Europa-Center**, whose Mercedes star can be seen from much of the rest of the city. It was built in 1965 – and it shows. Intended as the anchor for the development of a new western downtown, it was the first of Berlin's genuinely tall buildings; now, it's the grande dame of the city's shopping malls. The exterior looks best when neon-lit at night. The strange sculpture in front (erected in 1983) is officially called *Weltenbrunnen* (Fountain of the Worlds) but, like almost everything else in Berlin, it has a nickname: *Der Wasserklops* (Water Meatball).

Running along the south of the Europa-Center, **Tauentzienstrasse** is the westernmost piece of the Generalzug, a sequence of streets laid out by Peter Joseph Lenné to link the new west end of the city with Kreuzberg and points east. Constructed around 1860, they're all named after Prussian generals from the Napoleonic wars: Tauentzien, Kleist, Bülow and so on. The tubular steel sculpture in the central reservation was commissioned for the city's 750th anniversary in 1987 and represents the then-divided city.

Attempts to glam up the area continue apace with two large new developments to the north of Breitscheidplatz. The 1950s 'Zentrum am Zoo' complex overlooking the Zoo has been reimagined

Kaiser-Wilhelm-Gedächtnis-Kirche.

as the enormous new **Bikini Berlin**: a group of listed buildings that have become a sort of megahub combining shopping, work spaces, a cinema, a spa and the stylish **25hours Hotel** (*see p275*). West of it rises the 32-storey Zoofenster, which contains the luxury hotel **Waldorf Astoria Berlin** (*see p275*) on its upper floors.

Tauentzienstrasse continues east past **KaDeWe**, still the largest department store in continental Europe. Its full title is Das Kaufhaus des Westens (Department Store of the West), and it was founded in 1907 by Adolf Jandorf, acquired by Herman Tietz in 1926 and later 'Aryanised' and expropriated by the Nazis. KaDeWe is the only one of Berlin's famous turn-of-the-last-century department stores to survive the war intact, and has been extensively modernised over the last decade. Its most famous feature is the luxury food hall on the sixth floor; up yet another level is a cavernous glass-roofed restaurant with a fine view of Wittenbergplatz below.

Tauentzienstrasse ends at this large pedestrianised square. The 1911 neoclassical U-Bahn station here (by Alfred Grenander) is a listed building and has been wonderfully restored with wooden kiosks and old ads on the walls. A block further east is the huge steel sculpture at **An der Urania**, with its grim monument to children killed in in Berlin traffic. This marks the end, or the beginning, of the western 'downtown'.

Leading south-west from the Kaiser Wilhelm Memorial Church, the **Kurfürstendamm** (or Ku'damm, as it's universally known), West Berlin's tree-lined shopping boulevard, is named after the Prussian Kurfürst ('Elector') – and for centuries it was nothing but a track leading from the Elector's residence to the royal hunting palace in the Grunewald. In 1881, Bismarck insisted it be widened to 53 metres (174 feet) as Berlin's answer to the Champs-Élysées. Heaving with cafés, fashionable boutiques, bars and clubs, it was the focal point for decadent Berliners in the city's 1920s 'Babylon on the Spree' days.

At ground-level, the Ku'damm soon developed into an elegant shopping boulevard. It remains so today, with cinemas (mostly showing dubbed Hollywood fare), restaurants (from classy to burger joints) and upmarket fashion shops: the Ku'damm is dedicated to separating you from your cash. If you tire of shopping, check out the entertaining museum-cum-attraction **Story of Berlin**. Bleibtreustrasse to the north has more shops and several outrageous examples of 19th-century Gründerzeit architecture.

The side streets to the south are quieter but even more upmarket. Many villas were erected here; although few survive today, one sizeable exception on Fasanenstrasse contains the **Käthe-Kollwitz-Museum**, the Villa Griesbach auction house and the Literaturhaus Berlin, with its **Café im Literaturhaus**. The villas soon made way for upmarket tenement buildings with huge apartments. About half of the original buildings were destroyed in the war and replaced by functional offices, but many bombastic old structures remain.

At the north-west corner of the intersection of the Ku'damm and Joachimstaler Strasse is the **Neues Kranzler-Eck**, a Helmut Jahn-designed ensemble built around the famous old Café Kranzler, with a 16-storey tower and pedestrian courtyards including a habitat for parrots. Other notable new buildings include Josef Paul

SET SAIL

Exploring the city by boat.

While Berlin's claims to be the 'Prussian Venice' may meet with deserved scepticism, the German capital is still an engagingly watery place. The Spree meanders through the city on its journey from the Czech Republic to the Elbe. Beyond the Spree, the entire city and its surroundings is a maze of interlocking rivers, lakes and canals. For many areas of Berlin, boats are the ideal form of transport – indeed, in north-west Berlin, in and around Tegeler See, there are isolated houses on islands that can only be reached by ferry.

The regular BVG local transport tickets include ferry services across various lakes. For visitors on a budget, a normal AB zone ticket is enough to get you on the hourly year-round ferry link from Wannsee to Kladow. There's even a decent pub by the pier in a quasi-rural setting on the other side.

A fine range of city-centre tours is offered by **Stern und Kreisschiffahrt** (www.stern und kreis.de), **Reederei Winkler** (www. reederei winkler.de) and **Reederei Riedel** (www.reederei-riedel.de). Most operators offer circular tours, usually lasting three to four hours, which take in the Spree and the Landwehrkanal. Passengers can hop on and off at landing stages en route, and basic food and drink is served on board. For a complete tour, expect to pay around €19 per adult. There are convenient landing stages at the Schlossbrücke in Charlottenburg, at the Haus der Kulturen der Welt in Tiergarten, at Märkisches Ufer, at Jannowitzbrücke and

in the Nikolaiviertel. Many services operate only from mid March to late November.

A short train journey (20-30 minutes) to Wannsee offers more opportunities. Stern & Kreis's Seven Lakes Trip (7-Seen-Rundfahrt) gives a chance to ogle some of Berlin's poshest backyards as the boat slides gently past the handsome mansions surrounding the **Kleiner Wannsee** (see p164). The same tour takes in the Glienicker Brücke, cruises the Havel and stops at the **Pfaueninsel** (see p164). The service runs daily from late March to mid October, with departures at 10.30am and hourly thereafter. Boats leave from piers near Wannsee station.

Also with Stern & Kreis, a longer trip from Wannsee (daily in summer, less frequently the rest of the year) runs via Potsdam to quaint **Werder**, one of the most beautiful of Brandenburg villages, with a cluster of fish restaurants around the quay.

EXPLORE

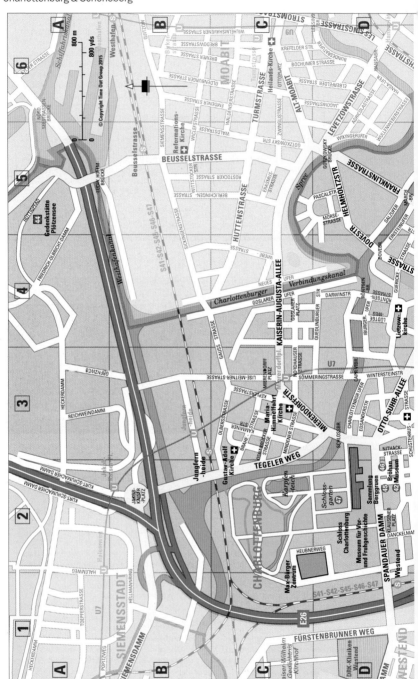

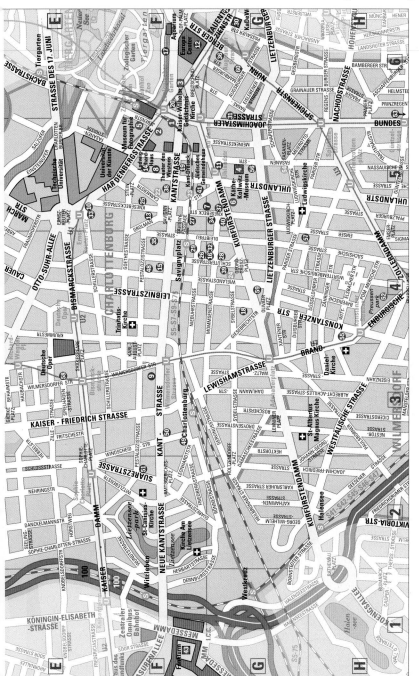

EXPLORE

Kleihues's **Kant-Dreieck** (Fasanenstrasse/ Kantstrasse), with its large metal 'sail', and Nicholas Grimshaw's **Ludwig-Erhard-Haus** for the Stock Exchange at Fasanenstrasse 83-84. Back towards the Kurfürstendamm end of Fasanenstrasse is the **Jüdisches Gemeindehaus** (Jewish Community House) and, opposite, the **Zille-Hof** flea market.

Kantstrasse runs more or less parallel to the Ku'damm at the Zoo end, and contains the grandiloquent **Theater des Westens**, Berlin's central venue for musicals, and more shops. Since the opening of the **Stilwerk** design centre, the stretch between Fasanenstrasse and Savignyplatz has become a centre for designer homewares shops. The environs of leafy **Savignyplatz**, meanwhile, are dotted with chic restaurants, cafés and shops, particularly on Grolmanstrasse and in the Savignypassage. Knesebeckstrasse includes the legendary **Marga Schoeller Bücherstube**, which secretly sold forbidden literature during the Nazi years.

Sights & Museums

Beate-Uhse Erotik-Museum

Joachimstaler Strasse 4 (886 0666, http:// erotikmuseum.beate-uhse.com). U2, U9, S5, S7, S75 Zoologischer Garten. **Open** 9am-10pm Mon-Wed; 9am-midnight Thur-Sat; 11am-10pm Sun. **Admission** (over-18s only) €9; €16 couples. **Map** p113 F5 ❶
This three floor collection (housed above a large Beate-Uhse store offering the usual videos and sex toys) contains oriental prints, some daft showroom-dummy tableaux, and glass cases displaying such delights as early Japanese dildos, Andean penis flutes, 17th-century chastity belts and a giant coconut that looks like an arse. There's a small, drab exhibit on pioneering sex researcher Magnus Hirschfeld, an inadequate item on bawdy Weimar illustrator Heinrich Zille, and a corner documenting the career of Frau Uhse herself, who went from Luftwaffe pilot to annual sex-aid sales of €50m. Bizarrely, it feels more like a dusty old regional museum than anything particularly racy.

C/O Berlin Amerika Haus

Hardenbergstrasse 22-24 (2844 4160, www. co-berlin.org). U2, U9, S5, S7, S75 Zoologischer Garten. **Open** 24hrs daily. **Admission** €10; €5 reductions. **Map** p113 F5 ❷
Berlin's art community rejoiced when much-loved photography gallery C/O Berlin announced it had found a new space at the Amerika Haus. Built by the US in the 1950s to promote transatlantic cultural exchange, it housed embassy offices until the new Pariser Platz site was completed in 2006. Today, following its reopening in 2014 after extensive renovations, it shows museum-quality photography from around the world.

FREE Kaiser-Wilhelm-Gedächtnis-Kirche

Breitscheidplatz (218 5023, www.gedaechtniskirche. com). U2, U9, S5, S7, S75 Zoologischer Garten. **Open** 9am-7pm daily. *Guided tours* 10.15am, 11am, noon, 1.15pm, 2pm, 3pm Mon, Fri, Sat; 1.15pm, 2pm, 3pm Tue-Thur. **Admission** free. **Map** p113 F6 ❸
The Kaiser Wilhelm Memorial Church is one of Berlin's best-known sights, and one of its most dramatic at night. The neo-romanesque structure was built in 1891-95 by Franz Schwechten in honour of – you guessed it – Kaiser Wilhelm I. Much of the building was destroyed during an Allied air raid in 1943. These days, the church serves as a stark reminder of the damage done by the war, although some might argue it improved what was originally a profoundly ugly building. Inside the rump of the church is a glittering art nouveau-style ceiling mosaic depicting members of the House of Hohenzollern on pilgrimage towards the cross. There's also a cross made from nails from Coventry's war-destroyed cathedral, and photos of the church before and after the war. The wrap-around blue stained glass in the chapel is quite stunning. Guided tours in English can be booked.

Museum für Fotografie.

IN THE KNOW I AM A BERLINER

Contrary to widely held belief, President Kennedy did not call himself a doughnut in front of half a million Berliners in 1963. A *Berliner* is only a doughnut in the north and west of Germany; in Berlin, they're known as *Pfannkuchen*, and his addition of the indefinite *ein* was grammatically correct in implying solidarity with the city's embattled citizens.

Käthe-Kollwitz-Museum

Fasanenstrasse 24 (882 5210, www.kaethe-kollwitz.de). U1, U9 Kurfürstendamm. **Open** 11am-6pm daily. **Admission** €6; €3.50 reductions. **No credit cards. Map** p113 G5 ④

Käthe Kollwitz's powerful, deeply empathetic work embraces the full spectrum of life, from the joy of motherhood to the pain of death (with a particular fascination for the latter). The collection includes her famous lithograph *Brot!*, as well as charcoal sketches, woodcuts and sculptures, all displayed to impressive effect in this grand villa off the Ku'damm. Some labelling is in English.

★ Museum für Fotografie

Jebenstrasse 2 (266 424242, www.smb.museum/mf). U2, U9, S5, S7, S75 Zoologischer Garten. **Open** 10am-6pm Tue, Wed, Fri-Sun; 10am-8pm Thur. **Admission** €10; €5 reductions. **Map** p113 F5 ⑤

Shortly before his death in 2004, Berlin-born Helmut Newton – who served his apprenticeship elsewhere in Charlottenburg at the studio of Yva – donated over 1,000 of his nude and fashion photographs to the city and provided funds towards the creation of a new gallery. This museum, doubling as a home for the Helmut Newton Foundation (www.helmutnewton.com), was the result. Housed in a former casino behind Bahnhof Zoo, it's now the largest photographic gallery in the city. The ground and first floors are dedicated to Newton's work. Six colossal nudes, modelled on 1930s Nazi propaganda photos, glare down at you on entering the building, and set the tone for the big, garish, confrontational pieces that dominate the exhibits. The top floor (renovated in 2010) has changing shows on the history of photography, drawn from the collection of the Berlin State Museums.

Story of Berlin

Kurfürstendamm 207-208 (8872 0100, www.story-of-berlin.de). U1 Uhlandstrasse. **Open** 10am-8pm daily; last entry 6pm. **Admission** €12; €5-€9 reductions. **Map** p113 G5 ⑥

If you're interested in the city's turbulent history, the Story of Berlin is a novel way of approaching it. The huge space is filled with well-designed rooms and multimedia exhibits created by a wide range of authors, designers and film and stage specialists, telling Berlin's story from its founding in 1237 to the present day. The 20 themed displays are labelled in both German and English. Underneath all this is a massive nuclear shelter. Built by the Allies during the 1970s, the low-ceilinged, oppressive bunker is still fully functional and can hold up to 3,500 people. Guided tours of the bunker are included in the price of the ticket.

Restaurants & Cafés

€ 1900 Café Bistro

Knesebeckstrasse 76 (8871 5871). S5, S7, S75 Savignyplatz. **Open** 8am-7pm Mon-Sat; 11am-7pm Sun. **Main courses** €3-€10. **No credit cards. Map** p113 G5 ⑦ Café

Booking is recommended for weekend breakfast at this kitschy café, when plates overflow with cold cuts, cheese and fruit. Traditional tray-baked crumble cakes and a salad menu are also available.

Arirang

Uhlandstrasse 194 (4502 1248). U2, U9, S5, S7, S75 Zoologischer Garten. **Open** noon-11pm daily. **Main courses** €6-€24. **No credit cards. Map** p113 F5 ⑧ Korean

This fabulous restaurant used to be a closely guarded secret in a shabby Wedding location, but in 2014 it moved to Charlottenburg. As is the norm in Korea, dishes are served with a selection of kimchi, pickled salads and rice, so take care not to over-order. The fiery kimchi and noodle stew and spring onion and seafood pancakes are perfect for sharing.

Aroma

Kantstrasse 58 (3759 1628). S5, S7, S75 Savignyplatz. **Open** noon-2.30am daily. **Dim sum** €4-€8.50. **No credit cards. Map** p113 F3 ⑨ Chinese

If you're hankering for a dim sum fix, head to Aroma in Berlin's mini Chinatown on Kantstrasse. You can enjoy assorted dumplings in the traditional, genteel tea-time style of *yum cha* or as part of a full dinner with more substantial plates. Go with classics such as *har gao* (steamed shrimp dumplings), fried turnip cakes or *cheong fun*, pillowy steamed rice noodle rolls stuffed with prawn or beef.

€ Brot & Butter

Hardenbergstrasse 4-5 (2630 0346). U1, U2 Ernst-Reuter-Platz. **Open** 8am-8pm Mon-Fri; 8am-6pm Sat. **Main courses** €3-€8. **No credit cards. Map** p113 E5 ⑩ Café

The on-site bakery of the magnificent Manufactum craft-oriented department store (*see p118*) does vast sourdough loafs and traditional crusty baguettes. The café serves almond croissants, small lunch specials and mixed plates of charcuterie. Don't miss the indulgent raw-milk butter.

EXPLORE

Café im Literaturhaus

Starters come impaled on smoking cinnamon sticks; soups are adorned with savoury sorbets; and, most impressively, the showpiece 'Candybox' dessert reimagines the staff's favourite childhood sweets – there's Snickers snow, passionfruit Gummy Bears, popping candy and a flash-frozen chocolate mousse.

€ Lon Men's Noodles
Kantstrasse 33 (3151 9678). S5, S7, S75 Savignyplatz. **Open** noon-midnight daily. **Main courses** €3-€6.50. **No credit cards.** **Map** p113 F4 ⑮ Taiwanese
This tiny hole-in-the-wall spot knocks out Taiwanese classics such as noodle soups and *gua bao* (rice buns filled with duck) as well as more esoteric plates of dressed beef tongue or pigs' ears sliced finely over rice noodles.

Marjellchen
Mommsenstrasse 9 (883 2676, www.marjellchen-berlin.de). S5, S7, S75 Savignyplatz. **Open** 5pm-midnight daily. **Main courses** €12-€20.50. **No credit cards.** **Map** p113 G4 ⑯ German
Not many places like Marjellchen exist any more. It serves specialities from East Prussia, such as Masurian jugged game or beef with prunes, in an atmosphere of old-fashioned *gemütlichkeit* (homely cosiness). The beautiful bar and great service are further draws, and the larger-than-life owner recites poetry and sometimes sings.

★ € Café im Literaturhaus
Fasanenstrasse 23 (882 5414, www.literaturhaus-berlin.de). U1 Uhlandstrasse. **Open** 9.30am-1am daily. **Main courses** €5.50-€11.50. **No credit cards.** **Map** p113 G5 ⑪ Café
This café is at the back of the late 19th-century Literaturhaus villa, which has a bookshop and runs lectures and readings. Sit in the greenhouse-like winter garden or the salon rooms, and tuck into a breakfast of scrambled eggs and smoked salmon, or a tramezzini sandwich at lunchtime.

First Floor
Hotel Palace, Budapester Strasse 45 (2502 1020, www.firstfloor.palace.de). U2, U9, S5, S7, S75 Zoologischer Garten. **Open** 6.30-11pm Tue-Sat. **Main courses** €43-€52. **Set meal** €109-€159. **Map** p113 F6 ⑫ Haute cuisine
In just a few years, chef Matthias Diether has scooped up a load of awards and a Michelin star at his First Floor restaurant. Come here for refined French dishes, such as Flaeming fawn with chervil and buckwheat, sea bass with Périgord truffle or étouffée dove with almond and pear. Book ahead.

Florian
Grolmanstrasse 52 (313 9184, www.restaurant-florian.de). S5, S7, S75 Savignyplatz. **Open** 6pm-3am daily. **Main courses** €14.50-€27. **Map** p113 F5 ⑬ German
Florian has served southern German classics on this quietly posh street for a couple of decades. The cooking is hearty, the decor impeccable. In typical bistro fashion, staff can switch from congenial to arctic at the drop of a hat.

Glass
Uhlandstrasse 195 (5471 0861, www.glassberlin.com). U2, U9, S5, S7, S75 Zoologischer Garten. **Open** 7-11pm Tue-Sat. **Set meal** €65-€85. **Map** p113 F5 ⑭ Haute cuisine
Inside a brutalist apartment building, chef Gal Ben-Moshe has been spinning straw into culinary gold.

Neni
25hours Hotel Bikini Berlin, Budapester Strasse 40 (120 2210, www.25hours-hotels.com). U2, U9, S5, S7, S75 Zoologischer Garten. **Open** noon-10.30pm Mon-Thur, Sun; noon-11.30pm Fri, Sat. **Main courses** €11-€21. **No credit cards.** **Map** p113 F6 ⑰ Middle Eastern
Yet another top-floor hotel restaurant, this time in Charlottenburg's newest boutique hotel. The menu encourages diners to share plates of Middle Eastern-style food, such as *sabich* (fried aubergine, houmous and salad), *chraime* (cod in tomato stew) and slow-roasted lamb shoulder.

Nussbaumerin
Leibnizstrasse 55 (5017 8033, www.nussbaumerin.de). U7 Adenauerplatz. **Open** 5pm-midnight Mon-Sat. **Main courses** €13-€20. **No credit cards.** **Map** p113 G4 ⑱ Austrian
Service is warm and welcoming at this old-fashioned Austrian restaurant, which is surprisingly good value for its interesting variations on the *Schnitzel* – the 'Salzburger' comes stuffed with feta, and the 'Kaiser' with cream sauce and potato dumplings.

Paris Bar
Kantstrasse 152 (313 8052, www.parisbar.net). S5, S7, S75 Savignyplatz. **Open** noon-2am daily. **Main courses** €17-€25. **Map** p113 F5 ⑲ Brasserie

EXPLORE

Owner Michel Wurthle's friendship with Martin Kippenberger and other artists of his generation is clear from all the art hanging here. Paris Bar, with its salon-like appeal, is one of Berlin's most established arty hangouts. It attracts a crowd of rowdy regulars, and newcomers can feel left out if seated in the rear. The pricey food, it has to be said, isn't nearly as good as the staff pretend. Book ahead.

★ Les Solistes by Pierre Gagnaire

Waldorf Astoria Berlin, Hardenbergstrasse 28 (814 000, www.waldorfastoriaberlin.com). U2, U9, S5, S7, S75 Zoologischer Garten. **Open** 6.30-10.30pm Tue-Sat. **Main courses** €52-€75. **Set meal** €115-€150. **Map** p113 F6 ㉑ **Haute cuisine**
The anodyne luxe-hotel interior is quickly forgotten once the splendid tasting menu begins. French classics, changing seasonally, are reinterpreted with panache by head chef Roel Lintermans – witness roasted pigeon in a blackcurrant and cherry compote, its leg served atop a heavenly dome of offal jelly, or a foie gras custard with sautéed squid. Pierre Gagnaire's signature showstopper 'grand' dessert course is a steady stream of jellied liquids, sorbets, caramels and reductions, involving everything from coconut milk laced with tapioca pearls to luxurious slabs of passionfruit fudge. Booking advised.

€ Witty's

Wittenbergplatz 5 (211 9496, www.wittys-berlin. de). U1, U2, U3 Wittenbergplatz. **Open** 11am-8pm daily. **Main courses** €2.80-€3.30. **No credit cards. Map** p113 G6 ㉒ **Imbiss**
Yearning for an authentic sausage fix, but concerned about the industrially processed content of your average Imbiss offering? Look no further. Witty's features a fully organic menu of Berlin staples, including Currywurst and fries.

Glass.

Bars & Pubs

Dicke Wirtin

Carmerstrasse 9 (312 4952, www.dicke-wirtin.de). S5, S7, S75 Savignyplatz. **Open** noon-2am daily. **No credit cards. Map** p113 F5 ㉒
The name means 'fat landlady', and this is a proper German pub: nine beers on tap, bizarre house schnapps (tiramisu liqueur, anyone?) and dirt-cheap prices for the area. If you get the munchies, try a plate of bread smothered in *Schmalz* (lard) for €2.60.

★ Diener Tattersall

Grolmanstrasse 47 (881 5329). S5, S7, S75 Savignyplatz. **Open** 6pm-2am daily. **No credit cards. Map** p113 F5 ㉓
Ex-boxer Franz Diener took this place over in 1954 and with his artist friends turned it into one of the central hubs of West Berlin cultural life. The chattering classes flocked here from concert halls and theatres to gossip and catch sight of off-duty actors drinking the night away. In a city fascinated with Ostalgie and the rapid rhythms of gentrification, raise a toast (or four) to this previous age of West Berlin bohemians.

Galerie Bremer

Wielandstrasse 29 (881 4908, www.galerie-bremer.de). S5, S7, S75 Savignyplatz. **Open** *Bar* 8pm-late Mon-Sat. *Gallery* 4-8pm Tue-Fri. **No credit cards. Map** p113 G4 ㉔
Supposedly Berlin's oldest cocktail bar, designed by Hans Scharoun and built as a salon to the adjoining art gallery in 1946, this is a great hidden spot for drinking in period style.

Shops & Services

Berliner Zinnfigurin

Knesebeckstrasse 88 (315 7000, www.zinnfigur. com). S5, S7, S75 Savignyplatz. **Open** 10am-6pm Mon-Fri; 10am-3pm Sat. **Map** p113 F5 ㉕ **Gifts & souvenirs**
Come here for armies of handmade tin soldiers, farm animals and historical characters, all painted in incredible detail, plus books on military history.

Bleibtreu-Antik

Schlüterstrasse 54 (883 5212, www.bleibtreu-antik.de). S5, S7, S75 Savignyplatz. **Open** noon-6.30pm Thur; or by appointment. **Map** p113 F4 ㉖ **Antiques**
In business since the early 1970s, this shop offers an impressive array of 19th-century antiques. Restored Biedermeier and Jugendstil furniture, glassware, silver and lamps are the focus, along with impressive costume jewellery from 1900 to 1960.

★ Bücherbogen

Stadtbahnbogen 593, Savignyplatz (3186 9511, www.buecherbogen.com). S5, S7, S75 Savignyplatz.

Open 10am-8pm Mon-Fri; 10am-6pm Sat. **No credit cards. Map** p113 F5 ❼ **Books & music**
An art-lover's dream, this massive bookshop takes up three whole railway arches, with rows of books on art, design and architecture, plus exhibition catalogues and lots of rare or out-of-print volumes.

★ Chelsea Farmer's Club
Schlüterstrasse 50 (8872 7474, www.chelsea farmersclub.de). U1 Uhlandstrasse. **Open** 11am-7pm Mon-Fri; 11am-6pm Sat. **Map** p113 G4 ❽ **Fashion**
Started by Hamburg dandy Christophe Tophinke, this shop stocks British gentlemen's classics: tweed suits, custom-made smoking jackets and shaving accessories. Their unofficial emblem is a knitted floral buttonhole.

Galerie Volker Diehl
Niebuhrstrasse 2 (2248 7922, www.diehlgalleryone. com). S5, S7, S75 Savignyplatz. **Open** 11am-6pm Mon-Sat. **Map** p113 F4 ❾ **Gallery**
The Berlin arm of the Russian-German gallery Volker Diehl has long been a prominent member of the international art world. It's the place to go for overseas talent, including Chinese-born artist Zhang Huan, Spanish sculptor Jaume Plensa and the Russian groups Blue Noses and AES+F.

KaDeWe
Tauentzienstrasse 21-24 (21210, www.kadewe. com). U1, U2, U3 Wittenbergplatz. **Open** 10am-8pm Mon-Fri; 10am-9pm Sat. **Map** p113 G6 ❿ **Department store**
KaDeWe stocks quite an impressive range of high-end designers and has recently tried to shed its stuffy image by bringing in upbeat, younger labels such as Alice+Olivia and London shoe brand Buffalo. It's still the quintessential luxury food-hall experience in a city otherwise teeming with budget supermarkets. The sixth floor has counter after counter of delicatessens, butchers, pâtisseries and grocers, with plenty of prepared foods to take away. The oyster bar is a perfect mid-shop pit stop.

Karstadt Sporthaus
Joachimstaler Strasse 5-6 (880 240, www.karstadt sport.de). U2, U9, S5, S7, S75 Zoologischer Garten. **Open** 10am-8pm Mon-Sat. **Map** p113 G6 ❿ **Sports**
A four-level megastore with a wide selection of big-brand international sportswear, German football memorabilia and children's clothes.

Klemke Wein
Mommsenstrasse 9 (8855 1260). S5, S7, S75 Savignyplatz. **Open** 9am-7pm Mon-Fri; 9am-2.30pm Sat. **No credit cards. Map** p113 G4 ❿ **Food & drink**
A respected specialist in French and Italian wines, from the smallest producer to the grandest château.

This typical Charlottenburg shop offers great wines at good prices, as well as digestifs and whiskies.

★ Manufactum
Hardenbergstrasse 4-5 (2403 3844, www. manufactum.de). U1, U2 Ernst-Reuter-Platz. **Open** 10am-8pm Mon-Fri; 10am-6pm Sat. **Map** p113 E5 ❸ **Department store**
Founded in 1988 by a high-profile Green Party politician as a counterpoint to cheap mass production, Manufactum quickly developed a cult following for its ironic catalogue blurbs and impeccable selection of products. It continues in the same vein today with an emphasis on high production quality, classic designs and sustainable materials, with a particular German focus. Prices reflect the quality.

Marga Schoeller Bücherstube
Knesebeckstrasse 33 (881 1112). S5, S7, S75 Savignyplatz. **Open** 9.30am-7pm Mon-Wed; 9.30am-8pm Thur, Fri; 9.30am-6pm Sat. **Map** p113 G5 ❹ **Books & music**
This bookshop (established 1930) won renown when owner Marga shook a fist at the Nazi regime by removing all Nazi-related texts from her shelves. It relocated in the '70s down the road from its original Ku'damm spot. English books are displayed in an inviting alcove. It goes further than most to provide new non-fiction titles, from philosophical and political texts to theatre studies.

P&T
Bleibtreustrasse 4 (9561 5468, www.paperandtea. com). S5, S7, S75 Savignyplatz. **Open** 11am-8pm Mon-Sat. **Map** p113 F4 ❺ **Food & drink**

KaDeWe.

A purpose-built central island displays the esoteric teas stocked at this beautiful shop. You'll find Japanese and Korean green teas, Taiwanese mountain tea and white jasmine-bud tea, as well as fine Asian ceramics for serving.

Solebox
Nürnberger Strasse 16 (9120 6690, www.solebox. de). U1, U2, U3 Wittenbergplatz. **Open** noon-8pm Mon-Sat. **Map** p113 G6 ⬤ **Accessories**
The place for reissues and limited-edition New Balance, Nike or Adidas, Solebox stocks a massive selection of exclusive sneakers, plus a few clothes. Staff are friendly and well informed.

Steiff Galerie in Berlin
Kurfürstendamm 38-39 (8862 5006, www. steiff.de). U1 Uhlandstrasse. **Open** 10am-8pm Mon-Fri; 10am-7pm Sat. **Map** p113 G5 ⬤
Gifts & souvenirs
Inventor of the teddy bear (so named in the US after a hunting story involving 'Teddy' Roosevelt), Steiff has been in business since the late 19th century. The company's whole range of artisan animals (not just bears) are here. Prices are aimed at adult hobbyists rather than kids.

Stilwerk
Kantstrasse 17 (315 150, www.stilwerk.de). S5, S7, S75 Savignyplatz. **Open** 10am-7pm Mon-Sat. **Map** p113 F5 ⬤ **Homewares**
This huge design marketplace offers high-end products from an array of retailers, including modern furnishings and kitchens, lighting and bathroom fittings, plus interior items. There's also a fourth-floor showcase for work from local design studios.

Taschen
Schlüterstrasse 39 (8870 8173, www.taschen.com). S5, S7, 75 Savignyplatz. **Open** 10am-7pm Mon-Sat. **Map** p113 G4 ⬤ **Books & music**
This wildly successful publishing house has made a name for itself producing books of alternative arts and erotica, and table-sized gift books. The Berlin flagship store has moved to these spacious – and recently renovated – premises.

Veronica Pohle
Kurfürstendamm 64 (883 3731, www.veronica pohle.de). U7 Adenauerplatz. **Open** 10.30am-7.30pm Mon-Fri; 11am-6.30pm Sat. **Map** p113 G5 ⬤ **Fashion**
Womenswear from top international labels such as Missoni, Roberto Cavalli, Vivienne Westwood, Diane von Fürstenberg and Alexander McQueen.

★ Viniculture
Grolmanstrasse 44-45 (883 8174, www.viniculture. de). S5, S7, 75 Savignyplatz. **Open** 11am-8pm Mon-Fri; 10am-6pm Sat. **Map** p113 F5 ⬤
Food & drink

Viniculture was pushing biodynamic and 'natural' wines years before they became fashionable. Stock comes from France, Germany, Austria and Italy, and there's a free Sunday tasting once a month.

SCHLOSS CHARLOTTENBURG & WEST

The palace that gives Charlottenburg its name lies about three kilometres (two miles) north-west of Bahnhof Zoo. In contrast to the commercialism and crush of the latter, this part of the city is quiet, wealthy and serene. **Schloss Charlottenburg** was built in the 17th century as a summer palace for Queen Sophie-Charlotte, wife of Friedrich III (later King Friedrich I), and was intended as Berlin's answer to Versailles. It's not a very convincing answer, but there's plenty of interest in the buildings and outside – the apartments of the New Wing and the gardens are the main attractions.

In front of the entrance is the **Museum Berggruen**, with work by Picasso and other modernists, and the art nouveau and art deco collection of the **Bröhan-Museum**. The arrival across the street a few years ago of the **Sammlung Scharf-Gerstenberg**, which traces the lines between fantastic and surrealist work, firmly established this corner of town as a stronghold for early 20th-century art.

There are few eating, drinking or shopping opportunities in the immediate vicinity of the palace, but if you head down Schlossstrasse and over Bismarckstrasse, the streets south of here, particularly those named after philosophers (Leibniz, Goethe) have many interesting small shops selling antiques, books and the traditional fashions worn by well-to-do locals.

A few kilometres north-east of Schloss Charlottenburg is a reminder of the terror inflicted by the Nazi regime on dissidents, criminals and anybody else they deemed undesirable. **The Gedenkstätte Plötzensee** (Plötzensee Memorial) preserves the execution shed of the former Plötzensee prison, where more than 2,500 people were killed between 1933 and 1945. A couple of kilometres southwest of the palace, at the western end of Neue Kantstrasse, stands the futuristic **International Conference Centre** (ICC). Built in the 1970s, it's used for pop concerts, political rallies and the like. Next door, the even larger **Messe- und Ausstellungsgelände** (Trade Fair & Exhibition Area) plays host to trade fairs ranging from electronics to food to aerospace. Within the complex, the **Funkturm** (Radio Tower) offers panoramic views. Nearby, Hans Poelzig's **Haus des Rundfunks** (Masurenallee 9-14) is an expressive example of brick modernism.

Another couple of kilometres to the northwest, the imposing columns and conjoined rings

EXPLORE

of the **Olympiastadion** loom large. One of the few pieces of Fascist-era architecture still standing in Berlin, it was extensively renovated for the 2006 World Cup Final. Immediately south of Olympiastadion S-Bahn station is the **Corbusierhaus**, a huge multicoloured apartment block. Designed by Le Corbusier, it was constructed for the International Building exhibition of 1957. From here, a ten-minute walk along Sensburger Allee brings you to the sculptures of the **Georg-Kolbe-Museum** and its charming garden café.

Sights & Museums

Bröhan-Museum

Schlossstrasse 1A (3269 0600, www.broehan-museum.de). U2 Sophie-Charlotte-Platz, or U7 Richard-Wagner-Platz. **Open** 10am-6pm Tue-Sun. **Admission** €6; €4 reductions; free under-18s. Special exhibitions varies. **Map** p112 D2 **42**

This quiet museum contains three well-laid-out floors of international art nouveau and art deco pieces that businessman Karl Bröhan began collecting in the 1960s and donated to the city of Berlin on his 60th birthday. The paintings, sculptures, furniture, porcelain, glass and silver dates from 1890 to 1939. Hans Baluschek's paintings of social life in the 1920s and '30s, and Willy Jaeckel's series of portraits of women are the pick of the fine art; the furniture is superb too. Labelling is in German only.

Funkturm

Messedamm (3038 1905, www.funkturm-messeberlin.de). U2 Theodor-Heuss-Platz or Kaiserdamm. **Open** 10am-8pm Mon; 10am-11pm Tue-Sun. **Admission** €5; €2.80 reductions. **No credit cards. Map** p113 F1 **43**

The 147m (482ft) high Radio Tower was built in 1926 and looks a bit like a smaller version of the Eiffel Tower. There's a zippy lift up to the observation deck, but challenge-seekers can attempt the 610 steps; vertigo sufferers can seek solace in the restaurant, only 55m (180ft) from the ground. The tower closes in summer for repairs, so ring ahead.

FREE Gedenkstätte Plötzensee

Hüttigpfad (344 3226, www.gedenkstaette-ploetzensee.de). U9 Turmstrasse then bus 123. **Open** *Mar-Oct* 9am-5pm daily. *Nov-Feb* 9am-4pm daily. **Admission** free. **Map** p112 A5 **44**

This site was the prison execution chamber where the Nazis murdered nearly 3,000 (largely political) prisoners. In just one night in 1943, 186 people were hanged. It was declared a memorial to the victims of Fascism in 1952, and a commemorative wall was built. There is little to see today, apart from the execution area behind the wall, with its meat hooks from which victims were hanged (many were also guillotined), and a small room with an exhibition. Excellent booklets in English are available. The

stone urn near the entrance is filled with earth from concentration camps. The rest of the prison is now a juvenile correction centre.

Georg-Kolbe-Museum

Sensburger Allee 25 (304 2144, www.georg-kolbe-museum.de). S3, S75 Heerstrasse, or bus X34, M49, X49. **Open** 10am-6pm Tue-Sun. **Admission** €5; €3 reductions. **No credit cards.**

Georg Kolbe's former studio has been transformed into a showcase for his work. The Berlin sculptor, regarded as Germany's best in the 1920s, focused on naturalistic human figures. There are examples of his earlier, graceful pieces, as well as his later, more sombre and bombastic works created in accordance with Nazi aesthetic ideals. His famous *Figure for Fountain* is in the sculpture garden, where there's also a great café for coffee and cake.

★ Museum Berggruen

Westlicher Stülerbau, Schlossstrasse 1 (266 424 242, www.smb.museum/mb). U2 Sophie-Charlotte-Platz, or U7 Richard-Wagner-Platz. **Open** 10am-6pm Tue-Sun. **Admission** €8; €4 reductions. **Map** p112 D2 **45**

Heinz Berggruen was one of Picasso's dealers in Paris, and went on to become a major modernist collector. He sold his entire collection to Berlin for a knockdown €100m in 2000. Displayed over an easily digestible three circular floors, it's inevitable that Pablo's works dominate – his astonishingly prolific and diverse output is well represented. Some of the many highlights include the 1942 *Redining Nude* and his late-period 1955 *The Woman of Algiers*. Works by Braque, Giacometti, Cézanne and Matisse also feature, and most of the second floor is given over to the wonderful paintings of Paul Klee.

★ Olympiastadion

Olympischer Platz 3 (2500 2322, www.olympia stadion-berlin.de). U2 Olympia-Stadion, or S5, S75 Olympiastadion. **Open** varies. **Admission** €7; €5 reductions. *Guided tours* €10; €8 reductions. **No credit cards.**

Built on the site of Berlin's original 1916 Olympic stadium, the current structure was designed by Werner March and opened in 1936 for the infamous 'Nazi Olympics' (you can see where the swastikas were removed from the old bell). The 74,000-seat stadium underwent a major and long-overdue refitting for the 2006 World Cup, including better seats and a roof over the whole lot. Home of Hertha BSC, it also hosts the German Cup Final, plus other sporting events and concerts. You can book a guided tour at the visitor centre by the Osttor (eastern gate).

Sammlung Scharf-Gerstenberg

Schlossstrasse 70 (266 424242, www.smb.museum/ssg). U2 Sophie-Charlotte-Platz. **Open** 10am-6pm Tue-Fri; 11am-6pm Sat, Sun. **Admission** €10; €5 reductions. **Map** p112 D2 **46**

Museum Berggruen.

Housed in the eastern Stüler building and in the Marstall (stables wing) opposite Charlottenburg Palace, this gallery exhibits works by the Surrealists and their forerunners. Artists featured run from Piranesi, Goya and Redon to Dali, Magritte and Ernst. The original collection was amassed by Otto Gerstenberg around 1910, and added to by his grandsons, Walter and Dieter Scharf.

Schloss Charlottenburg

Luisenplatz & Spandauer Damm (320 911, www.spsg.de). U2 Sophie-Charlotte-Platz, or U7 Richard-Wagner-Platz. **Open** *Apr-Oct* 10am-6pm Tue-Sun. *Nov-Mar* 10am-5pm Tue-Sun. **Admission** *Old Palace* €12; €8 reductions. *New Wing* €4; €3 reductions. *Belvedere* (Apr-Oct only) €3; €2.50 reductions. *Mausoleum* (Apr-Oct only) €2; €1. Combination ticket €15; €11 reductions. *Gardens* free. **Map** p112 D2 ㊼

Friedrich III (later King Friedrich I) built this sprawling palace and gardens in 1695-99 as a summer home for his queen, Sophie-Charlotte, who gave her name to both the palace and the wider district. Later kings also summered here, tinkering with and adding to the buildings. It was severely damaged during World War II, but has now been restored, and stands as the largest surviving Hohenzollern palace.

Each of the outbuildings has a separate admission charge, so the easiest option is to buy the combination ticket, which allows entrance to all parts of the palace, with the exception of the state and private apartments of King Friedrich I and Queen Sophie-Charlotte in the Altes Schloss (Old Palace), which are only accessible on a guided tour (€8, €5 reductions, in German only). This tour, through more than 20 rooms, some of staggering Baroque opulence, has its highlights (particularly the Porcelain Cabinet), but can be skipped – there's plenty of interest elsewhere. The upper apartments in the Old Palace can

be visited without a guided tour, but are a bit of a silver and porcelain overload.

The one must-see is the Neue Flügel (New Wing), also known as the Knobelsdorff Wing (after its architect). The upper floor contains the state apartments of Frederick the Great and the winter chambers of his successor, King Friedrich Wilhelm II. The contrast between the two sections is fascinating: Frederick's rooms are all excessive rococo exuberance (the wildly over-the-top Golden Gallery practically drips gilt), while Friedrich Wilhelm's far more modestly proportioned rooms reflect the more restrained classicism of his time. Frederick the Great was a big collector of 18th-century French painting, and some choice canvases hang from the walls, including Watteau's masterpiece *The Embarkation for Cythera*. Also worth a look are the apartments of Friedrich Wilhelm III in the New Wing.

By the east end of the New Wing stands the Neue Pavillon (New Pavilion), also known as the Schinkel Pavilion. It was built by Karl Friedrich Schinkel in 1824 for Friedrich Wilhelm III – the king liked it so much that he chose to live here in preference to the grandeur of the main palace. Inside is an excellent permanent exhibition on the architect's legacy.

The huge, impeccably kept gardens are one of the palace's main draws. Laid out in 1697 in formal French style, they were reshaped in a more relaxed English style in the 19th century. Within them, you'll find the Belvedere, a three-storey structure built in 1788 as a teahouse, now containing a collection of Berlin porcelain. Also in the gardens is the sombre Mausoleum, containing the tombs of Friedrich Wilhelm III, his wife Queen Luise, Kaiser Wilhelm I and his wife. Look out for temporary exhibitions in the Orangerie. There's a café and restaurant at the front of the palace. Note: the entire palace is closed on Mondays.

Restaurants & Cafés

Alt Luxemburg

Windscheidstrasse 31 (323 8730, www.alt-luxemburg.de). U2 Sophie-Charlotte-Platz. **Open** 5-10.30pm Mon-Sat. **Main courses** €27-€34. **Set meal** €50-€77. **Map** p113 F4 ㊽ German
Chef Karl Wannemacher combines classic German flavours with French techniques in his wonderfully romantic dining room. Expect generous helpings of the freshest sweetbreads on lentils and braised balsamic onions, or sea bass with a tapenade crust. The wine list could do with more moderately priced bottles, but there's 15% off all food from 5pm to 7pm.

€ Gasthaus Lentz

Stuttgarter Platz 20 (8871 5871, www.gasthaus-lentz-berlin.de). S5, S7, S75 Charlottenburg. **Open** 9am-1.30am daily. **Main courses** €3-€14.50. **No credit cards. Map** p113 F3 ㊾ Café
Bespectacled Charlottenburgers take their time with a newspaper and coffee here. Daily specials of

Time Out Berlin 121

German classics usually involve something porky with potatoes and salad.

Shops & Services

Go Asia
*Kantstrasse 101 (3151 8606, www.goasia.net).
S5, S7, S75 Charlottenburg.* **Open** 9am-9pm
Mon-Sat. **Map** p113 F3 ❀ **Food & drink**
There lots of small Asian supermarkets in Berlin, most dealing in South-east Asian essentials, but the vast GoAsia has a Sichuan chilli pastes, imported Japanese rice, kimchi varieties and plenty more.

Königsberger Marzipan
*Pestalozzistrasse 54A, Charlottenburg (323 8254).
U7 Wilmersdorfer Strasse.* **Open** 11am-6pm
Mon-Fri; 10am-1pm Sat. No **credit cards**.
Map p113 F2 ❀ **Food & drink**
Irmgard Wald and her late husband arrived in Berlin after the war, when the Soviets changed Prussian Königsberg to Kaliningrad, to begin their confectionery business anew. In 2005, Frau Wald handed over control to her charming American-born granddaughter. The company still produces fresh, soft, melt-in-your-mouth marzipan.

WILMERSDORF

Following Uhlandstrasse south of Kurfürstendamm, things get steadily quieter and leafier as you enter the traditionally middle-class residential area of **Wilmersdorf**. There are few sights of note – except for curiousities such as the ex-Nazi town hall at **Fehrbellinerplatz** and the **Künstlerkolonie Berlin**, a 1920s artists' commune on the border of Steglitz – but it's a great place to get a feel for how the other half of Berlin lives, away from the street art and piercings of the east. The area was farmland until the mid 19th century, when a property boom led to the phenomenon of the *Millionenbauern* (peasant millionaires), farmers handsomely paid off by developers. It rapidly developed into an affluent neighbourhood and was home to a large Jewish population during the Weimar years.

Sights & Museums

★ FREE Preussenpark
Konstanzer Strasse 46 (no phone). U7 Konstanzer Strasse. **Open** 24hrs daily. **Admission** free.
Map p113 H4 ❀
An ordinary local park is transformed in summer by numerous Thai street-food stalls beneath colourful parasols. The city authorities seem to turn a blind eye to the Thai community cooking fish cakes, soups, noodles, pad thai and other traditional dishes – all for sale. You can even have an open-air Thai massage, or head to the only non-Thai stand, where a Brazilian lady whips up a refreshing caipirinha.

Rogacki.

Restaurants & Cafés

Tian Fu
*Berliner Strasse 15 (8639 7780, www.tianfu.de).
U7, U9 Berliner Strasse.* **Open** 9am-1.30am
daily. Main courses €9-€17. No **credit cards**.
Map p113 H6 ❀ **Chinese**
Chilli-lovers can find it hard to get their fix in a spice-shy country, but Tian Fu provides some real Sichuan fire, of both the hot and numbing type. Kick things off with traditional cold starters such as tripe salad with Sichuan peppercorn or seaweed salad in black vinegar dressing, then dive into a fiery fish stew swimming in red chillies.
Other location Uhlandstrasse 142, Charlottenburg (861 3015).

Bars & Pubs

★ Rum Trader
*Fasanenstrasse 40 (881 1428). U3, U9
Spichernstrasse.* **Open** varies. No **credit
cards**. **Map** p113 G5 ❀
Subtitled the 'Institute for Advanced Drinking', this tiny bar is a Berlin classic, thanks to its eccentric owner, Gregor Scholl, who is ever present, smartly dressed in bow tie and waistcoat. There is no menu: Scholl will ask which spirit you like, and whether you want something *süss oder sauer* (sweet or sour). Don't waste his time (or talent) by asking for a mojito.

Shops & Services

★ Erich Hamann Bittere Schokoladen

Brandenburgische Strasse 17 (873 2085,
www.hamann-schokolade.de). U7 Konstanzer
Strasse. **Open** 9am-6pm Mon-Fri; 9am-1pm Sat.
Map p113 H4 ⑮ **Food & drink**
This beautiful Bauhaus building houses Berlin's
oldest functioning chocolate factory. Everything is
still done with an eye to period detail: chocolate thins
are boxed by hand in beautifully old-fashioned pack-
aging, while the signature chocolate 'bark' is still
made in the original purpose-built machine by Erich
Hamann's son Gerhard, now in his late seventies.

Galerie Daniel Buchholz

Fasanenstrasse 30 (8862 4056, www.galerie
buchholz.de). U1 Uhlandstrasse. **Open** 11am-
6pm Tue-Sat. **Map** p113 G5 ⑯ **Gallery**
A hushed repository of elegance and refinement,
this gallery left Cologne in 2008 after 20 years and
moved to Berlin. It represents a raft of well-known
names, such as 2006 Turner Prize winner Tomma
Abts, Wolfgang Tillmans and Richard Hawkins.

Maître Phillipe & Filles

Emser Strasse 42 (8868 3610, www.maitre
philippe.de). U1 Uhlandstrasse. **Open** 11am-
7pm Tue-Fri; 10am-2pm Sat. **Map** p113 G4
⑰ **Food & drink**
Master affineur Phillipe Causse, along with his
daughter Anaïs, make this a family affair, selecting
only the best cheeses France has to offer, plus other
French deli products. Enjoy nutty sheep's cheese
ardi grasna, crinkly-skinned goat's cheese chavignol
or dense aged comté, made from cow's milk.

★ Rogacki

Wilmersdorfer Strasse 145-146 (343 8250,
www.rogacki.de). U7 Bismarck Strasse. **Open**
9am-6pm Mon-Wed; 9am-7pm Thur; 8am-7pm Fri;
8am-4pm Sat. **Map** p113 E3 ⑱ **Food & drink**
A trip to Rogacki is like stepping back in time: beaming attendants in green, monogrammed uniforms
stand to attention behind rows of sparkling vit-
rines stuffed with all manner of prepared produce.
Smoked and pickled fish is the mainstay; specialities include *Bratherings* (fried and brined herring),
Rollmops (pickled herrings rolled around gherkin)
and *Senfgurken* (white gherkins from Spreewald).

V Kloeden

Wielandstrasse 24 (8871 2512, www.vonkloeden.
de). U7 Adenauerplatz. **Open** 10am-7pm Mon-Fri;
10am-4pm Sat. **Map** p113 G4 ⑲ **Children**
This charming shop proves that educational toys
don't need to be boring. There are shelves of picture books (some in both German and English), and
even Asterix comics in Latin. Toys include wooden
Brio train sets, eerily life-like Käthe Kruse dolls and
Kersa puppets, and rocking horses.

Weichardt Brot

Mehlitzstrasse 7 (873 8099, www.weichardt.de).
U7, U9 Berliner Strasse. **Open** 7.30am-6.30pm
Mon-Fri; 7.30am-2pm Sat. **No credit cards**.
Map p309 G11 **Food & drink**
Perhaps the best bakery in town, Weichardt Brot
grew out of a Berlin collective formed in the 1970s.
Demeter-certified (biodynamic) flour is stone-
ground daily on their three mills, making this a real
destination for bread-lovers. They also produce a
range of traditional German sweets.

SCHÖNEBERG

Geographically and atmospherically, Schöneberg
lies between Charlottenburg and Kreuzberg. It's
a diverse and vibrant part of town, mostly built
in the late 19th century. Though largely devoid
of conventional sights, Schöneberg is rich in
reminders of Berlin's recent history.

Schöneberg means 'beautiful hill' – oddly,
because the borough is flat. It does have an
'island', though: the triangular **Schöneberger
Insel**, carved out by the two broad railway
cuttings that carry S-Bahn line 1 and lines 2
and 25, with an elevated stretch of lines S41,
S42 and S45 providing the southern boundary.
In the 1930s, the area was known as the Rote
Insel ('Red Island'), because, socialistically
inclined and easy to defend as it was approached
mostly over a handful of bridges, it was one
of the last bits of Berlin to resist Nazification.
There's a fine view from Monumentenbrücke,
on the east side of the island going towards
Kreuzberg's Viktoriapark. On the north-west
edge of the island is **St Matthäus-Kirchhof**,

V Kloeden.

EXPLORE

a graveyard and the last resting place of the Brothers Grimm.

West along Langenscheidtstrasse leads you towards Kleistpark. Here, Schöneberg's main street is called Hauptstrasse to the south and Potsdamer Strasse to the north. Hauptstrasse leads south-west in the direction of Potsdam. David Bowie and Iggy Pop once resided at no.155. Further south, **Dominicuskirche** is one of Berlin's few Baroque churches.

North-west along Dominicusstrasse is **Rathaus Schöneberg**, outside which John F Kennedy made his famous 'Ich bin ein Berliner' speech. The square now bears his name. This was West Berlin's town hall during the Cold War, and the place where mayor Walter Momper welcomed East Berliners in 1989.

From here, Belziger Strasse leads back in the direction of **Kleistpark**. The entrance to Kleistpark from Potsdamer Strasse is an 18th-century double colonnade, moved here from near Alexanderplatz in 1910. The mansion in the park was originally a law court, and during the Cold War became headquarters for the Allied Control Council. After the 1972 treaty that formalised the separate status of East and West Germany, the building stood virtually unused. But there were occasional Allied Council meetings, before which the Americans, British and French would observe a ritual pause, as if expecting the Soviet representative, who had last attended in 1948, to show up. In 1990, a Soviet finally did wander in and the Allies held a last meeting to formalise their withdrawal from the city in 1994. This may be the place where the Cold War officially ended.

On the north-west corner of Potsdamer Strasse's intersection with Pallasstrasse stood the Sportpalast, site of many Nazi rallies and the scene of Goebbels' famous 'Total War' speech of 18 February 1943. In its place stands a shabby block of flats. One part of the complex straddles Pallasstrasse and rests on the huge concrete hulk of a Nazi air-raid shelter, which planners were unable to destroy.

At the west end of Pallasstrasse stands **St-Matthias-Kirche**. South from here, Goltzstrasse is lined with cafés, bars and interesting shops. To the north of the church is **Winterfeldtplatz**, site of bustling Wednesday- and Saturday-morning markets that help support the surrounding cafés and restaurants.

Nollendorfplatz to the north is the hub of Schöneberg's nightlife. The theatre on the square has had many incarnations. In the Weimar era, it was home to experimental director Erwin Piscator; under the Third Reich, Hitler came here to watch Zara Leander shows; in the 1980s, it was the infamous Metropol disco.

Outside Nollendorfplatz U-Bahn, the small memorial to homosexuals killed in concentration

---

IN THE KNOW
DAUGHTER OF SCHÖNEBERG

She may have once been reviled by Germans as a wartime traitor, but now Berlin is rightfully proud of Marlene Dietrich, the city's most iconic actress. Born in 1901 in the Rote Insel, she first found fame in silent films, then moved to the USA in the 1930s and, spurning the Nazis, was key in raising Allied war bonds. After a long career as a cabaret singer in Las Vegas, her will stated that she was to be buried in Schöneberg, but only after the Wall fell. Her wish came true; her grave is in the Städtischer Friedhof III cemetery.

---

camps is a reminder of the area's history. Christopher Isherwood chronicled Berlin from his rooming house at Nollendorfstrasse 17; Motzstrasse has been a major artery of Berlin's gay life since the 1920s. Gay Schöneberg continues around the corner and straddles Martin-Luther-Strasse along Fuggerstrasse.

Restaurants & Cafés

Café Aroma

Hochkirchstrasse 8 (782 5821, www.cafe-aroma. de). U7, S1, S2 Yorckstrasse. **Open** 6pm midnight Mon-Fri; 2pm-midnight Sat; 11am-midnight Sun. **Main courses** €8-€16. **Map** p310 K10 **Italian**

In a brunch-mad city, this lovely Italian trattoria is a Berlin foodie's favourite for its multi-course marathon of cold cuts, poached salmon, fried risotto balls and roast vegetables. One of the first restaurants to sign up to Germany's Slow Food association in the early 1990s, it takes pains to source sustainable and authentic produce.

Double Eye

Akazienstrasse 22 (0179 456 6960 mobile, www.doubleeye.de). U7 Eisenacher Strasse. **Open** 9.30am-6.30pm Mon-Fri; 10am-6.30pm Sat. **No credit cards. Map** p310 J11 **Café**

There's been a lot of competition recently among Berlin's third-wave coffee shops; Double Eye was one of the first, and still draws queues for its cheap but potent espressos and creamy custard tarts.

Habibi

Goltzstrasse 24, on Winterfeldtplatz (215 3332). U1, U2, U3, U4 Nollendorfplatz. **Open** 11am-3am Mon-Thur, Sun; 11am-5am Fri, Sat. **Main courses** €3-€12. **No credit cards. Map** p310 J9 **Middle Eastern**

Come here to enjoy freshly made Middle Eastern specialities including falafel, kibbeh, tabbouleh and various combination plates. Accompany with freshly squeezed orange or carrot juice, and finish with a complimentary tea and one of the wonderful pastries. The premises are light, bright and well run. It's deservedly busy and can get very full. **Other location** Akazienstrasse 9, Schöneberg (787 4428).

Ixthys

Pallasstrasse 21, on Winterfeldtplatz (8147 4769). U1, U2, U3, U4 Nollendorfplatz. **Open** noon-10pm Mon-Sat. **Main courses** from €7.50. **Map** p310 J10 **Korean**

Reams of handwritten scripture adorn the wall at this Christian Korean café and the menu has bizarre flow diagrams explaining man's relationship with original sin. Brisk service brings bulgogi marinated meats, or spicy broths, but the star of the show is the bibimbap, a classic dish of rice, layered with sautéed vegetables, chilli paste and sliced beef, crowned with a glistening fried egg and served in a scalding stone bowl so as to continue sizzling on the table.

Renger-Patzsch

Wartburgstrasse 54 (784 2059, www.renger-patzsch.com). U7 Eisenacher Strasse. **Open** 6pm-1am daily. **Main courses** €15-€20.50. **Map** p310 J11 **German**

The pan-German food – soup and salad starters, a sausage and sauerkraut platter, plus meat and fish dishes that vary daily – is finely prepared by versatile chef Hannes Behrmann, formerly of Le Cochon Bourgeois. House speciality is Alsatian tarte flambée: a crisp pastry base with toppings in seven variations. Communal seating is at long wooden tables, and in summer there's a nice garden on this beautiful corner.

Bars & Pubs

Green Door

Winterfeldtstrasse 50 (215 2515, www.green door.de). U1, U2, U3, U4 Nollendorfplatz. **Open** 6pm-3am Mon-Thur, Sun; 6pm-4am Fri, Sat. **No credit cards. Map** p310 J9.

Behind an actual green door (ring the doorbell) lies this popular cocktail bar. The heavily kitsch decor – oversized gingham wallpaper, curvy white walls and framed 1970s pictures – may grow on you after a few strong drinks. Playwright Fritz Müller-Scherz opened the bar 15 years ago, and it pulls a solid crowd of upmarket regulars as well as booze tourists on the Berlin quality cocktail trail. The impressive drinks menu runs the gamut from the basics to their house Green Door cocktail, a refreshing mix of champagne, lemon, sugar and mint.

Stagger Lee

Nollendorfstrasse 27 (2903 6158, www.stagger lee.de). U1, U2, U3, U4 Nollendorfplatz. **Open** 8pm-late (winter 6pm-late) daily. **No credit cards. Map** p310 J9.

This vaudeville bar takes its name from a 1920s folk song about the true-life exploits of a violent pimp from St Louis, Missouri. Low-hanging saloon lamps, Victorian wallpaper and an enormous mechanical till add to its faux-Americana charm. They serve excellent, if unusual, cocktails – the house special Julep mixes bourbon, mint and cherries, while the Robert Mitchum is simply a full glass of tequila, a box of matches and a Lucky Strike.

Shops & Services

Garage

Ahornstrasse 2 (211 2760, www.kleidermarkt.de). U1, U2, U3, U4 Nollendorfplatz. **Open** 11am-7pm Mon-Fri; 11am-6pm Sat. **Map** p310 J9 **Fashion**

Barn-like Garage sells cheap second-hand clothing priced by the kilo. The large selection is well organised, making it easy to root out last-minute party gear. On Wednesdays, there's a 30% discount 'happy hour' from 11am-1pm.

Michas Bahnhof

Nürnberger Strasse 24A (218 6611, www. michas-bahnhof.de). U3 Augsburger Strasse. **Open** 10am-6.30pm Mon-Fri; 10am-3.30pm Sat. **Map** p113 G6 **⑳ Gifts & souvenirs**

Unsurprisingly in such an engineering-mad country, Berlin has some fantastic model-train shops and Michas Bahnhof is one of the best. The small space is rammed with engines, old and new, from around the world – and everything that goes with them.

Pasam Baklava

Goebenstrasse 12A (2196 2383, www.pasam-baklava.de). U7, S1, S2 Yorckstrasse. **Open** 10am-8pm daily. **Map** p310 K10 **Food & drink**

A clear favourite among the Berlin food bloggerati, Pasam has a whiff of the faded grandeur of the Ottomans; it's a high-ceilinged brown-toned room with just one imposing cabinet displaying baklava. The eight or so varieties include pistachio, walnut and sobiyet (with semolina porridge), and there are also some rather dusty-looking biscuits stacked in a side cabinet.

Winterfeldtplatz Market

Winterfeldtplatz (0175 437 4303 mobile). U1, U2, U3, U4 Nollendorfplatz. **Open** 8am-2pm Wed; 8am-4pm Sat. **Map** p310 J9 **Food & drink**

In the leafy square surrounding St-Matthias-Kirche, this thriving farmers' market teems with life twice a week. There are more than 250 stalls; some stock traditional market tat, but most offer high-end gastronomic produce. The emphasis is on the local and seasonal, such as wild herbs and edible flowers, foraged mushrooms and local salami. Plenty of vendors serve cooked food; look out for Bauer Lindner, which sells pork bratwursts made from their own pigs raised organically in Brandenburg.

EXPLORE

Kreuzberg & Treptow

The ornate Oberbaumbrücke, renovated in the 1990s by Santiago Calatrava, is a road bridge crossing the River Spree to connect Kreuzberg with Friedrichshain. During the Cold War, it was a more serious crossing place: a border post and spy-exchange venue between West and East Berlin. Kreuzberg is also divided quite firmly into halves, according to its old postcodes – Kreuzberg 36, the eastern part, is scruffy and hip, great for a night out; Kreuzberg 61, in the west, is quieter, prettier, duller after dark but lovely during the day. Further east, Treptow is a quiet residential area concealing leafy Treptower Park, a huge war memorial and an abandoned amusement park.

Sowjetisches Ehrenmal am Treptower Park.

Don't Miss

1 Sowjetisches Ehrenmal am Treptower Park One of Berlin's most awesome public monuments (p145).

2 Jüdisches Museum Daniel Libeskind's masterful representation of the history of Judaism and Germany (p142).

3 Markthalle IX This bustling, covered farmers' market was created through sheer community effort (p136).

4 Marques Bar A cocktail bar evoking the luxury of 1920s New York (p135).

5 Hard Wax This vinyl shop is key to Berlin's techno history (p136).

EAST KREUZBERG

In the 1970s and '80s, the eastern half of
Kreuzberg north of the Landwehrkanal was
right at the edge of inner West Berlin. Enclosed on
two sides by the Wall, on a third by the canal, and
mostly ignored by the rest of the city, its decaying
tenements came to house Berlin's biggest, and
most militant, squat community. The area was
full of punky left-wing youths on a draft-dodging
mission – a loophole meant residents were exempt
from military service – and guest-worker Turks
who came to the area because rents were cheap
and people mostly left them alone.

No area of West Berlin has changed so much
since the fall of the Wall. This once-isolated
pocket found itself recast as desirable real
estate. Much of the alternative art scene shifted
north to Mitte, and even the May Day riots – long
an annual Kreuzberg tradition – began taking
place in Prenzlauer Berg. But gentrification
was slow to take off in this end of Kreuzberg,
unlike in Prenzlauer Berg, and now the riots
have moved back.

Kreuzberg has regained some of its appeal for
young bohemia, and enough of the anarchistic
old guard stayed behind to ensure that the area
retains a distinct atmosphere. It's an earthy kind
of place, full of cafés, bars and clubs, dotted with
independent cinemas, and is an important nexus
for the city's gay community.

Oranienstrasse is the area's main drag,
filled with bars and clubs, and is also home to
the quirky **Museum der Dinge**. The hideous
pre-fab development immediately to the north
of Kotbusser Tor U-Bahn station – Kotti for
short – has turned from night-time no-go area
into one of Berlin's most popular nightspots,
with popular bars such as **Möbel-Olfe**,
Monarch and the **Paloma Bar**. This scruffy
area is also the centre of Turkish Berlin (*see p139*
The Turkish Capital) and bustles with kebab
shops and Anatolian travel agents.

Rather more gentle these days is **Wiener
Strasse**, running alongside the old Görlitzer
Bahnhof, where more bars and cafés await.
A couple of blocks further south lies chi-chi
Paul-Lincke-Ufer, a canalside street lined with
smart cafés and restaurants and the district's
most desirable houses. South-west is Graefekiez,
a gentrified neighbourhood full of cafés and
boutique shops catering to hip young families.

Further north of Kotti is the innocuous
Moritzplatz roundabout, previously a no-
man's-land, which has seen several high-
profile openings, centred around the Aufbau
publishing building: the fantastic **Modulor**
craft shop, a Vietnamese *bahn mi* café and
the **Prince Charles** nightclub (*see p199*).
It's also the site of Europe's largest urban
garden, the **Prinzessinnengarten**

Museum der Dinge.

(www.prinzessinnengarten.net): a massive
community effort has transformed a wasteland
into an oasis of organic vegetables and beehives,
with regular workshops for children.

The U1 line runs overhead through the
neighbourhood along the middle of **Skalitzer
Strasse**. The onion-domed Schlesisches Tor
station was once the end of the line, but these
days the train continues one more stop across the
Spree to Warschauer Strasse. You can also walk
across the Oberbaumbrücke into Friedrichshain
and the post-industrial nightlife district around
Mühlenstrasse. But traffic is also coming the
other way. Courtesy of riverside development on
the Spree and an overspill from Friedrichshain,
the area around Schlesisches Tor station and
along **Schlesische Strasse** and over the canal
towards the next borough of Treptow is another
hotspot. Sometimes called the Wrangelkiez, this
buzzing area has become such a tourist draw that
local residents held a crisis meeting a few years
ago to complain about the noise levels.

Sights & Museums

FREE **FHXB Friedrichshain-
Kreuzberg Museum**
*Adalbertstrasse 95A (5058 5233, www.
fhxb-museum.de). U1, U8 Kottbusser Tor.*
Open noon-6pm Wed-Sun. **Admission** free.
Map p130 D4 ❶

A council-run museum about the area's turbulent history. The permanent exhibition catalogues both the area's Turkish immigrant heritage and its radical political legacy.

Museum der Dinge

Oranienstrasse 25 (9210 6311, www.museum derdinge.de). U1, U8 Kottbusser Tor. **Open** noon-7pm Mon, Thur-Sun. **Admission** €5; €3 reductions. **No credit cards.** **Map** p130 D3 ❷

On the top floor of a typical Kreuzberg apartment block, the 'Museum of Things' contains every kind of small object you could imagine in modern design from the 19th century onwards – from hairbrushes and fondue sets to beach souvenirs and Nazi memorabilia. It's not a musty collection, but a sleek, minimalist room organised by themes such as 'yellow and black' or 'functional vs kitsch', rather than by era or type, so that the 'things' appear in new contexts. It can get a little confused at times, which is hardly surprising with 20,000 objects, but this is a fascinating diversion. There's a great shop too.

Restaurants & Cafés

5 Elephant

Reichenberger Strasse 101 (9608 1527, www.fiveelephant.com). U1 Görlitzer Bahnhof. **Open** 8.30am-7pm Mon-Fri; 10am-7pm Sat, Sun. **No credit cards.** **Map** p131 F4 ❸ Café

You can feel the love at this café run by a charming Austro-American couple – she bakes the cakes, he roasts the beans. There's a selection of traditional cakes and tarts, but the Philadelphia cheesecake is transcendental: a wafer-thin layer of spice is all that separates the custardy interior from the velvety top.

Bar Raval

Lübbener Strasse 1 (5316 7954, www.barraval.de). U1 Görlitzer Bahnhof. **Open** 6-11pm Mon-Thur; 6pm-midnight Fri; 1pm-midnight Sat; 1-11pm Sun. **Main courses** €2.50-€12. **Map** p131 E4 ❹ Spanish

At the helm of Berlin's Spanish tapas wave is Bar Raval, owned by actor Daniel Brühl and restaurateur Atilano González. The open-plan kitchen serves classics such as salt-cod fritters, tortilla and succulent bellota ham. There's a weekly paella night, and the regional monthly specials feature the likes of Valencian monkfish in paprika sauce or Basque veal cheeks in red wine.

€ Baretto

Wrangelstrasse 41 (6162 7319). U1 Schlesisches Tor. **Open** 8am-7.30pm Mon-Sat; 9am-7.30pm Sun. **Main courses** €3-€6. **No credit cards.** **Map** p131 F4 ❺ Café

This lovely little spot was serving Italian espresso and fresh panini years before any of the hip third-wave cafés moved in. A proper locals' breakfast spot.

€ Burgermeister

Oberbaumstrasse 8 (0176 2153 0440 mobile, www.burger-meister.de). U1 Schlesisches Tor. **Open** 11am-3am Mon-Thur, Sun; 11am-4am Fri, Sat. **Main courses** €4-€6. **No credit cards.** **Map** p131 F3 ❻ Burgers

The hollowed-out remains of an old public toilet under the tracks of the U1 serve as the kitchen for this popular burger joint. A small glasshouse is erected in winter for people to fuel up on a cheeseburger and their famous chilli fries before going clubbing. You might have to queue to get in.

5 Elephant.

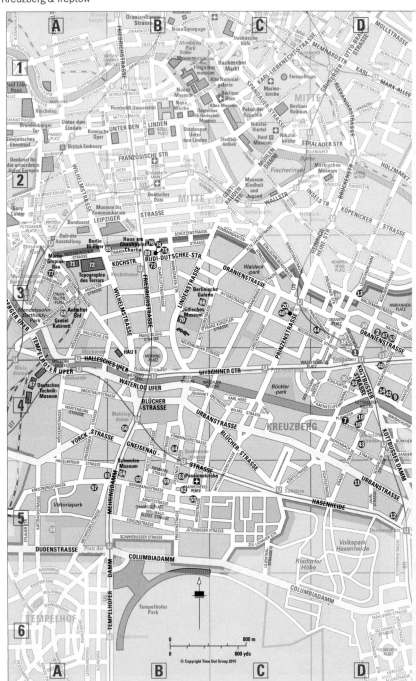

EXPLORE

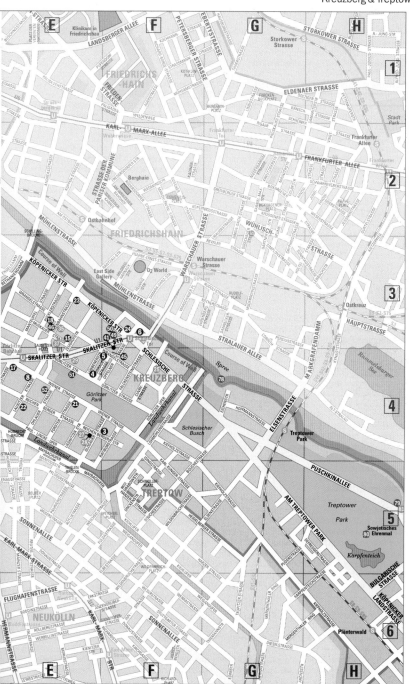

EXPLORE

Il Casolare

Grimmstrasse 30 (6950 6610). U1, U8
Kottbusser Tor. **Open** noon-midnight daily.
Main courses €8.50-€12. No credit cards.
Map p130 D4 **❼ Pizza**
Italian punks opened this pizzeria, which explains
all the old NoFX tour posters adorning the walls. It's
now a small chain, but the Kreuzberg branch is still
the best, with outdoor terrace seating on Planüfer
overlooking the canal. Service can be brusque, but
the thin, crispy pizza bases are great.
Other locations Il Ritrovo, Gabriel-Max-
Strasse 2, Friedrichshain (2936 4130); I Due Forni,
Schönhauser Allee 12, Prenzlauer Berg (4401 7333).

€ Chaparro

Wiener Strasse 14A (3036 8730, www.chaparro-
berlin.de). U1 Görlitzer Bahnhof. **Open** noon-10pm
Mon-Thur; noon-11pm Fri; 4-11pm Sat; 1-9pm Sun.
Main courses €4.30-€5.50. No credit cards.
Map p131 E4 **❽ Mexican**
Burritos, tacos, salsa, guacamole? Check, check,
check, check. This excellent Mexican eaterie does
it all, plus the requisite chilled beers and mezcal to
wash it all down with. It can get crowded.

€ Cocolo

Paul-Lincke Ufer 39-40 (0172 304 7584 mobile,
www.oliverprestele.de). U1, U8 Kottbusser Tor.
Open 6pm-midnight daily **Main courses**
€7.50-€10. No credit cards. Map p130 D4
❾ Japanese
The best ramen in Berlin. Originally just a tiny bar
in Mitte, it opened this spacious branch by the canal
in Kreuzberg. All the classic ramen styles are served,
but the cognoscenti always pick *tonkotsu*. The pork
stock is kicked up to a piggy 11 by the addition of
the milky liquid derived from hard-boiling bones,
collagen and fat for hours. It's then topped with a
soft-boiled egg, pickled ginger, crispy seaweed,
slices of roast pork and braised sweet pork belly.
Other location Gipsstrasse 3, Mitte (same phone).

€ Doyum Grillhaus

Admiralstrasse 36 (6165 6127). U1, U8 Kottbusser
Tor. **Open** noon-1am daily. **Main courses €3.50-**
€12. No credit cards. Map p130 D4 **❿ Turkish**
One of the best *ocakbasi* (Turkish grill house) around
Kotti is somehow hidden in plain sight. Tourists
flock to the overrated Hasir, but the Turkish locals
come to this beautifully tiled dining room for a plate
of *iskender* kebab smothered in yoghurt sauce, or
succulent minced lamb *adana*. No alcohol allowed.

Figl

Urbanstrasse 47 (7229 0850, www.gasthaus-figl.
de). U6, U8 Hermannplatz. **Open** 6pm-midnight
Tue-Sun. **Main courses €8.50-€17.50. No credit**
cards. Map p130 D5 **⓫ Pizza**
Figl occupies a former *Kneipe* (pub), and has kept
the beautiful original fittings: the dark wood bar,

a giant ceramic coal heater and, best of all, a two-lane
skittles alley in the basement. The menu is based
around beefed-up *Flammkuchen*: Alsatian flatbread
usually topped with crème fraiche, smoked bacon
and red onion. Here, they use the stone oven to full
effect, putting Tyrolean flavours (blood sausage,
ham, apple and *Bergkäse*) on what is more like a
pizza base, as well as offering Italian toppings of
artichoke, anchovies, taleggio or plain marinara.

€ Hamy Café

Hasenheide 10 (6162 5959, www.hamycafe.com).
U7, U8 Hermannplatz. **Open** noon-midnight
daily. **Main courses €4.90. No credit cards.**
Map p130 D5 **⓬ Vietnamese**
Don't panic if there's no room here: get others to
budge up and share their table, or wait – service is
so speedy it won't take long. There are three specials
a day, all priced at €4.90: glass noodle salad with
octopus, perhaps, or a golden chicken curry. Tofu
can be substituted for meat or fish. It's licensed, but
order a fresh lime juice or a lassi instead of beer.

€ Henne

Leuschnerdamm 25 (614 7730, www.henne-
berlin.de). U1, U8 Kottbusser Tor. **Open** 6pm-
midnight Tue-Sat; 5-10pm Sun. **Main courses €8.**
No credit cards. Map p130 D3 **⓭ German**
There's just one thing to order at Henne: half a crispy
fried chicken. The only decisions you need to make
after that are whether you want cabbage or potato
salad, and which beer to go for (try the Franconian
Landbier). Check out the letter over the bar from
JFK, regretting missing dinner here. The leafy beer
garden is pleasant in summer.

Horvath

Paul-Lincke-Ufer 44A (6128 9992, www.
restaurant-horvath.de). U1, U8 Kottbusser Tor.
Open 6-11pm Wed-Sun. **Main courses €33. Set**
meal €58-€119. Map p130 D4 **⓮ Haute cuisine**
Austrian chef Sebastian Frank gained a Michelin
star in 2011 outside of the usual Berlin luxury
hotel system at this canalside restaurant. Enjoy a
tasting menu of typical rustic German ingredients
transformed through novel techniques: onion,
pigeon and kohlrabi, or sturgeon, rib and celery,
are charred, abstracted and perfectly plated. The
Austrian wine list is excellent. Booking advised.

Jolesch

Muskauer Strasse 1 (612 3581, www.jolesch.de).
U1 Görlitzer Bahnhof. **Open** 11.30am-midnight
Mon-Fri; 10am-midnight Sat, Sun. **Main courses**
€13.50-€25. Map p131 E3 **⓯ Austrian**
All a proper *Wiener Schnitzel* (made with veal)
requires is a slice of lemon and a side of potato and
cucumber salad to cut through the fat. The classics
here are undisputed, but are also accompanied by a
chef's menu of seasonal and often adventurous dishes,
such as venison with quince, or hay-smoked lamb's

Jolesch.

tongue. For dessert, share a plate of *Kaiserschmarrn*; the fluffy, eggy pancake with plum sauce was an imperial favourite.

€ KaffeeBar Jenseits des Kanals

Graefestrasse 8 (no phone, www.kaffeebar-berlin. com). U8 Schönleinstrasse. **Open** 8am-7pm Mon-Fri; 9.30am-7pm Sat, Sun. **Main courses** €3.50-€7. **No credit cards. Map** p130 D4 ⑯ Café
Finally, leafy Graefekiez gets a well-pulled espresso. Freshly baked cakes, panini and free Wi-Fi make loitering at this comfy café most enjoyable.

Kimchi Princess

Skalitzer Strasse 36 (0163 458 0203 mobile, www.kimchiprincess.com). U1 Görlitzer Bahnhof. **Open** 6-11.30pm daily. **Main courses** €11-€24. **No credit cards. Map** p131 E4 ⑰ Korean
This sleek zinc and neon Korean barbecue joint has been chock-a-block with customers since it opened in 2010, despite shoddy service. The food is average, but it's a good place for large groups.

Markthalle

Pücklerstrasse 34 (617 5502, www.welt restaurant-markthalle.de). U1 Görlitzer Bahnhof. **Open** 10am-midnight daily. **Main courses** €10.50-€18.50. **Map** p131 E3 ⑱ German
This unpretentious *Schnitzel* restaurant and bar, with chunky tables and wood-panelled walls, is popular with locals and big groups. Breakfast is served until 4pm, lunch specials from noon, while dinner brings hearty dishes such as wild boar and red snapper. It's also fun just to sit at the long bar and sample the selection of grappas. After dinner, see what's on downstairs at the Auster Club. *Photos p134.*

€ Mo's King of Falafel

Graefestrasse 99 (7407 3666). U1, U8 Kottbusser Tor. **Open** 1-11pm daily. **Main courses** €3-€3.50. **No credit cards. Map** p130 D4 ⑲ Imbiss
It's actually Mo's wife who forms the little chickpea balls at this hole-in-the-wall joint. Enormous wraps stuffed with freshly fried falafel and salad cost just a few euros. Expect to queue in summer months. **Other location** Urbanstrasse 68, Neukölln (7407 3666).

Parker Bowles

Prinzenstrasse 85D (5527 9099, www.parker-bowles.com). U8 Moritzplatz. **Open** 9am-8pm Mon-Wed; 9am-late Thur-Sat. **Main courses** €12.50-€28.50. **Map** p130 C3 ⑳ Modern European
Cheekily named by the team behind the Prince Charles club next door, this low-key yet elegant supper club serves eclectic menu of vegetarian, paleo and meat and fish specialities, many sourced from local producers. Chef Sebastian Pfister tends towards the occasionally surreal in his juxtapositions and flavours – horseradish ice-cream, anyone? – but Parker Bowles is a welcome and delightful addition to the Berlin dining scene.

€ Pic Nic 34

Wiener Strasse 34 (0151 4774 3275 mobile). U1 Görlitzer Bahnhof. **Open** 12.30-10.30pm Tue-Sat. **Main courses** €3-€8. **No credit cards. Map** p131 E4 ㉑ Café
Overlooking Kreuzberg's alternative lifestyle hangout park of choice, Görlitzer Park, this Italian café boasts some of the best *salumi* (cured meats) in town. The main attraction, though, is the *piadina*, an

EXPLORE

Markthalle. *See p133.*

Schlesisch Blau

Köpenicker Strasse 1A (6981 4538). U1 Schlesisches Tor. **Open** noon-3pm, 7pm-midnight Mon-Fri; 7pm-midnight Sat. **Set meal** €20-€24. **No credit cards. Map** p131 F3 🟡 **German**
Another Kreuzberg curio, this homely restaurant offers a set menu that always features a salad, a soup, a few mains and a dessert. It's not fancy, but you can expect well-braised meats, tasty salads and warming root-based soups. Booking advised.

Bars & Pubs

Barbie Deinhoff's

Schlesische Strasse 16 (6107 3616, www.barbie deinhoff.de). U1 Schlesisches Tor. **Open** 7pm-6am daily. **No credit cards. Map** p131 F4 🟡
One of performance artist Lena Braun's many spaces, where the aesthetic is pitched somewhere between John Waters hyper-kitsch and retro-futuristic, with pink walls and shabby furnishings. It draws a mixed LGBT crowd, with statuesque drag queens rubbing shoulders with butch, tattooed girls. Tuesdays is an all-night happy hour.

Bei Schlawinchen

Schönleinstrasse 34 (no phone). U8 Schönleinstrasse. **Open** 24hrs daily. **No credit cards. Map** p130 D4 🟡
This dive situated just off Kottbusser Damm is a great example of a Berlin *Kneipe* (pub), with its bizarre decorations of toy dolls, old bicycles and instruments. High unemployment in the neighbourhood means that it's usually rammed all day, with rowdy characters propping up the bar or hammering away at the table football. Naturally, the beer is both cheap and plentiful.

Emilia-Romagna street-food favourite, somewhat akin to a folded pizza but grilled on a hotplate.

La Raclette

Lausitzer Strasse 34 (6128 7121, www.la-radette. de). U1 Görlitzer Bahnhof. **Open** 6pm-midnight daily. **Main courses** €15-€25. **No credit cards. Map** p131 E4 🟡 **French**
In the backstreets behind Görlitzer Park is this enchanting little French outpost. Go trad with a bottle of Burgundy and steak frites, or share their signature raclette with friends. There's a bar next door (open till 4am) where you can round things off with a cognac or Pernod.

Richard

Köpenicker Strasse 174 (4920 7242, www. restaurant-richard.de). U1 Görlitzer Bahnhof. **Open** 7pm-midnight Tue-Sat. **Main courses** €20-€28. **Set meal** €48-€78. **No credit cards. Map** p131 E3 🟡 **Haute cuisine**
Headed up by Swiss-born painter turned chef Hans Richard, this beautifully decorated dining room claims to 'look to Paris' for inspiration for its tasting menus. One menu is, refreshingly, vegetarian, a lifestyle choice often hard done by in the haute cuisine world, even if distinctly un-Parisian.

Feldman's

Reichenberger Strasse 86 (6128 0334). U1 Görlitzer Bahnhof. **Open** 6pm-late daily. **No credit cards. Map** p131 E4 🟡
Berlin does lighting well, from the gentle yellow haze of its sodium street lamps to an emphasis on candle-lit bars. Feldman's (previously Bellman's) is no exception. Inventive drinks include the Malcolm Lowry; named after the modernist writer deported from Mexico for his savage alcoholism, it's a potent blend of mezcal, triple sec, lime and white rum.

Das Hotel

Reichenberger Strasse 86 (6128 0334, www.das hotelclassic.blogspot.de). U1 Görlitzer Bahnhof. **Open** 6pm-late daily. **No credit cards. Map** p131 E4 🟡
Das Hotel occupies some attractive old *altbau* buildings, with an ice-cream parlour, brasserie, bar and dive club – pretty much everything except for actual hotel rooms. The bar is all candles and old pianos, and a Spanish DJ gets the downstairs dancefloor going on weekends. There are actually some 'secret' rooms to rent – contact them for details.

John Muir

Skalitzerstrasse 50 (0173 161 1141 mobile, www.johnmuirberlin.com). U1 Görlitzer Bahnhof. **Open** 6pm-late daily. **No credit cards. Map** p131 E4 ㉙

This bar aims to bring a Brooklyn flavour to SO36 (the area's postcode) with its mounted trophy heads and red-brick walls. It's craft beer night on Mondays, and the experimental cocktail menu changes monthly, featuring whimsical names such as Black Beer'd (cognac, black beer, lime, orange and bitters).

Luzia

Oranienstrasse 34 (8179 9958, www.luzia.tc). U1, U8 Kottbusser Tor. **Open** 10am-3am daily. **No credit cards. Map** p130 D3 ㉚

A favourite of Berlin club kids, this spot gets pretty rowdy on weekends. It's decorated with bizarre bric-a-brac, with murals by local artist Chin Chin pitched somewhere between gothic and the twee. The typical bar menu offers coffees and a selection of cakes during the day. The small smoking room in the back doubles up as a club on weekends.

Marques Bar

Graefestrasse 92 (6162 5906). U8 Schönleinstrasse. **Open** 6pm-late daily. **No credit cards. Map** p130 D4 ㉛

Below a rather average Spanish restaurant is this 1920s time-capsule of a cocktail bar. A host takes you to an available table – the decor is suitably solid and mahogany – and asks your preferred 'flavour profile' or what kind of drink you usually like. Then the bar staff do their magic, working with hundreds of booze varieties (plus over 30 tonics), vintage glassware and fist-sized rocks of ice.

Möbel-Olfe.

Möbel-Olfe

Reichenberger Strasse 177 (2327 4690, www.moebel-olfe.de). U1, U8 Kottbusser Tor. **Open** 6pm-late Tue-Sun **No credit cards. Map** p130 D4 ㉜

In the middle of a large housing estate, built in the 1960s and now occupied by lots of Turkish families, is this popular alternative gay bar (*see p180*).

Monarch

Skalitzer Strasse 134 (6165 6003, www. kottimonarch.de). U1, U8 Kottbusser Tor. **Open** 6pm-late Tue-Sun. **No credit cards. Map** p130 D4 ㉝

Finding this bar is part of the fun. It's directly above the Kaisers supermarket in an ugly prefab; you can see it from the overground platform of the U1 at Kottbusser Tor. To reach it, take the stairs to the right of Kaisers and follow the sound of the bass. It's an unpretentious place with regular rock concerts and cheap drinks, and dancing as the night wears on and the booze takes effect. The smaller and arguably cooler (but less fun) Paloma bar is next door at no.135, if you fancy moving on.

Roses

Oranienstrasse 187 (615 6570). U1, U8 Kottbusser Tor. **Open** 10pm-5am daily. **No credit cards. Map** p130 D4 ㉞

Whatever state you're in (the more of a state, the better), you'll fit in just fine at this boisterous den of glitter and furry walls. It draws customers of all sexual preferences, who mix and mingle and indulge in excessive drinking. No place for uptights, always full, very Kreuzberg-ish.

Schwarze Traube

Wrangelstrasse 24 (2313 5569). U1 Görlitzer Bahnhof. **Open** 7pm-late daily. **No credit cards. Map** p131 E3 ㉟

This bar on a quiet backstreet shot to fame when the slight but magnificently bearded owner, Atalay Aktasm represented Germany at the 2013 World Class Bartender of the Year final. Aktas describes his ideal ambience as 'noble trash'. It's all about the detail here – ask bar staff for a custom-made cocktail especially to your tastes, or request a classic cocktail.

Südblock

Admiralstrasse 1-2 (6094 1853, www.suedblock. org). U1, U8 Kottbusser Tor. **Open** 10am-late daily. **No credit cards. Map** p130 D4 ㊱

Aimed squarely at Kreuzberg's increasingly large gay population, this place (*see also p182*) was opened in 2010 by an ex-barman from Möbel-Olfe (*see above*).

Tante Lisbeth

Muskauer Strasse 49 (6290 8742, www.pyonen. de/tantelisbeth). U1 Görlitzer Bahnhof. **Open** 4pm-late Mon-Fri; 6pm-late Sat, Sun. **No credit cards. Map** p131 E3 ㊲

EXPLORE

For those wishing to give their lungs a break, this spacious bar has a separate smoking room, as well as a folksy granny-flat aesthetic, but hidden downstairs is the real reason to come: a 1970s bowling alley. Book it online and bring a group down to enjoy the wood-panelled clubhouse with original fittings. Make sure to order a *Herrengedeck* too – a 'gentlemen's menu' of a beer and schnapps.

Würgeengel

Dresdener Strasse 122 (615 5560, www. wuergeengel.de). U1, U8 Kottbusser Tor. **Open** 7pm-late daily. **No credit cards. Map** p130 D3 ㊳
It's a bit of a mouthful, but this sultry boozer is named after Luis Buñuel's absurdist movie masterpiece *The Exterminating Angel*, in which a group of bourgeois worthies find themselves inexplicably unable to leave a lavish dinner party. The smartly dressed waiting staff, glass-latticed ceiling and leather booths certainly evoke an Old World sensibility, but it's still accessibly priced.

Zur Kleinen Markthalle

Legiendamm 32 (614 2356, www.zur-kleinen-markthalle.de). U8 Moritzplatz. **Open** 4pm-1am Mon-Sat; noon-1am Sun. **No credit cards. Map** p130 D3 ㊴
Just across from Henne (*see p132*), this is the slightly less touristy choice, but it's no less of an old-school tavern with its dark wood interior. It's a great place to enjoy draught beers and a silky potato salad.

Shops & Services

Alimentari e Vini

Skalitzer Strasse 23 (611 4981, www.alimentari. de). U1, U8 Kottbusser Tor. **Open** 9am-8pm Mon-Fri; 9am-4pm Sat. **Map** p130 D4 ㊵ **Food & drink**
This well-established Italian delicatessen was one of the first places in Berlin to import goods direct from artisan producers. San Daniele hams, creamy burrata and fresh pastas are all stocked.
Other locations Marheinekeplatz 15, Kreuzberg (6953 9793); Arminiusstrasse 2-4, Moabit (3983 5088).

Chert

Skalitzer Strasse 68 (7544 2118, www.chert-berlin.com). U1 Schlesisches Tor. **Open** noon-6pm Tue-Sat. **Map** p131 F3 ㊶ **Gallery**
With a roster of around ten artists, including Mexico's Alejandro Almanza Pereda, British sculptor Carla Scott Fullerton and Swiss experimental installationist Jérémie Gindre, Chert is a small, perfectly formed and consistently rewarding experience.

Hard Wax

Paul-Lincke-Ufer 44A (6113 0111, www.hard wax.de). U1, U8 Kottbusser Tor. **Open** noon-8pm Mon-Sat. **Map** p130 D4 ㊷ **Books & music**

Up a staircase at the back of a Kreuzberg courtyard lies this vinyl mecca, famous for its flawless selection of dub, techno and reggae. It was opened by dub techno pioneers Basic Channel, and many of the city's biggest DJs (Marcel Dettmann, DJ Hell) started out by working here. Beware – it's infamous for its haughty service.

Kado

Graefestrasse 75 (6904 1638, www.kado.de). U8 Schönleinstrasse. **Open** 9.30am-6.30pm Tue-Fri; 9.30am-3.30pm Sat. **No credit cards. Map** p130 D4 ㊸ **Food & drink**
A mind-boggling selection of liquorice from all over the world is beautifully presented in row upon row of glass jars at Kado. All shapes, sizes and varieties are available.

Klemms

Prinzessinnenstrasse 29 (4050 4953, www. klemms-berlin.com). U8 Moritzplatz. **Open** 11am-6pm Tue-Sat. **No credit cards. Map** p130 D3 ㊹ **Gallery**
Sebastian Klemm and Silvia Bonsiepe's gallery, which was originally part of Mitte's once-happening Brunnenstrasse scene, now promotes offbeat and idiosyncratic shows from a range of photographers, painters and installation artists. Names to look out for include the likes of Viktoria Binschtok, Peggy Buth, Ulrich Gebert, Gwenneth Boelens, Falk Haberkorn and Adrian Sauer.

Kumru Kuruyemis

Wrangelstrasse 46 (3013 0216). U1 Schlesisches Tor. **Open** 9am-8.30pm Mon-Sat. **No credit cards. Map** p131 F4 ㊺ **Food & drink**
There are plenty of nut shops to feed the Turkish community's deep love of roasted sunflower seeds, pistachios and fried corn. But Kumru Kuruyemis is a step up, stocking unshelled salty almonds and *churchkhela*, a string of nuts dipped in grape must then dried like a sausage.

Markthalle IX

Eisenbahnstrasse 42-43 (577 094 661, www. markthalleneun.de). U1 Görlitzer Bahnhof. **Open** *Café* noon-4pm daily. *Market* 10am-6pm Fri, Sat. *Street food* 5-10pm Thur. **No credit cards. Map** p131 E3 ㊻ **Market**
During the late 19th century, 14 municipal covered markets were opened to replace traditional outdoor markets and improve hygiene standards. Local residents saved this one from closure in 2009, filling it with stalls serving heritage veg and locally sourced meats. It's also home to the excellent Heidenpeters microbrewery and the Sironi bakery from Milan. Aligned with the Slow Food movement, the market hosts regular themed events including street food on Thursday evenings, and Cheese Berlin, where'll you find a multitude of artisanal European cheeses.

Modern Graphics

Oranienstrasse 22 (615 8810, www.modern-graphics.de). U1, U8 Kottbusser Tor. **Open** 11am-8pm Mon-Fri; 10am-8pm Sat. **Map** p131 D3 ㊼ **Books & music**

Shelves of European and alternative comics, plus graphic novels, anime, T-shirts and calendars. **Other location** Europa-Center, Tauentzienstrasse 9-12, Charlottenburg (8599 9054).

Modulor

Prinzenstrasse 85 (690 360, www.modulor.de). U8 Moritzplatz. **Open** 9am-8pm Mon-Fri; 10am-6pm Sat. **Map** p130 C3 ㊽ **Gifts & souvenirs**

A paradise for the crafty, with everything laid out over several floors. There are rolls of synthetic materials for product designers or fashion students, but also more traditional art supplies – pencils, chalks, charcoals, oils and acrylics. Services include cutting, laser etching and tool rental.

Motto

Skalitzer Strasse 68 (4881 6407, www.motto distribution.com). U1 Schlesisches Tor. **Open** noon-8pm Mon-Sat. **Map** p131 F3 ㊾ **Books & music**

Tucked away in a disused frame factory in a courtyard off Schlesisches Tor, Motto is Swiss by origin and Swiss in its super design-consciousness. Fanzines, back issues, artists' books, posters, rare print-runs and cult classics are spread in a come-hither way across a long central table.

Overkill

Köpenicker Strasse 195A (6950 6126, www.overkillshop.com). U1 Schlesisches Tor. **Open** 11am-8pm Mon-Sat. **Map** p131 F3 ㊿ **Accessories**

At this urban culture hotspot, you'll find limited runs of Adidas, Asics and Nike shoes in unusual colourways, as well as sprays, markers and caps for the budding street artist.

Schwarzlicht Minigolf

Görlitzer Strasse 1 (6162 1960, www.indoor-minigolf-berlin.de). U1 Görlitzer Bahnhof. **Open** noon-10pm Mon-Thur; noon-midnight Fri; 10am-midnight Sat; 10am-10pm Sun. **Admission** €5.50; €4.50 reductions. **Map** p131 E4 (51) **Golf**

Five rooms of neon mini-golf situated beneath the Görlitzer Park café. The UV psychedelic extravaganza element is a little cheesy, but it's good fun for groups. Don't be put off by the zealous drug dealers: the park is perfectly safe after dark.

Tabac & Whisky Center

Ohlauer Strasse 4 (612 5168, www.whiskyund whiskey.de). U1 Görlitzer Bahnhof. **Open** 10am-7pm Mon-Sat. **Map** p131 E4 (52) **Food & drink**

Any lover of fine sipping spirits will get sucked into this great little shop, which stocks an excellent selection of single-malt whisky, bourbon and rare rums . Staff are extremely helpful.

Voo

Oranienstrasse 24 (6165 1119, www.vooberlin.com). U1, U8 Kottbusser Tor. **Open** 11am-8pm Mon-Sat. **Map** p130 D3 (53) **Fashion**

The Voo concept store brings sleek fashions to an area usually associated with punkier looks. Expect well-crafted outerwear from minimal Swedish favourite Acne, classic New Balance sneakers, colourful Kenzo print sweaters, and a selection of accessories. At the in-store coffee bar, Companion Coffee, you can get a fine macchiato while perusing upmarket magazines such as *The Travel Almanac*.

WEST KREUZBERG

The more sedate western part of Kreuzberg contains some of the most picturesque corners of West Berlin. **Viktoriapark** is the natural way to enter the area, and contains the actual Kreuzberg ('Cross Hill') after which the borough is named. A landscaped waterfall cascades down the hill in summer, and paths wind their way to the summit, where Schinkel's 1821 monument commemorates victories in the Napoleonic Wars – many of the streets nearby are named after battles and generals of that era. From this commanding view over a mainly flat city, the landmarks of both east and west spread out before you: Friedrichstrasse is dead ahead; the Europa-Center off to the left; the Potsdamer Platz high-rises in between; the Fernsehturm over to the right.

Viktoriapark.

Back on ground level, the streets north of the park lead to one of Berlin's most picturesque courtyard complexes. **Riehmers Hofgarten** is cobbled, closed to traffic and often used as a film location due to its 19th-century feel. It's also home to one of Berlin's nicest small hotels, the **Hotel Riehmers Hofgarten** (*see p279*).

Around the corner, on Mehringdamm, is the **Schwules Museum** (Gay Museum). **Bergmannstrasse**, which runs east from here, is the main hub of local activity. This street of cafés, junk shops, bookstores and record shops is livelier than ever by day, although uneventful by night. It leads to **Marheinekeplatz**, where the old Markthalle is now a sort of luxury mall full of speciality food stalls. **Zossener Strasse**, north from here, also bustles.

Bergmannstrasse continues east past a large cemetery to Südstern. Here is the entrance to the **Volkspark Hasenheide**, the other of the neighbourhood's large parks, with a good view from atop the Rixdorfer Höhe. The streets just south of Bergmannstrasse also resemble a movie set. Many buildings survived wartime bombing, and the area around **Chamissoplatz** has been immaculately restored – the cobbled streets are lined with houses still sporting their Prussian façades and illuminated by gaslight at night.

EXPLORE

Sights & Museums

Schwules Museum

Mehringdamm 61 (6959 9050, www.schwules museum.de). U6, U7 Mehringdamm. **Open** 2-6pm Mon, Wed-Fri, Sun; 2-7pm Sat. **Admission** €6; €4 reductions. **No credit cards. Map** p130 B5 (54)

The Gay Museum, opened in 1985, is still the only one in the world dedicated to homosexual life. The museum, its library and archives are staffed by volunteers, and it functions mostly thanks to private donations and bequests (such as the archive of GDR sex scientist Rudolf Klimmer). The museum is on the ground floor. On the third floor, the library and archives house 8,000 books (500 in English), 3,000 international periodicals, photos and posters, plus TV, film and audio footage, all available to borrow.

Restaurants & Cafés

Austria

Bergmannstrasse 30 (694 4440, www.austria-berlin.de). U7 Gneisenaustrasse. **Open** 6pm-midnight daily. **Main courses** €13.50-€18.50. **Map** p130 B5 (55) **Austrian**

With a collection of antlers, this place does its best to look like a hunting lodge. The *Schnitzel* famously spills over the edge of the plate. Literary types may recall it has a cameo in the Pulitzer prize-winning novel *Middlesex*, written by a regular diner, Jeffrey Eugenides, when the narrator declares, 'I don't like anyone who doesn't like Austria.' Book at weekends and in summer – when the outdoor seating on a tree-lined square comes into its own.

€ Mustafa's Gemüse Kebap

Mehringdamm 32 (no phone, www.mustafas.de). U6, U7 Mehringdamm. **Open** 10am-2am daily. **Main courses** €2.50-€4. **No credit cards. Map** p130 B4 (56) **Imbiss**

Easily the most popular kebab stall in town – don't be surprised by half-hour waits, especially for their chicken kebabs. But it's the vegetarian option that's really worth the wait: grilled peppers, aubergines and fried potatoes, finished with crumbled feta and a squirt of lemon juice to really make it sing.

Osteria No.1

Kreuzbergstrasse 71 (786 9162, www.osteria-uno.de). U6, U7 Mehringdamm. **Open** noon-2am daily. **Main courses** €8-€19. **Map** p130 A5 (57) **Italian**

Most of Berlin's best Italian chefs paid their dues at this 1977-founded establishment, learning their lessons from a family of restaurateurs from Lecce. There's an excellent lunch menu and, in summer, one of Berlin's loveliest garden courtyards. Kids eat free on Sundays. Booking recommended.

Bars & Pubs

Golgatha

Viktoria Park, entrance via Katzbachstrasse or Dudenstrasse (785 2453, www.golgatha-berlin.de). U6 Platz der Luftbrücke. **Open** Apr-Sept 10am-late daily. **Map** p130 A5 (58)

This legendary beer garden can do it all – breakfasts under dappled sunlight, hearty lunches, and drinking and dancing until the wee hours.

Shops & Services

Another Country

Riemannstrasse 7 (6940 1160, www.another country.de). U7 Gneisenaustrasse. **Open** 11am-8pm Mon-Fri; 11am-4pm Sat. **Map** p130 B5 (59) **Books & music**

This second-hand bookshop has a legendary status and a whiff of bohemia. It's a window into a Kreuzberg of the past – proprietor Sophia Raphaeline established it long before the area was laden with cafés, restaurants and shops. The rooms have the feel of a private study, with homely blue paintwork, piles of books laid out on tables, and a fridge for beers; a projector is set up for film nights, and quizzes and dinners are also held.

Colours

Bergmannstrasse 102 (694 3348, www.kleidermarkt.de). U7 Gneisenaustrasse. **Open** 11am-7pm Mon-Fri; noon-6pm Sat. **Map** p130 B5 (60) **Fashion**

THE TURKISH CAPITAL

From Gastarbeiter to German citizens.

Turkish food is a Berlin staple, but few realise that the döner kebab is only half an oriental import. A few people claim the stroke of genius of placing it in Turkish flatbread to increase portability – but it's most often attributed to the late Mehmet Aygun, founder of Kreuzberg's Hasir restaurant chain, who definitely profited most from the invention.

But Turkish culture stretches well beyond street food. Berlin is home to the world's largest Turkish community outside Turkey, with hubs in Kreuzberg and the fashionable Neukölln, where one in every three residents is of Turkish origin.

This meeting of cultures has had a difficult history. The fast flow of immigration began in 1961 as a direct consequence of the building of the Berlin Wall. With East German workers cut off from jobs in the West, thousands of *Gastarbeiter* ('guest workers') were recruited from Turkey to provide new cheap labour, and crammed together in purpose-built blocks. The West German authorities proved ungracious hosts. The 'guest workers' were considered no more

than a temporary necessity, and the Nationality Act (or 'Blood Law') of 1913, according to which German citizenship was based on heredity, was rigorously upheld. No person born of Turkish parents could be granted a German passport.

The Turkish community thus remained apart from mainstream society. As recently as 2004, a report found that up to 60 per cent of children in Kreuzberg nursery schools couldn't speak a single word of German. Popular antagonism peaked in 1990, when many feared that large numbers of foreign settlers would destabilise Germany's national identity and hinder a successful reunification. Then-Chancellor Helmut Kohl declared that Germany was 'not a land of immigration' – maligning the nine per cent of the population who had been born abroad. Some scandalous acts of anti-immigrant violence happened around this time.

But attitudes have softened. The basis of nationality on blood has come to be seen as inappropriate for a Germany that wants to transcend the less savoury aspects of its history. Since 2001, a new law grants citizenship to any child born on German soil, provided their parents have been legally resident for at least eight years, but dual nationality is still not allowed, a contentious issue for those not wanting to give up their Turkish passports. Tensions flared again in 2010, when a book criticising multiculturalism, by ex-senator Thilo Sarrazin, became a national bestseller, with Sarrazin accused of Islamophobia and racism.

In Kreuzberg, at least, there's a genuine desire for multiculturalism. The combination of Turkish families living side by side with punks and squatters has developed into a unique community and culture. The sound of *Turkendeutsche*, the hybrid language of the immigrant population, fills the air around Oranienstrasse, while Turkish-German rappers such as Cartel and Azziza-A spit lyrics on bar stereos.

The weekly **Turkischer Markt** (*see p153*) on the Maybachufer in Neukölln showcases the Turks' more traditional side, while Turkish gay nights at nightclub **SO36** (*see p182*) reveal a corresponding cosmopolitanism. Berlin's homegrown Turkish football club, Türkiyemspor, is also fêted as a model of integration.

EXPLORE

Berlinische Galerie.

Part of the Made in Berlin chain, this shop is mostly known for its gimmick of selling clothes by the 'kilo'. Up for grabs are jeans, leather jackets and dresses, including party stunners and fetching Bavarian dirndls, plus the odd gem from the 1950s.

Galerie Neu
Mehringdamm 72 (285 7550, www.galerieneu. net). U6, U7 Mehringdamm. **Open** 11am-6pm Tue-Sat. **Map** p130 B5 ⑥ **Gallery**
At this great little space, curators Thilo Wermke and Alexander Schröder show artists both emerging and established, working in various media, such as Florian Hecker, Kitty Krause and Cerith Wyn Evans.

Marheineke Markthalle
Marheinekestrasse 15 (6128 6146, meine-markthalle.de). U7 Gneisenaustrasse. **Open** 8am-8pm Mon-Fri; 8am-6pm Sat. **Map** p130 B5 ⑥ **Market**
A lovely covered market with French butchers, Italian charcuterie, flowers and organic produce, as well as plenty of prepared foods to take away.

Paul Knopf
Zossener Strasse 10 (692 1212, www.paulknopf. de). U7 Gneisenaustrasse. **Open** 9am-6pm Tue, Fri; 2-6pm Wed, Thur. **No credit cards.** **Map** p130 B5 ⑥ **Accessories**
A Kreuzberg institution stocking buttons in every shape, colour and style you can think of. Whatever you're seeking, Paul Knopf ('Button') will help you find it. His patient and untiring service is remarkable considering most transactions are for tiny sums.

Space Hall
Zossener Strasse 33 (694 7664, www.space-hall.de). U7 Gneisenaustrasse. **Open** 11am-8pm Mon-Sat. **Map** p130 B4 ⑥ **Books & music**

A favourite of Berlin's resident DJs and producers, Space Hall has a huge selection of new and second-hand CDs and vinyl. Techno, house and electronica are the mainstay, but there's also hip hop, indie and rock. Next door (no.35) specialises in vinyl.

NORTH-WEST KREUZBERG

The north-western portion of Kreuzberg, bordering Mitte, is not the prettiest, but it's where you'll find most of the area's museums and tourist sights. The most prominent is Daniel Libeskind's sensational **Jüdisches Museum** on Lindenstrasse, an example of architecture at its most cerebral, and a powerful sensory experience. Behind it, on Alte Jakobstrasse, is the **Berlinische Galerie**, home to Berlin's permanent collection of art, photography and architecture. West of here, close to the Landswehrkanal, is the enjoyable **Deutsches Technikmuseum Berlin** (German Museum of Technology) with a 1930s Junkers JU 52 plane mounted on the roof.

Over the canal to the north is the site of Anhalter Bahnhof, which was once the city's biggest and busiest railway station. Only a tiny section of façade remains, preserved in its bombed state near the S-Bahn station that bears its name. The **Gruselkabinett** ('Chamber of Horrors') occupies an old air-raid shelter on the Schöneberger Strasse side of the area where platforms and tracks once stood.

On Stresemannstrasse, the Bauhaus-designed **Europahaus** was heavily bombed during World War II, but the lower storeys remain. On the north side of the street, Berlin's parliament, the **Abgeordnetenhaus von Berlin** (Berlin House of Representatives), meets in what was formerly the Prussian parliament. Its surprisingly good

though there is an open-air exhibition in the dead space north of the old checkpoint. The actual site of the borderline is memorialised by Frank Thiel's photographic portraits of an American and a Soviet soldier. The small white building that served as gateway between East and West is now in the **Alliierten Museum** – the one in the middle of the street is a replica.

Just to the south is Kochstrasse. In 2008, the eastern stretch, containing the towering headquarters of right-wing media magnate Axel Springer, was renamed Rudi-Dutschke-Strasse in honour of one of Germany's most famous student revolutionaries. In April 1968, Dutschke was the victim of an attempted assassination, shot in the head and chest after various Springer publications had called on their readers to 'eliminate the troublemakers' and 'stop the terror of the young reds.' His supporters demonstrated outside the Springer building, claiming the publisher was partially responsible for the shooting. Dutschke died some years later of complications arising from his injuries.

canteen is open to the public when parliament is not sitting. Dating from the 1890s, the building was renovated in the early 1990s. Opposite stands the **Martin-Gropius-Bau**, a venue for major art shows. The building was modelled on London's South Kensington museums – the figures of craftspeople on the external reliefs reveal its origins as an applied arts museum.

Next to it is a mostly deserted block that once held the Prinz Albrecht Palais, which the Gestapo took over as its headquarters. In the basement's 39 cells, political prisoners were held, interrogated and tortured. The land was flattened after the war. In 1985, during an acrimonious debate over the design of a memorial to be placed here, a group of citizens staged a symbolic 'excavation'. To their surprise, they hit the Gestapo's basement, and plans were then made to reclaim the site. Today, there's an open-air exhibition about the rise of National Socialism and a documentation centre, the **Topographie des Terrors**.

Along the site's northern boundary on Niederkirchnerstrasse is one of the last few remaining stretches of the **Berlin Wall**, pitted and threadbare after thousands of 1990 souvenir-hunters pecked away at it with hammers and chisels. The stark building opposite is Hermann Göring's fortress-like Luftfahrministerium (Air Ministry), a rare relic of the Nazi past, which survived the allies' bombs and is now the Federal Finance Ministry.

Walking east, Niederkirchnerstrasse turns into Zimmerstrasse, which intersects Friedrichstrasse, where Checkpoint Charlie once stood and where the **Haus am Checkpoint Charlie** documents the history of the Wall. Most of the space where the border post once stood has been claimed by new buildings,

Sights & Museums

Berlin Hi-Flyer

Corner of Wilhelmstrasse & Zimmerstrasse (226 678 811, www.air-service-berlin.de). U6 Kochstrasse. **Open** *Apr-Oct* 10am-10pm daily. *Nov-Mar* 11am-6pm daily. **Admission** €19.90; €4.90-€14.90 reductions. **Map** p130 B3 ⑥⑤
This helium balloon has hovered 150m (490ft) above Berlin in various different guises since 1999 and, somewhat bewilderingly, is now one of the city's leading tourist attractions – as well as one of its most expensive. You do get a lovely view, but given that the panorama from the dome of the (free) Reichstag is almost as good, you might wish to give this one a miss.

Berlinische Galerie

Alte Jakobstrasse 124-128 (7890 2600, www.berlinischegalerie.de). U6 Kochstrasse. **Open** 10am-6pm Mon, Wed-Sun. **Admission** €8; €5 reductions; free under-18s. **Map** p130 B3 ⑥⑥
Founded in 1975, the Berlinische Galerie moved into this spacious renovated industrial building near the Jewish Museum in 2004. It specialises in art created in Berlin, dating from 1870 to the present, including painting, sculpture, photography and architecture. Its collections cover Dada Berlin, the Neue Sachlichkeit and the Eastern European avant-garde.
▶ *Visitors pay the reduced price if they have a ticket to the Jüdisches Museum (see p142) from the same day or two previous days.*

Deutsches Technikmuseum Berlin

Trebbiner Strasse 9 (902 540, www.sdtb.de). U1, U7 Möckernbrücke. **Open** 9am-5.30pm

EXPLORE

Tue-Fri; 10am-6pm Sat, Sun. **Admission** €6; €3.50 reductions. **Map** p130 A4 ⑤

Opened in 1982 in the former goods depot of the Anhalter Bahnhof, the German Museum of Technology is an eclectic, eccentric collection of new and antique industrial artefacts. The rail exhibits have pride of place, with the station sheds providing an ideal setting for locomotives and rolling stock from 1835 to the present. Other displays focus on the industrial revolution; street, rail, water and air traffic; computer technology; and printing technology. Behind the main complex is an open-air section with two functioning windmills and a smithy. Oddities, such as 1920s vacuum cleaners, make this a fun place for implement enthusiasts. The nautical wing has vessels and displays on inland waterways and international shipping, while another wing covers aviation and space travel. Electronic information points offer commentaries in English on subjects from the international slave trade to the mechanics of a space station. The Spectrum annex, at Möckernstrasse 26, houses over 200 interactive devices and experiments.

Gruselkabinett

Schöneberger Strasse 23A (2655 5546, www. gruselkabinett.com). S1, S2, S25 Anhalter Bahnhof. **Open** 10am-7pm Mon-Fri; noon-8pm Sat, Sun. **Admission** €9.50; €7 reductions. **No credit cards. Map** p130 A3 ⑥

This is the city's only visitable World War II air-raid shelter. Built in 1943, the five-level bunker was part of an underground network connecting various similar structures throughout Berlin. Today, it houses both the 'Chamber of Horrors' and an exhibit on the bunker itself. The 'horrors' begin at ground level with a display on medieval medicine (mechanical figures amputate a leg to the sound of canned screaming). Elsewhere, there's a patented coffin designed to demonstrate the effects of being buried alive. Upstairs is scarier: a musty labyrinth with a simulated cemetery, strange cloaked figures, spooky sounds and a few surprises. Kids love it, but not those under ten.

Haus am Checkpoint Charlie

Friedrichstrasse 43-45 (253 7250, www. mauermuseum.de). U6 Kochstrasse. **Open** 9am-10pm daily. **Admission** €12.50; €9.50 reductions. **Map** p130 B3 ⑥

A little tacky, but essential for anyone interested in the Wall and the Cold War. This private museum opened not long after the GDR erected the Berlin Wall in 1961, with the purpose of documenting the events that were taking place. The exhibition charts the history of the Wall, and details the ingenious and hair-raising ways people escaped from the GDR – as well as exhibiting some of the actual contraptions that were used, such as a home-made hot-air balloon.

★ Jüdisches Museum

Lindenstrasse 9-14 (2599 3300, guided tours 2599 3305, www.juedisches-museum-berlin.de). U1, U6 Hallesches Tor. **Open** (last entry 1hr before closing) 10am-10pm Mon; 10am-8pm Tue-Sun. **Admission** €5; €2.50 reductions. **Map** p130 B3 ⑦

The idea of a Jewish museum in Berlin was first mooted in 1971, the 300th birthday of the city's Jewish community. In 1975, an association was

EXPLORE

Deutsches Technikmuseum Berlin. See p141.

Haus am Checkpoint Charlie.

formed to acquire materials for display; in 1989, a competition was held to design an extension to house them. Daniel Libeskind emerged as the winner, the foundation stone was laid in 1992 and the permanent exhibition finally opened in 2001.

The ground plan of Libeskind's remarkable building is in part based on an exploded Star of David, in part on lines drawn between the site and former addresses of figures in Berlin's Jewish history, such as Mies van der Rohe, Arnold Schönberg and Walter Benjamin. The entrance is via a tunnel from the Kollegienhaus next door. The underground geometry is startlingly independent of the above-ground building. One passage leads to the exhibition halls, two others intersect en route to the Holocaust Tower and the ETA Hoffmann Garden, a grid of 49 columns, tilted to disorientate. Throughout, diagonals and parallels carve out surprising spaces, while windows slash through the structure and its zinc cladding like the knife-wounds of history. And then there are the 'voids' cutting through the layout, negative spaces that stand for the emptiness left by the destruction of German Jewish culture.

The permanent exhibition struggles in places with such powerful surroundings. What makes it engaging is its focus on the personal: it tells the stories of prominent Jews and what they contributed to their community, and to the cultural and economic life of Berlin and Germany. After centuries of prejudice and pogroms, the outlook for German Jews seemed to be brightening. Then came the Holocaust. The emotional impact of countless stories of the eminent and the ordinary, and the fate that almost all shared, is hard to convey adequately in print. The museum is undoubtedly a must-see, but expect long queues and big crowds. *Photos p144.*

▶ *Visitors pay the reduced price if they have a ticket to the Berlinische Galerie (see p141) from the same day or two previous days.*

Martin-Gropius-Bau
Niederkirchnerstrasse 7 (3025 4860, www. gropiusbau.de). S1, S2, S25 Anhalter Bahnhof. **Open** 10am-8pm Mon, Wed-Sun. **Admission** varies. **Map** p130 A3 ⓐ
Cosying up to where the Wall once stood (a short, pitted stretch still runs nearby along the south side of Niederkirchnerstrasse), the Martin-Gropius-Bau is named after its architect, uncle of the more famous Walter. Built in 1881, it has been renovated and is now used for large-scale art exhibitions, such as the David Bowie hit show that transferred from London's V&A.

★ FREE Topographie des Terrors
Niederkirchnerstrasse 8 (2545 0950, www.topographie.de). S1, S2, S25 Anhalter Bahnhof, or U6 Kochstrasse. **Open** *Outdoor exhibition* 10am-dusk daily. *Indoor exhibition* 10am-8pm daily. **Admission** free. **Map** p130 A3 ⓑ
Essentially a piece of waste ground that was once the site of the Prinz Albrecht Palais, headquarters of the Gestapo, and the Hotel Prinz Albrecht, which housed offices of the Reich SS leadership. This was the centre of the Nazi police-state apparatus and it was from here that the Holocaust was directed, and the Germanisation of the east was dreamed up. There's an outdoor exhibition that gives a pretty comprehensive chronology of Hitler's rise to power, as well as an indoor documentation centre. A segment of the Berlin Wall runs along the site's northern boundary.

EXPLORE

Restaurants & Cafés

Sale e Tabacchi

Rudi-Dutschke-Strasse 25 (252 1155, www. sale-e-tabacchi.de). U6 Kochstrasse. **Open** from 10am daily. **Main courses** €10.50-€40.50. **Map** p130 B3 ⑱ Italian
An old-school Italian restaurant, ideal for larger groups looking for some southern decadence and creaky, middle-aged Italian waiters. Food is simple and delicious rather than spectacular, but it's the ambience – a comfortable fug of cosiness and quiet affluence (the restaurant is owned by the left-leaning *Tageszeitung* newspaper) – that's the big draw.

Tim Raue

Rudi-Dutschke-Strasse 26 (2593 7930, www. tim-raue.de). U6 Kochstrasse. **Open** noon-1.30pm, 7-9.30pm Mon-Sat. **Main courses** €55-€96. **Set meal** €168. **Map** p130 B3 ⑭ Haute cuisine

Jüdisches Museum. See p142.

In contrast to many of Berlin's fine-dining establishments, this small restaurant, decorated with Chinese ceramics and dark wood furniture, prides itself on its informality. Not that this detracts from the exacting dishes. The tasting menu might include amuse-bouches of spicy cashews, prawn sashimi and marinated pork belly, moving on to main courses of wagyu beef, lobster, Australian winter truffle and tofu, all flaunting Japanese techniques and served with blobs, smears or foams of contrasting flavours and colours. Book ahead.

Shops & Services

Alexander Levy

Rudi-Dutschke-Strasse 26 (2529 2276, www. alexanderlevy.net). U6 Kochstrasse. **Open** 11am-6pm Tue-Sat. **Map** p130 B3 ⑮ Gallery
Scion of legendary Hamburg and Berlin dealers, Alex Levy took over this boxy space from his father in 2011, continuing the family trait of showcasing quality art with an experimental edge. Look out for up-and-coming local artist Julius von Bismarck and American-born installation whizz John von Bergen.

DAAD Galerie

Zimmerstrasse 90-91 (261 3640, www.daad galerie.de). U6 Kochstrasse. **Open** noon-6pm Tue-Sat. **Map** p130 B3 ⑯ Gallery
Something of a local institution, DAAD, founded with funding from the USA's Ford Foundation, is steeped in postwar Berlin history. Now financed by the city, the ongoing Berliner Künstlerprogramm sees 20 artists participate in a year-long residence, the fruits of which are exhibited in this space.

Johann König

Dessauerstrasse 6-7 (2610 3080, www.johann koenig.de). U2, S1, S2, S25 Potsdamer Platz. **Open** 11am-6pm Tue-Sat. **Map** p130 A3 ⑰ Gallery
Johann König is one of Berlin's bona fide iconoclasts. When he opened this gallery in 2002, at the age of 21, he invited his friend, artist Jeppe Hein, to install a wrecking ball, which swung about perilously, knocking chunks out of the walls whenever anyone entered the room. Nowadays, he's regarded as one of the leading lights in a scene that's certainly not short of wilful, eccentric and obstinate characters. His gallery represents some of the hottest artists around, including Monica Bonvicini, Tue Greenfort, Alicja Kwade and Michael Sailstorfer.

TREPTOW

The canal and lack of U-Bahn keeps this large district just east of Kreuzberg relatively isolated. From Schlesisches Tor U-Bahn station, walk down Schlesische Strasse, where you'll see the vast murals by Italian street artist Blu: on the left, two figures representing West and East Berlin de-masking each other; on the right, a besuited

Badeschiff.

man shackled in gold chains. Over the bridge is the canalside DJ bar **Club Der Visionaere** (*see p198*), open pretty much all hours in summer, while to the left is the Arena Berlin complex, which houses the **Badeschiff**, an urban 'beach' with a swimming pool suspended in the Spree. On the right is one of only three remaining GDR watchtowers, overlooking a former 'death strip' of the Wall that ran down the canal.

The grand tree-lined Puschkinallee with its 19th-century mansions neatly segues into the leafy **Treptower Park**. Slightly off the beaten track, the **Sowjetisches Ehrenmal** (Soviet War Memorial) gets fewer visitors than it deserves – it's easily the most impressive Communist monument in Berlin. The park runs alongside the Spree and ends with the charming **Insel der Jugend**, a tiny landscaped islet accessible by a bridge. Continue along the dirt tracks, popular with joggers and mountain bikers, to one of Berlin's best-known secrets, the abandoned **Spreepark** (www.berliner-spreepark.de). A massively popular amusement park in GDR days, it sank into debt after the Wall fell. Now the rides are all overgrown and the ferris wheel creaks eerily in the wind – it's wonderfully atmospheric. Security is tight, but guided tours are available from the main gate (check the websites). In early 2014 the site was purchased by the city, which has plans to return it to its former glory.

Sights & Museums

Badeschiff
Eichenstrasse 4 (533 2030, www.arena-berlin.de). S8, S9, S41, S42 Treptower Park. **Open** 8.30am-midnight daily. **Admission** €4; €3 reductions. **No credit cards. Map** p131 G4 ⑦
A former barge docked on the banks of the Spree has been converted into a heated swimming pool. It belongs to the Arena Berlin cultural centre, and has regular open-air parties. In winter, it becomes a covered sauna.

FREE Insel der Jugend
Treptower Park (8096 1850, www.insel berlin.de). S8, S9, S41, S42 Treptower Park. **Open** 24hrs daily. **Admission** free. **Map** p131 H5 ⑦
Connected to the mainland by German's first composite steel bridge, built in 1915, this wooded island has housed numerous leisure centres over the years, most recently a GDR youth centre. It's now a lovely small park, with a bar/café that hosts puppet-theatre workshops and other events, and open-air raves in summer. The old Neukölln coat of arms is displayed on the bridge's tower.

★ FREE Sowjetisches Ehrenmal
Treptower Park (901 393 000, www.stadtentwicklung.berlin.de). S8, S9, S41, S42 Treptower Park. **Open** 24hrs daily. **Admission** free. **Map** p131 H5 ⑧
This Soviet war memorial (one of three in Berlin) and military cemetery lies quietly in beautiful Treptower Park. Architect Yakov Belopolsky's design was unveiled just four years after World War II ended, on 8 May 1949, and its epic scale and brawny symbolism made it a war memorial for all East Germany. On entering, you're greeted by statues of two kneeling soldiers, and the view unfolds across a geometrical expanse flanked by 16 stone sarcophagi, which mark the burial site of the 5,000 Soviet soldiers who died in the final Battle of Berlin in spring 1945. At the end is a 12m (40ft) statue of a Soviet soldier holding a rescued German child and a massive sabre, a broken swastika crushed beneath his boot. It's an arresting image, whether surrounded by foliage in summer, or bleak snow in winter.

Bars & Pubs

Eierschale Zenner
Alt-Treptow 14-17 (533 7370, www.eierschale-zenner.com). S8, S9 Plänterwald. **Open** 10am-11pm Mon-Thur; 10am-4am Fri, Sat; 10am-10pm Sun. **Map** p131 H5 ⑧
On sunny weekends the terrace at this old-fashioned tavern turns into a greying disco, as elderly couples come to waltz and slow-dance the evening away. It has a great view over the River Spree. Steer clear of the grim food.

EXPLORE

Neukölln

Neukölln has gone from making headlines for rampant crime to being the city's hippest district. A vibrant ethnic mix, dominated by the Turkish community, draws the city's bohemians and artists, leading to an abundance of gritty bars and pubs as well as discreet but definite signs of gentrification. At its northernmost tip, the area hugging the canal is known as Kreuzkölln, and is fertile ground for charming cafés and restaurants. Following Weserstrasse south-east takes you past living-room bars and cocktail joints and towards the picturesque 18th-century 'village' of Rixdorf. Cross Karl-Marx-Strasse westwards and you'll be in Schillerkiez, another café and dining hotspot, and gateway to the vast expanse of Tempelhofer Feld.

Tempelhofer Feld.

Don't Miss

1 Rixdorf This 18th-century Bohemian village is an oasis of calm in the middle of the city (p154).

2 Tier A slinky 1920s vibe and killer cocktails make Tier a standout stop when Weserstrasse bar-hopping (p152).

3 Blutwurst Manufaktur Go full German with a taste of this award-winning blood sausage (p155).

4 Nansen This low-key canalside restaurant offers some of Berlin's most inventive farm-to-table cooking (p151).

5 Tempelhofer Feld Rent bikes to explore this decommissioned airport, now one of the largest urban parks in Europe (p154).

KREUZKÖLLN

The small strip bordering the canal just across from Kreuzberg was, until about ten years ago, a quiet, predominantly working-class area with a large Turkish population. But now, other languages are heard on the streets – French, Spanish, Swedish, Italian and Japanese, as well as English. The availability of space has led to a restaurant boom, with Prenzlauer Berg favourites such as the **Bird** (*see p73*) opening offshoots here. Pull up a chair, sip a flat white and watch the young and hopeful living their Berlin dream.

Home to the lively **Turkischer Markt** and **Nowkoelln Flowmarkt**, the canalside Maybachufer is just across the Kottbusser Brücke and makes for a jolly stroll. From here, head south for espresso bars, and vintage fashion and wooden-toy shops, making sure to stop for some of the city's best pistachio ice-cream at **Fräulein Frost** – after school hours, it's overrun by sugar-high toddlers. Quiet by day, Weserstrasse comes alive at night and is conveniently adjacent to the Levantine food paradise that is Sonnenallee.

Restaurants & Cafés

★ € Azzam
Sonnenallee 54 (3013 1541). U7, U8 Hermannplatz. **Open** 7am-midnight daily. **Main courses** €3.50-€6. **No credit cards.** **Map** p149 C3 ❶ Middle Eastern
People flock from all over the city to sample Azzam's houmous, made fresh throughout the day with chickpeas, tahini and seasonings. The grilled minced lamb is perfectly seasoned, and the falafel a crunchy, sesame-speckled delight. You get a lot for your money too: each dish comes with raw veg, bitter olives, garlicky mayo or tahini sauce, and a basket of stacked pitta bread, which doubles as cutlery.

€ Berlin Burger International
Pannierstrasse 5 (0160 482 6505 mobile, www.berlinburgerinternational.com). U7, U8 Hermannplatz. **Open** noon-midnight

---

**IN THE KNOW
NOSTALGIA FOR THE DDR**

These days, Sonnenallee is awash with shisha smoke and baklava, but 30 years ago it was home to a little known East–West border crossing. Check out Leander Haussmann's controversial 1999 film comedy *Sonnenallee*, about youth culture in the East, which kicked off the whole *Ostalgie* trend – a rose-tinted view of more 'innocent' times in the DDR.

Mon-Thur; noon-1am Fri, Sat; noon-10pm Sun. **Main courses** €5-€6.50. **No credit cards.** **Map** p149 B3 ❷ Imbiss
A proper hole-in-the-wall. The pavement tables are constantly packed, whatever the season: BBI has punters hooked on stacked hamburgers, served with three types of salad, and with a small amount of lamb mince in the patty for extra succulence.

★ € Bullys Bakery
Friedelstrasse 7 (2532 5500, www.bullysbakery. com). U7, U8 Hermannplatz. **Open** 7am-6pm Mon-Fri; 9am-6pm Sat; 10am-6pm Sun. **No credit cards.** **Map** p149 B3 ❸ Café
Daniel, the half-Spanish, half-German proprietor, bakes the best croissants in town, oozing butter and with just the right amount of flake to pair with a bracing macchiato. After breakfast, there are also various *Flammkuchen* – crisp pastries from Alsace topped with cheese and pear or ham – as well as fruity crumble cakes, tarts and a selection of muffins.

€ Burrito Baby
Pflügerstrasse 11 (3385 1520, www.burrito baby.de). U8 Schönleinstrasse. **Open** 1-10pm Wed-Fri; 4-10pm Sat; 4-9pm Sun. **Main courses** €4.50-€7.50. **No credit cards.** **Map** p149 C5 ❹ Mexican/Vegan
This cutesy Mexican canteen goes some way to rebalancing the area's coffee-shop to lunch-spot ratio. In a nod to neighbourhood trends, it's fully vegan. They even make their own lemonade.

California Breakfast Slam
Innstrasse 47 (686 9624, www.cabslam.com). U7 Karl-Marx-Strasse. **Open** 10am-midnight daily. **Main courses** €6.50-€15. **Map** p149 B3 ❺ North American
Cabslam has done much to popularise US-style brunch culture among the Berlin hip set, offering potent bloody marys alongside eggs benedict and Tex-Mex breakfast dishes. It started out as a pop-up, but has now opened a permanent space, serving weekday dinners too.

Chez Dang
Friedelstrasse 31 (5305 1205, www.chez-dang. com). U8 Schönleinstrasse. **Open** 11.30am-11.30pm Mon, Tue, Thur, Fri; 4-11.30pm Sat, Sun. **Main courses** €6-€11. **No credit cards.** **Map** p149 A3 ❻ Vietnamese
Steer clear of nearby Jimmy Woo and head to Chez Dang for a fresh and healthy Vietnamese fix. This family-run restaurant has pictures of the owner's grandparents on the walls, and the menu is far more inventive than the usual fast-food noodle joints.

€ City Chicken
Sonnenallee 59 (624 8600). U7 Rathaus Neukölln. **Open** 9am-1am daily. **Main courses** €3.50-€5.50. **No credit cards.** **Map** p149 C3 ❼ Rotisserie

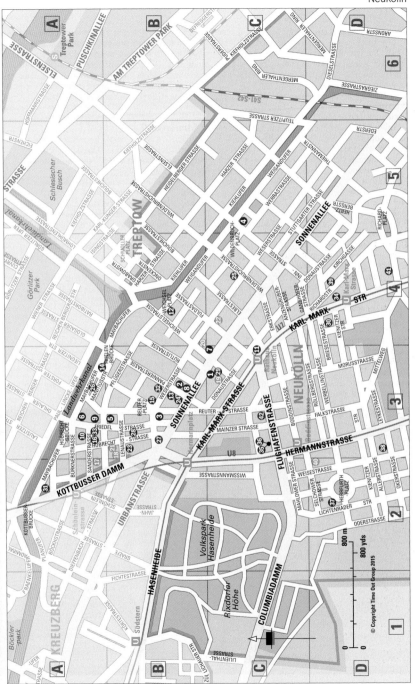

EXPLORE

Kreuzberg's Hühnerhaus gets a run for its money at City Chicken, the scene of frenzied rotisserie action. There's only really one option: a silver platter with half a roast chicken, a pile of fries, garlicky mayonnaise, assorted pickles and some pitta to mop up the juices.

€ Espera

Sonnenallee 35 (no phone). U7, U8 Hermannplatz. **Open** 7am-7pm Mon-Fri; 8.30am-7pm Sat, Sun. **Main courses** €2.50-€4.50. **No credit cards.** **Map** p149 B3 **8** Café
Sitting among the Syrian and Lebanese snack joints of Sonnenallee, this modern café offers filled focaccia and cakes. Enjoy an excellent cortado at an outdoor table fashioned from an old wine crate.

★ € Fräulein Frost

Friedelstrasse 39 (9559 5521). U8 Schönleinstrasse. **Open** 2-8pm daily. **No credit cards.** **Map** p149 A3 **9** Ice-cream
The opening of the city's numerous ice-cream parlours is Berliners' favourite herald of spring, and Fräulein Frost is one of the best. Yummy mummies flock here, and sleds provide outside seating (and fun) for kids. Refresh yourself with their signature GuZiMi (cucumber, lemon, mint) or go all out with a velvety pistachio.

Hamburger Heaven

Sanderstrasse 17 (6298 6070, www.hamburger heaven.de). U8 Schönleinstrasse. **Open** noon-10pm Mon-Thur, Sun; noon-11pm Fri, Sat. **Main courses** €5.50-€10. **No credit cards.** **Map** p149 A3 **10** Burgers

For a long time it was just a hole-in-the-wall near the Kottbusser Brücke, but Hamburger Heaven moved into its own digs in early 2014. Their recipe for success is clear: organic beef patties, excellent steaks cut to order and crisp fries – even if their home-made ketchup is a source of contention. **Other location** Graefestrasse 93, Kreuzberg (3761 4133).

★ € Imren Grill

Karl-Marx-Strasse 75 (no phone, www.imren-grill.de). U8 Schönleinstrasse. **Open** 9am-3am daily. **Main courses** €1.50-€7. **No credit cards.** **Map** p149 C3 **11** Imbiss
Part of a small chain, Imren Grill provides some of the best Turkish snacks in town. Lunch specials include baked fish with stew and rice – but first things first: order the classic *Döner im Brot* (kebab in toasted bread), with its stuffing of lamb grilled in neck fat, fresh salad, sesame sauce and chilli flakes. Then join the suited elderly gents at the park in front, who congregate to put the world to rights over cups of sweet black tea. **Other locations** Boppstrasse 4, Kreuzberg; Boppstrasse 10, Kreuzberg; Badstrasse 46, Wedding; Müllerstrasse 134, Wedding.

Kokolores

Weichselstrasse 3 (2574 4568, www.kokolores-neukoelln.de). U7 Rathaus Neukölln. **Open** 6-11pm Tue-Thur, Sun; 6pm-midnight Fri, Sat. **Main courses** €6.50-€14.50. **No credit cards.** **Map** p149 B4 **12** Polish
Very much a neighbourhood affair, this cosy place is packed every evening with the hip local youth

Geist im Glas.

EXPLORE

who come for the massive plates of Polish food at dirt-cheap prices. Wednesday is *pierogi* (steamed dumplings) night.

€ Melbourne Canteen

Pannierstrasse 57 (6273 1602, www.melbourne canteen.com). U7, U8 Hermannplatz. **Open** 9am-late daily. **Main courses** €4.50-€8. **No credit cards. Map** p149 B3 ⑬ **Café**

This Aussie café is most beloved for its rock-solid bloody mary, which will sledgehammer its way through even the most demonic of hangovers. They serve brunch classics, such as eggs benedict, and a tidy cocktail menu in the evenings.

★ Nansen

Maybachufer 39 (6630 1438, www.restaurant-nansen.de). U8 Schönleinstrasse. **Open** 6-11pm daily. **Main courses** €14.50-€23. **No credit cards. Map** p149 A3 ⑭ **German**

This long-time neighbourhood favourite is one of the city's best restaurants. Ingredients are locally sourced and quality is superb: braised and smoked meats, seasonal greens and pickled roots are some of the elements at play in the modern German dishes. The low-lit dining room is the perfect setting for a romantic evening.

Pizza a Pezzi

Weserstrasse 208 (no phone). U7, U8 Hermannplatz. **Open** 11am-midnight daily. **Main courses** €5-€9. **No credit cards. Map** p149 B3 ⑮ **Pizza**

This blue-tiled pizzeria has plenty of seating in its large corner location. They offer excellent *al taglio*-style pizzas – pre-made small squares finished to order in the oven – as well as standard whole pizzas, missable baked pastas and a fabulous tiramisu.

Sing Blackbird

Sanderstrasse 11 (no phone, www.singblackbird. com). U8 Schönleinstrasse. **Open** 10.30am-8pm daily. **No credit cards. Map** p149 A3 ⑯ **Café**

An instant hit on opening, this charming vegetarian café doubles up as an excellent vintage clothes shop, where you can bring in your clothes for trade or credit. They do cakes and are also home to the cold-pressed Daily Dose juice company.

Bars & Pubs

Black Lodge

Sanderstrasse 6 (no phone). U8 Schönleinstrasse. **Open** 9pm-late Tue-Sat. **No credit cards. Map** p149 A2 ⑰

Hidden behind the façade of a crusty old *Kneipe* (pub) lies this moody watering hole. The well-stocked bar knocks out sharp cocktails, and the back room is a perfect replica of the terrifying dream sequence room from *Twin Peaks*.

★ Geist im Glas

Lenaustrasse 27 (0176 5533 0450 mobile). U7, U8 Hermannplatz. **Open** 7pm-late daily. **No credit cards. Map** p149 B3 ⑱

The space here is built up with wooden platforms and great attention to detail, such as the Victorian curios laid into the bar or the esoteric toilet. They specialise in infused alcohols, shots of which are poured out of a giant bottle at the bar or mixed into their house cocktails, such as the Geist Russian, a rich blend of vodka infused with vanilla, cinnamon, Kahlúa and cream.

Das Gift

Donaustrasse 119 (no phone, www.dasgift.de). U7, U8 Hermannplatz. **Open** 5pm-late daily. **No credit cards. Map** p149 C3 ⑲

Famously owned by Mogwai's Barry Burns, Das Gift is his attempt at mashing a Glaswegian pub into a Berlin *Kneipe*. Lots of ales and single malts behind the bar, regular pie nights and a rowdy pub quiz go somewhat towards comforting the homesick Anglo expats that frequent the place.

Herz

Weichselstrasse 15 (0176 6476 0499 mobile). U7, U8 Hermnnplatz. **Open** 8pm-late Tue-Sat. **No credit cards. Map** p149 B4 ⑳

An experimental dance bar put together by a left-field French crew, Herz makes a welcome change from the usual Weserstrasse living-room bar. DJs play everything from glam rock to no wave, and there's a secret record/fashion shop in the back called Uni+Form.

EXPLORE

Mama

Hobrechtstrasse 61 (0157 7386 4042 mobile).
U7, U8 Hermannplatz. **Open** 7pm-late daily.
No credit cards. Map p149 B3 ㉑
Nearer to a grandmother in Neukölln years, Mama
was one of the area's first bars to nail down the look
with its GDR living-room furniture, intricate murals
and sound system veering towards Balkan beats.
The unpasteurised Svijany beer on tap is excellent.

★ Tier

Weserstrasse 42 (no phone). U7 Rathaus Neukölln.
Open 7pm-late daily. **No credit cards. Map**
p149 C4 ㉒
Seen through the frosted windows, Tier's long bar
could be a facsimile of Hopper's iconic *Nighthawks*.
The vinyl collection sticks to the trusted classics,
as does the cocktail menu, though there's a rotating
experimental special, such as 'Princess and the
Pea', a carbonated blend of vodka, lemon, pea syrup
and wheat beer.

Shops & Services

★ Azafran

Lenaustrasse 5 (6583 4970, www.azafran
gourmet.com). U7, U8 Hermannplatz. **Open**
2-8pm Tue-Sat. **No credit cards. Map** p149 B3
㉓ **Food & drink**
By far the best Spanish deli in the area (if not
town), Azafran carries only the finest produce
sourced directly from small farms, including potent
matured manchego, acorn-fed Domecq Ibérico
ham and Ramón Peña's fantastic line of canned
fish from Galicia. Prices reflect the quality. At the
adjoining Galatea wine bar, you can sample Spanish
tempranillos in the evening alongside some tapas.

Heil Quelle

Pannierstrasse 58 (6272 7822, www.heil-
quelle-berlin.de). U7, U8 Hermannplatz. **Open**
8am-8pm Mon-Fri; 9am-8pm Sat; 10am-4pm
Sun. **No credit cards. Map** p149 B3 ㉔
Convenience store/DIY

Oye Kreuzkölln.

This super-*Späti* (convenience store) amalgamated
with a local DIY shop and now offers not only bottled
foreign ales, English-language press and obscure
tobacco brands but also screws, paint and rope.

Let Them Eat Cake

Weserstrasse 164 (6096 5095, www.letthem
eat cake-berlin.tumblr.com). U7 Rathaus
Neukölln. **Open** 1-7pm Tue-Sat. **Map** p149 C4
㉕ **Fashion/Gallery**
This Swedish vintage shop with an adjoining
gallery space specialises in chunky 1990s clothing
and designer jewellery.

★ Nowkoelln Flowmarkt

Maybachufer (no phone, www.nowkoelln.de).
U8 Schönleinstrasse. **Open** *Mar-Nov* 10am-6pm
2nd Sun of mth. Closed Dec-Feb. **No credit cards.**
Map p149 A3 ㉖ **Market**
This massively popular canalside fleamarket has
grown considerably in recent years. Plenty of
local hipsters hawk vintage apparel, and there's a
strong food section with smoked fish sandwiches,
Käsespätzle and hot apple pie on offer. Note that the
market doesn't operate over winter.

EXPLORE

Other location Prinzessinnengarten, Kreuzberg (no phone, www.kreuzboerg.de).

Octopus Opticians
Sonnenallee 1 (693 4778). U7, U8 Hermannplatz. **Open** 10am-7pm Mon-Fri; 10am-3pm Sat. **No credit cards. Map** p149 B3 ㉗ **Health & beauty**
Germans take particular pride in their opticians, and this Hermannplatz shop stands out for its classic frames from New York's Moscot. As seen on Johnny Depp, no less.

Oye Kreuzkölln
Friedelstrasse 49 (8937 2815, www.oye-records. com). U7, U8 Hermannplatz. **Open** 1-8pm Mon-Sat. **Map** p149 B3 ㉘ **Books & music**
The southern branch of Oye Records, this small shop packs in a quality pick of house, techno and bass vinyl. Big-name DJs often do in-store events. **Other location** Oderbergerstrasse 4, Prenzlauer Berg (6664 7821).

Peppikäse
Weichselstrasse 65 (0176 5030 7656 mobile, www.peppikaese.de). U7 Rathaus Neukölln. **Open** 2-9pm Tue, Wed; 10am-9pm Thur-Sat. **No credit cards. Map** p149 C3 ㉙ **Food & drink**
Owner Georg, a local Slow Food champion, stocks Austrian and Swiss cheeses with a particular emphasis on raw-milk varieties.

★ Rag & Bone Man
Briesestrasse 9 (no phone). U7 Karl-Marx-Strasse. **Open** 1-7pm Mon, Wed-Fri; 1-6pm Sat. **Map** p149 D4 ㉚ **Fashion**
Rag & Bone Man is an excellent vintage clothes shop that also stocks a selection of young designers. Its racks are strong on velour, fake animal prints and silky things.

Turkischer Markt
Maybachufer (no phone, www.tuerkenmarkt. de). U8 Schönleinstrasse. **Open** 11am-6.30pm Tue, Fri. **No credit cards. Map** p149 A2 ㉛ **Market**
A lively market by the canal catering for the local Turkish community. You'll find fresh veg piled high, wonderful spices and, at the end of the day, whole crates of fruit sold off at bargain prices.

Vin Aqua Vin
Weserstrasse 204 (9405 2886, www.vinaquavin. de). U7, U8 Hermannplatz. **Open** 3-9pm Mon-Fri; 1-9pm Sat. **No credit cards. Map** p149 B3 ㉜ **Food & drink**
This wine bar and shop stocks an impeccable selection from all the trendiest regions (Ribera del Duero, Languedoc, Douro) and from plenty of small German vintners. Regular tasting events.

Vintage Galore
Sanderstrasse 12 (6396 3338, www.vintage galore.de). U8 Schönleinstrasse. **Open** 2-8pm Tue-Fri; noon-6pm Sat. **Map** p149 A3 ㉝ **Homewares**
Vintage Galore is one of the best places for authentic mid-century Danish furniture: it stocks everything from floor lamps to snack plates in the distinctive rounded teak style.

SCHILLERKIEZ & RIXDORF

As rents have shot up over the years, there's been consistent creep up and down Berlin's main artery of gentrification, the U8 metro line, and the effects are slowly making their way south to the Ringbahn (traditionally the limits of the city to 'real' Berliners). **Schillerkiez** is the newest area to come to life, as Spanish restaurateurs, Swedish fashion designers and English

Vintage Galore.

EXPLORE

Hufeisensiedlung.

bar-owners throw in their lot with the Turkish kebab shops and betting parlours. With leafy Herrfurthplatz at its heart, it ends at Hermannstrasse in the east and the awesome **Tempelhofer Feld** in the west. The city solved the problem of this enormous former airport (built by the Nazis) by turning it into a public park, but at time of writing there are controversial plans to build housing on its periphery.

Just past the Leinestrasse U-Bahn stop and hidden down Jonasstrasse, is the secluded baroque-style **Körnerpark**. Built on reclaimed land, it creates the wonderful illusion of being completely hidden from the rest of the city and makes for a perfect picnic spot.

Across the busy shopping street of Karl-Marx-Strasse is the historic and charming village of **Rixdorf**, centred around Richardplatz. Buildings dating from the original early 18th-century Bohemian settlement include a blacksmith and farmhouse, as well as the older 15th-century Bethlehemskirche. There's even a horse-and-carriage business still in operation, and the square regularly holds traditional events including a Christmas craft market.

Sight & Museums

Hufeisensiedlung
Lowise-Reuter-Ring (no phone). U7 Parchimer Allee. **Open** 24hrs daily. **Admission** free.
Heading far south into Britz, you'll find this vast housing estate, one of Berlin's six modernist estates listed as a UNESCO World Heritage Site. Built in the late 1920s by Bruno Taut and Martin Wagner, with some of the Garden City movement's ideals, the large horseshoe-shaped building contains 1,200 flats overlooking a large green space. Many of the flats retain their original Bauhaus fittings and distinctive brightly coloured doors.

Restaurants & Cafés

€ Café Rix
Karl-Marx-Strasse 141 (686 9020, www.caferix. de). U7 Karl-Marx-Strasse. **Open** 9am-midnight Mon-Thur; 9am-1am Fri, Sat; 10am-midnight Sun. **Main courses** €2-€9. **No credit cards.** **Map** p149 D4 ❷ Café
Hidden behind the noisy shopping street of Karl-Marx-Strasse is this oasis – a grand café housed in a former 19th-century ballroom. There's a lovely courtyard where you can enjoy a coffee and cake or their breakfast menu, which is served until 5pm.

€ Café Vux
Wipperstrasse 14 (no phone, www.vux-berlin. com). U7, S41, S42, S45, S46, S47 Neukölln. **Open** noon-7pm Wed-Sat; noon-6pm Sun. **No credit cards.** Café
This Brazilian-run café brings to mind a twee tea parlour. Enjoy incredible vegan versions of classics such as black forest gateau and coconut cheesecake.

Lava
Flughafenstrasse 46 (2234 6908, www.lava-berlin. de). U8 Boddinstrasse. **Open** 1-11pm daily. **Main courses** €7-€13.50. **Map** p149 C3 ❸ Bistro
Originally the deli of Lavanderia Vecchia (*see below*), this emerald-green offshoot has matured into a fine restaurant of its own under head chef Mathias Bartelmes. The artfully presented menu of classics includes the likes of french onion soup, salmon in an olive crust, or french toast with rhubarb ice-cream.

Lavanderia Vecchia
Flughafenstrasse 46 (6272 2152, www.lavanderia vecchia.de). U8 Boddinstrasse. **Open** noon-2.30pm, 7pm-midnight Tue-Fri; 7pm-midnight Sat. **Main courses** (lunch) €5.50-€13.50. **Set meal** (dinner) €40. **Map** p149 C3 ❸ Italian

This cute Italian joint has white linen strung along the ceiling, as a nod to the original occupant, a laundry house. Tricky to locate from the street, it's in a courtyard behind their newer trattoria, Lava (*see p154*). There's just one set menu for dinner (booking essential), costing a very reasonable €40 a head. Changing weekly, it features lots of classic antipasti (*vitello tonnato*, squid salad, sardines), followed by a pasta starter and homely mains, and accompanied by a choice of wines from the Sabina region of Italy.

La Pecora Nera

Herrfurthplatz 6 (6883 2676, www.pecoraberlin. de). U8 Boddinstrasse. **Open** 6pm-late Tue-Sun. **Main courses** €7.50-€13. **No credit cards.** **Map** p149 D2 ⓷ Italian

Schillerkiez really upped its restaurant game with the arrival of La Pecora Nera, a charming Venetian place with extremely reasonable prices. They make their own *bigoli*, a buckwheat pasta particular to the Veneto region, and Aperol spritz costs just €2.50 from 6pm to 7pm daily.

€ Rundstück Warm

Okerstrasse 40 (5485 6849). U8 Leinestrasse. **Open** 4-11pm Tue-Sun. **No credit cards.** **Main courses** €3.50-€5.50. **Map** p149 D3 ⓸ Burgers

Lava.

Headed by an excellent Guatemalan chef, this little burger place adjoins a larger bar next door. Spanish tiles line the wall, and charred padrón peppers are available as a side to the juicy burgers, as are homemade chilli sauces of varying intensity.

€ Zsa Zsa & Louis

Richardstrasse 103 (0157 7153 1002 mobile). *U7 Karl-Marx-Strasse.* **Open** noon-late daily. **Main courses** €6-€8.50. **No credit cards.** **Map** p149 D4 ⓺ Burgers

Started by one of the three owners of the ever-popular Kimchi Princess (*see p133*), this outfit serves doorstop sandwiches, including their spin on *vitello tonnato* – sliced veal, tuna mayo and cress – and Time for Fiesta, with chorizo, manchego, a fried egg and aïoli.

Bars & Pubs

Bierbaroness

Braunschweigerstrasse 46 (8669 1699). U7, S41, S42, S45, S46, S47 Neukölln. **Open** 9pm-3am daily. **No credit cards.**

This Canadian-owned dive bar attracts regulars heavy on the facial hair and even heavier on the bonhomie. There's free pool, a no-cocktails policy and the indie DJs double up as masseurs.

★ Circus Lemke

Selchower Strasse 31 (no phone). U8 Boddinstrasse. **Open** noon-10pm Mon-Fri; 10am-10pm Sat, Sun. **No credit cards.** **Map** p149 D2 ⓴

Doing double service as a café serving brunches by day and a cocktail bar come the evening, Circus Lemke's wooden furniture accommodates a crowd of welcoming regulars.

Shops & Services

★ Blutwurst Manufaktur

Karl-Marx-Platz 9-11 (687 2004, www.blutwurst manufaktur.de). U7 Karl-Marx-Strasse. **Open** 8am-6pm Mon-Fri; 8am-1pm Sat. **Map** p149 D4 ⓱ Food & drink

Rixdorf's award-winning butcher Markus Benser sells all sorts of pork products, both fresh and cured, and is also a great place to source game, but it's his creamy blood sausage that draws the crowds. He's even been inducted into the ancient French order of the Knights of the Boudin Noir.

Fantasiakulisse

Flughafenstrasse 32 (0178 335 7354 mobile, www.fantasiakulisse.de). U8 Boddinstrasse. **Open** 10am-6pm Mon-Fri; or by appointment **No credit cards.** **Map** p149 C3 ⓲ Gifts & souvenirs

Flughafenstrasse is junk-shop central, and Fantasiakulisse is a particular gem, rammed full of the eccentric owner's film memorabilia, theatre props and mannequin collection.

EXPLORE

Other Districts

As it consists of two cities – once divided and now fused back together – it's not surprising that Berlin sprawls for miles in every direction. Although most of the fun stuff is in the gentrified East and the key sites are in the centre, exploring the outlying boroughs – especially perennial upcomer Wedding and the bucolic Grünewald – is well worth the effort. Berlin's diversity is best appreciated by spending time at the peripheries. If the distances look daunting on a map, remember that the capital's late 19th-century expansion into a hinterland of lakes and forests coincided with the age of railways, which means that public transport will whisk you to most of the far-flung districts.

Gedenkstätte Berliner Mauer.

Don't Miss

1 **Vagabund Brauerei** Drink craft beer as it should be drunk: direct from the brewery pub (p159).

2 **Gedenkstätte Berliner Mauer** This memorial walk brings to life the awful trauma of a divided city (p158).

3 **Grunewald** Outdoor fun with forest, lakes and Cold War sites (p162).

4 **Berliner Teufelsberg** Abandoned ex-spy station with a stunning city view (p163).

5 **Du Bonheur** Macaroons in every flavour imaginable (p159).

North

WEDDING

The working-class industrial district of Wedding, formerly on the western side of the Wall, is now politically part of Mitte. Few visitors venture very far into its largely grim vastness. Continually being hailed as the next area for gentrification, its low rents have encouraged artists to move their studios here but it hasn't really seen anything like the restaurant or bar scene of places such as Neukölln.

Apart from a couple of low-key attractions, the big draw is one of the few remaining stretches of the Wall, at the **Gedenkstätte Berliner Mauer** (Berlin Wall Memorial). The area is home to a large African community and also Turkish, Chinese and Arabic residents, giving it a refreshingly multicultural feel.

Sights & Museums

FREE Anti-Kriegs-Museum

Brüsseler Strasse 21 (4549 0110, tours 402 8691, www.anti-kriegs-museum.de). U9 Amrumer Strasse. **Open** 4-8pm daily. **Admission** free. **Map** p305 H2.

The original Anti-War Museum was founded in 1925 by Ernst Friedrich, author of *War Against War*. In 1933, it was destroyed by the Nazis, and Friedrich fled to Brussels. He had another museum there from 1936 to 1940, when the Nazis again destroyed his work. In 1982, a group of teachers including Tommy Spree, Friedrich's grandson, re-established this museum in West Berlin. It now hosts films, discussions, lectures and exhibitions, as well as a permanent display that takes in World War I photos and artefacts from the original museum, children's war toys, information on German colonialism in Africa and pieces of anti-Semitic material from the Nazi era. Admission to the museum is free, but donations are welcome.

FREE Gedenkstätte Berliner Mauer

Bernauer Strasse 111 (467 986 666, www. berliner-mauer-gedenkstaette.de). U8 Bernauer Strasse, or S1, S2 Nordbahnhof. **Open** *Documentation centre* Apr-Oct 9.30am-7pm Tue-Sun. Nov-Mar 9.30am-6pm Tue-Sun. **Admission** free. **Map** p306 M4.

Immediately upon reunification, the city bought this stretch of the Wall on Bernauer Strasse to keep as a memorial. Impeccably restored, including death strip, watch tower and border fortifications, it's the best place to get a sense of just how brutally Berlin was severed in two. On this particular street, neighbours woke up one morning to find themselves in a different country from those on the opposite side of the road, as soldiers brandishing bricks and mortar started to build what the East German government referred to as the 'Anti-Fascist Protection Wall'.

Start off at the visitor centre by Nordbahnhof, but don't miss the excellent documentation centre across the street from the Wall, which includes a very good aerial video following the route of the Wall in 1990: it's the best chance you have of really getting your head around it. From the centre's tower, you can look down over the Wall and the Kapelle der Versöhnung (Chapel of Reconciliation). The Gedenkstätte is a work in progress; eventually, the trustees hope to extend along 1.4 kilometres (nearly a mile) of the former border strip.

Further down the road in the old Nordbahnhof station is an excellent exhibition, 'Border Stations and Ghost Stations in Divided Berlin', which tells the story of how East Germany closed down and then fiercely guarded stations through which West German trains travelled during the Cold War.

Restaurants & Cafés

€ Asia Deli

Seestrasse 41 (4508 4219). U6 Seestrasse. **Open** noon-11pm daily. **Main courses** €6-€8.50. **No credit cards. Map** p305 H2. **Chinese**

A closely guarded secret among chilli lovers, Asia Deli keeps unwary tongues away from its scorching dishes by having two menus. The watered-down version is given to non-Chinese diners, so make sure you ask for the 'real' menu. Then you can feast on the Hunanese and Sichuan dishes – steamed fish, pig offal, stir-fried greens – piled high with shredded red chilli and numbing Sichuan peppercorns.

L'Escargot

Brüsseler Strasse 39 (453 1563, www.l-escargot. net). U6 Seestrasse. **Open** 5pm-midnight Tue-Sat. **Main courses** €16-€25. **No credit cards. Map** p305 H2. **French/Italian**

L'Escargot is nothing much from the outside, but a warm welcome awaits within: chef-patron Martino frequently welcomes guests, and will discuss requirements and tastes before bustling into the kitchen. The cooking is a vague mix of French and Sicilian – the house speciality is a vast plate of garlicky snails – but the menu gallops cheerily across western Europe. Allow up to an hour for mains, as he cooks from scratch.

Volta

Brunnenstrasse 73 (0176 7755 6422 mobile, www.dasvolta.com). U8 Voltastrasse. **Open** 6pm-late Mon-Sat. **Main courses** €9.50-€16. **No credit cards. Map** p306 M3. **Gastropub**

The space ticks all the usual hipster boxes: exposed concrete walls, low-hanging industrial lamps and a long, makeshift wooden bar. Everyone raves about the Volta burger, a solid wodge of rare mince doused in a spicy barbecue sauce, tucked inside a sesame brioche bun. It comes crowned with a couple of onion rings and a local Spreewald gherkin, and hand-cut fries on the side.

Bars & Cafes

Moritz Bar

Adolfstrasse 17 (680 7670, http://moritzbar.com). U6, S41, S42 Wedding. **Open** 7pm-late daily. **No credit cards. Map** p306 K2.

Wedding's very own living-room bar, complete with upcycled wooden counter, Augustiner by the bottle and assorted vintage furniture. The south German brothers who run the place offer special events such as a weekly vegan food night, gay student Mondays and communal viewings of cult German TV detective series *Tatort*.

Vagabund Brauerei

Antwerpener Strasse 3 (5266 7668, www. vagabundbrauerei.com). U6 Seestrasse. **Open** 5pm-late daily. **No credit cards. Map** p306 J1.

Three old friends from Maryland have fulfilled their dream of starting a craft brewery thanks to a wildly successful crowdfunding initiative. They run a homely taproom at the microbrewery, with a rotating menu of beers that includes their own punchy Imperial IPA and unctuous Coffee Stout, as well as local guests from the likes of Heiden Peter and Eschenbräu.

Shops & Services

Du Bonheur

Brunnenstrasse 39 (5659 1955, www.dubonheur. de). U6 Französische Strasse. **Open** 8am-7pm Mon-Fri; 9am-7pm Sat, Sun. **Map** p307 N3. **Food & drink**

Anna Plagens trained under Pierre Hermé himself, the man credited with fetishising the macaroon at Fauchon, Ladurée and now under his own brand name. Unsurprisingly, Du Bonheur's macaroons are pretty spectacular, with fillings such as orange, salted caramel and liquorice. The buttery croissants are made daily, and they also do classics such as paris-brest, a circular choux ring filled with praline cream, as well as elegant birthday cakes with raspberry, chocolate cream and meringue.

West

SPANDAU

Berlin's western neighbour and eternal rival, Spandau is a little Baroque town that seems to contradict everything about the city of which it is now, reluctantly, a part. Spandauers still talk about 'going into Berlin' when they head off to the rest of the city. Berliners, meanwhile, basically consider Spandau to be part of west Germany, though travelling there is easy on the U7, alighting at either Zitadelle or Altstadt Spandau, depending on which sights you want to visit. There's nothing thrilling to see, but it makes for a low-key escape from the city.

The **Zitadelle** (Citadel) contains in one of its museums Spandau's original town charter, dating from 1232, a fact Spandauers have used ever since to argue their historical primacy over Berlin. The old town centre is mostly pedestrianised, with 18th-century townhouses interspersed with chain burger joints and department stores. One of the prettiest buildings is the former Gasthof zumStern

Zitadelle. *See p160.*

in Carl-Schurz-Strasse; older still are houses in Kinkelstrasse and Ritterstrasse – but the best preserved district is north of Am Juliusturm in the area bounded by Hoher Steinweg, Kolk and Behnitz. Steinweg contains a fragment of the old town wall from the first half of the 14th century; Kolk has the Alte Marienkirche (1848); and in Behnitz, at no.5, stands the elegant Baroque **Heinemannsche Haus**. In Reformationsplatz, the **Nikolaikirche** has a brick nave dating from 1410-50; the west tower was added in 1468, and there were later enhancements by Schinkel.

One of the most pleasant times to visit is Christmas, when the market square houses a life-size Nativity scene with real sheep and the famous Christmas market is in full swing.

Many will know the name Spandau from its association with Rudolf Hess. Hitler's deputy, who flew to Britain in 1940 for reasons that are still disputed, was held in the Allied prison here after the Nuremberg trials, and remained here (alone after 1966) until his suicide in 1987 at the age of 93. The prison, a 19th-century brick building at Wilhelmstrasse 21-24, was then demolished to make way for a supermarket for the British forces. Some distance south of Spandau is the **Luftwaffenmuseum der Bundeswehr Berlin-Gatow**.

Sights & Museums

FREE Luftwaffenmuseum der Bundeswehr Berlin-Gatow

Kladower Damm 182, Gatow (3687 2601, www.luftwaffenmuseum.de). U7 Rathaus Spandau then bus 135, then 20mins walk.
Open 10am-6pm Tue-Sun. **Admission** free.
For propeller heads only, this museum is on the far western fringes of the city at what was formerly the RAF base in divided Berlin; it's a long journey by public transport followed by a 20-minute walk from the bus stop (or you can get a cab from the U-bahn station). Then there's a lot more walking to take in more than 100 aircraft scattered around the airfield, plus exhibits in two hangars and the former control tower. The emphasis is on the history of military aviation in Germany since 1945, although there's also a World War I triplane, a restored Handley Page Hastings (as used during the Berlin Airlift) and a whole lot of missiles.

Zitadelle

Am Juliusturm 64 (354 9440, tours 334 6270, www.zitadelle-spandau.net). U7 Zitadelle. **Open** 10am-5pm daily. **Admission** €4.50; €2.50 reductions. **No credit cards**.
The bulk of the Zitadelle was constructed between 1560 and 1594, in the style of an Italian fort, to dominate the confluence of the Spree and Havel rivers. Since then it has been used as everything from a garrison to a prison to a poison-gas laboratory. The

Brauhaus Spandau.

oldest structure here (and the oldest secular building in Berlin) is the Juliusturm, probably dating back to an Ascanian fortress from about 1160. The present tower was home until 1919 to 120-million goldmarks, a small part of the five billion paid as French reparations to Germany in 1874 after the Franco-Prussian War. There are two museums within the Zitadelle: one tells the story of the building with models and maps; the other covers local history. *Photo p159.*

Restaurants & Cafés

Brauhaus Spandau
Neuendorferstrasse 1 (353 9070, www.brauhaus-spandau.de). U7 Altstadt Spandau. **Open** 4pm-midnight Mon; 11am-midnight Tue-Thur; 11am-1am Fri, Sat; 10am-midnight Sun. **Main courses** €6.50-€14.50. **German**
This large beer hall is about as German as they come: a large dining room with gallery, big hunks of pork and potato on the plate and mugfuls of frothy home-brewed beer. The food is stodgy but hits the spot, and they have dark, light and seasonal beers, which you can order in a gut-busting litre glass.

Satt & Selig
Carl-Schurz-Strasse 47 (3675 3877, www.satt-undselig.de). U7 Altstadt Spandau. **Open** 9am-11pm daily. **Main courses** €8-€18. **German**
Housed in an 18th-century inn, this restaurant with an outdoor terrace is a useful spot for a reviving coffee after a turn around Spandau's old town. The food is serviceable, with many meat, sauce and carb combos, as well as snacks such as nachos.

South-west

ZEHLENDORF & THE DAHLEM MUSEUMS

South-west Berlin contains some of the city's wealthiest suburbs, and in the days of division was the American sector, from which various landmarks survive. A major draw is the museums at Dahlem, including the world-class **Ethnologisches Museum** (Ethnological Museum). In the same building are the **Museum für Asiatische Kunst** (Museum of Asian Art) and the **Museum Europäischer Kulturen** (Museum of European Cultures).

Dahlem is also home to the **Freie Universität**, some of whose departments occupy former villas seized by the Nazis from their Jewish owners. North-west of the U-Bahn station, opposite the Friedhof Dahlem-Dorf (cemetery), is the **Domäne Dahlem** working farm – a great place to take kids.

Ten minutes' walk east from Dahlem along Königin-Luise-Strasse is the **Botanischer**

Botanischer Garten

Garten & Botanisches Museum (Botanical Garden & Museum), while following the same street for a kilometre or so westwards brings you to the edge of the **Grunewald** (*see p162*).

Sights & Museums

Botanischer Garten & Botanisches Museum
Königin-Luise-Strasse 6-8 (8385 0100, www.botanischergartenberlin.de). S1 Botanischer Garten then 15mins walk. **Open** *Garden* May-July 9am-9pm daily. Apr, Aug 9am-8pm daily. Sept 9-7pm daily. Mar, Oct 9am-6pm daily. Feb 9am-5pm daily. Nov-Jan 9am-4pm daily. *Museum* 10am-6pm daily. **Admission** *Garden & Museum* €6; €3 reductions. *Museum only* €2.50; €1.50 reductions. **No credit cards**.
The Botanical Garden was landscaped at the beginning of the 20th century. Today, it's home to 18,000 plant species, 16 greenhouses and a museum. The gardens make for a pleasant stroll, but the museum is a bit dilapidated and there's no information in English. Every Monday, they run a wild mushroom advice workshop, so feel free to forage away in the nearby forests.

Domäne Dahlem
Königin-Luise-Strasse 49 (666 3000, www.domaene-dahlem.de). U3 Dahlem-Dorf. **Open** *Museum* 10am-6pm Sat, Sun. **Admission** *Museum* €3; €1.50 reductions. **No credit cards**.
On this organic working farm, children can see how life was lived in the 17th century. Craftspeople preserve and teach their skills. It's best to visit during one of the several annual festivals, when kids can ride ponies, tractors and hay wagons. There's also a farm shop and, in good weather, a garden café.

Ethnologisches Museum

*Lansstrasse 8 (266 424242, www.smb.museum/
em). U3 Dahlem-Dorf.* **Open** 10am-5pm Tue-Fri;
11am-6pm Sat, Sun. **Admission** €6; €3 reductions.
The Ethnological Museum is a stunner: extensive,
authoritative, and beautifully laid out and lit.
It encompasses cultures from Oceania, Central
America and Africa to the Far East. Only the true
ethno-fan should attempt to see it all, but no one
should miss the Südsee (South Sea) room. Here,
you'll find New Guinean masks and effigies, and
a remarkable collection of original canoes and
boats – some huge and elaborate. The African
rooms are also impressive; look out for the superb
carvings from Benin and the Congo, and beaded
artefacts from Cameroon. An enlightening small
display explores the influence of African art on the
German expressionists.

Two other institutions are housed in the same
building. The Museum of Asian Art features
archaeological objects and works of fine art from
India, Japan, China and Korea, from the early Stone
Age to the present; while the Museum of European
Cultures covers European everyday culture from
the 18th century to the present. One highlight is a
mechanical model of the Nativity, displayed during
Advent. Audio guides in English are available.

Restaurants & Cafés

Krasselts

*Steglitzer Damm 22 (796 9147, www.krasselts-
berlin.de). U9, S1 Rathaus Steglitz.* **Open** 9am-
midnight Mon-Sat; 10am-midnight Sun. **Main
courses** €3-€5. Imbiss
Still family-run, Krasselts has been knocking out
the Berlin street-food classic of Currywurst for over
half a century. They closely guard their secret sauce
recipe and grind and stuff all their own sausages.
East Germans traditionally ate their sausage with
skin (pig intestine), but these days the distinction has
mostly disappeared. Enjoy at a standing table with a
side of fries or a crusty white roll.

Luise

*Königin-Luise-Strasse 40-42 (841 8880, www.
luise-dahlem.de). U3 Dahlem-Dorf.* **Open** 10am-
1am daily. **Main courses** €4-€15. Brasserie
This traditional Berlin brasserie does all sorts, with a
pizza menu (the buffalo mozzarella is made locally in
Brandenburg), German snacks such as Currywurst,
and breakfast too. It's near the Freie Universität, so
the large beer garden gets packed with students.

Xochimilco Café

*Steglitzer Damm 19 (6431 8770, www.xochimilco-
cafe.de). U9, S1 Rathaus Steglitz.* **Open** 8.30am-
6.30pm Mon-Fri; 9am-2pm Sat. **Main courses**
€3-€4.50. Café
Opened in 2013 by a German-Mexican couple, and
named after an area of Mexico City, Xochimilco has

planted the third-wave coffee flag firmly in Steglitz.
Colourful Aztec masks adorn the walls, and you can
snack on sandwiches, soup or fiery chilli con carne.

GRUNEWALD

The western edge of Zehlendorf is formed by
the Havel river and the extensive Grunewald, the
largest of Berlin's many forests. Due to its easy
accessibility by S-Bahn, its lanes and pathways
fill with walkers, runners, cyclists and horse
riders on weekends. There are several restaurants
next to the station, and on the other side of the
motorway at Schmetterlingsplatz, which are
open from April to October.

One popular destination is the **Teufelsee**,
a tiny lake packed with nudist bathers (and
mosquitos) in summer, reached by heading west
from the station along Schildhornweg for 15
minutes. Close by is the legendary **Teufelsberg**,
a by-product of wartime devastation – a railway
was laid from Wittenbergplatz to carry the 25
million cubic metres of rubble that eventually
became Berlin's highest point. There are great
views from the summit and the eerie abandoned
spy structure atop it. There has been talk of
replacing the Cold War-era, US electronic
listening post on it with some kind of hotel
and conference centre, but, for now, you can
take tours of the spooky site.

South of the station, at the far end of the
Grunewaldsee, the 16th-century **Jagdschloss
Grunewald** (Grunewald Hunting Lodge) is
an example of the kind of building that once
maintained the country life of the landed gentry,
the Prussian Junkers. A few kilometres away
is the **Alliierten Museum** (Allied Museum)
on Clayallee. A kilometre north of here is the
Brücke-Museum, housing a collection of
expressionist paintings and prints.

Further south, **Krumme Lanke** and
Schlachtensee are pleasantly clear urban
lakes along the south-eastern edge of the
Grunewald, perfect for picnicking, swimming
or rowing – and each with its own train station.
There's a particularly lovely beer garden and
restaurant at Schlachtensee.

On the west side of the Grunewald, halfway up
Havelchaussee, is the **Grunewaldturm**, a tower
built in 1897 in memory of Wilhelm I. It has an
observation platform 105 metres (344 feet) above
the lake, with expansive views as far as Spandau
and Potsdam. There's a restaurant at the base,
and another over the road, both with garden
terraces. A short walk south along Havelufer
leads to the ferry to **Lindwerder Insel** (island),
which also has a restaurant. To the north, a little
way into the forest, ex-Velvet Underground
singer Nico, who grew up in Schöneberg, is
buried among the trees in the **Friedhof
Grunewald-Forest**.

Sights & Museums

FREE Alliierten Museum

Clayallee 135, at Huttenweg (818 1990, www. alliiertenmuseum.de). U3 Oskar-Helene-Heim then 10mins walk, or bus 115. **Open** 10am-6pm Tue-Sun. **Admission** free.

The Allies arrived as conquerors, kept West Berlin alive during the 1948 Airlift and finally went home in 1994. In what used to be a US Forces cinema, the Allied Museum is mostly about the period of the Blockade and Airlift, documented with photos, tanks, jeeps, planes, weapons and uniforms. Outside is the former guardhouse from Checkpoint Charlie and an RAF Hastings TG 503 plane. Guided tours in English can be booked in advance.

Berliner Teufelsberg

Teufelsseechaussee 10 (0163 858 5096 mobile, http://berliner-teufelsberg.com). **Open** *Tours* noon-4pm daily. **Tickets** €7-€15; €8 reductions; free under-14s. Under-18s must be accompanied by an adult. **No credit cards**.

During the Cold War, the Allies built this listening station on the top of one of Berlin's highest hills to eavesdrop on what the East Germans were up to on the other side of the Wall. The site was abandoned when the Iron Curtain fell, and soon became a favourite spot for urban explorers and ravers looking for a trippy place to throw an open-air party. The days of illegally exploring the site are now over, with city-sanctioned guided tours taking you through the decrepit structure, its varied history, the stunning view over the city and the unnerving acoustics of the giant radar dome.

Brücke-Museum

Bussardsteig 9 (831 2029, www.bruecke-museum. de). U3 Oskar-Helene-Heim then bus 115. **Open** 11am-5pm Mon, Wed-Sun. **Admission** €5; €3 reductions. **No credit cards**.

This small but satisfying museum is dedicated to the work of Die Brücke (The Bridge), a group of expressionist painters that was founded in Dresden in 1905 before moving to Berlin. A large collection of oils, watercolours, drawings and sculptures by the main members of the group – Schmidt-Rottluff, Heckel, Kirchner, Mueller and Pechstein – is rotated in temporary exhibitions.

Restaurants & Cafés

Fischerhütte am Schlachtensee

Fischerhüttenstrasse 136 (8049 8310, www. fischerhuette-berlin.de). U1 Krumme Lanke or S1 Mexikoplatz. **Open** 10am-midnight daily. **Main courses** €14-€30. **German**

Overlooking the lake is the Fischerhütte, housing both a large beer garden and a more formal restaurant inside. It was built in the mid 18th century as a rest house on the road between Berlin and Potsdam (the official residence of the Prussian kings). The restaurant has plenty of old photos from its heyday in the 1920s, when these lakes were Berlin's answer to the French Riviera.

WANNSEE & PFAUENINSEL

At the south-west edge of the Grunewald, you'll find boats and beaches in summer, and castles and forests all through the year. **Strandbad Wannsee** is the largest inland beach in Europe. Between May and September, there are boats, pedalos and two-person hooded wicker sunchairs called *Strandkorb* for hire, a playground and a separate section for nudists. Service buildings house showers, toilets, cafés, shops and kiosks.

EXPLORE

Fischerhütte am Schlachtensee.

The waters of the Havel (the Wannsee is an inlet of the river) are extensive and in summer warm enough for comfortable swimming; there's a strong current, though, so don't stray beyond the floating markers. A small bridge north of the beach leads to Schwanenwerder, once the exclusive private island retreat of Goebbels and now home to the Aspen Institute, an international think-tank.

The town of Wannsee to the south is clustered around the bay of the Grosser Wannsee and is dominated by a long promenade, Am Grossen Wannsee, scattered with hotels and fish restaurants. On the west side of the bay is the **Gedenkstätte Haus der Wannsee-Konferenz**. At this elegant Gründerzeit mansion – now a museum – a group of prominent Nazis met in January 1942 to lay out their monstrous 'Final Solution' for the extermination of the Jewish race.

A short distance from S-Bahn Wannsee along Bismarckstrasse is a little garden where German dramatist Heinrich von Kleist shot himself in 1811; the beautiful view of Kleiner Wannsee was the last thing he wanted to see.

On the other side of the railway tracks is **Düppler Forst**, a forest with a nature reserve at Grosses Fenn at the south-western end. If you travel three S-Bahn stops to Mexikoplatz, then catch the 118 or 622, you'll reach the reconstructed 14th-century village at **Museumsdorf Düppel**.

From Wannsee, bus 218 scoots through the forest to a pier on the Havel, from where it's a brief ferry ride to **Pfaueninsel**. This island was inhabited in prehistoric times, but isn't mentioned in archives until 1683. In 1685, the Grand Elector presented it to Johann Kunckel von Löwenstein, a chemist who experimented with alchemy but instead of gold produced 'ruby glass' (examples of which are on view in the castle on the island).

It was only at the start of the Romantic era that the island's windswept charms began to attract more serious interest. In 1793, Friedrich Wilhelm II purchased it and built a castle for his mistress, but he died in 1797 before they had a chance to move in. Its first residents were Friedrich Wilhelm III and Queen Luise, who spent much of their time together on the island, even setting up a farm there. A royal menagerie was later developed. Most of the animals were moved to the new Tiergarten Zoo in 1842; now peacocks, pheasants, parrots, goats and sheep remain. Surviving structures include the Jakobsbrunnen (Jacob's Fountain), a copy of a Roman temple; the Kavalierhaus (Cavalier's House), built in 1803 from an original design by Schinkel; and the Swiss cottage, also based on a Schinkel plan. All are linked by winding paths laid out in the English manner by Peter Joseph Lenné. A walk around the island – with its monumental trees, rough meadows and views over the Havel – provides one of the most complete sensations of escape to be had within the borders of Berlin.

Back on the mainland, a short walk south along Nikolskoer Weg is the **Blockhaus Nikolskoe** (805 2914, www.blockhaus-nikolskoe.de), a huge wooden chalet built in 1819 by Friedrich Wilhelm II for his daughter Charlotte, and named after her husband, the future Tsar Nicholas of Russia. There's a magnificent view from the terrace, where you can sit back and enjoy some reasonable Berlin dishes or coffee and cakes.

Sights & Museums

FREE Gedenkstätte Haus der Wannsee-Konferenz
Am Grossen Wannsee 56-58 (805 0010, www.ghwk.de). S1, S7 Wannsee then bus 114. **Open** 10am-6pm daily. **Admission** free.
On 20 January 1942, a group of leading Nazis, chaired by Heydrich, gathered here to draw up plans for the Final Solution. Today, this infamous villa has been converted into the Wannsee Conference Memorial House, a place of remembrance, with a photo exhibit on the conference and its genocidal consequences. Call in advance if you want to join an English-language tour, though the information is in both English and German.

Museumsdorf Düppel
Clauertstrasse 11 (802 6671, www.dueppel.de). S1 Mexikoplatz then bus 118, 622. **Open** *Apr-Oct* 10am-5pm Sat, Sun. **Admission** €3; free-€1.50 reductions. **No credit cards.**
At this reconstructed 14th-century village, built around archaeological excavations, workers demonstrate medieval handicrafts, technology and farming techniques. Kids can enjoy ox-cart rides.

Strandbad Wannsee.

Köpenick.

GLIENICKE

West of Wannsee, and only a couple of kilometres from Potsdam, Glienicke was once the south-westernmost tip of West Berlin. The suspension bridge over the Havel here was named **Brücke der Einheit** (Bridge of Unity) because it joined Potsdam with Berlin. After the building of the Wall, it was painted different shades of olive green on the East and West sides, and used only by Allied soldiers and for top-level prisoner and spy exchanges – Anatoly Shcharansky was one of the last, in 1986.

The main reason to come here is **Park Glienicke**. Its centrepiece is **Schloss Glienicke** (not open to the public), originally a hunting lodge designed by Schinkel for Prinz Carl von Preussen, who adorned the garden walls with ancient relics collected on his Mediterranean holidays, and decided to simulate a walk from the Alps to Rome in the densely wooded park. The summer houses, fountains and follies are all based on original Italian models, and the woods and fields around them make an ideal place for a Sunday picnic, since this park is little visited. At the nearby inlet of Moorlake, there's a restaurant in an 1842 hunting lodge.

East

KÖPENICK

The name Köpenick is derived from the Slavonic *copanic*, meaning 'place on a river'. The old town, around 15 kilometres (nine miles) south-east of Mitte, stands at the confluence of the Spree and Dahme, and, having escaped bombing, decay and development by the GDR, still maintains much of its 18th-century character. This is one of the most sought-after areas of East Berlin, with handsome shops, cafés and restaurants clustered around the old centre. With its historic buildings and extensive riverfront, it's a fine place for a Sunday afternoon wander.

The imposing **Rathaus** (Town Hall) is a good example of Wilhelmine civic architecture. It was here in 1906, two years after the building's completion, that Wilhelm Voigt, an unemployed cobbler who'd spent half his life in jail, dressed up as an army captain and ordered a detachment of soldiers to accompany him into the Treasury, where they emptied the town coffers. He instantly entered popular folklore. Carl Zuckmeyer immortalised him in a play as Der Hauptmann von Köpenick (Captain of Köpenick) and the Kaiser eventually pardoned him because he'd proven the absolute obedience of the Prussian soldiery. His theft is re-enacted every June during the Köpenicker summer festival.

Close by, on a man-made island, is the grand white complex of **Schloss Köpenick** (1677-90), with a medieval drawbridge, Renaissance gateway and Baroque chapel.

Sights & Museums

Schloss Köpenick

Schlossinsel 1 (266 424242, www.smb.museum/sk). S47 Spindlersfeld. **Open** *Apr-Sept* 11am-6pm Tue-Sun. *Oct-Mar* 11am-5pm Thur-Sun. **Admission** €6; €3 reductions.
Items from the Kunstgewerbemuseum (Museum of Decorative Arts) are presented as Raumkunst (Room Art): furniture and decorative art from the Renaissance, Baroque and rococo eras are arranged according to period beneath carefully restored ceiling paintings. There's also an exhibition on the history of the island, plus a riverside café.

EXPLORE

IN THE KNOW
FRIEDRICHSHAGEN
& THE MÜGGELSEE

A couple of kilometres east of Köpenick, the village of Friedrichshagen has retained its independent character. The main street, Bölschestrasse, is lined with steep-roofed Brandenburg houses and ends at the shores of a large lake, the Grösser Müggelsee. Friedrichshagen is particularly enjoyable when the Berliner Burgerbräu brewery, family-owned since 1869, throws open its gates for its annual summer celebration. Stalls line Bölschestrasse, the brewery lays on music and people lounge about on the lake shore with cold beers. Boat tours are available, and the Bräustübl restaurant, next to the brewery, serves good Berlin cuisine.

Arts & Entertainment

Children

Despite its reputation for grown-up hedonism, Berlin is a remarkably child-friendly city. Apartment buildings dominate in Berlin, making gardens a costly luxury, but there are parks all over town – most with the usual swings and roundabouts, some with fantastic wooden adventure playgrounds. At all of Berlin's national museums, under-19s enjoy free admission. Many also have decent children's sections, and tickets to one kids' attraction often include a discount voucher for another. There are also superb indoor and outdoor swimming pools in which to cool off during the summer months, and cosy cafés with dry play areas for rainy days.

To find out what's on for children, pick up *Tip* or *Zitty*, Berlin's fortnightly listings magazines, and look under the 'Kinder' or 'Familie' section.

GETTING AROUND

Children under six travel free on Berlin's excellent public transport system. That's the good news. The bad news is that many stations still don't have lifts, so you'll either need to carry buggies upstairs yourself or rely on the kindness of strangers – and Berliners are not known for their altruism. Buses, however, are a breeze. They are designed to tilt towards the pavement at each stop, making it easy to get on with a pushchair or pram, and all vehicles have a designated parking area for *Kinderwagen*. The M100 and M200 buses are usually double-decker and run past all the key tourist destinations. Kids love sitting on the top deck and parents love the price – just the cost of a normal single transport ticket.

For older children, cycling is an option. There are cycle lanes all over town and off-road paths weaving through the city's parks. **Fat Tire Bikes** (Panoramastrasse 1A, Alexanderplatz, Mitte, 2404 7991, www.berlinfahrradverleih.com) rents out children's bikes, as well as bike trailers.

BABYSITTERS

The bigger hotels sometimes have a babysitting service, but there are also a number of English-speaking agencies operating in Berlin.

Babysitter-Express Berlin
4000 3400, www.babysitter-express.de.
This firm operates a 24-hour hotline for all your babysitting emergencies.

Kinderinsel
Eichendorffstrasse 17, Mitte (4171 6928, 4171 6938, www.kinderinsel.de/en). U6 Naturkundemuseum, or S1, S2, S25 Nordbahnhof. **Map** p306 M4.
This 'children's hotel' offers round-the-clock childcare for babes up to 14s. They can also send sitters to your hotel or home.

IN THE KNOW
QUIET AT THE BACK

Don't be surprised if you receive some unsolicited parenting advice. Berliners tolerate children, but do not indulge them like the Spanish or Italians, and will not be shy to tell you where you're going wrong – whether it's allowing your child to eat crisps or failing to keep them quiet on a bus.

BERLIN BY AREA
Mitte

There's no problem keeping children busy in Mitte. **Museumsinsel** (*see p44*), with its vast museums and weekend flea market, is a lively spot to visit. The **Bode Museum** (*see p48*) is particularly good for kids – it houses a special interactive children's museum (Kindermuseum) aimed at four- to ten-year-olds. Nearby **Monbijou Park** on Oranienburger Strasse – just over the pedestrian bridge by the Bode Museum – has playgrounds and, in summer, a great wading pool, the Kinderbad Monbijou.

For a different perspective, try a boat tour, many of which operate from the Museumsinsel and nearby. For a bird's-eye view, scan the city from the **Fernsehturm** (TV Tower; *see p58*) on Alexanderplatz. Down below, children cool off in the **Neptunbrunnen** (*see p55*) during the summer months. Also at 'Alex', in the otherwise grim Alexa Shopping Centre, is **Loxx Miniature Welten** (4472 3022, www.loxx-berlin.de, open 10am-8pm daily), featuring a working miniature railway that chugs around a scale model of Berlin.

Children will enjoy the dinosaur skeletons and multimedia displays at the **Museum für Naturkunde** (Museum of Natural History; *see p50*), the mummies at the Ägyptisches Museum in the **Neues Museum** (*see p50*) and the interactive exhibits at the **Museum für Kommunikation** (*see p50*). For a pricier treat, there's the **Legoland Discovery Centre** (www.legolanddiscoverycentre.de/berlin) in the

MountMitte.

basement of the Sony Center at Potsdamer Platz. Focused on kids aged three to ten and divided into seven themed areas, it's more of an indoor playground than an educational experience.

AquaDom & Sea Life (*see p56*) has 13 aquaria and plenty of hands-on gadgetry. Its centrepiece is the mighty AquaDom itself, a cylindrical saltwater tank with a glass lift rising through the centre, from which you can view numerous exotic fish. **MountMitte** (www.mountmitte.de), an outdoor rope course by Nordbahnhof, is ideal for sevens and up.

Many restaurants in Mitte have children's menus, but the area around Hackesche Höfe and Rosenthaler Strasse offers the richest pickings, with cafés and restaurants of every type. Most places are happy to do half-portions on request.

Prenzlauer Berg & Friedrichshain

Prenzlauer Berg has enjoyed something of a baby boom in recent years, although it has few specific attractions for kids. There are, however, plenty of cafés, restaurants, squares and playgrounds, particularly around Kollwitzplatz and Helmholtzplatz. **Das Spielzimmer** (Schliemannstrasse 37, 4403 7635, www.das-spielzimmer.net) is a very successful combination of indoor playground and café, complete with slides and a dressing-up box. North of Schönhauser Allee station is **Café Milchbart** (Paul-Robeson-Strasse 6, 6630 7755, www.milchbart.net), a family-oriented place with ballpond, climbing frame and excellent healthy food options.

Friedrichshain is slightly less kiddie-tastic, though there are plenty of family-friendly cafés – art centre-cum-café **Amitola** (Krossener Strasse 35, 2936 1871, www.amitola-berlin.de) comes highly recommended. **Paul & Paula** (Richard-Sorge-Strasse 25, 4208 9440, www.paul-und-paula.de), a café and shop rolled into one, is particularly geared up for babies. Older children will love the **Raw Tempel** (Revaler Strasse 99), a sports and arts complex housed in a dilapidated set of old factories that includes **Der Kegel** climbing centre (www.derkegel.de), **Neue Heimat**'s street-food market (www.neueheimat.com) and the **Skatehalle** indoor skateboarding centre (www.skatehalle-berlin.de). The **Computerspielemuseum** (Computer Games Museum; *see p84*) on Karl-Marx-Allee is fun for teenagers.

Die Schaubude (Greifswalder Strasse 81-84, 423 4314, www.schaubude-berlin.de) is a high-quality puppet theatre used by local and visiting troupes. **Machmit!** (Senefelderstrasse 5, 7477 8200, www.machmitmuseum.de) is a modern children's museum with arts and crafts sessions. **Volkspark Friedrichshain** (*see p84*) has half-pipes and skater routes for skaters, and the

Märchenbrunnen ('fairy tale fountain') features figures from stories by the Brothers Grimm. **Holzfabrik** (www.holzmarkt.com) has communal gardens and children's play areas by the river.

Kreuzberg

This vibrant borough has lots to offer kids. Older children will enjoy the **Haus am Checkpoint Charlie** (*see p142*), which displays the old cars and balloons that people used to circumvent the Wall. And they'll love the **Gruselkabinett** (*see p142*), a spooky chamber of horrors in an old World War II bunker. For an expensive but novel vertical adventure, there's the **Berlin Hi-Flyer** (*see p141*), a hot-air balloon that, weather permitting, floats 150 metres (500 feet) above ground near Checkpoint Charlie. The **Deutsches Technikmuseum Berlin** (*see p142*) has vintage locomotives and cars, computers and gadgets, and a maritime wing with boats. Entrance tickets include access to the superb Spectrum and its fantastic hands-on experiments.

Neue City Bowling Hasenheide (Hasenheide 107-109, 622 2038, www.bowling-hasenheide.de) offers a dozen ten-pin bowling lanes for children and is open from 10am daily. The Hasenheide park next door has a great adventure playground, crazy golf course and a small zoo. The little vale in the middle of the park is ideal for tobogganing when it snows.

Leafy **Viktoriapark** (*see p137*) is a landscaped hill with fine views, and another good place for tobogganing when weather permits. In summer, a waterfall cascades down to street level. The park also has playgrounds and a tiny zoo. Some of the best ice-cream in Berlin is just a few blocks north at **Vanille & Marille** (Hagelbergerstrasse 1, www.vanille-marille.de). Stroll down nearby Bergmannstrasse for a wide choice of food options. Close by is the huge supervised indoor playground **Jolo** (Am Tempelhofer Berg 7D, 6120 2796, www.jolo-berlin.de). Facilities include an inflatable mountain, mini bumper cars and a snack bar. One of the nicest children's cafés in Berlin is not far away – **Café Kreuzzwerg** (Hornstrasse 23, 9786 7609, www.cafe-kreuzzwerg.de) has fantastic coffee and loads to keep little ones amused.

A walk along the south bank of the canal on Carl-Herz-Ufer will take you to the **Brachvogel** beer garden (www.brachvogel-berlin.de), which has a crazy golf course and a playground next door. On the other side of the river is the slightly anarchic **Sommerbad Kreuzberg** lido complex (www.berlinerbaeder.de/118.html) with a big children's pool and slide. Further east, on the north bank, is **Statthaus Böcklerpark** with its small petting zoo. It organises a monthly children's flea market, as well as other events. Further east again and back on the south side is child-friendly Italian restaurant **Il Casolare** (Grimmstrasse 30, 6950 6610), which does great pizzas. For dessert, cross the road to **Isabel's Eiscafé** (Böckstrasse 51).

At the east end of the borough is **Görlitzer Park**, with playgrounds and another petting zoo to keep the little ones happy. Also in the

Berlin Hi-Flyer.

Labyrinth Kindermuseum. *See p172.*

park, the indoor glow-in-the-dark mini golf at **Schwarzlicht** (Görlitzer Strasse 1, 6162 1960, www.indoor-minigolf-berlin.de) is a good option for older children, especially in bad weather. Nearby is the **Cabuwazi Zirkus** (Wiener Strasse 59, 5446 9094, www.cabuwazi.de), a big top where children can learn circus skills. There are also performances by a young theatre troupe.

Schöneberg

Winterfeldtplatz is a pleasant focal point at the northern end of this huge district, with lots of cafés, restaurants and fast food places around the square and along Maassenstrasse to the north and Goltzstrasse to the south. There are plenty of parks and playgrounds here.

In the south of the borough, **Natur-Park Schöneberger Südgelände** (www.gruen-berlin.de) is an old railway shunting yard left for nature to reclaim. There's lots for the kids to explore – and no dog mess or crazy cyclists. Nearby is the **Planetarium am Insulaner** (Munsterdamm 90, 790 0930, www.wfs.be.schule.de), which has programmes for children.

The **Volkspark Wilmersdorf** has several good playgrounds (including one with a ski lift ride). Near the park's eastern end is **Stadtbad Schöneberg** (www.berlinerbaeder.de/105.html), a swimming pool that's ideal for kids. Inside the Schöneberg Museum is the **Jugend Museum** (Hauptstrasse 40/42, 902 776 163, www.jugend museum.de), a hands-on children's exhibition that offers small visitors the chance to play with everything from a Germanic sacrificial cow to a Barbie doll.

There are child-friendly restaurants all over Schöneberg. **Emma & Paul Familiencafé** Gleditschstrasse 47, www.emma-paul.de) is a great place to hang out with children and babies – there's a large play area with toys and cushions.

Tiergarten

The major draw in Tiergarten is the park itself, with its playgrounds and open spaces. Pedalos and rowing boats can be hired near the **Café am Neuen See** (*see p99*), which has a great beer garden in summer. Meanwhile, along Strasse des 17 Juni, the main road through the park, there's an interesting weekend flea market, the **Kunst und Trödel Markt** (*see p107*).

In the park's south-western corner is Berlin's beautiful **Zoo** (*see p105*), which used to be the home to the abandoned polar bear Knut (RIP), who is now morbidly stuffed at the Natural History Museum. On rainy days, head for the Zoo's sizeable Aquarium. The excellent **Gemäldegalerie** (*see p104*) runs Sunday afternoon tours for children.

Charlottenburg

Away from the bustle of Zoologischer Garten and the Ku'damm, the atmosphere is pleasant, with good restaurants, shops and markets.

The Saturday market at Karl-August-Platz is a gathering point for families, with a playground and plenty of cafés. If the sun's out, check out **Zwergenland** (Mommsenstrasse 48), a *Snow White and the Seven Dwarves*-themed playground, or **Piratenspielplatz** (Tegeler Weg 97, corner of Bonhoeffer Ufer, www.piraten restaurant.de), a pirate-inspired playground with pirate ship and pirate restaurant.

Fifteen minutes' walk west is the pretty **Lietzenseepark**, with a lake, playgrounds, cafés (open Apr-Oct) and sports areas. There are child-friendly restaurants all over Charlottenburg, particularly to the east. The kids will be welcome for Italian food at **La Cantina** (Bleibtreustrasse 17, 883 2156) or **Totò** (corner of Bleibtreustrasse & Pestalozzistrasse, 312 5449, www.trattoria-toto.de). At **Charlottchen** (Droysenstrasse 1, 324 4717, www.restaurant-charlottchen.de), parents eat in the dining room (the international food is nothing special) while kids let their hair down in a rumpus room. There are theatre performances on Sundays (11.30am, 3.30pm, €5).

The most child-friendly museum in the area is the **Story of Berlin** (*see p115*), probably the only history museum that youngsters won't tire of after ten minutes.

Neukölln

There's the lovely **Nowkoelln Flowmarkt** (*see p152*), the canals and plenty of kid-friendly cafés in Kreuzkölln. Further south is **Britzer Garten** (www.gruen-berlin.de), which is perfect for small children. The immaculately manicured gardens with their once-futuristic architecture look like something out of the *Teletubbies*, and there are farm animals, playgrounds, a narrow-gauge railway, a working 19th-century windmill and plenty of food and drink options.

Other Districts

Budding builders shouldn't miss the massive **Labyrinth Kindermuseum** (Osloer Strasse 12, 800 931 150, www.labyrinth-kindermuseum.de/en) in Wedding. It's an enormous DIY indoor maze made up of wooden walls filled with hands-on installations that help kids learn how things come together. They even teach children to use safety electrical tools.

Naturschutzzentrum Ökowerk.

The **ufaFabrik** cultural centre (Viktoriastrasse 10-18, 755 030, www.ufafabrik.de), in the southern district of Tempelhof, has a farm, several cafés and restaurants, a circus and a variety of courses and workshops. It's right by U-Bahn Ullsteinstrasse (U6).

South-west of the city, the vast **Grunewald** woods (*see p162*) are perfect for long walks, and the Kronprinzessinnenweg, which runs through the middle, is ideal for rollerblading and cycling. On a breezy day, fly a kite and enjoy the view from the **Teufelsberg** (*see p162*); on a sunny day, take a dip in the **Teufelsee** (*see p162*) or visit the wonderful nature park **Naturschutzzentrum Ökowerk** (www.oekowerk.de) just next door. **Strandbad Wannsee** (*see p163*) is Europe's largest inland beach; there's a playground, cafés and pedalos. The 204-step climb up the **Grunewaldturm** (Havelchaussee, 300 0730) is rewarded with a beautiful view of the Havel river and surroundings, and there's a restaurant and beer garden too.

To the east of the Grunewald, **Domäne Dahlem** (*see p161*) is a 1600s-style working farm with demonstrations by blacksmiths, carpenters, bakers and potters, and ponies, tractors and hay wagons to ride. **Museumsdorf Düppel** (*see p164*) is a reconstructed 14th-century village around archaeological excavations near the Düppel forest. From April to October, kids can ride ox carts or witness medieval technology, crafts and farming techniques.

To avoid summer crowds on the Havel and Wannsee, try the **Tegeler See** to the north-west of the centre. North-east of Tegel, in the quaint village of Alt Lübars, is **Jugendfarm Lübars** (415 7027, www.jugendfarm-und-familienfarm-luebars.de), with farm animals and traditional crafts such as bread baking or wool spinning.

South-east of the centre, the **Mellowpark** in Köpenick (Friedrichshagener Strasse 10-12, 652 603 771, www.mellowpark.de) offers supervised play for older children. Activities (daily from 2pm in summer) include skateboarding, basketball and BMX on the banks of the Spree.

Also to the east is the **Tierpark Berlin-Friedrichsfelde** (*see p93*), a lovely park and zoo, with playgrounds, a petting zoo and snack stands. Still further east, the **Müggelsee** (*see p165*) is another beautiful sailing and swimming area. There are day trips by boat from Mitte in the summer.

Out in Marzahn, the **Erholungspark** (Eisenacher Strasse, www.gruen-berlin.de) has oriental gardens, a 'garden of stones' with ponds, fountains and boulders, and a 'rhododendron grove' with statues of characters taken from Hans Christian Andersen and the Brothers Grimm. It's also dotted with playgrounds, kiosks and cafés.

Film

The first cinema opened in Berlin in 1895 and the city was soon full of movie palaces such as the Marmorhaus, with its huge white marble façade; the Lichtburg, which looked like a futuristic light sculpture; and the grandest of them all, the Ufa Palast Am Zoo. The last had an ever-changing façade designed to reflect whatever première it was hosting – sweeping searchlights for Fritz Lang's *Spione*, illuminated Nazi banners for Leni Riefenstahl's *Olympia*, or a spaceship flying across the starlit exterior for Lang's *Frau Im Mond*.

That was then. Now, like almost everywhere, the glory days of cinema-going in Berlin are over. While the city still has an impressive 280-plus screens, most of them show big blockbuster dross. But a healthy alternative film-going scene does exist.

THE CURRENT SCENE

Indie mainstays such as **Eiszeit** and **Central** have recently got their groove back, the **Moviemento** is better than ever, and **Babylon-Mitte** has shaken off its stodgy mindset and spiced up its schedule. And all seem to have English programming more in evidence. For monophones, there are the traditional all-English venues run by Yorck cinemas such as **Odeon**, **Babylon Kreuzberg** and **Rollberg**, and all eight screens at the **Cinestar Potsdamer Platz** show English-language fare.

IN THE KNOW CINE CITY

Every year, more than 100 films are shot on location in the German capital. *Das Leben der Anderen* (*The Lives of Others*) was shot at the old Stasi HQ in Lichtenberg. Jennifer Lawrence fought the system outside Tempelhof airport in *The Hunger Games: Mockingjay*. And when Matt Damon was supposed to be racing through the streets of Moscow in *The Bourne Supremacy*, he was actually legging it through the road tunnel beneath Tiergarten Park.

One surviving Berlin phenomenon is the city's fascination with silent films, often presented with live musical accompaniment. Favourites include historical hits such as *Metropolis* and *The Cabinet of Dr Caligari*. Babylon-Mitte has a regular silent film programme.

There are two film museums: the **Museum für Film und Fernsehen** (*see p104*) on Potsdamer Platz, which includes a special exhibition about Berlin's favourite daughter, Marlene Dietrich; and the **Filmpark Babelsberg**, near Potsdam. Since 2010, Berlin even has its own answer to the Hollywood Walk of Fame, the rather underwhelming Boulevard der Stars on Potsdamer Strasse.

FESTIVALS

The **Berlin International Film Festival**, or **Berlinale** (*see 30; photo p174*), in February, is the biggest and most prominent of the international film festivals, but it's far from the only game in town.

The ten-day **Fantasy Film Festival** (www.fantasyfilmfest.com) shows the latest in fantasy, splatter, horror and sci-fi from the US, Hong Kong, Japan and Europe. Films – most in English or with English subtitles – are often premières, with occasional previews, retrospectives and rarities. It takes place around late August/early September.

Berlinale. *See p173.*

With plenty of cultural subsidies going round, and a relatively international audience, Berlin is awash with film festivals focusing on specific countries. The **Israel Film Festival Berlin** (www.israelfilmfestivalberlin.com) is held in March, while **Alfilm** (www.alfilm.de), in April, represents Arabic cinema, with films from Egypt, Syria, Palestine and Iran. Australia has **Down Under Berlin** (www.downunderberlin.de) in September, and Latin America has the excellent **Lakino** (www.lakino.com) in October.

The **InterFilm Short Film Festival** (www. interfilm.de), in November, turned 30 in 2014 and has grown from a DIY affair into an international event with big buck prizes. It shows more than 500 short films from 88 countries. InterFilm is also responsible for **Going Underground**, a mini festival of 14 short silent films shown on LCD screens on the U-Bahn (and Seoul metro) in the first week of October. They claim to have Berlin's largest attendance – a (captive) audience of over 1.5 million passengers.

Unsurprisingly, the **Porn Film Festival Berlin** (www.pornfilmfestivalberlin.de) is extremely popular. It presents films, art videos and shorts that transgress the fine line between art and pornography. It's usually held in October and there are lots of related parties and talks.

Gay and lesbian films are put under the spotlight at the **Xposed International Queer Film Festival** (www.xposedfilmfestival.com), in June. The highest-profile LGBT film event is the Teddy Award (http://news.teddyaward.tv), which is presented as an official award during the Berlinale by an independent jury.

Transmediale (www.transmediale.de) is a five-day international programme of digital presentations, installations and performances, which leaves a month-long exhibition in its wake.

INFORMATION

Check listings in *Tip* and *Zitty*, as well as *(030)*, which is available free in many bars. A handy alphabetical film list that's searchable by language can be found online at www.berlinien. de/kino/kinoprogramm.html.

Watch for the notation OV or OF ('original version' or 'Originalfassung'), OmU ('original with subtitles') or OmE ('original with English subtitles'). But watch out – OmU could just as easily be a French or Chinese movie with German subtitles. The cinemas listed below are those most likely to be showing films in English. Various combinations of Monday, Tuesday and Wednesday are known as Kinotag, offering reduced admission, and some cinemas offer deals on pre-paid tickets. Even full-price tickets are generally cheaper than in London or New York.

CINEMAS

★ Arsenal

Potsdamer Strasse 2, Tiergarten (2695 5100, www.arsenal-berlin.de). U2, S1, S2, S25 Potsdamer Platz. **Tickets** €6.50; €5 reductions. **No credit cards.** Map p310 L7.

Berlin's own cinematheque continues to offer brazenly eclectic programming, ranging from classic Hollywood to contemporary Middle Eastern cinema, Russian art films to Italian horror movies, Third World documentaries to retrospectives of cinema's leading lights. Also check out its ongoing series of iconic films, Magical History Tour. The Arsenal shows plenty of English-language films and some foreign films with English subtitles. Its two state-of-the-art screening rooms in the Sony Center make it a welcome corrective to its multiplex neighbours.

▶ *The Arsenal is one of the core venues for the Berlin International Film Festival (see p30).*

Astor Film Lounge

Kurfürstendamm 255, Charlottenburg (883 8551, www.astor-filmlounge.de). U1, U9 Kurfürstendamm. **Tickets** €10-€18. Map p309 G8.

The first 'premium cinema' in Germany offers a luxury cinematographic experience complete with a welcome cocktail, doorman and valet parking. The building dates from 1948, when a café was converted into a small cinema called the KiKi (Kino im Kindl). It was later redesigned and renamed the Filmpalast, and become one of West Berlin's classiest *Kinos*. After thorough renovations and another name change, it's still a grand example of 1950s moviegoing luxury, with an illuminated glass ceiling, comfortable seats and a gong to announce the show.

★ Babylon Kreuzberg

Dresdener Strasse 126, Kreuzberg (6160 9693, www.yorck.de). U1, U8 Kottbusser Tor. **Tickets** €6.50-€8. **No credit cards.** Map p311 P9.

ARTS & ENTERTAINMENT

ESSENTIAL BERLIN FILMS

The city has played a starring role since the birth of film.

Cabaret.

DER BLAUE ENGEL
JOSEF VON STERNBERG
(1929)

Coinciding with the Wall Street Crash and the rise of Hitler, *The Blue Angel* was a turning point for German cinema, being the first sound picture produced at Berlin's Babelsberg Studios. A torrid story about a college professor obsessed with a nightclub singer (a then-unknown Marlene Dietrich), it still flickers alluringly.

CABARET
BOB FOSSE (1971)

The evergreen musical based on British expat Christopher Isherwood's sleazy account of life in 1930s Weimar Berlin, *Cabaret*'s blend of camp, theatricality and decadence is as vibrant as ever. Liza Minnelli is mesmerising as showgirl Sally Bowles, negotiating love amid the city's dives and music halls, against a creeping backdrop of Nazism.

CHRISTIANE F
ULI EDEL (1981)

Set in and around the bleak Gropiousstadt housing projects in West Berlin and the Zoo station, this hard-hitting movie recounts the descent of Christiane F, a teenage drug addict and prostitute, into the dark side of 1980s Berlin. The David Bowie soundtrack fits the mix of neon and squalor.

DER HIMMEL
ÜBER BERLIN
WIM WENDERS (1987)

One of the best-known films about the divided city, *Wings of Desire* sees angels descend from the skies to peer into the hearts and minds of everyday Berliners, soothing those in distress. One angel (Bruno Ganz) falls in love with a trapeze artist – becoming human in the process. Against a backdrop of a grimy Wall and austere monochrome views of Berlin, Wenders' masterpiece is a loving ode to the city.

GOODBYE LENIN!
WOLFGANG BECKER
(2003)

A devoted Socialist woman wakes up from a coma post-reunification. Her son, fearful of what the shock of discovering the demise of the DDR would do to her, goes to extraordinary lengths to pretend the world is the same as before 1989. A charming and affecting comedy, set almost entirely within former East Berlin.

DAS LEBEN
DER ANDEREN
FLORIAN HENCKEL VON
DONNERSMARCK (2006)

The Lives of Others is a gripping, heart-rending drama about an emotionally crippled Stasi officer detailed to spy on a renegade playwright and his girlfriend during the 1980s. Filmed on location around East Berlin, it captures the grim austerity and repression of the communist state in its final years.

Another Berlin perennial, this twin-screen theatre runs a varied programme featuring indie crossover and UK films. Once a local Turkish cinema, its films are almost all English-language and it offers a homely respite from the multiplex experience.

Babylon-Mitte

Rosa-Luxemburg-Strasse 30, Mitte (242 5969, www.babylonberlin.de). U2, U5, U8, S5, S7, S75 Alexanderplatz, or U2 Rosa-Luxemburg-Platz. **Tickets** €6.50; €3 reductions. **No credit cards.** **Map** p307 O5.

Housed in a restored landmark building by Hans Poelzig, the former Filmkunsthaus Babylon reinvented itself with a much more active programming policy. While it nominally focuses on new German independent cinema, English-language fare is on the up, particularly in its monthly Schräge Filme (Weird Films) programme; and its foreign film series tend to have English subtitles. It also hosts regular international film fests, such as Chilean Cinema Week and even a North Korean film festival.

Central

Rosenthaler Strasse 39, Mitte (2859 9973, www.kino-central.de). U8 Weinmeisterstrasse, or S5, S7, S75 Hackescher Markt. **Tickets** €7-€8. **No credit cards.** **Map** p307 N5.

Still hanging in there with a programming attitude that's uniquely its own, this place is worth a look for its various series spotlighting pop/trash culture and all forms of exploitation film. In summer, there's an outdoor cinema in the back courtyard.

CineStar IMAX Sony Center

Potsdamer Strasse 4, Tiergarten (2606 6400, www.cinestar.de). U2, S1, S2, S25 Potsdamer Platz. **Tickets** €9.50-€12; 3D films €12.50-€15. **Map** p310 L7.

CineStar has eight screens showing films exclusively in their original language, mostly English. Despite a few random sparks of creativity, what's shown is largely mainstream fare and all major releases tend to appear here, shown in both 3D and 2D versions on its massive IMAX screen. Counteract the high prices by buying the Five-Star ticket – five (2D) films for €32.50.

Colosseum

Schönhauser Allee 123, Prenzlauer Berg (4401 9200, www.uci-kinowelt.de/berlin_colosseum). U2, S8, S9, S41, S42 Schönhauser Allee. **Tickets** €5.20-€7.80; €4.30-€5 reductions. **Map** p307 O2.

Built in 1924 from a stable for the horses that pulled the first trams, the Colosseum was restored by the Soviets to become the finest cinema in East Berlin. Although it was turned into a multiplex in the late 1990s, the original auditorium is still in use, restored to its 1950s splendour. In the lobby you can still see the brick walls of the stables, complete with the rings used to tie up the horses.

Delphi Filmpalast am Zoo

Kantstrasse 12A, Charlottenburg (312 1026, www.delphi-filmpalast.de/kino/). U1 Uhlandstrasse. **Tickets** €6.50-€9. **Map** p309 F8.

The Delphi was originally a 1920s dance palace. Bombed out during the war, it was rebuilt as the Delphi Filmpalast and became a major Cinemascope and 70mm venue, where films such as *Ben Hur* and *My Fair Lady* would run for up to a year. It's the last cinema in the city still to have balcony seating. Now part of the excellent Yorck cinema group, it shows mainly new German arthouse films.

Eiszeit

Zeughofstrasse 20, Kreuzberg (611 6016, www. eiszeit-kino.de). U1 Görlitzer Bahnhof. **Tickets** €6.50-€7.50. **No credit cards.** **Map** p311 Q9.

Having started life as a squat cinema in the 1980s, Eiszeit offers a wide range of alternative cinema – with a recent accent on pop music films – and a good number of English-language films. It also hosts readings, performances and live music, and is home to several small film festivals.

Filmtheater Am Friedrichshain

Bötzowstrasse 1-5, Friedrichshain (4284 5188, www.yorck.de). Bus 200. **Tickets** €6.50-€8.50; 3D films €9.50-€11.50; children's films €4.50. **Map** p307 Q4.

This charming five-screen cinema is right on the park in Friedrichshain and has a lovely beer garden that's open during the summer.

FSK

Segitzdamm 2, Kreuzberg (614 2464, www.fsk-kino.de). U1, U8 Kottbusser Tor, or U8 Moritzplatz. **Tickets** €6-€7. **No credit cards.** **Map** p311 O9.

Named after the state film rating board, this two-screen cinema is deep in the heart of Turkish Kreuzberg. It shows a lot of foreign films, mostly with German subtitles, but occasionally has American or British indie films and documentaries.

Babylon-Mitte.

Zoo Palast.

Hackesche Höfe Kino
Rosenthaler Strasse 40-41, Mitte (283 4603,
www.hoefekino.de). U8 Weinmeisterstrasse, or
S5, S7, S75 Hackescher Markt. **Tickets** €7.50-€9.
No credit cards. Map p307 N5.
Being a four-storey walk up hasn't stopped this
place from becoming one of the area's best-attended
cinemas. It shows mostly foreign films, with documentaries and occasional indie features in English.

★ Kino International
Karl-Marx-Allee 33, Mitte (2475 6011, www.
yorck.de). U5 Schillingstrasse. **Tickets** €6.50-€8.
No credit cards. Map p307 P6.
The monumental post-Stalinist architecture of Kino
International belies a modest 551-seat auditorium,
but the real reason to come here is for the lobby, with
its crystal chandeliers and upholstered seating. A
first-class example of 1960s DDR chic, it overtook
the Colosseum as East Berlin's premier cinema, and
became a common venue for Communist Party functions and socialist shindigs.
▶ *Kino International is also the home of the gay*
and lesbian Club International, which shows LGBT
films every Monday ('Mongay') at 10pm.

Moviemento
Kottbusser Damm 22, Kreuzberg (692 4785,
www.moviemento.de). U7, U8 Hermannplatz,
or U8 Schönleinstrasse. **Tickets** €6.50-€7.50.
No credit cards. Map p311 P10.
This cosy upstairs cinema in Kreuzberg is one of the
last bastions of Berlin's original alternative cinema
scene. There's very imaginative programming, with
the occasional English film, but emphasis is placed
on foreign film weeks and themed festivals.

Odeon
Hauptstrasse 116, Schöneberg (7870 4019,
www.yorck.de). U4, S42, S46 Innsbrucker Platz,
or S1, S41, S42, S46 Schöneberg. **Tickets** €6.50-
€8.50. **No credit cards. Map** p309 H11.
The Odeon is a last hold-out of the big, old, single-
screen neighbourhood cinema and should be
supported just for that. Set deep in Schöneberg,
it's exclusively English-language, providing a

reasonably intelligent, though increasingly mainstream, selection of Hollywood and UK fare.

Rollberg
Rollbergstrasse 70, Neukölln (6270 4645, www.
yorck.de). U8 Boddinstrasse. **Tickets** €6.50-€8.
No credit cards. Map p311 Q12.
One of the three excellent cinemas in Neukölln run
by the Yorck group, Rollberg is hidden inside a nondescript shopping centre by a Kaisers supermarket.
It shows a healthy mix of Hollywood action flicks
and arthouse cinema, all in their original language.

Xenon
Kolonnenstrasse 5-6, Schöneberg (7800 1530,
www.xenon-kino.de). U7 Kleistpark. **Tickets** €5-€7.
No credit cards. Map p310 J11.
Only in Berlin would a dedicated gay cinema also
be a multiple award-winner for children's programming. Those who have come of age can find specific
gay and lesbian programming, as well as more mainstream independent films.

Zeughaus Kino
Deutsches Historisches Museum, Unter den Linden
2, Mitte (2030 4770, www.zeughauskino.de).
U6 Französiche Strasse. **Tickets** €5. **No credit**
cards. Map p307 N6.
The Zeughaus Kino has a variety of interesting
series and often hosts touring retrospective shows. It
makes a concerted effort to get the original versions
of movies, and foreign films sometimes appear with
English subtitles. The entrance is by the Spree river.

Zoo Palast
Hardenbergstrasse 29A, Charlottenburg (01805
222 966 premium phone, www.zoopalast-berlin.de).
U2, U9, S5, S7, S75 Zoologischer Garten. **Tickets**
€10.50-€11.50; 3D films €12.50-€16. **Map** p309 G8.
In the Cold War, West Berlin premières were always
held in this striking 1950s building, which in a different reincarnation during the Nazi era was the venue
for Albert Speer's most spectacular light shows.
Much like the surrounding Zoo area, it fell into disrepair; it reopened in late 2013 with seven new screens
showing traditional multiplex blockbuster fare.

Gay & Lesbian

Berlin's queer scene is one of the world's most active. In 2001, when he was elected mayor of Berlin, Klaus Wowereit declared: 'I am gay, and that's good the way it is!' (*Ich bin schwul, und das ist auch gut so!*'). Since then, 'Wowi', as he's known in Germany, has come to personify the permissive attitude of a city that has long cared more about a good party than labels such as 'gay' and 'straight'. Nothing is going to change that attitude. But as a slogan for the city's gay scene, his words constitute a vast understatement.

BERLIN'S GAY HISTORY

Historically, Berlin has acted as a tolerant, catch-all city for people of different religions, races and sexual orientations – even when the rest of Germany wasn't quite on board. Berlin was the capital of a kingdom whose 18th-century king, Frederick the Great, was rumoured to discuss and delve into homoerotic activities (just check out some of the art at his men-only summer retreat, **Sanssouci** – *see p220*). Later, in 1897, the first institution in the world with an emancipatory homosexual agenda was founded in Berlin – the Wissenschaftlich-Humanitäres Komitee (Scientific-Humanitarian Committee).

The 1920s accelerated and cemented Berlin's role as Europe's gay capital. The Weimar era (1918-33) brought an anything-goes spirit to the city: gay and lesbian bars flourished, drag performances were popular and an open sexual culture, not to mention a depressed national currency, attracted homosexual tourists from across the globe. The scene gave the world a first glimpse at what we might recognise as a modern gay community, and was frequented by Marlene Dietrich, Anita Berber and Christopher Isherwood. This freewheeling period ended with the election of the Nazis in 1933, after which homosexuals, especially in 'depraved' Berlin, were persecuted by the state. Thousands of gay men were forced to wear a pink triangle in concentration camps, many perishing in the bloody years of World War II. The gay victims of National Socialism are commemorated in a striking €600,000 memorial in the Tiergarten that was unveiled in 2008.

During the occupation and the Cold War (1945-89), gay culture existed on both sides of a divided Berlin, though mostly underground. West Berlin, in particular, saw a surge in its gay ranks, as many young men were attracted to the only city in West Germany where citizens were exempt from military service. In 1994, the notorious Paragraph 175, which had criminalised homosexual contact in Germany since 1871, was repealed by the newly unified nation. Civil partnerships between same-sex couples have been legal since 2001, and it is Berlin's politicians who are now leading the charge for full gay marriage. After such dramatic swings in acceptance, Berlin has adopted a never-again stance towards gay intolerance. Alternative lifestyles of all stripes are considered normal – even celebrated on giant pro-tolerance billboards in the U-Bahn stations.

THE SCENE TODAY

Schöneberg has the highest concentration of gay shops, bars, restaurants and organisations. But roving monthly parties and a constant turnover of gay bars have resulted in a diffusion of the scene into **Kreuzberg**, **Prenzlauer Berg**, **Mitte** and **Friedrichshain**. Even traditionally Turkish **Neukölln** has its share of go-to spots.

Summer is the most exciting time of year, when all contingents come together to play, party and protest. The **Lesbisch-Schwules Stadtfest** (*see p28*) on Nollendorfplatz in mid June is followed by the **Christopher Street Day** (*see p28*), Germany's version of Pride, which includes a flamboyant annual parade through Tiergarten. Alternative parades in other parts of town celebrate every shade of the queer rainbow.

The scene includes much more than the venues listed here, especially in terms of cultural events. For gay film culture, *see p174*. Gay art and history are documented at the **Schwules Museum** (*see p138*), which also has an archive. And, of course, the Berlin scene offers sex parties for every taste and perversion, as well as gay saunas, cruising parks and stigma-free darkrooms in many bars.

Tens of thousands of men have profiles on the wildly popular gay social – and sex-networking – site Gay Romeo (www.gayromeo.com) or its mobile-only competitor Grindr (www.grindr.com). Both provide excellent ways to learn about the latest gay happenings in the city.

Gays making contact in public is rarely of interest to passers-by, but bigots do exist and so does anti-gay violence. In the West, those responsible tend to be gangs of Turkish teenagers; in the East, right-wing skinhead Germans – but violence is rare and, compared to other cities, Berlin is an easy-going place.

INFORMATION

For gay and lesbian helplines, information and counselling services, *see p286*. The best way to find one-off events, parties and festivals is by checking *Blu* (www.blu.fm) and *Siegessäule* (www.siegessaeule.de), free monthly magazines that can be picked up at most LGBT venues. As well as a 'what's on' calendar, *Siegessäule* lists all gay and lesbian venues and pinpoints them on a map. It also publishes *Kompass* (www.siegessaeule-kompass.de), a classified directory in German of everything gay or lesbian. You can find English information in pocket-sized Gay City Guides for individual districts.

Mixed

In West Berlin's Schöneberg district, gays and lesbians trod separate paths for decades. Across the wall in East Berlin, though, homosexuals of both sexes shared bars and clubs, making common cause under the Communists. These traditions can still be felt today. The expansion of the gay scene into other parts of the city means that mixed venues predominate, though most places tend to lean one way or the other.

CAFES & BARS

Mitte

TheLiberate
Kleine Präsidentenstrasse 4 (8867 7778, www.theliberate.com). S5, S7, S75 Hackescher Markt. **Open** from 7pm Wed-Sun. **Map** p307 N5.
Not a card-carrying homo bar, but still, if well-to-do gays from the fashion world is your thing, TheLiberate should suit just fine. Slathered in gold-shimmering velvet and leather, it's a swanky and, for Berlin, expensive affair. Come the weekend, though, and all three rooms are chock-a-block with scenesters and champagne cocktails. *Photo p180.*

Friedrichshain

Himmelreich
Simon-Dach-Strasse 36 (2936 9292). U5 Frankfurter Tor, U1, S3, S5, S7, S75 Warschauer Strasse. **Open** from 6pm Mon-Fri; from 2pm Sat, Sun. **No credit cards. Map** p312 S7.

Christopher Street Day.

ARTS & ENTERTAINMENT

A colourful and comfortable lounge serving snacks and coffee during the day, as well as alcoholic drinks. Tuesday night is women-only (*see p191* **Women's Lounge**), although men in drag are welcome.

Charlottenburg

TortenheBär
Zauritzweg 9 (3454 0304). U2 Deutsche Oper. **Open** from noon Tue-Fri; from 3pm Sat, Sun. **Map** p309 E7.
A sedate but loveable coffee and wine bar in Charlottenburg. It's not explicitly gay, but its linen-draped tables are often filled with older, understated opera fans eating excellent tarts and discussing the latest production at the nearby Deutsche Oper.

Kreuzberg

Barbie Deinhoff's
Schlesische Strasse 16 (no phone, www.barbie deinhoff.de). U1 Schlesisches Tor or bus N29. **Open** from 7pm-late daily. **No credit cards**. **Map** p312 R9.
Sure, this is a queer performance space, but most people come to its bright casual rooms for the young, pan-sexual crowd, the top-notch local DJs and the hilarious art adorning the walls. Two-for-one Tuesdays are popular, attracting a particularly skint Kreuzberg crowd.

Café Melitta Sundström
Mehringdamm 61 (5484 4121, www.melitta-sundstroem.de). U6, U7 Mehringdamm. **Open** 1pm-late daily. **No credit cards**. **Map** p310 M10.
By day, this place serves as a cosy café for students; in the evening, it's full of gays who are too lazy to go to Schöneberg and lesbians who wouldn't go to Schöneberg anyway. It's no longer the entrance to legendary gay club Schwuz (*see p186*).

Möbel-Olfe.

TheLiberate. *See p179.*

Drama
Mehringdamm 63 (6746 9562). U6, U7 Mehringdamm. **Open** 2pm-late daily. **No credit cards**. **Map** p310 M10.
A schizophrenic but stylish café-bar on two floors: the pink palace at street level could only attract the unashamedly camp, while rowdy lesbians roll around on leopard-skin cushions and jungle colours upstairs. There is a small terrace in summer.

Möbel-Olfe
Reichenberger Strasse 177, corner of Dresdner Strasse (2327 4690, www.moebel-olfe.de). U1, U8 Kottbusser Tor. **Open** 6pm-late Tue-Sun. **No credit cards**. **Map** p311 P9.
The vast 1960s estate that houses a large number of Turkish families is also home to Möbel-Olfe, a popular alternative gay bar. Old chairs are glued to the ceiling as a cheeky nod to the space's original function as a furniture shop. Thursdays really get pumping – you can often see a foggy mass of bodies pressed against the large windows on either side of the building – while Tuesdays is more for the ladies.

Roses
Oranienstrasse 187 (615 6570). U1, U8 Kottbusser Tor. **Open** 10pm-5am daily. **No credit cards**. **Map** p311 P9.
Whatever state you're in (the more of a state, the better), you'll fit in just fine at this boisterous den of glitter. It draws customers of all sexual preferences, who mix and mingle and indulge in excessive drinking amid the plush, kitsch decor. No place for uptights, always full, very Kreuzbergish.

Tante Horst
Oranienstrasse 45 (3950 9022, www.tantehorst. de). U1 Moritzplatz. **Open** 6pm-late Tue-Sun. **Map** p311 O8.

This adorable, relaxed co-op bar and café promises an open atmosphere and an embrace of queer culture, making it an excellent place to warm up for a night out no matter where you fall on the sexuality spectrum. At this end of bustling Oranienstrasse, both the prices and the noise level drop considerably.

Schöneberg

Café Bilderbuch
Akazienstrasse 28 (7870 6057, www.cafe-bilderbuch.de). U7 Eisenacher Strasse. **Open** 9am-midnight Mon-Sat; 10am-midnight Sun. **Map** p310 J11.

Quaint and cosy, this venue serves as café, restaurant, gallery and library. Eclectic touches – a doll's house, vintage chairs and tables – tempt you to spend an afternoon people-watching or tinkering on a laptop. It's crowded at lunch and breakfast.

Neues Ufer
Hauptstrasse 157 (7895 7900). U7 Kleistpark. **Open** 11am-2am daily. **No credit cards.** **Map** p310 J10.

Established in the early 1970s, this is one of the city's oldest gay cafés. Formerly known as Anderes Ufer ('The Other Side'), it was an old haunt of David Bowie, who used to live just two doors away.

Neukölln

New on the scene is friendly bar **Club** (Biebricher Strasse 14, www.the-club-berlin.de), which hosts everything from Eurovision parties to screenings of RuPaul's *Drag Race*.

Silver Future
Weserstrasse 206 (7563 4987, www.silverfuture. net). U7, U8 Hermannplatz. **Open** 5pm-2am Mon-Thur; 5pm-3am Fri, Sat. **Map** p311 Q11.

Neukölln is the new frontier of cool in Berlin, and this is its longstanding queer destination. 'You are now leaving the heteronormative zone' announces a playful sign above the bar – and it's not kidding. Fun for groups of any sexual or gender definition, this neighbourhood bar is welcoming, witty and charmingly rough around the edges.

CLUBS & ONE-NIGHTERS
Friedrichshain

Berghain/Panorama Bar
Am Wriezener Bahnhof (no phone, www.berghain. de). U1, S3, S5, S7, S75 Warschauer Strasse. **Open** midnight-late Fri, Sat. **Admission** varies. **No credit cards.** Map p312 R7.

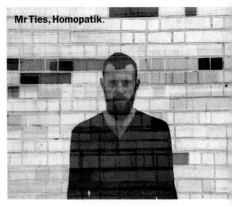

Mr Ties, Homopatik.

The hippest and hardest electronic music club in Berlin, if not Europe. The building is a Communist-era power station transformed into a concrete cathedral of techno on two floors, with the mixed Panorama Bar upstairs and Berghain below. The latter is awash with pumped-up, shirtless gay men sweating it out on the dancefloor (or in the darkroom at the back) from Saturday night well into Sunday afternoon. In summer, the party pours over into the garden chill-out area, bar and dancefloor. Arrive after 6am to avoid the massive queues. Once on Am Wriezener Bahnhof, just follow the stream of taxis to reach the door. Cameras are prohibited – they're taken at the door and returned later, but you won't need photos to remember it.

Die Busche
Warschauer Platz 18 (296 0800, www.die busche.de). U1, S5, S7, S75 Warschauer Strasse. **Open** from 10pm Fri, Sat. **Admission** €3.50-€6. **No credit cards.** Map p312 S8.

Die Busche (formerly Haus B) is an East German relic. Loud, tacky, mixed and packed, this is one of east Berlin's oldest discos and is full of loutish lesbians, gay teens and their girlfriends. The Friday and Saturday parties are musts for kitsch addicts and mainstream pop fans, and definitely a no-go area for guys who like a masculine atmosphere.

Homopatik
://aboutblank, Markgrafendamm 24C (no phone, www.homopatik.com). S3, S5, S7, S8, S9, S41, S42, S75, S85 Ostkreuz. **Open** midnight Fri-10pm Sat 3rd Fri of mth. **No credit cards.** Map p312 S8.

A cult party series that is gaining in popularity, thanks to marathon genre-hopping DJ sets from organiser and resident extraordinaire Mr Ties. Expect a wild and international crowd of gays, hetero-hipsters and young club rats. Ultimate summertime bonus: an expansive garden complete with blissed-out dancefloor, druggie trailer and even a ping-pong table.

ARTS & ENTERTAINMENT

Kreuzberg

Gutterslut
Chalet, Vor dem Schlesischen Tor 3 (no phone, www. gutterslut.net). U1 Schlesisches Tor. **Open** midnight-late Fri alt mth. **No credit cards. Map** p312 S9.
Not for the faint of heart. Once every two months or so, the self-titled Dalston Gay Mafia pitch up in Berlin for one of their trademark freak-outs. The tranny fabulous outfits might begin to falter as the party passes the ten-hour mark, but the good vibes last till the very end. Music-wise, it's ghetto electro and diet techno, or so they say. The location varies.

SO36
Oranienstrasse 190 (tickets 6110 1313, 6140 1306, www.so36.de). U1, U8 Kottbusser Tor. **Open** 8pm-late daily. **Admission** €3-€20. **No credit cards. Map** p311 P9.
A key venue for both gays and lesbians. The last Saturday of the month is Gay Oriental Night (Gayhane – House of Halay, from 11pm) with belly dancing, transvestites and Turkish hits. Sunday is Café Fatal, where gays and lesbians get into ballroom dancing with a lesson from a professional thrown in at the start of the evening. The last Friday of the month is gay-friendly My Ugly X, a blissfully trashy combo of pop music and drink specials. Roller Skate Disco (one undetermined Friday or Saturday per month, from 8pm) brings in boys and girls to hustle and shimmy to 1970s and '80s cheese. SO36 even makes bingo fun with its brash Super Sexy Bingo night (every second Tuesday, from 7pm).

Südblock
Admiralstrasse 1-2 (6094 1853, www.suedblock. org). U1, U8 Kottbusser Tor. **Open** from 10am. **Admission** varies. **No credit cards. Map** p311 P9.

A former beer-slinger from Möbel-Olfe (*see p180*) opened this bar for Kreuzberg's increasingly large gay population in 2010. Located under one of the wrap-around housing developments at Kottbusser Tor, the mixed (but girl-heavy) crowd enjoy nightly drinks and dancing, as well as many one-off rock parties. Popular party Creamcake has garnered acclaim beyond its queer fanbase for its progressive music policy. Südblock also serves food, ranging from breakfast to midnight snacks.

Gay
You don't need to look for the gay scene in Berlin. It'll find you in about ten minutes. Though events are spread throughout the city, some areas are gayer than others – especially the tourist-friendly concentration around Motzstrasse and Fuggerstrasse in Schöneberg, and the area around Schönhauser Allee S-Bahn and U-Bahn stations in Prenzlauer Berg.

CAFES, BARS & RESTAURANTS
Mitte

Betty F***
Mulackstrasse 13 (no phone, www.bettyf.de). U8 Weinmeisterstrasse. **Open** from 9pm daily (times vary in winter). **No credit cards. Map** p307 O5.
A quirky basement space near Hackescher Markt that offers everything from transsexual theatre performers to live classical music. Mostly, though, homosexuals of all ages gather here in the evening for an anything-goes atmosphere that strikes a good balance between edgy and casual.

ARTS & ENTERTAINMENT

Gutterslut.

Perle.

Delicious beverages abound at this small, austerely designed cocktail bar on Prenzlauer Berg's eastern fringe. Most nights, gay men line the bar gripping martinis or gather around the large table in the elevated back room. On Thursday nights, English is the predominant language as Perle becomes a hobnobbing party for gay expats and the Germans that love them. A streetside patio doubles the capacity in summer.

Friedrichshain

Grosse Freiheit 114
Boxhagener Strasse 114 (7072 8306, www.gay-friedrichshain.de/grosse-freiheit-114). **U5 Frankfurter Tor. Open** from 10pm Tue-Sun. **No credit cards. Map** p312 T7.
The name promises 'big freedom', and the bar delivers with a distinctly open policy to all kinds of gay fellows looking for a good time either at the bar or in the darkrooms. It's particularly popular with older locals, although the changing nature of the neighbourhood is slowly bringing in the under-40 crowd too. Note that the name only applies to men: no women allowed.

Zum Schmutzigen Hobby
Revaler Strasse 99 (no phone, www.ninaqueer.com). **U1, S5, S7, S75 Warschauer Strasse. Open** from 6pm daily. **No credit cards. Map** p312 T8.
In 2010, famed drag queen Nina Queer moved her popular watering hole from Prenzlauer Berg to this graffiti – and bottle-strewn party zone of reclaimed buildings next to the Spree. Nina has since left the bar, but it remains as good as ever. It's intensely fun, especially later in the night when loud US pop hits fill the air. The large outdoor patio hosts viewing parties for *Germany's Next Top Model*, Eurovision and other TV events of gay interest.
▶ *For more about Nina Queer, see p187 Nina Queer: Queen of Drag.*

Kreuzberg

Golden Finish
Wrangelstrasse 87 (0176 6688 2775 mobile, www.goldenfinish.de). **U1 Schlesisches Tor. Open** from 8pm daily. **No credit cards. Map** p312 R9.
A fun, if mercurial, bar near the swelling party zone of Schlesisches Tor. The crowd is a potpourri of Kreuzberg gays – punks, hipsters, bears-in-training – most under the age of 40. Take a whirl as the music-maker on the do-it-yourself DJ night, usually Saturdays. And the name, in case you're wondering, has nothing to do with dirty sex play.

Rauschgold
Mehringdamm 62 (7895 2668, www.rauschgold-berlin.de). **U6, U7 Mehringdamm. Open** 8pm-late daily. **No credit cards. Map** p310 M10.

Prenzlauer Berg

Flax
Chodowieckistrasse 41 (4404 6988, www.flax-berlin.de). **S8, S9, S41, S42, S85 Greifswalder Strasse, or tram M4, M10. Open** 5pm-3am Tue-Thur; 5pm-6am Fri, Sat; 10am-2am Sun. **No credit cards. Map** p307 Q4.
It may be on the edge of the Prenzlauer Berg gay scene, but Flax has developed into one of the most popular café/bars in the district, mainly pulling in a young mixed crowd. The excellent Sunday brunch (10am-5pm) costs €7.90 per person.

Greifbar
Wichertstrasse 10 (444 0828, www.greifbar.com). **U2, S8, S9, S41, S42, S85 Schönhauser Allee. Open** 10pm-late daily. **No credit cards. Map** p307 P2.
A thirty- to fortysomething Prenzlauer Berg crowd populates this cruisy bar looking for adventure and pleasure, either by picking someone up or by roaming about in the large darkrooms. There's also a decent retro-1980s atmosphere if you just want to drink and nibble on the free popcorn.

Marietta
Stargarder Strasse 13 (4372 0646, www.marietta-bar.de). **U2, S8, S9, S41, S42, S85 Schönhauser Allee. Open** 10am-2am Mon-Fri; 10am-4am Sat, Sun. **No credit cards. Map** p307 P2.
Hot hipster bartenders and a large room done up like a GDR office waiting room circa 1979 draw local gay boys and women to Marietta every night. On Wednesdays, the place is crammed with sexy young men gossiping, laughing and boozing.

Perle
Sredzkistrasse 64 (4985 3450, www.bar-perle.de) **U2 Eberswalder Strasse. Open** 7pm-late Tue-Sun. **Map** p307 P3.

Hafen.

This plush and somewhat tacky bar is a good place for those who feel like prolonging their night into morning or for taking a first drink on an evening out. Avoid the occasional cabaret performances.

Schöneberg

Café Berio

Maassenstrasse 7 (216 1946, www.cafeberio.de). U1, U2, U3, U4 Nollendorfplatz. **Open** 24hrs daily. **No credit cards. Map** p310 J9.

One of the best daytime cafés in Berlin, this Parisian-style café is full of attractive, trendy young men (including the waiters), with a good people-watching terrace in summer. Decent food is served all day – should you get hunger pangs at an ungodly hour.

Hafen

Motzstrasse 19 (211 4118, www.hafen-berlin.de). U1, U2, U3, U4 Nollendorfplatz. **Open** 8pm-late daily. **No credit cards. Map** p309 H9.

A red, plush and vaguely psychedelic bar in the centre of Schöneberg's gay triangle. It's popular with the fashion- and body-conscious, especially at weekends, when it provides a safe haven from nearby heavy cruising dens. It's usually very crowded, especially for Quizz-o-Rama, a pub quiz (in English) on the first Monday of the month.

Heile Welt

Motzstrasse 5 (2191 7507). U1, U2, U3, U4 Nollendorfplatz. **Open** 6pm-4am daily (from 8pm in summer). **No credit cards. Map** p309 H9.

A stylish café, lounge and cocktail bar for the fashionable: the front has a 1970s disco feel complete with furry wall; the back lounge offers plush leather seating. It's a good place to kick off an evening, practise some chat-up lines and decide whether or not to go clubbing. It's packed come 11pm on Friday and Saturday.

Mutschmanns

Martin-Luther-Strasse 19 (2191 9640, www.mutschmanns.de). U1, U2, U3, U4 Nollendorfplatz. **Open** 10pm-late Wed; 9pm-late Thur; 10pm-late Fri, Sat. **Admission** varies. **No credit cards. Map** p309 D5/6.

This well-frequented hardcore bar, with a large and hard darkroom in the basement, is suitable for cruising or just hanging out – albeit with a dress code of leather, rubber or uniform. Rubber Night is the first Saturday of the month.

Prinzknecht

Fuggerstrasse 33 (2362 7444, www.prinzknecht. de). U1, U2, U3 Wittenbergplatz. **Open** 3pm-2am Mon-Thur, Sun; 3pm-3am Fri, Sat. **No credit cards. Map** p309 H9.

With a large but underused darkroom out back, this huge, open bar draws in gays from the neighbourhood as well as leathermen and other hardcore customers. The place is somewhat provincial in feel, but nice for a chat and a beer. The crowd moves outside in summer.

Tom's Bar

Motzstrasse 19 (213 4570, www.tomsbar.de). U1, U2, U3, U4 Nollendorfplatz. **Open** 10pm-6am daily. **No credit cards. Map** p309 H9.

Once described by *Der Spiegel* as the climax of the night, Tom's is something of a cruising institution. The front bar is fairly chatty but the closer you get to the steps down to the darkroom, the more intense things become. It's very popular with men of all ages and styles, especially on Monday when you can get two drinks for the price of one.

Tramp's

Eisenacher Strasse 6 (no phone). U1, U2, U3, U4 Nollendorfplatz. **Open** 24hrs daily. **No credit cards. Map** p309 H9.

The name says it all. This back alley of a bar, complete with crazy paving on the walls, is open 24/7. Expect a random crowd of local soaks, rent boys and horny bucks looking for easy fun in the darkroom at the back.

Woof
Fuggerstrasse 37 (2360 7870, www.woof-berlin. com). U1, U2, U3 Wittenbergplatz. **Open** 10pm-4am Mon-Sat; 9pm-2am Sun. **No credit cards.** **Map** p309 H9.

Bears, daddies and leather lovers congregate around the bar or wander the sex rooms out back, especially on Tuesdays when drinks are two-for-one. The body-conscious and hairless should try other pastures.

CLUBS & ONE-NIGHTERS
Mitte

GMF
Avenue Club in Café Moskau, Karl-Marx-Allee 34 (2809 5396, www.gmf-berlin.de). U5 Schillingstrasse. **Open** 11pm-late Sun. **Admission** €10. **No credit cards. Map** p307 P6.

Berlin's ultimate and longstanding Sunday tea dance is located in the famed Café Moskau. The glass and concrete exterior gives way to a state-of-the-art basement club, split into two musical realms: pop and techno. The former, more sociable floor is rammed with twinks and gymgoers; the latter is more intense, complete with shirtless dancers and the occasional Paul van Dyk set.

Klub International
Kino International, Karl-Marx-Allee 33 (2475 6011, www.klub-international.com). U5 Schillingstrasse. **Open** 11pm-late 1st Sat of mth. **Admission** €7-€10. **No credit cards. Map** p307 P6.

In a landmark 1950s GDR cinema, this occasional club (usually once a month) is worth a look for the interior alone. It's one of the biggest parties in town, regularly attracting up to 1,500 youngish guests in their tightest T-shirts. There are two dancefloors, and DJs play a mix of house and mainstream music.

Propaganda
Imperial Club, Friedrichstrasse 101 (no phone, www.propaganda-party.de). U6, S1, S2, S5, S7, S25, S75 Friedrichstrasse. **Open** 11pm-late 1st Sat of mth. **Admission** €10. **No credit cards. Map** p306 M6.

Moving from one legendary 100-year-old building to another, Propaganda ditched its chandelier-laden Schöneberg home for a sultry basement beneath the Admiralspalast theatre in Mitte. Friendly boy-next-door types crowd on to the dancefloor for an untamed night of feel-good commercial house and dance music, the likes of which techno/electro fans would probably wish to avoid.

Prenzlauer Berg

Chantal's House of Shame
Bassy Club, Schönhauser Allee 176A (no phone, www.facebook.com/chantalshouseofshame). U2 Senefelderplatz. **Open** 11pm-8am Thur. **Admission** €7-€10. **No credit cards. Map** p307 O4.

A popular, friendly, electro dance night hosted by well-known local drag queen Chantal. The party has exchanged some of its underground cred for a larger space, but still packs in the party crew for an early weekend warm-up. You'll find a cross-section of Berlin's gay scene here, including some attractive transvestites and performers that put on a show around 1am.

Friedrichshain

CockTail D'Amore
0176 3823 0322 mobile, www.cocktaildamore. tumblr.com. **Open** midnight-late 1st Sat of mth. **Admission** varies. **No credit cards.**

This alternative party series keeps things fresh with frequent new locations and everlasting DJ sets from its organisers Discodromo and Boris (of Berghain fame). Sexy hairy boys in their twenties and thirties come here from across the city to dance to house music well into the next day. The vibe can be a bit snobby at first, but as the night wears on, it gets easier to befriend patrons on the dancefloor and in the outdoor chill-out space they usually have.

Kreuzberg

Irrenhouse
Comet Club, Falckensteinstrasse 47 (4400 8140). U1 Schlesisches Tor. **Open** 11pm-late 3rd Sat of mth. **Admission** €8-€10. **No credit cards. Map** p312 R9.

This popular one-nighter is true to its name: 'Madhouse'. Hostess Nina Queer (*see p187* **Nina Queer: Queen of Drag**) attracts a bizarre mixture of party kids, trashy drag queens and other flotsam of the night to dance to house and chart music under even more bizarre video installations. Popular and shrill, with candy distributed for free all night and a darkroom out back.

Horse Meat Disco
Prince Charles, Prinzenstrasse 85F (no phone, www.princecharlesberlin.com). U8 Moritzplatz. **Open** from 11pm 2nd Sat every other mth. **Admission** €10. **No credit cards. Map** p311 8O.

This DJ group may have been born in London's Vauxhall, but Horse Meat Disco has matured in Berlin. Once every two months, the city's hottest bearded, beefy men descend on Prince Charles to dance the night away to the group's signature disco-garage sound. Popular, packed and sexy.

ARTS & ENTERTAINMENT

Schöneberg

Connection

Fuggerstrasse 33 (218 1432, www.connection-berlin.com). U1, U2, U3 Wittenbergplatz. **Open** 11pm-6am Fri, Sat. **Admission** €8. **Map** p309 H9.

A popular weekend club, with DJs playing mainly electronic sounds. If you get bored of the dancefloor, you can cruise the vast flesh dungeons of Connection Garage (*see p190*) two floors below. After years of being men-only, it's now open to all.

Neukölln

SchwuZ

Rollbergstrasse 26 (5770 2270, www.schwuz.de). U7 Rathaus Neukölln. **Open & admission** varies. **No credit cards. Map** p311 Q12.

One of Berlin's longest-running dance institutions got a shot in the arm when it moved into the old Neukölln Kindl brewery in 2013. From mainstream to more underground, a mix of parties take place through the week, with Saturday being the main disco night at the Schwulen Zentrum ('gay centre'). The club attracts a mixed and ready-to-mingle crowd who take good advantage of the warehouse-like space and multiple dancefloors. Friday hosts an assortment of one-nighters, among them the wildly popular London Calling, on the first Friday of the month, with indie and pop music. L-Tunes (*see p191*) for lesbians and their friends, is on the last Friday of the month, with music ranging from classic pop to electronica. For a grittier vibe, Thursdays is reserved for a more experimental, techno soundtrack.

Wedding

Rose Kennedy

Brunnen 70, Brunnenstrasse 70 (no phone, www.brunnen70.de). U7 Voltastrasse. **Open** 11pm-late 4th Sat of mth. **No credit cards. Map** p306 M6.

Riding an industrial elevator down to a vast underground space juxtaposes nicely with the overload of pink-hued pop culture to follow. DJs serve up a saccharine diet of 1990s hits at this self-acknowledged 'bad taste party' hosted by drag queen deluxe Nina Queer. At the business end of proceedings, there's a porno cinema and an unverified claim to have 'Germany's biggest darkroom' – at 200sq m (2,150sq ft) they can't be far off.

LEATHER, SEX & FETISH VENUES

The hardcore and fetish scene in Berlin is huge. These days, leather gays are outnumbered by a younger hardcore crowd and skinhead types who prefer rubber and uniforms. Places to obtain your preferred garb are plentiful, as are opportunities to show it off, including the eternally crowded **Leather Meeting** over the Easter holidays, the annual **Gay Skinhead Weekend**, and various fetish parties and events. Most of the parties are men-only affairs and have a strict dress code.

Mitte

KitKatClub

Köpenicker Strasse 76 (278 9830, www.kitkatclub.org). U8 Heinrich-Heine-Strasse. **Open** 11pm-late Fri, Sat. **Admission** €10-€15. **No credit cards. Map** p311 P7.

This legendary mixed/straight sex and techno club has moved out of Schöneberg to Mitte, to take up residence every weekend in the same building as the Sage Club. The fourth Friday of the month is Piepshow; Saturday nights feature the club's flagship CarneBall Bizarre, with the Afterhour event to follow throughout Sunday. For pure polysexual hedonism, look out for cult party Gegen (http://gegenberlin.com) every two months. All nights are listed in the gay press, so make sure the crowd is the one you want. Most parties have a fetish dress code; the least you have to do is take off your shirt.

Prenzlauer Berg

Darkroom

Rodenbergstrasse 23 (no phone, www.darkroom-berlin.de). U2, S8, S9, S41, S42, S85 Schönhauser Allee. **Open** varies. **Admission** free-€2.50. **No credit cards. Map** p307 P1.

Yes, there is a darkroom in this small bar. In fact, it's more darkroom than bar. With the help of camouflage netting and urinals, the place pulls in a slightly hardcore clientele, but be warned that on less busy nights things can feel a bit desperate. The Naked Sex Party on Friday and Saturday's Golden Shower Party are particularly popular. Wednesday has an Underwear Sex Party from 7pm.

Stahlrohr 2.0

Paul-Robeson Strasse 50 (0170 803 7691 mobile, www.stahlrohr-bar.de). U2, S8, S9, S41, S42, S85 Schönhauser Allee. **Open** 10pm-6am Mon, Wed, Thur-Sat; 9pm-6am Tue; 6pm-6am Sun. **Admission** varies. **No credit cards. Map** p307 O1.

A small cruisy pub in front and a large darkroom in back. There are sex parties here for every taste, including but not limited to the Underwear Party, Slave Market, Sneaker Freaxx, Suck 'n' Blow and Karaoke Sex. The Youngster Party for those aged 18-28 is on Tuesday.

Friedrichshain

Lab.oratory

Am Wriezener Bahnhof (no phone, www.lab-oratory.de). U1, S3, S5, S7, S75 Warschauer Strasse. **Open & admission** varies. **No credit cards. Map** p312 R7.

NINA QUEER: QUEEN OF DRAG

The hostess with the mostest.

Berlin doesn't have a First Lady, but if it did, she would be Nina Queer. This self-declared 'most famous and successful drag queen in Germany' is at the centre of much that is fun and outrageous in the city's gay scene. One part Jodie Harsh, one part Grace Jones, Nina – or 'die Qveer' as her fans call her – claims to have been born in 1985 in a small mountain village in Carinthia, Austria. In 2000, so the story goes, she – then very much a he, called Daniel – escaped to Berlin and has been attracting attention here ever since.

'The last Austrian empress in Prussian exile' is another of her favourite taglines. Whether upstaging Hollywood stars on the red carpet during the Berlin Film Festival, saying the unsayable on her Radio Energy show or climbing the pop charts with songs such as 'Ficki Ficki Aua Aua' (Fuck Fuck Ouch Ouch), she is hard to ignore. In 2011, she even released an autobiography, *Dauerläufig* (*Long Running*), which quickly became a bestseller.

To meet the woman herself, just head to one of her gloriously over-the-top monthly parties. Nina runs the **Irrenhouse** club night (*see p185*) at the Comet Club, which has been packing in the punters since 2003. It's the place VIPs tend to show up looking for some harmless Berlin debauchery:

Justin Timberlake was here once and Nina has the photo to prove it. Or there's the more recent installment on the scene: **Rose Kennedy** (*see p186*). If you can actually find this underground kitsch fest, named after JFK's mother (for reasons only known to Nina), it ought to be well worth it.

In the same building as the Berghain nightclub (*see p195*), this sprawling hardcore sex den – complete with all the props: slings, beds, cages, pissoir, military zone, mock jail cells and so on – takes the sexual perversion on offer in Berlin to another level. In addition to the regular and hugely popular Naked Sex Party on Thursdays and the Friday Fuck with two drinks for the price of one, the venue also organises Saturday and Sunday night specials ranging from the relatively softcore Gummi (rubber outfits) and Athletes (sports gear), to harder stuff, such as Yellow Facts (watersports) and Scat (shit play). Check the website for dates and times.

Kreuzberg

Bodies in Emotion Erotik Party
AHA, Monumentenstrasse 13 (8962 7948, www.aha-berlin.de). U7 Kleistpark. **Open** 9pm-6am 2nd Fri of mth. **Admission** €6.50. **No credit cards. Map** p310 K11.
This sex party is popular with guys under 30 or who look it (you won't find many hairy chests here). What

you wear is up to you, but most put on shorts – which they then take off in the sex area, where mattresses and slings invite you to join in the fun. The rooms can get so packed that it's difficult to move (which can be good or bad, depending on your outlook).

Club Culture Houze
Görlitzer Strasse 71 (6170 9669, www.dub-culture-houze.de). U1 Görlitzer Bahnhof. **Open & admission** varies. **No credit cards. Map** p311 Q9.
Diverse sex parties (some of them mixed), ranging from Naked to SM and Fetish. Exclusive gay nights on Monday (Naked Sex) and Friday (Fist Factory). Mostly body-conscious night owls visit these kitsch rooms. Mattresses invite people to lie down, but most attendees hardly need encouragement.

Ficken 3000
Urbanstrasse 70 (6950 7335, www.ficken3000. com). U7, U8 Hermannplatz. **Open** 10pm-late daily. **Admission** varies. **No credit cards. Map** p311 P10.

A small, plucky sex club on the border with Neukölln, Ficken 3000 ('Fuck 3000') has both a sense of humour and an extensive basement cruising dungeon. On Sundays, young expats and hipsters pack the place for Pork, a night of fun pop remixes, pole dancing and sex. Porn is shown alongside old Joe Dallesandro movies.

Quälgeist

Mehringdamm 51 (788 5799, www.quaelgeist-berlin.de). U6, U7 Mehringdamm. **Open** varies. **Admission** €8-€15. **No credit cards.** **Map** p310 M10.

Quälgeist was the first institution established solely to organise SM parties, which include SM for beginners, bondage, slave markets and fist nights. You can pick up flyers at any leather bar. There's usually a dress code. The place can be tricky to find – walk through to the fourth courtyard and access is on the ground floor.

Triebwerk

Urbanstrasse 64 (6950 5203, www.triebwerk berlin.de). U7, U8 Hermannplatz. **Open** varies. **Admission** free (€10 minimum spend). **Map** p311 P10.

This small, comfortable bar with a huge video screen and a darkroom maze in the basement attracts Kreuzberg gays of every denomination. On Monday and Friday you can expect to find two-for-one drinks deals; Naked and Underwear parties feature on Tuesday, Saturday and Sunday, and Wednesday is the After Work Sex night.

Schöneberg

Ajpnia

Wartburgstrasse 18 (2191 8881, www.ajpnia.de). U4, U7 Bayerischer Platz. **Open** from 7pm Wed; from 9pm Sat. **Admission** €5-€6. **No credit cards.** **Map** p309 H11.

An intimate sex club frequented by men of all ages. Every first and third Saturday is PositHIV-Verkehr, a party by and for HIV-positive men; every second and fourth Saturday is Nacht-Verkehr (Night Traffic) and Wednesday is Feierabend-Verkehr (After Work Traffic). Verkehr also means 'intercourse', in case you were wondering. Check the website for the club's occasional women-only nights.

Böse Buben

Sachsendamm 76-77 (6270 5610, www.boesebuben-berlin.de). S1, S41, S42, S45, S46 Schöneberg. **Open** varies. **Admission** €6-€8. **No credit cards.** **Map** p310 J12.

A fetish sex party club with imaginatively furnished and decorated rooms. The tiled piss room, sling room, bondage cross and cheap drinks make this quite a grotto of hedonism. Wednesday is the After Work Sex Party; weekends have different parties such as hard SM, fist, bondage and spanking.

CDL-Club

Hohenstaufenstrasse 58 (3266 7855, www.cdl-club.de). U1, U2, U3, U4 Nollendorfplatz. **Open** varies. **Admission** free (€15 minimum spend). **Map** p309 H10.

One of Schöneberg's newest gay sex clubs brings some original elements to the scene, such as special treatment for the well endowed (there's cock and arse measuring; Fridays), a mandatory-mask party (white for tops, black for bottoms; Thursdays) and periodic gangbang events (check the website). The approach seems to be working: the place pulls in a decent crowd from across the age spectrum.

New Action

Kleiststrasse 35 (no phone, www.newactionberlin.de). U1, U2, U3, U4 Nollendorfplatz. **Open** 10pm-5am Mon-Thur; 10pm-7am Fri, Sat; 8pm-3am Sun. **Admission** varies. **No credit cards.** **Map** p309 H9.

Recently reopened, this fetish venue has a hardcore atmosphere. Early mornings, the bar and small darkroom can become quite a gathering of eccentrics who either don't want to go to bed yet or else just got up. Leather, rubber and uniforms rule the roost at this boozed-up spot, where Tuesday is 'Big Dick Nite' – a free drink for the well hung.

Scheune

Motzstrasse 25 (213 8580, www.scheune-berlin.de). U1, U2, U3, U4 Nollendorfplatz. **Open** from 9pm daily. **Admission** free. **No credit cards.** **Map** p309 H9.

A small, welcoming and cheap leather bar. Action in the cellar is late and heavy. There's a Naked Sex Party every Sunday afternoon (entrance 5.30-9pm), plus occasional rubber nights. It's very popular.

Touch Club

Courbierestrasse 13 (0179 152 8893 mobile). U1, U2, U3, U4 Nollendorfplatz. **Open** 8pm-5am daily. **Admission** varies. **No credit cards.** **Map** p309 H9.

An all-boys strip club in the classic style. The strippers are drawn from the predictable porntastic stereotypes – sporty athletes, barely legals, hot-blooded Latinos – and offer both public and private shows. VIP parties can be arranged for birthdays, bachelor parties and other special events.

SAUNAS

Saunas are not as popular as they used to be in Berlin, and remain most frequented after work. In-house bills are run up on your locker or cabin number and are settled on leaving. No open cabins, only personal ones.

Apollo Splash Club

Kurfürstenstrasse 101, Schöneberg (213 2424, www.apollosplashclub.com). U1, U2, U3

Wittenbergplatz. **Open** noon-7am Mon-Thur; noon Fri-7am Mon. **Admission** varies. **No credit cards. Map** p309 H8.

This huge labyrinth of sin with 250 lockers and 80 cabins has been given a major revamp in recent years – at least on the first floor. Upstairs has a spa feel, while downstairs retains elements of the place's former Brazilian theme. There is a bar, cinema, dry and steam saunas, a massage area, pool, plunge bath and jungle-style cruising area.

Der Boiler

Mehringdamm 34, Kreuzberg (5770 7175, www.boiler-berlin.de). U6, U7 Mehringdamm. **Open** noon-6am Mon-Thur; noon Fri-6am Mon. **Admission** €14.50-€19.50. **Map** p310 M10.

Mr B. *See p190.*

Tucked into an off-street courtyard (just beyond the queues for Mustufa's revered kebab), Der Boiler opened in 2011 and quickly became a big favourite. It's an ultra-modern expanse of saunas, steam rooms, whirlpools, cabins and glory holes, where most of the manhandling takes place in a dark maze. Attracting a hot variety of older and younger men, it's busier and kinkier on evenings and weekends.

CRUISING

Cruising is a popular and legal pursuit in Berlin. Most action takes place in parks, in the daytime, often just metres away from the general public, who don't seem to care. And don't panic or jump into a bush when encountering the police – they are actually there to protect you from gay bashers and they never hassle cruisers. There is no taboo about nudity in parks.

Grunewald

S7 Grunewald.

Go to the woods behind the car park at Pappelplatz. From the S-Bahn station, walk 500m (a third of a mile) south along Eichkampstrasse until it passes under the *Autobahn*, then turn to the right into the woods. From there it's about another 50m to the car park. This is a popular daytime spot but it's also well frequented at night, when bikers and harder guys mingle among the trees.

Tiergarten

S5, S7, S75 Tiergarten. **Map** p309 H7.

The Löwenbrücke (where the Grosser Weg crosses the Neuer See) is the cruising focal point – but the whole corner south-west of the Siegessäule becomes a bit of a gay theme park in summer, when daytime finds hundreds of gays sunning themselves on the Tuntenwiese ('faggot meadow') and taking periodic sex breaks in the woods.

Volkspark Friedrichshain

Tram M4. **Map** p307 Q5.

Offering friendlier, younger and more relaxed cruisers than Berlin's other hunting grounds, this outdoor sex patch was traditionally behind the Märchenbrunnen, but has now moved further east, to the slopes just off Friedenstrasse (just walk into the bushes behind the war memorial). Particularly active on sunny afternoons in the summer, when boys stroll over from the nearby meadow.

Wannsee

See p163.

Europe's largest inland beach is home to a patch of sand traditionally occupied by gay men – just walk all the way to the end of the beach and through to the far reaches of the FKK (nudist) zone. Sun-kissed men lounge here on their towels and use the nearest loos and shower rooms to cruise and have fun. Make sure there aren't any children about.

ARTS & ENTERTAINMENT

SHOPS & SERVICES
Books

Bruno's
Nollendorfplatz, corner of Bülowstrasse 106, Schöneberg (6150 0385, www.brunos.de). U1, U2, U3, U4 Nollendorfplatz. **Open** 10am-10pm Mon-Sat; 1-9pm Sun. **Map** p310 J9.
A large and plush shop with an extensive selection of reading and viewing material, plus cards, calendars, videos, condoms, lube and other paraphernalia.
Other location Schönhauser Allee 131, Prenzlauer Berg (6150 0387).

Prinz Eisenherz
Motzstrasse 23, Schöneberg (313 9936, www.prinz-eisenherz.com). U1, U2, U3, U4 Nollendorfplatz. **Open** 10am-8pm Mon-Sat. **Map** p309 H9.
One of the finest gay bookshops in Europe, including among its large English-language stock many titles unavailable in Britain. There's a good art and photography section, plus magazines, postcards and news of book readings and other events.

Toys & Fetish

Black Style
Seelower Strasse 5, Prenzlauer Berg (4468 8595, www.blackstyle.de). U2, S8, S9, S41, S42, S85 Schönhauser Allee. **Open** 1-6.30pm Mon-Wed; 1-8pm Thur, Fri; 11am-6pm Sat. **Map** p307 O1.
From black fashion to butt plugs, if it's made out of rubber or latex, Black Style has got it. High quality, reasonable prices and a big variety. Mail order too.

Butcherei Lindinger
Motzstrasse 18, Schöneberg (2005 1391, www.butcherei-lindinger.de). U1, U2, U3, U4 Nollendorfplatz. **Open** 2-8pm Mon-Sat. **No credit cards. Map** p309 H9.
A smart workshop producing tailor-made leather clothing, sportswear, kinky kecks and chainmail. It also offers a fantastic range of toys and rubber gear, including some of the biggest dildos on the market.

Connection Garage
Fuggerstrasse 33, Schöneberg (218 1432, www.connection-berlin.com). U1, U2, U3 Wittenbergplatz. **Open** 10am-1am Mon-Sat; 2pm-1am Sun. **Map** p309 H9.
Connection Garage stocks a huge selection of leather novelties, clothing, SM accessories and magazines. The cruising area comes alive at weekends when it amalgamates with the Connection club (*see p186*).

Jaxx
Motzstrasse 19, Schöneberg (213 8103, www.thejaxx.de). U1, U2, U3, U4 Nollendorfplatz.

Open noon-3am Mon-Sat; 1pm-3am Sun. **Admission** €8; €6 Tue. **Map** p309 H9.
Jaxx stocks a good selection of toys and videos, plus there are video cabins and a cruising area.

Leathers
Schliemannstrasse 38, Prenzlauer Berg (442 7786, www.leathers.de). U2 Eberswalder Strasse. **Open** noon-8pm Mon-Sat. **Map** p307 P2.
This workshop produces leather and SM articles of the highest quality. There's no smut here – just well-presented products and friendly, helpful staff. Extensive online shop for the lazy kinkster.

Mr B
Motzstrasse 22, Schöneberg (2199 7704, www.misterb.com). U1, U2, U3, U4 Nollendorfplatz. **Open** noon-8pm Mon-Fri; 11am-8pm Sat. **Map** p309 H9.
The Berlin outpost of this Dutch chain has everything for the hardcore crowd. It's known particularly for its leather and rubber outfits, metal accessories and toys, SM articles, lubricants and clothing. Occasional art exhibitions too. *Photo p189.*

RoB Berlin
Fuggerstrasse 19, Schöneberg (2196 7400, www.rob-berlin.de). U1, U2, U3, U4 Nollendorfplatz. **Open** noon-8pm Mon-Sat. **Map** p309 H9.
Like the RoB locations in other European capitals, Berlin's offers top-notch leather regalia and fetish items made uniquely for this chain in its own workshops. There are themed apartments for rent upstairs, and loads of information about upcoming events in the leather community.

Lesbian
Few cities can compete with Berlin's network of lesbian institutions, but there are few lesbian-only bars. For mixed bars and club nights, check *Siegessäule* (www.siegessaeule.de) or *L-mag* (www.l-mag.de), a quarterly free lesbian magazine. *Blattgold* (www.blattgold-berlin.de, in German) is a monthly lesbian mag. There are also relatively reliable listings at www.youngandlesbian.de/szene.html. Many young lesbians favour mixed venues such as **SchwuZ** (*see p186*), **SO36** (*see p182*), **Möbel-Olfe** (*see p180*) and **Die Busche** (*see p181*).

CAFES & BARS
Mitte

Café Seidenfaden
Dircksenstrasse 47 (283 2783, www.frausucht zukunft.de). U8 Weinmeister Strasse, or S5, S7, S75 Hackescher Markt. **Open** 10am-6pm Mon-Fri; noon-6pm Sat. **No credit cards. Map** p307 O5.

Sexclusivitäten.

This place is run by women from a therapy group of former addicts. There are readings and exhibitions, but absolutely no drugs or alcohol. It's packed at lunchtime, quiet at night.

Friedrichshain

Frieda Frauenzentrum
Proskauer Strasse 7 (422 4276, www.frieda-frauenzentrum.de). U5 Samariterstrasse. **Open** 9am-6pm Mon, Wed; 9am-8pm Tue, Thur; 2-8pm Fri; 11am-2pm 4th Sat of mth. **No credit cards.** **Map** p313 T6.
A centre for women's wellbeing and interests, with events aimed at lesbians, mothers and seniors.

Schöneberg

Begine
Potsdamer Strasse 139 (215 1414, www.begine. de). U2 Bülowstrasse. **Open** 5pm-late Mon-Fri; 7pm-late Sat. **No credit cards.** **Map** p310 J9.
This venerable women-only café frequented by lesbians is part of the 'Meeting Point and Culture for Women' centre. From concerts and cabaret to readings and yoga, it has a jam-packed programme.

CLUBS & ONE-NIGHTERS
Friedrichshain

Women's Lounge
Himmelreich, Simon-Dach-Strasse 36 (no phone, www.gay-friedrichshain.de/himmelreich). U5 Frankfurter Tor, or U1, S5, S7, S75 Warschauer Strasse. **Open** 6pm-late Tue. **Map** p312 S7.
Drink specials attract a casual crowd of Friedrichshain lesbians to this popular joint every Tuesday. Expect more socialising than dancing.
▶ *For more about Himmelreich, see p179.*

Kreuzberg

Girls' Dance
Serene Bar, Schwiebusserstrasse 2 (6904 1580, www.serenebar.de). U6 Platz der Luftbrücke. **Open** 10pm-late Sat. **No credit cards.** **Map** p311 M11.
Every Saturday, the girls come out to dance and play together at this long, narrow, amiable bar off the beaten track, near what used to be Tempelhof Airport. 'DJ(ane)s' play for the ladies, who take full advantage of the spacious dancefloor.

Neukölln

L-Tunes
SchwuZ, Rollbergstrasse 26 (5770 2270, www.schwuz.de). U7 Rathaus Neukölln. **Open** 10pm-late 4th Fri of mth. **Admission** €6-€8. **No credit cards.** **Map** p311 Q12.
On the fourth Friday of the month, at gay club SchwuZ (*see p186*), L-Tunes presents dance and electronica nights on two floors with a chill-out zone. It's primarily for young Kreuzberger girls, but the crowd varies in both age and demeanour.

SHOPS & SERVICES
Playstixx
Heimstrasse 6, Kreuzberg (6165 9500, www.playstixx.de). U7 Gneisenaustrasse. **Open** 1-7pm Tue-Fri; noon-5pm Sat. **No credit cards.** **Map** p311 N11.
The dildos on offer at this workshop, run by sculptress Stefanie Dörr, are more likely to come in the form of bananas, whales, fists and dolphins than phalluses. Most are made of non-allergenic, highly durable silicon.

Sexclusivitäten
Fürbringerstrasse 2, Kreuzberg (693 6666, www.sexclusivitaeten.de). U7 Gneisenaustrasse. **Open** noon-8pm Fri; also by appointment. **No credit cards.** **Map** p311 N10.
Laura Mérrit calls herself a feminist linguist and sexpert, offering sex counselling, conflict mediation and a big selection of sex toys. There's a variety of dildos, vibrators and other items.

Nightlife

World War II and the Berlin Wall aside, most people's clearest image of Berlin is of impossibly cool young people dancing moodily in some legendarily decadent nightclub. It's a reputation that has been dutifully fed by cinema over the years, whether it's Sally Bowles oozing sex in the Kit Kat Klub in *Cabaret* or sullen hipsters nodding their heads as Nick Cave thrashes his guitar in the classic Berlin flick *Wings of Desire*. The good news is, it's all true. Sort of. Berlin deserves its reputation as one of the world's best party cities: every taste is catered for here, all night long, in every kind of venue, from desperate dives in temporary locations to swanky premises where mirror balls make the world go round. There's even a KitKatClub (currently domiciled at Sage Club) that makes its celluloid namesake seem staid indeed.

BERLIN BY NIGHT

The landscape of the night is built on shifting sands as the cityscape continues to change. Mitte has seen the biggest number of casualties of late: the Scala has died a death, along with the Rodeo and, most recently, Cookies. Over towards Friedrichshain, two legendary haunts lost battles with developers: Maria am Ostbahnhof and Bar 25, the incredibly popular after-party spot by the Spree. Happily, though, their spirit lives on. Half of the Bar 25 crew moved to the other side of the river and opened the club **Kater Holzig**, but now, following a planning permission coup, they're back in their original spot with **Kater Blau**. Holzmarkt, as the location is now called, is a far grander cultural vision, but the new club is proof that the old debauched streak is alive and well. Reggae club **YAAM** was fortunate enough to take over Maria's old site and is doing its predecessor proud with its fun-time vibes from dusk till dawn and back again.

Meanwhile, Berlin's partygoers continue trekking further east in search of a good night out. Around Ostkreuz, the irritatingly punctuated **://about blank** has established a reputation as a cool place to go, along with the ramshackle **Salon zur Wilden Renate** and party neverland

Sisyphos. Northern Neukölln is also becoming a party centre, though there are more late bars than proper clubs in this residential area – particularly popular is **Sameheads**.

The area around Kottbusser Tor in Kreuzberg remains popular, but two stops east along the U1, around Schlesisches Tor, is where most of the action is these days. Here you'll find stalwarts such as **Magnet** and the riverside **Watergate**, while a €4 taxi ride up Köpenicker Strasse will bring you to **Tresor** and **Sage**. On the other (western) side of Kreuzberg, converted warehouse **Ritter Butzke** pulls a loyal crowd of younger Germans with its local DJs.

As for Berlin's most famous club, **Berghain**, there's little new to be said; it's easy enough to find and the best advice is just to dive in and formulate your own opinion of the city's highest-profile nightspot. At least it's not content to rest on its reputation. As well as installing a new sound system and developing its summer garden, Berghain hosts artistic shows and performances in a massive ground-floor space called Halle.

One thing remains the same in this sleepless city: techno still rules, and electronic beats of one kind or another remain the dominant sound of the city. But somewhere or other, you can find any type of music you like.

There is no clear boundary between some bars and clubs – in this guide, we've listed places such as **Trust**, **Tausend** and **Kingsize** in Mitte and **Monarch** in Kreuzberg under 'Bars & Pubs', but they could just as easily sit in this chapter.

WHEN TO GO

It's not unusual to head off to a party on Friday night and stumble into bed at some point on Sunday afternoon. The real party animals go out during the week too. While this approach is hardcore, the general attitude to clubbing is incredibly laid-back; no dressing up, no planning. Berliners let themselves go with the flow. Note that people don't head to clubs until 2am at the earliest. Admission prices are reasonable, hovering around €10-€12 for big clubs and half that for smaller DJ bars.

GETTING IN

An increasing number of Berlin clubs operate some sort of door policy. The brutal phrase *Gesichtskontrolle* (face control) is often bandied about. At peak times outside Berghain on a Saturday night, at least a third of the people in the queue won't get past the scary bouncer with a tattoo on his face – you'll know you're in if he nods; if he points to his left, hard luck. Argue the toss if you're feeling brave. If you want to increase your chances of getting in, there are a few simple rules. Don't be too loud. Don't be obviously off your face. Don't take pictures of one another in the queue. Don't have this guide in your hand. Use English sparingly. Learn the answer to '*Wie viele?*' (How many [people are you])? *Zwei, drei, vier*. Some clubs don't like people to try too hard; others will turn punters away who haven't made enough effort. Wear whatever you like, but bear in mind that Berliners tend not to dress up in a British sense – short frocks or high heels might be better left at home.

INFORMATION

To find out what's on where, pick up a copy of *Zitty* or *Tip*, Berlin's two fortnightly listings magazines, or their English-language monthly equivalent *Exberliner*. Discerning websites include www.iheartberlin.de, www.unlike.net/berlin and www.sugarhigh.de.

MITTE

Acud

Veteranenstrasse 21 (4435 9498, www.acud.de). U8 Rosenthaler Platz, or S1, S2, S25 Nordbahnhof. **Open & admission** varies. **No credit cards.** **Map** p307 N4.

A massive complex, containing a cinema, theatre and gallery, operated by a friendly Berlin arts collective. There's also a party floor with a playlist mainly devoted to reggae, breakbeat and drum 'n' bass; the

dingy bar is a popular spot for the city's stoners. The cinema programme is interesting, consisting mostly of independent and low-budget films. There's something going on here most nights of the week, and start times and prices vary accordingly.

Bohannon

Dircksenstrasse 40 (6950 5287, www.bohannon. de). U2, U5, U8, S5, S7, S75 Alexanderplatz. **Open** 10pm-late Mon, Thur-Sat. **Admission** €6-€10. **No credit cards.** **Map** p307 O5.

The club's name, a nod to US funk legend Hamilton Bohannon, indicates its driving musical principle. Billed as offering 'soulful electronic clubbing', this basement location features two dancefloors, regular sets by the likes of dancehall DJ Barney Millah and excellent Saturday night soul parties.

Clärchen's Ballhaus

Auguststrasse 24 (282 9295, www.ballhaus.de). S1, S2, S25 Oranienburger Strasse. **Open** 10am-late daily. **No credit cards.** **Map** p307 N5. *See p194* **Having a Ball.**

Golden Gate

Corner of Dircksenstrasse & Schicklerstrasse (5770 4278, www.goldengate-berlin.de). U8, S5, S7, S75 Jannowitzbrücke. **Open** midnight-late Thur-Sun. **Admission** varies. **No credit cards.** **Map** p307 P6.

Once home to a rather hit-and-miss music policy, with the occasional live show, this grimy little club has now settled firmly into a series of all-weekend techno parties. Its location – smack dab in the middle of a motorway – means it has no issue with noise. The Thursday night parties are particularly raucous, with the club carrying on until pretty much Monday afternoon. The dancefloor manages to contain a deceptive number of people in a Tardis-like feat; the crowd mixes hedonistic locals with an overspill of those who've fallen victim to the tough Berghain door policy. The atmosphere is extremely relaxed and positive, staying true to the Berlin party ethos of egalitarian fun with no fashion police or posing allowed. People mingle in the outdoor 'garden' space (really a small grimy patch with battered sofas – in winter covered by a marquee) that is comically visible to passers-by on the street.

House of Weekend

12th floor, Alexanderplatz 5 (2589 9366, www. houseofweekend.berlin). U2, U5, U8, S5, S7, S75 Alexanderplatz. **Open** varies. **Admission** €8-€15. **No credit cards.** **Map** p307 P5.

Situated right in the centre of activity of former East Berlin, Weekend's home is at the top of one of Alexanderplatz's many Communist-era tower blocks. The roof terrace is a big draw, combining a decent booking policy with spectacular views. It lost its cool factor long ago and recently rebranded itself as a VIP venue, which means upmarket barbecues on the terrace from 7pm and a buttoned-down club experience two floors below from 11pm.

Kaffee Burger & Old CCCP

Torstrasse 60 (2804 6495, www.kaffeeburger.de). U2 Rosa-Luxemburg-Platz. **Open** 9pm-late Mon-Sat; 7pm-late Sun. **Admission** €1-€5. **No credit cards. Map** p307 O5.

Proudly boasting 200 concerts and 364 parties a year, Kaffee Burger's programme runs the cultural gamut. Early evenings may see readings, lectures, films or live music. Later on, DJs play anything from old-school country to Balkan beats, or even flamboyant Israeli pop at the 'unkosher Jewish night' Meschugge. Adjoining Kaffee Burger is the

Russian-themed late bar, Old CCCP, with delightfully kitsch decor and lighting that's bright enough to facilitate interaction with strangers. At the weekend, you can bounce between the two for the same cover charge.

Sage Club

Köpenicker Strasse 76 (no phone, www.sage-club. de). U8 Heinrich-Heine-Strasse. **Open** 10pm-late Thur; 11pm-late Fri, Sat. **Admission** varies. **No credit cards. Map** p311 P7.

A labyrinthine complex of half a dozen dancefloors accessed via the north-side entrance to Heinrich-Heine-Strasse U-Bahn station, the Sage Club caters to a relatively young, rock-oriented crowd. It is

HAVING A BALL

The old-style dance hall is back in fashion.

Berlin has been famous for its substance-fuelled, all-night techno parties in cavernous raw spaces for the past few decades. But in the heart of Mitte, a decidedly old-school venue is giving the rave a run for its money in terms of popularity and downright fun.

And, in fact, it's nothing new: dance hall **Clärchen's Ballhaus** (*see p193*) has been frequented by fleet-footed Berliners since it was established by Clara Haberman in 1913. Since 2005, it's been under new management – the rakish duo of David Regehr and Christian Schulz – and is more popular than ever.

'People come here to find the love of their lives,' Schulz has said. These people can range from twentysomething hipsters to 75-year-old Ballhaus veterans to celebrities (such as German actress Heike Makatsch and even Charlotte Rampling) who've stopped in during Berlin Film Fest parties. Best of all, as the night wears on, these drastically divergent demographics start mixing. It's not unusual to see a geriatric Fred Astaire type teaching a young pink-haired artist how to tango or foxtrot.

The Ballhaus has two ballrooms. The vast ground-floor space is lined with silver tinsel streamers. Here, the dancefloor is ringed by wooden tables laid with white tablecloths and candles, while a huge disco ball spins overhead. But it's the room

upstairs that never fails to elicit gasps of awe from first-time visitors. Smaller, but with huge cracked mirrors, chandeliers, ornate mouldings and candlelight, the Spiegelsaal (Mirror Salon) transports guests straight back to the 1920s.

In fact, very little has changed since then. When Clärchen's was turned over to its new owners, Berliners who had danced here for decades feared it would fall prey to the homogenisation that 'renovation' in Berlin often brings. But Schulz and Regehr left the interior almost exactly as it was – both upstairs and downstairs have vintage fixtures and fittings, even wallpaper… as well as a heady smell of history that's hard to pin down. Is it all GDR, or is it the Weimar era?

Most regulars don't care (and more than a few were actually around during the GDR days). They're here to tango on Tuesdays, learn to swing on Wednesdays, attend the 'pasta opera' nights in the Mirror Salon, or even find the love of their lives on weekend nights. Some come to have an inexpensive oven-baked pizza, served inside or in the beautiful front garden. But the magic never fails: after midnight, both ballrooms teem with all types in a free-for-all that begins with live music and then segues into Michael Jackson, the Beach Boys, old German *Schlager* music, or all of the above. It's more cheesy than chic, but that's part of the charm.

only reliably open on Thursdays for rock night: an unpretentious affair where skinny jeans and leather jackets is the uniform of choice. At weekends you'll have better luck with some fetish gear, as Sage is the current home of the notorious KitKatClub (www.kitkatclub.de), complete with indoor swimming pool.

▶ *Further up Köpenicker Strasse, at nos.18-20, the owners operate Sage restaurant, serving tapas and pizza, as well as an outdoor beach bar in summer.*

Tresor

Köpenicker Strasse 70 (no phone, www.tresorberlin. de). U8 Heinrich-Heine-Strasse. **Open** 11pm-late Mon; midnight-late Wed-Sat. **Admission** €5-€12. **No credit cards. Map** p311 P7.

Berlin's original techno club is housed in what was formerly the main central-heating power station for East Berlin. The colossal location is breathtaking, but only a tiny portion of the vast space is in use; plans to create a huge centre of alternative art and culture have resulted so far in the Ohm performance space next door and large-scale experimental music festivals such as Berlin Atonal (www.berlin-atonal. com). The experience of the basement floor is one you'll not forget; a black hole occasionally punctuated by flashing strobes with some of the loudest, hardest techno it's humanly possible to hear.

PRENZLAUER BERG

Duncker

Dunckerstrasse 64 (445 9509, www.dunckerclub. de). U2 Eberswalder Strasse, or S8, S9, S41, S42 Prenzlauer Allee. **Open** 9pm-late Mon; 10pm-late Thur; 11pm-late Fri, Sat. **Admission** €5. **No credit cards. Map** p307 P2.

Duncker is located, aptly enough, in a neo-Gothic church on a nondescript side street. While the tail end of the week focuses on new wave, dark wave and indie, it's the Dark Monday goth party that is the club's bread and butter. Surprisingly, for a city the size of Berlin, venues catering for our friends in black are few and far between, making this a precious gem for fans of the genre.

Roadrunner's Paradise

Saarbrückerstrasse 24 (7808 2991, www. roadrunners-paradise.de). U2 Senefelderplatz. **Open** varies. **Admission** €8-€20. **No credit cards. Map** p307 O4.

Navigate your way through to the third courtyard of the former Königstadt brewery and you'll find Roadrunner's tucked away next to a motorcycle repair shop, a suitably greasy location for this butch venue. On offer is a tasty but irregular mixture of live shows and DJ sets, focusing on garage, bluesrock, rockabilly and surf. The tiny stage may seem a little lost in the wide-open concert space, but there's plenty of room to dance and the sound system is up to scratch. Alternatively, marvel at the array of 1950s American kitsch while sinking a beer.

IN THE KNOW BERGHAIN BLUES

Where should you go if you can't get into Berghain (or don't want to risk getting turned away)? For techno, try **Tresor** (see left); for electro, try **Watergate** (see p199) or **Ritter Butzke** (see p199); and for a grope in the dark, try the KitKatClub nights at **Sage Club** (see p194).

FRIEDRICHSHAIN

★ ://about blank

Markgrafendamm 24C (no phone, http:// aboutparty.net). S3, S5, S7, S8, S9, S41, S42, S75 Ostkreuz. **Open** midnight-late Thur-Sat. **No credit cards. Map** p312 T8.

Particularly famed for its open-air parties, this club near Ostkreuz station is a favourite with the city's more adventurous hedonists – not least for its monthly blowout Homopatik night (*see p181*).

★ Berghain/Panorama Bar

Am Wriezener Bahnhof (no phone, www.berghain. de). U1, S3, S5, S7, S75 Warschauer Strasse. **Open** midnight-late Fri, Sat. **Admission** €10-€14. **No credit cards. Map** p312 R7.

Easily the city's most famous club – and some would say the best club in the world – Berghain is not just a techno club: it's a way of life for many of the tireless regulars who call it 'church'. Housed within an imposing former power station, it emerged from the ashes of a legendary gay predecessor, Ostgut, which fell victim to the city's massive infrastructure projects. Even 'non-club' people will be intoxicated by the open atmosphere, liberal attitudes, eccentric characters, carefully preserved industrial fabric of the building and, of course, the gargantuan sound system. It's open, complete with darkrooms, from Saturday midnight until well into Monday morning. The club's reputation for a difficult and random door policy is not entirely undeserved: doorman Sven (recognisable by his facial tattoos) looms large all night with a seemingly haphazard attitude to who gets in. We recommend that you be calm, sober and respectful in the queue, and it goes without saying that drunken stag dos aren't welcome. Panorama Bar, up a flight of stairs from Berghain, is a smaller dancefloor that plays old-school house and features oversized artworks by Wolfgang Tillmans. *Photo 196.*

Kater Blau

Holzmarktstrasse 25 (no phone, www.katerblau.de). S5, S7, S75 Ostbahnhof. **Open** varies. **Admission** €5-€15. **Map** p311 Q7.

This is the X-rated part of the expansive, family-friendly Holzmarkt development. Now in its third incarnation, following previous lives as Bar 25 and Kater Holzig, it's back on the sunny north side of the

ARTS & ENTERTAINMENT

Berghain. See p195.

river. With a moored boat, roaring fire at night and many hammock-like structures, the potential for alfresco relaxing is very high. At the business end of proceedings, a fine roster of electronic DJs spin away unendingly – sometimes for four days straight. The vibe is more crusty than chic, and increasingly so as the weekend unravels. If you have the stamina (and courage) to last well into Monday afternoon, expect to encounter some of Berlin's strangest creatures.

K17
Pettenkofer Strasse 17A (4208 9300, www.k17-berlin.de). U5, S8, S9, S41, S42 Frankfurter Allee. **Open** 10pm-late Fri, Sat. **Admission** €6. **No credit cards. Map** p313 U6.
Goth, EBM, industrial and metal are undead and well in this three-floor club. Parties hit full pelt at the weekend and the occasional live shows feature hardcore, nu-metal and crossover bands. There's also a Dark Hostel within the same complex, offering goth-friendly accommodation.

Rosi's
Revaler Strasse 29 (no phone, www.rosis-berlin.de). S3, S5, S7, S8, S9, S41, S42, S75 Ostkreuz. **Open** 11pm-late Thur-Sat. **Admission** €2-€7. **No credit cards. Map** p312 T8.
A typical Berlin club, Rosi's is a tumbledown, DIY affair: all bare bricks and mismatched flea-market furniture. The atmosphere is very relaxed and the crowd tends to be young and studenty. Live acts are a regular feature, DJs spin mainly electro and rock, and the beer garden is popular on summer nights.

Salon zur Wilden Renate
Alt-Stralau 70 (2504 1426, www.renate.cc). S3, S5, S7, S8, S9, S41, S42, S75 Ostkreuz. **Open & admission** varies. **No credit cards. Map** p312 T9.
This knackered old house was perennially at risk of being torn down and turned into – of course – trendy

apartments. Once-sporadic parties follow a regular weekend rhythm these days, usually going till the last man standing. Students and wasted ravers press up against refugees from Mitte in the reliably crowded rooms, which are still set up like the flats they once were – complete with the odd bed. On languid summer afternoons, the club hops across the river to an intimate open-air wonderland called Else.

Urban Spree
Revaler Strasse 99 (7407 8597, www.urbanspree.com). U1, S5, S7, S75 Warschauer Strasse. **Open** noon-midnight Mon-Thur, Sun; noon-3am Fri, Sat. **Admission** varies. **Map** p312 S8.
This new arts centre is doing much to revive the somewhat moribund (and tacky) area by Revaler Strasse in Friedrichshain that's known as the 'clubbing mile'. Created by the French crew behind the much-missed .HBC complex, Urban Spree houses an art gallery, concert hall, studio spaces and food trucks. There are frequent performances and concerts, ranging from free-form jazz to acid-folk and improvised instrumental noise, with an emphasis on the experimental and DIY. Summertime bonus: an expansive suntrap of a beer garden.

YAAM
Schillingbrücke, at Stralauer Platz (no phone, www.yaam.de). S5, S7, S75 Ostbahnhof. **Open & admission** varies. **Map** p311 Q7.
Yet another victim of Berlin's Mediaspree development, YAAM was forcibly evicted from its previous home – but you can't keep a good reggae club down. It quickly found another riverside spot (formerly the location of club Maria), so it's business as usual for this legendary beach bar and cultural centre. By day, there might be kids playing and a laid-back game of volleyball in progress, with a jerk chicken stall on the side. Then, as the light fades, things ease up a notch or two with concerts and parties bouncing to an Afro-Caribbean beat. An ultra-friendly place.

TIERGARTEN

2BE

Klosterstrasse 44 (8904 87310, www.2be-club.de).
U2 Klosterstrasse. **Open** 11pm-late Sat.
Admission varies. **No credit cards.**
Map p306 K5.

The in-house DJs focus mainly on hip hop, with the odd reggae and dancehall tune thrown in for good measure, and there's also usually a live act or two playing each month. Big-name DJs such as Grandmaster Flash and LTJ Bukem have been known to put in an appearance. It's a spacious location, with outside seating and several bars. The crowd tends to be young and enthusiastic.

Adagio

Marlene-Dietrich-Platz 1 (258 9890, www.adagio.
de). U2, S1, S2 Potsdamer Platz. **Open** 11pm-late
Fri, Sat. **Admission** €10. **Map** p310 K8.

A spin-off from a swanky Zurich disco, Adagio has 'medieval' decor and Renaissance-style frescoes that are jarringly at odds with the Renzo Piano-designed theatre whose basement it occupies. Pricey drinks, abundant members-only areas and a music policy of disco, polite house and cheesy classics cater to forty-something tourists and after-work crowds willing to shell out for an illusion of exclusivity. There's a dress code (no jeans or sports shoes). Friday night is ladies' night – complete with male strip show.

KREUZBERG & TREPTOW

Arena Club

Eichenstrasse 4 (5332 0340, www.arena-berlin.de).
U1 Schlesisches Tor, or S8, S9, S41, S42 Treptower
Park. **Open & admission** varies. **No credit**
cards. Map p312 S9.

The bare brick walls and sparse lighting at this dingy and intimate venue in Treptow make it look more like a dungeon than a club. The sound system is adequate for the size, but the vibe does tend to get a bit sleazy towards the early hours. It's part of a larger riverside complex, Arena Berlin, and is also used as a theatre or concert venue. There are club-type events on the Hoppetosse boat and floating Badeschiff pool (*see p145*), both moored nearby on the Spree.

Chalet

Vor dem Schlesischen Tor 3 (6953 6290, www.
chalet-berlin.de). U1 Schlesisches Tor. **Open**
midnight-late Tue-Sun. **Admission** €10-€12.
No credit cards. Map p312 S9

Chalet was opened by some of the late, great Bar 25 crew – and these guys know a thing or two about getting their groove on. Located in a grand, 150-year-old townhouse, it has multiple levels and rooms to explore, as well as a large luscious garden in which to shoot the breeze when the beats get too much. An altogether stylish and sultry club with a party pretty much every night; more local on weekdays, more touristy at weekends.

Chesters

Glogauerstrasse 2 (8571 3255, www.chesters-
live.de). U1 Görlitzer Bahnhof. **Open** varies.
Admission €4-€8. **No credit cards.**
Map p312 R9.

Decor-wise, aside from a couple of drooping disco balls and a lonely stripper pole, there isn't much to write home about at this black-walled bunker of a club. It's the eclectic music policy that continues to pull in the painfully hip punters. Formerly an indie rock and hip hop concert venue, since two New York transplants took control of the booking, bass-heavy dance genres such as trap have become the order

ARTS & ENTERTAINMENT

Urban Spree.

of the day. For a compact space, the sound system packs a lot of heat, allowing for a head-spinning onslaught of bold new sounds until the wee hours.

Club der Visionaere

Am Flutgraben (6951 8942, www.clubder visionaere.com). U1 Schlesisches Tor, or S8, S9, S41, S42 Treptower Park. **Open** 2pm-late Mon-Fri; noon-late Sat, Sun. **Admission** €5. **No credit cards. Map** p312 S9

One of the first and best, this summer-only canalside club is a great way to find out what makes Berlin so special. Nestled under an enormous weeping willow, it's just out of sight of the road running between Kreuzberg and Treptower Park. There's a small indoor dancefloor and a rickety open-air area of wooden decking with a large jetty stretching out across the water. Due to intermittent fire regulation problems, the winter parties are now held in the nearby Hoppetosse boat. You can drop in during the week for a beer, but the place comes to life at the weekend, filling up with an after-hour crowd, happy to chill, drink and dance the day away.

★ Farbfernseher

Skalitzer Strasse 114 (5309 1711, www.farb fernseher.de). U1 Görlitzer Bahnhof. **Open** 10pm-late Wed-Sat. **Admission** €1-€3. **No credit cards. Map** p311 P9

Much more than a bar but not quite a club, Farbfernseher hits the mark for the in-betweeners of the Berlin night. Once an old television shop (hence the name, meaning colour TV), it has become a scenester favourite in recent years. Things quickly get hot and heavy on the dancefloor, which is usually marshalled by some rising local talent. Bloke-only groups: expect grief at the door on busier nights.

Gretchen

Obentrautstrasse 19-21 (2592 2701, www. gretchen-club.de). U1, U6 Hallesches Tor, or U6, U7 Mehringdamm. **Open & admission** varies. **No credit cards. Map** p310 M9

Coming straight out of left field, Gretchen has been soothing appetites for more experimental electronica in the city since 2011. It's run by the music heads behind the old Icon club, who put on an impressive array of nights that aren't afraid of forgoing Berlin's ubiquitous tech-house loops in favour of some trap, dubstep, drum 'n' bass or hip hop. The picturesque vaulted ceilings and intricate columns of this former Prussian stable create a wonderfully incongruous setting for the avant-garde sounds.

Lido

Cuvrystrasse 7 (6956 6840, www.lido-berlin.de). U1 Schlesisches Tor. **Open & admission** varies. **No credit cards. Map** p312 R9.

Lido is the HQ of famed Berlin indie-rocksters Karrera Klub, who have been champions of new music in the city for almost 20 years. This former theatre is a suitably spacious location in which to present upcoming new acts and artists, and it's got one of the best sound systems in Berlin. Friendly Fires, MGMT, Shitdisco and the Horrors have all graced the stage in the past. The rear courtyard is now equipped with a canopy, so even in inclement weather you can take a break from the dancefloor.

Magnet

Falckensteinstrasse 48 (4400 8140, www.magnet-club.de). U1 Schlesisches Tor. **Open & admission** varies. **No credit cards. Map** p312 R9.

Reborn from the old 103 Club, Magnet specialises in rock, indie and the occasional metal night, and, along

Club der Visionaere.

with Lido (*see above*), regularly hosts the popular Karrera Klub. It's a friendly, down-to-earth place that's as much a gig venue as a disco, having played host to all manner of acts including Death Cab For Cutie, Andrew WK, Xiu Xiu and LCD Soundsystem.

Prince Charles

Prinzenstrasse 85F (no phone, www.prince charlesberlin.com). U8 Moritzplatz. **Open** 11pm-late Thur-Sat. **Admission** varies. **No credit cards. Map** p311 O8.

Walking down the concrete underpass to the entrance, it feels more like the approach to a car park than a trendy little club. It's situated in a former swimming pool, and the tiled walls and soft lighting create an intimate atmosphere. Artfully dishevelled young things bop along to the house-heavy soundtrack, pausing for a breather outside on the extremely lounge-worthy wooden decking.

Ritter Butzke

Ritterstrasse 24 (no phone, www.ritterbutzke.de). U8 Moritzplatz. **Open** midnight-late Fri, Sat. **Admission** varies. **No credit cards. Map** p311 O8.

This enormous old factory is a current party hotspot thanks to its reliable booking policy (expect party faves such as Kollektiv Turmstrasse or Jake The Rapper) and imaginative decor. It held illegal parties for years but has now gone legit and even deigns to allow its parties to be promoted in listings mags from time to time. It's the antithesis of Berghain: a crowds of locals, and unsnooty and amiable bouncers (who are occasionally dressed as knights – *Ritter* means 'knight'). Brace yourself for a massive queue if you arrive between 1am and 3.30am.

Watergate

Falckensteinstrasse 49 (no phone, www.water-gate. de). U1 Schlesisches Tor. **Open** midnight-late Wed-Sat. **Admission** varies. **No credit cards. Map** p312 R9.

This slick two-level club was a driving force behind the rise of minimal techno in mid 2000s Berlin, as well as the first with a ceiling-mounted responsive LED lighting system, now copied all around the world. The downstairs Water Floor is particularly impressive with its panorama windows looking directly on to the Spree, and a floating deck terrace for watching the sunrise over Kreuzberg. It can feel too touristy on weekends and its increasingly populist bookings don't help, but pick the right night and you'll still feel the original magic. Wednesdays are for the professional ravers – there are few places where you can party well into a weekday morning with such a fine central view of the city. The music is usually some form of tech-house; Watergate does a lot to support smaller local labels such as Keinemusik and Souvenir, and legends (such as Kerri Chandler) often play too. Check the website for occasional events on Tuesdays and Sundays.

NEUKÖLLN

For legendary gay club **SchwuZ**, *see p186*.

Sameheads

Richardstrasse 10 (7012 1060, www.sameheads. com). U7 Karl-Marx-Strasse. **Open** 2pm-late Tue-Sat. **Admission** free-€3. **No credit cards. Map** p312 R12.

A friendly international hipster enclave that steadfastly refuses to be pigeonholed. What began as an offbeat fashion boutique quickly evolved into a bar and late-night party space. Vintage threads are still on sale in the day, while all manner of antics kick off as the sun goes down. You might stumble upon any or all of the following: comedy open mics, art shows, pub quizzes, film screenings and sweaty raves. It's all masterminded by three British brothers – Nathan, Leo and Harry – aka the Sameheads.

OTHER DISTRICTS

Sisyphos

Hauptstrasse 15, Lichtenberg (9836 6839, www.sisyphos-berlin.net). S3 Rummelsburg. **Open** midnight Fri-10am Mon. **Admission** €10. **No credit cards.**

You don't make the trek out to Sisyphos just for a snoop and a couple of beers. It's an 'in for a penny, in for a pound' sort of place, where the party begins on Friday and trundles on non-stop until Monday. Vast indoor and outdoor spaces at this former dog-biscuit factory help create a festival-like spirit that's pitch-perfect for sunny weekends. Music ranges from pumping techno inside to more housey tunes out by the 'lake' – more of a scummy pond, really. Crowd-wise, expect it all: fresh-faced student revellers and wizened ravers of a dreadlocked persuasion are among the regulars.

★ Stattbad

Gerichtstrasse 65, Wedding (4679 7350, www. stattbad.net). U6, S41, S42 Wedding, or S1, S2, S25 Humboldthain. **Open** midnight-late Sat. **Admission** €13. **No credit cards. Map** p306 K2.

Spearheading the forever-touted rise of Wedding, this imposing turn-of-the-century bathhouse is now a cultural centre. Like many of Berlin's ex-industrial buildings that have been earmarked for arty purposes, it's primarily used as a club and – with all the original fittings intact – is a particularly impressive place to party. You enter through various underground tunnels lined with giant pipes, emerging into the large, empty swimming pool. The DJ is literally in at the deep end, with the floor of the pool being the dancefloor. Acts come from the more indie side of the electronic spectrum. By day, it doubles as an urban art gallery. This is the location for the Berlin chapter of the massively popular Boiler Room DJ Livestream events, held monthly and filmed in – you guessed it – the old boiler room.

ARTS & ENTERTAINMENT

Performing Arts

Berlin's long division means the city has twice as many opera houses, orchestras and venues as most other German cities. Also, the country is blessed with incredibly generous subsidies across the entire spectrum of performing arts, so the city teems with musicians, dancers and directors. In the popular music arena, Berlin is nothing less than legendary as a one-time residence for David Bowie, Iggy Pop and Nick Cave, and as a spiritual home of electronic music. On stage, the city has one of the most exciting theatre cultures anywhere in the world, with five generously funded, multi-stage state theatres, surrounded and supplemented by a huge, thriving fringe scene. And the best thing about the huge amounts of accessible culture? Cheap seats are usually available on the day and there's none of the snootiness of grander German cities such as Munich.

Music

CLASSICAL & OPERA

No city in the world can compete with Berlin when it comes to the sheer number of orchestras and opera houses. This cultural richness is a legacy of not only the city's long artistic heritage, but also of its Cold War division. East and West Berlin were both awash with state subsidies in a bid to demonstrate the cultural supremacy of communist and capitalist philosophies. After reunification there was twice the amount of everything – so Berlin now boasts enough classical music for two (maybe three) cities. It's not just quantity, but quality too: the Berlin Philharmonic is arguably the world's finest symphony orchestra.

OPERA COMPANIES

The posters on the U-Bahn proclaim Berlin *Opernhauptstadt* ('opera capital') – and they aren't kidding. Not only does Germany have one-seventh of the world's opera houses, but Berlin alone has three state-subsidised opera houses – a record not matched even in Italy.

The three houses are now incorporated into one foundation, the Opernstiftung, but co-ordination of their programmes is still an issue, as is their simultaneous closure during summer.

The **Deutsche Oper** still lives under the shadow of its former long-time intendant (similar to general director), Götz Friedrich, who died in 2000. Since then, a revolving door of German opera luminaries have struggled to provide the house with a distinct artistic profile, with Dietmar Schwarz in charge since 2012.

The **Staatsoper Unter den Linden** has moved temporarily to the more utilitarian Schiller Theater, while its home undergoes a €240 million refurbishment that's due for completion in October 2015. Daniel Barenboim has been musical director since 1992; he signed another ten-year contract in 2011. Its orchestra, the Berliner Staatskapelle, founded in 1570, is one of the world's finest opera orchestras and has Barenboim as conductor for life. His presence ensures that performances are of the highest musical quality, even if they have sometimes been overshadowed by spectacular staging.

The **Komische Oper**, under intendant Andreas Homoki, prides itself on contemporary, even controversial, productions, and an outreach programme that includes Turkish subtitling. It doesn't shy away from sex and violence either, with a notorious version of Mozart's *Abduction of Seraglio* that used real prostitutes in the cast, who were graphically murdered on stage. Although it has the smallest budget of the three opera houses, it outshone the other two by winning the prestigious Opera House of the Year award in 2007 and 2013. Hungarian conductor Henrik Nánási took over from Patrick Lange as general music director in 2012.

For more independent operatic fare, don't neglect the down-at-heel but charming **Neuköllner Oper**, as well as **Novoflot** (www. novoflot.de), **Kiez Oper** (www.kiezoper.com) and **Home Opera** (www.homeopera.net). Expect innovative music and theatre of surprising quality, despite low budgets.

ORCHESTRAS

The mighty **Berliner Philharmoniker** (www.berliner-philharmoniker.de) goes from strength to strength under Sir Simon Rattle, appointed in 2002, with intendant Pamela Rosenberg joining in 2006. Rattle promised to bring adventure to the programme and attract younger audiences, and has introduced an emphasis on contemporary composers such as Thomas Adès and Marc Anthony Turnage. He went through a rocky patch around 2005-06, when he came in for criticism from some of the highbrow German press, suggesting he was not meeting the standards of his illustrious predecessors when it came to the German canon. However, in 2008 the orchestra voted to keep him in the post until 2018.

The **Deutsches Symphonie-Orchester Berlin** (www.dso-berlin.de) still garners fairly healthy subsidies and remains one of the finest places in town to hear avant-garde compositions and unusual programmes. However, chief conductor Ingo Metzmacher resigned in 2010 after disputes over financing, and his successor, Tugan Sokhiev, is also leaving, in 2016, to devote more time to his other job as musical director of the Bolshoi Theatre.

Groundbreaking 20th-century composers, from Hindemith to Prokofiev and Schönberg to Penderecki, have conducted their own work with the **Rundfunk-Sinfonieorchester Berlin** (www.rsb-online.de). Founded in 1923 to provide programming for the new medium of radio, the orchestra looks set to continue with its focus on contemporary work under lifetime musical director Marek Janowski.

Fans of the old masters are still well served by the **Konzerthausorchester Berlin** (www. konzerthausorchester.de), previously known as the Berliner Sinfonie-Orchester. The feisty group – founded after the building of the Wall as the East's answer to the Philharmonic – has a loyal

following, but one that prefers more familiar works. The unorthodox Hungarian conductor Ivan Fischer has been principal conductor since 2012, and has introduced some gimmicky policies such as surprise concerts, encore requests and the *Mittendrin* concerts, where audience members sit within the orchestra.

Berlin's chamber orchestras also offer a steady stream of first-rate concerts. A union of two older ensembles formed the **Berlin Opera Chamber Orchestra** (www.berlin operachamberorchestra.com), which, as the name suggests, plays opera music as well as contemporary classical at the Philharmonie. The **Kammerorchester Berlin** (www.koberlin.de) remains popular but predictable, with works ranging from Vivaldi to Mozart and back again. The **Deutsches Kammerorchester Berlin** (www.dko-berlin.de), founded in 1989, has acquired an excellent reputation for working with rising star conductors and soloists, and for offering innovative yet audience-friendly programmes. **Ensemble Mini** (www.mini mahler.com), formed by British director Joolz Gale, brings together 20 players who interpret the classics in surprising ways.

FESTIVALS

Music festivals pepper Berlin's calendar. The **Ultraschall** (*see p30*) festival of new music, every January, features many of the world's leading specialist ensembles. **MaerzMusik** (*see p27*), in March, showcases trends in contemporary music. The biennial **Zeitfenster** focuses on 17th-century baroque music for one week in April. Popular programmes, orchestras and soloists often kick off the **Classic Open Air** concert series (*see p29*) in July, while youth orchestras from all over Europe perform at **Young.euro.classic** (*see p29*) in August. The Berliner Festspiele (www.berlinerfestspiele. de) organises the annual **Musikfest Berlin** (*see p29*) in September, which brings some of the world's finest orchestras to Berlin.

TICKETS

Tickets are sold at concert hall box offices (generally up to one hour before the performance) or through ticket agencies (called *Theaterkassen*), though agency commissions can run as high as 17 per cent. **Hekticket** is probably the best bet, or you can try www.ticketonline.de. You can also make reservations by phone, except for concerts by the Philharmonie. Note that many Berlin venues do not accept credit cards.

Some of the former East Berlin venues remain more affordable than their western counterparts, but the days of dirt-cheap tickets are long gone. Getting seats at the Berlin Phil can still be difficult (although the website is easy to navigate). Standing-room at the top of the Konzerthaus

ARTS & ENTERTAINMENT

gives a decent view, but before buying cheap seats for the Staatsoper ask how much of the stage you can see.

Most venues offer student discounts. Under-30s should consider the **ClassicCard** (www.classiccard.de): it costs €15, is valid for a year and entitles the holder to excellent seats for a mere €8 for concerts and €10 for opera and ballet. Participating institutions include the Deutsche Oper, Komische Oper, Konzerthaus, Deutsches Symphonie-Orchester Berlin and the Staatsoper Unter den Linden. It can be purchased at these venues and online.

Hekticket

Hardenbergstrasse 29D, Charlottenburg (230 9930, www.hekticket.de). U2, U9, S5, S7, S75 Zoologischer Garten. **Open** noon-8pm Mon-Sat; 2-6pm Sun. **Map** p309 G8.

Discounts of up to 50% on theatre and concert tickets. For a small commission, staff will sell you tickets for the same evening's performance. Tickets for Sunday matinées are available on Saturday. You can check ticket availability online, though not everything is listed. **Other location** Karl-Liebknecht-Strasse 12, Mitte (2431 2431).

Major Venues

Deutsche Oper

Bismarckstrasse 35, Charlottenburg (343 8401, tickets 3438 4343, www.deutscheoperberlin.de). U2 Deutsche Oper. **Tickets** varies. **Map** p308 D7.

With roots dating from 1912, the Deutsche Oper built its present 1,900-seat hall in 1961, just in time to carry the operatic torch for West Berlin during the Wall years. Since reunification it has lost out in profile to the grander Staatsoper, but retains a solid reputation for productions of the classics. Discounted tickets are available half an hour before performances.

Komische Oper

Behrenstrasse 55-57, Mitte (202 600, tickets 4799 7400, www.komische-oper-berlin.de). U6 Französische Strasse. **Tickets** €12-€79. **Map** p306 M6.

Despite its name, the Komische Oper puts on a broader range than just comic works. Founded in 1947, it made its reputation by breaking with the old operatic tradition of 'costumed concerts' – singers standing around on stage – and putting an emphasis on 'opera as theatre', with real acting skill demanded of its young ensemble. Most of its productions are sung in German. Discounted tickets are sold just before performances.

Konzerthaus

Gendarmenmarkt 2, Mitte (2030 92101, www.konzerthaus.de). U6 Französische Strasse. **Tickets** €20.50-€51.50. **Map** p310 M7.

Formerly the Schauspielhaus am Gendarmenmarkt, this 1821 architectural gem by Schinkel was all but destroyed during the war. Lovingly restored, it reopened in 1984 with three main concert spaces. Organ recitals in the large hall are a treat, played on the massive 5,811-pipe Jehmlich organ. The Konzerthausorchester (*see p201*) is based here, and the Rundfunk-Sinfonieorchester Berlin and the Staatskapelle Berlin also play here.

★ Philharmonie

Herbert-von-Karajan Strasse 1, Tiergarten (254 880, tickets 2548 8999, www.berliner-philharmoniker.de). U2, S1, S2, S25 Potsdamer Platz. **Tickets** €10-€242. **Map** p310 K7.

Berlin's most famous concert hall, home to the world-renowned Berlin Philharmonic Orchestra, is also its most architecturally daring; a marvellous, puckish piece of organic modernism. Designed by Hans Scharoun, the golden building with its distinctive vaulting roof opened in 1963. Its reputation for superb acoustics is accurate, but it does depend on where you sit. Behind the orchestra, the acoustics leave much to be desired, but in front (where seats are much more expensive), the sound is heavenly. The same rules apply in the smaller Kammermusiksaal, which opened in 1987.

The Berliner Philharmoniker (www.berliner-philharmoniker.de) was founded in 1882 by 54 musicians keen to break away from the penurious Benjamin Bilse, in whose orchestra they played. It has been led by some of the world's greatest conductors, as well as by composers such as Peter Tchaikovsky, Edvard Grieg, Richard Strauss and Gustav Mahler. Its greatest fame came under the baton of Herbert von Karajan (1955-89), who was succeeded by Claudio Abbado; since 2002, it's been under the leadership of Sir Simon Rattle.

The Berlin Phil gives about 100 performances in the city during its August to June season, plus 20-30 concerts around the world. Some tickets are available at a discount immediately before performances.

Staatsoper Unter den Linden

Schiller Theater, Bismarckstrasse 110, Charlottenburg (203 540, tickets 2035 4555, www.staatsoper-berlin.de). U2 Ernst-Reuter-Platz. **Tickets** varies. **Map** p309 E7.

The Staatsoper – which is closed until at least October 2015 for a huge refurbishment – was founded as Prussia's Royal Court Opera for Frederick the Great in 1742 and designed by Knobelsdorff along the lines of a Greek temple. Although the present building dates from 1955, the façade faithfully copies the original, twice destroyed in World War II.

Until the renovations are complete, performances take place at the Schiller Theater (which itself recently benefited from a €24 million makeover). Unsold tickets are available for €13, half an hour before the performance.

Philharmonie.

Other Venues

Akademie der Künste

*Pariser Platz 4, Mitte (200 571 000, www.adk.de).
U55, S1, S2, S25 Brandenburger Tor.* **Tickets**
free-€10. **No credit cards. Map** p306 L6.
Founded by Prince Friedrich III in 1696, this is one
of the oldest cultural institutions in Berlin. By 1938,
the Nazis had forced virtually all its prominent members into exile. It was re-established in West Berlin in
1954 to serve as 'a community of exceptional artists'
from around the world. Post-reunification, it moved
into a new building at its pre-war address on Pariser
Platz, but some events are still held at its Tiergarten
address (Hanseatenweg 10). Events include performances of 20th-century compositions, jazz concerts,
poetry readings, film screenings and art exhibitions.

Berliner Dom

*Lustgarten 1, Mitte (tickets 2026 9136, www.
berliner-dom.de). S5, S7, S75 Hackescher Markt.*
Tickets *varies.* **Map** p307 N6.
Berlin's cathedral (*see p47*) holds good concerts, usually of the organ or choral sacred music variety.

Musikhochschule Hanns Eisler

*Charlottenstrasse 55, Gendarmenmarkt, Mitte
(688 305 700, tickets 203 092 101, www.hfm-
berlin.de). U2, U6 Stadtmitte.* **Tickets** *varies.*
Map p310 M7.
Founded in 1950, this musical academy is named
after the composer of the East German national
anthem. It offers students the chance to learn under
some of the stars of Berlin's major orchestras and
operas companies. Rehearsals and masterclasses
are often open to the public for free. Student performances, some of them top-notch, are held in the
Konzerthaus across the street; other events take
place at the Krönungskutschensaal in the Marstall,
a 300-seat venue blessed with perfect acoustics.
Other location Marstall, Schlossplatz 7, Mitte
(9026 9700).

Neuköllner Oper

*Karl-Marx-Strasse 131-133, Neukölln (6889 0777,
www.neukoellneroper.de). U7 Karl-Marx-Strasse.*
Tickets *€9-€24.* **Map** p312 R12.
No grand opera here, but a constantly changing
programme of chamber operas and music-theatre
works, much loved by the Neuköllners who come to
see lighter, bubblier, cheaper and much less formal
works than those offered by Berlin's big three opera
houses. Shame about the acoustics, though.

Nikolaisaal Potsdam

*Wilhelm-Staab Strasse 10-11, Potsdam (0331
288 8828, www.nikolaisaal.de). S7 Potsdam
Hauptbahnhof.* **Tickets** *€8-€45.*
Worth a trip out to Potsdam simply for the audito-
rium: behind a conventional baroque façade, the
white seating and space-age walls of white rubber
with protruding ovals is certainly eye-catching,
even distracting, but provides super acoustics.
Expect concerts by the Potsdam Chamber Academy,
Brandenburg State Orchestra, Brandenburg
Symphony Orchestra and German Film Orchestra
Babelsberg, as well as popular music events such as
Disney in Concert or an Elvis musical.

St Matthäus Kirche am Kulturforum

*Matthaeikirchplatz, Tiergarten (tickets 262 1202,
www.stiftung-stmatthaeus.de). U2, S1, S2, S25
Potsdamer Platz.* **Tickets** *varies.* **No credit
cards. Map** p310 K8.
Concerts range from free organ recitals to a chorus
of Russian Orthodox monks. Exquisite acoustics.

ROCK, WORLD & JAZZ

Berlin has always been a magnet for musicians – from the decadent Weimar years portrayed in *Cabaret*, to the Cold War-paranoia exile of David Bowie, Iggy Pop, and Nick Cave and the Bad Seeds, through the corporate career-reinventions of U2 (*Achtung Baby!*) and REM (*Collapse Into Now*), both recorded in the city, to West Berlin's adopted heroine Nico (buried in Grunewald cemetery) and East Berlin's Nina Hagen (who even composed the official club anthem of FC Union). The city seems to both like playing host to musicians, and be a city bands like playing.

But everything's not as rosy as it seems. The live music scene is not immune to ever-increasing gentrification, as developers tussle with locals to reclaim venues in Kreuzberg, Friedrichshain and Prenzlauer Berg for more corporate ends. Also, alternative music icons of the 1980s, '90s or last decade are now either heading towards pensionable age (Blixa Bargeld) or have achieved semi-establishment status (Peaches), or both.

Black music (reggae, hip hop, jazz) isn't quite as well represented as in London or Paris, reflecting Berlin's fairly white racial mix. On the other hand, other musical styles long out of fashion in other capitals (goth, thrash punk) steadfastly survive, even thrive, in Berlin. One field in which Berlin is still definitely leading the field is electronica. The capital is synonymous with the genre, which is now reinventing itself (again) as a result of the influx of foreign talent.

Ticket prices are still relatively cheap and – while the gargantuan warehouse techno parties of the 1990s may have faded into mythology – new venues continue to open. Holding out against the download tide, Berlin still has lots of good record shops, which are useful for finding out what's going on via flyers, posters and word of mouth.

And if you have an unquenchable desire to discover the Berlin backdrop to Bowie's *Low/Heroes* period or see the bar where Iggy Pop once ended a *Rolling Stone* interview by rolling around on the pavement, the **Fritz Music Tour** (www.musictours-berlin.com) is for you.

FESTIVALS

Late June sees 60,000 of Berlin's hardcore ravers descend upon the alternative **Fusion** festival (www.fusion-festival.de) – famous for having no advertising or line-up announcements. An 80-minute train ride away in the spectacular Ferropolis mining machinery museum, the **Melt! Festival** (www.meltfestival.de) presents indie-rock and electronica every July.

World music fans should head to the **Karnival der Kulturen** (*see p27*), a four-day celebration of multiculturalism in late spring. November brings the fantastic **JazzFest Berlin** (*see p30*).

Rock

Barbie Deinhoff's (*see p134*) in Kreuzberg is a bar, alternative art gallery and indie rock venue that embodies some of the most fun aspects of Berlin living.

Admiralspalast

Friedrichstrasse 101, Mitte (tickets 4799 7499, www.admiralspalast.de). U6, S1, S2, S5, S7, S25, S75 Friedrichstrasse. **Open & admission** varies. **Map** p306 M6.

One of the few original Weimar revue theatres left in Berlin, Admiralspalast was home to the GDR Berlin State Opera during the post-war years. Threatened with demolition in the late 1990s, it was restored and, in 2009, was the first venue in Germany to stage Mel Brooks' Nazi-lampooning *The Producers*. When it's not hosting theatre or cabaret performances, it presents sell-out gigs by the likes of PJ Harvey and James Blake.

Arena Berlin

Eichenstrasse 4, Treptow (5332 0340, www.arena-berlin.de). U1 Schlesisches Tor, or S8, S9, S41, S42 Treptower Park. **Open & admission** varies. **No credit cards.** **Map** p312 S9.

Inside a converted bus garage, Arena Berlin presents A-list artists such as Bob Dylan and Björk, as well as smaller acts. The surrounding entertainment complex includes a nightclub (*see p197*), the Badeschiff (a swimming pool anchored in the Spree river; *see p145*) and the party boat MS *Hoppetosse*.

★ Astra Kulturhaus

Revaler Stasse 99, Friedrichshain (2005 6767, www.astra-berlin.de). U1 Warschauer Strasse. **Open & admission** varies. **Map** p312 S8.

Berlin's premier alternative venue, this is part of the large RAW Tempel complex on old industrial warehouse grounds that's somewhat reminiscent of Christiania in Copenhagen. Arrive early as it gets crowded, and pillars can mean tricky sightlines. The likes of Bill Callahan, Godspeed You! Black Emperor, Death Cab for Cutie and Damon Albarn have played here.

Ausland

Lychener Strasse 60, Prenzlauer Berg (447 7008, www.ausland-berlin.de). U2 Eberswalderstrasse. **Open & admission** varies. **No credit cards.** **Map** p307 P2.

A small bohemian basement staging free jazz, avant-folk and live electronica, as well as films and art installations. Shows usually begin an hour later than the posted time (on principle, apparently). Nights often close with guest DJs, whose musical tastes can get pretty challenging.

Bassy Cowboy Club

Schönhauser Allee 176A, Prenzlauer Berg (281 8323, www.bassy-club.de). U2 Senefelderplatz. **Open** 9pm-late Tue, Fri; 10pm-late Sat. **Admission** from €3. **No credit cards.** **Map** p307 O4.

A move from Hackescher Markt to new premises in Schönhauser Allee, and a more diverse music programme, has done wonders for Bassy's reputation. It has a pre-1969 music policy, with concerts of rockabilly, beat, surf or hot jazz starting at 11pm.

C-Club

Columbiadamm 9-11, Tempelhof (tickets 8099 8715, www.c-dub-berlin.de). U6 Platz der Luftbrücke. **Open & admission** varies. **Map** p311 N11.

Once you get past its old-fashioned box office, this former US Forces cinema is a little characterless. It showcases mid-size acts of every genre, from Cannibal Corpse to the Horrors. Bigger draws usually play the Columbiahalle next door.

Columbiahalle

Columbiadamm 13-21, Tempelhof (tickets 6110 1313, www.c-halle.com). U6 Platz der Luftbrücke. **Open & admission** varies. **No credit cards.** **Map** p311 N11.

A roomy venue with a reputation for the best sound in town, Columbiahalle promotes larger acts that haven't made it to blockbuster status, such as Bon Iver or Manu Chao. Drinks are a little expensive, but it's a good-sized place to catch hip hop superstars such as A$AP Rocky and Snoop Dogg, who would probably be playing stadiums in other cities.

Frannz Club

Schönhauser Allee 36, Prenzlauer Berg (7262 7930, www.frannz.de). U2 Eberswalderstrasse. **Open** from 9pm daily. **Admission** varies. **No credit cards.** **Map** p307 O3.

A former DDR youth club, Frannz is a black box with decent sound, pricey drinks and unsmiling doormen. Musically, it's heavy on German acts that don't really translate culturally, though it has also booked rockabilly stars such as Wanda Jackson.

Fritzclub im Postbahnhof

Strasse der Pariser Kommune 8, Friedrichshain (698 1280, www.fritzclub.com). S5, S7, S75 Ostbahnhof. **Open & admission** varies. **No credit cards.** **Map** p312 R7.

This restored industrial building is relatively young in comparison to other venues, but its association with Radio Fritz gives it the clout to stage the likes of Arcade Fire, Paloma Faith and Fun Lovin' Criminals, as well as regular indie student parties.

Huxley's Neue Welt

Hasenheide 107-112, Neukölln (780 9980, www.huxleysneuewelt.com). U7, U8 Hermannplatz. **Open & admission** varies. **Map** p311 P11.

This early 20th-century ballroom on the corner of Hasenheide Park is now situated, somewhat incongruously, inside a modern retail park. It has a bit of a Wild West atmosphere and aesthetic, hosting poker championships and tattoo expos when not showcasing gigs by the likes of Elbow and Kasabian.

Junction Bar

Gneisenaustrasse 18, Kreuzberg (694 6602, café 6981 7421, www.junction-bar.de). U6 Gneisenaustrasse. **Open** *Café* 5pm-2am Mon-Fri; 2pm-2am Sat, Sun. *Bar* 8pm-5am daily. **Admission** €3-€6. **No credit cards.** **Map** p311 N10.

A Kreuzberg landmark that arranges 365 concerts a year of everything from jazz and swing to rock, with DJs keeping the party going into the early hours.

Kulturbrauerei

Schönhauser Allee 36, Prenzlauer Berg (4431 5100, www.kulturbrauerei.de). U2 Eberswalderstrasse. **Open** varies. **Admission** €5-€30. **Map** p307 O3.

With its assortment of venues, outdoor bars and barbecues, this cultural centre housed in an enormous former brewery can resemble a cross between a medieval fairground and a school disco. The two spaces operated by the Kulturbrauerei proper are Maschinehaus and the larger Kesselhaus, where concerts vary from reggae to Frank Zappa cover bands. There's an emphasis on German acts too.

★ Lido

Cuvrystrasse 7, Kreuzberg (6956 6840, tickets 6110 1313, www.lido-berlin.de). U1 Schlesisches Tor. **Open & admission** varies. **No credit cards.** **Map** p312 R9.

A true Kreuzberg institution, this indie concert venue was a cinema in the 1950s and retains its curved bar and neon signage. Saturday's Karrera Klub has championed guitar-driven music for over a decade, with a live gig followed by DJs playing indie dance classics. Other live music acts range from the avant-garde (Laibach, Lydia Lunch) to more contemporary bands (Kurt Vile, These New Puritans).

SO36.

Magnet

Falckensteinstrasse 48, Kreuzberg (4400 8140,
www.magnet-dub.de). U1 Schlesisches Tor. **Open**
9pm-late daily. **Admission** varies. **No credit**
cards. Map p312 R9.
Transplanted from Prenzlauer Berg to Kreuzberg,
this venue is one of the biggest bookers for the kind
of up-and-coming indie bands featured in the *NME*.
Catch them here before they hit the stadium circuit.

Passionskirche

Marheinekeplatz 1-2, Kreuzberg (tickets 6959
3624, 6940 1241, www.akanthus.de). U7
Gneisenaustrasse. **Open & admission** varies.
No credit cards. Map p311 N10.
Folk and world music acts mainly play here, but
Beck, Ryan Adams and Marc Almond have also
graced the stage of this deconsecrated church. Get
there early, as it's one of the few churches in Berlin
whose pews regularly overflow.

SO36

Oranienstrasse 190, Kreuzberg (tickets 6110
1313, 6140 1306, www.so36.de). U1, U8
Kottbusser Tor. **Open** 8pm-late daily. **Admission**
€3-€20. **No credit cards. Map** p311 P9.
Still going strong since the punk heyday of the
late 1970s, and with no sign of betraying its highly
politicised origins, SO36 is suitably scummy inside,
with decades of sweat, beer and blood ingrained
into the woodwork. While plenty of touring punk
and hardcore bands grace the black stage, the venue
embraces all forms of alternative lifestyle, including
the long-running gay and lesbian Turkish night,
Gayhane (*see p182*).

Soul Cat Music Club

Reichenberger Strasse 73, Kreuzberg (no phone,
www.soulcat-berlin.de). U1 Görlitzer Bahnhof.
Open from 8pm Tue-Sat. **Admission** usually free.
No credit cards. Map p311 Q10.
This two-room bar in Kreuzberg has nightly gigs of
soul, blues, folk and jazz, plus a small record shop
selling tapes and vinyl.

Tempodrom

Möckernstrasse 10, Kreuzberg (747 370, tickets
0180 555 4111 premium, www.tempodrom.de). U7
Möckernbrücke, or S1, S2, S25 Anhalter Bahnhof.
Open & admission varies. **Map** p310 L9.
Descendant of the legendary circus tent venue that
was pitched in various West Berlin locations, this
permanent space in tented form provides a beautiful
setting for more upmarket/middle-of-the-road acts
such as Chris Rea and the Pet Shop Boys. Plus, there
are sports events, comedy, musicals, classical concerts and the Liquidrom spa.

★ Urban Spree

Revaler Strasse 99, Friedrichshain (7407 8597,
www.urbanspree.com). U1, S5, S7, S75
Warschauer Strasse. **Open** noon-midnight Mon-
Thur, Sun; noon-3am Fri, Sat. **Admission** varies.
No credit cards. Map p312 S8.
Urban Spree houses an art gallery and bookshop
(*see p91*), concert hall, studio spaces and street-food
stalls, with an emphasis on the experimental and
DIY. Frequent gigs range from freeform jazz to acid-
folk and improvised instrumental noise. Look out
for gigs by far-out noiseniks Psychic Ills and ex-Can
frontman Damo Suzuki, as well as the occasional
curveball like hip-hop mega-producer Swizz Beatz.

Wabe

Danziger Strasse 101, Prenzlauer Berg (902 953
850, www.wabe-berlin.de). S8, S9, S41, S42
Greifswalder Strasse. **Open & admission** varies.
No credit cards. Map p307 Q3.
A DDR-era community centre in Ernst-Thälmann-
Park, Wabe's octagonal space encourages young
local groups with 'battle of the bands' contests and
MTV co-presentations. Plenty of German folk, nos-
talgia acts and some world music.

Wild at Heart

Wiener Strasse 20, Kreuzberg (6107 4701,
www.wildatheartberlin.de). U1 Görlitzer Bahnhof.
Open 8pm-late Thur-Sat. **Admission** €3-€12.
No credit cards. Map p311 Q9.

ARTS & ENTERTAINMENT

Wild at Heart imports artists and DJs from all over Europe to satisfy its enthusiastic, tattooed, rock, punk, rockabilly and ska regulars. It also has a jukebox to help you down one last shot of whiskey at daybreak while you ponder why your shirt is the only one with sleeves.

World

Berlin doesn't have quite the multicultural vibe of a London or New York – but it tries. World music artists also play at the **Kulturbrauerei** complex (*see p205*).

★ Haus der Kulturen der Welt
John-Foster-Dulles-Allee 10, Tiergarten (3978 7175, www.hkw.de). S5, S7, S75 Hauptbahnhof. **Open & admission** varies. **Map** p306 K6.
The 'House of World Cultures' was built in 1957 as a gift from the USA as part of the ambitious Interbau Exhibition of modernist architecture across West Berlin. With concerts, exhibitions and symposia that explore global cultural questions, it's a wonderful venue for world music, with performances from the likes of Rai superstar Khaled and desert blues musicians Amadou & Mariam.

Havanna
Hauptstrasse 30, Schöneberg (784 8565, www. havanna-berlin.de). U7 Eisenacher Strasse. **Open** 9pm-late Wed; 10pm-late Fri, Sat. **Admission** €4 Wed; €8 Fri, Sat. **No credit cards. Map** p310 J11.
Offering three dancefloors with salsa, merengue, reggaeton and R&B, it's a popular place with expat South Americans and Cubans. An hour before opening, you can pick up a few steps at a salsa class for €5.

Werkstatt der Kulturen
Wissmannstrasse 32, Neukölln (609 7700, www.werkstatt-der-kulturen.de). U7, U8 Hermannplatz. **Open & admission** varies. **No credit cards. Map** p311 P11.
This intimate venue presents trad ethnic music or local fusions blending jazz, trance or folk elements.

Jazz

For historical reasons, jazz venues tend to be clustered around the old West Berlin. It's also worth searching out galleries, social clubs and cultural houses. The famed DDR-era **JazzKeller Treptow** (www.jazzkeller69.de) continues to promote interesting shows in a variety of small spaces. Berlin also features Germany's only 24-hour jazz radio station, at 101.9 FM.

★ A-Trane
Bleibtreustrasse 1, Charlottenburg (313 2550, www.a-trane.de). S5, S7, S9, S75 Savignyplatz. **Open** 8pm-1am Mon-Thur, Sun; 8pm-5am Fri, Sat. **Admission** free-€20. **No credit cards. Map** p309 E8.
A-Trane usually lands at least one top-flight act a month for an extended run. Free entry on Mondays, except when there's a special performance. The late-night Saturday jam sessions, also free, are popular with students and tourists.

B-Flat
Rosenthaler Strasse 13, Mitte (283 3123, www. b-flat-berlin.de). U8 Rosenthaler Platz. **Open** 8pm or 9pm-late daily. **Admission** free-€13. **No credit cards. Map** p307 N5.

Haus der Kulturen der Welt.

ARTS & ENTERTAINMENT

Schaubühne am Lehniner Platz. See p210.

B-Flat pulls in a decent local hero once in a while, but its strongest nights tend to feature singers. Free Wednesday night jam sessions from 9pm.

Quasimodo
Kantstrasse 12A, Charlottenburg (312 8086, www. quasimodo.de). U2, U9, S5, S7, S75 Zoologischer Garten. **Open** from 10pm Tue-Sun. **Admission** €17-€25. **No credit cards**. **Map** p309 F8.
Privileging the 'jazzy' over jazz, this basement spot appears close to irrevocably severing connections to the music for which it was once noted. But it still promotes some good homegrown and international acts, such as American singer Terry Callier.

Yorckschlösschen
Yorckstrasse 15, Kreuzberg (215 8070, www. yorckschloesschen.de). U6, U7 Mehringdamm. **Open** 5pm-3am Mon-Sat; 10am-3am Sun. **Admission** free-€8. **Map** p310 L10.
A century-old *Eck-Kneipe*, Yorckschlösschen offers a faintly ridiculous mix of German Dixieland and vintage beat music. But in its old-world environment, it can get pretty groovy (after a few beers).

Theatre, Cabaret & Dance

THEATRE

Berlin has one of the most exciting theatre cultures anywhere in the world. The city has five generously funded, multi-stage state theatres, surrounded and supplemented by a huge, thriving fringe scene. The blessing and curse of the 'Big Five' – the **Berliner Ensemble**, **Deutsches Theater**, **Maxim Gorki Theater**, **Schaubühne** and **Volksbühne** – is that they run all their productions in an ever-changing, unpredictable repertory system. So if you want to catch a specific show, check the theatre's website before booking your flights. Conversely, off-scene shows, especially at main venues such as the **HAU** and **Sophiensaele**, tend to have quite short runs, although revivals are not uncommon.

While some performances have English surtitles (most frequently at the Schaubühne), it is equally possible to get a lot out of a show without speaking German, thanks to the frequently astonishing visual aspect of productions. Also, a lot of the repertoire – especially at the state theatres – includes much of the same Greek, Shakespeare and Chekhov that English audiences are used to, albeit presented with a radically different approach.

FESTIVALS
Perhaps the most important festival of the year is **Theatertreffen** at the **Berliner Festspiele** (www.berlinerfestspiele.de), which invites the ten productions that have been judged best of the season from the whole of Germany, as well as talks on contemporary theatre. Running alongside it is the **Stückemarkt** new plays festival, which presents readings (in German) of the best new national and international scripts. Berliner Festspiele also hosts the international **Foreign Affairs** in October, showcasing unusual international dance, theatre and music. The Schaubühne's **Festival for International New Drama (FIND)** in April provides new works from Germany and abroad.

On the fringe, perhaps the most ambitious festival is **100° Berlin – Festival des Freien Theaters** (www.100grad.wordpress.com) in February. A daily ticket (under €20) can get you admission to upwards of six hours of different performances across four sites with a choice of after-show late bars.

State Theatres

Berliner Ensemble
Bertolt-Brecht-Platz 1, Mitte (2840 8155, www.berliner-ensemble.de). U6, S1, S2, S5, S7, S25, S75 Friedrichstrasse. **Tickets** €5-€30; €9 reductions. **Map** p306 M6.
Probably Berlin's most famous theatre, thanks mainly to its historical association with Bertolt Brecht. Under current artistic director Claus Peymann, it is regarded by Germans as a little too comfortable and touristy, a place where older,

ARTS & ENTERTAINMENT

ESSENTIAL BERLIN ALBUMS

Sounds of the city.

HEROES
DAVID BOWIE (1977)

Heroes was recorded in the shadow of the Berlin Wall, with sonic terrorist Brian Eno, while Bowie was sharing a flat in Schöneberg with Iggy Pop. The centrepiece of the 'Berlin trilogy' of LPs that Bowie cut between 1976 and 1979, this slice of dark, futuristic art rock came to define a Berlin sound.

YOUR FUNERAL...
MY TRIAL
NICK CAVE & THE BAD
SEEDS (1986)

Recorded in Berlin's Hansa studios, this despairing epic summarised Nick Cave's drug-addled torpor at the time, with mournful elegies to longing and regret. The Bad Seeds appeared in *Wings of Desire*, playing the song 'The Carny' from the album.

BURN, BERLIN, BURN!
ATARI TEENAGE RIOT
(1997)

An angry, frenetic missive from techno-addled late '90s Berlin, ATR's debut album melded drum 'n' bass to industrial beats and sound collages. The new sound, 'digital hardcore', articulated perfectly the speed and anarchy of the city struggling to find a new identity.

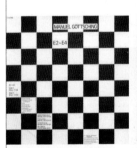

E2-E4
MANUEL GOTTSCHING
(1984)

Nine electro masterpieces blending hypnotic guitar motifs with drum machines and synths. The result was akin to primitive techno, forming the crucial link between German space rock of the 1970s with the booming Berlin techno scene of the '90s.

ACHTUNG BABY
U2 (1991)

If *Rattle and Hum* was U2's nod to the Rolling Stones, the band's decamping to Berlin's Hansa studios to garble synths and sequencers with Brian Eno was in deep homage to Bowie. In this sprawling, noisy, electro-rock creation, they captured the nervy, edgy atmosphere of post-reunification Berlin.

COME TO BERLIN
BARBARA
MORGENSTERN (2008)

Multi-instrumentalist Morgenstern emerged in the 2000s with a series of slick albums of acoustic ballads, electro, techno and skewed pop. From *BM*, the single 'Come to Berlin' was a catchy slice of deceptively sunny pop that wryly sent up the city's growing gentrification.

ARTS & ENTERTAINMENT

formerly radical directors go to work. You can still see the late Heiner Müller's 20-year-old staging of *The Resistable Rise of Arturo Ui*, along with productions by Robert Wilson and Peter Stein.

Deutsches Theater

Schumannstrasse 13A, Mitte (284 410, tickets 2844 1221, www.deutschestheater.de). U6, S1, S2, S5, S7, S25, S75 Friedrichstrasse. **Tickets** €5-€48; €9 reductions. **Map** p306 L5.

Of all the theatres in Berlin, the Deutsches Theater behaves most like a state theatre in any other German city, offering a *Spielplan* of new interpretations of works by Goethe and Schiller alongside Shakespeare, Aeschylus and a smattering of new plays. Productions vary enormously, from intensely exciting and innovative to more stately fare.

Maxim Gorki Theater

Am Festungsgraben 2, Mitte (2022 1115, www.gorki.de). U6, S1, S2, S5, S7, S25, S75 Friedrichstrasse. **Tickets** €10-€30. **Map** p307 N6.

Author and director Armin Petras became intendant in 2006, and with a fresh ensemble breathed new life into this landmark. Expect new interpretations of classical and modern dramas, as well as adaptations

from films and novels, with the result that the atmosphere alone is often enough to transcend the language barrier.

★ Schaubühne am Lehniner Platz

Kurfürstendamm 153, Charlottenburg (890 023, www.schaubuehne.de). U7 Adenauerplatz, or S5, S7, S75 Charlottenburg. **Tickets** €7-€43; €9 reductions. **Map** p308 D9.

Of the Big Five, the Schaubühne is most popular with English audiences and has a long history of anglophile collaboration. It was the theatre that essentially established Brits Mark Ravenhill and Sarah Kane as Germany's favourite playwrights. Under artistic director Thomas Ostermeier, the house style treads a happy medium between German radicalism and British realism, which, coupled with the frequent surtitling of performances in English, makes it an ideal starting point for anyone looking for an introduction to German theatre. *Photo p208.*

Volksbühne

Rosa-Luxemburg-Platz, Mitte (2406 5777, www. volksbuehne-berlin.de). U2 Rosa-Luxemburg-Platz. **Tickets** €6-€36; €6-€18 reductions. **Map** p307 O5.

Built in 1914, the Volksbühne is Berlin's most imposing theatre, and its austere exterior is well suited to the current regime under artistic director Frank Castorf, whose own productions seem to enrage as much as delight. That said, *Nach Moskau! Nach Moskau!*, his immense four-hour interpretation of Chekhov's *The Three Sisters*, was a critical hit. Also look out for idiosyncratic associate director René Pollesch, whose work might best be described as a kind of knockabout farce of critical theory wrapped up in dazzling stagecraft.

Ballhaus Naunynstrasse.

Sophiensaele.

Fringe Theatres

★ Ballhaus Naunynstrasse
Naunynstrasse 27, Kreuzberg (7545 3725, www.ballhausnaunynstrasse.de). U1, U8 Kottbusser Tor. **Tickets** €14; €8 reductions. **No credit cards. Map** p311 P8.

Thanks to artistic director Nurkan Erpulat's *Verrücktes Blut* winning best German play in 2011's Theatertreffen, Ballhaus Naunynstrasse is now the fringe theatre to visit. Located in the largely Turkish Kreuzkölln district, the company is gaining a strong reputation for investigating issues surrounding the immigrant experience and identity in Germany.

Ballhaus Ost
Pappelallee 15, Prenzlauer Berg (4799 7474, www.ballhausost.de). U2 Eberswalderstrasse. **Tickets** €15; €8 reductions. **Map** p307 P2.

This somewhat dilapidated ex-ballroom hosts art, performance art, dance and concerts, offering a unique and authentic cultural evening. There's also a lounge and bar populated by a very cool crowd.

Brotfabrik
Caligariplatz 1, Weissensee (471 4001, www.brotfabrik-berlin.de). Tram M2, M13. **Tickets** €12; €8 reductions. **Map** p307 Q1.

Located far from the centre of town, this former bread factory houses a cinema, gallery, café and small experimental theatre where productions by visiting companies are performed in a variety of languages. The café has a congenial summer courtyard.

English Theatre Berlin
Fidicinstrasse 40, Kreuzberg (691 1211, www.etberlin.de). U6 Platz der Luftbrücke. **Tickets** €6-€18. **No credit cards. Map** p310 M11.

Directors Günther Grosser and Bernd Hoffmeister, present a high-quality programme. Expect house productions, international guest shows and co-productions with performers from Berlin's lively

international theatre scene, all in English. Theater Thikwa, one of Europe's most renowned companies working with disabled actors, is also based here.

★ HAU
Main office: HAU2, Hallesches Ufer 32, Kreuzberg (259 0040, tickets 2590 0427, www.hebbel-am-ufer. de). U1, U7 Möckernbrücke, or U1, U6 Hallesches Tor. **Tickets** varies. **Map** p310 M9.

Since opening in 2003, HAU – the amalgamation of the century-old former Hebbel Theater (HAU1), Theater am Hallesches Ufer (HAU2) and Theater am Ufer (HAU3) – has gained an incredible reputation for hosting Berlin's most innovative and radical theatre programming, with work by the likes of Forced Entertainment, Nature Theater of Oklahoma, Alain Platel, Jerome Bel and long-standing HAU regulars Gob Squad and Rimini Protokoll.

Other locations HAU1, Stresemannstrasse 29, Kreuzberg; HAU3, Tempelhofer Ufer 10, Kreuzberg.

Sophiensaele
Sophienstrasse 18, Mitte (2789 0030, tickets 283 5266, www.sophiensaele.com). U8 Weinmeisterstrasse. **Tickets** €15; €10 reductions. **No credit cards. Map** p307 N5.

Hidden on a quiet side road near Hackescher Markt and set back behind a little courtyard, it's easy to miss Sophiensaele. Here, over four floors, you're likely to see some of the most cutting-edge performances in Berlin, and in some of the most atmospheric performance spaces the city has to offer.

Theaterdiscounter
Klosterstrasse 44, Mitte (2809 3062, www. theaterdiscounter.de). S1, S2 Oranienburger Strasse. **Tickets** €13; €8 reductions. **No credit cards. Map** p307 N5.

Opened a decade ago in an old telegraph office, this is where an intense group of ten actors and various directors performs new and experimental work. It's anti-illusion theatre with interactive possibilities – very casual and innovative.

ARTS & ENTERTAINMENT

Theater unterm Dach

Kulturhaus im Ernst-Thälmann-Park, Danziger Strasse 101, Prenzlauer Berg (902 953 817, www.theateruntermdach-berlin.de). S8, S41, S42, S85 Greifswalder Strasse. **Tickets** €12; €8 reductions. **No credit cards. Map** p307 Q3.
The large attic of a converted factory, situated well off the beaten path, is the place to see new German fringe groups. Productions are always full of energy and can be quite inspiring.

CABARET

Although today's cabaret bears little resemblance to the classic cabaret of the Weimar years, there are some great performers who can re-create an entire era in one night. The city is teeming with acts that can be more sexually adventurous (or ambiguous) than most other places and still manage to amuse the cool Berlin audiences.

Don't confuse cabaret with *Varieté*; the latter is more of a circus-like show, minus the animals but with lots of dancing girls. *Kabarett* is different again. A unique kind of German entertainment with a strong following in Berlin, it's basically political satire sprinkled with songs and sketches, sometimes intellectual, sometimes crass. Likely venues include Stachelschweine, Wühlmäuse or the Mehringhof Theater, but most of it will be over your head if you don't have perfect German and a thorough understanding of local politics.

When it comes to *Travestie* – drag revue – Berlin has some of the best on offer, from fabulous to tragic. Venues come in all sizes and styles, from small and dark to huge and glittery. For the more progressive and intelligent drag acts, the BKA Theater is a safe bet.

Varieté & Revue

Chamäleon

Hackesche Höfe, Rosenthaler Strasse 40-41, Mitte (tickets 400 0590, www.chamaeleonberlin.de). S5, S7, S75 Hackescher Markt. **Performances** 8pm Tue-Fri (July, Aug 9pm); 7pm, 10pm Sat. **Tickets** €37-€47. **Map** p307 N5.
This beautiful old theatre with a touch of decadence is located in the courtyards of the Hackesche Höfe. The focus is on stunning acrobatics combined with music theatre. As Hackesche Höfe becomes increasingly commercialised and touristy, there's a risk it may become a sort of Wintergarten (*see right*). For now, though, it attracts a diverse audience and is the most comfortable and affordable revue house.

Friedrichstadtpalast

Friedrichstrasse 107, Mitte (2326 2326, www.show-palace.eu). U6, S1, S2, S5, S7, S25, S75 Friedrichstrasse. **Performances** varies. **Tickets** €19-€117. **Map** p306 M5.

An East Berlin institution in a building that was originally designed to be the opera house in Damascus, this is the city's biggest revue theatre. Since reunification, it's mainly featured big, Vegas-style musical revues – with Vegas-style prices to match. Mostly packed with coachloads of German tourists.

Wintergarten Varieté

Potsdamer Strasse 96, Tiergarten (tickets 588 433, www.wintergarten-berlin.de). U1 Kurfürstenstrasse. **Performances & tickets** varies. **Map** p310 K8.
Prussia meets Disney with shows that are slick, professional and a little boring. Excellent acrobats and magicians, but some questionable comedy acts.

Cabaret

Bar jeder Vernunft

Spiegelzelt, Schaperstrasse 24, Wilmersdorf (883 1582, www.bar-jeder-vernunft.de). U3, U9 Spichernstrasse. **Performances** 7pm or 8pm daily. **Tickets** €12.50-€29.50. **Map** p309 G9.
Some of Berlin's most celebrated entertainers perform in this snazzy circus tent of many mirrors, which takes in shows, comedy, cabaret, literature and theatre. Dinner is an extra €29. It's not the cheapest night out, but it'll be worth it if the place revives its much-lauded production of *Cabaret*.

BKA Theater

Mehringdamm 34, Kreuzberg (202 2007, www.bka-theater.de). U6, U7 Mehringdamm. **Performances** usually 8pm daily. **Tickets** €18-€24. **Map** p310 M10.
With a long tradition of taboo-breaking acts, BKA still has some of the weirdest and most progressive performers in town: intelligent drag stand-up, freaky chanteuses, power-lunged divas. There are private tables and arena seats overlooking the stage.

Café Theater Schalotte

Behaimstrasse 22, Charlottenburg (341 1485, www.schalotte.de). U7 Richard-Wagner-Platz. **Performances** usually 8pm, days vary. **Tickets** €16; €12 reductions. **No credit cards. Map** p304 D6.
A nice café, dedicated staff and some excellent shows. The O-Tonpiraten, a very clever drag theatre troupe, often plays here. Look out for annual international a cappella festival in November.

Kleine Nachtrevue

Kurfürstenstrasse 116, Schöneberg (218 8950, www.kleine-nachtrevue.de). U1, U2, U3 Wittenbergplatz. **Performances** 9pm, 11.30pm Wed-Sat. **Tickets** €20-€30. **Map** p309 H8.
Used as a location for many films, this is as close as it gets to real nostalgic German cabaret – intimate, dark, decadent, but very friendly. Shows consist of short song or dance numbers sprinkled with

playful nudity and whimsical costumes. Special weekend performances vary from erotic opera to a four-course meal served to songs sung by the male 'reincarnation' of Marlene Dietrich.

Scheinbar

Monumentenstrasse 9, Schöneberg (784 5539, www.scheinbar.de). U7 Kleistpark. **Performances** 8pm most days. **Tickets** €8-€11. **No credit cards.** **Map** p310 K11.
Experimental, fun-loving cabaret in a tiny club exploding with fresh talent. If you like surprises, try the open-stage nights, where great performers mix with terrible ones, creating a surreal night for all.

Tipi am Kanzleramt

Grosse Querallee, between Bundeskanzleramt & Haus der Kulturen der Welt, Tiergarten (3906 6550, www.tipi-am-kanzleramt.de). Bus 100, 248. **Performances** 8pm Tue-Sat; 3pm, 7pm Sun. **Tickets** €16.50-€59.50. **Map** p306 K6.
A circus tent in the Tiergarten, near the Federal Chancellery, with cool international performers presenting various comedy, dance and cabaret shows. Fare is similar to Bar jeder Vernunft (*see p212*), except everything's twice the size.

Travestie

Theater im Keller

Weserstrasse 211, Neukölln (4799 7477, www.tik berlin.de). U7, U8 Hermannplatz. **Performances** 8pm Fri, Sat. **Tickets** €29. **Map** p311 Q11.
With seating for 43 people, this cosy neighbourhood drag club has a passable revue show.

DANCE

Berlin has a dynamic contemporary dance scene that cultivates fresh ideas while continuing to nurture the strong traditions of German dance theatre. Dance events, including international festivals and co-productions with foreign choreographers, are plentiful and there's a huge amount of highly experimental work on show, often attracting large audiences. **Sasha Waltz** (www.sashawaltz.de), the city's foremost and most famous choreographer, has contributed enormously to the aesthetic continuum of postmodern German dance theatre. Co-founder of the **Sophiensaele** (*see p211*) – a key venue for dance – she was also artistic director at the **Schaubühne** (*see p210*) for five years. Her pieces, always visually stunning, and often heavily dramatic, are performed in the biggest theatres in Europe and Asia. Other big names are Argentinian choreographer **Constanza Macras** and her DorkyPark company (www.dorkypark.org), and American choreographer **Meg Stuart** and her Damaged Goods company (www.damagedgoods.be).

For information on upcoming performances, pick up *TanzRaumBerlin* (www.tanzraumberlin.de), a Berlin periodical dedicated to dance.

FESTIVALS & TRAINING

The three-week festival **Tanz im August** (www.tanzimaugust.de) is one of Europe's leading dance festivals. It shows the most influential and cutting-edge choreography of the season, coupled with workshops for the public and lectures from artists and critics. There's also **Tanztage** (www.tanztage.de), held in the first two weeks of January and showcasing work by young local dancers. The **Lucky Trimmer** dance series (www.luckytrimmer.de) in April specialises in short pieces (ten-minute maximum) by established and emerging artists.

Dock 11 (www.dock11-berlin.de) is the city's most recognised dance school, providing training and rehearsal and production space. **Tanzfabrik** (www.tanzfabrik-berlin.de) is another reputable institution for training and rehearsals, which also holds international workshops and an innovative residency programme for dance-makers. **LaborGras** (www.laborgras.com), by the canal in Kreuzberg, is a small venue that frequently invites well-respected teachers from across the world to teach and perform.

Venues

★ Radialsystem V

Holzmarktstrasse 33, Friedrichshain (288 788 588, www.radialsystem.de). S5, S7, S75 Ostbahnhof. **Tickets** varies. **No credit cards.** **Map** p311 Q7.
This warren of rooms in a former pumping station by the river was opened in 2006 by Jochen Sandig, partner of choreographer Sasha Waltz, whose company, Sasha Waltz & Guests, is based here. It promotes a variety of one-off music and performance events, and attracts a well-heeled crowd.

Ballet

In 2004, what had been three main ballet companies became one, when half of the Deutsche Oper dancers and all but one at the Komische Oper lost their jobs. Those who were left joined the existing Staatsoper Ballet to form the **Staatsballett Berlin** (www.staatsballett-berlin.de). In late 2014, the Ukrainian 'dancer of the century', Vladimir Malakhov, handed over directorship to Spanish choreographer Nacho Duarte, who immediately began replacing some older dancers with fresh blood. Duarte's 88-member company performs from September to June at the Deutsche Oper, Komische Oper and the Staatsoper Unter den Linden, as well as at an experimental series at Berghain (*see p195*) called Shut Up and Dance.

ARTS & ENTERTAINMENT

Escapes & Excursions

Escapes & Excursions

There's enough in Berlin to occupy a lifetime, let alone a weekend visit, but a trip beyond the city limits is more than worthwhile. Travel less than an hour on the S-Bahn and you're in Brandenburg: a world where fields, lakes and dense woods are interrupted by a sparse scattering of little-visited towns and villages. This chapter features day trip destinations and escapes further afield. The most popular day trip is to Potsdam, which is to Berlin what Versailles is to Paris. Still only a few hours away, the seaside resort of Rügen is a classic holiday destination, and the cities of Leipzig and Dresden are ideal for a weekend break.

GETTING AROUND

Trains to all destinations depart from Berlin Hauptbahnhof, Europe's biggest and most futuristic train station. Depending on where they're going, trains also stop at Gesundbrunnen in the north, the new Südkreuz station (formerly Papestrasse) and also at Berlin-Spandau out west.

Regionalbahn trains – the red, double-decker ones – serve Berlin's hinterland, including many of the destinations in this chapter. They stop at larger stations such as Zoologischer Garten, Friedrichstrasse, Alexanderplatz and Potsdamer Platz, as well as Hauptbahnhof. **Deutsche Bahn** has an excellent timetable search facility in English at www.bahn.com.

POTSDAM & BABELSBERG

Potsdam is the capital of the state of Brandenburg. Located just outside Berlin's city limits to the south-west, it's the capital's most beautiful neighbour. Known for its 18th-century Baroque architecture, it's a magnet for tourists. The summer weekend crowds can be overwhelming.

For centuries, Potsdam was the summer residence of the Hohenzollerns, who were attracted by the area's gently rolling landscape, rivers and lakes. Despite the damage wrought during World War II and by East Germany's socialist planners, much remains of the legacy of these Prussian kings. The best-known landmark is Sanssouci, the huge landscaped park created by Frederick the Great – one of three royal parks flanking the town.

Potsdam has changed considerably since reunification. In East German times, its association with the monarchy was regarded with suspicion, and a lack of political will and economic means led to much of the town's historic fabric falling into disrepair or being destroyed. In 1990, though, Potsdam was assigned UNESCO World Heritage status and some 80 per cent of the town's historic buildings have since been restored.

The end of East Germany also marked the end of Potsdam's historic role as a garrison town. Until the Soviet withdrawal, some 10,000 troops were stationed here. With their departure, vast barracks and tracts of land to the north of the town were abandoned. The area is currently being redeveloped for civilian use, including the BUGA or Volkspark, with its **Biosphäre**.

The Old Town

One of the most dominant – if not the prettiest – buildings of historical interest in the Old Town

is the 19th-century **Nikolaikirche**. It's hard
to miss the huge dome, inspired by St Paul's
Cathedral in London. Rather more graceful is
the mid 18th-century **Altes Rathaus**, diagonally
opposite, whose tower was used as a prison until
1875. Nowadays, the former town hall is used
for exhibitions and lectures, and houses the
Potsdam Museum, with a permanent display
on the history of the city. Both the Nikolaikirche
and Altes Rathaus were badly damaged in World
War II and rebuilt in the 1960s. The two buildings
are all that remains of the original Alter Markt,
once one of Potsdam's most beautiful squares.

The **Stadtschloss**, in the centre of town, was
also substantially damaged during World War II,
and the East German authorities demolished the
rest of it in 1960. There are plans to rebuild it, but
funding problems mean this is unlikely to happen
soon. Private sponsors have already paid for the
reconstruction of the Fortunaportal, one of the
decorative former entrances to the palace, in the
Alter Markt. To get an impression of this square
before 1945, take a look at the model in the foyer
of the Altes Rathaus.

The area behind the vast Hotel Mercure was
once part of the palace gardens. Later, Friedrich
Wilhelm I, the Soldier King, turned it into a
parade ground. Now, it's a park. If you walk up
Breitestrasse, you can see all that's left of the old
Stadtschloss. The low red building that houses the
Filmmuseum Potsdam is the former Marstall,
or royal stables. Dating from 1685 and originally
an orangery, it's one of the oldest buildings in town.
The Filmmuseum explores nearly a century of
film-making at the Babelsberg studios, focusing
on DEFA, East Germany's sole film-making
company. The on-site cinema regularly shows
films, and guided tours are available in English.

Nearby Neuer Markt survived the war intact.
At no.1 is the house where Friedrich Wilhelm II was
born. The Kutschstall, originally a royal stables,
now houses the new **Haus der Brandenburgisch-
Preussischen Geschichte**, charting 800 years
of Brandenburg history.

Baroque & Dutch quarters

Potsdam's impressive Baroque Quarter is
bounded by Schopenhauerstrasse, Hegelallee,
Hebbelstrasse and Charlottenstrasse. Some of the
best houses can be found in Gutenbergstrasse and
Brandenburger Strasse, the city's pedestrianised
shopping drag. Note the pitched roofs with space
to accommodate troops – the Soldier King built
the quarter in the 1730s. Just around the corner is
Gedenkstätte Lindenstrasse, once the house
of a Prussian officer, later a Stasi detention centre
(you can now tour the cells).

Three Baroque town gates – Nauener Tor,
Jäger Tor and Brandenburger Tor – stand on the
northern and western edges of the quarter. East

from here, two churches bear witness to Potsdam's cosmopolitan past. The Great Elector's 1685 Edict of Potsdam promised refuge to Protestants suffering from religious persecution in their homelands, sparking waves of immigration. The **Französische Kirche** on Hebbelstrasse was built for the town's Huguenot community, while **St Peter & Paul's** in Bassinplatz was built for Catholic immigrants who came to this Protestant area in response to the Prussian kings' drive to bring in skilled workers and soldiers.

The Holländisches Viertel, or Dutch Quarter, is the most attractive part of Friedrich Wilhelm I's new-town extension. As part of a failed strategy to lure skilled Dutch immigrants to the town, the king had Dutch builders construct 134 gable-fronted houses. In **Jan Bouman Haus** on Mittelstrasse, you can see an original interior. Today, this area is filled with upmarket boutiques and restaurants.

Alexandrowka

Another Potsdam curiosity is the Russian colony of Alexandrowka, 15 minutes' walk north from the town centre. The settlement consists of 13 wooden-clad, two-storey dwellings with steeply pitched roofs laid out in the form of a St Andrew's Cross. There's even a Russian Orthodox church with an onion dome. Services are still held in the **Alexander-Newski-Kapelle**.

Alexandrowka was built in 1826 by Friedrich Wilhelm III to commemorate the death of Tsar Alexander I, a friend from the Wars of Liberation against Napoleon. The settlement became home to surviving members of a troupe of Russian musicians given into Prussian service by the Tsar in 1812. Two of the houses are still inhabited by the descendants of these men. Russian specialities are served by waitresses in folkloric costume at the **Teehaus Russische Kolonie** (Alexandrowka 1, 0331 817 0203, closed Mon). Nearby is the tiny **Alexandrowka Museum** (Russische Kolonie 2, 0331 817 0203, www. alexandrowka.de, closed Mon) with films and exhibits about the colony.

INSIDE TRACK CAR-SHARING

If you haven't got a car and want to travel to another city on the cheap, it's worth investigating the car-sharing service Mitfahrzentral. Drivers with space in their cars make offers via an easy-to-navigate website, listing their destination, when they're going and how much they want you to chip in. You have to sign up to the (German-language) site, www.mitfahrgelegenheit.de, but it's free – and much safer than hitching.

The area around and to the north of Alexandrowka became the focus of a different Russian presence during the Cold War. The late Wilhelmine villas served as offices for the Soviet administration or as officers' homes. Soviet forces took over buildings used by the Prussian army in the 19th century and later by the Nazis. One such building is the castle-like Garde-Ulanen-Kaserne in Jäger Allee, near the junction with Reiterweg.

The recently restored Belvedere, at the top of the hill to the north of Alexandrowka, is the town's highest observation point. It fell into disuse after the Wall went up in 1961, when people were banned from enjoying views over West Berlin.

Potsdam's royal parks

Back towards the town centre is Potsdam's biggest tourist magnet, **Park Sanssouci**. It's beautiful, but be warned: its main avenues can become overrun and it's not always easy to get into the palaces (guided tours are compulsory and numbers are limited).

The park is a legacy of King Frederick the Great, who was attracted to the area by its fine views. He initially had terraced gardens built here before adding a palace. *Sans souci* means 'without worry' and reflects the king's desire for a sanctuary where he could pursue his philosophical, musical and literary interests. Voltaire was among his guests. His nearby Bildergalerie was the first purpose-built museum in Germany.

After victory in the Seven Years' War, Frederick the Great built the huge **Neues Palais** on the park's western edge. Friedrich II's sumptuous suite, as well as the Grottensaal (Grotto Room), Marmorsaal (Marble Room) and Schlosstheater (Palace Theatre), are worth a visit. Parts of the Palais were renovated for Frederick the Great's 300th birthday in 2012, along with some of the surrounding park.

Attractions in the park include the **Orangery**; the **Spielfestung**, or toy fortress, built for Wilhelm II's sons, with a toy cannon that can be fired; the **Chinesisches Teehaus** (Chinese Teahouse), with its collection of Chinese and Meissen porcelain; and the **Drachenhaus** (Dragonhouse), a pagoda-style café. In the park's south-west corner lies **Schloss Charlottenhof**, with its copper-plate engraving room, built in the 1830s on the orders of crown prince Friedrich Wilhelm IV. Outside Sanssouci, on Breitestrasse, is the **Dampfmaschinenhaus**. It pumped water for Sanssouci's fountains, but was built to look like a mosque.

North-east of the town centre is another large park complex, the **Neuer Garten**, designed on the orders of Frederick the Great's nephew and successor to the throne, Friedrich Wilhelm II. The king died a premature death in the neoclassical **Marmorpalais**, allegedly as a result of his dissolute lifestyle. At the park's most northern corner is **Schloss Cecilienhof**, the last royal palace to be built in Potsdam. This incongruous, mock-Tudor mansion was built for the Kaiser's son and his wife. Spared wartime damage, in summer 1945 it hosted the Potsdam Conference, where Stalin, Truman and Churchill (later replaced by Clement Attlee) met to discuss Germany's future. Inside, you can see the round table where the settlement was negotiated.

During the conference, the Allied leaders lived across the Havel river in one of Babelsberg's secluded 19th-century villa districts. Stalin stayed in Karl-Marx-Strasse 27; Churchill stayed in Villa Urbig at Virchowstrasse 23, one of Mies van der Rohe's early buildings; and Truman stayed in Truman-Villa at Karl-Marx-Strasse 2. These buildings can be viewed from the outside only.

Potsdam's third and most recent royal park, **Park Babelsberg**, also makes for a good walk. In East German times it fell into neglect because it lay so near to the border. **Schloss Babelsberg**, a neo-Gothic extravaganza inspired by Windsor Castle, nestles among its wooded slopes. Another architectural curiosity is the **Flatowturm**, an observation point in mock medieval style close to the Glienicker See.

Also on the east side of the Havel river, not too far south of Potsdam's main station, is the Telegraphenberg – once the site of a telegraph station. In 1921, it became the site of Erich Mendelsohn's expressionist **Einsteinturm**, built to house an observatory that could confirm the General Theory of Relativity. A wonderfully whimsical building, it was one of the first products of the inter-war avant-garde.

On nearby Brauhausberg, there's one last reminder of Potsdam's complex, multi-layered past. The square tower rising up from the trees is the present seat of Brandenburg's state parliament. In East German days, the building was known as the 'Kremlin' because it served as local Communist Party headquarters. Originally, it was the Kriegsschule – 'the war school' – where young men trained to be officers in the German imperial army.

Babelsberg

The main attraction in Potsdam's eastern neighbour, Babelsberg, is the film-studio complex, sections of which are open to the public in theme-park form. In the 1920s, this was the world's largest studio outside Hollywood, and it was here that Fritz Lang's *Metropolis*, Josef von Sternberg's *The Blue Angel* and other masterpieces were produced. During the Nazi period, it churned out thrillers, light entertainment and propaganda pieces such as Leni Riefenstahl's *Triumph of the Will*. More than 700 feature films were made here during the Communist era.

The studios were privatised after reunification and now there are modern facilities for all phases of film and TV production. **Filmpark Babelsberg** has an assortment of attractions, ranging from themed restaurants and rides to set tours and stunt displays, but it's pretty tacky.

Biosphäre
Georg-Hermann-Allee 99 (0331 550 740, www. biosphaere-potsdam.de). Tram 96 Volkspark. **Open** 9am-6pm (last entry 4.30pm) Mon-Fri; 10am-7pm (last entry 5.30pm) Sat, Sun. **Admission** €11.50; €4.50-€7.80 reductions; free under-3s.

Filmmuseum Potsdam
Breitestrasse 1A (0331 271 8112, www. filmmuseum-potsdam.de). Tram 91, 92, 93, 96, 98, 99 Alter Markt. **Open** 10am-6pm Tue-Sun. **Admission** €4.50; €3.50 reductions. *Guided tours* €1. **No credit cards.**

Filmpark Babelsberg
Entrance on Grossbeerenstrasse (0331 721 2750, www.filmpark.de). S7 Babelsberg then bus 601, 619, 690 to Filmpark, or RE1 Medienstadt. **Open** *Easter to Halloween* 10am-6pm daily. Closed Halloween to Easter. **Admission** €21; €17 reductions.

Gedenkstätte Lindenstrasse
Lindenstrasse 54 (0331 289 6803, www. potsdam.de/potsdam-museum). Tram 91, 94, 96 Dortusstrasse. **Open** 10am-6pm Tue, Thur, Sat. **Admission** €1.50. **No credit cards.**

Haus der Brandenburgisch-Preussischen Geschichte
Kutschstall, Am Neuen Markt (0331 620 8550, www. hbpg.de). Tram 91, 92, 93, 96, 98, 99 Alter Markt. **Open** 10am-6pm Tue-Fri; 10am-5pm Sat, Sun. **Admission** €5; €4 reductions. **No credit cards.**

Jan Bouman Haus
Mittelstrasse 8 (0331 280 3773). Tram 92, 96 Nauener Tor. **Open** 1-6pm Mon-Fri; 11am-6pm Sat, Sun. **Admission** €2; €1 reductions; free under-12s. **No credit cards.**

Marmorpalais
Im Neuen Garten (0331 969 4200, www.spsg.de). Tram 92, 96, or bus 603 Reiterweg/Alleestrasse. **Open** *May-Oct* 10am-6pm Tue, Thur-Sun. *Nov-Apr* Guided tours only 10am-4.30pm Sat, Sun. **Admission** €5; €4 reductions. **No credit cards.**

FREE Nikolaikirche
Am Alten Markt (0331 270 8602, www.nikolai potsdam.de). Tram 91, 92, 93, 96, 98, 99 Alter Markt. **Open** *Jan-Mar, Nov, Dec* 9am-5pm Mon-Sat. *Apr, May, Sept, Oct* 9am-7pm Mon-Sat. *June-Aug* 9am-9pm Mon-Sat. **Services** 10am Sun. **Admission** free.

THE WILD SIDE

Wild swimming near Berlin.

Near Strausberg (35km east of Berlin).

Altlandsberger Chaussee 102, Eggersdorf. S5 S-Bahn to Strausberg, then bus 391 to Eggersdorf Mittelstrasse. The lake is a 1km walk (follow signs to Hotel Seeschloss – the lake is behind the hotel).
The waters of this lovely little lake are crystal clear. The directions given lead to the *strandbad* (beach), where you sometimes have to pay a small entry fee.

FLAKENSEE
Near Erkner (30km south-east of Berlin).

S3 S-Bahn to Erkner. From there, it's a 3.5km walk or cycle to the lake. Alternatively, get off the S3 at Rahnsdorf and take historic tram 87 to Woltersdorfer Schleuse.
There are lots of little bathing spots around this lake, which is surprisingly clean given the number of motorboats using it.

HELENESEE
Near Frankfurt/Oder (110km south-east of Berlin).

RE1 train from Berlin Hauptbahnhof to Frankfurt/Oder. From there, it's an 8km bike ride or bus 984 to the strandbad.
This large lake near the border with Poland is known by locals as Kleine Ostsee (Little Baltic Sea) thanks to its long white-sand beach and cooling clear water. There's a campsite and youth hostel if you fancy staying over.

SCHERMÜTZELSEE
Near Buckow (50km east of Berlin).

S5 S-Bahn to Strausberg, then bus 926 to Buckow.
This dreamy little lake is in the middle of the Märkische Schweiz nature park. In summer, it's a great way to cool off after a visit to Bertolt Brecht's summer house, now a museum (Bertolt-Brecht-Strasse 30, Buckow, www.brechtweigelhaus.de).

Potsdam Museum
Am Alten Markt 9 (0331 289 6821, www. potsdam.de/potsdam-museum). Tram 91, 92, 93, 96, 98, 99 Alter Markt. **Open** 10am-5pm Tue, Wed, Fri; 10am-7pm Thur; 10am-6pm Sat, Sun. **Admission** €5-€7.50.

★ Sanssouci
Maulbeerallee (0331 969 4200, www.spsg.de). Bus 606, 695. **Open** *Palace & exhibition buildings* varies. **Admission** *Palace & exhibition buildings* €12; €5-€8 reductions. *Park* free.

★ Schloss Cecilienhof
Im Neuen Garten (0331 969 4200, www.spsg.de). Bus 603. **Open** *Apr-Oct* 9am-6pm Tue-Sun. *Nov-Mar* 9am-4.30pm Tue-Sun. **Admission** €6; €5 reductions.

Where to eat & drink

B-West (Zeppelinstrasse 146, 0331 9792 013) attracts a lively, young crowd and serves simple German cuisine. **Café Heider** (Friedrich-Ebert-Strasse 29, 0331 270 5596) offers excellent coffee and cake, plus a wide range of main dishes. **Backstoltz** (Dortusstrasse 59, 0331 2012 929) is a cosy *croissanterie*, good for a light breakfast or lunch. There's also a range of cafés, pubs and restaurants along pedestrianised Brandenburger Strasse, most with tables outside in summer, and on nearby Lindenstrasse and Dortusstrasse.

Getting there

Potsdam and Babelsberg can be reached via the S7 S-Bahn line. It takes just under an hour from Mitte and you'll need a ticket that covers the C zone. From some parts of Berlin, it's easier to take the S1 to Wannsee and change to the S7 there. There's also a direct, hourly Regionalbahn train (RE1) from Mitte to Medienstadt Babelsberg (20mins), and a number of Regionalbahn trains to Potsdam Hauptbahnhof.

Getting around

Potsdam is too spread out to do everything on foot, but the tram and bus network covers everything. A Potsdam Card (from €9.50), available from the tourist office, provides free public transport and discounted entry to most attractions.

Tourist information

Potsdam Tourismus Service
Brandenburger Strasse 3 (0331 2755 8899, www.potsdamtourismus.de). Tram 91, 94, or bus 695 Luisenplatz. **Open** *Apr-Oct* 9am-7pm Mon-Fri; 9am-2pm Sat, Sun. *Nov-Mar* 10am-6pm Mon-Fri; 9am-2pm Sat.

SACHSENHAUSEN

Many Nazi concentration camps are open to the public as memorials and museums, and **KZ Sachsenhausen** is the nearest to Berlin. As soon as he came to power, Hitler set about rounding up and interning his opponents. From 1933 to 1935, an old brewery on this site was used to hold them. The present camp received its first prisoners in July 1936. It was a *schutzhaftlager* ('protective custody camp'). The first *schutzhaftlagern* were political opponents of the government: communists, social democrats, trade unionists. Soon, the range of prisoners widened to include gays, Jews and anyone guilty of 'anti-social' behaviour.

Around 6,000 Jews were brought here after Kristallnacht alone, with many later sent on to Auschwitz. Sachsenhausen saw some of the first experiments in organised mass murder: thousands of Russian POWs from the Eastern Front were killed at the camp's 'Station Z'.

The SS evacuated the camp in 1945 and began marching 33,000 inmates to the Baltic, where they were to be packed into boats and sunk in the sea. Some 6,000 died during the march before the survivors were rescued by the Allies. Another 3,000 prisoners were found in the camp's hospital when it was captured on 22 April 1945.

After the German capitulation, the Russian secret police, the MVD, reopened Sachsenhausen as 'Camp 7' for the detention of war criminals; in fact, it was filled with anyone suspected of opposition. On 23 April 1961, the partially restored camp was opened to the public as a national monument and memorial. Following the fall of the DDR, mass graves were discovered, containing the remains of an estimated 10,000 prisoners.

Behind the parade ground – where morning roll-call was taken, and from where inmates were required to witness executions on the gallows – stand the two remaining barracks blocks. One is now a museum and the other is a memorial hall and cinema, where a film about the history of the camp is shown. Next door stands the prison block. It's a good idea to hire an audio guide (€3; available in English) at the gate.

Perhaps the grimmest site at Sachsenhausen is the subsiding remains of Station Z, the small extermination block. A map traces the path the condemned would have followed, depending on whether they were to be shot (the bullets were retrieved and reused) or gassed. All ended up in the neighbouring ovens.

FREE KZ Sachsenhausen

Strasse der Nationen 22, Oranienburg (03301 2000, www.stiftung-bg.de). **Open** *Mid Mar-mid Oct* 8.30am-6pm Tue-Sun. *Mid Oct-mid Mar* 8.30am-4.30pm Tue-Sun. **Admission** free. The grounds of the camp are also open on Mondays, but the museum is closed.

Rügen.

Getting there

Oranienburg is at the northern end of the S1 S-Bahn line (40mins from Mitte). From the station, follow signs to 'Gedenkstätte Sachsenhausen' (20mins walk).

RÜGEN

The Baltic coast was the top holiday destination for DDR citizens; post-reunification, it's still the most accessible stretch of seaside for Berliners. The coast forms the northern boundary of the state of Mecklenburg-Vorpommern. Bismarck famously said of the area: 'When the end of the world comes, I shall go to Mecklenburg, because there everything happens a hundred years later.'

Many visitors head for the beautiful island of Rügen, with its white chalk cliffs, beech woods and beaches. Most people stay in the resorts on the east coast, such as Binz (the largest and best known), Sellin and Göhren. In July and August, Rügen can get pretty crowded (don't go without pre-booked accommodation), but the island's handful of restaurants and lack of late-night bars mean visitors are early to bed and early to rise.

Where to stay & eat

Most accommodation on Rügen is in private houses. Your best bet is to contact the local tourist office (*see p222*), which can help you find a room. Camping is also very popular. Binz offers the best selection of places to eat.

Getting there

There are some direct trains to Bergen on Rügen, but the journey usually involves changing trains at Stralsund. Journey time is 3-4hrs. Check www. bahn.com for timetables.

ESCAPES & EXCURSIONS

Tourist information

Bergen *Am Markt 25 (03838 807 780, www. ruegen.de).* **Open** *Mid Aug-June* 8am-6pm Mon-Fri. *July-mid Aug* 8am-6pm Mon-Fri; 8am-7pm Sat; 9am-4pm Sun.
Kurverwaltung Göhren *Poststrasse 9 (03830 866 790, www.ostseebad-goehren.de).* **Open** *Summer* 9am-6pm Mon-Fri; 9am-noon Sat. *Winter* 9am-noon, 1-4.30pm Mon, Wed, Thur; 9am-noon, 1-6pm Tue; 9am-noon, 1-3pm Fri.
Kurverwaltung Sellin *Warmbadstrasse 4 (03830 3160, www.ostseebad-sellin.de).* **Open** *July, Aug* 10am-6pm daily. *Sept-June* 8.30am-6pm Mon-Fri; 10am-2pm Sat, Sun.
Ostseebad Binz *Heinrich-Heine-Strasse 7 (03839 314 8148, www.ostseebad-binz.de).* **Open** *Summer* 10am-6pm daily. *Winter* 9am-4pm daily.

DRESDEN

Destroyed and rebuilt twice, the capital of Saxony – 100 kilometres (60 miles) south of Berlin – boasts one of Germany's finest art museums and many historic buildings. The most recent wave of rebuilding – including the restoration of the Frauenkirche – was completed in time for the city's 800-year anniversary in 2006.

Modern Dresden is built on the ruins of its past. A fire consumed Altendresden on the banks of the Elbe in 1685, and the city was subsequently reconstructed. Then, on the night of 13 February 1945, one of World War II's largest Allied bombing raids caused huge firestorms that killed between 25,000 and 40,000 people. After the war, Dresden was twinned with Coventry, and Benjamin Britten's *War Requiem* was given its first performance in the Hofkirche by musicians from both towns. Under the DDR, reconstruction was erratic, but a maze of cranes and scaffolding sprang up in the 1990s and Dresden has been making up for lost time ever since.

Its major attractions are the buildings from the reign of Augustus the Strong (1670-1733). The **Hofkirche** and **Zwinger** complex are fine examples of the city's Baroque legacy. Dresden's main draw for art-lovers is the **Gemäldegalerie Alte Meister** in the Zwinger, a superb collection of Old Masters, particularly Italian Renaissance and Flemish. There's also porcelain from nearby Meissen, and collections of armour, weapons, clocks and scientific equipment. There's more art at the newly refurbished **Albertinum**, with major paintings and sculpture on display from the Romantic period to the present day.

Building was continued by Augustus's successor, Augustus III, who then lost to Prussia in the Seven Years' War (1756-63). Frederick the Great destroyed much of the city during the war, though not the lovely **Brühlsche Terrasse** riverside promenade. A victorious Napoleon

Dresden.

ordered the demolition of the city's defences in 1809. By the Zwinger is the **Semperoper** opera house (1838-41), named after its architect, Gottfried Semper. It was fully restored in 1985.

The industrialisation of Dresden heralded a new phase of construction that produced the **Rathaus** (Town Hall, 1905-10) at Dr-Külz-Ring; the **Hauptbahnhof** (1892-95) at the end of Prager Strasse; the **Yenidze** cigarette factory (1912) on Könneritzstrasse, designed to look like a mosque; and the **Landtagsgebäude** (completed to plans by Paul Wallot, designer of Berlin's Reichstag, in 1907) at Heinrich-Zille-Strasse 11. The finest example of inter-war architecture is Wilhelm Kreis's **Deutsches Hygiene-Museum** (1929) at Lingner Platz 1, which houses the German Institute of Hygiene.

The **Neue Synagoge** in Rathenauplatz was dedicated in November 2001, 63 years after its predecessor (built by Semper in 1838-40) was destroyed in the Nazi pogroms. Reconstruction of the domed **Frauenkirche** at Neumarkt was completed and the restored cathedral was reconsecrated in October 2005. The communists had left it as a heap of rubble throughout the Cold War period as a reminder of Allied aggression. In the end, its restoration was funded partly by private donations from the UK and US. The golden orb and cross atop the dome were built by goldsmith Alan Smith, son of one of the British pilots who took part in the 1945 bombings.

The Striezelmarkt, founded in 1434, is the oldest Christmas market in Germany. It's held on Altstädtermarkt every December and is named after the savoury pretzel you see everyone eating. Dresden is also home to the best *stollen*, the German yuletide cake.

The Neustadt – on the northern bank of the Elbe – literally means 'new town', although it's more than 300 years old. Having escaped major damage during the war, the Neustadt has kept much of its original architecture intact. When Augustus the Strong commissioned the rebuilding of Dresden in 1685, he pictured a new Venice. The Neustadt doesn't quite measure up, but the 18th-century townhouses in Hauptstrasse and Königstrasse are charming.

Albertinum
Brühlsche Terrasse (0351 4914 2000, www. skd.museum). **Open** 10am-6pm Tue-Sun. **Admission** €10; €7.50 reductions.

Gemäldegalerie Alte Meister
Zwinger, Theaterplatz (0351 4914 6679, www. skd.museum). **Open** 10am-6pm daily. **Admission** €10; €7.50 reductions. **No credit cards**.

Semperoper
Tickets: Schinkelwache, Theaterplatz (0351 706 4911, www.semperoper.de). **Box office** 10am-6pm Mon-Fri; 10am-1pm Sat, Sun; also 1hr before performance. **Tickets** vary.

Where to eat & drink

Caroussel (Bülow-Residenz, Königstrasse 14, 0351 80030, closed Mon & Sun), a contemporary German restaurant with a Michelin star, has a leafy courtyard that's pleasant in summer. **Piccola Capri** (Alaunstrasse 93, 0351 801 4848, closed Sun) is one of the best Italians in the Neustadt. In the same part of town, there are plenty of good bars and cafés on and around Alaunstrasse in the area north-east of Albertplatz.

Where to stay

The **Artotel Dresden** (Ostra-Allee 33, 0351 49220, www.artotel.de) is decorated with 600 works by local artist AR Penck. **Ibis Hotel Bastei/Königstein/Lilienstein** (Prager Strasse, 0351 4856 2000, www.ibis-dresden.de) are three functional tower-blocks on Prager Strasse between the railway station and Altstadt. The **Hotel Bayerischer Hof Dresden** (Antonstrasse 33-35, 0351 829 370, www. bayerischer-hof-dresden.de) has comfy rooms and a personal feel. The **Hotel Taschenbergpalais Kempinski** (Taschenberg 3, 0351 49120, www. kempinski-dresden.de) provides indulgent luxury in a Baroque palace. Over in the Neustadt, the **Hostel Mondpalast** (Louisenstrasse 77, 0351 563 4050, www.mondpalast.de) is a decent budget

option. **Hotel Smetana** (Schlüterstrasse 25, 0351 256 080, www.hotel-smetana.de) is a pleasant three-star, east of the centre.

Getting there

Direct trains take about 2hrs from Berlin. Check www.bahn.com for the timetable.

Tourist information

Dresden Tourist-Information
QF-Passage, Neumarkt 2 (0351 501 501, www.dresden.de/tourismus). **Open** 10am-7pm Mon-Fri; 10am-6pm Sat; 10am-3pm Sun.

LEIPZIG

One of Germany's most important trade hubs and the former second city of the DDR, Leipzig is a centre of education and culture, and the place where East Germany's mass movement for political change began. It's also synonymous with Bach, who lived here for 27 years. The city, once one of Germany's industrial strongholds, has also been famed for its fairs for centuries; trade fairs (*messen*) are still its bread and butter. The pedestrianised, recently restored old centre is another attraction: with its Renaissance and Baroque churches, narrow lanes, old street markets and the ancient university, it's hard to believe that it was bombed to bits during World War II. The area is also crammed with enough sights, bars and restaurants to fill a day or two.

Located 130 kilometres (80 miles) south-west of Berlin, Leipzig traces its origins back to a settlement founded by the Sorbs, a Slavic people who venerated the lime tree, sometime between the seventh and ninth centuries. They called it Lipzk (Place of Limes).

Most visitors arrive at Leipzig Hauptbahnhof, the huge, renovated central train station. The station stands on the north-east edge of the compact city centre, which is surrounded by a ring road that follows the course of the old city walls. Much of the ring road is lined with parks; most of the city's attractions can be found within its limits.

The first place to head is the Leipzig tourist office, diagonally left across tram-strewn Willy-Brand-Platz from the front of the train station. Pick up a guide to the city in English (which includes a map) and head for Markt, the old market square, to get your bearings. The eastern side of the square is occupied by the lovely Renaissance **Altes Rathaus** (Old Town Hall), built in 1556-57. It now houses the **Stadtgeschichtliches Museum** (Town Museum). On the square's south side are the huge bay windows of the Könighaus, once a haunt of Saxony's rulers when visiting the city (the notoriously rowdy Peter the Great also once stayed here).

The church off the south-west corner of Markt is **Thomaskirche**, where Johann Sebastian Bach spent 27 years as choirmaster of the famous St Thomas's Boys' Choir; the composer is buried in the chancel and his statue stands outside the church. Opposite the church, in the Bosehaus, is the **Bach-Museum**. Documents, instruments and furniture illustrate the work and influence of the great man. South from Thomaskirche, towards the south-west corner of the ring road, is the **Neues Rathaus** (New Town Hall), whose origins date back to the 16th century, though the current buildings are only about 100 years old.

Immediately behind the Altes Rathaus is the delightful little **Alte Börse** (Old Stock Exchange). Built in 1687, it's fronted by a statue of Goethe, who studied at Leipzig University. Follow his gaze to the entrance to Mädlerpassage, Leipzig's finest shopping arcade, within which is **Auerbachs Keller** (*see p225*), one of the oldest and most famous restaurants in Germany. It was in Auerbachs, where he often used to drink, that Goethe set a scene in *Faust*.

North of the Alte Börse is Sachsenplatz, site of the city's main outdoor market, and new home of the **Museum der Bildenden Künste** (Museum of Arts Picture Gallery). Its 2,200-strong collection stretches from 15th- and 16th-century Dutch, Flemish and German paintings to DDR art. Artists featured include Dürer, Rembrandt and Rubens.

Just south-east of here is the **Nikolaikirche**, Leipzig's proud symbol of its new freedom. This medieval church, with its Baroque interior, is the place where regular free-speech meetings started in 1982. These evolved into the Swords to Ploughshares peace movement, which led to the first anti-DDR demonstration on 4 September 1989 in the Nikolaikirchhof.

West of here, on the edge of the ring road, is the **Museum in der 'Runden Ecke'** (Museum in the 'Round Corner'). The building once housed the local Stasi headquarters and now has an exhibition detailing its nefarious methods, such as collecting scents of suspected people in jars, as well as a hilarious section on Stasi disguises. Outside the ring road is **Leipzig Zoo**. All the usual family favourites are here.

In the south-east corner of the ring road rises the drab tower block of Leipzig University. Rebuilt in 1970 to resemble an opened book, this modern monstrosity is ironically one of Europe's oldest centres of learning. Alumni, besides Goethe, include Nietzsche, Schumann and Wagner. The university runs the **Äyptisches Museum**. Nearby is the **Grassi Museum für Angewandte Kunst** (Museum of Applied Art), founded in 1874; tours in English are available to book. Also here are the **Museum für Völkerkunde** (Ethnography Museum) and **Museum für Musikinstrumente** (Museum of Musical Instruments).

The university tower stands at the south-eastern corner of Augustplatz, a project of DDR Communist Party leader Walter Ulbricht, himself a Leipziger. Next door are the brown glass-fronted buildings of the **Gewandhaus**, home of the Leipziger Gewandhaus Orchester, one of the world's finest orchestras. On the square's northern side stands the **Opernhaus Leipzig**.

Ägyptisches Museum

Goethestrasse 2 (0341 973 7015, www.gko. uni-leipzig.de/aegyptisches-museum). **Open** 1-5pm Tue-Fri; 10am-5pm Sat, Sun. **Admission** €5; €3 reductions. **No credit cards.**

Bach-Museum

Thomaskirchhof 16 (0341 91370, www. bach-leipzig.de). **Open** 10am-6pm Tue-Sun. **Admission** €8; €6 reductions.

Gewandhaus

Augustusplatz 8 (0341 127 0280, www. gewandhaus.de). **Box office** noon-6pm Mon-Fri; 10am-2pm Sat. **Tickets** vary.

Grassi Museum für Angewandte Kunst

Johannisplatz 5-11 (0341 222 9100, www.grassi museum.de). **Open** 10am-6pm Tue-Sun. **Admission** €5-€8; €3.50-€5.50 reductions. **No credit cards.**

Leipzig Zoo

Pfaffendorfer Strasse 29 (0341 593 3500, www.zoo-leipzig.de). **Open** *Apr* 9am-6pm Mon-Fri; 9am-7pm Sat, Sun. *May-Sept* 9am-7pm daily. *Oct* 9am-6pm daily. *Nov-Mar* 9am-5pm daily. **Admission** €18.50; €11-€15 reductions. **No credit cards.**

Museum der Bildenden Künste

Katharinenstrasse 10 (0341 2169 9910, www. mdbk.de). **Open** 10am-6pm Tue, Thur-Sun; noon-8pm Wed. **Admission** €5; €3.50 reductions; free 2nd Wed of mth. *Temporary exhibitions* €6-€8; €4-€5.50 reductions.

FREE Museum in der 'Runden Ecke'

Dittrichring 24 (0341 961 2443, www.runde-ecke-leipzig.de). **Open** 10am-6pm daily. *Guided tours* 3pm daily. **Admission** free. *Guided tours* €4; €3 reductions. **No credit cards.**

FREE Nikolaikirche

Nikolaikirchhof 3 (0341 124 5380, www. nikolaikirche-leipzig.de). **Open** 10am-4.45pm Mon, Wed; 10am-6pm Tue, Thur, Fri; 10am-3.30pm Sat; 1-3.30pm Sun. **Admission** free.

Opernhaus Leipzig

Augustusplatz 12 (0341 126 1261, www.oper-leipzig.de). **Box office** 10am-7pm Mon-Fri; 10am-6pm Sat; 1hr before performance Sun. **Tickets** vary.

TAKE A PUNT

Paddling around the Spreewald.

This filigree network of tiny rivers, streams and canals, dividing patches of deciduous forest and farmland, is one of the loveliest excursions from Berlin. Author Theodor Fontane described the Spreewald as how Venice would have looked 1,500 years ago. It gets crowded in season, compromising its claim as one of the most perfect wilderness areas in Europe, but come out of season and you can have the area pretty much to yourself.

About 100 kilometres (60 miles) south-east of Berlin, the Spree bisects the area into the Unterspreewald and Oberspreewald. For the former, Schepzig or Lübben are the best starting points; for the latter, stay on the train a little further to Lübbenau. The Oberspreewald is the pick of the two, its 500 square kilometres (190 square miles) home to more than 300 natural and artificial channels, called *fliesse*. You can travel around these on punts or kayaks (rent your own or join a larger group), but motorised boats are forbidden.

The Haus für Mensch & Natur (Schulstrasse 9, Lübbenau, 03542 89210) is the visitor centre for the Spreewald Biosphere Reservation, with an exhibition about the environmental importance of the area. The tourist office in Lübbenau (Ehm-Welk-Strasse 15, 035 423 668,

www.luebbenau-spreewald.com) can provide various maps and walking routes, while www. spreewald-info.com and www.spreewald-online.de are good sources of information and allow you to book hotel rooms online. There are regular trains (www.bahn.com) to Lübben and Lübbenau, and journey times are around an hour to Lübben and an extra 15 minutes to Lübbenau.

The local population belongs to the Sorbish minority, a Slav people related to Czechs and Slovaks. Their own language is found in street names, newspapers and so on. This adds an air of exoticism, unlike the folk festivals laid on for tourists in the high season.

Stadtgeschichtliches Museum
Altes Rathaus, Markt 1 (0341 965 1320, www.stadtgeschichtliches-museum-leipzig.de). **Open** 10am-6pm Tue-Sun. **Admission** €6; €4 reductions. **No credit cards**.

FREE Thomaskirche
Thomaskirchhof 18 (0341 2222 4200, www.thomaskirche.org). **Open** 9am-6pm daily. **Admission** free.

Where to eat & drink

Apels Garten (Kolonnadenstrasse 2, 0341 960 7777, www.apels-garten.de) is a pretty restaurant with imaginative German cooking. **Auerbachs Keller** (Mädlerpassage, Grimmaische Strasse 2-4, 0341 216 100, www.auerbachs-keller-leipzig. de), located in a 1525 beer hall, has a gourmet menu and a cheaper version: both include classic Saxon cuisine. **Barthels Hof** (Hainstrasse 1, 0341 141 310, www.barthels-hof.de) offers hearty Saxon cooking in a cosy panelled *Gasthaus*.

Where to stay

The **Precise Hotel Accento Leipzig** (Taucher Strasse 260, 0341 92620, www.precisehotels.com) has stylish rooms. **Adagio Minotel Leipzig** (Seeburgstrasse 96, 0341 216 690, www.hotel-adagio.de) features individually furnished rooms and a central location. For art-nouveau luxury, try the **Seaside Park Hotel** (Richard-Wagner-Strasse 7, 0341 98520, www.park-hotel-leipzig.de).

Getting there

Regular trains from Berlin Hauptbahnhof take an hour to reach Leipzig.

Tourist information

Leipzig Tourist Service
Katharinenstrasse 8 (0341 710 4260, www.ltm-leipzig.de). **Open** *Mar-Oct* 9.30am-6pm Mon-Fri; 9.30am-4pm Sat; 9.30am-3pm Sun. *Nov-Feb* 10am-6pm Mon-Fri; 9.30am-4pm Sat; 9.30am-3pm Sun.

In Context

History

Occupation, imperialism, republicanism, fascism, communism, division and reunification: Berlin's seen it all.

TEXT: FREDERICK STUDEMANN

IN CONTEXT

Compared to other European capitals, such as Rome or London, Berlin is just a baby. The area where the city is now was so boggy that nobody bothered to settle there until the 12th century, when German knights under Albert the Bear wrested the swampland from Slavic tribes. The name Berlin is believed to come from the Slav word *birl*, meaning 'swamp'. Berlin and its twin settlement Cölln (on what is now the Museumsinsel) were founded as trading posts on the banks of the River Spree, halfway between the older fortress towns of Spandau and Köpenick. Today, the borough of Mitte embraces Cölln and old Berlin, and Spandau and Köpenick are peripheral suburbs. The town's existence was first recorded in 1237, when Cölln was mentioned in a church document. In the same century, construction began on the Marienkirche and Nikolaikirche, both of which still stand.

LAYING THE FOUNDATIONS

The Ascanian family, as Margraves of Brandenburg, ruled over the twin towns and the surrounding region. To encourage trade, they granted special rights to merchants, with the result that Berlin and Cölln – which were officially united in 1307 – emerged as wealthy trading centres linking east and west. Early prosperity ended in 1319 with the death of the last Ascanian ruler, leaving the city at the mercy of robber barons from outlying regions. Yet, despite political upheaval, Berlin's merchants continued their business. In 1359, the city joined the Hanseatic League of free-trading northern European cities.

The threat of invasion remained, however. In the late 14th century, two powerful families, the Dukes of Pomerania and the brutal von Quitzow brothers, vied for control of the city. Salvation came in the guise of Friedrich of Hohenzollern, a southern German nobleman sent by the Holy Roman Emperor in 1411 to bring peace to the region. Initially, Friedrich was well received by the local people. The bells of the Marienkirche were melted down and made into weapons for the fight against the aggressors. Friedrich officially became Margrave. In 1416, he took the title of Elector of Brandenburg, denoting his right to vote in the election of the Holy Roman Emperor – titular head of the German-speaking states. Gradually, Berlin was transformed from an trading post to a small-sized capital. In 1442, foundations were laid for Berlin Castle and a royal court was established. By 1450, the city's population was 6,000.

With peace and stability came the loss of independent traditions, as Friedrich consolidated power. Disputes rose between the patrician classes and the craftsmen's guilds. Rising social friction culminated in the 'Berlin Indignation' of 1447-48, when the population rose up in rebellion. Friedrich's son, Friedrich II, and his courtiers were locked out of the city and the castle foundations were flooded, but the uprising soon collapsed and the Hohenzollerns returned triumphant. Merchants faced new restrictions and the economy suffered.

The Reformation arrived in Berlin and Brandenburg during the reign of Joachim I Nestor (1535-71), the first Elector to embrace Protestantism. He strove to improve Berlin's cultural standing by inviting artists, architects and theologians to the city. In 1538, Caspar Theyss and Konrad Krebbs, two master-builders from Saxony, began work on a Renaissance-style palace. Taking 100 years to complete, it evolved into the bombastic Stadtschloss, which stood on what is now Museumsinsel in the Spree until the East German government demolished it in 1950.

Joachim's studious nature was not reflected in the self-indulgent behaviour of his subjects. Attempts to clamp down on drinking, gambling and loose morals had little effect. Visiting the city, Abbot Trittenheim remarked that 'the people are good, but rough and unpolished; they prefer stuffing themselves to good science.' After stuffing itself with another 6,000 people, Berlin left the 16th century with a population of 12,000.

The outbreak of the Thirty Years War in 1618 dragged Berlin on to the wider political stage. Although initially unaffected by the conflict between Catholic forces loyal to the Holy Roman Empire and the Swedish-backed Protestant armies, the city was eventually caught up in the war, which left the German-speaking states ravaged and divided for two centuries. In 1626, imperial troops occupied Berlin and plundered the city. Trade collapsed and the city's hinterland was laid waste. Four serious epidemics between 1626 and 1631 killed thousands. By the end of the war, in 1648, Berlin had lost a third of its housing and the population had fallen to less than 6,000.

Painstaking reconstruction was carried out under Friedrich Wilhelm, the 'Great Elector'. He succeeded his father in 1640, but sat out the war in exile. Influenced by Dutch ideas on town planning and architecture, Wilhelm embarked on a policy that linked urban regeneration, economic expansion and solid defence. New city fortifications were built and a garrison of 2,000 soldiers established as Friedrich expanded his 'Residenzstadt'. In the centre of town, the Lustgarten was laid out opposite the Stadtschloss. Running west from the palace, the first Lindenallee ('Avenue of Lime Trees' or Unter den Linden) was created.

To revive the city's economy, a sales tax replaced housing and property taxes. With the money raised, three new towns were built – Friedrichswerder, Dorotheenstadt and Friedrichstadt. (Together with Berlin and Cölln, these now form the district of Mitte.) In the 1660s, a canal was constructed

Frederick the Great

linking the Spree and Oder rivers, confirming Berlin as an east–west trading centre.

But Friedrich Wilhelm's most inspired policy was to encourage refugees to settle. First to arrive were over 50 Jewish families from Vienna. In 1672, Huguenot settlers came from France. Both groups brought with them vital new skills. The growing cosmopolitan mix laid the foundations for a flowering of intellectual and artistic life. By the time the Great Elector's son Friedrich III took the throne in 1688, one in five Berliners spoke French. Today, French words still pepper Berlin dialect, among them *boulette* (hamburger) and *étage* (floor). In 1701, Elector Friedrich III had himself crowned Prussian King Friedrich I (not to be confused with the earlier Elector).

The common association of Prussia with militarism can broadly be traced back to the 18th century and the efforts of two men in particular: King Friedrich Wilhelm I (1713-40) and his son Friedrich II (also known as Frederick the Great). Although father and son hated each other, and had different sensibilities (Friedrich Wilhelm was boorish and mean, Friedrich II sensitive and philosophical), together they launched Prussia as a major military power and gave Berlin the character of a garrison city.

The obsession with all things military did have some positive effects. The king needed competent soldiers, so he made school compulsory; the army needed doctors, so he set up medical institutes. Berlin's economy also picked up, and skilled immigrants arrived. The result was a population boom – from 60,000 in 1713 to 90,000 in 1740 – and a growth in trade.

FREDERICK THE GREAT

Frederick the Great (Friedrich II) took Prussia into a series of wars with Austria and Russia (1740-42, 1744-45 and 1756-63; the last known as the Seven Years War) in a bid to win territory in Silesia in the east. Initially, the wars proved disastrous. The Austrians occupied Berlin in 1757, the Russians in 1760. However, thanks to a mixture of good fortune and military genius, Frederick emerged victorious from the Seven Years War.

When not fighting, the king set about forging a modern state apparatus and transforming Berlin and Potsdam. This was achieved partly through conviction – the king was friends with Voltaire and saw himself as an aesthetically minded Enlightenment figure – but it was also a political necessity. He needed to convince enemies and subjects that even in times of crisis he was able to afford grand projects. So Unter den Linden was transformed into a grand boulevard. At the palace end, the Forum Fredericianum, designed and constructed by the architect von Knobelsdorff, comprised the Staatsoper, Sankt-Hedwigs-Kathedrale, Prince Heinrich Palace (now housing Humboldt-Universität) and the Staatsbibliotek. Although it was never completed, the Forum is still one of Berlin's main attractions. The Tiergarten was landscaped and a new palace, Schloss Bellevue (now the German president's official residence), built. Frederick also replaced a set of barracks at Gendarmenmarkt with a theatre, now called the Konzerthaus.

To encourage manufacturing and industry, advantageous excise laws were introduced. Businesses such as the KPM (Königliche

Porzellan-Manufaktur) porcelain works were nationalised and turned into prestigious and lucrative enterprises. Legal and administrative reforms saw religious freedom enshrined in law and torture abolished. Berlin also became a centre of the Enlightenment. Cultural and intellectual life blossomed around figures such as philosopher Moses Mendelssohn and poet Gottfried Lessing. By the time Frederick died in 1786, Berlin had a population of 150,000 and was the capital of one of Europe's great powers.

Frederick's death marked the end of the Enlightenment in Prussia. His successor, Friedrich Wilhelm II, was more interested in spending money on classical architecture than wasting time debating the merits of various political philosophies. Censorship was stepped up and the king's extravagance sparked an economic crisis. By 1788, 14,000 Berliners were dependent on state and church aid. The state apparatus crumbled under the weight of greedy administrators. When he died in 1797, Friedrich Wilhelm II left his son with huge debts.

However, the old king's love of classicism gave Berlin its most famous monument: the Brandenburger Tor (Brandenburg Gate). It was built by Karl Gottfried Langhans in 1789, the year of the French Revolution, and modelled on the Propylaea in Athens. Two years later, Johann Schadow added the Quadriga, a sculpture of Victoria riding a chariot drawn by four horses. Originally one of 14 gates, the Brandenburger Tor is now Berlin's geographical and symbolic centre.

If the king did not care for intellect, then the emerging bourgeoisie did. Towards the turn of the century, Berlin became a centre of German Romanticism. Literary salons flourished; they were to remain a feature of the city's cultural life into the middle of the 19th century.

THE NAPOLEONIC WARS

In 1806, Berlin came face to face with the effects of revolution in France: following the humiliating defeat of the Prussian forces in the battles of Jena and Auerstadt on 14 October, Napoleon's army headed for Berlin. The king and queen fled to Königsberg and the garrison was removed from the city. On 27 October, Napoleon and his army marched through the Brandenburger Tor. Once again, Berlin was an occupied city.

Napoleon set about changing the political and administrative structure. He called together 2,000 prominent citizens and told them to elect a new administration, which ran the city until the French troops left in 1808. Napoleon also ordered the expropriation of property belonging to the state, the Hohenzollerns and many aristocratic families. Priceless artworks were removed from palaces and shipped to France. Even the Quadriga was taken from the Brandenburg Gate and sent to Paris. At the same time, the city was hit by crippling war reparations.

When the French left, a group of energetic, reform-minded aristocrats, grouped around Baron vom Stein, moved to modernise the moribund Prussian state. One key reform was the separation of state and civic responsibility, which gave Berlin independence to manage its own affairs. A new council was elected (though only property owners and the wealthy were entitled to vote). In 1810, the philosopher Wilhelm von Humboldt founded the university. All remaining restrictions on the city's Jews were removed.

Although the French occupied Berlin again in 1812 on the way back from their infamous Russian campaign, this time they were met with stiff resistance. A year later, the Prussian king finally joined the anti-Napoleon coalition and thousands of Berliners signed up to fight. Napoleon was defeated at nearby Grossbeeren. This, together with a later defeat in the Battle of Leipzig, marked the end of Napoleonic rule in Germany.

In August 1814, General Blücher brought the Quadriga back to Berlin, restoring it to the Brandenburg Gate with one highly symbolic addition: an Iron Cross and Prussian eagle were added to the staff in Victoria's hand.

The burst of reform was, however, fairly short-lived. Following the Congress of Vienna (1814-15), which established a new political and strategic order for post-Napoleonic Europe, King Friedrich Wilhelm III reneged on promises of constitutional reform. Instead of a greater unity among the German states, a loose alliance came into being; dominated by Austria, the German Confederation was distinctly anti-liberal in its tenor. In Prussia, state power increased. Alongside the normal police, a secret service and a vice squad were established. The police president even had the power to issue directives to the city

'9 November is the anniversary of the establishment of the Weimar Republic (1918), the Kristallnacht pogrom (1938) and the fall of the Wall (1989).'

council. Censorship increased and the authorities sacked von Humboldt from the university he had created.

With their hopes for change frustrated, the bourgeoisie withdrew to their salons. It's one of the ironies of this time that, although political opposition was quashed, a vibrant cultural movement flourished. Academics such as Hegel and Ranke lectured at the university, enhancing Berlin's reputation as an intellectual centre. The period became known as Biedermeier, after a fictional character embodying bourgeois taste, created by Swabian comic writer Ludwig Eichrodt. Another legacy is the range of neoclassical buildings designed by Schinkel, such as his Altes Museum and the Neue Wache.

For the majority, however, it was a period of frustrated hopes and bitter poverty. Industrialisation swelled the ranks of the working class. Between 1810 and 1840, the city's population doubled to 400,000. But most of the newcomers lived in conditions that would later lead to riot and revolution.

REVOLUTION & THE IRON CHANCELLOR

Prussia was ideally equipped for the industrial age. By the 19th century, it had grown dramatically and boasted one of the greatest abundances of raw materials in Europe. It was the founding of the Borsig Werke in 1837 that established Berlin as the workshop of continental Europe. August Borsig was Berlin's first big industrialist. His factories turned out locomotives for the new railway between Berlin and Potsdam, which opened in 1838. Borsig also left his mark through

the establishment of a suburb (Borsigwalde) that still carries his name. The other great pioneering industrialist, Werner Siemens, set up his electrical engineering firm in a house near Anhalter Bahnhof. The Siemens company also created a new suburb, Siemensstadt.

Friedrich Wilhelm IV's accession to the throne in 1840 raised hopes of an end to repression; and, initially, he appeared to share the desire for change. He declared an amnesty for political prisoners, relaxed censorship, sacked the hated justice minister and granted asylum to refugees. Political debate thrived in coffeehouses and wine bars. The university was another focal point for discussion. In the late 1830s, Karl Marx spent a term there, just missing fellow alumnus Otto von Bismarck. In the early 1840s, Friedrich Engels did his military service in Berlin.

The thaw didn't last. It soon became clear that Friedrich Wilhelm IV shared his father's opposition to constitutional reform. Living and working conditions worsened for most Berliners. Rapid industrialisation brought sweatshops, 17-hour days and child labour. This misery was compounded in 1844 by harvest failure, and food riots broke out on Gendarmenmarkt.

Things came to a head in 1848, the year of revolutions. Political meetings were held in beer gardens and the Tiergarten, and demands made for reform and a unification of German-speaking states. On 18 March, the king finally conceded to allowing a new parliament, and vaguely promised other reforms. Later that day, the crowd of 10,000 that gathered to celebrate the victory were set upon by soldiers. Shots were fired and the revolution began. Barricades went up throughout central Berlin and demonstrators fought with police for 14 hours. Finally, the king backed down for a second time. In exchange for the dismantling of barricades, he ordered his troops out of Berlin. Days later, he took part in the funeral service for the 'March Dead' – 183 revolutionaries who had been killed – and promised more freedoms.

Berlin was now ostensibly in the hands of the revolutionaries, and the king seemed to embrace liberalism and nationalism. Prussia, he said, should 'merge into Germany'. But the revolution proved short-lived. When pressed on unification, he merely suggested that the other German states send representatives

IN CONTEXT

to the Prussian National Assembly, an offer that was rebuffed. Leading liberals instead convened a German National Assembly in Frankfurt in May 1848, while a new Prussian Assembly met in what is now the Konzerthaus to debate a new constitution. At the end of 1848, reforming fervour took over Berlin.

Winter, however, brought a change of mood. Using continuing street violence as the pretext, the king ordered the National Assembly to be moved to Brandenburg. In November, he brought troops back into Berlin and declared a state of siege. Press freedom was restricted. The Civil Guard and National Assembly were dissolved. On 5 December, the king delivered his final blow by unveiling a new constitution fashioned to his own tastes. Throughout the winter of 1848-49, thousands of liberals were arrested or expelled. A new city constitution, drawn up in 1850, reduced the number of eligible voters to five per cent of the population. The police president became more powerful than the mayor.

By 1857, the king had gone senile. His brother Wilhelm acted as regent until becoming king on Friedrich's death in 1861. Once again, the people's hopes were raised: the new monarch began by appointing liberals to the cabinet. The building of the Rotes Rathaus (Red Town Hall), completed in 1869, gave the city council a headq uarters to match the size of the royal palace. But by 1861, the king was locked in a dispute with parliament over proposed army reforms. He wanted to strengthen his control of the armed forces. Parliament refused, so the king went over its members' heads and appointed a new prime minister: Otto von Bismarck.

An arrogant genius and former diplomat, Bismarck was well able to deal with unruly parliamentarians. Using a constitutional loophole to rule against the majority, he quickly pushed through the army reforms. Extra-parliamentary opposition was dealt with in the usual manner: oppression and censorship. Dissension thus suppressed, Bismarck turned his mind to German unification. Unlike the bourgeois revolutionaries of 1848, who desired a Germany united by popular will and endowed with political reforms, Bismarck strove to bring the states together under the authoritarian dominance of Prussia. His methods involved astute foreign policy and outright aggression.

Otto von Bismarck.

Wars against Denmark (1864) and Austria (1866) brought post-Napoleonic order to an abrupt end. Prussia was no longer the smallest Great Power, but an initiator of geopolitical change. Austria's defeat confirmed Prussia's primacy among German-speaking states. Victory on the battlefield boosted Bismarck's popularity across Prussia – but not in Berlin itself. He was defeated in his constituency in the 1867 election to the new North German League. This was a Prussian-dominated body, linking the northern states, and a stepping stone towards Germany's overall unification.

Bismarck's third war – against France in 1870 – revealed his scope for intrigue and opportunism. Exploiting a dispute over the Spanish succession, he provoked France into declaring war on Prussia. Citing the North German League and treaties signed with the southern German states, Bismarck brought together a united German army under Prussian leadership. Following the defeat of the French army on 2 September, Bismarck turned a unified military into the basis for a unified nation. The Prussian king would be German emperor: beneath him would be four kings, 18 grand dukes and assorted princes from the German states, which would retain some regional powers. (This arrangement formed the basis for the modern federal system of regional Länder.)

On 18 January 1871, King Wilhelm was proclaimed German Kaiser ('Emperor') in the Hall of Mirrors in Versailles. In just nine years, Bismarck had united Germany and forged an empire that dominated central Europe. The political, economic and social centre of this new creation was Berlin.

IMPERIAL BERLIN

The coming of empire threw Berlin into its greatest period of expansion and change. The economic boom (helped by five billion gold francs extracted from France as war reparations) fuelled a wave of speculation. Farmers in Wilmersdorf and Schöneberg became millionaires overnight as they sold off their fields to developers.

During the following decades, Berlin emerged as Europe's most modern metropolis. This period was dubbed the Gründerzeit (Foundation Years) and was marked by a move away from traditional Prussian values of thrift and modesty towards the gaudy and bombastic. The mood change manifested itself in monuments and buildings. The Reichstag, the Kaiser-Wilhelm-Gedächtniskirche, the Siegessäule (Victory Column) and the Berliner Dom were all built in this period. Superficially, the Reichstag (designed by Paul Wallot, and completed in 1894) represented a commitment to parliamentary democracy. But in reality, Germany was still in the grip of conservative, backward-looking forces. The Kaiser's authoritarian powers remained, as demonstrated by the decision of Wilhelm II to sack Bismarck in 1890 following policy disagreements.

When Bismarck began his premiership in 1861, his offices on Wilhelmstrasse looked over fields. By the time he lost his job, they were in the centre of Europe's most congested city. Economic boom and growing political and social importance attracted hundreds of thousands of new inhabitants. At unification in 1871, 820,000 people lived in Berlin; by 1890 this number had nearly doubled.

The working class was shoehorned into tenements – Mietskasernen, 'rental barracks' – that sprouted across the city, particularly in Kreuzberg, Wedding and Prenzlauer Berg. Poorly ventilated and overcrowded, the Mietskasernen (many of which still stand) became a breeding ground for unrest.

The Social Democratic Party (SPD), founded in 1869, quickly became the voice for the have-nots. In the 1877 general election, it won 40 per cent of the Berlin vote. With that was born the left-wing reputation of Rotes Berlin ('Red Berlin') that persists to the present day. In 1878, two assassination attempts on the Kaiser gave Bismarck an excuse to classify socialists as enemies of the state. He introduced restrictive laws to ban the SPD and other progressive parties. The ban lasted until 1890 – the year of Bismarck's sacking – but did not stem support for the SPD. In the 1890 general election, the SPD dominated the vote in Berlin; in 1912, it won more than 70 per cent of the vote, becoming the largest party in the Reichstag.

Kaiser Wilhelm II, famed for his ridiculous moustache, was crowned in 1888, and soon came to personify the new Germany: bombastic, awkward and unpredictable. Like his grandmother Queen Victoria, he gave his name to an era. Wilhelm's epoch is associated with showy militarism and foreign policy bungles leading to a world war that cost the Kaiser his throne and Germany its stability.

The Wilhelmine years were also notable for the explosive growth of Berlin (the population rose to four million by 1914) and a blossoming of cultural and intellectual life. The Bode-Museum was built in 1904. In 1912, work began on the Pergamonmuseum, while a new Opera House was unveiled in Charlottenburg (destroyed in World War II; the Deutsche Oper now stands on the site). Expressionism took off in 1910 and the Kurfürstendamm filled with galleries – Paris was still Europe's art capital, but Berlin was catching up. By Wilhelm's abdication in 1918, Berlin had become a centre of scientific and intellectual development. Six Berlin scientists, including Einstein and Max Planck, were awarded the Nobel Prize. But by 1914, Europe was armed to the teeth and ready to tear itself apart. In June, the assassination of Archduke Franz Ferdinand provided the excuse.

IN CONTEXT

IN CONTEXT

WORLD WAR I & THE WEIMAR REPUBLIC

No one was prepared for the disaster to follow. After Bismarck, the Germans had come to expect quick, sweeping victories. The armies on the Western Front settled into their trenches for a war of attrition that would cost over a million German lives. Meanwhile, the civilian population faced austerity. After the 1917 harvest failed, there were outbreaks of famine. Soon, dog and cat meat started to appear on the menu in Berlin restaurants.

The SPD's initial enthusiasm for war evaporated, and in 1916 the party refused to pass the Berlin budget. A year later, members of the party's radical wing broke away to form the Spartacus League. Anti-war feeling was voiced in mass strikes in April 1917 and January 1918. These were brutally suppressed, but, when the Imperial Marines in Kiel mutinied on 2 November 1918, the authorities were no longer able to stop the anti-war movement. The mutiny spread to Berlin, where members of the Guards Regiment came out against the war. On 9 November, the Kaiser was forced into abdication and, later, exile. This date is weirdly layered with significance in German history: it's the anniversary of the establishment of the Weimar Republic (1918), the Kristallnacht pogrom (1938) and the fall of the Wall (1989).

On this day in 1918, Philip Scheidemann, a leading SPD parliamentarian and key proponent of republicanism, broke off his lunch in the second-floor restaurant of the Reichstag. He walked to a window overlooking Königsplatz (now Platz der Republik) where a crowd had massed and declared: 'The old and the rotten have broken down. Long live the new! Long live the German Republic!' At the other end of Unter den Linden, Karl Liebknecht, who co-led the Spartacus League with Rosa Luxemburg, declared Germany a socialist republic from a balcony of the occupied Stadtschloss. Liebknecht and the Spartacists wanted a communist Germany; Scheidemann and the SPD favoured a parliamentary democracy. Between them stood those still loyal to the vanished monarchy. All were prepared to fight; street battles ensued throughout the city. It was in this climate of turmoil and violence that the Weimar Republic was born.

The revolution in Berlin may have brought peace to the Western Front, where hostilities were ended on 11 November, but in Germany it unleashed political terror and instability. Berlin's new masters, the SPD under Friedrich Ebert, ordered renegade battalions returning from the front (known as the Freikorps) to quash the Spartacists, who launched a concerted bid for power in January 1919.

Within days, the uprising was bloodily suppressed. Liebknecht and Luxemburg were arrested, interrogated in a hotel near the Zoo, and then murdered by the Freikorps. A plaque marks the spot on the Liechtenstein Bridge from which Luxemburg's body was dumped into the Landwehr Canal. Four days later, national elections returned the SPD as the largest party: the Social Democrats' victory over the far left was complete. Berlin was deemed too dangerous for parliamentary business, so the government decamped to the provincial town of Weimar, which gave its name to the first German republic.

Germany's new constitution ended up being full of good liberal intentions, but riddled with technical flaws, leaving the country wide open to weak coalition government and quasi-dictatorial presidential rule. Another crippling blow was the Versailles Treaty, which set the terms of peace. Reparation payments (set to run until 1988) blew a hole in an already fragile economy. Support for the right-wing nationalist lobby was fuelled by the loss of territories, and restrictions placed on the military led some on the right to claim that Germany's soldiers had been 'stabbed on the back' by Jews and left-wingers.

In March 1920, a right-wing coup was staged in Berlin under the leadership of Wolfgang Kapp, a civil servant from east Prussia. The recently returned government fled the city. For four days Berlin was besieged by roaming Freikorps. Some had taken to adorning their helmets with a new symbol: the *Hakenkreuz* or swastika. Ultimately, a general strike and the army's refusal to join Kapp ended the putsch. But the political and economic chaos in the city remained.

Political assassinations were commonplace, and food shortages led to bouts of famine. Inflation started to escalate. There were two main reasons for the precipitate devaluation of the Reichsmark. To pay for the war, the desperate imperial government had resorted to printing more money, a policy continued by the new

Declaration of the Weimar Republic, 9 November 1918.

republican rulers. The burden of reparations also led to an outflow of foreign currency.

In 1923, the French government sent troops into the Ruhr industrial region to take by force reparation goods that the German government said it could no longer afford to pay. The Communists planned an uprising in Berlin for October, but lost their nerve.

THE MUNICH BEER HALL PUTSCH

In November, a young ex-corporal called Adolf Hitler, who led the tiny National Socialist Party (NSDAP or Nazi Party), launched an attempted coup from a Munich beer hall. He called for armed resistance to the French, an end to the 'dictatorship of Versailles' and punishment for those – especially the Jews – who had 'betrayed' Germany at the war's end. Hitler's first attempt to seize power came to nothing. Instead of marching on Berlin, he went to prison. Inflation was finally brought down with the introduction of a new currency. But the overall decline of moral and social values that had taken place in the five years since 1918 was not so easy to reverse.

Josef Goebbels came to Berlin in 1926 to take charge of the local Nazi Party. On arriving, he noted: 'This city is a melting pot of everything that is evil – prostitution, drinking houses, cinemas, Marxism, Jews, strippers, negroes dancing and all the offshoots of modern art.' The city overtook Paris as Europe's arts and entertainment capital, and added its own decadent twist. 'We used to

have a first-class army,' mused Klaus Mann, the author of the novel *Mephisto*, '…now we have first-class perversions.'

By 1927, Berlin boasted more than 70 cabarets and nightclubs. While Brecht's *Dreigroschenoper* (*Threepenny Opera*) played at the Theater am Schiffbauerdamm, Dadaists gathered on Tauentzienstrasse at the Romanisches Café (which was later one of the victims of the Allied bombing campaign – the Europa-Center mall now stands on the site). Avant-garde magazines proliferated, focusing on these exciting new forms of art and literature. But the flipside of all the frenetic enjoyment was poverty, substance addiction and seething social tension, reflected in the works of artists such as George Grosz and Otto Dix. In the music halls, Brecht and Weill used a popular medium to ram home points about social injustices.

In architecture and design, the revolutionary ideas of the Bauhaus school in Dessau (it moved to Berlin in 1932, but was closed down by the Nazis a year later) were taking concrete form in projects such as the Shell House on the Landwehr Canal, the Siemensstadt new town and the model-housing project Hufeisensiedlung in Britz.

The Wall Street Crash and the onset of global depression in 1929 ushered in the brutal end of the Weimar Republic. The fractious coalition governments that had clung to power in the prosperous late 1920s were no match for rocketing unemployment

FALSE ECONOMY

Hyperinflation turned the economy – and society – upside down.

Of all the disasters that have befallen Berlin, nothing was as mad as the hyperinflation of 1923. It wasn't a sudden catastrophe: the German government had been dallying with inflation for years, funding its war effort by printing bonds. In 1914, a dollar was buying 4.2 German marks; by late 1922, it was buying 7,000. Then the French occupied the Ruhr and things went haywire. By 20 November 1923, the rate was a whopping 4,200,000,000,000 marks to the dollar.

Images from the time are vaguely comic: children using bundles of notes as building blocks; a wheelbarrow of currency for a loaf of bread. At the height of the crisis, over 300 paper mills and 2,000 printing presses worked around the clock to supply the Reichsbank with notes – in denominations of one million, then one billion, then a hundred billion. Some companies paid their employees twice a day, so they could shop at lunch to beat afternoon inflation.

A little hard currency could buy anything – or anyone. Foreign visitors splashed out in an orgy of conspicuous consumption.

Entrepreneurs created whole business empires from ever cheaper marks. And the homes of peasants in nearby villages filled up with Meissen porcelain and fine furniture as Berliners traded valuables for eggs or bread.

People starved as their possessions vanished. The suicide rate shot up, as did infant mortality. Teenagers prostituted themselves after school, often with parental approval. Nothing made sense anymore. And as the fabric of everyday life was seen to unravel, so did people's faith in government. Among the worst hit were those who had most trusted the idea of the German state: the middle-class patriots who had sunk their money into war bonds, only to be paid back in worthless paper. The crisis was eventually brought under control, but the result had been a mass transfer of wealth to a handful of opportunists, big businesses and government. And as a pauperised people wondered who to blame, the hard right had found a cause. Nothing prepared the ground for Hitler better than the literal and moral impoverishment of the inflationary period.

Children playing with banknotes, 1919.

and a surge in support for extremist parties. By the end of 1929, nearly one in four Berliners was out of work. The city's streets became a battleground for clashes between Nazi stormtroopers (the SA), Communists and Social Democrats. Increasingly, the police relied on water cannon, armoured vehicles and guns to quell street fighting. One May Day demonstration left 30 dead and several hundred wounded.

In 1932, the violence in Berlin reached crisis level. In one six-week period, 300 street battles resulted in 70 people dead. In the general election in July, the Nazis took 40 per cent of the general vote, becoming the largest party in the Reichstag. Hermann Göring, one of Hitler's earliest followers and a wounded veteran of the Beer Hall Putsch, was appointed Reichstag president. But the prize of government still eluded the Nazis. In November elections, they lost two million votes across Germany and 37,000 in Berlin, where the Communists emerged as the strongest party. The election was held against the backdrop of a strike by 20,000 transport employees protesting against wage cuts. The strike had been called by the Communists and the Nazis, who vied with each other to capture the mass vote and bring the Weimar Republic to an end. Under orders from Moscow, the KPD (Communist Party) shunned all co-operation with the SPD, ending any possibility of a broad left-wing front.

As Berlin headed into another winter of depression, almost every third person was out of work. A survey recorded that almost half of Berlin's inhabitants were living four to a room, and that a large proportion of the city's housing stock was unfit for human habitation. Berlin topped the European table of suicides.

The new government of General Kurt von Schleicher ruled by presidential decree. Schleicher had promised President von Hindenburg that he could tame the Nazi Party into a coalition. When he failed, his rival Franz von Papen manoeuvred the Nazi leader into power. On 30 January 1933, Adolf Hitler was named chancellor. That evening, the SA staged a torchlight parade through the Brandenburg Gate. Watching from the window of his house, the artist Max Liebermann remarked to his dinner guests: 'I cannot eat as much as I'd like to puke.'

> '*Hitler ordered that the lime trees on Unter den Linden be chopped down to give the boulevard a cleaner, more sanitised form.*'

HITLER TAKES POWER

Hitler's government was a coalition of Nazis and German nationalists, led by the media magnate Alfred Hugenberg. Together, their votes fell just short of a parliamentary majority, so another election was called for March, while Hitler continued to rule by decree. Weimar's last free election was also its most violent. Open persecution of communists began. The Nazis banned meetings of the KPD, closed left-wing newspapers and broke up SPD election rallies. On 27 February, a fire broke out in the Reichstag. It was almost certainly started by the Nazis, who used it as an excuse to step up the persecution of opponents. Over 12,000 communists were arrested. Spelling it out in a speech at the Sportspalast two days before the election, Goebbels said: 'It's not my job to practise justice, instead I have to destroy and exterminate – nothing else.'

The Nazis still didn't achieve an absolute majority (in Berlin they polled 34 per cent), but that didn't matter. With the support of his coalition allies, Hitler passed an Enabling Act that gave him dictatorial powers. By summer, Germany had been declared a one-party state. The SS established itself in Prinz Albrecht Palais, where it was later joined by the secret police, the Gestapo. To the north of Berlin near Oranienburg, the Sachsenhausen concentration camp was set up. Along the Kurfürstendamm, squads of SA stormtroopers would go 'Jew baiting', and on 1 April 1933 the first boycott of Jewish shops began. A month later, Goebbels, who became Minister for Propaganda, organised a book-burning, which took place in the courtyard of the university on Unter den Linden. Books by Jews or writers deemed degenerate or traitors were thrown on

IN CONTEXT

Olympiastadion, built for the 1936 Olympic Games.

to a huge bonfire. The Nazis began to control public life. Party membership became obligatory for doctors, lawyers, professors and journalists. Unemployment was tackled through public works programmes, conscription to an expanding military and by 'encouraging' women to leave the workplace.

During the Night of the Long Knives in July 1934, Hitler settled old scores with opponents within the SA and Nazi Party. At Lichterfelde barracks, officers of the SS shot and killed over 150 SA members. Hitler's predecessor as chancellor, General von Schleicher, was shot with his wife at their Wannsee home. After the death of President von Hindenburg in August, Hitler had himself named Führer ('Leader') and made the armed forces swear an oath of allegiance to him. It had taken the Nazis less than two years to subjugate Germany.

A brief respite came with the Olympic Games in August 1936. To persuade foreign spectators that all was well in the Reich, Goebbels ordered the removal of anti-Semitic slogans from shops. 'Undesirables' were moved out, and the pavement display cases for the racist Nazi newspaper *Der Stürmer* (*The Stormtrooper*) were dismantled. The Games, centred on the newly built Olympiastadion, were not such a success for the Nazis. Instead of blond Aryans sweeping the field, Hitler had to watch the African-American Jesse Owens clock up medals and records. The Games did work, however, as a public relations exercise. Foreign visitors left with reports of a strident and healthy nation.

As part of a nationwide campaign to cleanse cultural life of what the Nazis considered *Entartete Kunst* ('degenerate art'), works of modern art were collected and brought together in a touring exhibition designed to show the depth of depravity in contemporary ('Jewish-dominated') culture. But Nazi hopes that these 'degenerate' works would repulse the German people fell flat. When the exhibition arrived at the Zeughaus in early 1938, thousands queued for admission. People loved the paintings. After the exhibition, the artworks were auctioned in Switzerland. Unsold works were burnt in the fire station on Köpenicker Strasse – more than 5,000 were destroyed.

After taking power, Hitler ordered that the lime trees on Unter den Linden be chopped down to give the boulevard a cleaner, more sanitised form – the first step in Nazi urban planning. Hitler's plans for the redesign of Berlin reflected the hatred the Nazis felt for the city. Hitler entrusted young architect Albert Speer with the job of creating a metropolis to 'out-trump Paris and Vienna'.

The heart of old Berlin was to be demolished, and its small streets replaced by two highways stretching 37 kilometres (23 miles) from north to south and 50 kilometres (30 miles) from east to west. Each axis would be 90 metres (295 feet) wide. Crowning the northern axis would be a domed Volkshalle ('People's Hall') nearly 300 metres (1,000 feet) high, with space for 150,000 people. Speer and Hitler also had grand plans for a triumphal arch three times the size of the Arc de Triomphe, and a Führer's Palace 150 times bigger than the one occupied by Bismarck. The new city was to be called Germania.

Little of this was built. The new Chancellery, completed in early 1939, went up in under a year – and was demolished after the war. On the proposed east–west axis, a small section around the Siegessäule was widened for Hitler's 50th birthday in April 1939.

Of the half a million Jews living in Germany in 1933, over a third were in Berlin. For centuries, the Jewish community had played an important role in Berlin's development, especially in financial, artistic and intellectual circles. The Nazis wiped all this out in 12 years of persecution and murder. Arrests followed the boycotts and acts of intimidation. During 1933 and 1934, many of Berlin's Jews fled. Those who stayed were subjected to legislation (the 1935 Nuremberg Laws) that banned Jews from public office, forbade them to marry Aryan Germans and stripped them of citizenship. Jewish cemeteries were desecrated and the names of Jews chipped off war memorials. Berlin businesses that had been owned by Jews – such as the Ullstein newspaper group and Jonass department store (now the Soho House hotel) – were 'Aryanised'. The Nazis expropriated them or forced owners to sell at absurdly low prices.

On 9 November 1938, Kristallnacht, a wave of 'spontaneous' acts of vandalism and violence against Jews, was staged in response to the assassination of a German diplomat in Paris by a young Jewish émigré. Jewish properties across Berlin were stoned, looted and set ablaze. A total of 24 synagogues were set on fire. The Nazis rounded up 12,000 Jews and took them to Sachsenhausen concentration camp.

WORLD WAR II

Since 1935, Berliners had been taking part in air-raid drills, but it was not until the Sudeten crisis of 1938 that the possibility of war became real. Hitler was able to get his way and persuade France and Britain to let him take over the German-speaking areas of northern Czechoslovakia, but a year later, his plans to repeat the exercise in Poland were met with resistance. Following Germany's invasion of Poland on 1 September 1939, Britain and France declared war on the Reich. Despite the propaganda and early victories, most Berliners were horrified by the war. The first air raids came with the RAF bombing of Pankow and Lichtenberg in early 1940.

In 1941, after the German invasion of the Soviet Union, the 75,000 Jews remaining in Berlin were required to wear a yellow Star of David and the first systematic deportations

to concentration camps began. By the end of the war, only 5,000 Jews remained in Berlin. Notorious assembly points for the deportations were Putlitzstrasse in Wedding, Grosse Hamburger Strasse and Rosenstrasse in Mitte. On 20 January 1942, a meeting of the leaders of the various Nazi security organisations at a villa by the Wannsee lake agreed on a 'final solution' to the Jewish question: genocide.

The turning point in the war came with the surrender at Stalingrad on 31 January 1943. By summer, women and children were being evacuated from Berlin; by the end of 1943, over 700,000 people had fled. The Battle of Berlin, which the RAF launched in November 1943, reduced much of the city centre to rubble. Nearly 5,000 people were killed and around 250,000 made homeless.

On 20 July 1944, a group of officers, civil servants and former trade unionists launched a last-ditch attempt to assassinate Hitler. But Hitler survived the explosion of a bomb placed at his eastern command post in East Prussia by Colonel Count von Stauffenberg.

In early January 1945, the Red Army launched a major offensive that carried it on to German soil. On 12 February, the heaviest bombing raid yet on Berlin killed over 23,000 people in little more than an hour. As the Russians moved into Berlin's suburbs, Hitler celebrated his last birthday on 20 April in his bunker behind Wilhelmstrasse. Three days later, Neukölln and Tempelhof fell. By 28 April, Alexanderplatz and Hallesches Tor were in the hands of the Red Army.

The next day, Hitler called his last war conference. He then married his companion Eva Braun and committed suicide with her the day after. As their bodies were being cremated by SS officers, a few streets away a red flag was raised over the Reichstag. The city officially surrendered on 2 May 1945.

When Bertolt Brecht returned to Berlin in 1948, he found 'a pile of rubble next to Potsdam'. Nearly a quarter of all buildings had been destroyed. The human cost of the war was equally startling – around 80,000 Berliners had been killed, not including the thousands of Jews who would not return from the concentration camps. There was no gas or electricity and only the suburbs had running water. Public transport had broken down. In the weeks after capitulation, Red Army

IN CONTEXT

'In the Cold War, Berlin was the focal point for stand-offs between the United States and the Soviet Union.'

soldiers went on a rampage of looting, murder and rape. Thousands of men were transported to labour camps in the Soviet Union. Food supplies were used up and later the harvest failed in the land around the city. Come winter, the few remaining trees in the Tiergarten and other parks were chopped down for firewood.

Clearing the rubble was to take years of dull, painstaking work. The *Trümmerfrauen* ('rubble women') cleared the streets and created literal mountains of junk – such as the Teufelsberg, one of seven hills that now exist as a result. The Soviets stripped factories across Berlin as part of a programme to dismantle German industry and take it back home. As reparation, whole factories were moved to Russia.

Under the terms of the Yalta Agreement, which divided Germany into four zones of control, Berlin was also split into sectors, with the Soviets in the East and the Americans, British and French in the West. A Kommandatura, made up of each army's commander and based in the building of the People's Court in Kleistpark, dealt with the administration of the city. Initially, the administration worked well in getting basics such as public transport back in running order. But tensions between the Soviets and the Western Allies began to rise as civilian government of city affairs returned. In the Eastern sector, a merger of the Communist and Social Democratic parties (both refounded in summer 1945) was pushed to form the Socialist Unity Party (SED). In the Western sector, the SPD continued as a separate party. Events came to a head after elections for a new city government in 1946. The SED failed to get more than 20 per cent of the vote, while the SPD won nearly 50 per cent of all votes cast. The Soviets vetoed the appointment of the SPD's mayoral candidate, Ernst Reuter, a committed anti-communist.

THE BERLIN AIRLIFT & THE COLD WAR

The situation worsened in spring 1948. In response to the decision by the Western Allies to merge their respective zones in Germany into one administrative entity and introduce a new currency, the Soviets quit the Kommandatura. In late June, all transport links to West Berlin were cut off and Soviet forces began a blockade of the city. Three 'air corridors' linking West Berlin with Western Germany became lifelines as Allied aircraft transported food, coal and industrial components to the beleaguered city.

Within Berlin, the future division of the city began to take permanent shape as city councillors from the West were drummed out of the town hall. They moved to Rathaus Schöneberg in the West. Fresh elections in the Western sector returned Reuter as mayor. The Freie Universität was set up in response to communist dominance of the Humboldt-Universität in the East.

Having failed to starve West Berlin into submission, the Soviets called off the blockade after 11 months. The Berlin airlift also convinced the Western Allies that they should maintain a presence in Berlin and that their sectors of the city should be linked with the Federal Republic, founded in May 1949. The response from the East was the founding of the DDR (Deutsche Demokratische Republik – German Democratic Republic, or GDR) on 7 October. With the birth of the 'first Workers' and Peasants' State on German soil', the formal division of Germany into two states was complete.

During the Cold War, Berlin was the focal point for stand-offs between the United States and the Soviet Union. Far from having any control over its own affairs, the city was wholly at the mercy of geopolitical developments. Throughout the 1950s, the 'Berlin Question' remained prominent on the international agenda. Technically, the city was still under Four-Power control, but since the Soviet departure from the Kommandatura, and the setting up of the German Democratic Republic with its capital in East Berlin (a breach of the wartime agreement on the future of the city), this counted for little in practice. In principle, the Western Allies adhered to these agreements by retaining ultimate authority in West Berlin, while letting the city integrate into the West German system. Throughout

Berlin airlift, March 1949.

the 1950s, the two halves of Berlin began to develop separately as the political systems in East and West evolved.

In the East, Communist leader Walter Ulbricht set about creating Moscow's most hardline ally in eastern Europe. Work began on a Moscow-style boulevard – called Stalinallee – running east from Alexanderplatz. Industry was nationalised and subjected to rigid central planning. Opposition was kept in check by the new Ministry for State Security: the Stasi.

West Berlin landed the role of 'Last Outpost of the Free World' and, as such, was developed into a showcase. As well as the Marshall Plan, which paid for much of the reconstruction of West Germany, the US poured millions of dollars into West Berlin to maintain it as a counterpoint to communism. The prominence accorded West Berlin was later reflected in the high profile of its politicians (Willy Brandt, for example), who were received abroad by prime ministers and presidents.

Yet despite the emerging divisions, the two halves of the city continued to co-exist in some abnormal fashion. City planners on both sides of the sectoral boundaries initially drew up plans with the whole city in mind. The transport system crossed between East and West, with the underground network being controlled by the West and the S-Bahn by the East. Movement between the sectors (despite 'border' checks) was relatively normal, as Westerners went East to watch a Brecht play or buy cheap books. Easterners travelled West to work, shop or see the latest Hollywood films. The secret services of both sides kept a high presence in the city. Berlin became the espionage capital of the world.

As the effects of US money and the West German 'economic miracle' took hold, West Berlin began to recover. Unemployment dropped from 30 per cent in 1950 to virtually zero by 1961. The labour force also included about 50,000 East Berliners who commuted over the inter-sector borders. In the East, reconstruction was slower. Until the mid 1950s, East Germany paid reparations to the Soviet Union. To begin with, there seemed to be more acts of wilful destruction than positive construction. The old Stadtschloss, slightly damaged by bombing, was blown up in 1950 to make way for a parade ground, which later evolved into a car park.

In 1952, the East Germans sealed off the border with West Germany. The only way out of the 'zone' was through West Berlin and consequently the number of refugees passing through from the East rose dramatically from 50,000 in 1950 to 300,000 in 1953. Over the decade, one million refugees from the East came through West Berlin.

In June 1953, partly in response to the rapid loss of skilled manpower, the East German government announced a ten per cent increase in working 'norms' – the number of hours and volume of output that workers were required to fulfil each day. In protest, building workers on Stalinallee (now Karl-Marx-Allee) downed tools on 16 June and marched to the government offices on Leipziger Strasse. The government refused to relent, and strikes soon broke out across the city. Crowds stormed Communist Party offices and tore red flags from public buildings. By noon, the government had lost control of the city and it was left to the Red Army to restore order. Soviet tanks rolled into the centre of East Berlin, where they were met by stones thrown by demonstrators. By nightfall the uprising was crushed. Officially, 23 people died, though other estimates put the figure at over 200.

The 17 June uprising only furthered the wave of emigration. And by the end of the 1950s, it seemed likely that East Germany would cease to function as an industrial state due to the loss of skilled labour. Estimates put the loss to the East German economy through emigration at some 100 billion Deutschmark. Ulbricht increased his demands on Moscow to take action.

In 1958, Soviet leader Nikita Khrushchev tried to bully the Allies into relinquishing West Berlin by calling for an end to military occupation and a 'normalisation of the situation in the capital of the DDR, by which he meant Berlin as a whole. The ultimatum was rejected and the Allies made clear their commitment to West Berlin. Unwilling to provoke a world war, but needing to prop up his ally, Khrushchev backed down and sanctioned Ulbricht's alternative plan for a solution to the Berlin question.

A TALE OF TWO CITIES

During the early summer of 1961, rumours spread that Ulbricht intended to seal off West Berlin with a barrier or reinforced border. Emigration had reached a high point, as 1,500 East Germans fled to the West each day. However, when in the early hours of 13 August

units of the People's Police (assisted by Working Class Combat Groups) began to drag bales of barbed wire across Potsdamer Platz, Berlin and the world were caught by surprise. In a finely planned and executed operation, West Berlin was sealed off within 24 hours. As well as a fence of barbed wire, trenches were dug, the windows of houses straddling the new border were bricked up, and tram and railway lines were interrupted: all this under the watchful eyes of armed guards. Anyone trying to flee to West Berlin risked being shot; in the 28 years the Wall stood, nearly 80 people died trying to escape. Justifying their actions, the East Germans said they had erected an 'Anti-Fascist Protection Rampart' to prevent a world war.

Days later, the construction of a wall began. When it was completed, the concrete part of the 160-kilometre (100-mile) fortification ran to 112 kilometres (70 miles); 37 kilometres (23 miles) of the Wall ran through the city centre. Previously innocuous streets such as Bernauer Strasse (where houses on one side were in the East, on the other in the West) suddenly became the location for one of the world's most deadly borders.

The initial stunned disbelief of Berliners turned into despair as it became clear that (as with the 17 June uprising) the Western Allies could do little more than make a show of strength. President Kennedy dispatched American reinforcements to Berlin and, for a few tense weeks, American and Soviet tanks squared off at Checkpoint Charlie. Vice-President Johnson came to show moral support a week after the Wall was built. Two years later, Kennedy himself arrived and spoke to a crowd of half a million in front of Rathaus Schöneberg. His speech linked the fate of West Berlin with that of the free world and ended with the now famous statement, 'Ich bin ein Berliner!' – which, contrary to popular belief, was correct: doughnuts are actually known as *Pfannkuchen* in Berlin.

In its early years, the Wall was the scene of many daring escape attempts. People abseiled off buildings, swam across the Spree, waded through sewers or tried to climb over. But as the fortifications were improved with mines, searchlights and guard dogs, and as the guards were given orders to shoot on sight, escape became nearly impossible. By the time the Wall finally fell in 1989, it had been 'updated' four times to render it more or less completely impermeable.

In 1971, the Four Powers met and signed the Quadripartite Agreement, which formally recognised the city's divided status. Border posts (such as Checkpoint Charlie) were introduced and designated to particular categories of visitors – one for foreigners, another for West Germans, and so on.

During the 1960s, with the Wall an infamous and ugly backdrop, the cityscape of modern Berlin (both East and West) began to take shape. On Tauentzienstrasse in the West, the Europa-Center was built, and the bomb-damaged Kaiser-Wilhelm-Gedächtnis-Kirche was given a partner – a new church made up of a glass-clad tower and squat bunker. Hans Scharoun laid out the Kulturforum in Tiergarten as West Berlin's answer to the Museumsinsel complex in the East. The first building to go up was Scharoun's Philharmonie, completed in 1963. Mies van der Rohe's Neue Nationalgalerie was finished in 1968. In the suburbs, work began on concrete mini-towns, Gropiusstadt and Märkisches Viertel. Conceived as solutions to housing shortages, they would develop into alienating ghettos. Alexanderplatz in the

East was rebuilt along totalitarian lines, and the Fernsehturm (Television Tower) was finished. The historic core of Berlin was mostly cleared to make way for parks or new office and housing developments. On the eastern outskirts of the city in Marzahn and Hohenschönhausen, work started on soulless mass-scale housing projects.

In 1965, the first sit-down was staged on the Kurfürstendamm by students protesting against low grants and expensive accommodation. This was followed by several student political demonstrations against the state in general and the Vietnam War in particular. The first communes were set up in Kreuzberg, sowing the seeds of a counterculture that would make the district famous. The student protest movement came into violent confrontation with the police in 1967 and 1968. One student, Benno Ohnesorg, was shot dead by police at a demonstration against the Shah of Iran. A year later, the students' leader, Rudi Dutschke, was shot by a right-winger. Demonstrations were held outside the offices of the Springer newspaper group, whose papers were blamed for inciting the shooting. It was out of this movement that the murderous Red Army

IN CONTEXT

Constructing the Berlin Wall, 6 June 1961.

Faction (also known as the Baader-Meinhof Gang) was to emerge, making headlines in the 1970s with kidnaps and killings.

The signing of the Quadripartite Agreement confirmed West Berlin's abnormal status and ushered in an era of decline, as the frisson of Cold War excitement and 1960s rebellion petered out. More than ever, West Berlin depended on huge subsidies from West Germany to keep it going. Development schemes and tax breaks were introduced to encourage businesses to move to the city (Berliners also paid less income tax), but still the economy and population declined. At the same time, there was growth in the number of *Gastarbeiter* (guest workers) who arrived from southern Europe and Turkey. Today, there are over 120,000 Turks in the city, largely concentrated in Kreuzberg.

By the late 1970s, Berlin was in a serious malaise. In the West, the city government was discredited by a number of scandals. In East Berlin, where Erich Honecker had succeeded Ulbricht in 1971, a regime that began in a mood of reform became repressive. Some of East Germany's best writers and artists, previously supporters of socialism, emigrated. From its headquarters in Normannenstrasse, the Stasi directed its policy of mass observation and permeated every part of East German society. Between East and West there were squalid exchanges of political prisoners for hard currency. The late '70s and early '80s saw the rise of the squatter movement, which brought violent political protest back on to the streets.

THE FALL OF THE WALL & BEYOND

The arrival of perestroika in the USSR had been ignored by Honecker, who stuck hard to his Stalinist instincts. Protest was strong and only initially beaten back by the police. By the spring of 1989, the East German state was no longer able to withstand the pressure of a population fed up with communism and closed borders. Throughout the summer, thousands fled the city and the country via Hungary, which had opened its borders to the West. Those who stayed began demonstrating for reforms.

By the time Honecker was hosting the celebrations in the Volkskammer (People's Chamber) to mark the 40th anniversary of the DDR on 7 October 1989, crowds were outside, chanting 'Gorby! Gorby!' to register their opposition. Honecker was ousted days later. His successor, Egon Krenz, could do little to stem the tide of opposition. In a bid to defend through attack, he decided to grant the concession East Germans wanted most: freedom to travel.

On 9 November 1989, the gates of the Berlin Wall were opened, just over 28 years after it had been built. As thousands of East Berliners raced through to the sound of popping corks, the end of East Germany and the unification of Berlin and Germany had begun.

With the Wall down, Berlin found itself once again at centre stage. Just as the division of the city defined the split of Europe, so the freedom to move again between East and West marked the dawn of the post-Cold War era. For a year, Berlin was in a state of euphoria. Between November 1989 and October 1990, the city witnessed the collapse of communism and the first free elections (March 1990) in the East for more than 50 years; economic unification, with the swapping of the tinny Ostmark for the Deutschmark (July 1990); and the political merger of East into West, with formal political unification on 3 October 1990. (It was also the year West Germany won its third football World Cup. The team may have come from the West, but in a year characterised by outbursts of popular celebration, Easterners cheered too.)

Unification also brought problems, especially for Berlin, where the two halves of the city now had to be quickly made whole again. While Western infrastructure in the form of roads, telephones and other amenities was in decent working order, in the East it was falling apart. Challenges also came from the collapse of a command economy where jobs were provided regardless of cost or productivity. The Deutschmark put hard currency into the wallets of Easterners, but it also exposed the true state of their economy. Within months, thousands of companies cut jobs or closed down altogether.

Responsibility for restructuring Eastern industry was placed with the Treuhandanstalt, a state agency that, for a while, was the world's largest industrial holding company. The Treuhand gave high-paid employment to thousands of Western yuppies and put hundreds of thousands of Easterners on

THE ALL-SEEING STASI

The DDR's surveillance operation covered all aspects of life.

It's claimed that at some point in their lives, one in three citizens had worked as unofficial informers for East Germany's Ministerium für Staatssicherheit, better known as the Stasi. There were around 90,000 full-time agents and 175,000 *Inoffizielle Mitarbeiter* (unofficial employees, aka informers) – that's around 2.5 per cent of those aged between 18 and 60. One thing's for sure: the secret police apparatus was the most pervasive in the history of state-sponsored repression; in its 1940s heyday, the Gestapo only had about 30,000 members.

Though its grip on everyday life in the DDR was exhaustive, the Stasi must go down in history as a flawed institution. In spite of its secret prisons, hidden cameras and microphones, and burgeoning network of IMs, the Stasi ultimately failed to prevent the peaceful revolution of 1989.

A few weeks after the Wall was breached, crowds fell on the Stasi headquarters at Normannenstrasse, venting anger and frustration at their former tormentors. In the preceding days, Stasi agents had been working overtime, using shredders to destroy documents. They barely put a dent in the six million or so files, which are now administered by a special authority charged with reviewing them and making them available to prosecutors and everyday people who are simply curious to know what the Stasi knew about them.

Not surprisingly, the files contained embarrassing revelations for many politicians, journalists, athletes and others trying to get on with life in reunited Germany. Most of the charges involved people being listed as unofficial informers, a status hard to dispute or verify. Many could have been falsely implicated by over-ambitious Stasi career types, whose rank and pay were pegged to their success at recruiting spies.

Thousands of Germans readily own up to their double lives with the Stasi. They have to, in fact, to get their pensions – one major function of the agency minding the Stasi files is to determine who is eligible for retirement payments. One of those qualifying was Erich Mielke, the Stasi supremo, who collected about €400 a month until his death in 2000. His former office is now part of the **Forschungs- und Gedenkstätte Normannenstrasse** (*see p92*), otherwise known as the Stasi Museum; a new exhibition providing an overview of the Stasi's structure, methods and activities opened here in early 2015. You can also take a guided tour of a Stasi prison at the **Gedenkstätte Berlin-Hohenschönhausen** (*see p92*) – it's grim.

IN CONTEXT

Gedenkstätte Berlin-Hohenschönhausen.

'Unification brought problems, especially for Berlin, where the two halves of the city now had to be quickly made whole again.'

the dole. Easterners soon turned on the Treuhand, vilified as the agent of a brutal Western takeover. The situation escalated when Detlev Karsten Rohwedder, a Western industrialist who headed the agency, was assassinated in spring 1991 – probably by members of the Red Army Faction. The killing of another state employee, Hanno Klein, an influential city planner, drew attention to another dramatic change brought about by unification: the property boom. With the Wall down and – after a 1991 parliamentary decision – the federal government committed to moving from Bonn to Berlin, a wave of construction and investment swept the city.

The giddy excitement of the post-unification years soon gave way to disappointment. The sheer amount of construction work, the scrapping of federal subsidies and tax breaks to West Berlin, rising unemployment and a delay in the arrival of the government all contributed to dampening spirits. In 1994, the last Russian, US, British and French troops left the city. With them went its unique Cold War status. After decades of being different, Berlin was becoming like any other big European capital.

The 1990s were characterised by the regeneration of the East. In the course of the decade, the city's centre of gravity shifted towards Mitte. Government and commercial districts were revitalised. On their fringes, especially around Oranienburger Strasse, the Hackesche Höfe and into Prenzlauer Berg, trendy bars, restaurants, galleries and boutiques sprouted in streets that under communism had been grey and crumbling.

Fast-track gentrification in the East was matched by the decline of West Berlin. Upmarket shops and bars began to desert Charlottenburg and Schöneberg. Kreuzberg,

once the inelegantly wasted symbol of a defiant West Berlin, degenerated to near slum-like conditions in places, while a new bohemia developed across the Spree in Friedrichshain. Westerners did, however, benefit from the reopening of the Berlin hinterland. Tens of thousands of them swapped the city for greener suburbs in the surrounding state of Brandenburg.

THE BERLIN REPUBLIC

Having spent the best part of a decade doing what it had done so often during its turbulent past – regenerating itself out of the wreckage left by history – Berlin ended the 20th century with a flourish. Many of the big, symbolic construction projects had already sprouted: the new Potsdamer Platz, a Reichstag remodelled by Norman Foster. Other major landmarks such as Daniel Libeskind's Jüdisches Museum and IM Pei's extension to the Deutsches Historisches Museum on Unter den Linden followed.

The turn of the century also saw Berlin return to its position at the centre of German politics. Parliament, the government and the accompanying baggage of lobbyists and journalists arrived from Bonn. From Chancellor Gerhard Schröder down, everyone sought to mark the transition as the beginning of the 'Berlin Republic' – for which, read: a peaceful, democratic and, above all, self-confident Germany, as opposed to the chaos of the Weimar years or the self-conscious timidity of the Bonn era.

In the early 2000s, Berlin's financial problems – brought on by rocketing demands on expenditure, decline in central government handouts and the collapse of traditional industries – grew steadily worse. Matching this was the ineptitude of the city's political establishment, desperate to hang on to old privileges and unwilling to face up to tough, new choices. This was all encapsulated in the collapse of the Bankgesellschaft Berlin, a bank largely owned by the city. In the summer of 2001 it was felled by a raft of dud and corrupt real-estate loans. As well as sparking further deterioration in public finances, the scandal brought down the Senate – a grand coalition of Christian Democrats (CDU) and SPD that had governed since 1990. The resulting elections went some way towards a new start. Klaus Wowereit, head of the SPD, broke one of the great post-unification taboos and invited the Party of Democratic Socialism – successor party to East Germany's Communists and winners of half the Eastern vote – into a Social Democrat-led coalition.

At national level, Schröder's second term was far from happy. A brave attempt at welfare reform saw the chancellor attacked from all sides, including the left of his own SPD. Defeats in regional polls forced Schröder in May 2005 to make one last bold move: early elections. Schröder entered the bitter campaign trailing his opponent Angela Merkel and the Christian Democrats in the opinion polls, but came within a whisker of winning the September general election. The result was a mess. Both the main parties – CDU and SPD – lost votes; neither was able to form its preferred coalition. Instead, they were forced into a CDU-led grand coalition with Merkel as chancellor. As the first woman and first Easterner to hold the chancellorship, Merkel ensured her place in the history books when she took office in November 2005.

Meanwhile, the final pieces of Berlin's structural reunification puzzle tumbled into place. The following year was to see the colossal new Berlin Hauptbahnhof take a bow as one of Europe's largest stations, while the renovated Olympiastadion would play host to the World Cup Final. Peter Eisenman's grand Denkmal für die ermordeten Juden Europas (Memorial to the Murdered Jews of Europe) was unveiled with the usual whiff of controversy. The hexagon of Leipziger Platz took final shape as the city centre's reception room. And after years of argument, demolition of the Palast der Republik finally began. The former communist parliament is to be replaced by a reconstruction of the old Stadtschloss that once stood on the site, to house the Humboldt Forum cultural centre.

The improvement of Germany's international standing was confirmed by the 2006 FIFA World Cup. Berlin was the centrepiece for what was widely judged to be one of the best-organised and – for the fans – most enjoyable competitions in the event's history. Key to the success was the bold decision to welcome all fans – ticket-holders or not – to Germany to take part in the wider experience of the event. It was also the first time that Germans felt comfortable overtly displaying signs of national pride, with flags sprouting up everywhere. Germany may have failed to scoop the cup that year at the Olympiastadion, but their youthful team under Joachim Löw finally clinched it in 2014.

On the political front, Angela Merkel's relations with the SPD became more strained as the Social Democrats adopted more left-wing positions in a bid to stem a catastrophic collapse in the party's support. When the grand coalition broke down in 2009, fresh federal elections were called. After a hard-fought battle, the CDU remained the biggest party but were forced into a coalition with the pro-business FDP. The Euro crisis, and its ensuing German-led austerity policy, has demonstrated Merkel's position as the most powerful leader of the trading bloc. Re-elected in 2013, the CDU formed another 'grand coalition' with the SDP, their previous FDP partners having been voted out of parliament for the first time since 1948.

In Berlin, the Social Democrats have had more to cheer about. Mayor Klaus Wowereit and his 'Red-Red' senate was returned to office by elections in 2006 that saw the SPD increase its share of the vote, while support for the CDU fell. The Left Party, which included the PDS, saw its vote slump by more than nine per cent. Wowereit was re-elected in 2011, and after coalition talks with the Greens failed, also entered a 'grand coalition' with the CDU, under a ministry-sharing deal. Accusations of cronyism and the humiliating delay of the new Berlin-Brandenburg Airport led to him resigning as mayor from December 2014.

Relations between Berlin and the federal government remained strained as the two haggled over who should meet the debt-laden city's 'national' costs. Agreement on some issues was matched by bitter wrangling on others, such as the ultimate future of the Tempelhof airport site, which was co-owned by local and national governments. The decision to close the airport – in the face of vocal protest – as part of a consolidation of the city's airports at Schoenefeld was made in 2007. Since autumn 2010, it's become a hugely popular park and attempts by the city to develop it were met with enormous popular opposition in 2014. But for all the political wrangling, commentators can agree on one thing: for all its coalitions, development and new city landmarks, Berlin still hasn't quite settled down yet.

IN CONTEXT

Architecture

*The city's many styles reflect
a complicated history.*

TEXT: MICHAEL LEES, HELEN PIDD

Following its rapid elevation in the late 19th century to European capital, near obliteration during World War II (from above by the RAF, and on the ground by Soviet forces), and 40 years of straddling the frontline between capitalism and communism, it's hardly surprising that Berlin in 2015 is a barely coherent mish-mash of architectural styles. But while the German capital lacks the consistency (or immediate beauty) of a Paris or an Edinburgh, it is a curate's egg of great individual buildings, from the Baroque to the Stalinist, from DDR-tastic communist follies to elegant masterpieces of 20th-century modernism, and bravura restorations (often by British architects) of ruined landmarks, such as Norman Foster's Reichstag dome, and David Chipperfield's supremely subtle resurrection of the bomb-damaged Neues Museum. With the city coffers running low, the two-decade-long building boom that followed the fall of the Wall is over – and, sadly, what continues is mostly generic commercial and office space, such as the vast Mall of Berlin in Leipziger Platz.

But Berlin has re-emerged as a cultural and creative metropolis to match its heyday under the Weimar Republic. It always had a long history of architectural development and experimentation. During the 1910s and '20s, Berlin was home to some of the century's greatest architects and designers, such as Peter Behrens, Bruno Taut, Ludwig Mies van der Rohe and Walter Gropius. But the path to modernism had been launched a century earlier by Karl Friedrich Schinkel, perhaps Berlin's greatest builder.

It wasn't until the late 19th century that Berlin was able to hold its own with grander European capitals, thanks to a construction boom known as the Gründerzeit, triggered by the rapid progress in industry and technology that followed German unification in 1871. The young country was eager for its new capital to achieve the *Weltstadt* (world city) status of Paris or London and so widened its streets and installed large blocks. These followed a rudimentary geometry and were filled in with five-storey *Mietskaserne* (rental barracks) built around linked internal courtyards. The monotony was partially relieved by a few public parks, while later apartment houses gradually became more humane and eventually rather splendid. During the 1920s, this method of development was rejected in favour of Bauhaus-influenced slabs and towers, which were used to fill out the peripheral zones at the edge of the forests. The post-war years saw even more radical departures from the earlier tradition in all sectors of the city.

The post-Wall building boom deposited a new layer, a mixture of contemporary design and historic emulation. The spirit of historic revival has even taken in the city's most famous landmark, the Wall. Speedily dismantled after 1989, it is now commemorated in public art, from the **Gedenkstätte Berliner Mauer** (see p158) at Bernauer Strasse to Frank Thiel's portraits of the last Allied soldiers, suspended above **Checkpoint Charlie** (see p142). The former line of the Wall is also marked in places by a cobblestone strip, visible just west of the Brandenburg Gate. But its memory is fading. 'Where was the Wall?' is the first question on many visitors' lips, and the answer is surprisingly nebulous, as the course of the Wall twisted and dog-legged at the most convoluted angles. The Wall was rarely straight for long.

Marienkirche.

EARLY DAYS

Berlin's long journey to world-city status began in Berlin and Cölln, two Wendish/Slavic settlements on the Spree that were colonised by Germans around 1237. Among their oldest surviving buildings are the parish churches **Marienkirche** (see p58) and **Nikolaikirche** (see p58). The latter was rebuilt in the district known as the Nikolaiviertel, along with other landmarks such as the 1571 pub Zum Nussbaum and the Baroque **Ephraim-Palais** (see p56). The Nikolaiviertel, between Alexanderplatz and the Spree, is the only part of central Berlin to give any idea of how the medieval city might have felt – except it's a kitsch fake, rebuilt by the East Germans in 1987, just a few decades after they had levelled the original district.

The massive **Stadtschloss** (City Palace, 1538-1950), badly damaged in the war, was replaced by the DDR's infamous Palast Der Republik, which was itself demolished in 2008. A controversial campaign to reconstruct the palace was finally won; work has begun at a frenetic pace, and the new building is set to open in 2019 as an art museum. The Schlossbrücke crossing to Unter den Linden, adorned with sensual figures by Christian Daniel Rauch, and the Neptunbrunnen (Neptune Fountain, now relocated south of Marienkirche), modelled on Bernini's Roman fountains, were designed to embellish the original palace.

Zeughaus

The economy now catered to an army comprising 20 per cent of the population (a fairly constant percentage until 1918). To spur growth in gridded Friedrichstadt – and to quarter his soldiers cheaply – the king forced people to build new houses, mostly in a stripped-down classical style. He permitted one open square, later renamed the Gendarmenmarkt, where twin churches were built in 1701, one of which now houses the **Hugenottenmuseum** (*see p49*). The square and churches were Baroque-ified with the addition of grandiose porticoes and domed towers in the 1780s.

After the population reached 60,000 in 1710, a new customs wall enclosed four new districts – the Spandauer Vorstadt, Königstadt, Stralauer Vorstadt and Köpenicker Vorstadt; all are now part of Mitte. The 14-kilometre (nine-mile) border remained the city limits until 1860.

Geometric squares later marked three of the 14 city gates in Friedrichstadt. At the square-shaped Pariser Platz, Carl Gotthard Langhans built the **Brandenburger Tor** (Brandenburg Gate) in 1789, a triumphal arch later topped by Johan Gottfried Schadow's Quadriga (*see p40*). The stately buildings around the square were levelled after World War II, but have now largely been rebuilt or replaced, including the **Adlon Kempinski** hotel (Patzschke, Klotz, 1997; *see p265*), on an expanded version of its original site, and the buildings flanking the gate, Haus Sommer and Haus Liebermann (Kleihues, 1998).

Even with the army, Berlin's population did not reach 100,000 until well into the reign of Frederick the Great (1740-86). Military success inspired him to embellish Berlin and Potsdam; many of the monuments along Unter den Linden stem from his vision of a 'Forum Fredericianum'. Though never completed, the unique ensemble of neoclassical, Baroque and rococo monuments includes the vine-covered **Humboldt-Universität** (Knobelsdorff, Boumann, 1748-53); the **Staatsoper** (Knobelsdorff, Langhans, 1741-43); the **Prinzessinnenpalais** (1733, now the Operncafé) and the **Kronprinzenpalais** (1663, expanded 1732; Unter den Linden 3).

Set back from the Linden on Bebelplatz are the **Alte Bibliothek** (Unger, 1775-81, part of Humboldt-Universität), reminiscent of the curvy Vienna Hofburg; and the pantheon-like,

THE RESIDENZSTADT

In 1647, the Great Elector Friedrich Wilhelm II (1640-88) hired Dutch engineers to transform the route to the Tiergarten, the royal hunting forest, into the tree-lined boulevard of Unter den Linden. It led west toward **Schloss Charlottenburg** (*see p121*), built in 1695 as a summer retreat for Queen Sophie-Charlotte. Over the next century, the Elector's 'Residenzstadt' expanded to include Berlin and Cölln. Traces of the old stone Stadtmauer (city wall) that enclosed them can still be seen on Waisenstrasse in Mitte. Two further districts, Dorotheenstadt (begun 1673) and Friedrichstadt (begun 1688), expanded the street grid north and south of Unter den Linden. Andreas Schlüter built new palace wings for Elector Friedrich Wilhelm III (1688-1713, crowned King Friedrich I of Prussia in 1701) and supervised the building of the **Zeughaus** (Armoury, Nering and de Bodt, 1695-1706; now home to the Deutsches Historisches Museum; *see p49*), whose bellicose ornamentation embodies the Prussian love of militarism.

Wilhelm I, the Soldier King (1713-40), imposed conscription and subjugated the town magistrate to the court and military elite.

copper-domed **Sankt-Hedwigs-Kathedrale** (Legeay and Knobelsdorff, 1747-73; see p51). Not long after the Napoleonic occupation, Karl Friedrich Schinkel became Berlin's most revered architect under Prince Friedrich Wilhelm IV. Drawing on classical and Italian precedents, his early stage-sets experimented with perspective, while his inspired urban visions served the cultural aspirations of an ascendant German state.

He designed the colonnaded **Altes Museum** (1828; see p47), regarded by most architects as his finest work, and the **Neue Wache** (New Guardhouse, 1818; see p44), next to the Zeughaus, whose Roman solidity lent itself well to Tessenow's 1931 conversion into a memorial to the dead of World War I. Other Schinkel masterpieces include the **Schauspielhaus** (1817-21, now the Konzerthaus; see p202); the neo-Gothic brick **Friedrichswerdersche Kirche** (1830) and the cubic **Schinkel-Pavillon** (1825; see p53) at Schloss Charlottenburg.

After his death in 1841, his many disciples continued working. Friedrich August Stüler satisfied the king's desire to complement the Altes Museum with the **Neues Museum** (1841-59 and 1997-2009; see p50), mixing new wrought iron technology with classical architecture. By 1910, Museumsinsel comprised the neoclassical **Alte Nationalgalerie** (Stüler, 1864; see p47), with an open stairway framing an equestrian statue of the king; the triangular **Bode-Museum** (von Ihne, 1904; see p48); and the sombre grey **Pergamonmuseum** (Messel and Hoffmann, 1906-09; see p50). These are a stark contrast to the neo-Renaissance polychromy of the **Martin-Gropius-Bau** across town (Gropius and Schmieden, 1881; see p143).

ERA OF EXPANSION

As the population boomed after 1865, doubling to 1.5 million by 1890, the city began swallowing up neighbouring towns and villages. Factory complexes and worker housing gradually moved to the outskirts. Many of the new market halls and railway stations used a vernacular brick style with iron trusses, such as **Arminiushalle** in Moabit (Blankenstein, 1892, still an indoor food market; Bremer Strasse 9) and Franz Schwechten's romanesque **Anhalter Bahnhof** (1876-80, now a ruin; Askanischer Platz).

Brick was also used for civic buildings, such as the neo-Gothic **Berliner Rathaus** (1861-69; see p56), while the orientalism of the gold-roofed **Neue Synagoge** on Oranienburger Strasse (Knoblauch, Stüler, 1859-66; see p58) made use of colourful masonry and mosaics.

Restrained historicism gave way to wild eclecticism as the 19th century marched on, in public buildings as well as apartment houses with plain interiors, dark courtyards and overcrowded flats behind decorative façades. This eclectic approach is also reflected in the lavish Gründerzeit villas in the fashionable suburbs to the south-west, especially Dahlem and Grunewald. In these areas, the modest yellow-brick vernacular of Brandenburg was rejected in favour of stone and elaborate stucco.

Foreshadowing a new age of rationality and mechanisation, an attempt at greater stylistic clarity was made after 1900, in spite of the bombast of works such as the new **Berliner Dom** (Raschdorff, 1905; see p47) and the **Reichstag** (Wallot, 1894; see p98). The Wilhelmine era's paradoxical mix of reformism and conservatism yielded an architecture of Sachlichkeit ('objectivity') in commercial and public buildings. In some cases, such as Kaufmann's **Hebbel-Theater** (1908, now part of HAU; see p211), or the **Hackesche Höfe** (Berndt and Endell, 1906-07; see p54), Sachlichkeit meant a calmer form of art nouveau (or Jugendstil); elsewhere, it was more sombre, with heavy, compact forms, vertical ribbing and low-hanging mansard roofs. A very severe example is the stripped-down classicism of Alfred Messel's Pergamonmuseum.

The style goes well with Prussian bureaucracy in the civic architecture of Ludwig Hoffmann, city architect from 1896 to 1924. Though he sometimes used other styles for his many schools, courthouses and city halls, his towering **Altes Stadthaus** in Mitte (1919; Jüdenstrasse, corner of Parochialstrasse) and the **Rudolf-Virchow-Krankenhaus** in Wedding (1906; Augustenburger Platz 1), then innovative for its pavilion system, epitomise Wilhelmine architecture.

Prior to the incorporation of Berlin in 1920, many suburbs had full city charters and sported their own town halls, such as the massive **Rathaus Charlottenburg** (1905; Otto-Suhr-Allee 100) and **Rathaus Neukölln** (1909; Karl-Marx-Strasse 83-85). Neukölln's Reinhold Kiehl also built the **Karl-Marx-Strasse Passage** (1910, now home of the Neuköllner Oper; see p203), and the **Stadtbad Neukölln** (1914; Ganghoferstrasse 3), with niches and mosaics evoking a Roman atmosphere. Special care was also given to suburban rail stations, such as the **S-Bahnhof Mexikoplatz** (Hart and Lesser, 1905) in Zehlendorf, set on a garden square with shops and restaurants, and the **U-Bahnhof Dahlem-Dorf**, whose half-timbered style aims for a countrified look.

ARCHITECTURAL PIONEERS
The work of many pioneers brought modern architecture to life in Berlin. One of the most important was Peter Behrens, who reinterpreted the factory with a new monumental language in the façade of the **Turbinenhalle** at Huttenstrasse in Moabit (1909) and several other buildings for AEG. After 1918, the turbulent birth of the Weimar Republic offered a chance for a final aesthetic break with the Wilhelmine style. The humming metropolis gave birth to a new gothic-industrial style known as Brick Expressionism, used in electricity power stations (HH Müller's 1926 **Abspannwerk**, or transformer station, on the canal in Kreuzberg at the junction of Ohlauerstrasse and Paul-Lincke Ufer), breweries (the original **Berliner Kindl brewery**, now a gay club; Rollbergstrasse, Neukölln)

and churches (Fritz Höger's 1932 **Kirche am Hohenzollerndamm**, 202 Hohenzollerndamm).

A radical new architecture gave formal expression to long-awaited social and political reforms. The Neues Bauen ('new buildings') began to exploit the new technologies of glass, steel and concrete, inspired by the early work of Tessenow and Behrens, Dutch modernism, cubism and Russian constructivism. Berlin architects could explore the new functionalism, using clean lines and a machine aesthetic bare of ornament, thanks to post-war housing demand, and a new social democrat administration that put planner Martin Wagner at the helm after 1925.

The city became the pioneer of a new form of social housing. The *Siedlung* (housing estate) was developed within the framework of a 'building exhibition' of experimental prototypes – often collaborations among architects such as Luckhardt, Gropius, Häring, Salvisberg and the brothers Taut. Standardised sizes kept costs down and amenities such as tenant gardens, schools, public transport and shopping areas were offered when possible. Among the best-known 1920s estates are Bruno Taut's **Hufeisen-Siedlung** (1927; Bruno-Taut-Ring, Britz), arranged in a horseshoe shape around a communal garden, and **Onkel-Toms-Hütte** (Häring, Taut, 1928-29; Argentinische Allee, Zehlendorf), with Salvisberg's linear U-Bahn station at its heart. Most *Siedlungen* were housing only, such as the **Ringsiedlung**

IN CONTEXT

Hufeisen-Siedlung.

BERLIN BUNKERS

Hard-to-remove relics of war, now repurposed.

Next to the railway lines on the Schöneberg–Tempelhof border (General-Pape-Strasse, corner of Dudenstrasse) stands a huge, featureless cylinder of concrete. Built in 1942 as part of the planning for Germania, the Nazi imperial capital that never was, it's a *Grossbelastungskörper* (heavy load testing body) designed to gauge the resilience of Berlin's sandy geology near the site for a proposed triumphal arch.

Sammlung Boros.

This artless, seldom-noticed lump is the lone physical trace of the north–south axis whose overblown structures were intended to wow the world.

But it's not the only huge hulk of reinforced concrete that the Nazis left behind, and is tiny compared to some of the bunkers, flak towers and air raid shelters that outlasted the regime they were intended to protect. The question of how to integrate them into the urban landscape has sparked a variety of answers.

Berlin's Zoo flak tower was the biggest bunker in the world when the royal engineers began trying to blow it up in July 1947. One year and 66 tonnes of explosives later, they finally broke the thing open, causing extensive damage to the zoo. It took many further detonations before the foundations were finally cleared in 1969-70.

Given the difficulty of demolition, most of these structures have simply been left where they were. On Pallasstrasse in Schöneberg, an air-raid shelter, formerly part of the otherwise demolished Sportspalast complex, has been used to support one end of an apartment block that bridges the street. After the war, two enormous concrete towers in what is now Volkspark Friedrichshain were blown open, then filled in and covered with rubble from the bombed-out city. Result: the park now has two attractively landscaped

hills, and only a few visible segments of balustrade hint at what lies beneath.

A bit more can be seen of a similarly blasted and buried Nazi flak tower in Wedding's Humboldthain park. Climbers practise on its north face, several species of bat dwell in its recesses, a viewing platform on the top offers a panorama of the Berlin skyline, and guided tours of the interior are offered by the Berliner Unterwelten association (www.berliner-unterwelten.de).

There are two other bunkers you can get inside. Kreuzberg's **Gruselkabinett** (see *p140*) is housed in a five-storey concrete hulk, and includes an exhibition about the structure itself, which was once an air-raid shelter for the long-destroyed Anhalter Bahnhof. A bunker on the corner of Reinhardtstrasse and Albrechtstrasse in Mitte, previously a not-very-convenient air-raid shelter for Friedrichstrasse station, was repurposed as a techno club in the early 1990s and today houses the fabulous **Sammlung Boros** art collection (see *p66*).

But of Berlin's most infamous bunker, the one where Hitler spent his frenzied last days, there's no longer any trace – it was demolished in the late 1980s. A sparse information board on Gertrud-Kolmar-Strasse (opposite the junction with An Der Ministeriumsgarten) is all that marks its former location.

(Goebelstrasse, Charlottenburg) and **Siemensstadt** (Scharoun et al, 1929-32). Traditional-looking 'counter-proposals' were made by more conservative designers at **Am Fischtal** (Tessenow, Mebes, Emmerich, Schmitthenner et al, 1929; Zehlendorf).

Larger infrastructure projects and public works were also built by avant-garde architects under Wagner's direction. Among the more interesting are the rounded U-Bahn station at **Krumme Lanke** (Grenander, 1929), the totally rational **Stadtbad Mitte** (1930; Gartenstrasse 5), the **Messegelände** (Poelzig, Wagner, 1928; Messedamm 22, Charlottenburg), the ceramic-tiled **Haus des Rundfunks** (Poelzig, 1930; Masurenallee 10, Charlottenburg), and the twin office buildings on the southern corner of Alexanderplatz (Behrens, 1932).

Beginning with his expressionist Einsteinturm in Babelsberg, Erich Mendelsohn distilled his own brand of modernism, characterised by the rounded forms of the Universum Cinema (1928; now the **Schaubühne**; see p210) and the elegant corner solution of the **IG Metall** building (1930; Alte Jacobstrasse 148, Kreuzberg).

> 'The Berlin Wall, put up in a single night in 1961, has claim to be the most iconic structure of the 20th century.'

FASCIST FANTASY

In the effort to remake liberal Berlin in their image, the Nazis banned modernist trademarks such as flat roofs and slender columns in favour of traditional architecture. The Bauhaus was closed down and modern architects fled Berlin as Hitler dreamt of refashioning it into the fantastical mega-capital 'Germania', designed by Albert Speer. The crowning glory was to be a grand axis with a railway station at its foot and a massive copper dome at its head, some 16 times the size of St Peter's in Rome. Work was halted by the war, but not before demolition was begun in Tiergarten and Schöneberg.

Hitler and Speer's fantasy was that Germania would someday leave picturesque ruins. Those ruins came sooner than expected. Up to 90 per cent of the inner city was destroyed by Allied bombing. Mountains of rubble cleared by women survivors rose at the city's edge, such as the Teufelsberg in the West and Friedrichshain in the East. During bombing and reconstruction, many apartment buildings lost their decoration, resulting in the bare plasterwork and blunted lines characteristic of Berlin today.

Fascism also left a less visible legacy of bunker and tunnel landscapes. The more visible fascist architecture can be recognised by its stripped-down, abstracted classicism, typically in travertine: in the West, **Flughafen Tempelhof** (Sagebiel, 1941; see p154) and the **Olympiastadion** (March, 1936; see p120); in the East, the marble-halled **Reichsluftfahrtministerium** (Sagebiel, 1936, now the Bundesministerium der Finanzen; Wilhelmstrasse 97, Mitte) and the **Reichsbank** (Wolff, 1938, now the Auswärtiges Amt; Werderscher Markt, Mitte).

AFTER THE WAR

The **Berlin Wall**, put up in a single night in 1961, introduced a new and cruel reality, and has claim to be the most iconic structure of the 20th century. Very little of the original survives, save for a stretch at **Bernauer Strasse**, and the **East Side Gallery** murals (see p84). The city's centre of gravity shifted as the Wall cut off the historic centre from the West, suspending the Brandenburger Tor and Potsdamer Platz in no-man's land, while the outer edge followed the 1920 city limits.

Post-war architecture is a mixed bag, ranging from the crisp linear brass of 1950s storefronts to concrete 1970s mega-complexes. Early joint planning efforts led by Hans Scharoun were scrapped, and radical interventions cleared out vast spaces. Among the architectural casualties in the East were Schinkel's Bauakademie and much of Fischerinsel, clearing a sequence of wide spaces from Marx-Engels-Platz to Alexanderplatz. In West Berlin, Anhalter Bahnhof was left to stand in ruins and Schloss Charlottenburg narrowly escaped demolition.

Though architects from East and West shared the same modernist education, their work became the tool of opposing ideologies,

IN CONTEXT

and housing was the first battlefield. The DDR adapted Russian socialist realism to Prussian culture in projects built with great effort and amazing speed as a national undertaking. First and foremost was **Stalinallee** (1951-54, now Karl-Marx-Allee; Friedrichshain) with its colossal Stalinist twin towers. The Frankfurter Tor segment of its monumental axis was designed by Herman Henselmann, a Bauhaus modernist who briefly agreed to switch styles.

In response, West Berlin called on leading International Style architects such as Gropius, Niemeyer, Aalto and Jacobsen to build the **Hansaviertel**. A loose arrangement of inventive blocks and pavilions at the edge of the Tiergarten, it was part of the 1957 Interbau Exhibition for the 'city of tomorrow', which included Le Corbusier's Unité d'Habitation in Charlottenburg (Corbusierhaus, just south of Olympiastadion S-Bahn station).

Stylistic differences between East and West diminished in the 1960s and '70s, as new *Siedlungen* were built to even greater dimensions. The **Gropiusstadt** in Britz and **Märkisches Viertel** in Reinickendorf (1963-74) were mirrored in the East by equally massive (if shoddier) prefab housing estates in Marzahn and Hellersdorf.

To replace cultural institutions then cut off from the West, Dahlem became the site of various museums and of the new **Freie Universität** (Candilis Woods Schiedhelm, 1967-79). Scharoun conceived a 'Kulturforum' on the site cleared for Germania, designing two masterful pieces: the **Philharmonie** (1963; *see p202*) and the **Staatsbibliothek** (1976; *see p287*). Other additions were Mies van der Rohe's sleek **Neue Nationalgalerie** (1968; *see p105*) and the **Gemäldegalerie** (Hilmer & Sattler, 1992-98; *see p104*).

The US presented Berlin with Hugh Stubbins' **Kongresshalle** in the Tiergarten (1967, now the Haus der Kulturen der Welt; *see p98*), a futuristic work, which embarrassingly required seven years' repair after its roof collapsed in 1980. East German architects brewed their own version of futuristic modernism in the enlarged Alexanderplatz with its **Fernsehturm** (TV Tower, 1969; *see p58*); the nearby **Haus des Lehrers** (Henselmann, 1961-64; Grunerstrasse and Karl-Marx-Allee, Mitte),

Kino International.

with its wonderfully restored frieze; the next-door **Congress Hall** (ICC – and as elegant as anything achieved by Oscar Niemeyer in Brasilia); and the impressive cinemas **Kino International** (Kaiser, 1964; Karl-Marx-Allee 33, Mitte) and **Kosmos** (Kaiser, 1962; Karl-Marx-Allee 131, Friedrichshain). The 1970s even saw a brief burst of Soviet sci-fi architecture, with the bronze-glass and brown marbled **Czech Embassy to the DDR** (Vera & Vladimir Machonin, 1978; Wilhelmstrasse 44).

Modernist urban renewal gradually gave way to historic preservation after 1970. In the West, largely in response to the squatting movement, the city launched a public-private enterprise within the Internationale Bauausstellung (IBA – International Architecture Exhibition), to conduct a 'careful renewal' of the *Mietskaserne* and 'critical reconstruction' with infill projects to close the gaps left in areas along the Wall.

It is a truly eclectic collection: the irreverent organicism of the prolific Hinrich and Inken Baller (1982-84; Fraenkelufer, Kreuzberg) contrasts sharply with the neo-rationalist work of Peter Eisenman (1988; Kochstrasse 62-63, Kreuzberg) and Aldo Rossi (1988; Wilhelmstrasse 36-38, Kreuzberg). A series of projects was also placed along Friedrichstrasse. IBA thus became a proving-ground for contemporary architectural theories. (Much of the IBA is explored in Jim Hudson's blog, now archived at architectureinberlin.wordpress.com.)

In the East, urban renewal slowed to a halt when funds for the construction of new housing ran dry; and towards the end of the 1970s, inner-city areas again became politically and economically attractive. Most East-bloc preservation focused on run-down 19th-century buildings on a few streets and squares in Prenzlauer Berg. Some infill buildings were also added on Friedrichstrasse in manipulated grids and pastel colours, so that the postmodern theme set up by IBA architects on the street south of Checkpoint Charlie was continued over the Wall. But progress was slow, and when the Wall fell in 1989 many sites still stood half-finished.

UNITING THE CITY

Rejoining East and West became the new challenge, requiring work of every kind, from massive infrastructure to commercial and residential projects. There were two key decisions. The first was to eradicate the Wall's no-man's land zone with projects that would link urban structures on either side. The second was to pursue a 'critical reconstruction' of the old city block structure, using a contemporary interpretation of Prussian scale and order.

The historic areas around Pariser Platz, Friedrichstrasse and Unter den Linden were peppered with empty sites and became a primary focus for this critical reconstruction. The first major commercial project in Friedrichstrasse stuck with the required city scale but took the game rules lightly. The various buildings of the **Friedrichstadt-Passagen** (1996; Friedrichstrasse 66-75, Mitte), despite their subterranean mall link, offer separate approaches. Pei Cobb Freed & Partners' **Quartier 206** (see p46) is a gaudy confection of architectural devices reminiscent of 1920s Berlin, while Jean Nouvel's **Galeries Lafayette** (see p53) is a smooth and rounded glass form. Only the third building, **Quartier 205**, by Oswald Mathias Ungers, uses a current German style, with its sandstone solidity and rigorous square grid.

Good examples of the emerging Berliner Architektur, based on the solidity of the past but with modern detail and expressive use of materials, are to be found in Thomas van den Valentyn and Matthias Dittmann's monumental **Quartier 108** (1998; Friedrichstrasse and Leipziger Strasse,

Mitte) and in the **Kontorhaus Mitte** (1997; Friedrichstrasse 180-190, Mitte) by Josef Paul Kleihues, Vittorio Magnago Lampugnani, Walther Stepp and Klaus Theo Brenner.

On both sides of the city, much historic substance was lost in World War II and the sweeping changes that followed. Today, the rebuilding of the former imperial areas near Unter den Linden, the Museumsinsel and Schlossplatz revolve around a choice between critical reconstruction or straightforward replicas of the past. The Kommandantenhaus, next to the Staatsoper on Unter den Linden, rebuilt by Thomas van den Valentyn as the **Stiftung Bertelsmann** (2004), is an example of the tendency towards historical replication, as is the mooted reconstruction of Friedrich Schinkel's Bauakademie next door. Thankfully, some decisions have been taken in favour of contemporary architecture, particularly the entrance building to the **Auswärtiges Amt** (Foreign Office, 1999; Werdescher Markt 1) by Thomas Müller and Ivan Reimann, and IM Pei's triangular block for the **Deutsches Historisches Museum** (2003; see p49), with its curved foyer and cylindrical stair tower.

Berlin's return to capital city status has brought with it a number of interesting new embassies and consulates in and around a revived diplomatic quarter. Notable on Tiergartenstrasse are the solid red stone **Indian Embassy** by Leon Wohlhage Wernik (2001) and the extension of the existing **Japanese Embassy** by Ryohei Amemiya (2000). There are other intriguing examples around the corner in Klingelhöferstrasse: the monumental, louvre-fronted **Mexican Embassy** by Teodoro Gonzalez de Leon and J Francisco Serrano (2000); and the encircling copper wall of the five **Nordic embassies**, containing work by various Scandinavian architects after a plan by Alfred Berger and Tiina Parkkinen (1999).

There are four main sites now linking East and West: the area around Potsdamer Platz and Leipziger Platz; the government quarter and 'Band des Bundes'; the new Berlin Hauptbahnhof; and the reinstatement of the Reichstag and Pariser Platz, the historical formal entrance to the city. These are mostly stand-alone projects outside the discussion on critical reconstruction; their architecture reflects this in a greater freedom of approach.

IN CONTEXT

Jüdisches Museum.

Potsdamer Platz (*see p40*) was the first of the four, designed as a new urban area based on the old geometries of Potsdamer Platz and Leipziger Platz. This former swathe of no-man's land was redeveloped not only to forge a link between Leipziger Strasse to the East and the Kulturforum to the West, but also to supply Berlin with a new central focus in an area that was formerly neither one side or the other.

The twin squares of Potsdamer Platz and Leipziger Platz have been reinstated and five small quarters radiate to the south and west. **Leipziger Platz** has risen again as an enclosed octagonal set-piece, with modern terrace buildings. Potsdamer Platz is by contrast once more an open intersection, entrances to the various quarters beyond staked out with major buildings by Hans Kollhoff, Hilmer & Sattler and Albrecht, Helmut Jahn, Renzo Piano and Schweger and Partner (1999-2003). The closed metal and glass block of Helmut Jahn's **Sony Center** (2000) is a singular piece, organised around a lofty central forum with a tented glass and textile roof as its spectacular focus. Offices and apartments look down on to a public space with cinemas, bars, restaurants and the glass-encased remnants of the old Esplanade Hotel.

The Daimler (formerly DaimlerChrysler) area on the other side of Potsdamer Strasse is a network of tree-lined streets with squares and pavement cafés. It's also the work of various architects, though Renzo Piano got all the key pieces, notably the **Arkaden** shopping mall, the **Debis** headquarters, and the **Musicaltheater** and **Spielbank** on Marlene-Dietrich-Platz (all 1999), all in a language of terracotta and glass. The quarter's south-west flank facing on to Tilla-Durieux-Park is a rich architectural mix, with Richard Rogers' two

buildings of cylinders, blocks and wedges (1998; Linkstrasse) and Arata Isozaki's concoction of ochre and brown stripes topped with a wavy glass penthouse (1998; Linkstrasse). It's often said of the Potsdamer Platz project that 'the world's best architects came – and did their worst buildings'. Not quite fair, as their original plans were watered down by the city's conservative building commissioner, but not far off either.

The 'Band des Bundes', the linear arrangement of new government buildings north of the Reichstag, is another project linking East and West. The result of a competition won by Axel Schultes and Charlotte Frank, it straddles the Spree and the former border, resembling a paper clip that binds the two halves of the city. The centrepiece is the **Bundeskanzleramt** (Federal Chancellery, Schultes and Frank, 2000; Willi-Brandt-Strasse, Tiergarten) flanked by buildings with offices for parliamentary deputies. The arrangement reads like a unity thanks to a common and simple language of concrete and glass.

North of this across the Spree is the new central station, **Berlin Hauptbahnhof** (Von Gerkan Marg, 2006; *see p282*), now Europe's largest rail intersection. The 321-metre (1,053-feet) east–west overground platforms are covered by a barrel vault of delicately gridded glass. This is crossed in a north–south direction by a station hall 180 metres (590 feet) long and 40 metres (131 feet) wide, which gives access to the trains on each intersecting level and to the shopping centre. Each side of the station hall is framed by buildings spanning the east–west vault. The building stands as a functional and symbolic link between East and West Germany, and as a hub of the whole European rail network.

Finally, there are the historical links. To the south of the Bundeskanzleramt is the **Reichstag** (see p98), sitting on the old threshold to the East, gutted, remodelled and topped with a new glass dome by Norman Foster (1999) to bring a degree of public access and transparency to a building with a dark past. **Pariser Platz** (see p40) has been almost entirely built to its old proportions. The utterly bland **US Embassy**, unveiled on 4 July 2008 in the south-west corner, completes the set piece. Some of the buildings are a pale blend of modern and historic but there are exceptions, such as the **DG Bank** by Frank Gehry (2000; Pariser Platz 3) with its witty use of a rational façade in front of the spectacular free forms in its internal court, or Christian de Portzamparc's **French Embassy** (2002; Pariser Platz 5), which plays with classical composition but uses contemporary materials. In the opposite corner is the **Akademie der Künste** (Behnisch and Partner; 2005), an exception to its neighbours with a welcoming and open glass façade. Round the corner, Michael Wilford's **British Embassy** (2000; see p40) also came to terms with the city's strict planning limitations by raising a conformist punched stone façade, which he then broke open to expose a rich and colourful set of secondary buildings in the central court. When the last bits of Leipziger Platz are filled in, all the major symbolic linking projects planned in the reunification period will be complete.

The last 15 years has also produced work that had nothing to do with reunification. Daniel Libeskind's **Jüdisches Museum** (1999; see p142) in Kreuzberg is a symbolic sculpture in the form of a lightning bolt. Peter Eisenmann's **Denkmal für die ermordeten Juden Europas** (2005; see p48), south of Pariser Platz, is a departure from a traditional memorial, with its open and sunken grid of 2,700 steles. Nicholas Grimshaw's **Ludwig-Erhard-Haus** for the stock exchange (1998; see p114) breaks with convention by taking the form of a glass and steel armadillo, though a city-required fire wall obscures the structure. Dominique Perrault's **Velodrom** (1997; Paul-Heyse-Strasse 26) sinks into the landscape in the form of a disc and a flat box of glass, concrete and gleaming steel mesh. Sauerbruch and Hutton's striking HQ for the **GSW** (1999; Kochstrasse 22A, Kreuzberg), with its translucent sailed top and colourful and constantly changing façade, shows how singular buildings can take the city's urban quality to the next level.

IN CONTEXT

CHIPPERFIELD'S MUSEUM ISLAND

A tapestry of textures.

Considering it catapulted David Chipperfield from merely the front rank of the world's architects into the celebrity realm of the 'starchitect', won the 2011 Mies van der Rohe Award for Architecture and saw its mastermind awarded both a knighthood and a RIBA prize, what's surprising about the restoration of the **Neues Museum** (see p50) is how understated and unassuming it is. It's the first triumph in Chipperfield's masterplan for the Museuminsel, which has taken more than 15 years.

Badly damaged by Allied bombing in World War II, the Neues Museum was left to rot under the communist regime despite its prominent location on the capital's Museum Island. Its makeover is breathtakingly elegant, chaste and discreet. The biggest single intervention is a gargantuan, blank, modernist staircase, but perhaps the most beautiful space is the top deck of the five-storey concrete 'cage' of slim pillars, inserted into an existing courtyard without touching the sides; a light-filled atrium containing a handful of Egyptian busts.

Chipperfield is so beloved in Berlin, he's been described as 'one of Germany's greatest architects' – even though he's British. He continues work on the **James Simon Gallery**, which will act as a new unified entrance and ticket hall for all the museums on the island, and has begun a redesign of the **Neue Nationalgalerie**. His own stark office on Joachimstrasse was awarded a RIBA award in 2013, and fans of his work should check out the imposing, ten-storey **Parkside** apartment block, right on the edge of the Tiergarten, behind Potsdamer Platz.

Essential Information

Hotels

With an average room price hovering at just over €100 per night, Berlin still ranks among the least expensive western cities in which to stay – in stark comparison to London at €161 a night and New York's average of a whopping €217. There are so many places to choose from now that hoteliers are going the extra mile to stand out: the excellent-value Amano near Hackescher Markt has its own iPhone app with themed walking tours and city guide, while the 304-room Nhow by the river in Friedrichshain touts itself as a 'music and lifestyle hotel', complete with two recording studios and a spa – and Gibson guitars available on room service. Meanwhile, in trendy Neukölln, you can sleep in vintage caravans parked in an old vacuum cleaner factory at the Hüttenpalast.

CITY ROUND-UP

On the luxury front, the **Adlon**, **Sofitel** and the newer **Das Stue** steal the show, with extremely convenient central locations, though the very fashionable **Casa Camper** hotel in Hackescher Markt is snapping at their heels. So too is **Soho House**, which has opened a Berlin outpost in an old Jewish department store, and installed a swimming pool on the roof. For a taste of more refined elegance, head out to the **Schlosshotel Grünewald**, which is located just outside the city near a large forest nature reserve.

At the other end of the price spectrum, there seems to be a new hostel opening every month, and standards are generally high. The current trend is for boutique hostels, with arty DIY interiors, private rooms and affordable prices:

IN THE KNOW DOUBLE DUVETS

Don't be surprised if your double bed comes with two single duvets. It's a German thing: they think we're crazy for fighting over one between two. And as for why the pillows are so big and square? We've never figured that one out.

the **Michelberger** in Friedrichschain is extremely popular with visiting creatives, while **Generator Mitte** is a great base for sightseeing. The tourist boom in Berlin has resulted in hundreds of new hotel beds becoming available, but there's also been a huge rise in people renting out rooms via websites such as Airbnb – something that has got local residents up in arms about rising prices and rowdy tenants.

PRICES AND INFORMATION

Hotels are graded according to an official star rating system designed to sort the deluxe from the dumps – but we haven't followed it in this guide, as the ratings merely reflect room size and amenities such as lifts or bars, rather than other important factors such as decor, staff or atmosphere. Instead, we've divided the hotels by area, then listed them in four categories, according to the standard prices (not including seasonal offers or discounts) for one night in a double room with en suite shower/bath. As a rule of thumb: **Deluxe** starts from €190 and goes up and away; **Expensive** means €120-€190; **Moderate** €60-€120; while rooms marked as **Budget** cost less than €60.

Many of the larger hotels now refuse to publish any rates at all, depending instead on direct booking over the internet (often at a discount), which enables them to vary their prices daily. In addition to hotels' own websites, discount specialists such as www.expedia.com and www.hotels.com are worth a look too. Check if breakfast is included in the room price. Most hotels offer it as a buffet, which can be as simple as coffee and bread rolls (called *schrippen* in Berlin) with cheese and salami, or the full works, complete with smoked meats, muesli with fruit and yoghurt, and even a glass of sparkling wine.

It's wise to reserve in advance whenever possible: on any given weekend in Mitte or Prenzlauer Berg, many hotels are extremely busy. Be wary of cancellation policies too: it's best to ask before you book.

Note that, since 1 January 2014, visitors have to pay a new city tax, amounting to 5 per cent of the price of their room per night. Business travellers are exempt, but have to prove they're in Berlin on business.

Booking.com
Reservations +44 20 3320 2609,
www.booking.com.
With offices Europe-wide, this English-language booking service has pre-reserved beds in hotels of all categories in the city, and guest information can be sent directly to the hotel as a confirmed booking. Check for special offers too.

VisitBerlin
Reservations & information 2500 2333,
www.visitberlin.de.
This privatised tourist service can sort out hotel reservations, tickets for shows and travel arrangements to Berlin.

MITTE

The city's historic administrative quarter is thriving, with an ever-growing number of hotels in all price brackets. While many hipper tourists have started to defect towards less trafficked areas, the faded post-Wall charm of one of the city's oldest quarters is still popular with many. You may not find much of the historic pension charm of Charlottenburg here, but for gallery-hopping, shopping and sightseeing, it's one of the more exciting parts of Berlin.

Deluxe

Adlon Kempinski Berlin
Unter den Linden 77 (226 10, www.hotel-adlon.de).
U6 Französische Strasse, or S1, S2 Brandenburger
Tor. **Map** p306 L6.
Not quite the Adlon of yore, which burned down after World War II, this new, more generic luxury version was rebuilt by the Kempinski Group in 1997 on the original site next to the Brandenburg Gate.

Apart from a few original features, you're really paying for the prime location and the superlative service: bellboys who pass you a chilled bottle of water when you return from a jog in nearby Tiergarten; as well as dining at Tim Raue's Thai concept Sra Bua and the extremely formal Lorenz Adlon Esszimmer, which received a second Michelin star in 2013. If you want to rent out one of the three bulletproof presidential suites (from where Michael Jackson once dangled his child), it will set you back around €15,000, but you do at least get a 24-hour private butler and limousine for your money.

Casa Camper
Weinmeisterstrasse 1 (www.casacamper.com/
berlin, 2000 3411). U8 Weinmeisterstrasse.
Map p307 O5.
In 2011, the Spanish shoe company opened this luxury boutique hotel right in the heart of the Scheunenviertel. Tired shoppers and partygoers alike can take a break and grab some refreshments any time at the hotel's free 24-hour snack bar, which is included in the price of the room in lieu of room service. Full meals are served at the restaurant, Dos Paillos, which specialises in fusion Asian-style cuisine served as a tapas-sized tasting menu with delicacies such as toro sushi (the fatty neck of tuna) on offer. One of the chief attractions of this stylishly minimalistic joint are the light-flooded showers with their stunning views over the city.

Casa Camper

Hotel de Rome

Behrenstrasse 37 (460 6090, www.hotelderome. com). U6 Französische Strasse. **Map** p307 N6.
In 2006, this 19th-century mansion, originally built to house the headquarters of Dresdner Bank, was transformed by Rocco Forte into its present sumptuous state. Despite the intimidating grandeur, the young staff are surprisingly friendly. All 146 rooms push the limits of taste, with plenty of polished wood, marble and velvet. The former basement vault now houses a pool, spa and fully equipped gym. The lobby restaurant, La Banca, specialises in upscale Mediterranean cuisine with alfresco dining in the summer; cocktails and lighter fare are available at the Rooftop Terrace or the Opera Court, where high tea is served every afternoon.

Sofitel Berlin Gendarmenmarkt

Charlottenstrasse 50-52 (203 750, www.sofitel. com). U2, U6 Stadtmitte. **Map** p310 N6.
'Design for the senses' is the motto here. This is a truly lovely hotel, and rooms are often difficult to come by, but it's well worth the fight. So much attention has been paid to the details: from the moment you enter the lobby, with its soothing colour scheme and wonderful lighting, the atmosphere is intimate and elegant. This carries into the rooms, each beautifully styled, with perhaps the best bathrooms in the city. Even the conference rooms are spectacular, and the hotel's 'wellness' area includes plunge pools, a gym and a meditation room. In summer, you can wind down on the sun deck, which perches high above the surrounding rooftops overlooking the splendid domed cathedrals of Gendarmenmarkt.

Expensive

Albrechtshof

Albrechtstrasse 8 (308 860, www.hotel-albrechtshof. de). U6, S1, S2, S5, S7, S25, S75 Friedrichstrasse. **Map** p306 M6.
Located a stone's throw from the Berliner Ensemble and Friedrichstrasse station, the Albrechtshof is a member of Verband Christlicher Hotels (Christian Hotels Association). They don't make a song and dance about it, but it has its own chapel, named after former guest Martin Luther King. The rooms are comfy and clean, if not particularly stylish, and staff are friendly. The restaurant offers pedestrian north German cuisine, and in summer breakfast is served in the courtyard garden.

Dude

Köpenicker Strasse 92 (411 988 177, www. thedudeberlin.com). U8 Heinrich-Heine-Strasse. **Map** p311 O7.
Housed in an elegant 19th-century townhouse, this 30-room boutique hotel was created by an advertising executive to provide an antidote to identikit design and a sense of good humour befitting Berlin. There are a number of house rules – no photography,

ringing a doorbell for access, no large groups – to help foster an atmosphere of anything-goes discretion. The rooms are quite stark, with brass-knobbed beds offset by block-coloured walls, and Molton Brown goodies in the bathroom. Breakfast is served in the all-day deli, and the high-end Brooklyn Beef Club steak restaurant specialises in rare whiskies and Napa Valley wines.

Gendarm

Charlottenstrasse 61 (206 0660, www.hotel-gendarm-berlin.de). U2, U6 Stadtmitte. **Map** p310 M7.
If you fancy a five-star location but don't want to spend a fortune, this place is just the ticket. Aside from a few pink frills, it doesn't have a lot of extras, but the 21 rooms and six suites are smart and comfortable, and it's close to the restaurants of Gendarmenmarkt, shopping on Friedrichstrasse and the State Opera. At rates around half those of the nearby Sofitel or Hilton, you can't really go wrong – unless you bring a car, that is: parking around here can end up costing as much as your room.

Hackescher Markt

Grosse Präsidentenstrasse 8 (280 030, www.classik-hotel-collection.de). S5, S7, S75 Hackescher Markt. **Map** p307 N5.
This elegant hotel in a nicely renovated townhouse avoids the noise of its central Hackescher Markt location by cleverly having many rooms face inwards on to a tranquil green courtyard. Some have balconies, all have their own bath with heated floor, and the suites are spacious and comfortable. The pleasant, helpful staff speak good English. While

THE BEST HOTELS

Amano
Style on a budget. *See p268.*

Grand Hostel
Clean, airy and no bunk beds. *See p279.*

Hotel Pension Funk
For turn-of-the-century glam out west. *See p277.*

Hüttenpalast
Camping – but not as you know it. *See p280.*

Michelberger
Weird and wonderful. *See p272.*

Motel One
Smart chain that's great value. *See p279.*

Soho House
Sumptuous yet cosy. *See p267.*

you don't necessarily get the most atmosphere for the money, you can't beat the address.

Honigmond Garden Hotel

Invalidenstrasse 122 (2844 5577, www.honigmond.de). U6 Oranienburger Tor. **Map** p306 M4.

Along with its nearby sister Honigmond Restaurant-Hotel (*see p269*), this is one of the most charming hotels in Berlin, and it doesn't cost an arm and a leg. Choose between large bedrooms facing the street, smaller ones overlooking the fish pond and Tuscan-style garden, or spacious apartments on the upper floor. As with all great places, the secret is in the finer detail. The rooms are impeccably styled with polished pine floors, paintings in massive gilt frames, antiques and iron bedsteads. There's also a charming sitting room overlooking the garden. Highly recommended.

Lux 11

Rosa-Luxemburg-Strasse 9-13 (936 2800, www.lux-eleven.com). U2 Rosa-Luxemburg-Platz. **Map** p307 O5.

A member of the Design Hotels group, this former apartment house for the DDR secret police is a stylish, no-nonsense apartment-hotel with an emphasis on well-being. The cool, modern, white-walled apartments are elegant and nicely appointed, with everything from intercom for visiting guests to microwave and dishwasher in the kitchen, and queen-sized beds in between. The location is perfect for the fashionable sites of Mitte, or a night at the Volksbühne, and there's also the Prince bar and Type Hype concept store in the building. Rates drop dramatically the longer the stay.

Maritim proArte Hotel Berlin

Friedrichstrasse 151 (203 35, www.maritim.de). U6, S1, S2, S5, S7, S25, S75 Friedrichstrasse. **Map** p306 M6.

Despite the fact that its status as one of Berlin's first 'designer hotels' has been overshadowed by newcomers, this is still popular with businessmen and air stewards, who congregate in the mall-like lobby and like to soak up the posh bar, restaurants and boutiques. Each of the 403 rooms, apartments and suites has free internet, air-conditioning and marble bathrooms. Staff are polite and helpful, and it's just a short walk to the shops on Friedrichstrasse or to the Brandenburg Gate.

Meliá Berlin

Friedrichstrasse 103 (2060 7900, www.melia berlin.com). U6, S1, S2, S5, S7, S25, S75 Friedrichstrasse. **Map** p306 M6.

Just across the street from Friedrichstrasse station, this shiny corner building on the banks of the Spree is a huge link in the Spanish Sol Meliá chain. All 364 rooms are similarly and tastefully appointed, many with fine views of the river and the

Reichstag beyond, but the rich wood units and headboards seem a little incongruous. The rooftop Café Restaurant Madrid offers reasonably priced theatre and business-lunch menus, while the tapas bar off the lobby provides lighter fare and entertainment. The helpful staff are pleasant, making this an ideal and convenient stop-over for the harried business traveller; but for simple folk in search of atmosphere, there's better value for money elsewhere.

Radisson Blu Hotel Berlin

Karl-Liebknecht-Strasse 3 (238 280, www.radisson blu.com/hotel-berlin). S5, S7, S75 Hackescher Markt. **Map** p307 N6.

With interiors by German designer Yasmine Mahmoudieh (responsible for the cabins of the Airbus A380), the 427 rooms here are fresh, uncluttered and free of the normal blandness typical of big hotel chains. The Radisson's claim to fame, however, is 'the tank' – a 25m (82ft) high aquarium with a million litres of saltwater housing 2,500 varieties of fish. Many of the bedrooms even have a view of it. If you're tempted to take a dip, though, we suggest the pool in the hotel spa, or dive into a drink in the Atrium Lobby Lounge bar.

★ Soho House

Torstrasse 1 (405 0440, www.sohohouseberlin. com). U2 Rosa-Luxemburg-Platz. **Map** p307 P5.

The average Berliner has a healthy scepticism towards anything 'private' or 'exclusive', so eyebrows were raised when Soho House opened its branch in the German capital in 2010. But even the toughest critic would have to admit that the building and its history are too unique to be dismissed out of hand. The imposing Bauhaus structure has an incredible history: it initially housed a Jewish-owned department store before it was taken over first by the Nazis, then by the communist regime. These days, Soho House occupies eight floors, and has installed one of their excellent Cowshed spas, a library and its own cinema. In the rooms, beautiful old wooden floors and 1920s furniture mix with raw concrete walls. There's a touch of Britishness too, with a kettle and biscuits in each room (unusual in Germany); together with the artfully selected furniture and warm atmosphere, this gives it a much greater sense of *Gemütlichkeit* (cosy homeliness) than its rivals. A swim in the rooftop pool overlooking east Berlin rounds off the experience. *Photo p268.*

Westin Grand

Friedrichstrasse 158-164 (202 70, www.westin grandberlin.com). U6 Französische Strasse. **Map** p306 M6.

Despite its East German prefabricated exterior, the Westin Grand is pure five-star international posh (the Stones stay here when they're in town). The decor is gratifyingly elegant, with lots of polished crystal and brass and a grandiose foyer and staircase. The rooms are tastefully traditional, and the 35

Soho House. *See p267.*

suites are individually furnished with period decor themed after their names. There's also a garden, bar and restaurant, and the civilised haunts of the Gendarmenmarkt are just outside the door.

Moderate

Amano

Auguststrasse 43 (809 4150, www.hotel-amano. com). U8 Rosenthaler Platz. **Map** p307 N5.

The nice thing about Amano is that it doesn't try too hard – and it doesn't need to, given its perfect location right in the centre of Berlin. The rooms and apartments are modern and unpretentious with free Wi-Fi. Other perks are the backyard garden and a roof-terrace lounge where older hotel guests mingle with young preppy professionals. Bikes are also available to rent.

Arte Luise Kunsthotel

Luisenstrasse 19 (284 480, www.arte-luise.com). U6, S1, S2, S5, S7, S25, S75 Friedrichstrasse. **Map** p306 L6.

Housed in a neoclassical former residential palace just a short walk from the Reichstag and Brandenburger Tor, this 'artist home' is one of the city's more imaginative small hotels, with each of its 50 rooms decorated by a different renowned artist. There's graffiti artist Thomas Baumgärtel's 'Royal Suite', a golden room spray-painted with bananas; and Guido Seiber's 'Berlin Society', covered in the artist's humorous renditions of Berlin celebrities and streetlife. Some rooms get a little noise from the S-Bahn trains, but that shouldn't deter you: this is a great place to stay.

Art'otel Berlin Mitte

Wallstrasse 70-73 (240 620, www.artotels.de). U2 Märkisches Museum. **Map** p311 O7.

A real gem on the Spree. This delightful hotel is a creative fusion of old and new, combining restored rococo reception rooms with ultra-modern bedrooms designed by Nalbach & Nalbach. As well as highlighting the artwork of George Baselitz – originals hang in the corridors and all 109 rooms – the hotel's decor has been meticulously thought out to the smallest detail, from the Philippe Starck bathrooms to the Breuer chairs in the conference rooms. Staff are pleasant, and the views from the top suites across Mitte are stunning.

Honigmond Restaurant-Hotel

Tieckstrasse 12 (284 4550, www.honigmond.de). U6 Oranienburger Tor. **Map** p306 M4.

The 40 rooms in this beautiful 1899 building are spacious and lovely, and although some of the less expensive ones lack their own shower and toilet, don't let that put you off: this is probably the best and prettiest mid-price hotel east of the Zoo. The reception area has comfy chairs around a gas fireplace, and breakfast is served in the Honigmond restaurant, open since 1920. The friendly staff speak English, and the hotel is perfectly sited, within walking distance of the Scheunenviertel and Hackescher Markt. More affordable luxury would be hard to find.

Hotel Pension Kastanienhof

Kastanienallee 65 (443 050, www.kastanienhof. biz). U8 Rosenthaler Platz. **Map** p307 O4.

Ideally located at the bottom of Kastanienallee, this is a warm, cosy, old-fashioned hotel. The pastel-coloured rooms are generously proportioned and well equipped, and there are three breakfast rooms and a bar. The English-speaking staff are friendly. It's especially popular at weekends, so book ahead.

Miniloftmitte

Hessische Strasse 5 (847 1090, www.miniloft.com). U6 Naturkundemuseum. **Map** p306 L5.

A brilliant alternative to the hotel hustle, these 14 flats – housed in a combined renovated apartment building and award-winning steel/concrete construction – are modern, airy and elegant. Each comes with a queen-sized bed, couch and dining area (the frosted-glass panels separating bath and kitchen are an interesting touch), with warm-coloured fabrics, organic basics in the kitchen, and lots of space and light. The owners/designers/architects are a young, friendly couple who live and work on the premises. Rates are greatly reduced the longer the stay, and free cleaning is provided weekly for long-term visitors.

Park Inn Hotel

Alexanderplatz 7 (238 90, www.parkinn.de). U2, U5, U8, S5, S7, S75 Alexanderplatz. **Map** p307 O5.

With 1,012 rooms overlooking Alexanderplatz, Berlin's largest (and tallest) hotel is something of a mixed bag. Although the views are spectacular, and most of the rooms have been renovated with extra windows, the vibe is a little cold and impersonal considering the price. There are special package deals – and a casino – for the convention groups that fill the lobby in busloads, and easy access to public transport for a business stopover, but for the traveller in search of warmth and atmosphere, there are better choices nearby.

Platte Mitte

Rochstrasse 9 (0177 283 2602 mobile, www. plattemitte.de). S5, S7, S75 Hackescher Markt. **Map** p307 O6.

Proudly calling itself a 'No Hotel', these three apartments on the 21st floor of a 1967-built *Plattenbau* are airy and well designed, each with spectacular views of the city around Alexanderplatz. Colourfully decorated and eclectic to say the least, the furnishings mix original pieces of the period with artfully fanciful touches such as poster-plastered walls and mannequins by the bed. Babysitting services are available, as well as a personal Pilates trainer. And as most of the neighbours are original tenants, this is a wonderfully unique way to experience Berlin. The prices listed are for up to two nights only, and are greatly reduced for longer stays. Rates include bedlinen and weekly cleaning.

Budget

Baxpax Downtown Hostel Hotel

Ziegelstrasse 28 (2787 4880, www.baxpax.de). U6, S1, S2, S5, S7, S25, S75 Friedrichstrasse. **No credit cards. Map** p306 M5.

This new, third addition to the Baxpax hostel empire is an excellent place to stay, in a brilliant location. Clean, contemporary and well designed, it has all the usual amenities, from a luggage room to darts, with the additional luxury of a fireplace lounge, courtyard and rooftop terrace. There's a dorm just for women, 24-hour reception and keycard access for security, and a friendly, relaxed atmosphere.
Other locations Baxpax Mitte, Chausseestrasse 102, Mitte (2839 0965); Baxpax Kreuzberg, Skalitzer Strasse 104, Kreuzberg (6951 8322).

★ Circus

Weinbergsweg 1A (2839 1433, www.circus-berlin. de). U8 Rosenthaler Platz. **Map** p307 N4.

Almost the standard by which other hostels should be measured, the Circus is a rarity – simple but stylish, warm and comfortable. And the upper-floor apartments have balconies and lovely views. The laid-back staff can help get discount tickets to almost anything, or give directions to the best bars and clubs, of which there are plenty nearby. The place is deservedly popular and is always full, so be sure to book ahead. Just across the Platz, the owners also run the moderately priced Circus Hotel, whose 63 double rooms, each with private bath, surround a central terraced winter garden and café. Their breakfast buffets are bountiful, with an excellent choice of organic granolas, and useful things such as laptops are available to rent, as well as bikes, Segways and even electric motorbikes. *Photo p270.*

CityStay

Rosenstrasse 16 (2362 4031, www.citystay.de). S5, S7, S75 Hackescher Markt. **No credit cards. Map** p307 O6.

On a small, quiet street – but as central as you can get – this is a great modern hostel for the price. The rooms are clean and simple, and there are showers on every floor. Security is top-notch, with access cards for the video-monitored entrance and floors. The breakfast buffet features fresh organic bread, and the kitchen will fix your eggs any way you like 'em.

EasyHotel

Rosenthaler Strasse 69 (no phone, www.easyhotel. com). U8 Rosenthaler Platz. **Map** p307 N5.
The 125 rooms at this hotel are as you would expect from the budget airline – small and cheap. But they're also smart and clean, and not aggressively orange as you might imagine. Plus, the hotel is brilliantly located for the shops, bars and restaurants of the most exciting bit of Mitte. Book far enough in advance and a room here is a real bargain, though beware that, just like flying with a low-cost carrier, the extras soon mount up. It's €8 to get your room cleaned, €3 for 24-hour internet access and €3 for luggage storage.

Generator Mitte

Oranienburger Strasse 65 (921 037 680, www.generatorhostels.com). S1, S2, S25 Oranienburger Strasse. **Map** p306 M5.
The Generator hostel empire continues its spread across Europe, with two locations in Berlin: this funky flagship on Oranienburger Strasse, and a larger but blander site in Prenzlauer Berg. It positions itself somewhere between a traditional backpackers' hostel and a boutique hotel. There are plenty of useful services, such as a 24-hour laundry, luggage storage and an affordable daily menu dished out in the evenings. It's definitely geared towards a younger crowd, with urban art on the walls and a late-night bar with DJs at weekends. As well as the usual bunk dorms, there are a number of private rooms (sleeping up to four), as well as female-only dormitories.
Other locations Storkower Strasse 160, Prenzlauer Berg (417 2400).

Heart of Gold Hostel Berlin

Johannisstrasse 11 (2900 3300, www.heartofgold-hostel.de). S1, S2, S25 Oranienburger Strasse. **Map** p306 M5.
The prime location aside (it's only 50m from Oranienburger Strasse), this member of the Backpacker Germany Network (www.backpacker-network.de) is loosely themed on Douglas Adams' *The Hitchhiker's Guide to the Galaxy.* Rooms are bright and cheerful, with parquet floors. Lockers are free; individual bathrooms and showers, and a keycard system guarantee security. The laundry is cheap, as are the shots in the bar; and with rentable 'Sens-O-matic' sunglasses and Squornshellous Zeta mattresses to help you recover, what more could a backpacker (or hitchhiker) need? Towels, of course, which are available for free at reception.

Wombat's City Hostel Berlin

Alte Schönhauserstrasse 2 (8471 0820, www. wombats-hostels.com/berlin). U2 Rosa-Luxemburg-Platz. **Map** p307 O5.
Situated virtually on Berlin's hipster heaven of Torstrasse, Wombat's City Hostel Berlin is minutes from Alexanderplatz and the scuzzier surroundings of Mitte's bar drag, leading up to Rosenthalerplatz. A colourful, cosy spot, it's well equipped with a laundry, coffee shop, computers and free Wi-Fi; best of all is the seventh-floor bar with its outdoor terrace. Next door is a Cajun restaurant.

ESSENTIAL INFORMATION

Circus. *See p269.*

Ackselhaus & Bluehome.

PRENZLAUER BERG

From the cool of Kastanienallee to the funky chic of Helmholtzplatz, this neighbourhood just north of Mitte may be charming, but it has a dearth of decent hotels – surprising, considering the number of visitors the area attracts.

Expensive

Ackselhaus & Bluehome

Belforter Strasse 21 & 24 (4433 7633, www.ackselhaus.de). U2 Senefelderplatz. **Map** p307 P4.

Just doors apart, what ties these two establishments together – aside from their shared reception desk – is a wonderfully realised, luxurious 'modern colonial' style. Each room is lovingly decorated, with much attention to detail; themes range from China to Maritime to Movie, so there should be a room for every taste. The delightful Kairo Suite will make you feel as if you've been transported away from the hustle and bustle of Prenzlauer Berg on to the set of *The English Patient*. Bluehome (at no.24), with its blue façade, and balconies overlooking Belforter Strasse, houses the Club del Mar restaurant, which offers a breakfast buffet. There's also a lovely back garden, complete with lawn chairs in summer.

Moderate

Myer's Hotel

Metzer Strasse 26 (440 140, www.myershotel.de). U2 Senefelderplatz, or tram M2. **Map** p307 P4.

This renovated 19th-century townhouse sits on a tranquil street. There's a garden and a glass-ceilinged gallery, and the big leather furniture seems to beg you to light up a cigar. In addition, the beautiful Kollwitzplatz is just around the corner, as are a bunch of decent bars and restaurants. Although the tram stop is just down the street, it's a lovely walk from here into Mitte.

Budget

Lette'm Sleep Hostel

Lettestrasse 7 (4473 3623, www.backpackers.de). U2 Eberswalder Strasse. **Map** p307 P2.

Just off Helmholtzplatz, this small hostel has new floors and bathrooms, and a beer garden in the back for summer barbecues. Free tea and coffee are provided, but not breakfast – so you can either make it yourself in the kitchen or visit one of the many decent cafés around the corner. All rooms have hand basins, and hot showers are always available. Each of the three large apartments sleeps up to ten people, and there are reduced rates for longer stays.

Transit Loft

Immanuelkirchstrasse 14A (4849 3773, www. transit-loft.de). Tram M2, M4. **Map** p307 Q4.

This loft hotel in a renovated factory is ideal for backpackers and young travellers. All the rooms have en suite bathrooms, and there's a private sauna, gym and billiard room with special rates for hotel guests. Staff are friendly and well informed, and there's good wheelchair access too.

FRIEDRICHSHAIN

Friedrichshain hasn't quite panned out as the city's new bohemia, but with decent transport connections, a still somewhat 'Eastie' alternative feel, good cafés and lots of nightlife, it continues to be a great area to stay in, especially if you're on a tight budget.

Moderate

Almodovar Hotel

Boxhagener Strasse 83 (692 097 080, www. almodovarhotel.com). U5 Samariterstrasse. **Map** p324 T1.

This new boutique hotel is 'Berlin' through and through: fully vegetarian, with organic products

Michelberger.

in the rooms and even a complimentary yoga mat. Rooms are bright and spacious, and the penthouse suite even boasts its own sauna – but there's also a spa with ayurvedic treatments that's available to all guests. The lovely rosewood furniture was sustainably made specifically for the hotel.

★ Michelberger

Warschauer Strasse 39-40 (2977 8590, www.michelbergerhotel.com). U1, S5, S7, S75 Warschauer Strasse. **Map** p312 S8.

With its purposefully unfinished look and effortlessly creative vibe, Michelberger might seem like Berlin in a nutshell to some. While the cheaper rooms are characterised by a stylish simplicity reminiscent of a school gym, the pricier rooms have an air of tongue-in-cheek decadence – decked out in gold from floor to ceiling or in the style of a mountain resort – complete with sunken bathtubs and movie projectors. Michelberger might not be as spotlessly clean as other hotels (though it's far from being dirty), but it's much more fun. The downside of the convenient location (right across from Warschauer Strasse U-Bahn station) is that some rooms are quite noisy; the quieter ones face the courtyard.

Nhow

Stralauer Allee 3 (290 2990, www.nhow-hotels. com). U1, S5, S7, S75 Warschauer Strasse. **Map** p312 S9.

If you're allergic to pink, you'd be well advised to check in elsewhere. In a huge modern building right by the River Spree, New York designer Karim Rashid

has implemented his eye-popping vision of a music and lifestyle hotel. Even the elevators are illuminated by different coloured lights, and some are decorated with photos of Rashid and his wife. As you'd expect from a music hotel, all rooms are equipped with iPod docking stations, and if you're in the mood for a spontaneous jam, you can order a Gibson guitar or an electric piano up to your room. The river view is beautiful and the breakfast buffet leaves no wish unfulfilled. There's a pleasant sauna too.

Budget

Eastern Comfort

Mühlenstrasse 73-77 (6676 3806, www.eastern-comfort.com). U1, S5, S7, S75 Warschauer Strasse. **Map** p312 R8.

Berlin's first 'hostel boat' is moored on the Spree by the East Side Hotel, across the river from Kreuzberg. The rooms – or, rather, cabins – are clean and fairly spacious (considering it's a boat), and all have their own shower and toilet. The four-person room can feel a little cramped, but if you need to get up and stretch there are two common rooms, a lounge and three terraces offering lovely river views. The owners have now done up a second boat, the Western Comfort, which is moored across the river on the Kreuzberg bank.

Industriepalast Hostel

Warschauer Strasse 43 (7407 8290, www.ip-hostel.com). U1, S5, S7, S75 Warschauer Strasse. **No credit cards. Map** p312 S8.

This vast red-brick hostel on bleak Warschauer Strasse, next to Michelberger (*see p272*), was once an industrial works. Renovated in a pleasingly functional and colourful way, it's a popular spot. With 400 beds over 90 rooms, accommodation options are manifold, from dorms to an entire apartment, plus a disabled-access room. A good choice if you're after a clean, warm bed and a cheery atmosphere.

Ostel Das DDR Design Hostel

Wriezener Karree 5 (2576 8660, www.ostel.eu). S5, S7, S75 Ostbahnhof. **Map** p312 R7.

The four clocks on the wall read: Berlin, Moscow, Peking and Havana. There's a stern-looking poster of Erich Honecker on the wall. But there's no political message at this budget East German-themed hostel: just a cheap bed for the night. For an additional €3.50, guests are given a *Lebensmittelmarke* (food-ration coupon) for breakfast at the Ossi Hof pub out front. And for those who just can't get enough of *Ostalgie* (nostalgia for the East), there's a hotel *Konsum* (state-run market), which sells everything from plaster egg cups to chocolate DDR coins. There's even a rare roll of original toilet paper – but it's not for sale. Nearby is the Ostel's DDR-Ferienwohnung (holiday apartment), which sleeps up to six in DDR style, with everything from TV to washing machine, great views and a Trabant-driven tour of the city.

TIERGARTEN

Tiergarten is now officially part of Mitte, but don't tell the locals. There are a few notable establishments dotting the edges of the park that gives the district its name, as well as big modern embassies and a complex of cultural institutions located by the New National Gallery – and rising like a plasticky Oz beyond it, the glitz and glare of Potsdamer Platz.

Deluxe

Grand Hyatt Berlin

Marlene-Dietrich-Platz 2 (2553 1234, www.berlin. grand.hyatt.com). U2, S1, S2, S25 Potsdamer Platz. **Map** p310 K8.

This is a classy joint, just far enough off the beaten tourist path to keep its cool. The lobby is all matt black and sleek wood panelling – a refreshing change from the usual five-star marble or country villa look. The rooms, which are decorated without a floral print in sight, are spacious and elegant; the internet TV is also a nice touch. The rooftop spa and gym has a splendid swimming pool with views across the city. The sushi restaurant, Vox, is one of the best places to enjoy fresh fish in the city.

InterContinental Berlin

Budapester Strasse 2 (260 20, www.berlin. intercontinental.com). U2, U9, S5, S7, S75 Zoologischer Garten. **Map** p309 H8.

The extremely plush and spacious 'Interconti' exudes luxury. The airy lobby, with its soft leather chairs, is ideal for browsing the papers, and the rooms, overlooking the zoo and western edges of the new diplomatic quarter, are large and tastefully decorated, right down to the elegant bathrooms. Thomas Kammeier, Berlin master chef, whips up Michelin-starred marvels with a view at the restaurant Hugos (*see p106*), while the huge gym and spa has everything a body could possibly need to exercise off the meal.

Mandala

Potsdamer Strasse 3 (590 050 000, www.the mandala.de). U2, S1, S2, S25 Potsdamer Platz. **Map** p310 L7.

This privately owned addition to the Design Hotels portfolio is, given the address, an oasis of calm, luxury and taste. The 144 rooms and suites, most of which face their glass walls upon an inner courtyard, are perfectly designed for space and light, decorated in warm whites and beiges, with comfortable

Nhow.

minimalist furnishings and TVs. A sheltered path through the Japanese garden on the fifth floor leads to Facil (*see p106*), the ultra-modern restaurant that was awarded its second Michelin star in 2013. The Qiu lounge offers lighter fare, and the rooftop spa, windowed from end to end, offers spectacular city views. Reduced rates are available for longer stays.

Ritz-Carlton
Potsdamer Platz 3 (337 777, www.ritzcarlton.com). U2, S1, S2, S25 Potsdamer Platz. **Map** p310 L7.
It's flashy, it's trashy, it's Vegas-meets-Versailles. The Ritz-Carlton is so chock-a-block with black marble, gold taps and taffeta curtains that the rooms seem somewhat stuffy, small and cramped. It's supposedly art deco in style, but feels more like a Dubai shopping mall. Still, the oyster and lobster restaurant is deliciously decadent, and the service is fantastic: the technology butler will sort out the bugs in your computer connection, and the bath butler will run your tub. Bring a fat wallet and get ready to be pampered. The Curtain Club cocktail bar even has a perfume-matching menu.

★ Das Stue
Drakestrasse 1 (311 7220, www.das-stue.com). S5, S7, S75 Tiergarten. **Map** p309 H7.
The newest (and hippest) member of Berlin's luxury hotel family, Das Stue has restored the 1930s Royal Danish Embassy to its former splendour with the help of Spanish designer Patricia Urquiola. There's a long list of reasons to stay at this Design Hotel,

including a pearl-white spa, rooms overlooking the Tiergarten, the original three-storey library, and the Michelin-starred Cinco restaurant (*see p105*) with a menu provided by superstar Catalan chef Paco Pérez. The central location means it's a short walk to most of Berlin's major sights. Some rooms overlook Berlin Zoo, with binoculars provided for close-up views of your four-legged neighbours.

Expensive

Sheraton Berlin Grand Hotel Esplanade
Lützowufer 15 (254 780, www.esplanade.de). U1, U2, U3, U4 Nollendorfplatz. **Map** p310 J8.
With an entry wall of gushing water lit overhead by glittering lights, this is one of Berlin's better luxury hotels, overlooking the Landwehr Canal and close to the Tiergarten. The lobby is equally grand, spacious and beautifully decorated, while the rooms are tasteful and gratifyingly free of frilly decor. There's also a fitness centre and a triangular swimming pool, plus three restaurants to choose from. Just as important is the fact that it's within stumble-back-to-bed distance of Harry's New York Bar on the ground floor.

CHARLOTTENBURG

This is the smart end of town, with fine dining and elegant shopping, and where five-star luxury hotels sit happily alongside the traditional charms of pensions housed in grand 19th-century Gründerzeit townhouses.

Das Stue.

25hours Hotel Bikini Berlin.

Deluxe

Waldorf Astoria Berlin
Hardenbergstrasse 28 (814 0000, www.waldorf astoriaberlin.com). U2, U9, S5, S7, S75 Zoologischer Garten. **Map** p309 G8.

Part of the regeneration of the area surrounding Zoo station (which includes Hotel Bikini Berlin, *see below*), is this 32-storey skyscraper. Completed in 2013, it houses Germany's first Waldorf Astoria hotel, one of the most valuable brands in the Hilton empire. The decor leaves a little to be desired – only the Lang bar truly reflects the desired art deco aesthetic, with the rooms being quite bland and corporate – but the Michelin-starred Pierre Gagnaire restaurant, Les Solistes (*see p117*), is already one of the best in the city. The hotel boasts all the usual five-star amenities, as well as unrivalled city views from the top-floor suites and an award-winning Guerlain spa. Extras can add up though – Wi-Fi access costs €25 a day and breakfast is a whopping €36.

Expensive

★ 25hours Hotel Bikini Berlin
Budapester Strasse 40 (120 2210, www.25hours-hotels.com). U2, U9, S5, S7, S75 Zoologischer Garten. **Map** p309 G8.

Breathing new life into the iconic 1950s Bikini-Haus office block that adjoins the Tiergarten, the revamped shopping mall also features a 149-room branch of Design Hotels' funky 25hours brand. The design is a mix of exposed brick and industrial lighting, plenty of greenery and brightly coloured furnishings. There's great attention to detail, such as rooms that come with window-side hammocks, free Mini rental and the fab Middle Eastern restaurant Neni (*see p116*). The West is finally getting hip.

Art Nouveau Berlin
Leibnitzstrasse 59 (327 7440, www.hotelart nouveau.de). U7 Adenauerplatz, or S5, S7, S75 Savignyplatz. **Map** p309 E8.

This is one of the most charming small hotels in Berlin. The rooms are decorated with flair, in a mix of Conran-modern and antique furniture, each with an enormous black and white photo hung by the bed. The en suite bathrooms are cleverly integrated into the rooms without disrupting the elegant townhouse architecture. Even the TVs are stylish. The breakfast room has a fridge full of goodies, should you feel peckish in the wee hours, and the staff are sweet.

Bleibtreu
Bleibtreustrasse 31 (884 740, www.bleibtreu.com). U1 Uhlandstrasse, or S5, S7, S75 Savignyplatz. **Map** p309 E9.

The Bleibtreu is a friendly, smart and cosy establishment popular with the media and fashion crowds. Although on the smaller side, the rooms are all very modern, and decorated with environmentally sound materials. The restaurant is famed for its no-sugar menu, and there's also Deli 31 for a bagel and coffee. Private yoga classes are offered, as well as reflexology. A wonderful choice for the health-conscious, certainly, but good service with lots of pampering and attention means it should appeal to anyone.

Ellington
Nürnberger Strasse 50-55 (683 150, www. ellington-hotel.com). U1, U2, U3 Wittenbergplatz, or U3 Augsburger Strasse. **Map** p309 G9.

This is one of the classiest, most sophisticated joints in Berlin. Hidden within the shell of a landmark art deco dance hall, it combines cool contemporary elegance with warmth and ease. The rooms, mostly white with polished wood accents, are brilliantly simple, with modern free-standing fixtures and half-walls, and absolute calm behind the original double windows. The staff are helpful and remarkably cheerful given the daft flat caps they're made to wear. An ambitious menu is served in the Duke restaurant, and there are Sunday jazz brunches in the central courtyard. All this and KaDeWe around the corner… the Duke himself would have been proud.
▶ *For more about shopping at KaDeWe, see p118.*

Kempinski Hotel Bristol Berlin

Kurfürstendamm 27 (884 340, www.
kempinskiberlin.de). U1, U9 Kurfürstendamm.
Map p309 F8.

This famous Berlin hotel was first a celebrated restaurant before being rebuilt in its present form in 1951. While the rooms aren't as plush as you might expect at these prices, the grand atmosphere, friendly staff, original Berlin artwork, wonderful pool and saunas make up for it. A newish restaurant, Reinhard's, has added a regional menu to the proceedings, or you can try the dubious-sounding 'Currywurst with a twist' at the Kempinski Grill.

Savoy Hotel Berlin

Fasanenstrasse 9-10 (311 030, www.hotel-savoy.
com). U2, U9, S5, S7, S75 Zoologischer Garten.
Map p309 F8.

Erected in 1929, and a favourite of author Thomas Mann, this is a smart, stylish hotel with lots of low-key flair. The rooms are elegant and understated, but the suites jazz it up a bit, such as the white Greta Garbo suite and black marble Henry Miller suite. The Weinrot restaurant serves a well-thought-out modern menu. A further bonus is the location, set back just far enough from the hustle and bustle of Zoologischer Garten to be quiet and convenient.

Sofitel Berlin Kurfürstendamm

Augsburger Strasse 41 (800 9990, www.
sofitel.com). U1, U9 Kurfürstendamm.
Map p309 G8.

Designed by Berlin architect Jan Kleihues, this five-star establishment changed hands from the French Concorde hotel group to Sofitel, another French luxury hotel chain. It's grandly proportioned, with a refreshingly minimalist and contemporary approach resembling the bow of an ocean liner. The 311 rooms (including 44 huge suites) are decorated in warm woods and colour tones, with intimate lighting and modern art, to elegant and understated effect. The Restaurant Saint Germain will serve your breakfast, the Brasserie Le Faubourg your French dinner – after cocktails in the Lutèce Bar – and for those staying in the suites, there's even an 'Executive' Club Sofitel on the top floors offering a wonderful panorama of the city. The complimentary gym and sauna may come in handy after all this indulgence.

Moderate

Berlin Plaza

Knesebeckstrasse 62 (884 130, www.plazahotel.de).
U1 Uhlandstrasse. **Map** p309 F9.

Despite a rather plain minimalist decor and colour scheme in the rooms, there's an understated poshness about the Plaza. All double rooms, and even some singles, have both a shower and bath. The restaurant and bar serve regional German specialities, and the breakfast buffet is excellent. Under-13s can stay with parents for free.

Hotel-Pension Dittberner

Wielandstrasse 26 (884 6950, www.hotel-
dittberner.de). U7 Adenauerplatz, or S5, S7,
S75 Savignyplatz. **Map** p309 E9.

From the ride up the 1911 elevator and into the sitting room, this is a grand place, stylish and eclectic, and an obvious labour of love. It's filled with fine original artworks, enormous chandeliers and handsome furnishings. Everywhere, including the beautiful breakfast room, is airy and elegant, and some of the rooms and suites are truly palatial (one has a winter garden around the courtyard, for example). But the main draw here is comfort. Frau Lange, the owner, is friendly and helpful, and goes out of her way to make her guests feel at home. Truly one of the best pensions in the city.

Midi Inn City West

Wielandstrasse 26 (885 7010, http://kudamm.
midi-inn.de). U7 Adenauerplatz, or S5, S7, S75
Savignyplatz. **Map** p309 E9.

Just one floor below the Dittberner (*see above*), this thoroughly unassuming 19-room pension is charming, sweet and nicely priced. The mainly white rooms, with stripped floorboards or parquet, are calm, and the atmosphere is relaxed. Staff are very friendly, accommodating and speak English. A top choice if you're travelling as part of a group and want to be in the West End. Added bonus: the price gets lower the longer you stay.

Budget

JETpak Flashpacker

Pariserstrasse 58 (784 4360, www.jetpak
berlin.com). U1, U2, U3, U9 Spichernstrasse.
Map p309 F9.

A great choice for those wishing to strike camp in the heart of West Berlin, not far from the shopping mecca of Ku'damm and the charming jumble of cafés, bars and boutiques of Savignyplatz. This clean, well-equipped 'upmarket' edition of Berlin's three JETpak hostels is definitely the best of the bunch and especially recommended for couples on a budget. Staff are known for their friendly, helpful attitude (not always a given in Berlin).
Other locations JETpak Alternative, Görlitzer Strasse 38, Kreuzberg (6290 8641); JETpak Ecolodge, Pücklerstrasse 54, Grunewald (832 5011).

★ Hotel Pension Funk

Fasanenstrasse 69 (882 7193, www.hotel-pensionfunk.de). U1 Uhlandstrasse.
Map p309 F9.

In the area around the Gedächtniskirche, not a lot is left of the charm and glamour that made the Ku'damm the most legendary street of pre-war Berlin. That makes this wonderful pension, which is hidden away on a quiet side street, a real gem. The house, built in 1895, used to be home to the Danish silent movie star Asta Nielsen and has been lovingly restored. The 14 rooms have elegant dark wood furniture and art deco detailing, and everything is spotless. The owner has done his best to make the bathrooms match modern standards without destroying the overall feel – in one room, the bathroom is hidden inside a replica of an antique wardrobe – but some fall slightly short of the standards you would expect from a newer hotel. However, the very reasonable prices make up for this. And the breakfast served in the cosy dining room is as good as anywhere more expensive.

Pension-Gudrun

Bleibtreustrasse 17 (881 6462, www.pension-gudrun-berlin.de). S5, S7, S75 Savignyplatz.
No credit cards. Map p309 E8.

This simple, tiny pension has huge rooms and friendly, helpful owners who speak English, French, Arabic and German. The rooms are decorated with lovely turn-of-the-century Berlin furniture, and for families or small groups, it's a marvellous deal.

WILMERSDORF

Wilmersdorf may not be the most interesting of areas, but it does play host to Berlin's most decadent luxury hotel (Schlosshotel im Grunewald Berlin), its most discreet hotel (Brandenburger Hof Hotel), its coolest designer hotel (Ku'Damm 101) and its wackiest hotel (Propeller Island).

Deluxe

Brandenburger Hof Hotel

Eislebener Strasse 14 (214 050, www.brandenburger-hof.com). U1, U9 Kurfürstendamm, or U3 Augsburger Strasse. **Map** p309 G9.

This discreet, privately owned gem, tucked down a quiet street behind KaDeWe, is the epitome of modern luxury without the stuffiness. Staff are friendly, and the 72 rooms, all done out in a contemporary-elegant style, are warm and relaxing. There's a beautiful Japanese garden in the middle, surrounded by individually decorated salons available for meetings and special occasions. Chef Bobby Bräuer helms the Quadriga restaurant, famous for its extensive German wine cellar. For a real treat, however, avail yourself of the hotel's 'Exquisit Program', which includes limousine service from the airport, flowers, afternoon tea and open bar till 6.30pm. Highly recommended.

★ Schlosshotel im Grunewald Berlin

Brahmsstrasse 10 (895 840, www.schlosshotel berlin.com). S7 Grunewald. **Map** p308 A12.

Designed down to the dust ruffles by Karl Lagerfeld, this restored 1914 villa on the edge of Grunewald is a luxury that mere mortals can only dream of. There are 12 suites and 54 rooms with elegant marble bathrooms, a limousine and butler service, and well-trained staff to scurry after you. R&R is well covered too, with a swimming pool, a golf course, tennis courts and two restaurants (with summer dining on the lawn, of course). This is a beautiful place,

Hotel Pension Funk.

ESSENTIAL INFORMATION

Schlosshotel im Grunewald Berlin. See p277.

in a beautiful setting, but so exclusive that it might as well be on another planet. It's worth checking the internet for deals, nonetheless.

Expensive

Ku'Damm 101

Kurfürstendamm 101 (520 0550, www.kudamm 101.com). U7 Adenauerplatz, or S41, S42, S45, S46 Halensee. **Map** p308 C9.

This hotel is a huge hit with style-conscious travellers. The lobby, created by Berlin designers Vogt and Weizenegger, is enjoyably more funk than functional, while the 170 rooms, with lino floors and Le Corbusier colour palette, were designed by Franziska Kessler, whose mantra is clarity and calm. There's also a breakfast garden terrace, and the Lounge 101 is good for daytime snacks or a late-night cocktail.

Moderate

Propeller Island City Lodge

Albrecht Achilles Strasse 58 (891 9016, www.propeller-island.com). U7 Adenauerplatz. **Map** p308 D9.

More than just a hotel, Propeller Island City Lodge is a work of art. Artist-owner Lars Stroschen has created 32 incredible rooms, each themed, and decorated like jaw-dropping theatre sets. The Flying Room, for example, has tilted walls and floors, and a large bed seemingly suspended in air. The Therapy Room, all in white with soft, furry walls, has adjustable coloured lights to change with your mood. While each room has six channels of piped-in music, they also have more functional mod cons such as room service and phones. Reservations can be made via the website, where you can view each room, then choose your favourite three.

SCHÖNEBERG

This very pleasant leafy area is full of cafés, restaurants and shops, as well as the traditional gay area of Nollendorfplatz, but has a dearth of decent accommodation. You're better off staying further east in Kreuzberg.

Moderate

Axel Hotel Berlin

Lietzenburger Strasse 13-15 (2100 2893, www. axelhotels.com). U1, U2, U3 Wittenbergplatz. **Map** p309 H9.

Describing itself as 'hetero-friendly', this hotel is part of a chain catering towards the LGBT market. Sleek, modern rooms decked out in in glass and black walls are comfortable and spotless, plus it's on the doorstep of gay Schöneberg with plenty of saunas, bars and shops within walking distance.

Lindemanns

Potsdamer Strasse 171-173 (526 854 909, www. lindemanns-hotel.de). U7 Kleistpark. **Map** p310 J10.

The strict monochrome palette in rooms here can become monotonous, but they are well proportioned, with big windows and some even have circular tubs. The hotel itself is efficiently run and is the perfect base for gallery-hopping in the new art hotspot of Potsdamer Strasse.

KREUZBERG

The former centre of (West) Berlin's alternative scene, Kreuzberg has some of the city's most picturesque streets, liveliest markets, best bars and most interesting alternative venues. The area around Schlesisches Tor is a particular party hotspot.

Expensive

Riehmers Hofgarten

Yorckstrasse 83 (7809 8800, www.hotel-riehmers-hofgarten.de). U6, U7 Mehringdamm. **Map** p310 M10.

In a historic building with one of Berlin's prettiest courtyards, this is a wonderful hotel. The 22 exquisitely styled rooms are airy and elegant (the furniture was custom-designed), the staff are charming, and Thomas Kurt, the larger-than-life chef at the hotel restaurant, e.t.a. hoffmann, is widely praised. Although the location is somewhat off the beaten track, the neighbourhood has many charms of its own, with Victoria Park and Bergmannstrasse's shops and cafés nearby. Reasonably priced for what you get, and recommended.

Moderate

Johann

Johanniterstrasse 8 (225 0740, www.hotel-johann-berlin.de). U1, U6 Hallesches Tor. **Map** p311 N9.

This spotlessly clean – if slightly utilitarian – hotel is located in the sleepiest bit of Kreuzberg, one block from the canal and the great Brachvogel beer garden. It's a ten-minute stroll to the Jewish Museum and a pleasant 20-minute walk by the water to reach the restaurants and bars of eastern Kreuzberg. The rooms are big and airy; some (like room 301 – the pick

Die Fabrik.

of the crop) retain original arched ceilings that date from the building's original use as an army barracks in the 19th century. The simple buffet breakfast can be taken in the lovely courtyard and there's also an honesty bar. The owners, Rainer and Katrin, provide free cots for babies, and most rooms can accommodate a third bed.

Budget

★ Die Fabrik

Schlesische Strasse 18 (611 7116, www.diefabrik. com). U1 Schlesisches Tor. **No credit cards**. **Map** p312 R9.

Smack bang in the middle of a newly invigorated Schlesische Strasse, this former telephone factory (hence the name) with turn-of-the-century charm intact, has 50 clean and comfortable no-frills rooms. There's no kitchen, no TV and no billiards. Just a bed and a locker. But with a café next door for breakfast, and plenty of restaurants, bars and galleries nearby, you don't need much more. It also produces its own solar-powered heating and hot water, and the bed-linen is free.

★ Grand Hostel

Tempelhofer Ufer 14 (2009 5450, www. grandhostel-berlin.de). U1, U7 Möckernbrücke. **Map** p310 M9.

This fantastic hostel is located in a suitably grand 19th-century building with high ceilings and plenty of period character. The rooms are spacious and spotless, and there are no bunks, even in the dorms, just comfy real beds with good-quality linen. There are bikes for hire, and the cheerful, well-informed staff know everything from the best kebab shops in Berlin to where to do karaoke on a Wednesday. The only possible downer is that it's situated in one of the less happening parts of Kreuzberg, albeit with great transport links to the hotspots.

Lekker Urlaub

Graefestrasse 89 (3730 6434, www.lekkerurlaub. de). U8 Schonleinstrasse. **No credit cards**. **Map** p311 P10.

This charming bijoux B&B is in one of the prettiest and buzziest bits of Kreuzberg. Set on the ground floor of a typical Berlin tenement, the rooms are small but clean. Each is unique: the bed in one is only reachable by a ladder, so avoid if you're scared of heights. The lovely café attached serves meals from 9am to 6pm and even accepts payment by Bitcoin, but there are also dozens of bars and restaurants within a two-minute radius.

Motel One Berlin-Mitte

Prinzenstrasse 40 (7007 9800, www.motel-one. com). U8 Moritzplatz. **Map** p311 O8.

Who'd have thought that such a seemingly anonymous chain could produce such a smart hotel? The 180 rooms, relatively recently remodelled and

ESSENTIAL INFORMATION

refreshed, are basic but done with flair: check out the large dark wood headboards, flat-screen TVs and modern free-standing sinks. Even the appliqué on the curtains and pillows is bearable. Your dog can enjoy it as well for only €5 a night extra. Throw in the bargain rates and top location (in Kreuzberg, despite the name) and you have a winner.

Rock 'n' Roll Herberge
Muskauer Strasse 11 (6162 3600, www.rnr herberge.de). U1 Görlitzer Bahnhof. **No credit cards.** **Map** p311 Q9.
As the name suggests, this budget hotel is aimed particularly at bands on tour and for music lovers to feel at home. It's a great place, on a quiet stretch just blocks from the main drags of Kreuzberg. The downstairs rooms are small, but some have bathrooms. Staff are friendly, there's a Currywurst party every Thursday with vegan and vegetarian sausages, and the bar-restaurant is popular with colourful locals. Extras include free Wi-Fi.

Transit
Hagelberger Strasse 53-54 (789 0470, www.hotel-transit.de). U6, U7 Mehringdamm. **Map** p310 M10.
Located in one of the most beautiful parts of Kreuzberg, this former factory is now a bright and airy hotel with 49 basic but clean rooms, each with a shower and toilet. There's also a 24-hour bar, and the staff speak good English. With Victoria Park around the block and a wealth of bars, cafés and restaurants in the area, it's often full – so it's wise to book ahead. Women-only dorms are also available.

NEUKÖLLN

For all sorts of hip newcomers, this is the place to be in today's Berlin, where artisan espresso bars, late-night cocktail bars and living-room galleries

have sprouted in the past few years. The influx has been met with a huge increase in subletting and Airbnb usage – which has got residents increasingly irritated. Most accommodation options here are still very affordable.

Budget

Cat's Pajamas Hostel
Urbanstrasse 64 (6162 0534, www.thecats pajamas hostel.com). U7, U8 Hermannplatz. **Map** p311 P10.
A brand-new, light and airy hostel, with new wooden furniture and en suite bathrooms throughout its dorms and private rooms. The location is extremely convenient too, in the middle of Kreuzkölln and a direct metro ride from Schönefeld airport.

Hüttenpalast
Hobrechtstrasse 65-66 (3730 5806, www. huettenpalast.de). U7, U8 Hermannplatz. **Map** p311 Q10.
The Hüttenpalast (literally 'Cabin Palace') is a large hall that was once the factory floor of an old vacuum cleaner company. Since 2011, it's been home to three vintage caravans and three little cabins, each sleeping two people. It's set out like a mini indoor campsite, with separate male and female shower rooms and a tree in the middle. Each morning, guests emerge from their boltholes to discover the tree has borne fruit – well, little bags containing croissants. There's fresh coffee on hand and the streetfront café does an à la carte menu for those with particularly grumbling stomachs. Each caravan is different – Kleine Schwester (Little Sister) is decked out with white wood panelling and matching linen; the Herzensbrecher (Heartbreaker) has a domed metal ceiling; the Schwalbennest (Swallow's Nest) is big enough to squeeze in a table. If you're at all

Hüttenpalast.

claustrophobic, the huts, each one unique in design and decoration, are slightly better – but they also have regular rooms of varying sizes. Free Wi-Fi too.

Rixpack Hostel

Karl-Marx-Strasse 75 (5471 5140, www.rixpack. de). U7 Rathaus Neukölln. **Map** p311 Q11.
Located near the lovely medieval village of Rixdorf, this hostel was one of the first in the area. It's a no-frills affair with metallic bunk beds and industrial carpeting, and one room fitted into the back of an old firetruck. It's about as cheap as it gets.

Scube Parks

Columbiadamm 160 (6980 7841, www.scubepark. berlin). U8 Boddinstrasse. **Map** p311 P12.
The irritating attempt to make 'Scubeing' a verb aside, this is an interesting alternative to a hostel, with 30 Scubes laid out over a couple of square kilometres of greenery behind the Hasenheide park. Essentially a wooden hut, each Scube comes with two to four beds (and bedding), electrical outlets, windows and not much else. There's a cosy common room with shower and also a shared kitchen.

OTHER DISTRICTS
Moderate

Hotel Benn

Ritterstrasse 1A, Spandau (353 9270, www.hotel-benn.de). U7 Altstadt Spandau.
This sweet little hotel is situated smack dab in the middle of Spandau's beautiful old town in a 16th-century red-brick townhouse. The decor isn't exactly period, but it's full of light and the furnishings are comfortable enough. A generous breakfast buffet and free Wi-Fi are bonuses.

Hotel De France

Müllerstrasse 74, Wedding (417 290, www.hotel-francais-berlin.de). U6 Ruhrberge.
There's very little Parisian glamour about this functional business hotel: the only things relating to its name are the brasserie seats in the restaurant and a crude Eiffel Tower replica in the garden. Located near the Centre Français de Berlin with its cinema and meeting rooms, it's still cheap and relatively cheerful.

CAMPING

If you want to explore the campsites of Berlin or surrounding Brandenburg, ask for a camping map from one of the **VisitBerlin** information offices (*see p292*). The campsites are far out of the city, so check timetables for last buses if you want to enjoy the city's nightlife. Prices don't vary much between sites: for tents, you'll pay about €5; for caravans about €8 (plus around €6.50 per person). More information can be obtained from the Deutscher Camping Club.

Landesverband des Deutscher Camping Club

Kladower Damm 213-217, Gatow 14089 (218 6071, 218 6072, www.dccberlin.de). **Open** 10.30am-6pm Mon; 8am-4pm Wed; 8am-1pm Fri.

YOUTH HOSTELS

As well as the hostels listed by area above, there are three official YHA hostels in Berlin: **Jugendgästehaus-International** (261 1097), **Jugendgästehaus am Wannsee** (803 2034) and **Jugendherberge Ernst Reuter** (404 1610). All have single-sex dormitories. They're rammed most of the year, so you'll need to reserve in advance.

You can book online or call the hostels directly. You have to be a member of the YHA to stay in them; to obtain a membership card, go to the Mitgliederservice des DJH Berlin International (also known as the Jugend-Zentrale). Take your passport and a passport-sized photo. Junior membership (under-26s) costs €12.50; family membership is €21. Individual hostels also have a day membership deal – an extra €3.10 per day.

Mitgliederservice des DJH Berlin International

Kluckstrasse 3, Tiergarten (261 1097, www. jh-berlin-international.de). U1, U7 Möckernbrücke, or U1, U2 Gleisdreieck. **Open** 24hrs daily. **Map** p310 L9.

LONGER STAYS

For a longer stay, try calling a *Mitwohnagentur* (flat-seeking agency). Agencies listed below can find you a room in a shared house or furnished flat for anything from a week to a couple of years. Start looking at least a month ahead, especially at holiday times. This is all private accommodation: you will be living in someone's home.

If you're staying for a couple of weeks and find something through a *Mitwohnagentur*, you will probably pay €50-€80 a night. For longer stays, agencies charge different rates. Ask for the total figure, including fees, before booking. You can also book direct, via Airbnb or similar websites (*see p276* **In the Know**).

Erste Mitwohnzentrale

Prenzlauer Allee 52, Prenzlauer Berg (324 3031, www.mitwohn.com). U2 Eberswalder Strasse, or tram M10. **Open** 9am-7pm Mon-Fri; 10am-3pm Sat. **No credit cards. Map** p309 E8.

HomeCompany

Bundesallee 34-40, Charlottenburg (194 45, www.homecompany.de). U9 Güntzelstrasse. **Open** 9am-6pm Mon-Thur; 9am-5pm Fri; 9am-1pm Sat. **Map** p309 G10.

Getting Around

ARRIVING & LEAVING

By air

The new **Berlin Brandenburg Willy Brandt Airport (BER)** should have opened some years ago. But, following years of confusion and controversy, no one seems to know exactly when it will open, with current estimates stretching to 2018 and beyond. Until then, Berlin remains served by two airports: **Tegel** and **Schönefeld**. Information in English on all airports (including live departures and arrivals) can be found at www.berlin-airport.de. Both Tegel and Schönefeld are likely to close as soon as BER opens, just south of the Schönefeld site.

Flughafen Tegel (TXL)

Airport information 0180 5000 186, www.berlin-airport.de. **Open** 4am-midnight daily. **Map** p304 C1.
The more upmarket scheduled flights from the likes of BA and Lufthansa use the compact Tegel airport, just 8km (5 miles) north-west of Mitte.
  Buses 109 and **X9** (the express version) run via Luisenplatz and the Kurfürstendamm to Zoologischer Garten (also known as Zoo Station, Bahnof Zoo or just Zoo) in western Berlin. Buses run every 5-15 minutes, and the journey takes 30-40 minutes. Tickets cost €2.70 (and can also be used on U-Bahn and S-Bahn services). At Zoo you can connect to anywhere in the city.
  From the airport, you can also take bus 109 to Jacob-Kaiser-Platz U-Bahn (U7), or bus 128 to Kurt-Schumacher-Platz U-Bahn (U6), and proceed on the underground from there. One ticket (€2.70) can be used for the combined journey.
  The **JetExpressBusTXL** is the direct link to Berlin Hauptbahnhof and Mitte. It runs from Tegel to Alexanderplatz, with useful stops at Beusselstrasse S-Bahn (connects with the Ringbahn), Berlin Hauptbahnhof (regional and inter-city train services as well as the S-Bahn), Unter den Linden S-Bahn (north and south trains on the S1 and S2 lines). The service runs every 10 or 20 minutes, 4.30am-12.30am (5.30am-12.30am at weekends) and takes 30-40 minutes; a ticket is €2.70.

A **taxi** to anywhere central will cost around €20-€25 and take 20-30 minutes.

Flughafen Schönefeld (SXF)

Airport information 0180 5000 186, www.berlin-airport.de. **Open** 24hrs daily.
The former airport of East Berlin is 18km (11 miles) south-east of the city centre. It's small, and much of the traffic is to eastern Europe and the Middle East. Budget airlines from the UK and Ireland also use it – EasyJet flies in from Bristol, Gatwick, Glasgow, Liverpool, Luton and Manchester; Ryanair from Dublin, East Midlands, Edinburgh and Stansted.
  Train is the best means of reaching the city centre. S-Bahn Flughafen Schönefeld is a five-minute walk from the terminal (a free S-Bahn shuttle bus runs every ten minutes, 6am-10pm, from outside the terminal; at other times, bus 171 also runs to the station). From here, the **Airport Express train** runs to Mitte (25 minutes to Alexanderplatz), Berlin Hauptbahnhof (30 minutes) and Zoo (35 minutes) every half hour from 5am to 11.30pm. You can also take S-Bahn line **S9**, which runs into the centre every 20 minutes (40 minutes to Alexanderplatz, 50 minutes to Zoo), stopping at all stations along the way. The **S45** line from Schönefeld connects with the Ringbahn, also running every 20 minutes.
  Bus X7, every 10 or 20 minutes, 4.30am-8pm, runs non-stop from the airport to Rudow U-Bahn (U7), from where you can connect with the underground. This is a good option if you're staying in Kreuzberg, Neukölln or Schöneberg. When it's not running, bus 171 takes the same route.
  Tickets from the airport to the city cost €3.30, and can be used on any combination of bus, U-Bahn, S-Bahn and tram.
  A **taxi** to Zoo or Mitte is quite expensive (€30-€35) and takes around 45 minutes.

Flughafen Berlin Brandenburg Willy Brandt (BER)

www.berlin-airport.de.
The airport's operators promise a fast train shuttle that will transport passengers to the city centre in just 20 minutes.

Airlines

Air Berlin *0180 573 7800, www.airberlin.com.*
Air France *0180 583 0830, www.airfrance.de.*
Alitalia *0180 507 4747, www.alitalia.de.*
British Airways *0180 526 6522, www.britishairways.com.*
EasyJet *01805 666 000, www.easyjet.com.*
German Wings *0906 294 1918, www.germanwings.com.*
Iberia *0180 544 2900, www.iberia.com.*
Lufthansa *01803 803 803, www.lufthansa.de.*
Ryanair *0900 116 0500, www.ryanair.com.*

By rail

Berlin Hauptbahnhof
0180 599 6633, www.bahn.de. **Map** p306 K5.
Berlin's central station is the main point of arrival for all long-distance trains, with the exceptions of night trains from Moscow and Kiev, which usually start and end at Berlin Lichtenberg (S5, S7, S75).
  Hauptbahnhof is inconveniently located in a no-man's land north of the government quarter, and is linked to the rest of the city by S-Bahn (S5, S7, S9, S75), and by the new U55 underground line that runs to the Bundestag and, in 2016, the Brandenburger Tor only (connecting there with S-Bahn lines S1, S2, S25). Eventually, the line will extend to connect to the U5 at Alexanderplatz, via Museumsinsel and Unter den Linden, but not until at least 2019.
  On their way in and out of town, inter-city trains now also stop at Gesundbrunnen, Südkreuz and Spandau, depending on their destinations.

By bus

Zentraler Omnibus Bahnhof (ZOB)
Masurenallee 4-6, Charlottenburg (301 0380, www.iob-berlin.de). **Open** 6am-9pm Mon-Fri; 6am-3pm Sat, Sun. **Map** p308 B8.
Buses arrive in western Berlin at the Central Bus Station, opposite the Funkturm and the ICC. From here, U-Bahn line U2 runs into the city centre.

PUBLIC TRANSPORT

Berlin is served by a comprehensive and interlinked network of buses, trains, trams and ferries. It's efficient and punctual, but not that cheap.

With the completion of the inner-city-encircling Ringbahn in 2002, the former East and West Berlin transport systems were finally sewn back together, though it can still sometimes be complicated travelling between eastern and western destinations. But services are usually regular and frequent, timetables can be trusted, and one ticket can be used for two hours on all legs of a journey and all forms of transport.

The Berlin transport authority, the BVG, operates bus, U-Bahn (underground) and tram networks, and a few ferry services on the outlying lakes. The S-Bahn (overground railway) is run by its own authority, but services are integrated within the same three-zone tariff system.

Information

The **BVG** website (www.bvg.de) has a wealth of information (in English) on city transport, and there's usually someone who speaks English at the 24-hour **BVG Call Center** (194 49). The **S-Bahn** has its own website at www.s-bahn-berlin.de.

The Liniennetz, a map of U-Bahn, S-Bahn, bus and tram routes for Berlin and Potsdam, is available free from info centres and ticket offices. It includes a city-centre map. A map of the U- and S-Bahn can also be picked up free at ticket offices or from the grey-uniformed *Zugabfertiger* – passenger-assistance personnel.

Fares & tickets

The bus, tram, U-Bahn, S-Bahn and ferry services operate on an integrated three-zone system. Zone A covers central Berlin, zone B extends out to the edge of the suburbs and zone C stretches into Brandenburg.

The basic single ticket is the €2.70 *Normaltarif* (zones A and B). Unless going to Potsdam or Flughafen Schönefeld, few visitors are likely to travel beyond zone B, making this in effect a flat-fare system.

Apart from the longer-term *Zeitkarten*, tickets for Berlin's public transport system can be bought from the yellow or orange machines at U- or S-Bahn stations, and by some bus stops. These take coins and sometimes notes, give change and have a limited explanation of the ticket system in English. You can

often pay by card, but don't count on it (if you do, don't forget to collect your card – infuriatingly, the machines keep the card until all the tickets are printed, making it very easy to forget). An app, FahrInfo Plus, is also available for iOS and Android, which allows you to purchase and carry tickets on your smartphone; details on www.bvg.de/en/travel-information/mobile.

Once you've purchased your ticket, validate it in the small red or yellow box next to the machine, which stamps it with the time and date. (Tickets bought on trams or buses are usually already validated.)

There are no ticket turnstiles at stations, but if an inspector catches you without a valid ticket, you will be fined €40. Ticket inspections are frequent, and are conducted while vehicles are moving by pairs of plain-clothes personnel.

Single ticket (Normaltarif)

Single tickets cost €2.70 (€1.70 6-14s) for travel within zones A and B, €3 (€2) for zones B and C, and €3.30 (€2.40) for all three zones. A ticket allows use of the BVG network for two hours, with as many changes between bus, tram, U-Bahn and S-Bahn as necessary, travelling in one direction.

Short-distance ticket (Kurzstreckentarif)

The *Kurzstreckentarif* (ask for a *Kurzstrecke*) costs €1.60 (€1.20 reductions) and is valid for three U- or S-Bahn stops, or six stops on the tram or bus. No transfers allowed.

Day ticket (Tageskarte)

A *Tageskarte* for zones A and B costs €6.90 (€4.70 reductions), or €7.40 (€5.30) for all three zones. A day ticket lasts until 3am the morning after validating.

Longer-term tickets (Zeitkarten)

If you're in Berlin for a week, it makes sense to buy a *Sieben-Tage-Karte* ('seven-day ticket') at €29.50 for zones A and B, or €36.50 for all three zones (no reductions). A stay of a month or more makes it worth buying a *Monatskarte* ('month ticket'), which costs €79.50 for zones A and B, and €98.50 for all three zones.

Tourist travelcards

There are two excellent-value travelcards aimed at tourists, which pack in unlimited transport within designated zones, with a bundle of other attractive perks – discounts and deals with partnering tourist and cultural attractions, shops, bars and clubs. For zones A and B, the **Berlin CityTourCard** (www.citytourcard.com) costs €17.40 for a 48-hour pass, €24.50 for 72 hours and €31.90 for

five days, while the **Berlin WelcomeCard** (www.berlin-welcomecard.de) is €19.50 for 48 hours, €26.70 for 72 hours (€40.50 including access to museums and Museum Island) and €34.50 for five days.

U-Bahn

The U-Bahn network consists of ten lines and 170-plus stations. The first trains run shortly after 4am; the last between midnight and 1am, except on Fridays and Saturdays when most trains run all night at 15-minute intervals. The direction of travel is indicated by the name of the last stop on the line.

S-Bahn

Especially useful in eastern Berlin, the S-Bahn covers long distances faster than the U-Bahn and is a more efficient means of getting to outlying areas. The Ringbahn, which circles central Berlin, was the final piece of the S-Bahn system to be renovated, though there are still disruptions here and there.

Buses

Berlin has a dense network of 150 bus routes, of which 54 run in the early hours. The day lines run from 4.30am to about 1am the next morning. Enter at the front of the bus and exit in the middle or at the back. The driver sells only individual tickets, but all tickets from machines on the U- or S-Bahn are valid. Most bus stops have clear timetables and route maps.

Trams

There are 21 tram lines (five of which run all night), mainly in the east, though some have been extended a few kilometres into the western half of the city, mostly in Wedding. Hackescher Markt is the site of the main tram terminus. Tickets are available from machines on the trams, at the termini and in U-Bahn stations.

Other rail services

Berlin is also served by the **Regionalbahn** ('regional railway'), which once connected East Berlin with Potsdam via the suburbs and small towns left outside the Wall. Run by **Deutsche Bahn** (www.bahn.de), it still circumnavigates the city. The website has timetable and ticket information in English.

ESSENTIAL INFORMATION

Travelling at night

Berlin has a comprehensive *Nachtliniennetz* ('night-line network') that covers all parts of town, with more than 50 bus and tram routes running every 30 minutes between 12.30am and 4.30am.

Maps and timetables are available from BVG kiosks at stations, and large maps of the night services are found next to the normal BVG map on station platforms. Ticket prices are the same as during the day. Buses and trams that run at night have an 'N' in front of the number.

On all buses travelling through zones B and C after 8pm, the driver will let you off at any point along the route via the front door.

Truncated versions of U-Bahn lines U1, U2, U3, U5, U6, U7, U8 and U9 run all night on Fridays and Saturdays, with trains every 15 minutes. The S-Bahn also runs at 30-minute intervals.

Boat trips

Getting about by water is more of a leisure activity than a practical means of navigating the city, but the BVG network has a handful of boat services on Berlin's lakes. There are also several private companies offering tours of Berlin's waterways; *see also p111* **Das Boot**.

Reederei Heinz Riedel
Planufer 78, Kreuzberg (693 4646, www.reederei-riedel.de). U8 Schönleinstrasse. **No credit cards. Map** p323 P9.
A tour through the city's network of rivers and canals costs €4.50-€18.

Stern und Kreisschiffahrt
Puschkinallee 15, Treptow (536 3600, www.sternundkreis.de). S8, S9, S41, S42 Treptower Park. **Open** *Apr-early Oct* 9am-6pm Mon-Fri; 9am-2pm Sat.
Around 25 cruises along the Spree and around the lakes. A 3hr 30min tour costs €18.50.

TAXIS

Berlin taxis are pricey, efficient and numerous. The starting fee is €3.40 and thereafter the fare is €1.79 per kilometre for the first seven kilometres, and €1.28 per kilometre thereafter. The rate remains the same at night. For short journeys, ask for a *Kurzstrecke* – up to two kilometres for €4, but only available when you've hailed a cab and not from taxi ranks.

Taxi stands are numerous, especially in central areas near stations and at major intersections.

You can phone for a cab 24 hours daily on 261 026. Most firms can transport people with disabilities, but require advance notice. Cabs accept all credit cards except Diners Club, subject to a €1.50 charge.

If you want an estate car (station wagon), request a *combi*. As well as normal taxis, **Funk Taxi Berlin** (261 026) operates vans that can carry up to seven people (ask for a *grossraum Taxi*; same rates as for regular taxis) and has two vehicles for people with disabilities.

DRIVING

Despite some congestion, driving in Berlin presents few problems. Visitors from the UK and US should bear in mind that, in the absence of signals, drivers must yield to traffic from the right, except at crossings marked by a diamond-shaped yellow sign. Trams always have right of way. An *Einbahnstrasse* is a one-way street.

Breakdown services

ADAC
Bundesallee 29-30, Wilmersdorf (0180 222 2222). **No credit cards.** 24hr assistance for about €65/hr.

Fuel stations

Aral
Holzmarktstrasse 12, Mitte (2472 0748). **Open** 24hrs daily. **Map** p311 P7.
Kurfürstendamm 128, Wilmersdorf (8909 6972). **Open** 24hrs daily. **Map** p308 B9.

Parking

Parking is usually metered in Berlin side streets (residents get an *Anwohnerplakette* pass), but spaces are hard to find. Buy a parking ticket from a nearby machine; if you don't have one, or park illegally, you risk having your car clamped or towed.

There are long-term car parks at Schönefeld and Tegel airports, and many Parkgaragen and Parkhäuser (multi-storey and underground car parks) around the city, open 24 hours, that charge around €2/hr.

Vehicle hire

Car hire is not expensive and all major companies are represented in Berlin, with car hire desks at all the city's airports. Car-sharing services such as **DriveNow** (https://de.drive-now.com) are increasingly popular.

CYCLING

West Berlin is wonderful for cycling – flat, with lots of cycle paths, parks and canals to cruise beside. East Berlin has fewer cycle paths and more cobblestones and tram lines.

Cycles can be taken on the U-Bahn (except during rush hour, 6-9am and 2-5pm), up to a limit of two at the end of carriages that have a bicycle sign. More may be taken on S-Bahn carriages, and at any time of day. In each case an extra ticket (€1.80 for zones A and B) must be bought for each bike. A good guide to cycle routes is the *ADFC Fahrradstadtplan* (€6.90), available in bike shops.

Berlin's bike rental scheme, **Call-A-Bike**, operates in summer only. The bikes are parked in designated docking stations. You have to register to use the system; you can register at a docking station terminal, via the website (www.callabike-interaktiv.de, in German only) or by calling 0700 0522 5522. There's a one-off registration fee of €12 and a charge of 8c per minute, up to a maximum of €15 per 24 hours. The Pauschal annual subscription (€36) allows unlimited journeys of up to 30 minutes for free, and make sense for those making longer visits.

Bike hire

Fahrradstation
Dorotheenstrasse 30, Mitte (2838 4848, www.fahrradstation.de). U6, S1, S2, S5, S7, S9, S75 Friedrichstrasse. **Open** 10am-7.30pm Mon-Fri; 10am-6pm Sat; 10am-4pm Sun. **Rates** from €15 per day; €35 3 days. **Map** p306 M6.
Other locations Auguststrasse 29A, Mitte (2250 8070); Leibzigerstrasse 5, Mitte (6664 9180); Kollwitzstrasse 77, Prenzlauer Berg (9395 8130); Bergmannstrasse 9, Kreuzberg (215 1566); Goethestrasse 46, Charlottenburg (9395 2757).
Pedalpower
Grossbeerenstrasse 53, Kreuzberg (7899 1939, www.pedalpower.de). U1, U7 Möckernbrücke. **Open** 10am-6.30pm Mon-Fri; 11am-2pm Sat. **Rates** from €10/day. **No credit cards. Map** p310 L10.
Other location Pfarrstrasse 115, Lichtenberg (5515 3270).

WALKING

Berlin is a good walking city, but it's spread out. Mitte is most pleasant on foot, but if you then want to check out Charlottenburg, you'll need to take a bus or train.

Resources A-Z

ADDRESSES

German convention dictates that the house/building number follows the street name (eg Friedrichstrasse 21), and numbers sometimes run up one side of the street and back down the other side. *Strasse* (street) is often abbreviated to *Str*, and is not usually written separately but appended to the street name, as in the example above. Exceptions are when the street name is the adjectival form of a place name (eg Potsdamer Strasse) or the full name of an individual (eg Heinrich-Heine-Strasse).

Within buildings: EG means *Erdgeschoss*, the ground floor; 1. OG (*Obergeschoss*) is the first floor; VH means *Vorderhaus*, or the front part of the building; HH means *Hinterhaus*, the part of the building off the *Hinterhof*, the 'back courtyard'; SF is *Seitenflügel*, stairs that go off to the side from the *Hinterhof*. In big, industrial complexes, stairwells are often numbered or lettered. Treppenhaus B, or sometimes just Haus B, would indicate a particular staircase off the courtyard.

AGE RESTRICTIONS

The legal age for drinking in Germany is 16 for beer and wine, 18 for hard liquor; for smoking it's 18; for driving it's 18. The age of consent for both heterosexual and homosexual sex is 16.

CUSTOMS

EU nationals over 17 years of age can import limitless goods for personal use, if bought with tax paid on them at source. For non-EU citizens and for duty-free goods, the following limits apply:
● 200 cigarettes or 50 cigars or 250 grams of tobacco
● 1 litre of spirits (over 22 % by volume) or 2 litres of fortified wine (under 22% by volume)
● 4 litres of non-sparkling wine
● 16 litres of beer
● Other goods to the value of €300 for non-commercial use, up to €430 for air/sea travellers.

Travellers should note that the import of meat, meat products, fruit, plants, flowers and protected animals is restricted and/or forbidden.

DISABLED

Many but not all U-Bahn and S-Bahn stations have ramps and/or elevators for wheelchair access; the map of the transport network (*see p314*; look for the wheelchair symbol) indicates which ones. These stations are equipped with folding ramps to allow passengers in wheelchairs to board the trains. These passengers are required to wait at the front end of the platform to signal to the driver their need to board. All bus lines and most tram lines are also wheelchair-accessible.

Public buildings and most of the city's hotels have disabled access. However, if you require more specific information about access, try either of the following organisations:

Beschäftigungswerk des BBV
Weydemeyerstrasse 2A, Mitte (5001 9100, www.bbv-tours-berlin. de). U5 Schillingstrasse. **Open** 9am-8pm Mon-Fri; 10am-6pm Sat. **Map** p307 P6.
The Berlin Centre for the Disabled provides legal and social advice, together with a transport service and travel information.

Touristik Union International
0511 5678 0105, www.tui.com.
The TUI provides information on accommodation and travel in Germany for the disabled.

DRUGS

Berlin is relatively liberal in its attitude towards drugs. In recent years, possession of hash or grass has been effectively decriminalised. Anyone caught with an amount under ten grams is liable to have the stuff confiscated, but can otherwise expect no further retribution. Joint smoking is tolerated in some of Berlin's younger bars and cafés – a quick sniff will tell whether you're in one. Anyone caught with small amounts of hard drugs will net a fine, but is unlikely to be incarcerated.

For **Drogen Notdienst** (emergency drug service), *see p287*.

ELECTRICITY

Electricity in Germany runs on 230V, the same as British appliances. You will require an adaptor (G to F) to change the shape of the plug. US appliances (120V) require a voltage converter.

EMBASSIES & CONSULATES

Australian Embassy
Wallstrasse 76-79, Mitte (880 0880, www.germany.embassy.gov.au). U2 Spittelmarkt. **Open** 8.30am-5pm Mon-Thur; 8.30am-4.15pm Fri. **Map** p310 M7.

British Embassy
Wilhelmstrasse 70, Mitte (204 570, www.gov.uk/government/world/ germany). S1, S2 Unter den Linden. **Open** 9.30am-noon Mon, Tue, Thur, Fri. **Map** p306 L6.

Embassy of Ireland
Jägerstrasse 51, Mitte (220 720, www.embassyofireland.de). U2, U6 Stadtmitte. **Open** 9.30am-12.30pm Mon-Fri, by appointment only. **Map** p310 M7.

ESSENTIAL INFORMATION

US Embassy
Clayallee 170, Zehlendorf (83050, visa enquiries 032 221 093 243, www.germany.usembassy.gov). U3 Oskar-Helene-Heim. **Open** *US citizen services* By phone 2-3pm Mon-Thur (visits by appointment only). *Visa enquiries* By phone 8am-8pm Mon-Fri.
A new US embassy building opened in 2008 on Pariser Platz, next to the Brandenburg Gate, but consular services still operate out of the original embassy in Zehlendorf.

EMERGENCIES

See also p287 **Helplines.**
Police 110.
Ambulance/Fire Brigade 112.

GAY & LESBIAN

See also pp178-191.

Help & information

Lesbenberatung
Kulmer Strasse 20A, Schöneberg (215 2000, www.lesbenberatung-berlin.de). U7, S2, S25 Yorckstrasse. **Open** 2-5pm Mon, Wed, Fri; 10am-7pm Tue; 2-7pm Thur. **Map** p310 K10.
Counselling in all areas of lesbian life, as well as self-help groups, courses, cultural events and an 'info-café'.

Mann-O-Meter
Bülowstrasse 106, Schöneberg (216 8008, www.mann-o-meter.de). U2, U3, U4 Nollendorfplatz. **Open** 5-10pm Mon-Fri; 4-8pm Sat, Sun. **Map** p310 J9.
Drop-in centre and helpline. Advice about AIDS prevention, jobs, accommodation and gay contacts, plus cheap stocks of safer-sex materials. English spoken.

Schwulenberatung
Niebuhrstrasse 59-60, Charlottenburg (2336 9070, www.schwulenberatungberlin.de). U7 Wilmersdorfer Strasse. **Open** 9am-8pm Mon-Fri. **Map** p308 D8.
The Gay Advice Centre provides information and counselling about HIV and AIDS, crisis intervention and advice on all aspects of gay life.

HEALTH

EU countries have reciprocal medical treatment arrangements with Germany. EU citizens will need the **European Health Insurance Card (EHIC)** – from the UK, this is available by phoning 0845 606 2030

or online (www.ehic.org.uk). You'll need to provide your name, date of birth and national insurance number. It doesn't cover all medical costs (dental treatment, for example), so private medical insurance is not a bad idea too. Citizens from non-EU countries should take out private medical insurance. The British Embassy (*see p285*) has a list of English-speaking doctors and dentists, as well as lawyers and interpreters.
Should you fall ill in Berlin, you can take your EHIC to any doctor or hospital emergency department and get treatment. All hospitals have a 24-hour emergency ward. Otherwise, patients are admitted to hospital via a physician. Hospitals are listed in the *Gelbe Seiten* (*Yellow Pages*) under 'Krankenhäuser/ Kliniken'.

Accident & emergency

These are the most central hospitals. All have 24-hour emergency wards.

Charité
Schumannstrasse 20-21, Mitte (45050, www.charite.de). U6 Oranienburger Tor. **Map** p306 L5.

Klinikum Am Urban
Dieffenbachstrasse 1, Kreuzberg (130 210, www.vivantes.de/kau). U7 Südstern, or bus M41. **Map** p311 O10.

St Hedwig Krankenhaus
Grosse Hamburger Strasse 5, Mitte (23110, www.alexius.de). S5, S7, S75 Hackescher Markt, or S1, S2 Oranienburger Strasse. **Map** p307 N5.

Complementary medicine

There is a long tradition of alternative medicine (*Heilpraxis*) in Germany, and your medical insurance will usually cover treatment costs. For a full list of practitioners, look up 'Heilpraktiker' in the *Gelbe Seiten* (*Yellow Pages*). There you'll find a complete list of chiropractors, osteopaths, acupuncturists, homeopaths and healers of various kinds. However, note that homeopathic medicines are harder to get hold of and much more expensive than in the UK, and it's generally more difficult to find an osteopath or a chiropractor.

Contraception & abortion

Family-planning clinics are thin on the ground in Germany, and generally you have to go to a

gynaecologist (*Frauenarzt*). The abortion law was amended in 1995 to take into account the differing systems that had existed in East and West. East Germany had abortion on demand; in the West, abortion was only allowed in extenuating circumstances, such as when the health of the foetus or mother was at risk. In a complicated compromise, abortion is still technically illegal, but is not punishable. Women wishing to terminate a pregnancy can do so only after receiving certification from a counsellor. Counselling is offered by state, lay and church bodies.

Feministisches Frauen Gesundheits Zentrum (FFGZ)
Bamberger Strasse 51, Schöneberg (213 9597, www.ffgz.de). U4, U7 Bayerischer Platz. **Open** 10am-noon Mon, Tue, Fri; 10am-noon, 4-6pm Thur. **Map** p309 G10.
Courses and lectures are offered on natural contraception, pregnancy, cancer, abortion, AIDS, migraines and sexuality. Self-help and preventative medicine are stressed. Information on gynaecologists, health institutions and organisations can also be obtained.

ProFamilia
Kalckreuthstrasse 4, Schöneberg (3984 9898, www.profamilia-berlin de). U1, U2, U3 Wittenbergplatz. **Open** 3-6pm Mon, Tue, Thur; 9am-noon Sat. **Map** p309 H9.
Free advice on sex, contraception and abortion. Call for an appointment.

Dentists

Dr Andreas Bothe
Kurfürstendamm 193D, Charlottenburg (882 6767). U1 Uhlandstrasse. **Open** 8am-2pm Mon, Wed, Fri; 2-8pm Tue, Thur. **Map** p309 F8.

Doctors

If you don't know of any doctors in Berlin, or are too ill to leave your bed, phone the *Ärztlicher Bereitschaftsdienst* (emergency doctor's service, 310 031). This service specialises in dispatching doctors for house calls. Charges vary according to the treatment required.
The British Embassy (*see p285*) can provide a list of English-speaking doctors, although you'll find that most doctors speak some English. All will be expensive, so be sure to have either your EHIC or your private insurance documents at hand

if seeking treatment. The doctors listed below speak excellent English.

Dr Joseph Francis Aman

Franziskus Krankenhaus, Budapester Strasse 15-19, Tiergarten (2638 3503). U2, U9, S5, S7, S75 Zoologischer Garten. **Open** 8am-6pm Mon, Tue, Thur; 8am-1pm Fri. **Map** p309 H8.
Dr Aman is an American GP with a practice in the Roman Catholic hospital that is opposite the InterContinental Hotel.

Dr Christine Rommelspacher

Oldenburger Strasse 37, Tiergarten (391 1701). U9 Turmstrasse. **Open** 9am-noon, 4-7pm Mon, Thur; 9am-noon Tue, Wed. **Map** p305 G5.

HIV & AIDS

Berliner Aids-Hilfe (BAH)

Kurfürstenstrasse 130, Tiergarten (885 6400, advice line 19411, www. berliner-aidshilfe.de). U1, U2, U3, U4 Nollendorfplatz. **Open** noon-6pm Mon; noon-2.30pm Wed; noon-3pm Thur, Fri. *Advice line* noon-10pm Mon-Wed. **Map** p310 J9.
Information on all aspects of HIV and AIDS. Free consultations, condoms and lubricant are also provided.

Pharmacies

Prescription and non-prescription drugs (including aspirin) are sold only at pharmacies (*Apotheken*). You can recognise these by a red 'A' outside the front door. A list of the nearest pharmacies open on Sundays and in the evening should be displayed in the window of every pharmacy. A list of emergency pharmacies (*Notdienst-Apotheken*) is available online at www.akberlin. de/notdienst.

HELPLINES

Berliner Krisendienst

www.berlinerkrisendienst.de.
Mitte, Friedrichshain, Kreuzberg, Tiergarten & Wedding 390 6310. Neukölln 390 6390. Charlottenburg & Wilmersdorf 390 6320. Prenzlauer Berg, Weissensee & Pankow 390 6340. Schöneberg, Tempelhof, Steglitz 390 6360. *All* **Open** 24hrs daily.
For most problems, this is the best service to call. They offer help and/or counselling on a range of subjects, and if they can't provide exactly what you're looking for, they'll put you in touch with someone who can. The phone lines, organised by

district, are staffed 24 hours daily. Counsellors will also come and visit you in your house if necessary.

Drogen Notdienst

Genthiner Strasse 48, Schöneberg (19237, www.drogennotdienst.org). U1 Kurfürstenstrasse. **Open** 8.30am-9.30pm Mon-Fri; 2-9.30pm Sat, Sun. *Phone line* 24hrs daily. **Map** p309 G9.
At the 'drug emergency service', no appointment is necessary if you're coming in for advice.

Frauenkrisentelefon

615 4243, www.frauenkrisentelefon. de. **Open** 10am-noon Mon, Thur; 3-5pm Tue; 7-9pm Wed, Fri; 5-7pm Sat, Sun.
Offers advice and information for women, on anything and everything.

ID

By law you are required to carry some form of ID, which – for UK and US citizens – means a passport. If police catch you without one, they may accompany you to wherever you've left it.

INTERNET

Many cafés, bars and restaurants will offer free wi-fi, though the networks are usually password-protected. For longer stays, a number of local mobile networks offer affordable data plans.

Sidewalk Express Internet Point

Dunkin' Donuts, Sony Center, Tiergarten (www.sidewalkexpress. com). U2, S1, S2, S25 Potsdamer Platz. **Open** 7am-1am Mon-Fri; 8am-1am Sat. **Map** p310 K7/L7.
Dozens of computers, no staff, mechanised system to buy time online, and plenty of doughnuts to hand. Some other branches are similarly lodged with Dunkin' Donuts.
Other locations Potsdamer Platz Arkaden, Potsdamer Platz; Bahnhof Alexanderplatz Dunkin Donuts; Bahnhof Zoologischer Garten; Bahnhof Friedrichstrasse (ground floor, and Dunkin Donuts basement); Hauptbahnhof Burger King.

LEFT LUGGAGE

Airports

There is a left luggage office at Tegel (4101 2315; open 5am-10.30pm daily) and lockers at Schönefeld (in the Multi Parking Garage P4). *See p282.*

Rail & bus stations

There are left luggage lockers at Bahnhof Zoo, Friedrichstrasse, Alexanderplatz, Potsdamer Platz, Ostbahnhof and Hauptbahnhof. In addition, Zentraler Omnibus Bahnhof (ZOB) also provides left luggage facilities.

LEGAL HELP

If you get into legal difficulties, contact your embassy (*see p285*): it can provide you with a list of English-speaking lawyers in Berlin.

LIBRARIES

Berlin has hundreds of *Bibliotheken/ Büchereien* (public libraries). To borrow books, you will be required to bring two things: an *Anmeldungsformular* ('certificate of registration'; *see p292*) and a passport.

Amerika-Gedenkbibliothek

Blücherplatz 1, Kreuzberg (9022 6401, www.zlb.de). U1, U6 Hallesches Tor. **Open** 10am-9pm Mon-Fri; 10am-7pm Sat. **Membership** €10/yr; €5 students. **Map** p310 M9.
This library only contains a small collection of English and American literature, but it has an excellent collection of English-language videos and many DVDs.

Staatsbibliothek zu Berlin – Haus Potsdamer Strasse

Potsdamer Strasse 33, Tiergarten (266 433 888, http://staatsbibliothek-berlin.de). U2, S1, S2, S25 Potsdamer Platz. **Open** 9am-9pm Mon-Fri; 10am-7pm Sat. **Map** p310 K8.
Books in English on every subject are available at this branch of the state library – as seen in Wim Wenders' film *Wings of Desire.*

Staatsbibliothek zu Berlin – Haus Unter den Linden

Dorotheenstrasse 27, Mitte (266 433 888, http://staatsbibliothek-berlin.de). U6, S1, S2, S5, S7, S9, S75 Friedrichstrasse. **Open** 9am-9pm Mon-Fri; 10am-7pm Sat. **Map** p306 M6.
A smaller range of English books than the branch above, but it's still worth a visit, not least for the café.

LOST/STOLEN PROPERTY

If any of your belongings are stolen while in Germany, you should go immediately to the police station nearest to where the incident occurred (listed in the *Gelbe Seiten/ Yellow Pages* under 'Polizei') and report the theft. There you will be required to fill in report forms for insurance purposes. If you can't speak German, don't worry: the police will call in one of their interpreters, a service that is provided free of charge.

If you leave something in a taxi, call the number that's on your receipt (if you remembered to ask for one), and tell them the time of your journey, the four-digit *Konzessions-Nummer* that will be stamped on the receipt, a number where you can be reached, and what you've lost. They'll pass this information to the driver, and he or she will call you if they have your property.

For information about lost or stolen credit cards, *see p290*.

BVG Fundbüro

Potsdamer Strasse 180, Schöneberg (194 49). U7 Kleistpark. **Open** 9am-6pm Mon-Thur; 9am-2pm Fri. **Map** p310 J10.
Contact this office if you have any queries about property lost on Berlin's public transport system. If you're robbed on one of their vehicles, you can ask about the surveillance video.

Zentrales Fundbüro

Platz der Luftbrücke 6, Tempelhof (902 773 101). U6 Platz der Luftbrücke. **Open** 9am-2pm Mon; Tue, Fri; 1-6pm Thur. **Map** p310 M11.
This is the central police lost property office.

MEDIA

Foreign press

A wide variety of international publications are available at larger railway stations and **Internationale Presse** newsagents around town. Bookshops **Dussmann** (*see p53*) also carries international titles. The monthly *Exberliner* magazine (*see p289*) has listings, as well as articles on cultural and political topics in English.

National newspapers

Bild

www.bild.de
The flagship tabloid of the Axel Springer group. Though its credibility varies from story to story, *Bild* leverages the journalistic resources of the Springer empire and its three-million circulation to land regular scoops.

Frankfurter Allgemeine Zeitung

www.faz.net
Germany's de facto newspaper of record. Stolid, exhaustive coverage of daily events, plus lots of analysis, particularly on the business pages.

Handelsblatt

www.handelsblatt.com
The closest thing Germany can offer to the *Wall Street Journal*, the *Handelsblatt* co-operates with that paper's European offshoot.

Süddeutsche Zeitung

www.sueddeutsche.de
Based in Munich, the *Süddeutsche* blends first-rate journalism with enlightened commentary and uninspired visuals. On Fridays, there's an English-language feature supplement called *The New York Times International Weekly*.

Die Tageszeitung

www.taz.de
Set up in rebellious Kreuzberg in the 1970s, the 'taz' attempts to balance the world view of the mainstream press and give coverage to alternative political and social issues.

Die Welt

www.welt.de
Once a lacklustre mouthpiece of conservative, provincial thinking, *Die Welt* has widened its political horizons, though it's still thought of as a yuppy paper. Not very popular in Berlin.

Local newspapers

Berliner Morgenpost

www.morgenpost.de
This rather staid broadsheet is the favourite of the petty bourgeois. Reasonable local coverage, and it's gained readers in the East through the introduction of neighbourhood editions, but there's no depth on the national and international pages.

Berliner Zeitung

www.berliner-zeitung.de
This East Berlin paper has passed through the hands of a number of owners since it was relaunched in the early 1990s. Though it is profitable and its journalistic ambitions less sullied than of its West Berlin competitor, *Der Tagesspiegel*, it remains a local read, with a circulation largely confined to the Eastern districts.

BZ

www.bz-berlin.de
The daily riot of polemic and pictures hasn't let up since it was demonised by the left in the 1970s – but its circulation has.

Der Tagesspiegel

www.tagesspiegel.de
Owned by the conservative Holtzbrinck publishing empire

from West Germany, this paper has fallen from the pre-eminent position it once held in West Berlin. The paper has dumbed down to boost circulation, losing the intellectual underpinnings that once attracted well-educated, upmarket readers.

Weekly newspapers

Freitag

www.freitag.de
'The East-West weekly paper' is a post-1989 relaunch of a GDR intellectual weekly. Worth a look for its political and cultural articles.

Jungle World

www.jungle-world.com
Defiantly left, graphically switched-on and commercially undaunted, this Berlin-based weekly can be relied on to mock the comfortable views of the mainstream press. Born of an ideological dispute with the publishers of *Junge Welt*, a former East Berlin youth title, it lacks sales but packs a punch.

Die Zeit

www.zeit.de
Every major post-war intellectual debate in Germany has been carried out in the pages of *Die Zeit*, the newspaper that proved that a liberal tradition was alive and well in a country best known for excesses of intolerance. The style of its elite authors makes a difficult read.

Magazines

Focus

www.focus.de
Once, its spare, to-the-point articles, four-colour graphics and service features were a welcome innovation. But the gloss has faded, and *Focus* has established itself as a non-thinking man's *Der Spiegel*, whose answer to the upstart was simply to print more colour pages and become warm and fuzzy by adding bylines.

Der Spiegel

www.spiegel.de
Few journalistic institutions in Germany possess the resources and clout to pursue a major story in the way that *Der Spiegel* can, making it one of the best and most aggressive news weeklies in Europe. After years of firing barbs at ruling Christian Democrats, *Der Spiegel* was caught off guard when the Social Democrats were elected in 1999, but remains a must-read for anyone interested in Germany's power structure. There's substantial English content on its website.

Stern

www.stern.de

The heyday of news pictorials may have long gone, but *Stern* still manages to shift around a million copies a week of big colour spreads detailing the horrors of war, the beauties of nature and the curves of the female body. Nevertheless, some say its reputation has never really recovered from the Hitler diaries fiasco in the early 1980s.

Listings magazines

Berlin is awash with free listings magazines, notably **[030]**(www.berlin030.de; music, nightlife, film) and **Partysan** (www.partysan.net; a pocket-sized club guide) and their gay cousins **Siegessaeule** (www.siegessaeule.de) and **Blu** (www.blu.fm). These can be picked up in bars and restaurants. Two newsstand fortnightlies, **Zitty** and **Tip**, come out on alternate weeks and, at least for cinema information, it pays to get the current title.

Exberliner
www.exberliner.com
Berlin's current English-language monthly is a lively mix of listings, reviews and commentary, mostly written by youngish American expats.

Tip
www.tip-berlin.de
A glossier version of *Zitty* in every respect, *Tip* gets better marks for its overall presentation and readability, largely due to higher-quality paper, full colour throughout and a space-saving TV insert.

Zitty
www.zitty.de
Having lost some countercultural edge since its founding in 1977, *Zitty* remains a vital force on the Berlin media scene, providing a fortnightly blend of close-to-the-bone civic journalism, alternative cultural coverage and comprehensive listings. The Harte Welle ('hardcore') department of its Lonely Hearts classifieds is legendary.

Television

Germany cabled up in the late 1970s, so there is no shortage of channels. But television has never been viewed as an art form. That means programming revolves around bland, mass-market entertainment, except for political talk shows, which are pervasive, but often very good.

At its worst, there are cheesy 'erotic' shows, vapid folk-music programmes with studio audiences that clap in time, and German adaptations of reality TV and casting shows such as *Big Brother* and *Star Search*. Late-night TV, in particular, is chock-a-block with imported action series and European soft porn, interspersed with finger-sucking adverts for telephone sex numbers.

There are two national public networks, **ARD** and **ZDF**, a handful of no-holds-barred commercial channels, and a load of special-interest channels. ARD's daily *Tagesschau* at 8pm is the most authoritative news broadcast nationally.

N-tv is Germany's all-news cable channel, owned partly by CNN, but lacking the satellite broadcaster's ability to cover a breaking story. **TVBerlin** is the city's experiment with local commercial television, but it's still catching up with ARD's local affiliate **RBB** (a merger of Berlin and Brandenburg stations SFB and ORB), which covers local news with more insight.

RTL, **Pro 7** and **SAT.1** are privately owned services offering a predictable mix of Hollywood re-runs and imported series, plus their own sensational magazine programmes and, sometimes, surprisingly good TV movies.

Special interest channels run from **Kinderkanal** for kids to **Eurosport**, **MTV Europe** and its German-language competitor **Viva**, to **Arte**, an enlightened French-German cultural channel with high-quality films and documentaries.

Channels broadcasting regularly in English include **CNN**, **NBC**, **MTV Europe** and **BBC World**. British or American films on ARD or ZDF are sometimes broadcast with a simultaneous soundtrack in English for stereo-equipped TV sets.

Radio

Some 29 stations compete for audiences in Berlin, so even tiny shifts in market share have huge consequences for broadcasters. The race for ratings in the greater metropolitan area is thwarted by a clear split between the urban audience in both East and West and a rural one in the hinterland. The main four stations in the region have their audiences based in either **Berlin (Berliner Rundfunk**, 91.4; **r.s.2**, 94.3) or Brandenburg (**BB Radio**, 107.5; **Antenne Brandenburg**, 99.7). No single station is able to pull in everyone.

Commercial stations **104.6 RTL** (104.6) and **Energy 103.4** (103.4) offer standard chart pop spiced with news. **RadioEins** (95.8) is the most adventurous, offering mostly new and old indie music, while **Fritz** (102.6) plays things a little safer. Jazz is round the clock on **Jazz Radio** (106.8). Information-based stations such as **Info Radio** (93.1) are increasing in popularity. The **BBC World Service** (90.2) is available 24 hours a day.

MONEY

One euro (€) is made up of 100 cents. There are seven banknotes and eight coins. The notes are of differing colours and sizes (€5 is the smallest, €500 the largest) and each of their designs represent a different period of European architecture. They are: €5 (grey-green), €10 (red), €20 (blue), €50 (orange), €100 (green), €200 (yellow-brown), €500 (purple).

The eight denominations of coins vary in colour, size and thickness – but not enough to make them easy to tell apart. They share one common side; the other features a country-specific design (all can be used in any participating state). They are: €2, €1, 50 cents, 20 cents, 10 cents, 5 cents, 2 cents, 1 cent.

At the time of going to press, the exchange rate was £1 = €1.36 and US$1 = €0.91.

ATMs

ATMs are found throughout the centre of Berlin, and are the most convenient way of obtaining cash. Most major credit cards are accepted, as well as debit cards that are part of the Cirrus, Plus, Star or Maestro systems. You will normally be charged a fee for withdrawing cash.

Banks & bureaux de change

Foreign currency and travellers' cheques can be exchanged in most banks. *Wechselstuben* (bureaux de change) are open outside normal banking hours and give better rates than banks, where changing money often involves long queues.

Reisebank AG
Zoo Station, Hardenbergplatz 1, Charlottenburg (881 7117, www.reisebank.de). U2, U9, S5, S7, S75 Zoologischer Garten. **Open** 8am-9pm daily. Map p309 G8.
The *Wechselstuben* of the Reisebank offer good exchange rates, and can be found at the bigger stations.
Other locations Bahnhof Friedrichstrasse, Mitte (2045 5096); Berlin Hauptbahnhof, Tiergarten (2045 3761); Ostbahnhof, Friedrichshain (296 4393).

ESSENTIAL INFORMATION

ESSENTIAL INFORMATION

Credit cards

In general, German banking and retail systems are less enthusiastic about credit than their UK or US equivalents, though this is gradually changing. Many Berliners prefer to use cash for most transactions, although larger hotels, shops and restaurants often accept major credit cards (American Express, Diners Club, MasterCard, Visa).

If you want to draw cash on your credit card, some banks will give an advance against Visa and MasterCard cards. However, you may not be able to withdraw less than the equivalent of US$100. A better option is using an ATM.

LOST/STOLEN CARDS

If you've lost a credit card, or had one stolen, phone the relevant 24-hour emergency number:

American Express 069 9797 2000.
Diners Club 0180 5070 704.
MasterCard 0800 819 1040.
Visa 0800 811 8440.

Tax

Non-EU citizens can claim back German value-added tax (*Mehrwertsteuer* or *MwSt*) on goods purchased in the country (it's only worth the hassle on sizeable purchases). Ask the shop to provide a Tax-Free Shopping Cheque for the amount of the refund and present this, with the receipt, at the airport's refund office before checking in bags.

OPENING HOURS

Most **banks** are open 9am to noon Monday to Friday, and 1pm to 3pm or 2pm to 6pm on varied weekdays. Shops can stay open from 6am to 10pm, except on Sundays and holidays, though few take full advantage of the fact. Big stores tend to open at 9am and close between 8pm and 10pm. Most smaller shops will close around 6pm.

An increasing number of all-purpose neighbourhood **shops** (*Späti*) stay open until around midnight. Many Turkish shops are open on Saturday afternoons and on Sundays from 1pm to 5pm. Many bakers open to sell cakes on Sundays from 2pm to 4pm. Many 24-hour petrol stations and many internet cafés also sell basic groceries.

The opening times of **bars** vary, but many are open during the day, and most stay open until at least 1am, if not through until morning.

Most **post offices** are open 8am to 6pm Monday to Friday and 8am to 1pm on Saturdays.

POLICE STATIONS

You are unlikely to come in contact with the *Polizei* unless you commit a crime or are the victim of one. There are few patrols or traffic checks.

The central police HQ is at Platz der Luftbrücke 6, Tempelhof (46640), and there are local stations at: Kruppstrasse 2, Mitte; Charlottenburger Chausee 67, Charlottenburg; Friesenstrasse 16, Kreuzberg; Eiswaldtstrasse 18, Schöneberg. But police will be dispatched from the appropriate office if you just dial 46640. For emergencies, dial 110.

POSTAL SERVICES

Most post offices (*Post* in German) are open from 8am to 6pm Monday to Friday, and 8am to 1pm Saturday.

For non-local mail, use the *Andere Richtungen* ('other destinations') slot in postboxes. Letters of up to 20g to anywhere in Germany cost €0.60 in postage. For postcards it's €0.45. For anywhere outside Germany, a 20g airmail letter or postcard costs €0.75.

Postamt Friedrichstrasse
Georgenstrasse 14 18, Mitte (0228 4333 111). U6, S1, S2, S5, S7, S25, S75 Friedrichstrasse. **Open** 6am-10pm Mon-Fri; 8am-10pm Sat, Sun. **Map** p306 M6. Berlin has no main post office. However, this branch, which is to be found inside Friedrichstrasse station, keeps the longest opening hours of the Berlin offices.

Poste restante

Poste restante facilities are available at the main post offices of each district. Address them to the recipient 'Postlagernd', followed by the address of the post office, or collect them from the counter marked *Postlagernde Sendungen*. Take your passport with you.

SAFETY & SECURITY

Though crime is increasing, Berlin remains a safe city by Western standards. Even for a woman, it's pretty safe to walk around alone at night in most central areas of the city. However, avoid the Eastern working-class suburbs if you look gay or non-German. Pickpockets are not unknown around tourist areas. Use some common sense.

SMOKING

Many Berliners smoke, though the habit is in decline. Smoking is banned on public transport, in theatres and many public institutions. Many bars and restaurants have closed-off smoking rooms. Smaller, one-room establishments (under 75sq m/800sq ft) may allow smoking if they want to, but must post a sign outside denoting a Raucherkneipe (smoker pub). There's no problem with smoking at outside tables – which means that, even in winter, lots of places have outside tables.

STUDY

Germany's university system is currently in a state of flux. Under the Bologna Process (the EU's initiative to create a unified standard of education throughout Europe), the traditional *Magister* degree – which lasts between nine and 12 terms, during which time students can take a wide variety of courses – is being replaced by internationally recognised bachelor's and master's degrees. Confusion reigns among lecturers, and the gradual changeover has created a two-tiered system, with students on different courses at the same university receiving discrepant levels of education. *Magister* students are often favoured by employers because of the length and depth of the degree compared to the three-year bachelor.

Berlin retains its pull on scholars from across the world. There are currently almost 150,000 students in the city – approximately ten per cent of whom are foreigners – divided between four universities and 16 subject-specific colleges.

Language classes

Goethe-Institut
Neue Schönhauser Strasse 20, Mitte (259 063, www.goethe.de). U8 Weinmeisterstrasse, or S5, S7, S75 Hackescher Markt. **Map** p307 O5. Although considerably more expensive than most of its competitors, a four-week course costs €1,070, or €1,580 with accommodation), the Goethe-Institut offers the most systematic and intensive language courses in the city. Enrolled students can benefit from extra-curricular conversation classes, as well as a cultural extension programme that organises regular cinema, theatre and museum visits. Exams can be taken (with certificates awarded) at the end of every course.

Tandem

Bötzowstrasse 26, Prenzlauer Berg (441 3003, www.tandem-berlin. de). U2 Eberswalder Strasse. **Map** p307 O3/P3.

For a €5 administrative fee, Tandem will put you in touch with German speakers interested in conversation exchange. Formal language classes are also available at €370 a month.

Universities

Freie Universität Berlin

Central administration, Kaiserswerther Strasse 16-18, Dahlem (information 8381, www. fu-berlin.de). U3 Dahlem-Dorf.
Germany's largest university was founded in 1948, after the Humboldt fell under East German control. Centre of the 1969 student movement, the FU was for a long time a hotbed of romantic left-wing dissent. Sadly, though, not much of this idealism remains. Since the Wall came down, the FU lost much of its prestige and influence to its fierce rival, the newly restructured Humboldt, and the vast, anonymous campus is embroiled in the same bureaucratic structures as any other modern (and German) university. However, the FU got one up on the Humboldt with its relatively new 'elite university' status. The resulting €21 million a year for proposed new research projects is welcome in the strapped-for-cash capital.

Humboldt-Universität zu Berlin (HUB)

Unter den Linden 6, Mitte (20930, www.hu-berlin.de). U6, S1, S2, S5, S7, S25, S75 Friedrichstrasse.
Map p306-7 N6/M6
Humboldt was founded in 1810 by the humanist Willem von Humboldt. Hegel and Schopenhauer both taught there, Karl Marx was a student, and other departments have included the likes of Albert Einstein, Werner Heisenberg, Heinrich Heine and Max Planck. The HU entered a dark period in the 1930s, when professors and students joined enthusiastically in the Nazi book-burning on Bebelplatz. After 1945, the university fell into decline under Communism. Since 1989, the HU has regained much of its former reputation.

Sprach- und Kulturbörse an der TU Berlin

Raum 411, Fraunhoferstrasse 33-36, Charlottenburg (3142 2730, www.skb.tu-berlin.de). U2 Ernst-Reuter-Platz. **Map** p305 F6.
The TU's Language and Cultural Exchange Programme for foreigners,

the SKB is open to students from any university in Berlin. It offers a range of services, including language courses and seminars on international issues.

Technische Universität Berlin (TU)

Strasse des 17 Juni 135, Tiergarten (3140, www.tu-berlin.de). U2 Ernst-Reuter-Platz. **Map** p309 F7.
The TU began life in 1879 and is strong in chemistry, engineering and architecture. In the 1930s, the emphasis on development, business and construction made the TU a priority for the Nazi government, which allocated it more funds than any other university in the country. After the war, the TU was reopened under its current name and expanded to include philosophy, psychology and the social sciences. It is now (with some 30,000 students, 19 per cent of whom are foreigners) one of Germany's largest universities.

Universität der Künste Berlin (UdK)

Hardenbergstrasse 33, Charlottenburg (31850, www. udk-berlin.de). U2, U9, S5, S7, S75 Zoologischer Garten.
Map p309 F7.
Formerly the Hochschule der Künste (a name most Berliners still use), this founded in 1975 as a single vocational academy comprising the former Colleges of Art, Drama, Music and Printing. The range of subjects has been broadened over the years, and courses are now offered in everything from fashion design to experimental film and media. The eclectic variety of artistic and academic disciplines, along with the appointments of some high-profile teachers, has secured the UdK a well-deserved reputation as one of the best establishments of its kind in Europe.

Useful organisations

Studentenwerk Berlin

Behrenstrasse 40-41, Mitte (939 3970, www.studentenwerk-berlin.de). U6 Französische Strasse. **Open** *InfoPoint* 8am-4pm Mon-Wed; 10am-6pm Thur; 8am-3pm Fri.
Map p309 F7.
The central organisation for students in Berlin will give advice and provide information about accommodation, finance, employment and various other essentials.
Other locations InfoPoints: Hardenbergstrasse 34, Charlottenburg; Otto-von Simson-Strasse 26, Dahlem.

TELEPHONES

All phone numbers in this guide are local Berlin numbers (other than in the Escapes & Excursions chapter). Numbers beginning 0180 have higher tariffs, and numbers beginning 015, 016 or 017 are mobiles.

Dialling & codes

To phone Berlin from abroad, dial the international access code (00 from the UK, 011 from the US, 0011 from Australia), then 49 (for Germany) and 30 (for Berlin), followed by the local number.

To phone another country from Germany, dial 00, then the relevant country code: Australia 61; Canada 1; Ireland 353; New Zealand 64; United Kingdom 44; United States 1. Then, dial the local area code (minus the initial zero) and the local number.

To call Berlin from elsewhere in Germany, dial 030 and then the local number.

Making a call

Numbers prefixed 0180 are service numbers charged at €0.04-€0.14 per minute when calling from a land-line telephone, and up to €0.42 per minute when calling from a mobile, depending on the network's policies.

Public phones

Most public phones give you the option of cards or coins, and from Telekom phones (the ones with the magenta 'T') you also can send SMSs. Phonecards can be bought at post offices and newsagents for various sums from €5 to €50.

Operator services

For online directory enquiries, go to www.teleauskunft.de.

International directory enquiries 118 34.
Operator assistance/German directory enquiries 118 33 (118 37 in English).
Phone repairs 080 0330 2000.
Time 0180 4100 100 (automated, in German).

Mobile phones

Check with your service provider before leaving about service while you're in Germany. US mobile phone users should call their phone provider before departure to check their mobile's compatibility with GSM bands.

ESSENTIAL INFORMATION

TIME

Germany is on Central European Time – one hour ahead of Greenwich Mean Time. When summer time is in effect, London is one hour behind Berlin, New York six hours behind, San Francisco nine hours behind, and Sydney nine hours ahead.

Germany uses a 24-hour system. 8am is '8 Uhr' (usually written 8h), noon is '12 Uhr Mittags' or just '12 Uhr', 5pm is '17 Uhr' and midnight is '12 Uhr Mitternachts' or just "Mitternacht'. 8.15 is '8 Uhr 15' or 'Viertel nach 8'; 8.30 is '8 Uhr 30' or 'halb 9'; and 8.45 is '8 Uhr 45' or 'Viertel vor 9'.

TIPPING

A ten per cent service charge will already be part of your restaurant bill, but it's common to leave a small tip too. In a taxi, round up the bill to the nearest euro.

TOILETS

Coin-operated, self-cleaning 'City Toilets' are becoming the norm. The toilets in main stations are looked after by an attendant and are pretty clean. Restaurants and cafés have to let you use their toilets by law, and legally they can't refuse you a glass of water either.

TOURIST INFORMATION

EurAide

DB Reisezentrum, Hauptbahnhof, Tiergarten (www.euraide.de). S5, S7, S75 Hauptbahnhof. **Open** *Mar, Apr* 11am-7pm Mon-Fri. *May-July* 10am- 8pm Mon-Fri. *Aug-Oct* 10am-7pm Mon-Fri. *Nov* 11am-6.30pm Mon-Fri. *Dec* 10am-7.30pm Mon-Fri. **Map** p306 K5.
Staff advise on sights, hostels, tours and transport, and sell rail tickets.

VisitBerlin

250 025, www.visitberlin.de.
Berlin's official (if private) tourist organisation has information points at Kurfürstendamm 22, Charlottenburg; Brandenburg Gate; Hauptbahnhof (ground floor, Europaplatz exit); Tegel Airport (next to gate 1); and at the base of the TV Tower at Alexanderplatz. All are open daily.

VISAS & IMMIGRATION

A passport valid for three months beyond the length of stay is all that is required for UK, EU, US, Canadian and Australian citizens for a stay in Germany of up to three months. Citizens of EU countries with valid national ID cards need only show their ID cards.

Citizens of other countries should check with their local German embassy or consulate whether a visa is required. As with any trip, confirm visa requirements well before you plan to travel.

Residence permits

For stays of longer than three months, you'll need a residence permit. EU citizens, and those of Andorra, Australia, Canada, Cyprus, Israel, Japan, South Korea, Malta, New Zealand and the US, can obtain one by doing the following.

First, you need to register at your local *Anmeldungsamt* (registration office) – there's one in the *Bürgeramt* (citizens office) of every district. A list can be found at www.berlin. de/politik-und-verwaltung/ buergerservice. You don't need an appointment, but expect to wait. Bring your passport and proof of a Berlin address. You'll be issued with an *Anmeldungsbestätigung* – a form confirming you have registered at the *Anmeldungsamt*.

At this point, take your *Anmeldungsbestätigung* to the **Landesamt für Bürger und Ordnungsangelegenheiten Ausländerbehörde** in the Moabit district of Tiergarten. Also bring your passport, two passport photos and something to read. There are always huge queues and it takes forever – people start queuing hours before the office opens – but all you can do is take a number and wait. Eventually, you will be issued with an *Aufenthaltserlaubnis* – a residence permit. If you have a work contract, bring it – you may be granted a longer stay.

If you're unsure about your status, contact the German Embassy in your country of origin, or your own embassy or consulate in Berlin (*see p285*).

Landesamt für Bürger und Ordnungsangelegenheiten Ausländerbehörde

Friedrich-Krause-Ufer 24, Tiergarten (information 902 690, www.berlin.de/labo/auslaender/ dienstleistungen). U9, S41, S42 Westhafen. **Open** 7am-2pm Mon, Tue; 10am-6pm Thur (or by appointment via email). **Map** p305 H3.

WHEN TO GO

Berlin has a continental climate, which means that it's hot in summer and cold in winter. In January and February, the city often ices over. Spring begins in late March/early April. May and June are the most beautiful months.

On public holidays (*Feiertagen* – for a list, *see p29*), it can be difficult to get things done in Berlin. However, most cafés, bars and restaurants stay open – except on the evening of 24 December, when almost everything closes.

WOMEN

See also p287 **Helplines** and *p286* **Health**.

Women's centres

EWA Frauenzentrum

Prenzlauer Allee 6, Prenzlauer Berg (442 5542, www.ewa-frauenzentrum.de). U2 Senefelderplatz. **Open** 11am-10pm Mon-Thur; varies Fri-Sun. **Map** p307 P4.
Website in German only.

THE LOCAL CLIMATE

Average monthly temperatures and rainfall in Berlin.

	High (°C/°F)	Low (°C/°F)	Rainfall (mm/in)
Jan	2 / 36	-3 / 27	43 / 0.17
Feb	3 / 37	-2 / 28	38 / 0.15
Mar	8 / 46	0 / 32	38 / 0.15
Apr	13 / 55	4 / 39	43 / 0.17
May	18 / 64	8 / 46	56 / 0.22
June	22 / 72	11 / 52	71 / 0.28
July	23 / 73	13 / 55	53 / 0.21
Aug	23 / 73	12 / 54	66 / 0.26
Sept	18 / 64	9 / 48	46 / 0.18
Oct	13 / 55	6 / 43	36 / 0.14
Nov	7 / 45	2 / 36	51 / 0.20
Dec	3 / 37	-1 / 30	56 / 0.22

Vocabulary

PRONUNCIATION

z – pronounced 'ts'
w – like English 'v'
v – like English 'f'
s – like English 'z', but softer
r – like a throaty French 'r'
a – as in father
e – sometimes as in bed, sometimes as in day
i – as in seek
o – as in note
u – as in loot
ch – as in Scottish loch
ä – combination of 'a' and 'e', like 'ai' in paid or like 'e' in set
ö – combination of 'o' and 'e', as in French 'eu'
ü – combination of 'u' and 'e', like true
ai – like pie
au – like house
ie – like free
ee – like hey
ei – like fine
eu – like coil

USEFUL PHRASES

Greetings

hello/good day guten Tag; **goodbye** auf Wiedersehen, (informal) tschüss; **good morning** guten Morgen; **good evening** guten Abend; **good night** gute Nacht.

Basic words & requests

yes ja, (emphatic) jawohl; **no** nein, nee; **maybe** vielleicht; **please** bitte; **thank you** danke; **thank you very much** danke schön; **excuse me** entschuldigen Sie mich, bitte; **sorry!** Verzeihung!; **I'm sorry, I don't speak German** Entschuldigung, ich spreche kein Deutsch; **do you speak English?** sprechen Sie Englisch?; **can you please speak more slowly?** können Sie bitte langsamer sprechen?; **my name is…** ich heisse…; **I would like…** ich möchte…; **how much is…?** wieviel kostet…?; **please can I have a receipt?** darf ich bitte eine Quittung haben?; **please can you call me a cab?** können Sie bitte mir ein Taxi rufen?; **open/closed** geöffnet/geschlossen; **with/without** mit/ohne; **cheap/expensive** billig/teuer; **big/small** gross/klein; **entrance/exit** Eingang/Ausgang; **bureau de change** die Wechselstube; **help!** Hilfe!

Directions

left links; **right** rechts; **straight ahead** gerade aus; **corner** ecke; **far** weit; **near** nah; **street** die Strasse; **square** der Platz; **city map** der Stadtplan; **how do I get to…?** wie komme ich nach…?; **how far is it to…?** wie weit ist es nach…?; **where is…?** wo ist…?

Travel

arrival/departure Ankunft/Abfahrt; **airport** der Flughafen; **railway station** der Bahnhof; **ticket** die Fahrkarte, der Fahrschein; **airline ticket** die Flugkarte, der Flugschein; **passport** der Reisepass; **petrol** das Benzin; **lead-free** bleifrei; **traffic** der Vehrkehr.

Health

I feel ill ich bin krànk; **doctor** der Arzt; **dentist** der Zahnarzt; **pharmacy** die Apotheke; **hospital** das Krankenhaus; **I need a doctor** ich brauche einen Arzt; **please call an ambulance** rufen Sie bitte ein Krankenwagen; **please call the police** rufen Sie bitte die Polizei.

NUMBERS

0 null; **1** eins; **2** zwei; **3** drei; **4** vier; **5** fünf; **6** sechs; **7** sieben; **8** acht; **9** neun; **10** zehn; **11** elf; **12** zwölf; **13** dreizehn; **14** vierzehn; **15** fünfzehn; **16** sechszehn; **17** siebzehn; **18** achtzehn; **19** neunzehn; **20** zwanzig; **21** einundzwanzig; **22** zweiundzwanzig; **30** dreissig; **40** vierzig; **50** fünfzig; **60** sechszig; **70** siebzig; **80** achtzig; **90** neunzig; **100** hundert; **101** hunderteins; **110** hundertzehn; **200** zweihundert; **201** zweihunderteins; **1,000** tausend; **2,000** zweitausend.

DAYS & TIMES OF DAY

Monday Montag; **Tuesday** Dienstag; **Wednesday** Mittwoch; **Thursday** Donnerstag; **Friday** Freitag; **Saturday** Samstag, Sonnabend; **Sunday** Sonntag; **morning** Morgen; **noon** Mittag; **afternoon** Nachmittag; **evening** Abend; **night** Nacht; **today** Heute; **yesterday** Gestern; **tomorrow** Morgen.

FOOD & DRINK

Basics

breakfast Frühstück; **lunch** Mittagessen; **dinner** Abendessen; **snack** Imbiss; **appetiser** Vorspeise; **main course** Hauptgericht; **dessert** Nachspeise; **fried, roasted** gebraten; **boiled** gekocht; **breaded, battered** paniert; **egg, eggs** Ei, Eier; **cheese** Käse; **noodles/pasta** Nudeln/Teigwaren; **sauce** Sosse.

Phrases

I'd like to reserve a table for… people Ich möchte einen Tisch für… Personen reservieren; **I am a vegetarian** Ich bin Vegetarier; **The menu, please** Die Speisekarte, bitte; **We'd/I'd like to order** Wir möchten/Ich möchte bestellen; **The bill, please** Bezahlen, bitte.

Meat (Fleisch)

meatball Boulette; **mince** Hackfleisch; **venison** Hirsch; **chicken** Huhn, Huhnerfleisch; **rabbit** Kaninchen; **chop** Kotelett; **lamb** Lamm; **liver** Leber; **kidneys** Nieren; **turkey** Puten; **beef** Rindfleisch; **ham** Schinken; **pork** Schweinefleisch; **bacon** Speck; **sausage** Wurst.

Fish (Fisch)

eel Aal; **trout** Forelle; **prawns** Garnelen; **lobster** Hummer; **cod** Kabeljau; **crab** or **shrimp** Krabbe; **salmon** Lachs; **haddock** Schellfisch; **tuna** Thunfisch; **squid** Tintenfisch; **clams** Venusmuscheln.

Vegetables (Gemüse) & fruit (Obst)

pineapple Ananas; **apple** Apfel; **pear** Birne; **cauliflower** Blumenkohl; **beans** Bohnen; **green beans** Brechbohnen; **mushrooms** Champignons, Pilze; **green peas** Erbsen; **strawberries** Erdbeeren; **cucumber** Gurke; **raspberries** Himbeeren; **potato** Kartoffel; **cherry** Kirsch; **garlic** Knoblauch; **cabbage** Kohl; **carrots** Möhren; **peppers** Paprika; **chips** Pommes; **lettuce** Salat; **asparagus** Spargel; **onions** Zwiebeln.

Further Reference

BOOKS

Fiction

Baum, Vicki *Berlin Hotel*
Written in 1944, this pulp thriller
anticipates the horror of the
collapsing Reich via the story of a
German resistance fighter trapped in
a hotel with a cast of Nazi bigwigs.
Deighton, Len *Berlin Game,*
Mexico Set, London Match Epic
espionage trilogy set against an
accurate picture of 1980s Berlin.
Döblin, Alfred *Berlin-*
Alexanderplatz Devastating
expressionist portrait of the inter-
war underworld in the working-
class quarters of Alexanderplatz.
Eckhart, Gabriele *Hitchhiking*
Short stories viewing East Berlin
through the eyes of street cleaners
and a female construction worker.
Fallada, Hans *Every Man Dies*
Alone Classic tale of a middle-aged
couple in wartime Berlin who begin a
campaign of resistance to the Third
Reich – with tragic consequences.
Grass, Gunther *Local Anaesthetic*
The angst of a schoolboy threatening
to burn a dog in the Ku'damm in
protest at the Vietnam War is firmly
satirised, albeit in Grass's irritating
schoolmasterly way.
Harris, Robert *Fatherland*
Alternative history and detective
novel set in a 1964 Berlin as the
Nazis might have built it.
Isherwood, Christopher *Mr*
Norris Changes Trains, Goodbye to
Berlin Isherwood's two Berlin novels,
the basis of the movie *Cabaret*, offer
a sharp picture of the city as it tipped
over into Nazism.
Johnson, Uwe *Two Views* Love
story across the East-West divide,
strong on the mood of Berlin in the
late 1950s and early 1960s.
Kaminer, Wladimir *Russian Disco*
Bestselling collection of short tales
from the Russian émigré and DJ.
Kästner, Erich *Emil and the*
Detectives Classic children's book,
set mostly around Bahnhof Zoo
and Nollendorfplatz.
Kerr, Philip *Berlin Noir* The Bernie
Gunther trilogy, about a private
detective in Nazi Berlin.
McEwan, Ian *The Innocent*
A naive young Englishman is
recruited into Cold War plotting
with tragi-comic results.
Nabokov, Vladimir *The Gift*
Written and set in 1920s Berlin,

where an impoverished Russian
émigré dreams of writing a book.
Porter, Henry *Brandenburg*
Decent fall-of-the-Wall spy thriller,
even if the author does get some of
the street names wrong.
Regener, Sven *Berlin Blues*
Irresponsibility and childhood's end
in the bars of late 1980s Kreuzberg.
Ryan, Robert *Dying Day* Readable
espionage thriller with the Berlin
Airlift as backdrop.
Vermes, Timur *Look Who's Back*
Adolf Hitler wakes up one morning
in a patch of Berlin wasteland, the
site of the former *Führerbunker*, to
find it's 2011 and life is very different.

Biography & memoir

Anonymous *A Woman in Berlin*
Extraordinary diary of a woman
fighting to survive at the end of
World War II in the ruins of Berlin.
Funder, Anna *Stasiland* Brutal
stories of individuals and the East
German state, retold through the
author's conversations with friends.
Newton, Helmut *Autobiography*
Begins with an absorbing account of
growing up Jewish in Weimar Berlin,
and Newton's apprenticeship with
fashion photographer Yva.
Parker, Peter *Isherwood* Vast
biography includes a well-researched
section on the author's Berlin trouble.
Rimmer, Dave *Once Upon a Time in*
the East The collapse of communism
seen stoned and from street level –
tales of games between East and West
Berlin and travels through assorted
East European revolutions.
Schirer, William L *Berlin Diaries*
Foreign correspondent in Berlin
1931-1941 bears appalled witness to
Europe's plunge into Armageddon.

History

Beevor, Antony *Berlin: The*
Downfall 1945 Bestselling narrative
history of the Third Reich's final,
desperate collapse.
Friedrich, Otto *Before the Deluge*
Vivid portrait of 1920s Berlin,
based on interviews with those
who survived what followed.
Garton Ash, Timothy *We the*
People Instant history of the 1989
revolutions by on-the-spot academic.
Kellerhoff, Sven Felix *The*
Führer Bunker The bare facts
about Hitler's last refuge and what
became of it.

Levenson, Thomas *Einstein in*
Berlin Absorbing tale of the historical
deal between physicist and city.
Maclean, Rory *Berlin: Imagine*
a City A rich history of lives lived
in Berlin, real and imagined, from
Konrad von Cölln in 1649 to Knut
the late, lamented polar bear.
Metzger, Rainer *Berlin in the*
'20s A wonderful pictorial record
of Berlin's most creative era.
Richie, Alexandra *Faust's*
Metropolis The best one-volume
history of Berlin.
Taylor, Frederick *The Berlin Wall*
Now the definitive history of the
notorious border. Taylor's book on
Dresden is well worth a read too.

Architecture

Ladd, Brian *The Ghosts of Berlin:*
Confronting German History in the
Urban Landscape Erudite and
insightful look into the relationship
between architecture, urbanism and
Berlin's violent political history.

FILM

Cabaret (Bob Fosse, 1972) Liza
Minelli as Sally Bowles, the very
definition of the Berlin myth.
Christiane F (Uli Edel, 1981) To hell
and back in the housing estates and
heroin scene of late 1970s West
Berlin, with Bowie soundtrack.
The Edukators (Hans
Weingartner, 2004) Sinister crime
comedy caper with three would-be
radicals in the heart of Berlin getting
more than they bargained for when
they take a wealthy hostage.
A Foreign Affair (Billy Wilder,
1948) Marlene Dietrich sings 'Black
Market' among the romantically
rendered ruins of postwar Berlin.
Goodbye, Lenin! (Wolfgang
Becker, 2003) Ostalgia, the movie
– a comic eulogy for the GDR, in
which socialism gets a different
kind of send-off.
The Good German (Steven
Soderbergh, 2006) Clooney and
Blanchett are old flames in a black-
and-white pastiche of Wilder and
Reed, set in a cynical 1945.
The Legend of Paul and Paula
(Heiner Carow, 1974) Cult GDR love
story banned by the unromantic
regime. Soundtrack by the also
legendary Pudhys.
The Lives of Others (Florian
Henckel von Donnersmarck, 2006)

Stasi agent watches writer and silently changes sides in this award-winning thriller.

M (Fritz Lang, 1931) Paedophilia and vigilantism as Peter Lorre's child murderer stalks Weimar Berlin.

The Man Between (Carol Reed, 1953) James Mason stars in *The Third Man*'s Berlin cousin.

Olympia (Leni Riefenstahl, 1937) In filming the 1936 Olympics, the Nazis' favourite director invented the conventions of modern sportscasting.

One, Two, Three (Billy Wilder, 1961) James Cagney is brilliant as the Pepsi exec whose daughter falls for East Berlin communist Horst Buchholz.

Possession (Andrzej Zulawski, 1981) Sam Neil and Isabel Adjani star in cult psychosexual horror flick, which uses its West Berlin backdrop to compellingly weird effect.

The Spy Who Came in from the Cold (Martin Ritt, 1965) Intense atmosphere, excellent Richard Burton performance, and an ending that shatteringly brings home the obscenity of the Wall.

Wings of Desire (Wim Wenders, 1987) Bruno Ganz in love, Peter Falk in a bunker, Nick Cave in concert, and an angel on the Siegessäule – Wenders has never surpassed his (double) vision of the divided city.

MUSIC

AG Geige *Raabe?* (Zensor) One of the first post-1989 discs to emerge from the East Berlin underground came from this bizarre electronica outfit.

Ash Ra Tempel *Join Inn* (Temple/ Spalax) The 1972 hippy freakout incarnation of guitarist Manuel Göttsching, before he was reborn as techno's most baffling muse.

The Birthday Party *Mutiny/ The Bad Seed EP* (4AD) Nick Cave and cohorts escaped to early 1980s Berlin to record their most intense EPs, here compressed into one CD.

David Bowie *"Heroes"* (EMI) In which Bowie romanticises the Wall and captures the atmosphere of [SIC] Neuköln.

David Bowie *Low* (EMI) The album that soundtracked Bowie's new career in a new town.

Caspar Brötzmann/FM Einheit *Merry Christmas* (Blast First/Rough Trade Deutschland) Guitarist son Caspar is no less noisy than père Brötzmann, especially on this frenzy of feedback and distortion.

Peter Brötzmann *No Nothing* (FMP) Uncharacteristically introspective recording from the sax colossus of German improvisation.

Ernst Busch *Der Rote Orpheus/Der Barrikaden Tauber* (BARBArossa) Two-CD survey of the revolutionary tenor's 1930s recordings.

Nick Cave *From Her To Eternity* (Mute) Cave in best *Berlinerisch* debauched and desperate mode.

Comedian Harmonists *Ihre grossen Erfolge* (Laserlight) Sublime six-part harmonies from the Weimar sensations whose career was cut short during the Third Reich.

Crime & the City Solution *Paradise Discotheque* (Mute) Underrated Berlin-Australian group's finest disc (1990) is an oblique commentary on the heady amorality of the immediate post-1989 era.

DAF *Kebabträume* (Mute) Exhilarating German punk satire of Berlin's Cold War neuroses, culminating in the coda 'We are the Turks of tomorrow'.

Marlene Dietrich *On Screen, Stage And Radio* (Legend) From 'I Am the Sexy Lola' to 'Ruins of Berlin', the sultry Schöneberg singer embodies the mood of decadent Berlin.

Einstürzende Neubauten *Berlin Babylon Soundtrack* (Zomba) More Neubauten 'Strategies Against Architecture' accompanying a highly watchable documentary about the changes in Berlin's landscape and the movers and shakers behind them.

Alec Empire *The Geist Of…* (Geist) Wonderful triple CD compilation of ATR mainman Empire's less combative electronica explorations.

Manuel Göttsching *E2-E4* (Racket) Great lost waveform guitar album by ex-Ash Ra Tempel leader.

Malaria! *Compiled* (Moabit Musik) With suffocating synth swirls, heavy-stepping beats and songs such as 'Passion' and 'Death', Malaria! was '80s girl-pop, Berlin-style.

Maurizio *M* (M) Essential CD compilation of Basic Channel mainman Moritz Von Oswald's vinyl releases, which lights up Chicago house with streaming beats diverted from the Berlin-Detroit techno grid.

Iggy Pop *The Idiot* (Virgin America) With Bowie in the producer's chair, Iggy begins to absorb the influence of early German electronica and the city of bright, white clubbing.

Iggy Pop *Lust For Life* (Virgin America) Way back in West Berlin, Iggy the passenger cruises through the divided city's ripped-back sides.

Stereo Total *My Melody* (Bungalow) Demented *chansons* with cheesy lounge backing – Mitte's kitsch aesthetic plus a Francophone spin.

Tangerine Dream *Zeit* (Jive Electro) Where cosmic consciousness and electronic minimalism first met by the Wall.

Ton Steine Scherben *Keine Macht Für Niemand* (David Volksmund) Ernst Busch reincarnated as the early 1970s rock commune that provided Kreuzberg's anarchists with their most enduring anthems.

U2 *Achtung Baby!* (Island) It took Zoo station and post-Wall Berlin to inspire the U2 album for people who don't like U2.

Christian van Dorries *Wagnerkomplex* (Masse und Macht) Spooky examination of 'music and German national identity' carried out in the shell of the Palast der Republik.

Various *Das Beste Aus Der DDR Parts I-III* (Amiga) Three-part DDR rock retrospective, divided into rock, pop and 'Kult', including Puhdys, Silly and Karat, plus Sandow's 'Born in the GDR'.

Various *Berlin 1992* (Tresor) Berlin techno in its early, apocalyptic phase. Includes Love Parade anthem 'Der Klang der Familie' by 3Phase.

Various *Pop 2000* (Grönland/ Spiegel Edition) Eight-CD companion to TV chronicle of postwar German culture in East and West.

Various *Tranceformed From Beyond* (MFS) Compilation that defined Berlin trance.

Westbam *A Practising Maniac At Work* (Low Spirit) The peak of Berlin's best-known DJ, veering from stomping techno to twisted disco.

WEBSITES

www.alt-berlin.info Archive of searchable historic Berlin maps, from 1738 to 1989.

www.berlin-info.de Essentially a hotel booking site, but also contains information for visitors. Operated by the official tourist board BTM.

www.berlin.de Berlin's official site – run by the tourist board (BTM) – is inevitably not its most objective, but is nonetheless well written.

www.bvg.de Timetable and public transport information for Berlin/ Brandenburg, in English/German.

http://dict.leo.org Simply the best English-German online dictionary.

www.ostberlin.de Everything you wanted to know about life in the former East Berlin.

www.smb.museum Bilingual site with detailed information on around 20 major Berlin museums.

www.timeout.com/travel/berlin General information and history, plus shop, restaurant, café, bar and hotel reviews, written by residents.

www.zitty.de The online sister of one of Berlin's two listings fortnightlies. In German only.

www.tip-berlin.de Zitty's competition, with similar functions.

ESSENTIAL INFORMATION

Index

INDEX

INDEX

INDEX

Maps

Charlottenstraße

81 - 83

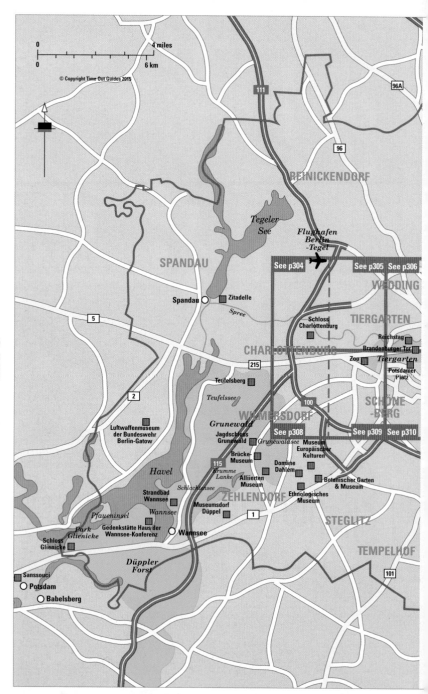

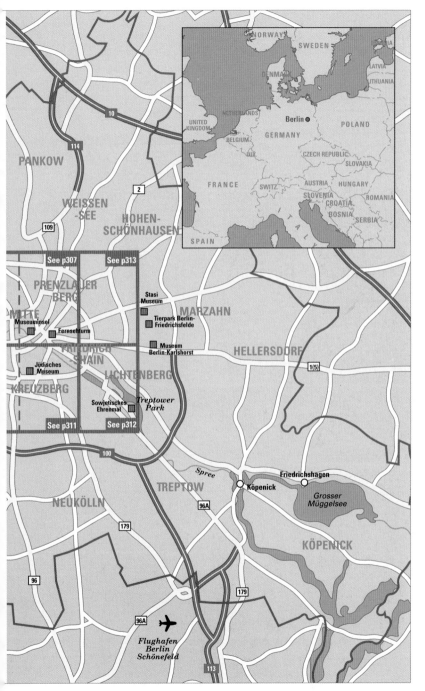

PANKOW

10

114

WEISSEN
-SEE

2

109

HOHEN-
SCHÖNHAUSEN

NORWAY

SWEDEN

DENMARK

LATVIA

LITHUANIA

NETHERLANDS

Berlin

POLAND

UNITED
KINGDOM

BELGIUM

GERMANY

CZECH REPUBLIC

SLOVAKIA

FRANCE

SWITZ

AUSTRIA

HUNGARY

SLOVENIA

ROMANIA

CROATIA

BOSNIA

SERBIA

SPAIN

ITALY

See p307

See p313

PRENZLAUER
BERG

Stasi
Museum

MARZAHN

MITTE

Museuminsel

Fernsehturm

Tierpark Berlin-
Friedrichsfelde

FRIEDRICHS
HAIN

Museum
Berlin-Karlshorst

HELLERSDORF

Jüdisches
Museum

LICHTENBERG

1(5)

KREUZBERG

Sowjetisches
Ehrenmal

Treptower
Park

See p311

See p312

100

Spree

Friedrichshagen

TREPTOW

Köpenick

Grosser
Müggelsee

NEUKÖLLN

96A

179

KÖPENICK

96

179

96A

Flughafen
Berlin
Schönefeld

113

MAPS

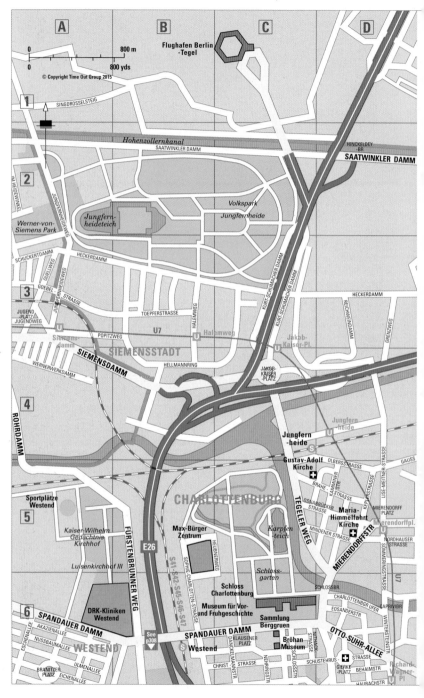

MAPS

A B C D

0   800 m
0   800 yds

Flughafen Berlin
-Tegel

SINGDROSSELSTEIG

Hohenzollernkanal
SAATWINKLER DAMM

HINCKELDEY
-BR

SAATWINKLER DAMM

IM HEIDEWINKEL

JUNGFERNHEIDEWEG

Werner-von-
Siemens Park

Jungfern-
heideteich

Volkspark
Jungfernheide

SCHUCKERTDAMM

HECKERDAMM

HECKERDAMM

KURT-SCHUMACHER DAMM

KURT-SCHUMACHER DAMM

RECHNERDAMM

GRENZWEG

QUELLWEG

GOEBEL
STRASSE

JUNGFERNHEIDEWEG

JUGEND
PLATZ
JUGENDWEG

TOEPFERSTRASSE

HALEMWEG

Siemens-
damm

POPITZWEG

U7

Halemweg

Jakob-
Kaiser-Pl.

SIEMENSDAMM

SIEMENSSTADT

WERNERWERKDAMM

HELLMANNRING

JAKOB-
KAISER-
PLATZ

ROHRDAMM

Jungfern
-heide

Jungfern
-heide

Gustav-Adolf
Kirche

OLBERSSTRASSE

GAUSS

Sportplätze
Westend

BRAHE

KAMMINER
STR

KEPLERSTRASSE

LISE-MEITNER-STRASSE

MIERENDORFF
PLATZ

CHARLOTTENBURG

OSNABRÜCKER
STRASSE

Maria-
Himmelfahrt
Kirche

Mierendorffpl.

Kaiser-Wilhelm
Gedächtnis
Kirchhof

Max-Bürger
Zentrum

Karpfen
-teich

TEGELER WEG

MINDENER STRASSE

NORDHAUSER
STRASSE

SOMMERINGSTRASSE

U7

Luisenkirchhof III

FÜRSTENBRUNNER WEG

E26

S41·S42·S45·S46·S47

HEUBNERWEG

SOPHIE-CHARLOTTEN-STRASSE

Schlossgarten

MIERENDORFFSTR

SCHLOSSBR.

CHARLOTTENBGR UFER

CAPRIVIBR.

DRK-Kliniken
Westend

SPANDAUER DAMM

Schloss
Charlottenburg

Museum für Vor-
und Frühgeschichte

Sammlung
Berggruen

EOSANDERSTR

OTTO-SUHR-ALLEE

WINTERSTEINSTR

ESCHENALLEE

AKAZIENALLEE

NUSSBAUMALLEE

ULMENALLEE

See
p308

SPANDAUER DAMM

KLAUSENER
PLATZ

DANCKELMANNSTR

Westend

Bröhan
Museum

NEHRINGSTR

SCHUSTEHRUSSTR

STRASSE

BRANITZER
PLATZ

EICHENALLEE

WESTEND

CHRIST STRASSE

STRASSE

SEELINGSTR

GIERKE
PLATZ

BEHAIMSTR

Richard-
Wagner-
Pl.

HAUBACHSTR

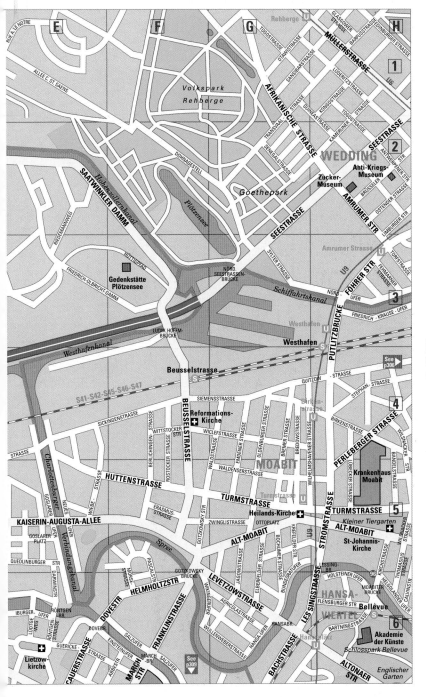

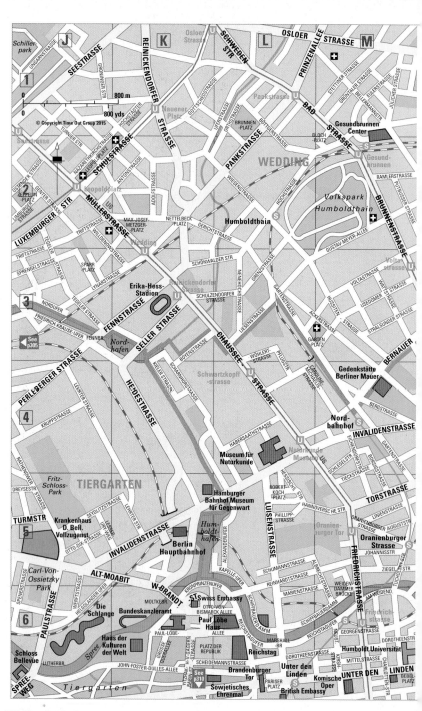

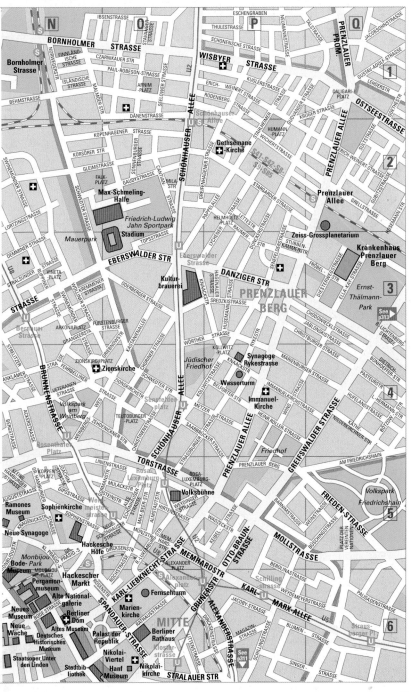

MAPS

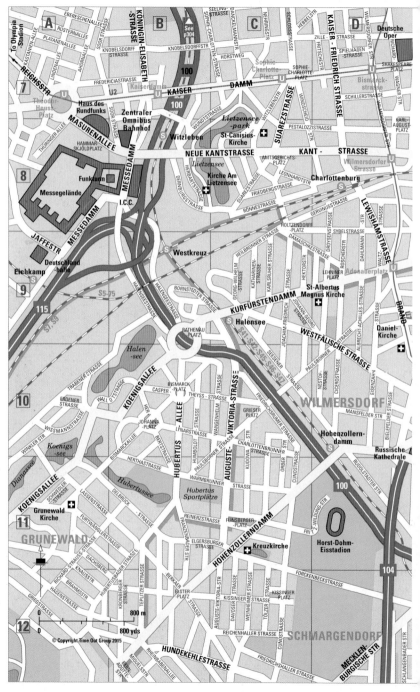

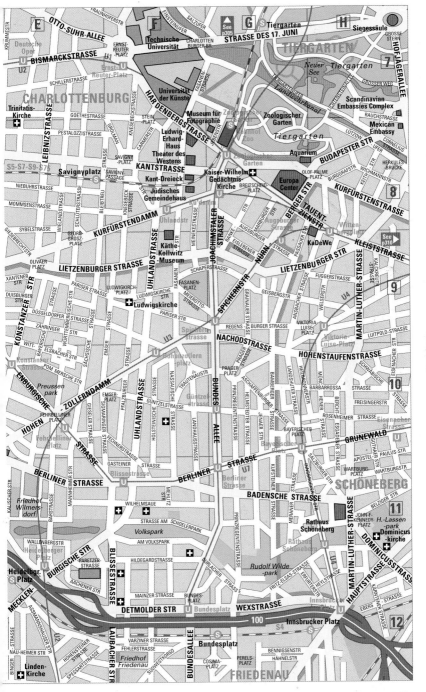

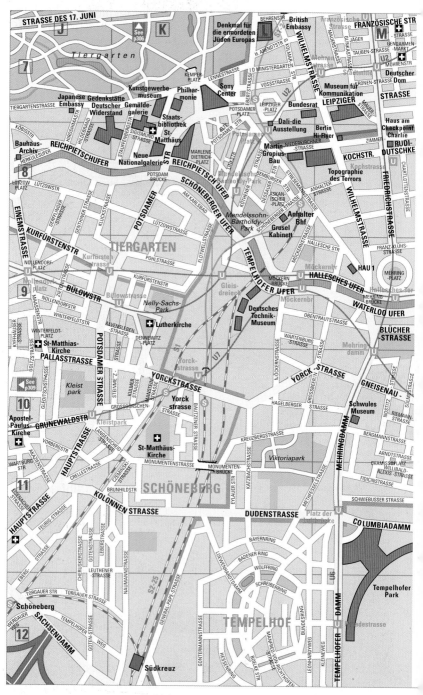